ANCIENT BORINQUEN

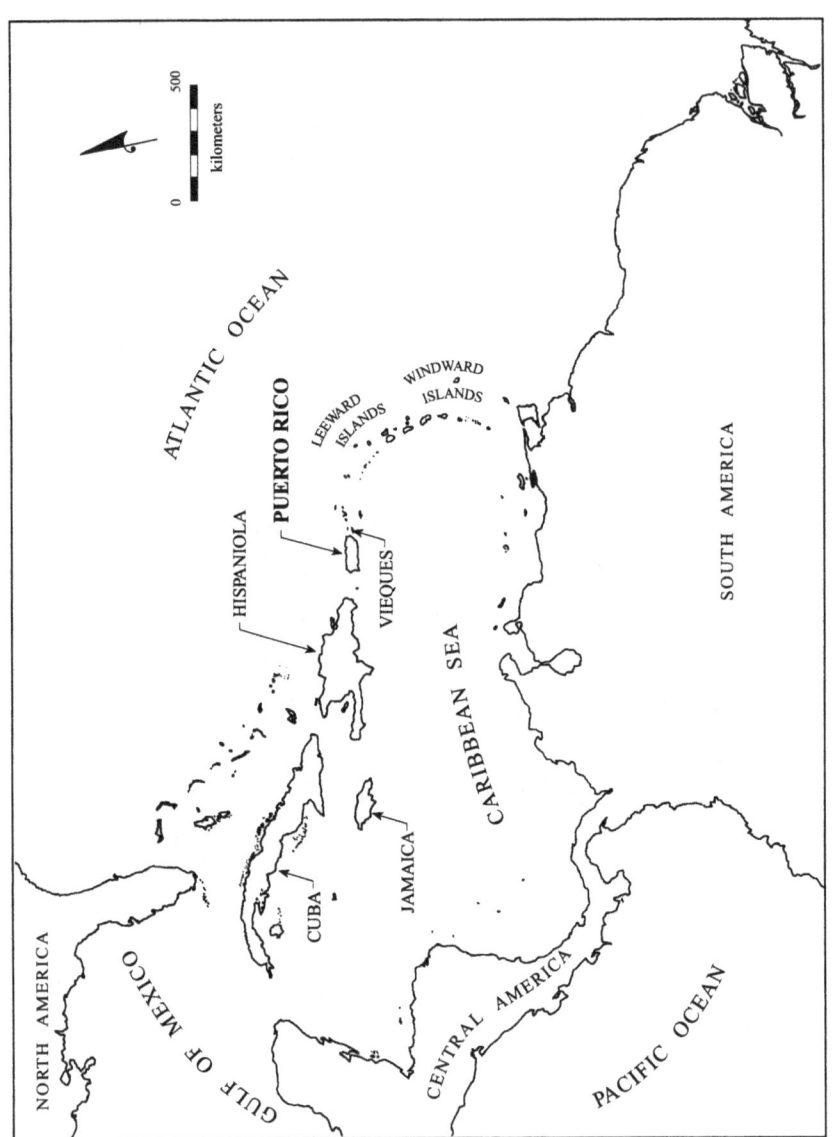

Map of the Caribbean Basin.

ANCIENT BORINQUEN

Archaeology and Ethnohistory
of Native Puerto Rico

Edited by Peter E. Siegel

The University of Alabama Press
Tuscaloosa

The University of Alabama Press
Tuscaloosa, Alabama 35487-0380
uapress.ua.edu

Copyright © 2005 by the University of Alabama Press
All rights reserved.

Inquiries about reproducing material from this work should be addressed to the University of Alabama Press.

Typeface: AGaramond

Cover image: Side of Hacienda Grande–style effigy bowl from Mounded Midden I, Maisabel site, Puerto Rico; illustration by Peter E. Siegel
Cover design: Ander Monson

E-ISBN: 978-0-8173-8150-9

Cataloging-in-Publication data is available from the Library of Congress.
ISBN: 978-0-8173-5238-7 (paper)
ISBN: 978-0-8173-1471-2 (cloth)

To Ricardo E. Alegría and Irving Rouse, Caciques of
Puerto Rican Archaeology

In memory of James B. Peterson

CONTENTS

List of Illustrations
ix

Preface
xv

1 The Crab-Shell Dichotomy Revisited: The Lithics Speak Out
RENIEL RODRÍGUEZ RAMOS
1

2 The Paso del Indio Site, Vega Baja, Puerto Rico: A Progress Report
JEFF WALKER
55

3 Environmental and Cultural Correlates in the West Indies:
A View from Puerto Rico
PETER E. SIEGEL, JOHN G. JONES,
DEBORAH M. PEARSALL, AND DANIEL P. WAGNER
88

4 The Status of Paleoethnobiological Research on Puerto Rico
and Adjacent Islands
SUSAN D. DEFRANCE AND LEE A. NEWSOM
122

5 Ceramic-Age Dietary Patterns in Puerto Rico:
Stable Isotopes and Island Biogeography
ANNE V. STOKES
185

6 Deconstructing the Polity: Communities and Social Landscapes of
the Ceramic-Age Peoples of South Central Puerto Rico
JOSHUA M. TORRES
202

7 The Proto-Taíno Monumental *Cemís* of Caguana:
A Political-Religious "Manifesto"
JOSÉ R. OLIVER
230

8 Rivers of Stone, Rivers within Stone: Rock Art in Ancient Puerto Rico
PETER G. ROE
285

9 The Aftermath of Conquest:
The Indians of Puerto Rico during the Early Sixteenth Century
KAREN F. ANDERSON-CÓRDOVA
337

10 Multiple Visions of an Island's Past and Some Thoughts for
Future Directions in Puerto Rican Prehistory
PETER E. SIEGEL
353

References Cited
365

Contributors
415

Index
419

ILLUSTRATIONS

Figures

Frontispiece Map of the Caribbean Basin.

Figure 1.1. General core-flake lineal reduction model. 20

Figure 1.2. Percentages of flakes by technique of extraction in the selected subsample for each lithostratigraphic unit. 25

Figure 1.3. Bipolar cores in the Cuevas component of the site (LU-III). 30

Figure 1.4. Percentages of collapsed raw materials by lithostratigraphic unit in the flake products related to core-flake reduction in the selected subsample. 31

Figure 1.5. Flakes made by the cobble slicing technique. 32

Figure 1.6. Cores made by the cobble slicing technique. 33

Figure 1.7. Chert flakes made by parallel flaking. 35

Figure 1.8. Maximum dimension of freehand flakes in the selected subsample by lithostratigraphic unit. 36

Figure 1.9. Maximum dimension of flint freehand flakes in the selected subsample. 37

Figure 1.10. Archaic celt (LU-I). 39

Figure 1.11. Cross sections of celts and adzes. 40

Figure 1.12. Necked specimens. 42

Figure 2.1. Locations of excavation units in Pilasters 5 through 8. 59

Figure 2.2. Mechanized and manual excavation of Pilaster 8. 60

Figure 2.3. Post molds, burials, and other features in Pilaster 6. 66

Figure 2.4. Woman, infant, and offering. Death during childbirth. 72

Figure 2.5. Man holding another man's skull. 73

Figure 3.1. Details of the Manatí, P.R. and Vega Alta, P.R. 7.5-minute quadrangles. 91

Figure 3.2. Photograph of the pond while Core LM-2 is in process. 92

Figure 3.3. Topographic map of the Maisabel setting. 95

Figure 3.4. Representative soil profiles across the Maisabel site. 98

Figure 3.5. Pollen diagram of the Río Cibuco mangrove core. 109

Figure 3.6. Pollen diagram of the LM-2 pond core. 110

Figure 3.7. Phytolith diagram of the LM-2 pond core. 112

Figure 4.1. Map of Puerto Rico showing the locations of sites discussed in the text. 123

Figure 5.1. General range of isotope values of potential prehistoric food items. 187

Figure 5.2. Source of protein in the diet of individuals from Paso del Indio. 194

Figure 5.3. Whole diet of individuals from Paso del Indio. 194

Figure 5.4. Mean $\delta^{13}C$ values for human bone collagen and apatite, Paso del Indio. 195

Figure 5.5. Apatite to collagen spacing from Paso del Indio individuals. 195

Figure 5.6. Source of protein in the diet of individuals from Maisabel. 196

Figure 5.7. Whole diet of individuals from Maisabel. 196

Figure 5.8. Mean $\delta^{13}C$ values for human bone collagen and apatite, Maisabel. 197

Figure 5.9. Apatite to collagen spacing from Maisabel individuals. 198

Figure 5.10. Temporal change in diet in Puerto Rico. 200

Figure 6.1. Study area. 204

Figure 6.2. Period II site distributions, cost boundaries, and village clusters. 216

Figure 6.3. Period III site distributions, cost boundaries, and village clusters. 217

Figure 6.4. Period IV site distributions, cost boundaries, and village clusters. 218

Figure 6.5. Site type frequencies through time. 221

Figure 6.6. General trends in ceramic distributions through the region. 223

Figure 6.7. Territory associated with villages through time.   224

Figure 7.1. Locations of sites with stone-demarcated precincts in Puerto Rico.   232

Figure 7.2. Locations of archaeological sites in the vicinity of Caguana.   233

Figure 7.3. View to the three-pointed karst hills northwest from the oval Plaza C, Caguana.   234

Figure 7.4. Two perspectives of a three-pointed stone carved from metavolcanic rock.   235

Figure 7.5. Map of the stone-demarcated precincts of Tibes, Ponce.   239

Figure 7.6. Contour map of Caguana.   240

Figure 7.7. A pair of igneous stone *guaízas* (masks) from Puerto Rico.   243

Figure 7.8. An incised necklace separator made from *Strombus* spp. shell from Site Utu-27.   244

Figure 7.9. A limestone monolith from Site Utu-27.   250

Figure 7.10. The "Duho Oliver," from Dos Bocas Region, Utuado.   253

Figure 7.11. An anthropomorphic *cohoba* inhalator from La Cucama cemetery.   254

Figure 7.12. Oblique aerial photograph of Caguana.   259

Figure 7.13. Close-up plan view of Plaza A and immediate structural features as mapped by Mason in 1915.   261

Figure 7.14. Petroglyph 24.   262

Figure 7.15. Photo of northern end of Plaza A marking the locations of Petroglyphs 1, 11, and 17–22, and oval Precinct C and its sole petroglyph (23).   262

Figure 7.16. A simple face and a doglike zoomorphic being related to the Domain of the Nonliving.   265

Figure 7.17. Petroglyph 3.   266

Figure 7.18. Petroglyph 4.   268

Figure 7.19. Ornithomorphic petroglyphs.   269

Figure 7.20. Petroglyphs 9, 10, 11, 12, and 13.   270

Figure 7.21. Petroglyph 17.   273

Figure 7.22. Petroglyph 18.   273

Figure 7.23. Petroglyph 19.   274

Figure 7.24. Petroglyph 21.   275

Figure 7.25. Petroglyph 22.   275

Figure 7.26. A dual and quadripartite structural model of the iconography and their respective domains.   277

Figure 7.27. A model of the spatial cosmic domains within the central Plaza A, Caguana.   279

Figure 7.28. An iconic image from Caguana.   281

Figure 8.1. A map of Puerto Rico situating the rock art sites discussed in the text.   286

Figure 8.2. A close-up of northern ledge pictographs from Chamber 2, Cueva de Mora, Comerío.   287

Figure 8.3. A ball park petroglyph, Caguana.   288

Figure 8.4. Anatropic imagery in Puerto Rican prehistoric pottery and rock art.   290

Figure 8.5. A proposed three-phase seriation of Puerto Rican petroglyphs.   292

Figure 8.6. A selection of beach rock petroglyphs from the site of Maisabel Playa.   293

Figure 8.7. River boulder petroglyphs, Río Caguitas.   294

Figure 8.8. A cave petroglyph of a "wrapped ancestor," Cueva del Indio   295

Figure 8.9. Group A beach rock petroglyphs from Maisabel Playa.   296

Figure 8.10. Stalagmite petroglyphs from Cueva de la Momia, Comerío.   303

Figure 8.11. The petroglyphic assemblage from the Pueblito Carmen river boulder.   304

Figure 8.12. A componential approach to the somatic components of anthropomorphic petroglyphs in Puerto Rico.   305

Figure 8.13. The beginnings of a generative grammar for Puerto Rican anthropomorphic petroglyph design.   306

Figure 8.14. Two versions of an El Bronce crowned anthropomorphic head.   309

Figure 8.15. Cross-media isomorphisms in Chican Ostionoid (Taíno) incised ceramics and petroglyphs.   311

Figure 8.16. The Cueva la Mora, Comerío, as cosmogram.   312

Figure 8.17. A planimetric map of all 12 chambers of la Mora cavern.   313

Figure 8.18. The peripheral "portal guardian" petroglyphs from Cueva la Mora.   314

Figure 8.19. The "wrapped ancestor" group from the northern ledge of Chamber 2, Cueva la Mora.   317

Figure 8.20. A selection of the northern ledge pictographs from Chamber 2, Cueva la Mora.   318

Figure 8.21. A group of "wrapped ancestors" from Chamber 2, Cueva la Mora.   319

Figure 8.22. The central "shamanic" male figure pictograph from the southern ceiling, Cueva la Mora.   320

Figure 8.23. A selection of the southern ceiling pictographs, Cueva la Mora.   321

Figure 8.24. The "living dead" and their ancestors.   322

Tables

Table 1.1. Frequency Distribution of Gross Types by Pilaster in the Analyzed Collection.   14

Table 1.2. Flake Subtypes by Collapsed Raw Materials in the Selected Subsample of Core-Flake Products for Each of the Lithostratigraphic Units.   15

Table 1.3. Core Types by Collapsed Raw Materials in the Different Lithostratigraphic Units of the Selected Subsample.   21

Table 1.4. Flake Type Frequencies by Reduction Protocol and Lithostratigraphic Unit in the Selected Subsample.   26

Table 2.1. Paso del Indio Site Radiocarbon Dates.   79

Table 3.1. Maisabel Coring Project Radiocarbon Dates.   102

Table 3.2. Sedimentation Rates and Inferred Landscape and Pond Conditions during Major Cultural Periods.   103

Table 3.3. Documented Prehistoric Sites in the Vicinity of Maisabel.   116

Table 4.1. Sources of Prehistoric Archaeobotanical and Zooarchaeological Assemblages from Puerto Rico and Vieques.   124

Table 4.2. Archaeobotanical and Zooarchaeological Assemblages from Commonwealth of Puerto Rico.   128

Table 4.3. Macrophytic Identifications from Archaeological Sites on Puerto Rico and Vieques.   132

Table 4.4. Ethnobotany of Plant Taxa from Puerto Rican Sites.   138

Table 4.5. Seed and Other Nonwood Plant Remains from Puerto Rico and Vieques.   142

Table 4.6. Wood Remains from Ceramic-Age Sites on Puerto Rico and Vieques. 145

Table 4.7. Zooarchaeological Identifications from Archaeological Sites on Puerto Rico and Vieques. 151

Table 4.8. Taxa Totals for Zooarchaeological Assemblages from Puerto Rico and Vieques. 176

Table 5.1. Isotope Data for Human Skeletal Samples from Paso del Indio and Maisabel in Puerto Rico. 192

Table 6.1. Chronological Model for Prehistoric Puerto Rico. 206

Table 6.2. Site Data. 212

Table 7.1. The Quadripartite Structure of the *Cemís* of Hispaniola. 252

Table 7.2. Precinct Measurements and Number of Associated Petroglyphs. 260

PREFACE

A book on the prehistory and ethnohistory of a modern geopolitical entity is artificial. It is unlikely that prehistoric occupants recognized the same boundaries and responded to the same political forces that operated in the formation of current nations, states, or cities. Yet archaeologists traditionally have produced such volumes, and they generally represent anchors for ongoing research in a region for years to come. A book on the prehistory of Puerto Rico may be especially contrived. How do we separate events and processes that occurred in the past on Puerto Rico from immediate neighbors, the wider Caribbean Basin, lowland South America, and, perhaps, Central America? We don't. To varying degrees, all of the chapters in this book at least address issues and in some cases draw on data from beyond the boundaries of Puerto Rico. As Irving Rouse observed long ago, often the passageways between islands were the logical units of analysis and loci of intense cultural activity (Rouse 1951).

The intensity and quality of archaeological research on Puerto Rico has skyrocketed over the past two decades. Compliance-driven cultural resource management investigations combined with ongoing academic studies have resulted in a body of data that may be unique in the Caribbean. Visits to the archives and site files of the State Historic Preservation Office and the Institute of Puerto Rican Culture, both located in San Juan, reveal thousands of survey and excavation reports and documented archaeological sites. In addition, graduate students and researchers from Puerto Rico and abroad have been keeping apace with innovative methods of analysis and theoretical perspectives.

Archaeologists actively addressing a broad range of topics were invited to prepare chapters for this book on the prehistory and ethnohistory of Puerto Rico. The book is not meant to supplant previous synthetic studies of the island. Rouse's two-volume survey will always be a crucial source of information (Rouse 1952a, 1952b). However, ideas about what happened in the past are constantly changing as theoretical frameworks change, methodological advances are developed, and new data are recognized and acquired.

These three domains of research have been progressing in tandem at a rapid pace in Puerto Rico. Others and I felt that it was time to take stock and to evaluate a range of issues and datasets currently positioned at center stage in the archaeology of the island. Most of the authors invited to contribute to this volume are known for their long-term involvement in Puerto Rican archaeology. Others are relatively new to the field but are actively conducting cutting-edge research. In total, this book provides a comprehensive overview of recent trends in the prehistoric archaeology of Puerto Rico. The substance of the volume offers a combination of new data, synthesis, and new insights on topics that are of fundamental importance in current Puerto Rican archaeology. And, issues that are crucial to Puerto Rico both reflect and illuminate similar concerns elsewhere in the West Indies, lowland South America, and Central America.

This book concentrates on issues and data of the ceramic age. Although researchers use different beginning dates for the ceramic age in Puerto Rico, it is generally agreed to be around 200 B.C. (Rouse 1992; Siegel 1991a). Early ceramic-age groups began colonizing the Caribbean islands by approximately 400–500 B.C. (Siegel 1991b). These people originated in the Orinoco Valley of Venezuela. As a group, the colonists are recognized by a distinctive material culture tradition, including thin-walled elaborately painted, incised, and modeled ceramic vessels and figurines and carved and ground shell, bone, stone, and coral objects (Roe 1989a; Rouse 1992). Similarities in material culture across sites and through time provide the basis for assigning the groups to a single series of Saladoid cultures, named after the Saladero type site excavated by Rouse and Cruxent (1963). A source of considerable debate is the nature and extent of interactions between the resident Archaic populations of the West Indies and the Saladoid colonists (Chanlatte Baik 1995; Siegel 1989a). Further, it has been suggested that some Archaic groups, especially on Hispaniola, may have developed pottery prior to or in connection with the arrival of the Saladoid colonists (Rouse 1992:90–92; Veloz Maggiolo et al. 1974). New information, some of which is explored in this book, indicates that Archaic people may have been managing and modifying the landscape more than what was traditionally recognized. Another book will be needed to explore the dynamics and complexity of the Archaic cultures of Puerto Rico.

The 16 or more centuries of ceramic-age occupations on Puerto Rico reveal dramatic shifts in how people related to one another, the environment, and the cosmos. The earliest Saladoid colonists, referred to as the Hacienda Grande complex (ca. 200 B.C.–A.D. 400), occupied large seemingly self-contained villages dispersed around the periphery of the island in coastal or near-coastal settings. All evidence indicates that these people were egalitarian horticulturalists, who brought to the West Indies a conception of the universe derived from Amazonian cosmology (Alegría 1986b; López-Baralt 1985; Roe 1982, 1997; Siegel 1997; Stevens-Arroyo 1988; Wilbert 1981, 1987). By late Saladoid times (Cuevas complex, ca. A.D. 400–600/700), groups began occupying mid to upper drainage locations. The trend toward settling the interior foothills and mountains continued during the post-Saladoid, or Ostionoid, occupations (Monserrate [ca. A.D. 600/700–900], Santa Elena [A.D. 900–1200], and Esperanza [A.D. 1200–1500] complexes). By approximately A.D. 700, formally designed ball courts and ceremonial plazas were included in the repertoire of village or settlement types constructed by the occupants of Puerto Rico (Alegría 1983; Siegel 1999). The idea for formally recognized ceremonial spaces was deeply rooted in the early Saladoid period, apparent in the structural organization of many early ceramic-age sites on Puerto Rico and the Lesser Antilles (Chanlatte Baik and Narganes Storde 1983; Rainey 1940; Rodríguez López 1991; Rouse 1974; Rouse and Morse 1999; Siegel 1996; Versteeg 1989).

During the Santa Elena period, there was a significant increase in the number and variety of sites documented for Puerto Rico, compared to earlier periods. This observation has generally been interpreted to be a product of demographic factors, although recently social and political considerations have been evaluated (Curet 1992a; Rodríguez López 1990; Siegel 2004). Demographic, social, and political factors have also been reviewed in the context of increasingly competitive and territorial chiefly polities, most notably during the Santa Elena and Esperanza periods (Siegel 2004). Culture change during the ceramic age of Puerto Rico has been investigated from a range of perspectives, broadly subsumed within the realms of subsistence, ecology, social and political organization, and cosmology. In one way or another, all of these realms are addressed in the current book.

The chapters in the volume are generally organized by scope of analysis. Studies of artifacts and individual sites are presented at the beginning and more general thematic overviews at the end. Reniel Rodríguez opens the book with his careful analysis of lithic distinctions between early and late ceramic-age groups as represented in the large stratified Paso del Indio site. Rodríguez addresses the venerable crab-shell "dichotomy" using a line of evidence heretofore not considered. Jeff Walker then examines the larger context of Paso del Indio, reviewing the excavation history and major classes of data collected from this large intensively occupied late Saladoid and Ostionoid village. A few kilometers to the north of Paso del Indio, situated on the Atlantic coast, is the Maisabel site. This site was the center of considerable research during the 1980s and early 1990s, resulting in numerous publications and theses, one of which was my dissertation (Siegel 1992). John Jones, Deborah Pearsall, Daniel Wagner, and I present results of a sediment coring project that we conducted in the environs of Maisabel and offer suggestions into Late Archaic and ceramic-age land-use history and cultivation practices. Susan deFrance and Lee Newsom provide an island-wide summary of subsistence research, from the respective disciplines of zooarchaeology and archaeobotany. Anne Stokes addresses dietary patterns during the ceramic age by examining carbon and nitrogen isotope ratios in a series of human skeletons. Her study was performed within the framework of biogeography and thus she evaluates skeletal remains from other sections of the Caribbean in addition to Puerto Rico.

Joshua Torres reviews changes in the social landscape of south-central Puerto Rico. Combining data generated from compliance-mandated investigations with academic research Torres traces settlement patterns from the early to late ceramic periods and constructs models of political and social organization for this region. José Oliver addresses political and ideological organization using settlement and iconographic data in Caguana and the surrounding landscape. Peter Roe reviews the current state of rock art studies on the island. Rock art is a particularly difficult medium to address beyond simple description. Roe presents a good balance between tight description and interpretation, offering an example of how explanatory research may proceed using rock art. Karen Anderson closes the book in her discussion of Taíno life during the century following Spanish colonization, thus marking the end of prehistory in Puerto Rico.

The title of the book, *Ancient Borinquen,* acknowledges the indigenous name for Puerto Rico. When the Spanish arrived, they observed that the Native American occupants called the island Borinquen (variously Boriquén, Boriquen, Buriquén, Borinquén, Burenquén) (Arrom 2000:131–145). Many of the early Spanish accounts refer to the Native Americans of Puerto Rico as *borinqueños.* Today, residents of the island frequently refer to *Borinquen* to evoke a link with the past and to assert a sense of independent identity.

This book came to fruition because of the hard work and support of many people and institutions. John Milner Associates provided infrastructural support and Margy Schoettle helped in matters of formatting. I thank the authors for sending me their chapters, working through various rewrites, and responding to numerous requests, comments, and questions. Finally, Rosa, Diana, and David put up with a lot during the process, when I spent many long evenings and weekends at the office and carried my laptop to piano and violin lessons, the dentist, and shopping.

ANCIENT BORINQUEN

I

The Crab-Shell Dichotomy Revisited
The Lithics Speak Out

Reniel Rodríguez Ramos

In the early 1930s, Froelich Rainey was sponsored to pursue excavations in Puerto Rico as part of the Caribbean Archaeology Program of the Peabody Museum of Yale University. As stated by the program director, Cornelius Osgood (1942:6–7), these excavations were made in an "attempt to improve the methodology of archaeology through intensive research in a particular area, as well as to resolve the Historic problems of the aboriginal populations of the West Indies." Following these objectives, Rainey conducted fieldwork at eight sites in Puerto Rico, along the coast and in the mountainous interior. As a result of this work, Rainey indicated that there was a generalized disruption in the cultural sequence of Puerto Rico; he consistently observed the presence of a layer dominated by crab claws in midden deposits, thus named the Crab culture, overlaid by a cultural stratum that evidenced the intensive exploitation of shells and other marine dietary elements, which he termed the Shell culture. He also noted that the ceramics belonging to the Crab culture were well fired, had hard paste, and their surfaces were painted. In contrast, pottery from the Shell culture was unpainted and coarse-tempered. Rainey concluded that these two cultures reflected two different migrations from South America. Furthermore, even though by that date there had not yet been any formal discovery of a preceramic component in Puerto Rico, he indicated that "The recent excavations have had no bearing on this Ciboney culture except to show that some of the traits by which it is characterized according to Harrington are found in the late, Shell Culture, deposits in Porto Rico" (Rainey 1940:180). The existence of these two cultures, which among other things presented contrasting protein bases, gave rise to the highly discussed crab-shell dichotomy.

A couple of years later, Irving Rouse arrived in Puerto Rico to continue the work initiated by Rainey as part of the Scientific Survey of Puerto Rico and the Virgin Islands. Rouse's (1940:49) initial impression of West Indian ceramics, based primarily on his typological analysis of materials from Puerto Rico and Haiti available at the Peabody Museum, was "that pottery-making in the West Indies had a multiple origin, from both North and South America, rather than a single origin from the latter continent." However, a decade later in his extensive publication of the results of his work on the island he presented a markedly different perspective (Rouse 1952a, 1952b). Based on the latter studies, Rouse concluded that there was a "continuum of ceramic modes" between the Crab and Shell culture pottery, suggesting that there was only one migration of pottery makers to the Antilles. Since then, Rouse's model has become the most widely used chrono-cultural framework in Caribbean archaeology. In the latest version of his model, Rouse (1992) indicated that there were two migrations to Puerto Rico: the Archaic peoples followed by the Saladoids. The Saladoids were divided into two subseries, the Huecan and the Cedrosan Saladoid; the Archaics as well as the Huecan Saladoid were quickly absorbed or pushed west to the Greater Antilles by the earliest Cedrosans (represented by the Hacienda Grande ceramic style), who then evolved in Puerto Rico into the Ostionoid series; this series presented two major subseries on the eastern and western halves of the island (Elenan and the Ostionan Ostionoid, respectively), which eventually developed into the Chican Ostionoid, the subseries that represents the remains of the Taínos.

There seems to be general agreement on two points: that Archaic cultures "contributed little to the subsequent peoples and cultures of the Greater Antilles" (Rouse and Alegría 1990:80) and that the Cedrosan Saladoid peoples represent the "ancestors of the Taínos" (e.g., Rouse 1992:37, 49). During the last three decades, with the upsurge of processual concerns concomitant with the generalized decrease in emphasis on chronology building, studies dealing with the ceramic age in Puerto Rico such as those on settlement patterns (Curet 1992a, 1992b; Torres 2001), sociopolitical organization (Curet 1992a; López 1975; Siegel 1992), religious development (Curet and Oliver 1998; Rouse 1982; Walker 1993), and dietary shifts (deFrance 1989; Keegan 1989a; Stokes 1998), among others, have commonly presumed the presence of a single cultural series operating on the island at any point in time. Following this argument, it has been proposed that intra-societal dynamics of Cedrosan populations led to increasing social complexity and shifts in material culture, resulting in the Ostionoid series and eventually culminating in the development of the Taíno culture that Columbus encountered upon his arrival to the islands. Thus, with a few notable exceptions (Alegría 1988; Chanlatte Baik and Narganes Storde 1983, 1990; Oliver 1999), most of the studies that have explored different aspects of the crab-shell dichotomy have focused on explaining the structural causes for the reported changes that resulted in the transformation from the Saladoid to the Ostionoid series, assuming the existence of a mono-cultural landscape on the island represented by the sole presence of Saladoid peoples. In cases where the existence of strong interactions between competing cultures during Period II has been mentioned as a cause for these changes (e.g., Rouse 1992; Siegel 1992), the antagonistic groups (e.g., La Hueca complex, Archaic groups) that have ignited such changes have been limited to a marginal function prior to their riddance, therefore not contributing important elements of their culture to the post-Saladoid cultural scenario of the island.

The cultural transformation from Saladoid to Ostionoid has been primarily documented on the basis of the supposed continuum of modes observed in ceramic production on the island. This use of ceramics as the primary analytical unit for establishing a cultural sequence for the ceramic age of Puerto Rico, as well as in the West Indies in general, has perhaps inadvertently resulted in a lack of systematic studies of other artifacts that might indicate the influence of other cultures or the operation of other processes of interaction. Because of this, material classes such as stone artifacts have usually taken the back seat in ceramic-age culture-historic studies, especially those related to the flaked lithic subsystem, based on the generalized notion that "The ceramic-age flaked-stone industry does not produce temporally-diagnostic artifacts" (Siegel 1992:111). The lack of emphasis on lithic studies is especially intriguing in issues such as the nature of the contact situation between the Archaic peoples and the earliest ceramic bearers, when one takes into consideration that their interaction (i.e., the demise or displacement of Archaic populations), has been traditionally addressed by the ubiquity of pottery rather than on methodically studied lithic sets, which was one of the types of material employed by the two.

In an effort to expand the baseline used to address the crab-shell dichotomy, I framed the present study within two main objectives. The first of these was to determine if there is a "continuum of modes" in the lithic industries between the Saladoid and the Ostionoid series in Puerto Rico. The primary database consists of 2,907 lithic artifacts obtained from the Paso del Indio site (PDI) (see Walker, this volume). PDI offers a unique opportunity to address long-term changes in lithic patterning. In particular, I have investigated changes in raw material selection and tool production through time.

Sealed contexts within the site correspond to the major subseries identified for the ceramic age of the island, thus data on inter-assemblage variability from PDI can be used to examine the degree of continuity in lithic production. An underlying hypothesis is the conservative nature of lithic technology, whose processual templates seem to be more stable than those observed in the production of other items of material culture such as ceramics, as has been repeatedly argued for the West Indies (Bartone and Crock 1993; Crock and Bartone 1998; Rodríguez Ramos 1999a, 2001a; Walker 1980a, 1997a) and for other contexts as well (e.g., Parry and Kelly 1987; Ranere 1975).

A comparison of the data on inter-assemblage variability generated by the technological analysis of the lithics from this site, coupled with that reported from other sites on the island will serve as the basis for the second objective, which will encompass a revisit to Rainey's notion of the persistence of Archaic elements in the post-Crab culture of Puerto Rico. In the present work I will argue that this crab-shell dichotomy is at least partly the result of the influence of Archaic populations in the articulation of a post-Saladoid cultural scenario of the island. Thus, I consider that this dichotomy, instead of being simply a consequence of the development of Cedrosan populations, is to a great extent the result of the ways in which the interactions between the Archaic cultures and the ceramics bearers were framed.

The Crab-Shell Dichotomy in Context: The Case of Puerto Rico

Puerto Rico presents the longest continuous span of occupation in the Antilles. Until the 1970s, the earliest occupations of the island were dated to approximately uncalibrated 2275 ± 85 B.P. (Veloz Maggiolo et al. 1975). The general view of these "preceramic" societies considered them to have been fairly stationary following their initial occupation of Puerto Rico to their demise by the earliest ceramic-bearing migrants, which was estimated then to be around the time of Christ. The static character of these societies was partly based on the information provided in the Spanish chronicles regarding the cave dwellers that inhabited Cabo San Antonio in western Cuba and the Guacayarima peninsula in southwestern Haiti (Dávila 1985b; Keegan 1989b, 1992). Conventional wisdom regarding preceramic peoples of Puerto Rico was that they lived in caves, were exclusively hunters and gatherers, were marginal to agro-ceramic societies when coexisting in proximate areas, and that they did not evolve much through time. The chronicles were cited to support the notion that the Archaic peoples were pushed by the Saladoid colonists into isolated refugia of Cuba and Haiti (e.g., Rouse and Allaire

1978). Notions of Archaic social arrangements were also based on analogies with hunting and gathering groups from continental contexts, which basically consisted of nuclear units who tended to shift their residential locations periodically in response to the movement of their protein sources or due to the differential food availability resulting from seasonal changes (Pantel 1996).

The dates for and ideas about the initial entrance of these pre-Arawak peoples to the island have changed markedly during the past two decades. The Angostura and Maruca sites have extended the initial peopling of Puerto Rico to at least 4000 B.C., approximately three millennia earlier than previously thought. Further, our notions about preceramic adaptive strategies have been revised. For instance, Angostura and Maruca are open-air habitation sites, in contrast to the assumption that caves were the primary residential locations. The assumption that Archaic societies were "largely circumscribed to island boundaries" (Oliver 1992a:25) has been questioned by the documentation of interisland circulation of stone raw materials (Febles 1998, citing Jeff Walker [personal communication]; Rodríguez Ramos 2001b).

Assumptions about Archaic subsistence patterns have been challenged recently. Plants recovered from Archaic deposits may have originated in Belize (Newsom 1993). Siegel et al. (this volume) obtained evidence for considerable forest clearing in the vicinity of the Maisabel site as early as uncalibrated 3820 ± 70 B.P. Horticultural practices in the area from which these groups supposedly originated were already established at the time of their migration, indicating their capacity of manipulating the natural landscape (Siegel et al., this volume; Wilson et al. 1998).

There is evidence for considerable subsistence variability on the island during the Archaic period; in some places terrestrial resources were emphasized, especially in interior rockshelter sites (e.g., Cueva Tembladera [Martínez 1994]; Cueva Gemelos [Dávila 1981]; Sabana Seca [Sanders et al. 2001]), while in coastal open-air contexts littoral and/or maritime resources were favored (e.g., Maruca [Rodríguez López 1997]; Cayo Cofresí [Figueroa 1991; Veloz Maggiolo et al. 1975]). A great part of the protein obtained from the sea was generated by the collection of mollusks from both coastal and open-sea sources. Some of these sites also present the development of techniques for increasing the effectiveness of fish capture, such as the use of tended facilities (i.e., cast nests), as has been indirectly observed by the recovery of netweights both in Puerto Rico (Ayes Suárez 1988, 1989), as well as in other sites in the Greater Antilles (e.g., El Curro in the Dominican Republic [Ortega and Guerrero 1981]; Caimanes III in Cuba [Navarrete 1989]). Other fish-capture techniques were based on the use of spears tipped by shell and bone points. The fact that Archaic peoples had well-established techniques for protein capture from terrestrial and riverine sources indicates that they had mastered one of the greatest challenges of living in an insular setting lacking macrofauna: consistent meat obtainment in inland contexts.

Identifying Archaic cultural complexes has become a debatable topic on the island. Some scholars have indicated that the dissimilarities in artifact assemblages are the result of culturally distinct traditions (i.e., Rouse 1992), while others have argued that the observed variability might indicate functional rather than cultural differences (Lundberg 1980). Pantel (1988, 1991) suggested that differences might relate to variability in raw material sources instead of distinct stone-working traditions. There is also no clear evidence for separating Lithic from Archaic assemblages, as most preceramic contexts bear indications of pecking and grinding techniques from the earliest phases of occupation. Despite these classificatory dilemmas, pre-Saladoid assemblages of Puerto Rico present a fairly conservative flaked-stone repertoire, comprised of freehand flakes used in a wide variety of ways, mostly in activities such as scraping, cutting, or drilling. Flakes were produced using cherts as well as river-rolled metavolcanics. Assemblages indicate that flake production occurred in most cases offsite, rather than transporting raw materials to the places where tools were needed and used (Rodríguez Ramos 2002). There is no evidence for the manufacture of bifacially flaked-stone tools; flaking operations have been mostly limited to core reduction for producing flakes as final products. Based on his analysis of the Cerrillos assemblages, Pantel (1991:160) observed that flakes from preceramic sites are characterized by "the absence of cortex, a perpendicular striking platform and [the] absence of secondary flaking." Therefore, flake production tends to ascribe to parallel freehand flaking formats over cores with single or inverted platforms. By following this reduction format, pre-Arawak knappers were able to extract some of the massive flakes that have commonly been ascribed to chopping functions. These flakes show little, if any, secondary modification, primarily limited to abrupt unifacial retouch along the tool margins to create incurbate or denticulate working edges.

In addition to chipped stone, Archaic assemblages on the island contain ground stone tools (e.g., Angostura [Moscoso et al. 1999]; Cayo Cofresí [Veloz Maggiolo et al. 1975]). Among the most chrono-diagnostic ground tools are conical manos. These tools present a three-pointed morphology and a high degree of polishing on most of their body surfaces; they are tantalizingly similar to some simple *cemís* found in the Dominican Republic. Preceramic sites have also presented small mortars in the form of discoid stones with a central depression on one of their faces. From the Angostura site, Ayes Suárez (Moscoso et al. 1999) recovered a necked, bifacially ground specimen identified by him as a hoe. Preceramic contexts in Puerto Rico present a remarkable array of use-modified stones, of which the most distinctive is the edge grinder. These handheld pieces tend to present faceted ablations in one or two opposing margins and battering wear at their extremes. Their faceted margins usually have a convex outline thus leading some to suggest their use in a rocking motion (Walker 1985a). In addition to edge grinders, Archaic sites have also produced a large array of grain and, probably, tuber-processing tools, such as manos and end-battered stones. Also, these sites often contain discoid nutting stones with a pitted depression in the center of one or both of their faces, coupled with peripheral battering around its margins. Archaic contexts on the island have also produced evidence of bead production, varying from undecorated forms to complexly shaped examples. Other artifacts from preceramic sites are made from shell, especially celts, gouges, plates, and picks. These have been found in a range of settings, from the interior of the island to coastal locations, and present reduction protocols that to a great degree overlap with those evidenced among the lithic materials.

The pre-Saladoid cultural landscape of Puerto Rico and the Greater Antilles has become even more complex with the discovery of sites that present ceramic evidence in association with otherwise Archaic assemblages similar to those previously described. These sites have been named in different ways, depending on whether the classificatory focus resides either on their cultural or structural aspects. For instance, those that have named them on the basis of a cultural terminology have termed them "Caimitoide" (Veloz Maggiolo 1993) and "Cedeñoide" (Zucchi 1984), while others who have focused on societal aspects have labeled them "protocerámico," "apropiadores ceramistas," or "protoagrícolas," among other terms (see Brito and Pereira 2001; Ulloa and Valcárcel 2002). In the Dominican Republic, the earliest documented evidence of this process was found at Honduras del Oeste (Rímoli and Nadal 1980), el Caimito and Musiepedro sites (Veloz Maggiolo 1993). Initially, when ceramic sherds were found at those sites, Veloz Maggiolo and Ortega (1973) indicated they were either intrusive material or were imported from another location. However, a year later Veloz Maggiolo et al. (1974) revisited this evidence and concluded that the presence of ceramics seemed to indicate a group that presented a transitional lifeway from hunting and gathering to a formative organization.

When confronted with this evidence, Rouse (1992) indicated that the presence of ceramics in these sites was the result of diffusion of ceramic production from the Saladoid invaders who were occupying the islands around that time. However, recent evidence of the wide distribution of these sites both in Cuba and the Dominican Republic, their technological and decorative differences to Saladoid wares, and their early dates have provided clear indications that pottery production was not necessarily a product of transculturation with Cedrosan populations, but rather of either independent invention and/or the presence of cultural contacts or direct migrations from other circum-Caribbean areas, as had been postulated by Kozlowski as early as 1975. This evidence has prompted some scholars to revisit the postulations of Zucchi (1984) and Evans and Meggers (1976), who indicate the possibility of migrations directly from northwestern South America and the Intermediate area, a feasible possibility according to Callahan's (1995) model of potential navigational routes to the Caribbean. Evidence of people producing ceramics prior to when they are supposed to and in otherwise Archaic contexts, has also been documented in northern Puerto Rico (Martínez 1994; Moscoso et al. 1999; Rodríguez and Ayes Suárez 1997).

There is general agreement that around 500 B.C. the first waves of Saladoid migrants began their movement into the Antilles. This migration of Saladoid peoples throughout the islands has been a widely analyzed topic in Caribbean archaeology. However, the nature of the interaction that took place between the preceramic inhabitants of Puerto Rico and the ceramic-making newcomers is a very complex topic that has scarcely been addressed. One of the few arguments about this contact situation was provided by Rouse and Alegría (1990), on the basis of the data generated from Alegría's excavations on the neighboring sites of María de La Cruz and Hacienda Grande. The scenario confronted by these scholars was one in which two adjacent sites presented Archaic and Cedrosan Saladoid occupations that overlapped in time for more than a century, based on the earliest dates gathered from Hacienda Grande (uncalibrated 2060 ± 80 B.P.; Beta 9970) and the latest date associated with the Archaic component of María de la Cruz (uncalibrated 1910 ± 100 B.P., Y-1235) (Rouse and Alegría 1990; Rouse and Allaire 1978). On the basis of the presence of several edge grinders at Hacienda Grande, these authors concluded that there had been a process of acculturation of the Archaic societies into the Hacienda Grande culture. For these authors the drastic absorption of Archaic societies into the ceramic-age groups resulted in a general lack of integration of their elements in the Saladoid bearing society. This rapid and one-way process has since then been recognized as the major form of interaction registered between these groups in the island. The generalized notion of this contact situation is best reflected by Oliver (1992a:38), who indicates that "Wherever they settled, the Cedrosan Saladoid peoples interacted with and eventually replaced the resident Archaic peoples and their cultures. It appears that the rate of population replacement must have been fairly quick in the Antilles, except for the larger islands of Cuba and Hispaniola."

Others such as Chanlatte Baik and Narganes Storde (1990) have proposed alternative scenarios for this interaction on the island, which have not received enough attention by Caribbeanist researchers. These authors suggest that Archaic peoples, when being in contact with La Hueca (see below) and then Cedrosan populations, adopted from them the ability to produce ceramics and the techniques for agriculture, which permitted them to continue their path toward higher social complexity. These developed Archaic populations then became pivotal for the further configuration of the late prehispanic setting of the island.

The issue of the ways in which these contact situations were framed is not the only aspect that has been the subject of intense debate. Even though there was general agreement that the one and only subseries represented in all the Antilles during this early ceramic period was the Cedrosan Saladoid, the discovery of the La Hueca site in 1979 led Chanlatte Baik and Narganes Storde (1980, 1983) to argue for the presence of another migration of ceramic-bearing societies that predated the Cedrosans. These peoples, who for Chanlatte Baik and Narganes Storde were more closely related to Andean societies than to those from the Orinocan corridor, were called by them the "Huecoides" (from La Hueca [LH]). In contrast to the earliest Cedrosan peoples, who presented the use of white over red painting as the most widely applied decorative element on inverted bell-shaped vessels, the LH wares presented a lack of painting, while ceramics were adorned basically by the use of plastic decoration of which the most diagnostic variety was the application of zone-incised crosshatching (ZIC), in some cases filled with white or pink paint. In addition to the differences in ceramics, the LH peoples presented distinctive dietary orientations (Narganes Storde 1985) as well as lapidary iconography that had never been found in any other ceramic complex on the island. According to Rouse (1992, 1999), the LH manifestation represents a subseries that was an offshoot of the Cedrosan Saladoid, separating from them in the northern Lesser Antilles. Roe (1999) argued that the existence of these LH peoples was short-lived, as they were raided by the Cedrosans who captured their women and eliminated their men, thus explaining why ZIC wares have been found in Hacienda Grande components on the island.

Based on a comparative analysis that I conducted on the lithics from these two early ceramic components, I concur with Chanlatte Baik's view, and concluded that their lithic production behaviors indicated the presence of mutually distinct traditions of stone working (Rodríguez Ramos 1999a, 2001a). Tools that are distinctive of these LH peoples, which have never been found in any Cedrosan context up to this point, include the channeled stone, the LH adze, and the edge-ground biface. I also documented the application of flake extraction procedures employing a centripetal flaking format, which produced discoid cores and flakes with converging dorsal scar patterns, similar to the recurrent Levallois technique defined in other contexts (Boëda 1993). These people were also more dependent on freehand flaking strategies for flake extraction, some of which were based on a parallel flaking approach, presenting a secondary emphasis in bipolar reduction. This contrasted with the Cedrosan knapping procedures, which were almost exclusively dominated by the application of multidirectional freehand flaking in a continuum with the bipolar technique as the main reduction approach, applied almost invariably over fine-grained materials. This reduction continuum, which was originally documented by Walker (1980a, 1980b) in St. Kitts, has also been observed in other Cedrosan Saladoid contexts of the island as well (Rodríguez Ramos 2001a; Walker 1985a). In addition to the freehand bipolar continuum, the most diagnostic lithic artifact found in Cedrosan components of the island has been the plano-convex adze. This tool type is often associated with burials, suggesting that it may have had ritual value (Roe 1985a).

Regardless of the debates concerning this early ceramic context on the island, there is a generalized acceptance that around A.D. 600 there were marked changes in its cultural landscape, which resulted in the development of the Ostionoid series, Rouse's term for what Rainey identified as the Shell culture. In fact, the changes that were observed when compared to the Cedrosan Saladoid manifestations of the island prompted Rouse to consider these post-Saladoid cultural manifestations within a new series, while others such as Alegría (1988) and Rainey (1940) indicated that what they interpreted as abrupt changes were the result of the migration of another group of Arawak people from South America. Others like Chanlatte Baik and Narganes Storde (1990) have argued that these changes reflect the development of Archaic populations on the island and the result of their interactions with the LH and the Cedrosan peoples. For them, the different manifestations within this series in the island were the result of the distinct ways in which these relationships were configured in different areas.

In contrast, for Rouse (1986, 1992) the development of the Ostionoid series resulted from the gradual evolution of Cedrosan Saladoid society. He understands that Rainey saw dramatic changes in the ceramic repertoire because he focused on decorated sherds, thus not contemplating the gradual nature of the changes between these two series, which were separated by a period when plain pottery was dominant. Furthermore, he understands that the changes in diet observed by Rainey that comprised a shift from a terrestrial diet based mainly on crabs to a marine diet primarily based on shells, were simply the result of the seasonal runs of crabs that tended to skew the composition of the dietary remains in midden deposits.

The fact that there were marked changes between these two series in the island has promoted a great deal of investigations, trying to explain these shifts from different perspectives. For instance, Carbone (1980) indicated that the transformations observed in post-Saladoid contexts were the result of drastic climatic changes. However, this notion has been disfavored because of the temporally disparate rate of cultural change observed across the Antilles (i.e., Curet 2003). Others such as Keegan (1989a), based primarily on bone isotope data, indicated that the changes observed in diet reflected an expansion in "diet breadth," in which the increasing scarcity of terrestrial protein sources concomitant with an increasingly high protein demand, made necessary the exploitation of other biotic sources. Relying also on bone isotope data, Stokes (1998:196) presented contrasting results with those from Keegan, as she indicated that "It appears that both Saladoid and Ostionoid populations in Puerto Rico were relying heavily on terrestrial resources." Another explanation provided from the zooarchaeological perspective (deFrance 1989) was that the observed dietary changes responded to the gradual decimation of the crab communities of the island, which demanded the exploitation of other food sources for sustaining the necessary protein provision for a growing human population. Based on data from St. Kitts, Goodwin (1979:473) indicated that the major variable for these changes was a demographic explosion that "triggered intensification in resource use." Others have looked at these changes from a sociopolitical standpoint, indicating that the observed changes were partly the result of "institutionalized stratification" that repercuted in the overall post-Saladoid scenario (Curet 2003:13; see also Siegel 1992 and Torres 2001 for alternative approaches to this issue).

Regardless of the different approaches for explaining the reasons for the changes resulting in the post-Saladoid cultural scenario of the island, there is general consensus that the major cultural manifestation configured after the end of the Cedrosan Saladoid subseries in Puerto Rico resulted eventually in the development of Taíno society. Interestingly enough, besides Chanlatte Baik and Narganes Storde (1990) and Oliver (1999), no other major work that has dealt with different aspects of the crab-shell dichotomy or with the reasons for the development of the Ostionoid series has considered the possibility of Archaic societies operating on the island as an important agent in that process. As was stated earlier, one of the main reasons for the lack of exploration of this possibility has been the scarcity of systematically studied data sets to deal with this issue. In the following section I will outline the nature of the sample that served as our basis to explore this possibility as well as the analytical framework that was used in its analysis.

Nature of the Sample

The present study considers the production of utilitarian stone items at Paso del Indio (PDI). This site is adequate for addressing the issue at hand for several reasons. First of all, it contains a representation of the latest phases of occupation of the Cedrosan Saladoid (Cuevas style) overlaid by materials that date to the Early Ostiones period (also commonly named as "transitional," e.g., Oliver 2001; Rouse 1992; Siegel 1992), thus offering an opportunity to deal with this period from a diachronic perspective. Also, by comparing these materials at a single location, one is able to eliminate differential availability of raw materials as a source for artifactual variation since the same local material sources were equally accessible for all the peoples that occupied this valley through time. Finally, this site was chosen because of the high lithic quantity and representativeness of lithics at a single site, thus providing a unique opportunity to look at long-term trends from a site-level scale, which up to this point has never been done on the island.

Based on the evidence generated thus far, the occupational history of the site is contained within seven major lithostratigraphic units (LU), which were used to define each of the assemblages (for a complete list of the radiocarbon assays from this site refer to Walker, this volume). The first of these (LU-I) developed around 4120 ± 60 B.P. (Beta 77165; charcoal), comprising its Early Archaic component. Around 1920 ± 80 B.P. (Beta 87611; charcoal), there was a Late Archaic deposit that overlaid the earliest occupation of the site by more than a meter of sediment (LU-II). Then, between 1550 ± 60 B.P. (Beta 87610; charcoal) and 1350 ± 70 B.P. (Beta 77164; charcoal), the site presented its Cedrosan occupation associated with the Cuevas style (LU-III). Following the Cuevas occupation of the site, a stratum that contained ceramic wares that presented both Cedrosan and Ostionan elements was identified (LU-IV) (the so-called transitional, Elvis Babilonia and Miguel Rodríguez, personal communication 2001). Then, a date of around 1210 ± 70 B.P. (Beta 77185; charcoal) is the earliest assay associated with the Elenan Ostionoid component of the site, which spans two lithostratigraphic units (LU-V and VI), extending up to 640 ± 60 B.P. (Beta 77177; charcoal). The last lithostratigraphic unit corresponds to the Chican Ostionoid subseries (LU-VII).

The excavation of the site was spatially segmented on the basis of six pilasters, namely Pilasters 6-North, 6-South, 7, 8-North, 8-South, and 8-Intermediate (for more information regarding fieldwork at PDI see Walker, this volume; García et al. 1995). The selection of artifacts that composed the analyzed lithic collection adhered to the general sampling protocols defined for the project in general, which included all of those recovered from ten recovery units (five from Pilaster 6-North, three from Pilaster 7, and two from Pilaster 8-South) as well as the ones collected from features defined in the field (Table 1.1). I considered only those artifacts with known stratigraphic provenience or elevation, with the exception of nine items recovered on the surface, which were included in the present analysis due to their relative typological absence in the sample.

Due to the fact that the LU-III and IV contained a markedly lower concentration of lithic artifacts in the sample than the overlying layers, I decided to include the materials retrieved from all the excavated units that corresponded to those two lithostratigraphic units (III and IV). This was also done for the primary purpose of obtaining a better panorama of the transitional period that I wish to explore in the present work. This same procedure was applied to formal artifacts that were not represented in enough quantities in the general sample, which included celts, beads, *cemís,* netweights, stone collar fragments, and other singular artifact types. In order to address the issue of flint management through time, I also included all of the artifacts made from this material recovered from definite contexts in the site.

In the mitigation of the site, recovery methods varied; some artifacts were collected during monitoring, others were unearthed employing manual excavations and sieved using 6.4 mm meshes, others were collected from the surface, while the rest were obtained from the coarse portion of flotation samples. This obviously had implications for the constitution of the assemblages in different parts of the site and thus prompted me to reconsider the sampling scope, especially that related to the analysis of the flaked materials. Because of the higher sampling rigor that is needed to address patterning in core-flake reduction protocols, I selected a subsample for analysis from this lithic subsystem, based on the materials recovered exclusively from the selected units from Pilasters 6 and 7. I framed most of the analysis of the core-flake reduction portion of this collection on the basis of this selected subsample. Table 1.2 shows the composition and provenience of the flakes and cores selected for analysis. The format for flake and core analysis was immensely nurtured by the insights of Jeff Walker and Stan Ahler, whom I thank for their comments.

The present analysis followed standard lithic classification procedures for the initial separation of the materials into three general categories: flaked, use-modified, and pecked and ground materials. As expected, many artifacts crosscut these categories as these are not necessarily mutually exclusive since

Table 1.1. Frequency Distribution of Gross Types by Pilaster in the Analyzed Collection.

Gross Type	Total		Pilaster												
			6N		6S		7		8N		8I		8S		Other	
	n	%	n	%	n	%	n	%	n	%	n	%	n	%	n	%
Flakes	2036	70.0	1489	73.1	135	6.6	377	18.5	2	.1	32	1.6	1	.04	-	-
Cores	184	6.3	100	54.3	31	16.8	51	27.7	-	-	2	1.0	-	-	-	-
Celt/Adze	63	2.2	33	52.4	13	20.6	10	15.9	-	-	5	11.6	-	-	2	3.2
O. Formal[a]	169	5.8	97	57.4	40	23.7	28	16.6	2	1.2	2	1.2	-	-	-	-
Use Mod.[b]	455	15.7	300	65.9	86	18.9	52	11.4	4	.9	11	2.4	2	.4	-	-
Total	2907	100.0	2019	69.5	305	10.5	518	17.8	8	.3	52	1.8	3	.1	2	.08

[a] Other formal ground artifacts, such as *cemis*, bends, and stone collars.
[b] Use modified (e.g., hammerstones and edge-ground cobbles).

Table 1.2. Flake Subtypes by Collapsed Raw Materials in the Selected Subsample of Core-Flake Products for Each of the Lithostratigraphic Units.

Type	Collapsed Raw Material	Statistical	Lithostratigraphic Unit					Total
			III	IV	V	VI	VII	
Complete-freehand	Flint	Count	4		3	4		11
		% within COLRM[a]	36.4%		27.3%	36.4%		100.0%
	River metavolcanic	Count	2	5	43	279	56	385
		% within COLRM	.5%	1.3%	11.2%	72.5%	14.5%	100.0%
	River sedimentary	Count				1		1
		% within COLRM				100.0%		100.0%
	Other imported	Count	2					2
		% within COLRM	100.0%					100.0%
	Angular limestone	Count			1	2	1	4
		% within COLRM			25.0%	50.0%	25.0%	100.0%
Complete-bipolar	Flint	Count	23		3	1		27

Continued on the next page

Table 1.2 Continued

Type	Collapsed Raw Material	Statistical	Lithostratigraphic Unit					Total
			III	IV	V	VI	VII	
	River metavolcanic	% within COLRM	85.2%		11.1%	3.7%		100.0%
		Count	1	1	13	83	12	110
		% within COLRM	.9%	.9%	11.8%	75.5%	10.9%	100.0%
	River sedimentary	Count			1	1		2
		% within COLRM			50.0%	50.0%		100.0%
	Other imported	Count	1					1
		% within COLRM	100.0%					100.0%
	Angular limestone	Count			2			2
		% within COLRM			100.0%			100.0%
Complete-indeterminate	River metavolcanic	Count				3	1	4
		% within COLRM				75.0%	25.0%	100.0%
Orientable flake fragments	Indeterminate	Count	1					1
		% within COLRM	100.0%					100.0%

			4		3	5	1	13
	Flint	Count	4		3	5	1	13
		% within COLRM	30.8%		23.1%	38.5%	7.7%	100.0%
	River metavolcanic	Count		1	8	58	7	74
		% within COLRM		1.4%	10.8%	78.4%	9.5%	100.0%
	River sedimentary	Count				1		1
		% within COLRM				100.0%		100.0%
	Other imported	Count				1		1
		% within COLRM				100.0%		100.0%
Undifferentiated flake fragments	Flint	Count	2			2	1	5
		% within COLRM	40.0%			40.0%	20.0%	100.0%
	River metavolcanic	Count			10	54	7	71
		% within COLRM			14.1%	76.1%	9.9%	100.0%
	Other imported	Count				2		2
		% within COLRM				100.0%		100.0%
Radially split flakes	River metavolcanic	Count				3		3
		% within COLRM				100.0%		100.0%

Continued on the next page

Table 1.2 Continued

Type	Collapsed Raw Material	Statistical	Lithostratigraphic Unit					Total
			III	IV	V	VI	VII	
	Angular limestone	Count	1					1
		% within COLRM	100.0%					100.0%
Shatter	Indeterminate	Count	1					1
		% within COLRM	100.0%					100.0%
	Flint	Count	11	1	4	7	1	24
		% within COLRM	45.8%	4.2%	16.7%	29.2%	4.2%	100.0%
	River metavolcanic	Count	14	4	45	286	40	389
		% within COLRM	3.6%	1.0%	11.6%	73.5%	10.3%	100.0%
	River sedimenary	Count			1	4		5
		% within COLRM			20.0%	80.0%		100.0%
	Other imported	Count	4	1	2			7
		% within COLRM	57.1%	14.3%	28.6%			100.0%

[a]Collapsed Raw Material.

any combination of reduction techniques can be present in a single item. Therefore, I classified tools in either of these based on the last reduction technique applied during their manufacture. That is, if a celt preform was manufactured by bifacial thinning but in later stages was pecked and then ground, it was classed as a ground artifact.

The Lithics from Paso del Indio

Flaked Materials

As is the case in most West Indian assemblages, the overwhelming majority of the analyzed lithic materials consisted of the products of the core-flake reduction subsystem, being comprised basically of flakes, shatter, and cores. The discussion regarding these materials will be framed on a general core-flake reduction flowchart (Figure 1.1), which will be used to diagram the different reduction protocols and their sequence. This diagram is based on a linear reduction model in which the reductive and dynamic nature of lithic related behaviors is an integral assumption, as has been discussed previously by Collins (1975) and Shafer (1973), among many others, and applied to West Indian collections by Walker (1980a, 1997a).

Most of the core-flake products of this site were obtained from its ceramic-bearing components. The preceramic deposits (LU-I and II) revealed little evidence of flake production; a single flake core was unearthed from the earliest cultural deposit of the site (LU-I) and one flake was collected from LU-II. The core from LU-I was made from flint and consists of a thick flake or nodule segment that presents four discontiguous flake removals parallelly struck from its ventral portion (IIA-1). In this particular case it is not clear if the objective piece was a bipolarly split nodule segment of a thick freehand flake, as no diagnostic ventral features were observed because flakes were detached from both its bulbar and distal portions. The flake negatives are rather small, measuring around 3 cm in maximum dimension, and are wedge-shaped with feather terminations. LU-II presented a single basalt freehand flake. This flake presented a flat striking platform modified by trimming, as well as a feathered termination. It was most likely extracted from a single platform core (IIA-1), as reflected by its flat platform and parallel dorsal scar pattern. This flake showed scraping wear in one of its margins as was observed at a 4x magnification level with an Optivisor.

In LU-III, which contains the Cuevas component of the site, the flaked lithic repertoire was quite similar to others described on the island. First of all, there was a marked emphasis on flint obtainment for flake production as observed in the raw material distributions of both flakes and shatter (Table

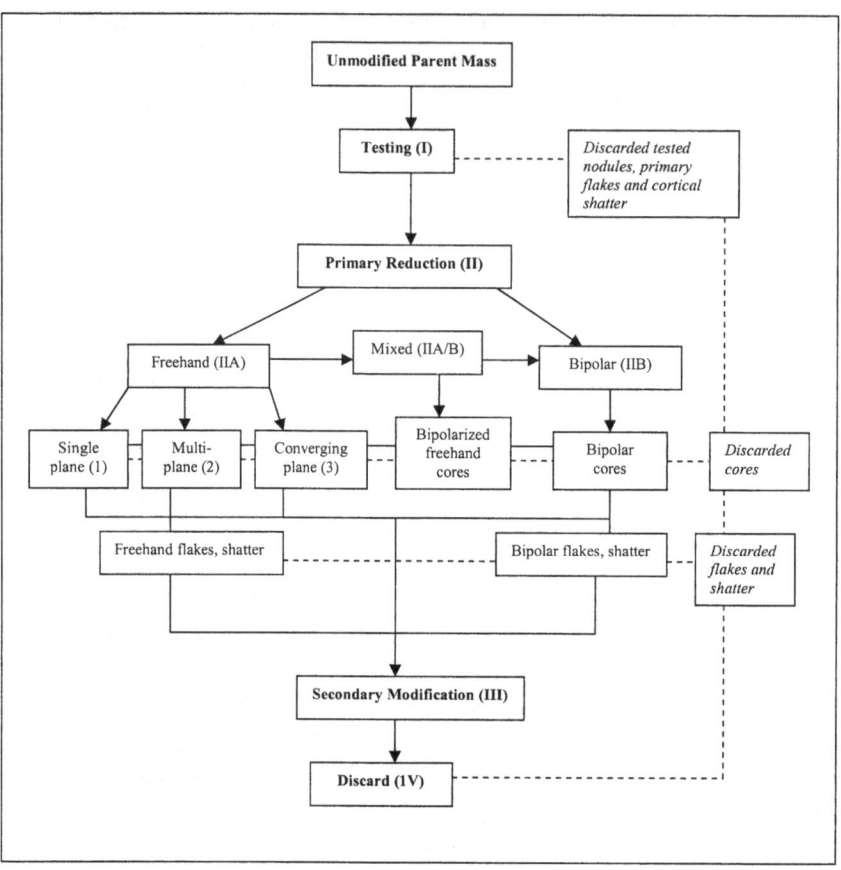

Figure 1.1. General core-flake lineal reduction model.

1.2) as well as cores (Table 1.3). In this component around 67 percent (16 cores and 44 flakes and shatter pieces) of the products of flaking consisted of different varieties of flints, most of which seem to proceed from Flinty Bay in Antigua, as was indicated by a macroscopic comparison with materials that I recently collected from that source. These flints were imported in nodular form as is evidenced by the high incidence of nodule segments, primary flakes, and cortex-bearing shatter recovered from this lithostratigraphic unit. This component also contains evidence of other fine-grained cherts similar to those identified by Walker et al. (2001) in the northwestern part of the island (San Sebastian Formation). This emphasis on the import of raw material in nodular form to Cedrosan contexts is a common element in both Hacienda Grande and Cuevas sites in Puerto Rico (Knippenberg 1999; Rodríguez Ramos 2001a, 2002).

Table 13. Core Types by Collapsed Raw Materials in the Different Lithostratigraphic Units of the Selected Subsample.

Core type	Collapsed Raw Material	Statistical	Lithostratigraphic Unit					Total
			III	V	VI	VII		
Tested piece	Metavolcanics	Count	-	-	2	1		3
		% within COLRM[a]			66.7%	33.3%		100.0%
Crystal core[b]	Mined calcite	Count	-	1	1	1		3
		% within COLRM		33.3%	33.3%	33.3%		100.0%
Single platform	Metavolcanics	Count	-	5	13	3		21
		% within COLRM		23.8%	61.9%	14.3%		100.0%
Inverted platform	Metavolcanics	Count	-	-	3	1		4
		% within COLRM			75.0%	25.0%		100.0%
Bidirectional	Metavolcanics	Count	-	-	2	-		2
		% within COLRM			100.0%			100.0%
Multidirectional	Metavolcanics	Count	1	2	8	1		12
		% within COLRM	8.3%	16.7%	66.7%	8.3%		100.0%

Continued on the next page

Table 1.3 *Continued*

Core type	Collapsed Raw Material	Statistical	Lithostratigraphic Unit					Total
			III	V	VI	VII		
Centripetal	Flint	Count	-	1	1	-		2
		% within COLRM	-	50.0%	50.0%	-		100.0%
	Flint	Count	-	-	1	-		1
		% within COLRM	-	-	100.0%	-		100.0%
Flake core[c]	Metavolcanics	Count	-	-	1	-		1
		% within COLRM	-	-	100.0%	-		100.0%
Bipolar	Metavolcanics	Count	-	1	4	3		8
		% within COLRM	-	12.5%	50.0%	37.5%		100.0%
	Flint	Count	5	-	4	-		9
		% within COLRM	55.6%	-	44.4%	-		100.0%
Exhausted bipolar	Metavolcanics	Count	-	-	2	1		3
		% within COLRM	-	-	66.7%	33.3%		100.0%
	Flint	Count	9	2	1	-		12
		% within COLRM	75.0%	16.7%	8.3%	-		100.0%

			1	-	1	-	2
	Unknown	% within COLRM	50.0%	-	50.0%	-	100.0%
Bipolarized flake[d]	Metavolcanics	Count	-	-	2	1	3
		% within COLRM	-	-	66.7%	33.3%	100.0%
	Flint	Count	2	-	1	-	3
		% within COLRM	66.7%	-	33.3%	-	100.0%

Note. No cores were recovered from this subsample of Lithostratigraphic Unit IV.

[a] Core Raw Material.

[b] Core derived from quartz or calcite. This material was frequently smashed, and the small crystal fragments may have been used as temper inclusions in potting production. In addition, crystal fragments may have served as bead blanks.

[c] Flake that served as a freehand core.

[d] Flake that was further reduced, bipolarly, for the purpose of producing microflakes.

Once these nodules were brought to the site, they were reduced in a continuum from the freehand to the bipolar technique, as has been documented in other Cedrosan contexts. Freehand flaking was done as an initial step, either to obtain flakes with suitable edge angles to be used in a wide variety of tasks or to create the necessary core setup for their further reduction by bipolar flaking. Freehand flaking was accomplished mostly by random flaking (IIA-2). Random flaking is defined as the opportunistic application of force to a core, taking advantage of suitable flaking conditions during nonsystematic knapping operations. This use of nonstandardized freehand flaking strategies resulted in a rather amorphous set of flakes, which commonly presented hinge and step terminations. Most of these did not have any platform preparation or any other technical procedure indicative of the search for standard flake morphologies, thus indicating that the overall form of the finished products played a secondary role in their production. This form of flaking resulted in multidirectional cores and flakes with randomly oriented dorsal scar patterns, unprepared striking platforms, and diverse morphologies. The cores that were randomly reduced were usually discarded because of the high incidence of step and hinged negative scars as well as by the generalized absence of suitable platform angles for flaking.

Most cores and freehand flakes were further reduced by bipolar flaking (IIB). In the Cuevas component there is a marked emphasis in bipolar flaking comprising around 76 percent (n = 28) of the flakes and 94 percent (n = 17) of the cores attributable to any of these two reduction techniques (Figure 1.2; Tables 1.3 and 1.4). Bipolar flaking was applied by resting the objective pieces over a rigid surface (i.e., anvil) and applying force over it at a 90 degree angle. According to the cortex content of bipolar flakes and the presence of nodular segments that were produced using this technique, it is evident that the bipolar application of force might have started early in the reduction sequence on some occasions. However, other pieces seemed to have been initially reduced using freehand flaking and were then bipolarly reduced (IIA/B). This transition from freehand to bipolar flaking was observed in cores and flakes that presented traits of both reduction strategies. Bipolar flakes and cores seem to have been continually reduced, resulting in some cores as small as 7 mm (Figure 1.3). Judging from the small sizes of the exhausted bipolar cores and their respective negative flake scars, the purpose of bipolar flaking seems to have been to produce microflakes, perhaps to be inserted in grater boards as initially argued by Walker (1980a) or in other types of composite tools. Unfortunately, the end products of this reduction operation were not retrieved from this site due to the coarse recovery methods employed.

Starting in LU-IV, the so-called transitional period, marked changes were

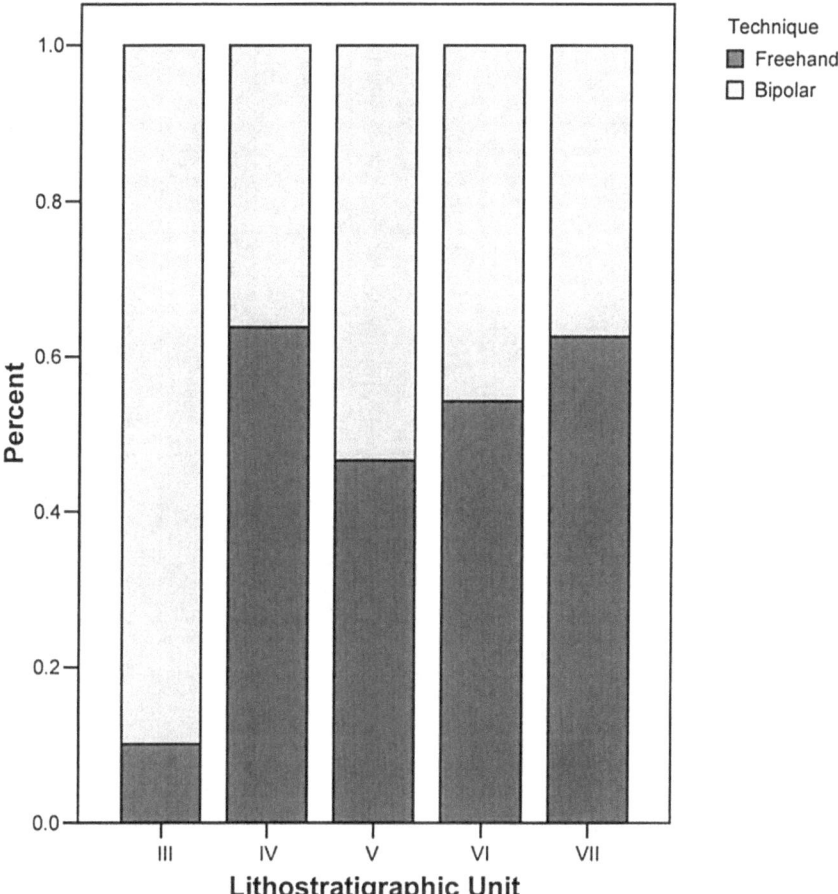

Figure 1.2. Percentages of flakes by technique of extraction in the selected subsample for each lithostratigraphic unit.

observed in core-flake reduction at PDI. One of these is a dramatic increase in the use of river rolled metavolcanics for flake production, in contrast to an emphasis in the import of flints that was observed in the Cuevas component (Figure 1.4). Flint was still imported to the site, but the emphasis seems to have changed from the import of nodules to the procurement of freehand flakes seemingly reduced at other locations. I did observe some evidence of the import of flint nodules for onsite reduction, but not all of these bore resemblance to the raw materials from which some of the flakes were produced, thus indicating that at least some of these were extracted at other locations and then brought to the site.

Table 1.4. Flake Type Frequencies by Reduction Protocol and Lithostratigraphic Unit in the Selected Subsample.

Reduction protocol	Type	Statistical	Lithostratigraphic unit						Total
			III	IV	V	VI	VII		
Core-flake reduction	Complete-freehand	Count	8	5	47	286	57		403
		% within SPECIFIC TYPE	2.0%	1.2%	11.7%	71.0%	14.1%		100.0%
		% within LU[a]	11.3%	38.5%	33.8%	35.9%	44.9%		35.1%
	Complete-bipolar	Count	25	1	19	85	12		142
		% within SPECIFIC TYPE	17.6%	.7%	13.4%	59.9%	8.5%		100.0%
		% within LU	35.2%	7.7%	13.7%	10.7%	9.4%		12.4%
	Complete-indeterminate	Count				3	1		4
		% within SPECIFIC TYPE				75.0%	25.0%		100.0%
		% within LU				.4%	.8%		.3%
	Orientable flake fragment[b]	Count	5	1	11	65	8		90
		% within SPECIFIC TYPE	5.6%	1.1%	12.2%	72.2%	8.9%		100.0%
		% within LU	7.0%	7.7%	7.9%	8.2%	6.3%		7.8%

		2	6	10	58	8	78
Undifferentiated flake fragment	Count	2		10	58	8	78
	% within SPECIFIC TYPE	2.6%		12.8%	74.4%	10.3%	100.0%
	% within LU	2.8%		7.2%	7.3%	6.3%	6.8%
Radially split flakes	Count	1			3		4
	% within SPECIFIC TYPE	25.0%			75.0%		100.0%
	% within LU	1.4%			.4%		.3%
Shatter	Count	30	6	52	297	41	426
	% within SPECIFIC TYPE	7.0%	1.4%	12.2%	69.7%	9.6%	100.0%
	% within LU	42.3%	46.2%	37.4%	37.3%	32.3%	37.1%
Total	Count	71	13	139	797	127	1147
	% within SPECIFIC TYPE	6.2%	1.1%	12.1%	69.5%	11.1%	100.0%
	% within LU	100.0%	100.0%	100.0%	100.0%	100.0%	100.0%
Crystal Extraction	Quartz or calcite shatter	Count	59	3	18	33	29	142
		% within SPECIFIC TYPE	41.5%	2.1%	12.7%	23.2%	20.4%	100.0%
		% within LU	100.0%	100.0%	100.0%	100.0%	100.0%	100.0%

Continued on the next page

Table 1.4 Continued

Reduction protocol	Type			Lithostratigraphic unit						
				III	IV	V	VI	VII	Total
	Total	Count		59	3	18	33	29	142
		% within SPECIFIC TYPE		41.5%	2.1%	12.7%	23.2%	20.4%	100.0%
		% within LU		100.0%	100.0%	100.0%	100.0%	100.0%	100.0%
Tool use related	Resharpening ground tool	Count		2			3		5
		% within SPECIFIC TYPE		40.0%			60.0%		100.0%
		% within LU		18.2%			13.0%		10.6%
	Fine-grained hammerstone flake	Count				2	1		3
		% within SPECIFIC TYPE				66.7%	33.3%		100.0%
		% within LU				28.6%	4.3%		6.4%
	Use flake ground tool	Count		3		3	10	2	18
		% within SPECIFIC TYPE		16.7%		16.7%	55.6%	11.1%	100.0%
		% within LU		27.3%		42.9%	43.5%	66.7%	38.3%
	Use flake pounding tool	Count		6	3	2	9	1	21
		% within SPECIFIC TYPE		28.6%	14.3%	9.5%	42.9%	4.8%	100.0%

		% within LU	54.5%	100.0%	28.6%	39.1%	33.3%	44.7%
	Total	Count	11	3	7	23	3	47
		% within SPECIFIC TYPE	23.4%	6.4%	14.9%	48.9%	6.4%	100.0%
		% within LU	100.0%	100.0%	100.0%	100.0%	100.0%	100.0%
Counts by lithostratigraphic unit			**141**	**19**	**164**	**853**	**159**	**1036**

[a] Lithostratigraphic unit.
[b] Either a proximal or distal end of a flake and with only one margin present.
[c] Flake removed from the bit of a celt or an adze in order to resharpen the tool.

Figure 1.3. Bipolar cores in the Cuevas component of the site (LU-III).

Freehand flaking strategies also shifted in this so-called transitional period from an emphasis on multidirectional flake removals to the systematic detachment of parallel flakes (IIA-1). Parallel flaking consists of the scaled removal of flakes from single (single platform cores) or opposed (inverted platform cores) flaking platforms along a single core axis. In this reduction format, the main focus is to detach flakes in sequence with the aim of delineating the trajectories of subsequent flake removals. Within this reduction approach I have identified several varieties, which seem to have been applied when reducing different types of raw materials, although some of these indeed overlapped across raw material categories. Within this reduction format I included single platform cores, inverted platform cores, and flake cores. Blade cores would also fall in this class if they were present.

One of the parallel flake extraction processes consisted of the reduction of river-rolled metavolcanics. I labeled this process of cobble reduction by parallel flaking the cobble slicing technique. It consists of the systematic detachment of flakes sequentially from one end of a cobble toward its other extreme. It usually starts with the selection of a suitable ovoid cobble, almost invariably a river-rolled volcanic or metamorphic rock, with one (single platform) or two (inverted platform) flat surfaces that serve as its natural striking plat-

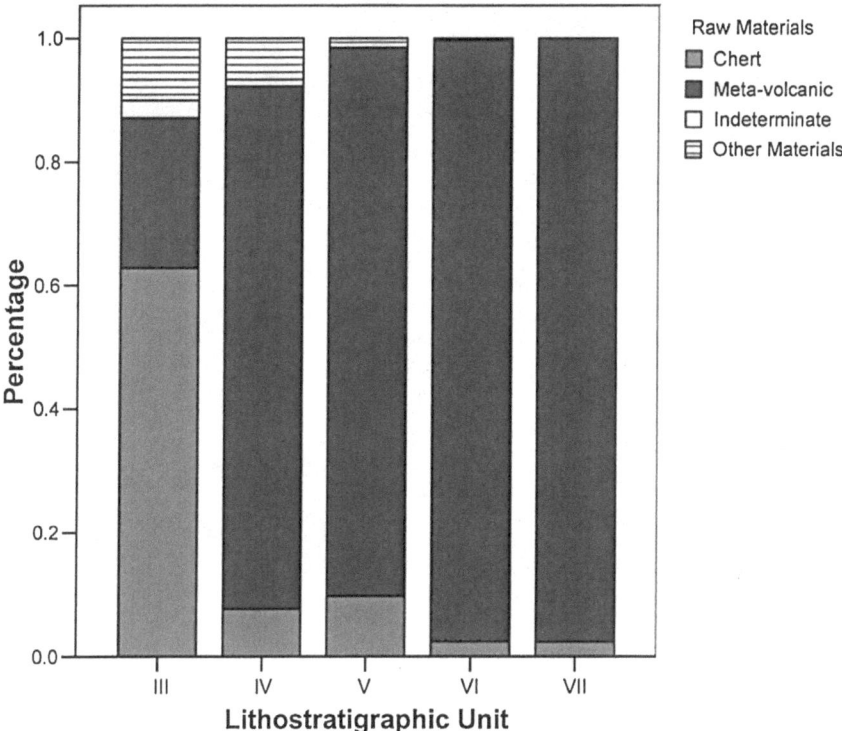

Figure 1.4. Percentages of collapsed raw materials by lithostratigraphic unit in the flake products related to core-flake reduction in the selected subsample.

forms. Some of these cobbles seem to have been broken along an internal fissile plane, and then used that natural flat facet as a striking platform. Then, a sequence of flakes is detached in slices along the perimeter of the thinner face of the core rather than on its longest axis. This explains why both single and inverted platform cores are always of lesser length than width. The first slice begins with the detachment of a primary flake from the ridge that marks the confluence of two adjacent cobble faces (corner struck flakes). In some cases in which there was a projecting thin section of the cobbles, it was removed by a single blow creating a rather massive, short, and thick primary flake with a convex platform. This initial flake extraction procedure creates the path for further flake removal across the face of the core.

When moving from the corners to the center of the cores, the flakes from the first removal sequence tend to contain cortical platforms with partially cortical dorsal surfaces, while the ones from the second sequence present cor-

Figure 1.5. Flakes made by the cobble slicing technique.

tical platforms and no dorsal cortex cover, with the exception of the flakes that are removed from the two ends of the cobble face, which preserve cortex in either one of their margins. The flakes that can be attributed to this process present a combination of features that include: cortical or naturally faceted flat platforms, in a small number of cases prepared by trimming; dorsal surfaces with flake scars that run parallel to their longitudinal axis; and a relatively high incidence of flakes with axially split bulbs of force (Figure 1.5). The cores that were used in their pristine state almost invariably presented an ovoid or cylindrical morphology while the ones that were first split and then reduced were usually conical in form (Figure 1.6).

In limited experimentation with similar material to that found in the present collection, I have noted that in order to extract some of the rather massive freehand flakes that were found among the analyzed materials it is necessary to support the cores on the ground or some other soft surface (i.e., wood) rather than stone. An advantage of this practice would have been the lessening of the cushioning effect (Shafer 1973) created when flaking hard materials handheld, thus minimizing hinge and step fracturing of the pieces. By resting the cores over a surface, the knappers also increased flaking efficiency by having more control over the flaking angle. In fact, this floor resting might explain why some of these massive freehand flakes presented a rather

Figure 1.6. Cores made by the cobble slicing technique.

straight profile and diffuse bulbs. In this case, I do not think this core support was actually done on a stone anvil, as distal crushing was not observed in the cores or the flakes.

As previously stated, there was a relatively common occurrence of flakes that presented axially split bulbs of force in the cobble slicing technique. The causes for this are not certain. However, Baena (1998:184) offers an explanation, attributing it mostly to the stress retention capacities of the reduced materials that are subjected to core-flake reduction (he understands that this is uncommon in bifacial thinning processes). Recently Ahler (personal communication 2002) has also noted the effect of raw materials on this axial splitting and has suggested that the use of hard and massive percussors as well as the application of overly forceful blows as probable causes for this to occur. In my limited tests, I have also observed other processes that might produce axially split flakes, which include the placement of the percussive blow too near the edge of the core, the inclination of the percussion plane excessively close to a 90 degree angle, and the presence of material flaws in the proximal or bulbar area. In some cases, this splitting did not extend to the end of the flakes, being confined only to their proximal portions. Finally, it is worth noting that in our experimental work I observed that this axial splitting process is totally imperceptible in the negative flake scars left on the cores.

Another form of parallel reduction was that reflected in nodular ovoid flint materials, in which the ventral surface of a bipolarly split nodule segment or a thick freehand flake served as the striking platform. As previously noted (Walker et al. 2002), the purpose of this reduction protocol seems to have been threefold. First of all, it served for economizing purposes, as it resulted in the creation of two potential cores with straight platforms from only one parent mass, and as a result the amount of flakes that could be obtained from a single nodule could be doubled. Also, the process of splitting a nodule into two halves served for creating two decorticated surfaces, in which the applied blows were much more predictable and, thus, efficient, because their trajectory nor their force was diffused by the pillow effect which is created by cortex on percussion platforms. Finally, another purpose could have been that the process of segmenting an ovoid nodule produces two potential conical segments, a morphology that eases flaking operations.

After splitting the nodule into two segments, flakes were extracted following a parallel flaking format similar to the one previously described for the cobble slicing technique. In this case, flakes tend to present flat decorticated platforms usually prepared by trimming, with parallel dorsal scar patterns and different degrees of cortex content depending on their reduction state (Figure 1.7). As was the case in the core slicing technique, flakes tend to be extracted by applying the blow in line with a ridge producing flakes with plano-convex cross sections. It is very important to note that although the mechanics of this flaking protocol operate in a similar fashion as a "true-blade technology" (Collins 1999; Kooyman 2000), its purpose was not necessarily aimed at producing flakes with blade proportions (length twice its width) but rather to extract flakes with straight and parallel durable edges. This mode of flaking, however, seemed to have as an effect an increase in overall length, as is shown in Figure 1.8, where complete freehand flakes seem to increase in size starting in LU-IV and continuing through the last occupational periods of the site. The fact that this flaking format was what contributed to this increase in size, rather than it being the result of the differing physical properties of the raw materials, is also indicated by the trends observed only on flint freehand flakes, as indicated in Figure 1.9.

The extraction of flakes following parallel flaking formats remained the primary mode of core-flake reduction from LU-IV (transitional period) to LU-VII (Chican Ostionoid occupation). In addition to parallel flaking protocols, post-Saladoid contexts in this site contained evidence of multidirectional flaking as a secondary flake extraction approach. This was represented both by the production of bidirectional and multidirectional cores, as well as by freehand flakes with randomly oriented dorsal scar patterns (IIA-3). These

Figure 1.7. Chert flakes made by parallel flaking.

seem to have been produced in the same fashion already described in the Cuevas component.

Another form of flaking, which was the most uncommon of the freehand flaking techniques evidenced in this site, followed a centripetal flaking format (IIA-2). This flaking technique was applied to fine-grained materials such as flint and silicified tuff, extracting flakes from the margins of the cores toward their center. This resulted in the production of discoid cores that presented converging flake patterns in opposite faces. Unfortunately, I did not observe any direct evidence of this flaking format on the flakes included in our sample, but according to my previous description of this knapping approach, evidenced in the LH materials from the La Hueca and Punta Candelero sites (Rodríguez Ramos 2001a), the flakes should present dorsal scar patterns that meet around the center of their dorsal portions, and a predominantly wedge-shaped morphology. The only one of these cores that was included in the selected subsample was unearthed from LU-VI (Elenan Ostionoid), but I also observed another one from LU-V (also Elenan Ostionoid).

Starting in LU-V (Elenan Ostionoid), there was an increase in freehand flakes that present retouch (III). Even though the percentage of flakes that present postextraction manipulations remains fairly small, there seems to be a slight increase in post-Saladoid contexts. The major form of retouch ob-

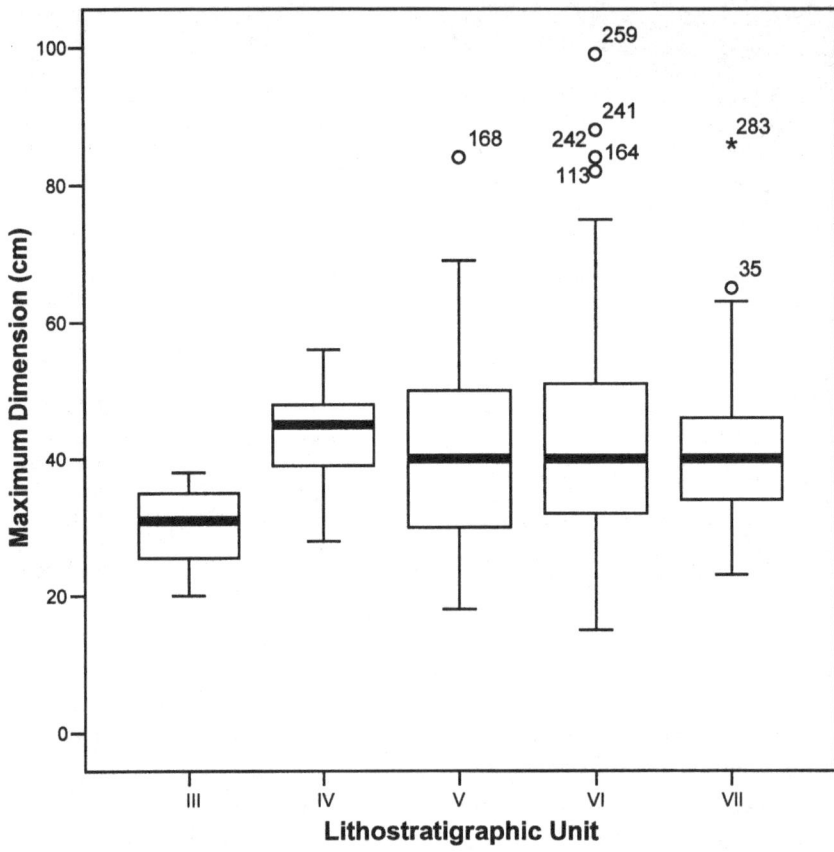

Figure 1.8. Maximum dimension of freehand flakes in the selected subsample by lithostratigraphic unit.

served in post-Saladoid lithics was the unifacial-abrupt. This retouch seems to have been applied using a small hammer to knap around one edge of the flakes. Some of the flakes presented a unifacial-abrupt continuous retouch applied to their distal ends to create rather flat working edges when seen in plan view, producing pieces that are similar to those described as end scrapers in other contexts. In other cases, this abrupt retouch was applied in a discontinuous fashion, leaving a space of the lateral margins of the flakes between each of the retouch blows, thus producing a serrated working edge. Other flakes were also retouched by the application of a confined abrupt blow with the purpose of isolating a concave working edge, probably to use them in a spoke-shaving action as has been described elsewhere. Finally, some of the

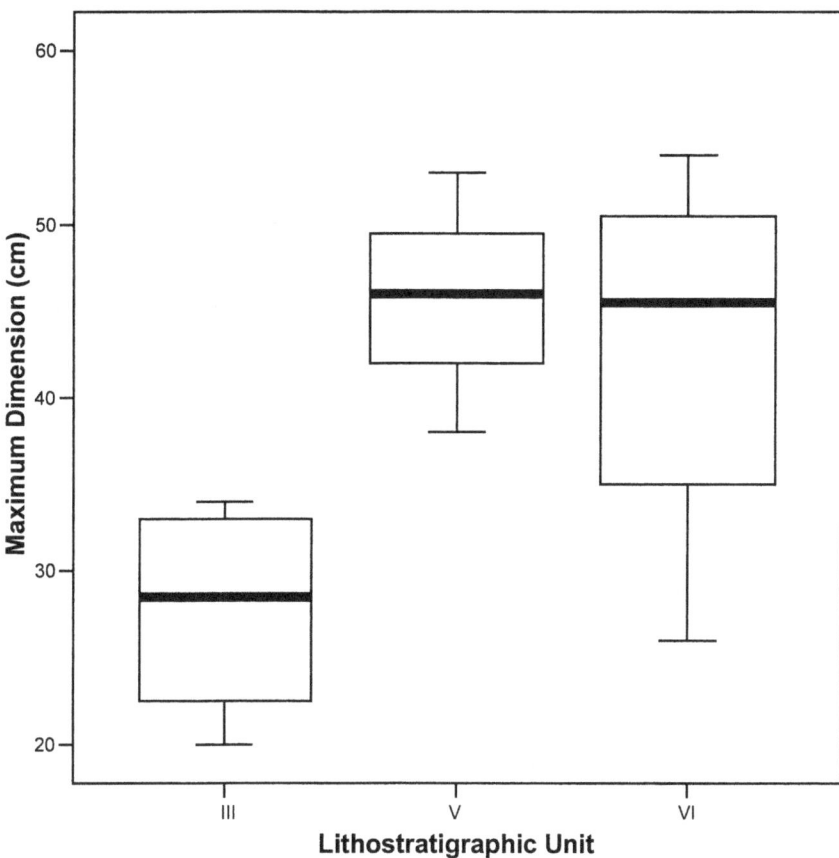

Figure 1.9. Maximum dimension of flint freehand flakes in the selected subsample.

flakes, usually those that were radially split or other flake fragments, presented retouch done with the purpose of isolating a pointed projection.

Starting in LU-IV (transitional period) I also observed a continuity in the application of bipolar flaking, which was documented earlier in the Cuevas materials (IIB). However, in contrast to the ways in which it was applied in the Cedrosan component of the site, the bipolar reduction observed in post-Saladoid contexts did not necessarily occur in a continuum with freehand flaking. In the case of post-Saladoid contexts, nodules were imported to the site and were then bipolarly reduced seemingly from their nodular state. In addition to the contrast in the forms in which bipolar flaking was applied, I also observed the adaptation of this mode of reduction for reducing metavolcanic cobbles in post-Saladoid contexts, which was not observed in the

Cuevas materials. Another interesting trend observed in post-Saladoid assemblages was that, in contrast to the Cuevas context where bipolar products were observed dispersed around the sampled area, there were clusters of bipolar flakes and cores, seemingly indicating discrete areas where this reduction approach was applied. For instance, in the Elenan Ostionoid (LU-V) component of the site, I identified a locus of clustered flakes, cores, and shatter from what seems to represent a single knapping episode in unit 12 of Pilaster 8-Intermediate, and another in unit 3 of Pilaster 7. This seems to indicate that bipolar flaking was becoming a more specific activity, corresponding to the increasing segmentation of social space into functionally discrete units evidenced during the later phases of occupation of the site.

Pecked and Ground Materials

Paso del Indio also has a good representation of celts and adzes, totaling 63 in the analyzed sample. The discussion of these implements will be based mostly on their morphological criteria, as the site did not present concrete evidence of their local reduction. The only type of evidence of their production came from surficial traces found in some of the polished specimens, which presented striations running parallel to the longitudinal axis of the tool, while around their distal ends these marks were parallel to their bits. The first evidence of the use of ground items was found in the earliest lithostratigraphic unit of the site (LU-I). There we found a highly weathered massive celt, measuring 190 mm in maximum length and weighing 1,430 g (Figure 1.10). This piece was made of fine-grained basalt and presented a tear-drop plan view, with curved-divergent margins gradually converging with their bit as well as a lenticular cross section. This tool is very similar in overall morphology to one of the types presented by Herrera Fritot (1964:125, Plate 1 [Artifact 3]). This specimen was reused after its uselife as a celt had expired, as one of its lateral margins was normalized by pecking, seemingly to be submitted to a use similar to that described for edge grinders (see below). The unearthing of this celt is very important as it is one of the earliest bifacial ground tools that has been identified on the island, besides the biface obtained by Ayes Suárez (Moscoso et al. 1999) in his excavations at the Angostura site.

The Cuevas component of this site presents the array of ground bifacial core tools that have been commonly associated with the Cedrosan subseries on the island. Among these is the plano-convex adze, initially termed "rectangular axe" by Rainey (1940), which, as previously mentioned, has been identified as a *fossil directeur* of Cedrosan occupations on the island. The two basalt plano-convex pieces unearthed from this site consisted of medial frag-

Figure 1.10. Archaic celt (LU-I).

ments that presented the characteristic parallel straight lateral margins, tapering gradually from the bit toward their proximal ends. One aspect that seems to be common to plano-convex adzes recovered from other sites is that they tend to be consistent, with a width approximately twice their thickness.

The Cedrosan component of the site presented not only plano-convex adzes but also biconvex celts, usually classed under the term "petaloid celts." The celts obtained from this component tended to be well ground, some presenting almost a polished surface. They have a biconvex cross section and a

Figure 1.11. Cross sections of celts and adzes (top row: left, plano-convex adze, right, biconvex celt; bottom row, both petaloid adzes).

bifacially beveled symmetrical bit. One interesting aspect that distinguished these celts from others obtained in later contexts was that they tended to present straighter lateral margins, presenting a distinct boundary with their rounded bit when seen in plan view. One of the celts found in this component was rather massive and displayed wear in the central portion of one of its faces, seemingly as a result of its use as an anvil.

There was an interesting trend in the production of ground bifaces for adze functions (wood shaving) starting in LU-IV. I observed the use of pieces with a petaloid outline used in adze functions, indicated by the offsetting of the tool's center plane to alter their bit angle, providing them with an asymmetrical cross section, in contrast to the plano-convex cross section of the plano-convex adzes (Figure 1.11). I termed these pieces petaloid adzes. This altering of the tool's center plane obviously had implications for the articulation of the haft element as well as for the orientation in which the tool was employed on the wooden object, which should be further explored in the future. These pieces presented a conical poll. Unfortunately, all of the recovered items ascribed to this type were fragmented, being devoid of their bits. There were four pieces assigned to this type, one of which was recovered from LU-IV, two from LU-V, and one from LU-VI.

A continuous production of the biconvex celts occurred from LU-IV onward. However, in contrast to the overall form of those recovered from the Cedrosan component of the site, their lateral margins tend to become more rounded and to present a less drastic boundary with their bits. Also, these pieces tend to have increasingly finer terminations, putting more emphasis in polishing as one moves upward in the lithostratigraphic sequence of this site. In fact, some of these celts were highly sophisticated in their manufacture and do not present any evidence of use, perhaps indicating their sumptuary value, as has been observed by Siegel (1992) in the Maisabel site.

A tool form that marks its appearance in the Elenan Ostionoid (two were found in LU-VI) component of the site is that identified as a "buril" by Herrera Fritot (1964). These pieces are basically cigar-shaped bifaces, usually presenting extremely well polished terminations. They tend to present a cross section that varies from ovoid to circular and convex-divergent lateral margins, presenting a slight tapering from their bits to their proximal ends. These pieces present a rather flat bit in plan view, which is symmetrically beveled, and their poll ends are of a conical form. These pieces do not show clear indications of being hafted so it is a possibility that they were handheld during use, perhaps in a chisel-like mode.

Other interesting artifacts recovered from the Ostionoid component were two necked specimens (Figure 1.12). These were roughly shaped items manufactured simply by pecking at the poll end. Their bits, however, did not present any evidence of further manufacture and, more interestingly, no evidence of usewear. These pieces tend to be rather large, measuring 113 cm in maximum length, and weighing around 440 g. One of these was found in LU-V, and the other in LU-VI.

Other Ground Tools

A stationary version of the channeled stone associated with the Elenan components of the site (LU-V) was recovered. I originally identified this tool type among the LH materials at La Hueca site. In PDI, the channeled stone was produced from a large fossiliferous limestone slab, presenting a linear incision with a round bottom that extended across one of its faces. This incision was around 10 mm in width, 6 mm in depth, and 42 cm long presenting similar dimensions to those obtained from the LH context of La Hueca site, which had an average width of 7 mm and depth of 5 mm (Rodríguez Ramos 2001a). These items contrast with the handheld specimens that are found in Cedrosan contexts, in which there is usually more than one orientation to their incisions. Babilonia (personal communication 2001) has identified these handheld specimens produced over ceramic body sherds among the ceramic repertoire of PDI.

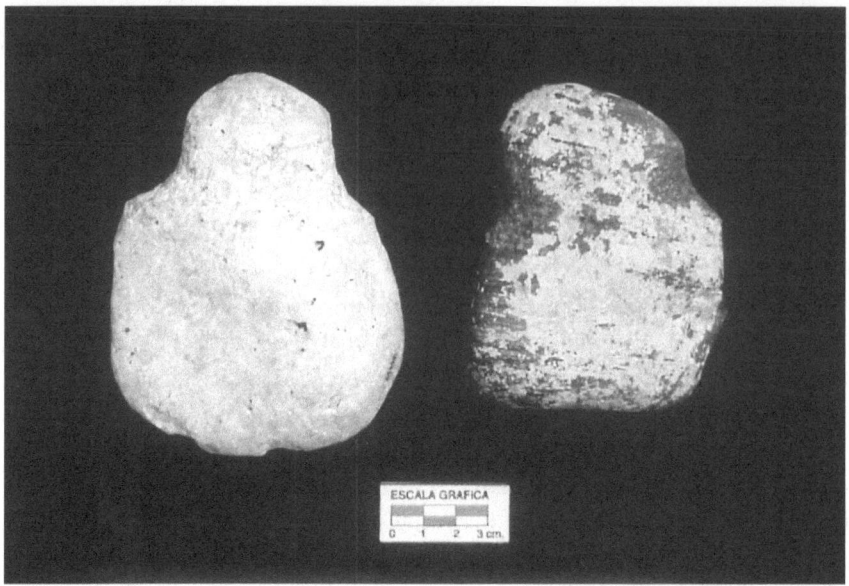

Figure 1.12. Necked specimens.

Another item found at this site that was produced by pecking was a rim fragment from a stone bowl. This piece was found in LU-V, and according to ceramic criteria it presents a convex-out orientation. It seems to have been globular in outline, similar to some of the predominant shapes observed in Ostionoid wares from the site. It did not show any form of decoration such as incisions or pecked inflections, but presented a great degree of grinding that provided it with its overall form. This piece was made of rhyolite.

A conical mano was unearthed from LU-VII. This piece was made from calcarenite and presents the classic three-pointed form, although its proximal end is not as conical as that observed in some of the Archaic specimens found on the island. It was produced by pecking but its incipient cones were not reduced enough by grinding, giving it a somewhat coarse texture. It presented a maximum length of 83 cm and weighed 188 g.

This site also presented evidence of the production of netsinkers, starting from LU-IV. Two different processes were used in the production of these items at PDI. The first of these consisted of the collection of flat discoid pebbles that were alternately flaked at two opposite extremes in order to isolate notched sections, which were then ground. Walker (1985b) has indicated that these pieces were anvil-rested during their production, but I have also produced them simply by handheld freehand flaking. The other process consisted of using thick freehand flakes, which were notched in a similar fashion to that previously described. In the case of PDI, the netweights that were produced from flakes seem to be restricted to the latest occupation of the site (LU-VII). In fact, around the southeastern portion of the site we observed a cluster of these artifacts associated with the Chican Ostionoid component.

Use-Modified Materials

Paso del Indio presented a vast array of pieces with modifications resulting strictly from use. Establishing formal types in these use-modified materials was difficult due to the suite of activities that might be represented in a single item. With the aid of Ahler and Walker, we devised a system called the "combo analysis." This system was designed to address the co-occurrence of different activities in multifunctional use-modified artifacts and reutilized formal tools, which might signal a suite of related functions. An advantage of this method is in determining recurrent patterns that might inform on artifact function that previous typologies did not, based strictly on macroscopic observations. It also provides a systematic vocabulary for expressing the different types of traces observed that may be used in future studies. Even though I will not go into detail on the results of this analysis, the following description of these artifacts will apply this terminology, which was originally articulated by Ahler for the present study. I want to state at this point that the following section will be very brief in comparison to the great degree of variability found among these use-modified materials from PDI, and I hope to expand on these in the future.

The most distinctive of the use-modified artifacts found at this site was the edge grinder, also known as pebble grinder (Alegría et al. 1955) or the edge-ground cobble (Ranere 1976; Rodríguez Ramos 2001a). As previously indicated, these pieces tend to present a faceted ablation on one or more of their margins, as well as percussion marks on their broadly convex edges or angular projections. Even though I consider that the faceted margins of these tools could have been strictly a result of use in pieces that presented an original flat surface, I also think that in some cases this ablation was produced by pecking and then finished either by use or by intentional grinding (Rodríguez Ramos 2001a). At this site, evidence of the use of this sort of tool was found in LU-I, LU-II, LU-IV, LU-V, and LU-VII. The earliest of these items was a highly weathered piece (with a similar weathering rind as that observed in the Archaic celt) that presented one faceted margin. Unfortunately, this piece was fragmented, thus impeding its description in greater detail. The next context with this tool form was the aceramic deposit from LU-II. The edge grinder found there presented one major faceted margin, with incipient cone marks on one of its marginal projections. It was made from a fine-grained tuff cobble. Starting in LU-IV, there was a resurgence of this tool type presenting similar attributes and comparable dimensions to those described earlier. One piece deviated from the norm, which presented a confined symmetrical concavity within one of its faces similar to those observed in nutting stones, in addition to a marginal facet and area with confined incipient cones indicative of pounding activities.

This site presented an interesting assortment of what seem to be grain and/or tuber processing tools. Among these were the end-pitted stones. These were usually of an elongated shape and presented pitted attrition in one or both of their extremes. These tools seem to have been used for pounding materials over flat surfaces, as evidenced by the straightness of their working surfaces. In fact, it was very hard to differentiate these from pecking tools associated with the production of ground items. However, the fact that these were mostly made of soft materials such as fossiliferous limestones leads me to infer that they were probably not used for tool manufacturing but rather to process softer substances. This tool was widely used in all of the ceramic occupations of the site. Another form of food-processing tool was a mano-like rock made mostly from basalt and andesite cobbles, which presented two main variations on the basis of the configuration of their used surfaces. One of these presented rounded working surfaces, similar to those identified for manos, while the others presented two major faceted areas that converged in a ridge located on this working surface, such as those identified as pestles by Ranere (1976). These differences in the morphology of their working surfaces resulted from specific uses; those described as pestles were "apparently held at an angle of approximately 60 degrees to the mortar and used for pounding or grinding without being rotated" as noted by Ranere (1976:114) in other contexts, while the manos that present the rounded working surface seem to have been used in a circular motion over the worked material. These tools were found exclusively starting from LU-V.

Among these use-modified materials I also observed some items identified as mortars. These consisted of handheld specimens that presented a broad concavity on one of their faces. These depressions, which varied in depth from very deep to rather shallow, expanded across most of their faces. Some of these pieces were of a discoid form, while others were ovoid in shape, morphologies that were also projected in the ground surface area. The earliest of these tools was found in LU-IV, being continually observed in LU-V and VI. According to Ahler (personal communication 2002), some of these pieces are similar to the trough metates found in the southwestern United States.

I also identified several metates. In contrast to the mortars previously described, these pieces were floor supported and were much larger and thicker. These did not present intentional modification to their natural morphology, as their major feature was a broad concavity in their central portions of one of their faces. All of the specimens found at this site were fragmented. In contrast to the previously described grain-processing tools, metates were observed in all the ceramic-bearing lithostratigraphic units from the site.

Another tool type identified in the present study was the edge-faceted handheld cobbles. These flat cobbles presented a faceted margin that either encircled the piece or was confined to specific sections of the tool, usually in curved areas. These were rather small, measuring an average of 6 mm in maximum length. This is another tool type that was found starting in LU-IV.

The rest of the use-modified materials included many of the common ones usually found in most archaeological excavations of the island, which include single- and double-sided anvils, hammerstones, nuttingstones, grinding slabs, and other subtypes of grinding tools. As previously mentioned, I hope to expand on these in the future.

Discussion of the Lithic Evidence

The lithic assemblages recovered from PDI have provided a good picture of diachronic changes in stone tool production that might be used for comparative purposes in the future. First, the uncovering of a ground petaloid celt dating to approximately 2580 B.C. (LU-I) is, along with the hoe identified at Angostura (Moscoso et al. 1999), the earliest direct evidence of the production of bifacial ground tools in the island. The Early Archaic context of PDI also contained other artifacts that have been considered characteristic of the earliest occupations of Puerto Rico such as the edge grinder, a single platform core, and a basalt freehand flake seemingly extracted from a single platform core. Although limited, the finding of the single platform core in the Archaic deposit of the site seems to be consonant with flake production patterns indicated by Pantel (1988) for the preceramic period of the island.

The Late Archaic component of this site (LU-II) poses the same problems that have been identified by Lundberg (1980) for establishing definite cultural affiliations in contexts devoid of pottery. The fact that this deposit contained an edge grinder is not by itself enough evidence for defining it as an Archaic context. However, the fact that the flake tool found in association with it was produced following reduction protocols that are not related to those characteristic of Cedrosan occupations might serve as further evidence for assigning these pieces to an Archaic component. If one were to accept that this is an Archaic context, then it would be one of the latest known dates for this component on the island (A.D. 90), corresponding well with the latest date from the Archaic deposit of María de la Cruz, which was A.D. 40 (Rouse and Alegría 1990; Rouse and Allaire 1978).

The Cedrosan artifactual repertoire of this site presents the classic trends observed for this component at other sites in Puerto Rico. First, it presents a marked emphasis in the import of fine-grained sedimentary rocks for the production of flakes and a core-flake organization that primarily showed a continuum from freehand to the bipolar techniques, which corresponds well with the knapping sequence observed by Walker (1980a) in a Cedrosan Saladoid component from St. Kitts, as well as with that observed in Puerto Rico for both Hacienda Grande (Rodríguez Ramos 2001a; Walker 1985a) and Cuevas components (Rodríguez Ramos 2001a). The application of the bipolar technique stands in sharp contrast to the emphasis on freehand flaking observed in earlier Archaic contexts, as has been already noted by Walker (1980a). In addition, freehand flaking in the Cedrosan component of this site is dominated by opportunistic flaking operations producing multidirectional cores and randomly shaped flakes, which also contrast markedly with the more patterned parallel flaking formats associated with Archaic contexts on the island. The Cuevan context of PDI also shows the traditional manufacture of the plano-convex adze, which seems to be present on the island since the earliest phases of this component, and its production appears to have extended well into its latest stages. All this corroborates my previous indication that Cedrosan Saladoid occupations of the island present very cohesive stone-working traditions that span across its two styles: Hacienda Grande and Cuevas (Rodríguez Ramos 2001a).

This Cedrosan lithic tradition, which appeared fairly stable through time, seems to change dramatically beginning in LU-IV (transitional period). For instance, flaking protocols begin to show greater emphasis on the procurement of local resources for stone working. These pieces were usually obtained from riverine sources that were brought back to the site for reduction. This emphasis on the procurement of local materials has been documented in Ostionan sites across the island (Futato 1995; Goodwin and Walker 1975; Pantel 1986; Rodríguez Ramos 1999b, 2001b; Walker 1985b, 1997a). However, raw materials such as chert continue to be imported in two major forms: Nodules were brought to the site to be reduced by bipolar flaking, arguably to produce the microchips that were to be inserted in cassava grater boards; the other form in which these pieces were brought to the site was as flakes that perhaps were reduced at other locations. In a limited number of cases, I also observed the import of flint nodules for their intrasite reduction into single-platform cores, although these cases seem to have been rather limited.

Once the raw material entered the site, freehand flaking strategies showed a retroduction to the emphasis on core-flake reduction operations focused primarily on following parallel flaking formats, as has been repeatedly observed in Archaic sites in Puerto Rico, the Dominican Republic, and Cuba (Kozlowski 1975; Pantel 1988, 1991; Veloz Maggiolo and Ortega 1973). This form of flaking surpassed raw material boundaries, as it was applied to flint as well as to basic rocks. This technological shift was not necessarily a response to the limitations imposed by the more frequently incorporated local raw materials, but was a strategy aimed at producing flakes with predetermined morphologies. Interestingly, none of the Cuevas components documented on the island have presented such a procedure for freehand flake reduction. In fact, the only ceramic-bearing contexts that have evidenced this parallel reduction format were those related to the LH component (Rodríguez Ramos 2001a). Although limited in occurrence, another interesting flaking format present in the post-Saladoid context of this site is centripetal flaking. This mode of flaking has never been found in any Cedrosan component in Puerto Rico or the Lesser Antilles. The only context that has presented such a core-flake reduction procedure has been the LH context of La Hueca and Punta Candelero sites (Rodríguez Ramos 2001a).

In addition to the marked changes in flaking protocols documented at PDI, I also noted shifts in other segments of the lithic spectrum. The planoconvex adze makes its dramatic disappearance at the end of the Saladoid, never to be found again in later cultural complexes of the island. The supposed function of this tool, which is related to wood shaving, is replaced in later contexts by the petaloid adze. The lack of recognition of this tool type in earlier studies was a result of looking at ground woodworking tools strictly in plan view, which usually led to their classification as petaloid celts. This pattern of offsetting the tool's center plane to create irregularly beveled bits has been previously observed among the LH materials of La Hueca and Punta Candelero in a tool form that I labeled the LH adze (Rodríguez Ramos 1999a, 2001a). As was the case in PDI, this tool form presents a petaloid outline and thus had also been previously misidentified as a petaloid celt.

Paso del Indio also presented the traditional finely shaped and polished petaloid celts made of varying sizes and raw materials, labeled initially as the "hacha Taína" by Coll y Toste (1897). In addition to these nicely finished celts, the Elenan Ostionoid component of the site presents the incorporation of the "buril," a tool form that has never been found among the Cedrosan materials of the island but has been identified previously in association with

Elenan Ostionoid deposits (Rodríguez Ramos 2001c). Also, this component presented necked specimens that are almost indistinguishable from some presented by Veloz Maggiolo (1993:61) recovered from the Banwary Trace site.

I also identified the production of several tool forms traditionally related to the Archaic period of the island in the post-Saladoid component of the site, while they have never been found in any Cedrosan context. Among these were stone bowls, handheld mortars, edge grinders and netweights, among others. The stone bowls have been one of the items identified in the Dominican Republic as part of the Casimiroid artifactual repertoire (Rouse 1992; Veloz Maggiolo 1993). The handheld mortars are almost indistinguishable from those presented by Rouse (1992:Figure 18a) among the diagnostic artifacts of the Coroso peoples of Puerto Rico, as well as by Harris (1976) among the Archaic materials from Trinidad. The edge grinders, in contrast to Pantel's (1986:49) argument that "the pebble grinder can be regarded now as a preceramic and early Hacienda Grande ceramic phase tool type," were present from the "transitional" phase of this site to the Chican Ostionoid component. I have also identified these items in what Oliver (2001) called a transitional horizon in the Salto Arriba site in Utuado (Rodríguez Ramos 2001d). Finally, the netsinker is another item that marks its retroduction from Archaic deposits (Ayes Suárez 1988, 1989; Ortega and Guerrero 1981:33). This tool type has been totally absent from any of the Cedrosan components of the island studied so far, while it has been a common tool type among the artifactual repertoire of post-Saladoid contexts, located both in inland and coastal settings (Futato 1995; Rodríguez Ramos 1999b, 1999c; Walker 1985b, 1997a; Weaver et al. 1995). These are rather important tools, as they are indicative of the use of tended facilities such as castnets, which dramatically increased fish capture by procurement event.

Even though this study has focused strictly on utilitarian materials, I have also observed some interesting trends in ideotechnic artifacts. For instance, in PDI is registered the continuous production of beads from the Cuevas to Chican Ostionoid component of the site. However, their manufacture seems to present some changes around LU-IV. For instance, starting in the "transitional" layer there was an incorporation of the biconical form in bead manufacture, which was not observed in the Cedrosan context of this site. I also noted the incorporation of incised decorative elements on these beads, as well as the manufacture of bi-incised beads, which presented the major longitudinal incision transversed by an additional incision located at one of its extremes. In addition, especially starting in LU-V, there was an explosion of ritual artifacts that were made from hard rocks. Interestingly, I did not observe evidence of hard-rock sculpting among the Cuevan materials from this site. Among the sculpted items, we observed the classic three-pointed *cemís*. Most of the *cemís* found at this site would fall in Fewkes's (1907:111) type 4 category, identified as "smooth specimens, destitute of head, face, legs, or incised superficial ornamentation." I made a distinction among these based primarily on their geometric configuration between those that were bidimensional vs. those that were three-dimensional. Bidimensional *cemís* tended to be made of flat, fossiliferous limestone cobbles, with pecking applied mostly to isolate their conoid projection. These were rather coarse, and in most cases were not finished by grinding. I have produced similar items in around two minutes of work, so little effort was put into their production. I also noted clear evidence of the production of three-dimensional trigonoliths that presented the classic bimodal distribution in size discussed by Walker (1993). Interestingly, the *cemís* that presented the highest degrees of elaboration were rather small, some of which were made from such materials as hematite, marble, calcarenite, and calcie-rudite, the famous *cemí*-stone from St. Martin (Crock 2000). It was among these small *cemís* that I found the only evidence of a decorated three-pointer, which presented the representation of two lateral eyes, nostrils, and a mouth. Another *cemí* representation found in the Elenan Ostionoid component of the site was a zoomorphic figurine made of fine-grained basalt, depicting a reptilian (boalike) image. Finally, two stone belt fragments were recovered from the Chican Ostionoid component, among the rare specimens obtained from systematic excavations on the island. These were roughly shaped, and both seem to have corresponded to undecorated shoulder panels. This rich ritual paraphernalia, evidenced in this site starting mostly from LU-V, seems to indicate a marked superstructural continuum from the Elenan to the Chican Ostionoid component, not only in the types of sumptuary artifacts but also in the techniques of hard rock sculpturing that were applied for their production, as has been noted by Sued Badillo (1979a).

Conclusions

As I have established in this study, there are marked discontinuities in the utilitarian lithic production protocols between the Saladoid and the Ostionoid series in Paso del Indio, evidenced in other sites of the island as well, which indicate the advent in the latter series of distinct stone-working traditions. These changes were not limited to specific segments of the lithic spectrum but were generalized across each of the major lithic subsystems. My interpretation of the implications of these shifts and their possible explanation will be addressed to the extent possible in the following paragraphs. The single site perspective limits the degree to which issues at the level of series or even subseries may be addressed. Nonetheless, I consider the trends observed in PDI's collection, coupled with the information generated at other sites on the island, to be adequate for making inferences that may be addressed in future studies.

Paso del Indio presents one of the latest dates gathered for a Cedrosan Saladoid component on the island, corroborating Siegel's (1992) suggestion that the Cuevas style extended to around A.D. 700, approximately 100 years later than previously estimated. The materials indicate that the lithic assemblages associated with this subseries remained stable through time, as they show marked continuities when compared to the lithics from both Hacienda Grande and Cuevas style deposits recovered from other sites (Knippenberg 1999; Rodríguez Ramos 1999a, 2001a; Walker 1985a). Therefore, the lithic evidence seems to corroborate the noted cultural continuum that exists between these two Cedrosan styles on the island, as has been suggested by Rouse (1992), among others. Its ground tool technology presents the manufacture of the plano-convex adze as its most diagnostic lithic constituent, while flake production procedures are amply dominated by the application of bipolar force over the objective pieces, which are most commonly fine-grained isotropic materials. The Cedrosan peoples of Puerto Rico were well connected to Lesser Antillean Cedrosan groups, evidenced by the import of flint nodules from islands like Antigua and, in earlier contexts, the production of bifacial ground tools of radiolarian limestone that originated in St. Martin (Knippenberg 1999; Rodríguez Ramos 1999a, 2001a).

The Cuevas context of PDI also indicates the possibility that weak interactions existed with other cultures such as the La Hueca peoples, evidenced by the edge-ground biface in the Cedrosan layer. This tool form was imported to the site in finished form, as no evidence of preforms or flake residues associated with its production were unearthed. Rather, the flakes that could be attributed to this artifact type presented ground dorsal portions, thus indicating that they were the product of recycling rather than production behaviors. The only evidence for the production of this lithic item has been found in LH contexts, suggesting that this tool form was obtained as a trade commodity from those peoples. If we accept this assumption, we would also have to concur that LH peoples coexisted in the island with Cedrosan populations to at least A.D. 670, as has been postulated by Chanlatte Baik and Narganes Storde (1990), which contrasts to their quick demise as argued by Roe (1999) and Rouse (1992).

According to the evidence from PDI, the lithic continuity that existed in the Cedrosan Saladoid subseries across its two styles was dramatically altered after A.D. 700. Around that time, flaked, use-modified, and ground utilitarian lithic materials began to be produced following different reduction templates from those observed in Saladoid societies for around a thousand years in Puerto Rico, indicating the advent of distinct traditions of stone working. Some of these changes include the greater emphasis on freehand flake production following parallel reduction formats, the incorporation of basic rocks among the raw materials that were used for core-flake reduction, the relative decay in the interaction spheres that promoted the import of raw materials from the Lesser Antilles concomitant with the intraisland emphasis on flint obtainment, the replacement of the plano-convex adze with the petaloid adze, the incidence of the stone bowl, the production of necked specimens, the presence of the conical mano, the reincorporation of the distinctive edge grinder that has never been found in Cuevas deposits, the presence of a vast array of grain and/or tuber processing tools, and the retroduction of the netweights. PDI also presents other artifact types in post-Saladoid contexts that have been commonly absent from Cedrosan deposits, as for instance the bone points. These post-Saladoid artifacts indicate a great degree of overlap with those described for Archaic cultures of the island. This leads me to suggest that the incorporation of Archaic traditions coincided with the advent of the Ostionoid series in the site, referring us back to Rainey's (1940) indication of the persistence of Archaic elements in the post-Crab cultural setting of the island and perhaps accounting for Rouse's (1940) original impression of the existence of two distinct cultures of different origins in the Antilles. This proposition obviously implies that the Archaic peoples would have coexisted with both the Cedrosan and La Hueca cultures, and thus were not quickly displaced as traditionally argued. On the basis of these assumptions, the cultural landscape of the island during this period would have been characterized by a multiethnic scenario rather than by a single major cultural manifestation spanning across all of its territory. But, if we accept this situation, where is the evidence for the persistence of Archaic cultures to such a late date on the island?

A possible explanation, consistent with Chanlatte Baik and Narganes Storde's (1990) arguments, could be that some of the aforementioned protoceramic or developed-Archaic peoples continued to evolve, eventually acquiring higher degrees of complexity. The capacity of evolution of these societies is obvious when one considers the evidence that is slowly but steadily accumulating, which, in addition to their knowledge of ceramic production, includes their probable practice of horticultural activities, their ability to build formal living units, and, in what I believe to be one of the most important aspects, their great knowledge of inland and coastal protein sources and their capture mechanics. This, in combination with the natural richness of Puerto Rico coupled with the accumulated experience of living on the islands for many generations, should have made them adept at dealing with the particular unforeseen events that might arise due to intense climatic perturbations, among other contingencies that are an integral part of living in an insular setting. According to the evidence gathered thus far from these cultures, their archaeological deposits should be constituted by artifactual repertoires that, if we were to eliminate the ceramic materials, would remain with a lithic and shell complex that would otherwise be considered Archaic, which is basically the case in many of the so-called Ostionoid contexts of the island. I believe this evidence might have not been observed thus far due to the generalized lack of detailed studies about these other elements of material culture, which are the ones most appropriate in dealing with this relative persistence of Archaic elements on the island. I also think it would be very short-minded to assume that the influence of Archaic societies was limited to the technomic level, and thus we should try to begin rethinking our interpretations of the superstructural elements of post-Saladoid societies by taking them into consideration. In stating this I am by no means pretending to imply that the development of these people explains the advent of the Ostionoid series, but only that their interactions with the Cedrosans and the LH might have been much more consequential, symmetrical, and long-lived than formerly suggested.

The main weakness in this argument is the scarcity of dates associated with non-Cedrosan wares that predate the end of the Saladoid series on the island. However, when we take into consideration the generalized scarcity of absolutely dated sites, coupled with the emphasis ascribed in fitting archaeological deposits to the existing chrono-cultural units already established in Rouse's model based strictly on ceramic-based criteria, it is obvious that such a possibility should not be discarded a priori. In fact, this could explain why some sites that have been identified within the Ostionoid series have dated earlier than what they are supposed to as was the case of LO-23 (Grossman et al. 1990:133), which was associated with the Elenan Ostionoid subseries disregarding the fact that one of its assays dated between A.D. 350 and A.D. 500 (1525 ± 75 B.P.; Gx-14042) and thus was discarded because it did not fit the established model. Additional examples of these "anomalous" dates have been reported for other Ostionoid sites such as La Iglesia de Maragüez (Weaver et al. 1995; A.D. 420 ± 90, Beta 45287), PO-38 (Weaver et al. 1992; A.D. 170 ± 30, Beta 33260), PO-39 (Weaver et al. 1992; A.D. 420 ± 90, Beta 45287), PO-23 (Krause 1989; A.D. 340 ± 70, Beta 23282), and Palmar de Animas (Siegel and Joseph 1993; 130 ± 70 B.C., Beta 64388), among others. Moreover, this might be one of the reasons for the chronological dilemma of Cerrillos (Pantel 1975), which supposedly presents Archaic lithic assemblages dating as recently as A.D. 625. This chronological issue is particularly important when we consider that the vast majority of the sites in Puerto Rico present ceramics identified within different styles of the Ostionoid series, which are the ones that might present the greatest degree of overlap with the wares that have been identified with the protoceramic cultures.

Another issue is what type of interaction occurred between these developed-Archaic people and the late Cedrosan Saladoids. This is a matter well beyond our explanatory capabilities, based on evidence currently available. When one considers the upheaval of sorts that marked the end of the Saladoid series, as is reflected in many respects beyond the lithic realm, one is inclined to consider that strong interactions were in effect as has been argued by Rouse (1992). However, in contrast to his arguments, which indicate that the Archaic societies that were antagonistic to the Cedrosans were settled in the Dominican Republic, I consider that the initial and longest-lived interaction between these people was registered in Puerto Rico, which might partly explain the reasons for the surgence of the Ostionoid series on the island.

Another aspect that becomes evident when analyzing the lithic evidence is the need to further evaluate the west-to-east influence corridor for dealing with some of the processes that have been observed on the island. For instance, most of the raw materials employed for the manufacture of utilitarian as well as sumptuary items originate from western sources, located both in areas such as Cerro Las Mesas (serpentinite and limonite) (Rodríguez Ramos 2001b), the Bermeja complex of the southwest of the island (Moya 1989; Pantel 1988; Rodríguez Ramos 2001b) and the San Sebastian formation of northwestern Puerto Rico (Rodríguez et al. 2003; Walker et al. 2002). Other western sources such as the Dominican Republic have been considered as well, in deposits associated with the La Hueca complex (Rodríguez Ramos 1999, 2001a) as well as to later ones dating to the Ostionoid series (Weaver et al. 1995). In fact, within this context it is intriguing why cultural manifestations such as the La Hueca complex present lithic reduction protocols such as the centripetal flaking format, which is similar to a recurrent Levallois technique, which are more similar in many respects to those that have been documented in Cuba (Febles 1988; Febles and Baena 1995; Martínez et al. 1993) rather than to those viewed in contexts of the Lesser Antilles. This, together with the import of raw materials that probably proceeded from extra-Antillean sources that are not necessarily related to the Orinoco–Lesser Antillean corridor, should make us reconsider the probability of a circum-Caribbean sphere of influence in the development of prehispanic cultures on the island, as well as the rest of the Greater Antilles, as has been indicated before (Evans and Meggers 1976; Veloz Maggiolo 1993; Zucchi 1984).

The present study is not intended to be the final word on many issues raised here or an all-encompassing solution to explain the pre-Columbian cultural scenario of the whole island. Our aim was to revisit assumptions that have guided our perceptions of the prehispanic panorama of Puerto Rico, with the purpose of indicating that it was much more complex than previously thought due to the culturally plural context in which it was developed. This complexity has not been considered in sufficient detail due to the emphasis in ascribing archaeological deposits to the established chrono-cultural entities based primarily, if not exclusively, on ceramic-based criteria. Evidently, the big question of who were the ancestors of the Taínos needs to be rethought in light of this scenario, where other cultures besides the Cedrosans might have been more prominent in the articulation of the late prehispanic cultural setting than was originally thought. It is within this context of constant chaos rather than normative progressions that our conceptions about the prehispanic landscape of the island should be framed in the future.

Acknowledgments

During the course of this work I was fortunate to receive the input and overall assistance of many friends and colleagues. First of all, I would like to thank Jeff Walker for his support during the Paso del Indio project and for always sharing his lithic vision with me. Also, the friends who worked with me in the PDI project and with whom I discussed many of the topics presented in this paper over and over ("labia A-B-C") merit my deepest gratitude. These are Elvis Babilonia, Rosa Martinez, Soraya Serra, and Boanerges Pérez. Carlos Solís, from Law-Caribe, provided much administrative support and contributed immensely by incorporating Stan Ahler in the course of my analysis, who was a great mentor during his stay in Puerto Rico. This paper received comments by my two colleagues from the Oficina Estatal de Conservación Histórica de Puerto Rico (PR SHPO), Miguel Bonini and Sharon Meléndez, and a detailed editorial review by Hugh Tosteson. I would also like to express my gratitude to other colleagues who took the time to read and comment on this paper that include José Oliver, Sebastian Knippenberg, Luis Chanlatte, Yvonne Narganes, William Keegan, Jaime Pagán, Samuel Wilson, Jorge Ulloa, Lourdes Dominguez, Marisol Rodríguez, Emily Lundberg, and Antonio Curet. Finally, I would like to thank Peter Siegel for his invitation to participate in this publication.

2

The Paso del Indio Site, Vega Baja, Puerto Rico
A Progress Report

Jeff Walker

The Paso del Indio site in Vega Baja is the deepest, best-stratified site found to date in Puerto Rico, and possibly in the Caribbean. Archaeological material was found to a depth of nearly 5 m below surface. Lighter colored flood-deposited sediments separate the darker occupational layers from each other. The light-colored flood sediments make all the darker intrusive features readily evident, so the site has a wealth of clearly distinguishable post molds, hearths, burials, and other features. The occupation layers begin with a small Archaic component, and after a hiatus begin again with a late Cedrosan Saladoid (Cuevas style) component that gradually develops into an Elenan Ostionoid component, culminating in a Chican Ostionoid component. At least 11 distinct occupational horizons were identified within the more than 30 stratigraphic layers, and in these the Elenan Ostionoid component is the best represented. More than 40 radiocarbon dates from the site range from 2580 B.C. to A.D. 1655. The abundance of recognizable post molds and other household features is remarkable. These will be analyzed to determine the size and shape of the structures, household composition, and intrasite patterning. The site contains over 150 human burials.

Geographic Setting

The Paso del Indio site, at an elevation of 10 to 15 m above sea level, is located on the west bank of the Río Indio in Vega Baja on the north-central coast of Puerto Rico (see Figure 3.1). The Río Indio joins the Río Cibuco less than 2 km downstream, which in turn empties into mangrove swamps along the Atlantic Ocean about 5 km farther downriver. The confluence of the Río Indio and the Río Cibuco is on the coastal plain. The site lies on the right bank of the Río Indio floodplain. This lower section of the Río Indio is hemmed in on either side by steep limestone hills, known as *mogotes*, rising 50 to 100 m above the river valley, and is deeply incised, narrow, and slow meandering with sandbars and steep-sided banks over 5 m high. Upriver, the valley is narrow and tightly restricted by limestone topography, and the river is swifter-moving with gravel bars and a broader channel. Just 4 km upstream from the site, the Río Indio cuts through formations with volcanic rocks, which can be found in the river gravels. The river tends to rise rapidly after heavy rains, and on several occasions it jumped its banks and flooded the excavation units nearest its course. The sediments encountered during the excavations testify that this pattern of flooding was the norm throughout much of the Paso del Indio site occupation (Clark et al. 2003).

At the time of excavation the site was abandoned pastureland, and prior to that it had been planted in sugarcane for at least 50 years. Plowing resulted in a disturbed zone, approximately 30 to 40 cm below surface, but there is surprisingly little archaeological material visible on the surface. The original vegetation on the floodplain was probably dense forest, which presumably was cleared in prehistoric times for planting crops and building dwellings. The surrounding steep-sided limestone hills today are a combination of residential areas and dense vegetation probably little different from the past. There are a few small rockshelters with petroglyphs in the surrounding cliffs that apparently were used occasionally in the past, but no major cave system. The thin soils of the steep limestone hills would have supported a different type of vegetation from the floodplain, placing the site on an ecotone, thus increasing the variety of available resources.

Overland, the Atlantic coast is only 6 km north of Paso del Indio, but easiest access would have been via the Río Cibuco, a short 7-km paddle by canoe. The Saladoid/Elenoid site of Maisabel excavated in 1980 by Ovidio Dávila Dávila of the Institute of Puerto Rican Culture in conjunction with the Sociedad Arqueológica Cibuco de Vega Baja, then by Peter Siegel (1989a, 1992) and Peter Roe (1991a) lies to the west of that river mouth and was apparently contemporaneous with the Paso del Indio site for at least part of the two sites' occupations.

Archaeological History of the Site

The Paso del Indio site was originally recorded as VB-4 in 1979. However, the site went unnoticed by Jesús Figueroa Lugo (1988) during his Phase IA survey of the route for PR 22, a four-lane toll road between San Juan and Arecibo. In 1993, Carlos Ayes Suárez alerted the authorities that excavations for a footing of one of the highway's bridges had impacted the site. The Puerto Rico Highway and Transportation Authority (PRHTA) responded quickly and in May of 1993 initiated Phase II site evaluation using soil borings to determine the horizontal and vertical limits of the site, followed by limited Phase III data recovery excavations and monitoring, all directed by Osvaldo García Goyco and Adalberto Maurás Casillas (1993a). García Goyco and Maurás Casillas were then contracted to conduct more extensive data recovery mitigations, with Edwin Crespo Torres as the physical anthropologist. Soon thereafter I was asked by PRHTA to participate in the development of the research design and to provide expert technical assistance during the fieldwork. The conditions for the archaeological mitigation plan were set forth in various 1993 documents (García Goyco and Maurás Casillas 1993b, 1993c), which were ultimately approved by the review agencies through a Memorandum of Agreement signed in mid-1994. The large-scale data recovery operation that started in 1993 lasted until August of 1995 under the direction of García Goyco and Maurás Casillas, with my technical assistance, and with Crespo as the physical anthropologist.

Deep Testing and Remote Sensing

Deep Testing

In 1993, when the construction impacts revealed a deep site, the archaeological project began with intensive systematic deep testing to determine the horizontal and vertical limits of the site (García Goyco and Maurás Casillas 1993b). In total, 450 soil borings were drilled at 10-m intervals, most of them to between 3 to 4 m deep. This proved to be essential in developing the data recovery plan for the site. A standard commercial soil-coring rig was used. Split spoon cores were extracted, analyzed, and recorded onsite. These soil logs were used to plot the absence, presence, and type of cultural material, enabling the horizontal extent of the site to be determined. García and Maurás were able to plot the depths and presumed cultural affiliations of three different components at the site. They also dug three rectangular units (2 by 12 m, 2 by 6 m, and 2 by 3 m, all less than 3 m deep) in the vicinities of Pilasters 5, 6, and 7 (see Figure 2.1); originally these were to be the entire excavation.

No Archaic component was detected during this first phase of the mitigation. The deepest material they located with the soil borings and initial excavations were classified as "Igneri"; in horizontal area, this component measured about 225 by 125 meters. Above this was the "pre-Taíno" component, far larger, with an estimated area of 450 by 200 meters. The uppermost "Taíno" component had the same approximate size as the pre-Taíno. Spatially, the ceramic-age occupations did not shift significantly over time, which is remarkable considering that the village was probably abandoned on several occasions during the millennia under consideration.

Although García and Maurás did record the density and types of cultural material in the boring logs, which can be used in the future to conduct excavations on particular cultural components, the location of the subsequent large-scale data recovery units was dictated by the pre-established locations for the highway bridge footings (pilasters). The earlier excavation units, and the profiles of the Pilaster 7 bridge footing excavated during construction operations, helped greatly in designing additional data recovery. Based on these data it was possible to exclude from further archaeological consideration all but Pilasters 5, 6, 7, and 8, and to demonstrate that there were no significant archaeological deposits on the east side of the river.

Remote Sensing

In June 1993, courtesy of Kent Schneider, the Regional Archaeologist of the Southern Region of the USDA Forest Service, in partnership with Ervan Garrison (Garrison and Schneider 1994) of the University of Georgia, three different types of remote-sensing techniques were attempted at the Paso del Indio site. The instruments used included a terrain conductivity meter, a gradiometer, and a ground penetrating radar (GPR) unit. A testing grid was established over the site, concentrating on the blocks to be excavated.

At first, the results seemed promising, especially those of the GPR; however, as the excavations proceeded it became apparent that the remote-sensing projections were not so useful. This had more to do with our naïveté about the complexity of the site, than with the remote-sensing methods themselves. GPR readings were taken at 3-m intervals. This should have been adequate to identify large-scale features such as house floors, plaza surfaces, and stone rows of plazas. However, the site was far too complex to use GPR effectively at this interval; during excavation we soon discovered that there could be more than a half dozen burials, or dozens of post molds and other features within a 3-m^2 area. Not only were cultural features extremely concentrated, but also the site was quite deep. A reanalysis of the GPR data in conjunction with the GIS-mapped excavation data would refine our understanding of the GPR-registered soil anomalies. In turn, this would allow us to offer reliable projections for those unexcavated portions of the site that were tested by GPR.

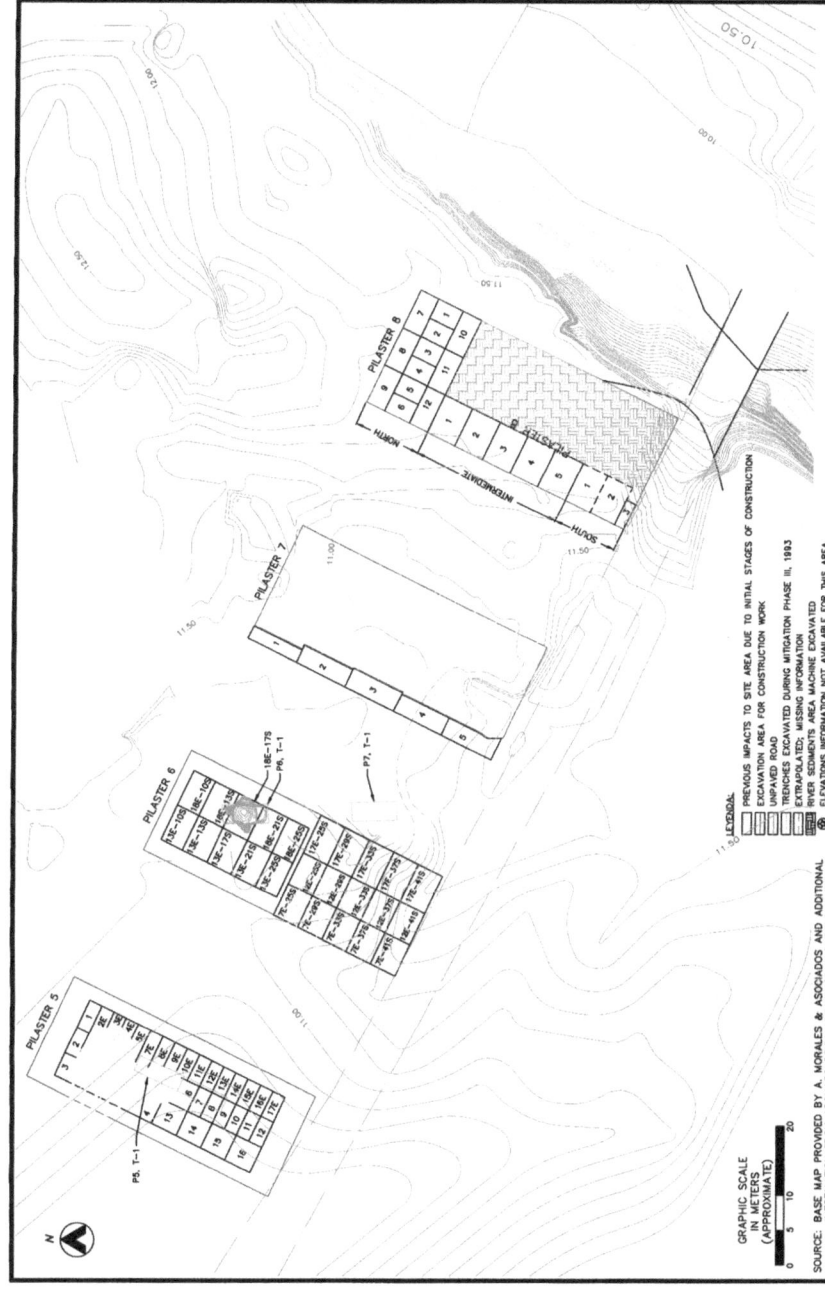

Figure 2.1. Locations of excavation units in Pilasters 5 through 8.

Figure 2.2. Mechanized and manual excavation of Pilaster 8.

Data Recovery Excavations

The main excavation comprised four bridge footings: Pilasters 5, 6, 7, and 8 (Figure 2.1). The soil borings showed that Pilaster 5 contained little archaeological material, so it was excavated by machine and monitored during excavation. Earlier in 1993 the construction excavation of Pilasters 3 and 4 to the west were also monitored. The monitoring confirmed that Pilasters 3, 4, and 5 did not contain substantial archaeological deposits, indicating that these areas were marginal to all prehistoric occupations of the site.

Pilasters 6 and 7 showed the highest densities of cultural material in the soil borings, and these were identified for a combination of hand excavation and controlled machine stripping of noncultural layers. The uppermost layers of these excavation blocks were stripped mechanically; when numerous features became apparent excavations continued by hand. All 10 units in the northern Pilaster 6, an approximately 18 by 10 meter area, were excavated by hand. In southern Pilaster 6, part was impacted by prior construction activity, part was excavated by hand, and part by machine.

The Pilaster 7 excavation block was a roughly 40 by 3 meter strip along the western side of the construction-impact area. The western side of the construction excavation was the eastern side of the archaeological excavation block. This entire exposed eastern profile was drawn "in reverse," before the archaeological excavation started, and this exposed profile was used to guide the stratigraphic excavations. In order to allow the driving of pilings, this block was excavated in two stages separated by several months, resulting in some discrepancies in the final western stratigraphic profile because the two sections of profile were not matched in the field.

Pilaster 8 with its lower artifact density was slated for monitored controlled mechanical excavation (Figure 2.2). This was implemented, but again, the presence of many archaeological features that were not discernable in the soil borings resulted in considerable hand excavation. The eastern side of Pilaster 8 turned out to be recent river deposits that sloped at about a 45 degree angle into the riverbed. The over 40-meter-long western side of the block, however, provided the oldest dates and some of the most interesting stratigraphy in the entire site. During excavation of Pilaster 8, several deep aceramic features, which had not been detected in previous stages of testing and excavation, were discovered. Some of these deeply buried deposits were thought to be Archaic in age, which has since been confirmed by radiocarbon dates.

Public Archaeology

As excavation progressed, the press was alerted to the discoveries, and at certain points during the project television newscasts highlighted the day's finds. Numerous newspaper articles were written about the site, including several front-page stories in the island's leading newspapers. Toward the end of the project a small museum was built onsite, in which a short video produced by the PRHTA was screened, followed by a guided tour through cases displaying artifacts in chronological order, culminated by a walk along a boardwalk overlooking the excavators at work. Thousands of island school children were brought to the site, as well as hundreds of drop-in visitors. While excavations were in progress Paso del Indio was certainly the island's most visited prehistoric site, and because of the extensive media attention it was definitely the best promotion for archaeology the island has experienced in decades.

During excavation, the public became very interested in the site. Although Puerto Ricans are taught from a young age that they are descended from the mixing of three races (Spanish colonizers, African slaves, and Taíno Indians), the Taíno people ceased to exist as a cultural entity not long after Europeans arrived in the New World. The enthrallment with the Paso del Indio site reflects a heartfelt desire to rediscover, understand, and reconnect with this broken Taíno branch of the Puerto Rican heritage tree.

This project was exemplary in its coordination with the construction activities and the concentration required by the field crew and staff. Because of urgency to complete the toll road, the construction of the bridge continued during the entire archaeological excavation. From the beginning, the data recovery excavations were under severe time constraints because the highway was near completion and this particular bridge was critical. The PRHTA and Las Piedras Construction Company provided engineering support in the form of onsite structures, sidewall shoring, heavy machinery, surveying, and other logistical services. The two main excavation blocks were covered with semipermanent roofs of zinc sheeting so that excavation could proceed rain or shine. During the initial phases the construction activity was simply nondistracting surveying and an occasional truck driving across the site, but by the middle of the project thunderous oil-spewing pile drivers operated all day long within 50 meters of ongoing archaeological excavations, and during the final phase of the project the highway bridge spans were being constructed directly overhead. Time constraints and distractions were surmounted, and the archaeological data recovery excavations were completed in August of 1995.

Over 10,000 cubic meters of the site were excavated. Much of this was monitored while it was excavated by heavy equipment, which was used to strip away the plow zone, flood deposits, and in some cases strata with low artifact density. García reported that 20 units were excavated by hand and 58 dug by machine; the units were not equal-sized, but roughly one-fifth of the entire volume was excavated by hand. At its peak, over 100 people were involved in the excavation and simultaneous laboratory processing.

Gaps in the Data

There were some major gaps in the archaeological field data. For instance, though a survey crew was onsite throughout the excavation, and daily they recorded hundreds of points—features, stratigraphy, artifact elevations, and such—and some of these data were entered into a computer, much of the original field documentation was less than optimal. For the final analyses this necessitated revisiting stratigraphic profiles, plan view drawings of excavation units, and many of the drawings of features in order to clarify the original field observations. Although field records were often sketchy, it was possible to reconstruct much of the data using the extensive photographic record, the summaries compiled by the excavation unit crew bosses, and field notebooks and by patching together wall profiles and plan views. Certainly, pressures of time, long hours, inexperienced crew, and the distraction of media and visitors to the site resulted in much of the missing or poor-quality data.

Meticulous plan views of the excavation floors were routinely drawn, and hundreds of thousands of artifacts and ecofacts were point-plotted, but they were rarely assigned artifact numbers in the field. Unfortunately, after they were drawn, all the artifacts and ecofacts from a particular feature or floor were simply picked up and bagged together. Therefore, it is usually impossible to know precisely where any particular artifact came from. It was not until they were processed in the field laboratory that artifacts were finally assigned catalog numbers, so the provenience data for individual items was lost. This procedure resulted in the loss of horizontal provenience at a microscale, though it has been preserved at a less precise scale—at the level of feature, or excavation unit and stratum. As a result, it will be impossible to analyze the positional relationship between specific artifacts, and they must be treated as if they were artifact lots from excavation units rather than individual artifacts with precise coordinates.

The most precise provenience data ironically come from the most disturbed contexts, from intrusive features. Intrusive features such as post molds, when originally dug by the prehistoric site occupants would have penetrated deep into underlying cultural layers, resulting in the mixing of these various horizons when in prehistory they pushed the dirt back into the hole. Centuries later, archaeologists meticulously plotted the features and routinely bagged their contents separately.

Because each excavation layer (usually a natural stratum, but sometimes when strata were thick they were subdivided into 10 cm artificial levels) of nonfeature material was bagged by excavation unit, the vertical control is relatively accurate, usually within a 5 to 10 cm vertical context. The horizontal control is less precise because the excavation units measured anywhere from 1 to 8 meters on a side, resulting in imprecise spatial data.

This has important implications for the types of analysis that can be conducted using these data. Chronological inferences should be reliable because they rely on the vertical dimension. Analyses that rely on the horizontal dimension are compromised, with the exception of the features. As a result, though we can clearly define a house by its post molds using the available feature data, we will be unable to distinguish what went on inside vs. outside this structure, except in rare cases where the house floor and some exterior features surrounding the structure were specifically identified in the field and excavated and bagged as distinct entities.

Post-field revelations have made it necessary to lower expectations on the precision of the information, critically rethink much of the research design, and to seriously reconsider how to handle certain categories of data. Fortunately, the in-field laboratory ran smoothly and the records are more complete. There are many cases where the field documentation is missing critical information, but by using the laboratory records, inventory forms, artifact catalog, site sketches, and the photographs we have been able to clear up many doubts.

Laboratory Analyses

The amount of archaeological material recovered from the site is truly staggering. Concurrent with the excavation, laboratory processing in the form of washing and sorting materials, flotation of soil samples for archaeobotanical remains, and some preliminary analyses were conducted in the onsite field laboratory under the supervision of Lydia Peraza Muñoz. This proved to be significant in the ultimate preservation of the artifacts because of a long delay in starting the laboratory analyses. Most of the material was crammed into truck trailers without climate control for two years, but because it had been washed and processed in the field, it did not deteriorate.

After completion of almost 16 months of fieldwork in August of 1995, García began organizing the data, and with a reduced staff he began limited laboratory analysis and curation efforts. A research design for the laboratory analysis phase was presented in 1998 (Solís Magaña and García Goyco 1998), nearly three years following fieldwork; an "End of Fieldwork Report" was completed a year later (García Goyco and Solís Magaña 1999). Osvaldo García Goyco eventually resigned from the project, while Law Environmental continued the laboratory analysis, with Carlos Solis Magaña as the Project Manager. During this period Miguel Rodríguez López and I were asked by the PRHTA to serve as Acting Co-Principal Investigators, roles that we continue to occupy as the laboratory analysis approaches completion.

The general trend of the laboratory research design has been followed, with noteworthy modifications in methods and particulars. As with any research, it has been dynamic, so the focus has changed during the course. As we became more familiar with the data—and particularly as we became more familiar with *gaps* in the data—the direction and methods of analysis were adapted to the data available and to integrate fresh perspectives. Due to the changes in project leadership, and the available data, the original research design was refocused toward an integrated technological analysis.

A cadre of specialists is in various stages of completion with their respective analyses. Elsewhere in this volume some of these specialists present detailed analysis of material from the Paso del Indio site.

Geomorphology

From early in the data recovery excavation, geomorphologist Jeff Clark was recruited to analyze the stratigraphy. He visited the site on several occasions between 1993 and 1995 and processed sediments from soil columns; nine locations were used for his observations. Clark's initial report from his first field analysis of the stratigraphy in 1993 served as baseline data for all subsequent excavation at the site. He described the 40-plus-meter profile on the west wall of construction Pilaster 7, roughly in the center of the site. He has since completed and published his analysis (Clark et al. 2003). The archaeologists working the site benefited greatly from Clark's geomorphological analysis.

Archaeologists tend to think of a site as a series of depositional episodes, fast or slow, but always cumulative. Clark reminds us that stratigraphic sequences are not limited to deposition, but when floodwaters are raging, devastating episodes of erosion may strip away cultural and natural layers as well, and he points out cases of this in Paso del Indio. When Clark and I attempted to cross-reference the stratigraphic profile drawings of the three main excavation blocks—an exercise best done in the field—we found that all the numbered soil layers did not necessarily coincide precisely from one block to the next. Reniel Rodríguez Ramos, using field notes, photographs, and profiles, was largely able to clarify this, and the resulting sequence is being used as the backbone for the relative chronology of the site. We will integrate this geomorphological interpretation with archaeological observations to arrive at stratigraphic interpretations for different parts of the site.

Clark confirms that periodic floods constituted the major depositional process at the site, and that the frequency and intensity of floods varied during different periods of occupation. He states that the flooding probably did not endanger many lives, but he does feel that during those periods when flooding was more frequent it probably caused substantial damage to residences, loss of property, severe disruption of village life, and interruptions to subsistence activities such as agriculture. From the evidence, it is not possible to tell whether these floods were the result of very intense rains, or associated with hurricanes. However, at Paso del Indio we have multiple opportunities to analyze the effects that catastrophic floods had on prehistoric village life.

House Patterns

Post Molds

Post molds were abundant and easily recognized (Figure 2.3). They are being entered in a GIS database, along with other features, and used to determine the shapes, sizes, orientations, and locations of the prehistoric structures. Using the GIS layers processed, when observing the post mold patterns we can tentatively distinguish several dwellings and smaller structures. This allows us to make inferences about interior and exterior use-areas and the position of

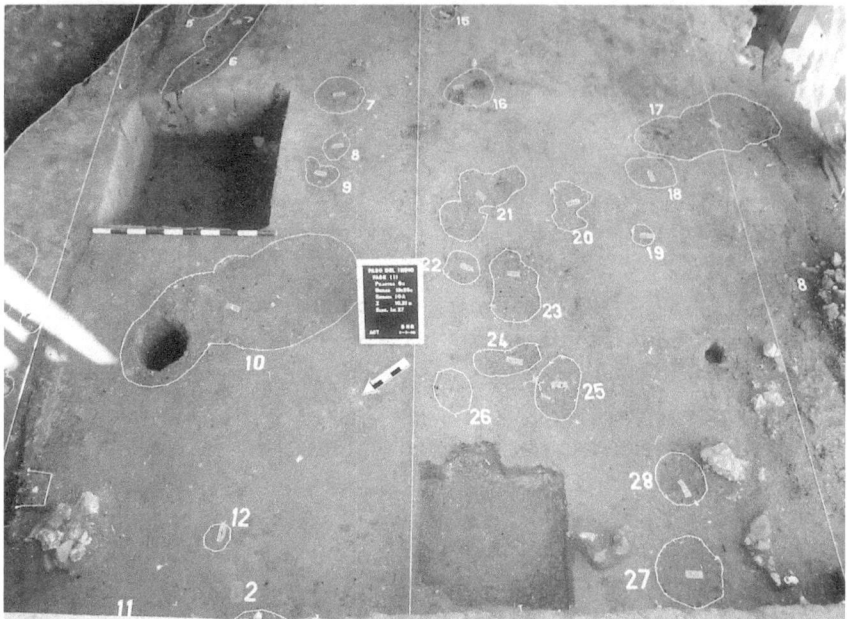

Figure 2.3. Post molds, burials, and other features in Pilaster 6.

dwellings in relation to other major site features such as the stone pavements, to estimate household size, and to explore the manner in which these factors behave over time. Using GIS, we are able to quickly display contemporaneous post molds by selecting only those that originate in given stratigraphic units. Selecting sets of features, based on stratigraphy, allows for more accurate interpretations than previously has been possible on poorly stratified sites where post mold patterns from later houses overlap and mask the patterns from earlier houses. The GIS database includes tabular information on the depth and content of the features, which helps to establish associations, and to use diagnostic artifacts to independently validate the relative chronology of the house-post features.

Living Floors

There are areas confined within patterns of post molds that have been identified as possible living floors. Sometimes these were considered features in the field, and so they can be analyzed as discrete units. Identifying activity areas within living floors is far more difficult because of the poor horizontal control discussed herein. We are using field drawings, field notes, and laboratory observations to refine the analysis and identify internal use areas to the extent possible.

Hearths

There are several features provisionally identified as hearths, but they are not common. These are being analyzed both independently and in conjunction with post mold patterns to determine if they are interior house fires (such as smudge-pits) or cooking hearths, or outside of structures and therefore presumably used for other purposes. One notable example is a small burned area with a group of fire-cracked rocks from deep in Pilaster 8. This discrete feature is not associated with post molds or other features and is interpreted as an outdoor hearth on the bank of the river. Charcoal from an Archaic-age hearth in Pilaster 8 provides one of the earliest dates for the site.

Site Features

Rock Pavements and Ditches

A wide band of limestone cobbles several layers deep was encountered in the northern end of Pilaster 7 in Stratum 8, placing it near the top of the Elenan Ostionoid cultural component. This extensive feature is clearly anthropogenic. García Goyco and Maurás Casillas (1993b) thought this might be one side of a ball court plaza, but no second rock feature parallel to it was found in the part of the site they excavated, so this is still an unproven hypothesis. Because the precise nature of this pavement is not yet understood, it simply is called a "rock pavement." During the spatial analysis of this stratigraphic level it will be possible to establish the relationship between this rock pavement and house floors, burials, and other features, and hopefully determine its function.

A second, but different type of rock pavement is located a bit deeper in Pilaster 6, also from the late Elenan Ostionoid component. Along with the limestone cobbles, this feature contained a significant amount of cultural material, including pot sherds that were wedged vertically between the rocks, indicating this pavement was intentionally constructed, and not simply a layer of discarded rocks and sherds. In association with this second pavement was a shallow ditch that apparently served to drain water from this low-lying part of the site. These two features are associated with what appears to be a house floor and may be related to the structures' roof run-off and drip-line. The interpretation is that the ditch and pavement were concerted efforts to remedy a muddy area in front of the dwelling where roof run-off water puddled up. After study of the associated post molds and apparent house floor, the precise relationship and purpose of these interrelated features will be apparent.

Production Areas

At least one feature from near the riverbank in Pilaster 8 is unambiguous evidence that discrete production areas are preserved at the site. It consists of a concentration of chipped-stone flakes and shatter, all from the same mass of raw material—a clear sign that this was a single flaking episode. We are watching for additional production areas as the analysis proceeds, and are using the GIS mapping and database for this purpose. Certain features and artifact concentrations can indicate prehistoric production areas. However, as discussed, due to the imprecise recording of the artifact locations at the site, it will not be possible to address this at the microlevel as was initially planned, though using GIS it is possible to distinguish larger production areas on the basis of artifact distributions, refuse patterns, and associated features.

Intrasite Patterns

Distribution of features is being used to investigate the spatial organization of activities within the village. In particular, we are examining the location of structures in relation to each other and to nearby open areas. We are identifying specific functions of nonstructural areas, especially the possible ball court or plaza mentioned above. It is essential to look at the location of burials vis-à-vis such site features as dwellings and the possible central plaza. We will be looking at these intrasite patterns in all of the occupation levels, because these patterns might have changed over time. Ultimately we will compare our findings with other sites in Puerto Rico, focusing on other north coast sites in the vicinity. Of particular interest, are possible relationships between the coastal ceramic-age Maisabel site (Siegel 1989a, 1992; Roe 1991a) and the Archaic-age Angostura site (Ayes Suárez 1988), which were both apparently contemporaneous with Paso del Indio during portions of their occupations.

Human Burials

Osteology

Edwin Crespo's (2000) recent doctoral dissertation compares the Paso del Indio population with the Cuevas population from Punta Candelero. Crespo (2001) has written a detailed report on the osteology and pathologies of the Paso del Indio human remains, which will be a chapter in the final report. A chapter on funerary practices is also in progress. Together these certainly will contribute significantly to our knowledge of prehistoric populations in Puerto Rico.

Crespo (2000, 2001) analyzed 138 burials from Paso del Indio; in addition, 14 individuals were detected in wall profiles but were left unexcavated. Although the cultural affiliation of every burial is not absolutely clear, we do know the overwhelming majority of them date to the pre-Taíno Elenan Ostionoid layers. In earlier reports, a few burials were attributed to the "Igneri" late Saladoid layers, and others assigned to the Taíno Chican Ostionoid cultural components. We will continue to reexamine the available data to ascertain the stratigraphic context of each burial pit, thereby assigning each inhumation to its proper cultural component. So far, the reevaluation suggests that all of the burials are from the Elenan Ostionoid component. In addition, we are analyzing the pottery found with the burials to establish ceramic chronology as well as funerary practices; 18 individuals had one pot, and three individuals had two pots buried with them. In his analyses, Crespo considered all 138 burials to represent a single population. Of this group, he determined that 66 were adults and 72 were subadult infants and juveniles. He determined that 32 of the adults were male and 30 were female; sex determination was not possible for the 72 subadults or for four adults in poor states of preservation.

Crespo determined there was an approximate 30 percent rate of infant mortality in the Paso del Indio population, stating that this percentage is about normal for Precolumbian and preindustrial populations elsewhere. Although this seems high when compared to other Puerto Rican sites, one reason for such a seemingly elevated incidence of death of younger individuals in this population might be the result of excellent preservation at the Paso del Indio site. The bones of infants and children are thin and fragile, and as a rule do not preserve as well as those of adults. However, the site formation processes, the sandy sediments, and the soil chemistry appear to have provided a more favorable environment for preservation of these delicate human remains than we find at many other sites on the island. I argue that the seemingly high infant mortality rate at Paso del Indio is closer to the actual prehistoric mortality rate than the lower percentages we generally see in Puerto Rican sites.

There are also 26 well-documented instances of tabular oblique frontal-occipital cranial deformation at the site. Fully 62 percent of the 42 individuals where it was possible to make this determination had cranial deformation, with almost the same incidence regardless of sex or age. The fact that over one-third of the population did not have cranial deformation indicates that the practice is plausibly related to social factors, such as status or affinity.

Crespo also identified a number of notable pathologies in the Paso del Indio human remains. The most noteworthy is the occurrence of syphilis (treponematosis) in one female aged between 20 and 25 years at her death. She was found with a complete late Ostiones-style pot. According to Crespo, this is the first irrefutable case of prehistoric syphilis in the Antilles.

Stable Isotope Analysis

Anne Stokes presents her findings on the possible diet of 11 individuals from the Paso del Indio site in her doctoral dissertation (1998) and in a chapter in this volume. Her analysis indicates that though seven of these individuals had similar diets, the other four ate different foods. We are looking closely at the group of seven to see what they had in common, and at the other four to see how they differed from the larger group. As we continue our analyses we are scrutinizing these individuals to detect any discernable patterns in funerary practices, cranial deformation, stature, sex or age distributions, and chronology that coincide with the dietary differences Stokes identified. We are interested in social and health implications. Stokes's findings that maize might have been a regular part of the diet of certain individuals at Paso del Indio are intriguing. Broader statements beyond those based on the human bone await the outcome of the archaeobotanical work being conducted by Lee Newsom, and zooarchaeological analyses by Irvy Quitmyer and Nathalie Serrand.

Funerary Practices

Because of the large number of burials recovered from Paso del Indio, it will be possible to recognize funerary practices that have gone unnoticed, or were only cautiously interpreted at other sites. So far, a few distinct patterns have emerged on the treatment of the dead. The majority of the burials at the site are fully articulated and flexed, with the individuals arranged in a fetal position when they died, possibly wrapped in hammocks or other bindings. There are numerous secondary burials, including several instances where bones from one individual were placed with the complete and fully articulated burial of a second individual. Secondary burials, often arranged in what appear to have been bundles, were disarticulated post-cranial bones, some with crania, and some without. A few instances might have been multiple burials. It was recently recognized that several individuals in Pilaster 7 might have been interred one after another within a very close time span. The details of this quick succession of burials are under investigation, but deaths during an epidemic are one likely explanation.

Two other burials are women with infants lodged in their birth canal, indicating that they died during childbirth (see Figure 2.4). According to

Crespo (2000, 2001), this will be the first time death during childbirth has been reported in the archaeological literature for the Caribbean.

Grave goods were relatively uncommon, but when present show distinct patterns. In cases where the sex of the individual can be determined, Crespo made two significant observations. He found that in all cases when the grave goods are ceramic pots, the individuals are females; and, in all cases when a second cranium accompanies a primary burial, these primary burials are males.

In the cases of the ceramics that accompany the female burials we have looked closely at these artifacts to determine whether they were pottery originally made for common household or routine ceremonial use, and simply interred with the deceased women, or whether they were intentionally manufactured vessels, made exclusively for inclusion with these women at burial. What we see strongly suggests that at least some of the vessels buried with these women were quickly and intentionally made at the time of death, and therefore are grave goods directly related to the funeral, and arguably, intimately reflective of the deceased or their circumstance.

To illustrate this point, one of the women who died during childbirth was accompanied by a small ceramic vessel near her left shoulder (Figure 2.4). This miniature pot is complete, but unlike all but one other example, this one has designs incised on the exterior base, the outside bottom surface on which a pot would normally rest. The only other similar example was a design incised on the exterior base of a pot buried with a child of indeterminate sex. The uncommon and impractical location for these designs seems to result from the pot-builders' desire to express something vital. In this case, the symbolism, the "message" if you will, apparently was more essential than following the customary decorative norms, or possibly the norms for "decorating" a pot to accompany a burial differed substantially from those for decorating daily wares. Technologically, this is a small, simple restricted-mouthed pot with molded protuberances at the ends, with paired perforations at one end, useful for hanging by a string, or attaching decorative objects such as feathers. The incisions are carefully made and narrow, though there is evidence that this miniature pot was fired soon after it was fashioned; it has pot-lid spalls, which are a result of blistering during firing when the clay is not allowed to dry sufficiently. Carefully built, miniature in size, distinctively decorated, and hurriedly fired are indications that the production of this pot was atypical and apparently rushed, possibly doing in a day what would normally be a two- to three-day process. A combination of factors we might expect under unusual circumstances, in this case a healthy, young, pregnant woman who died unexpectedly—along with her child, during a dreadful labor. Possibly a

Figure 2.4. Woman, infant, and offering. Death during childbirth.

grieving family member, wanting to include a token, a gift, a symbol for the unborn child and its mother, in their sorrow fashioned a small pot to place with these two unfortunate beings when they were laid to rest.

Giving birth is a time of extreme risk for both the mother and the child; a moment when a new life or a sudden death are in precarious balance. The

Figure 2.5. Man holding another man's skull.

possibility of a woman dying during childbirth must have been a serious concern in prehistoric times. Citing ethnohistoric references from Mexico, Crespo (2001:52–53) argues that women who died during childbirth were held in extreme reverence and experienced "divine" deaths. The second case of a childbirth burial from Paso del Indio lends support to his arguments. This woman also died along with her child, apparently during a premature birth; in this case Crespo puts the age of the fetus at 7 to 8 months. The mother's skull and mandible were removed postmortem. As will be seen from other burials discussed below, for the inhabitants of Paso del Indio, this was probably not an act of desecration, but an act of supreme reverence.

At Paso del Indio there are three irrefutable cases where adult males were interred with the skull of another adult male held in their hands or cradled in their arms (Figure 2.5). There are a considerable number of other examples at the site where primary burials have secondary burials consisting of cranial and post-cranial remains in direct association with them, but none are as obvious as these three cases. The other cases will be detailed in the final report, but let us focus here on the three particularly evocative cases.

All three are mature adult males, and each holds the skull of another mature adult male. The unresolved questions are: "Whose heads are they holding? Were they enemy or kin? Were these men buried holding a skull taken from a slain adversary or from an honored ancestor?"

There are various references in the ethnohistoric record to ancestor worship practiced among the Taíno. Therefore, these burials could well be evidence that the practice extended back to Elenan Ostionoid times. Solely on the basis of the positioning of the secondary skulls in the hands and arms of the primary individuals, I am willing to venture that these three pairs of burials are evidence of ancestor worship. The primary individuals were positioned holding or cradling the skulls close to their bodies—as if they were treasured and dear—not what I would expect to see when a man was buried with a trophy head of a mortal enemy. I would expect an enemy's skull to be treated like a nonhuman object, possibly modified and arranged less intimately in relation to the victor's body. For instance they would have been treated more along the lines of the perforated human frontal bone pectorals and hollow ceramic effigy heads that Roe (1991b) argues were raiding trophies, not ancestral relics.

We should be able to address these questions by conducting DNA analysis of the individuals in each pair. The underlying assumption is that a relative is usually not a mortal enemy. On the one hand, if the two individuals are unrelated we will assume they were enemies; consequently these cases could represent some manner of trophy-head taking—a well-documented ethnographic practice in Amazonia. On the other hand, if the analyses show that the holder and the holdee are genetically related, we have a quite different, and to me, a far more fascinating situation involving prehistoric ancestor worship. Crespo and Antonio Curet are running initial tests on a handful of burials from the site to determine if they retain suitable DNA for analysis; once this has been confirmed, more in-depth analysis will certainly follow.

Crespo describes similar cases in detail, but in synopsis, it is clear from these three instances and the treatment of other secondary burials, that the Paso del Indio people engaged in postmortem manipulation of their dead. The nearby Maisabel site also had secondary burials (Siegel 1992), and we will be looking closely at how these compare chronologically and in funerary treatment. By comparison, there are several examples reported by Menno Hoogland (1995:148) of infants' skulls and long bones removed from Taíno burials at the Kelbey's Ridge 2 site on Saba. In addition to describing the burials, Hoogland provides comprehensive ethnographic and ethnohistoric references supporting the argument that the Antillean practice of manipulating human bones is related to *cemíism* and ancestor worship. Regardless of the final interpretation, whether they were ancestors or enemies, these three

Paso del Indio cases of men holding other men's skulls are apparently the first definitive reporting in the Caribbean literature of this particular funerary practice.

Lithic Artifacts

The stone artifacts from the site are abundant and varied; because of the sheer volume of site excavation, this lithic collection is perhaps one of the largest and most representative ever analyzed from Puerto Rico. Rodríguez Ramos conducted the lithic analysis, and he presents his major findings elsewhere in this volume. Stanley Ahler and I provided occasional guidance and comments during different phases of the analysis. Ahler was particularly helpful in conceptualizing the technological analysis of multiuse tools for percussion/grinding, which I believe will be a significant breakthrough in recognizing and interpreting the complexity of this suite of tools. A full range of utilitarian and ceremonial stone artifacts was recovered from the site, including attractive items for personal adornment; a variety of large and small three-pointer stones; a stone-collar fragment; as well as thousands of flakes, cores, hammerstones, choppers, celts, adzes, and classic edge grinders. Artifacts were fashioned from both locally available and foreign stone, for example flint from Antigua and possibly some from Hispaniola was identified, with other material coming from possibly even farther away.

In addition, the local limestone was used for structural purposes. It was found in post molds, it was found filling a ditch, and it was found in a band several layers deep and meters wide as a stone pavement—possibly the stone wall of a plaza or a paved walkway. Fire-cracked rock of local stone was also abundant. All the lithic material has been fully analyzed by Rodríguez, so the reader is referred to his chapter herein, and for a more thorough treatment, ultimately to his section in the final site report.

Ceramic Artifacts

The ceramic artifacts are under analysis by several specialists. Miguel Rodríguez has coordinated the analyses of these materials by Antonio Curet, who will be looking at the ceramic attributes from diachronic, synchronic, and manufacturing perspectives; and by Richard Krause who concentrated on the technological and decorative aspects of the ceramic artifacts. Elvis Babilonia Acevedo has done the bulk of the laboratory analyses of the ceramics under the supervision of these various specialists. It is our expectation that because of the excellent context for the Elenan Ostionoid period at Paso del Indio, that detailed analysis of the ceramics will greatly refine our understanding of the changes that took place in vessel forms, decorative motifs, and ceramic technology during this time period. This in itself will be a major contribution.

Shell Artifacts

Initial identification of shell artifacts was conducted in the field laboratory. Marines Colón undertook the subsequent analysis of the shell tools and ornaments, discovering that numerous shell artifacts were still included with the nonartifactual shell. To date, Colón has studied over 500 shell tools and ornaments. These include: simple clam-shell scraping tools; conch whorl gouges and bowls; olive shell tinklers; small shell beads; and a variety of more delicately carved shell items, which probably served as teeth and eye inserts for larger pieces sculpted in wood, stone, or cotton, as well as other purely decorative purposes.

The shell is being analyzed from both technological and stylistic perspectives. As pointed out by Ramón Dacal Moure (2001), when we know the species of shell from which the artifact was made, we know its precise shape at the beginning of the production process. This is a quality that shell technology holds in common with bone technology, but which contrasts sharply with artifacts fashioned in stone or wood where the initial shape of the raw material can vary considerably. This helps in understanding shell artifact production, and prehistorically probably resulted in a more formal approach to producing shell artifacts. We expect to see shell artifact production sequences like those described by Dacal Moure (1978), Serrand (1995), and Carlson (1995) on other islands.

We will seek to determine whether the designs carved into the shell artifacts show any stylistic similarities to those carved into the stone and incised into the ceramic artifacts. Similarities or differences in the symbols portrayed in these diverse media should be edifying. Although shell tools are utilitarian in function, carved shell was also used for personal adornment, such as the olive shell tinklers found at the site. Shell also had sacred ceremonial uses. For instance, a set of carved shell "teeth," like those often affixed to the mouths of some stone three-pointers and wooden *duhos,* was found inside the mouth of one of the human burials.

Archaeobotanical Remains

Charcoal was common at the site, so water flotation of countless samples was undertaken in the field. A field-built barrel and sieve device was used. Lee

Newsom has since demonstrated that this type of process can be very destructive of the charred remains, and that dry sieving of archaeobotanical samples would probably have been better. Nonetheless, Newsom was able to draw some conclusions from what she identified. Elsewhere in this volume, Newsom discusses some of her early findings based on the charred plant and wood remains from Paso del Indio. From her ongoing research, we expect to learn about charred food remains; the kinds of locally available wood; and the types of habitats that surrounded the site which were exploited by its inhabitants.

While fieldwork was still in progress, preliminary tests were run on soil samples sent to John Jones of Texas A&M University (now of Washington State University); he found that pollen grains were preserved. These initial results led to taking additional samples, both from stratigraphic columns and from feature and burial contexts. These samples have not yet been analyzed for pollen or phytoliths, but potentially will provide additional information concerning the native vegetation surrounding the site, crops planted prehistorically, and changes in the local environment during occupation of the site. These data will be especially useful to compare to the study conducted at the nearby Maisabel site (Siegel et al., this volume).

Faunal Remains

The faunal remains potentially will provide insights into the range of environments exploited by the Paso del Indio occupants. Quitmyer will be looking at the animal bone, and Serrand at some of the shell. We will be interested to see if there were changes through time, or if exploitation patterns remain static. When complete, these studies will be combined with the other biological and environmental data. We will pay particular attention to the macrobotanical and, when available, palynological data to investigate relationships between different sources of environmental information. We are also interested in comparing the results of the faunal analyses with the dietary study, based on Stokes's analysis of stable isotopes extracted from human bone collagen.

Chronology and Radiocarbon Dates

Cultural Chronology

At the project's inception, García Goyco and Maurás Casillas (1993a) employed Ricardo Alegría's cultural chronology, thus the designations of Igneri, pre-Taíno, and Taíno cultural components, a system they continued to follow until fairly late in the project, when Solis and García (1998) switched to Irving Rouse's (1992) cultural nomenclature. We occasionally use Alegría's designations to maintain consistency with the earlier published reports from the site. The earliest documented occupation in the site was a small Archaic component, followed by a long hiatus, and then a late Cedrosan Saladoid (Cuevas complex or Igneri) component that gradually developed into an Elenan Ostionoid (Santa Elena and Ostiones complexes or pre-Taíno) component. The occupational history culminated in a Chican Ostionoid (Capá complex or Taíno) component. Once Curet's ceramic modal analysis is completed, and we are able to state clearly which ceramic attributes predominate in specific strata, we will be able to present a more precise cultural history for Paso del Indio, to be directly correlated with Rouse's greater Caribbean chronology.

Radiocarbon Dates

The radiocarbon dates from Paso del Indio are presented in Table 2.1. In total, 44 dates, all derived from charcoal, were processed by Beta Analytic. Charcoal samples were submitted in several batches over the course of the project. This chronology will be among the most extensive in Puerto Rico for the Elenan Ostionoid, solidly positioned within a Cuevas-Elenan-Capá sequence. The dates are presented by strata; remarkably, of the 44 samples only four fall outside of the expected sequence. We will assess the contexts of the four seemingly anomalous samples for indications of disturbances that may not have been recognized in the field.

Technological Analyses

Part way through the laboratory analysis it was recognized that there was no all-embracing research design beyond reconstructing culture history. We also recognized that several specialists were employing technological analyses of the lithic, ceramic, and shell artifacts—that is, the bulk of the collections. With the encouragement of two renowned colleagues—ceramic technologist Richard Krause and lithic technologist Stanley Ahler—a revised research design focusing on artifact technology was initiated. Integrating the analyses of the specific artifact sets will enable us to identify broad technological patterns; this will be the final step of the laboratory investigation. Issues related to intersite interaction, intrasite structure, cultural chronology, geomorphology, archaeobotany, zooarchaeology, and osteology will not be slighted, but will follow more traditional paths, contributing to the systematic technological approach when appropriate.

Table 2.1. Paso del Indio Site Radiocarbon Dates.

Pilaster-Unit	Elevation (m, ASL)	Conventional Radiocarbon Age (BP)	Calibrated Date Range 2 Sigma	Calibrated Date Range 1 Sigma	Intercept	Beta Analytic Sample Number	Analysis
7-1	10.78	560 ± 60	A.D. 1290–1440	A.D. 1310–1360 A.D. 1390–1420	A.D. 1410	178671	STANDARD
6N-13/21	10.685	630 ± 40	A.D. 1290–1410	A.D. 1300–1400	A.D. 1310 A.D. 1370 A.D. 1380	178664	AMS
6S-17/25	10.51	260 ± 50	A.D. 1505–1595 A.D. 1620–1680 A.D. 1745–1805 A.D. 1935–1950	A.D. 1640–1670	A.D. 1655	77166	AMS
7-2	9.56/9.46	640 ± 60	A.D. 1275–1420	A.D. 1290–1400	A.D. 1310 A.D. 1365 A.D. 1375	77177	AMS
7-4	10.500	730 ± 40	A.D. 1240–1300	A.D. 1270–1290	A.D. 1280	178675	AMS
6N-13/17	10.480	940 ± 60	A.D. 990–1230	A.D. 1020–1180	A.D. 1040	178661	STANDARD

Continued on the next page

Table 2.1 Continued

Pilaster-Unit	Elevation (m, ASL)	Conventional Radiocarbon Age (BP)	Calibrated Date Range 2 Sigma	Calibrated Date Range 1 Sigma	Intercept	Beta Analytic Sample Number	Analysis
6N-13/21	10.330	840 ± 60	A.D. 1035–1285	A.D. 1170–1265	A.D. 1220	81849	STANDARD
6S-17/33	10.300	830 ± 80	A.D. 1025–1300	A.D. 1165–1275	A.D. 1225	77175	STANDARD
6S-17/33	10.3 +/-	870 ± 80	A.D. 1010–1290	A.D. 1040–1260	A.D. 1195	87604	STANDARD
6N-13/17	10.16	910 ± 40	A.D. 1020–1220	A.D. 1040–1180	A.D. 1160	178662	AMS
6S-17/37	10.28/10.0	940 ± 60	A.D. 995–1235	A.D. 1020–1180	A.D. 1045 A.D. 1105 A.D. 1115	77174	STANDARD
6N-13/17	10.170	1180 ± 70	A.D. 685–1005	A.D. 780–970	A.D. 880	81848	STANDARD
6N-18/10	10.147	910 ± 60	A.D. 1010–1260	A.D. 1035–1215	A.D. 1165	87600	STANDARD
6N-13/13	10.02	1030 ± 50	A.D. 900–1150 A.D. 1100–1140	A.D. 980–1030	A.D. 1010	178660	STANDARD
6S-17/29	9.980	950 ± 60	A.D. 990–1225	A.D. 1020–1175	A.D. 1040	87603	STANDARD
6N-18/13	9.834	970 ± 50	A.D. 990–1195	A.D. 1015–1065 A.D. 1065–1155	A.D. 1035	81845	STANDARD

6S-17/25	9.440	980 ± 50	A.D. 985–1180	A.D. 1010–1055 A.D. 1090–1150	A.D. 1030	77168	AMS
6N-13/21	9.24/8.992	1050 ± 50	A.D. 890–1040	A.D. 975–1020	A.D. 1000	81850	STANDARD
6N-18/13	10.033	1060 ± 60	A.D. 880–1045 A.D. 1105–1115	A.D. 960–1020	A.D. 995	81843	
7-4	10.180	1010 ± 40	A.D. 980–1050 A.D. 1100–1140	A.D. 1000–1030	A.D. 1020	178676	AMS
8I-3	10.560	930 ± 40	A.D. 1020–1200	A.D. 1030–1170	A.D. 1050 A.D. 1100 A.D. 1140	178679	AMS
7-5	10.118	630 ± 50	A.D. 1285–1420	A.D. 1295–1400	A.D. 1310 A.D. 1355 A.D. 1385	77183	STANDARD
6N-18/21	9.860	1230 ± 60	A.D. 670–960	A.D. 700–880	A.D. 780	178667	Extended counting
6N-18/13	9.763	1080 ± 60	A.D. 865–1035	A.D. 895–1015	A.D. 985	81846	STANDARD
6N-18/13	9.740	960 ± 50	A.D. 995–1205	A.D. 1020–1165	A.D. 1035	81844	STANDARD
6N-13/25	9.606	950 ± 60	A.D. 990–1220	A.D. 1020–1170	A.D. 1040	178665	Extended counting
6N-18/10	9.546	990 ± 50	A.D. 980–1175	A.D. 1005–1045 A.D. 1105–1115	A.D. 1025	81841	STANDARD

Continued on the next page

Table 2.1 Continued

Pilaster-Unit	Elevation (m, ASL)	Conventional Radiocarbon Age (BP)	Calibrated Date Range 2 Sigma	Calibrated Date Range 1 Sigma	Intercept	Beta Analytic Sample Number	Analysis
7-2	9.440	960 ± 40	A.D. 1000–1180	A.D. 1020–1060 A.D. 1080–1150	A.D. 1030	178672	AMS
6N-18/21	9.410	970 ± 40	A.D. 1000–1170	A.D. 1020–1050 A.D. 1100–1140	A.D. 1030	178668	STANDARD
6N-13/17	9.350	1060 ± 40	A.D. 900–1030	A.D. 970–1010	A.D. 990	178663	AMS
6N-13/10	9.230	960 ± 130	A.D. 790–1290	A.D. 980–1220	A.D. 1030	178669	Extended counting
7-2	9.260	1270 ± 70	A.D. 670–870	A.D. 690–780	A.D. 720 A.D. 740 A.D. 760	178673	AMS
8I-2	9.607	1350 ± 70	A.D. 600–855	A.D. 645–720 A.D. 735–760	A.D. 670	77164	STANDARD
6S-17/37	9.050	1450 ± 40	A.D. 540–660	A.D. 580–650	A.D. 620	178666	AMS
6N-13/21	8.900	1440 ± 60	A.D. 535–685	A.D. 590–660	A.D. 635	87601	STANDARD
6N-13/13	8.800	1470 ± 40	A.D. 530–650	A.D. 560–640	A.D. 610	178674	AMS
8I-2	9.607	1550 ± 60	A.D. 405–640	A.D. 435–600	A.D. 540	87610	STANDARD

8I-4	9.386	1520 ± 40	A.D. 430–630	A.D. 530–600	A.D. 550	178681	AMS
6N-13/13	8.710	1580 ± 90	A.D. 250–650	A.D. 400–580	A.D. 450	178670	STANDARD
8I-3	9.189	1920 ± 80	B.C. 60–A.D. 260	A.D. 15–210	A.D. 90	87611	STANDARD
8I-2	8.971	2330 ± 110	B.C. 780–160	B.C. 520–360 B.C. 290–230	B.C. 390	178677	Extended counting
8S-2	8.790	2520 ± 40	B.C. 800–520	B.C. 790–760 B.C. 680–550	B.C. 770	178678	AMS
8I-5	7.452	4110 ± 40	B.C. 2870–2570 B.C. 2520–2500	B.C. 2860–2810 B.C. 2690–2580	B.C. 2630	178680	AMS
8I-4	7.198	4060 ± 60	B.C. 2870–2800 B.C. 2760–2460	B.C. 2845–2830 B.C. 2620–2485	B.C. 2580	77165	AMS

Underlying the premise of the overarching technological framework is the goal to address the manner in which the technological strategies utilized in the site were interconnected and interdependent. In doing so, it should be possible to evaluate the relative expenditures of energy and effort, and, ideally, to identify shifts in emphasis through time. By considering technological complexity, it should be possible to identify methods used to save time in some domains, thereby allowing more time to be spent in other pursuits.

Although complex, the technological framework potentially will enable us to identify "invisible" technologies. These are traditionally acknowledged by archaeologists as having been used prehistorically but are rarely preserved (see for example the underwater finds at Manantial de la Aleta [Ortega and Atiles 2003]); they are "invisible" because these artifacts were made of perishable materials such as cordage, cotton textiles, basketry, gourds, and wood. The cross-technological analysis will help us understand the integration of prehistoric technologies.

For example, the prehistoric preparation of manioc bread might involve two technological sequences that are archaeologically invisible. The construction of a wood-backed grater board is an archaeologically "invisible" technological process unless seen in the light of other material technologies. Graterboard teeth (microliths) are physical remains of this stone-working technology (Walker 1980b), but woodworking tools do not directly testify to the presence of the grater board. The same is true of the basketry squeezer (tipiti) and sieves, which can only be inferred from the stone-grater teeth and the ceramic griddles, indicators that manioc bread was indeed being made. Too often, archaeological reports tend to compartmentalize the analysis of different material types, so a comprehension of the truly integrated functioning of multiple prehistoric technologies is sacrificed.

Geographic Information System (GIS)

GIS is most often used in archaeology as a sophisticated mapping tool and less often to manage tabular data or to integrate spatial and tabular data. We are employing GIS to process spatial and tabular data together. A modest plan to utilize GIS was included in the original proposal for the laboratory phase of the project. However, early on it was recognized that this technology would be more productive if applied to a broad range of data and in plotting of the features. Guidance was provided by Jessica Granell, an expert in GIS who reviewed our methods and assumptions to assure that the full potential of this tool would be exploited. Although using GIS as an island-wide site inventory tool was recently initiated by the Puerto Rico State Historic Preservation Office, to our knowledge, this is the first time GIS will be used for an intrasite analysis in Puerto Rico.

When studying the features, it became apparent many of them were not cultural, but were in fact anomalous discolorations or natural differences in soil color or texture. This prompted our reassessment of the feature identifications, their defining characteristics, and eventually a lengthy reanalysis of the field-recorded features from two of the four major excavation blocks. Richard Krause aided in no small measure in reconceptualizing what constitutes a legitimate archaeological feature, and Reniel Rodríguez, and later Elvis Babilonia with the help of Rosa Martínez took on the enormous task of reanalyzing all the data on the features in order to winnow out nonfeatures from the database before digitizing them in GIS. They meticulously researched each feature using field notes, photographs, drawings, and data files before making each individual decision. Those deemed to be features following the more restricted definition were highlighted and color-coded on copies of the field plan views and then digitized for GIS.

GIS has some distinct advantages over traditional archaeological mapping techniques when viewing a site as complex as Paso del Indio. Traditionally, when an archaeologist draws a plan view of an excavation floor, he/she draws all the features and artifact concentrations visible at that level. Thus in multicomponent sites we are often combining different periods of information—younger features intrusive from higher in the profile are mapped together with the older, deeper features appearing for the first time in the level. This practice tends to complicate any visual analysis by presenting features from different periods on a single plane. Cleaning up these drawings by eliminating the earlier intrusive features will provide an accurate picture of the events, but involves extremely time-consuming redrawing of the plan views. This hindrance may be overcome using GIS. By digitizing layers for each stratum of a site and codifying them in a manner that specifies the stratum each feature was first recognized, it is possible to select only those features that are truly contemporaneous. Because GIS has the ability to "turn on" or "turn off" the outlines of individual features, or sets thereof, it is feasible to quickly view an excavation floor as it appeared in the field—with all the features visible simultaneously—or to instruct the program to display those features that originated from specified excavation floors. Further, specified feature types may be selected for display. For example, post molds, fire hearths, or burials may be depicted by class or in various combinations for a given layer(s). This requires careful planning when developing the database so that it is structured and codified in a format suitable for manipulation and recognition by the GIS program, but the enormous time savings and the exceptional analytical power this provides are well worth the initial time investment.

Closing Remarks

Research Contributions to Date

The research to date has resulted in an extensive published and unpublished record about the Paso del Indio site. It is the first time remote sensing such as GPR has been used on a Puerto Rican archaeological site. It leads the way in using geomorphology to interpret archaeological stratigraphy and flood sequences. It presents vast amounts of raw data on burials, some very tantalizing initial interpretations of funerary practices, and evidence that ancestor worship was practiced prehistorically through the manipulation of human remains. The large number of radiocarbon dates—including two from the Archaic age—is invaluable for refined stratigraphic interpretations. The project has introduced GIS as an analytical tool capable of data manipulation and interpretation. Arguably one of the greatest contributions is to public archaeology, providing a captivating live educational stage to highlight archaeology and to teach the public in ways that books and documentaries never will.

The transitions in key personnel and the consequent loss of "corporate knowledge" were truly unfortunate. Hopefully we will continue to make meaningful contributions using the records and collections we were provided. We inherited major logistical handicaps, but it must be emphasized that the bulk of the data are sound. We have an excellent photographic record, a fairly complete set of profiles and plan views, and abundant field notes. These documents have helped immensely in sorting out most of the questions that have arisen. And, most importantly, those specialists and staff who were willing to continue throughout the long and strenuous ordeal of the project, and are just beginning to publish their findings, must be congratulated for their professional dedication to seeing this project through to the end.

Anticipated Research Contributions

We have nearly completed the laboratory analyses, but there are numerous tantalizing leads yet to follow. Once the data from all of the specialists becomes available, the weaving together of all their findings will be a distinct challenge. We are optimistic the effort we have taken to enter this information into a GIS database will pay off. We expect to reach additional insights in intersite spatial analysis, house size and patterns, processing areas, and public spaces. Environmental interpretations should blossom when data on the macrobotanical remains, pollen, and fauna become available. We also expect to greatly refine the ceramic technology and stylistic analysis during the key transition periods represented at the site. Personally, I am looking forward to testing my ideas about interrelated technological strategies, and to see if I can indeed identify "invisible" and broad-scale technologies. Some of the research that might prove to be the most significant contribution in the long run is only now beginning: research focusing on the human population, such as diet and health, and DNA analysis that might lead to revelations about social status, differential treatment of the dead, and more complex sociopolitical patterns. Whatever tomorrow's research topics turn out to be, the Paso del Indio site has immense potential for future research.

3

Environmental and Cultural Correlates in the West Indies
A View from Puerto Rico

*Peter E. Siegel, John G. Jones,
Deborah M. Pearsall, and Daniel P. Wagner*

Observations made by the early Spanish chroniclers of the Greater Antilles reflect Native American societies that were hierarchically organized, with lesser chiefs providing personnel for labor and warfare to more powerful chiefs (Colón 1947; Joyce 1916; Rouse 1948). The geographic and size distributions of the late prehistoric/protohistoric ball courts in Puerto Rico provide evidence for locally based centralized polities (Siegel 1999). At the macroregional scale of the entire island, political organization was not centralized. Archaeological and ethnohistoric data reveal interpolity competition (Siegel 2004).

Archaeological data derived from ceramic styles, iconography, settlement organization, and distinctive artifacts reflect linkages between the Saladoid cultures that dispersed into the West Indies by approximately 500 B.C. and the Taínos, who were well established in the fifteenth century A.D. (Oliver, this volume; Rouse 1986, 1992; Siegel 1992, 1996; Walker 1993). In previous research, Siegel has constructed an argument for the importance of ideology and cosmology in the development of Taíno complex society, focusing specifically on the relations between settlement structure and ideology (Siegel 1989a, 1991c, 1996; see also Curet 1996; Curet and Oliver 1998; Oliver 1998, this volume). At this stage of research it is critical to explore systematically the potential linkages between society, economy, and environment when discussing culture change.

Two sections of the chronological spectrum are of increasing interest in Caribbean archaeology with regard to continuity and change in adaptations and group interactions. In Puerto Rico these are the Archaic/ceramic-age transition, dating to approximately 200 B.C., and the Saladoid/Ostionoid transition, which dates to ca. A.D. 600. To what extent did Archaic groups modify the landscape and, perhaps, introduce cultivation, after which later ceramic-age populations imported their own horticultural practices? What was the nature of interactions between the Archaic and ceramic-age populations? What was the timing and rate of introduction of new species of plants and animals to the West Indies by Native Americans? For obvious reasons, researchers think of the current landscapes of the West Indies as a product of recent "human disturbances and influences," resulting from such practices as overgrazing and strip farming (Newsom and Pearsall 2003:360). As observed by Newsom and Pearsall (2003), it is useful to consider, too, landscape modifications at various times in prehistory, and implications for contemporaneous groups as well as successive populations.

In this chapter we focus on the environmental and cultural contexts of the Maisabel site. This site was occupied continuously from approximately 200 B.C. to A.D. 1200, spanning the full range of the Saladoid period and much of the Ostionoid period. Importantly, this occupational history spans the transition from tribal egalitarian communities to chiefdoms in Puerto Rico.

The original goals of the current investigation were to obtain direct baseline information for the environmental context, subsistence economy, and land-use practices of the people who occupied the Maisabel location prior to, during, and following the transition from egalitarian to ranked society. The Ostionoid period (ca. A.D. 600–1500) witnessed the development of site hierarchies and the gradual narrowing of political power to small subsets of the population (Rodríguez López 1990; Siegel 1992, 1996, 1999; Wilson 1990). During this time Maisabel was a hamlet or village (Siegel 1995). Hamlets undoubtedly were of fundamental importance in the flow of goods through emerging tributary networks (Johnson and Earle 1987). The primary production and initial preparation of goods may have occurred at the hamlet level in a settlement hierarchy. Several questions provide structure for the current research. When did clearing occur that resulted in significant increases in the amount of arable land? Which cultigens appear first in the microbotanical record, and in what combinations? Does the emphasis on specific crops shift to more easily storable food (i.e., maize, manioc) in relation to changes in requirements for tribute?

These questions were addressed through a program of coring and augering within and around the Maisabel site. Sediment cores were taken from a small pond defining one edge of the site and from a mangrove located to the east of the site (Figures 3.1 and 3.2).

Holocene Environment in the West Indies

It is difficult to address issues of culture and environment in any island of the West Indies without considering the larger context of the archipelago (Watters and Rouse 1989). As such, results of the present study may be compared to other paleoenvironmental reconstructions in the Caribbean Basin. A 7.5-meter-long core taken from Lake Miragoane on Haiti provides a detailed environmental record for the northern Caribbean (Brenner and Binford 1988; Curtis and Hodell 1993; Higuera-Gundy 1989, 1991; Higuera-Gundy et al. 1999; Hodell et al. 1991). This reconstruction reveals a series of changing climates beginning in the early post-Pleistocene, and which is associated with distinct pollen zones, vegetational changes, and fluctuating lake levels. The general pattern is characterized by a xeric environment from 10,400–8200 cal B.P., giving way to an increasingly mesic clime from 8200–3900 cal B.P. There was a "sudden onset of dry conditions at 3.2 kyr BP," which culminated in a "sharp increase" in aridity, marking a dry episode from 2400 to 1500 cal B.P. (Hodell et al. 1991:792). This was followed by a "period of wetter conditions" between approximately 1500 and 900 cal B.P., and reverting to a dry setting from 900 cal B.P. to the present (Hodell et al. 1991:792, Table 2, Figure 2). Within the broad pattern of evaporation and precipitation ratios there are numerous wiggles in the climate curve, reflecting short-term environmental fluctuations that may have been of considerable importance to human groups occupying the region (Hodell et al. 1991:Figure 2). Indeed, some of these fluctuations may have been a product of human activities.

For Andros Island in the Bahamas, Kjellmark (1996) documented a dry period from approximately 3260–1390 cal B.P., followed by a mesic climate supporting tropical hardwoods. Berman and Pearsall (2000:233) suggest that the earlier xeric environment may explain the lack of human occupation in the Bahamas at this time.

Nyberg et al. (2001a) examined lithological and mineral magnetic parameters and foraminifer data from a set of sediment cores obtained off the south and west coasts of Puerto Rico to discuss changing precipitation patterns and climate variability over the past 2,000 years in the region. Prior to approximately A.D. 850 to 1000, Nyberg et al. (2001a) indicate that relatively dry conditions prevailed. More humid conditions are inferred in the sediment core data following this period. Their inferences for elevated precipitation

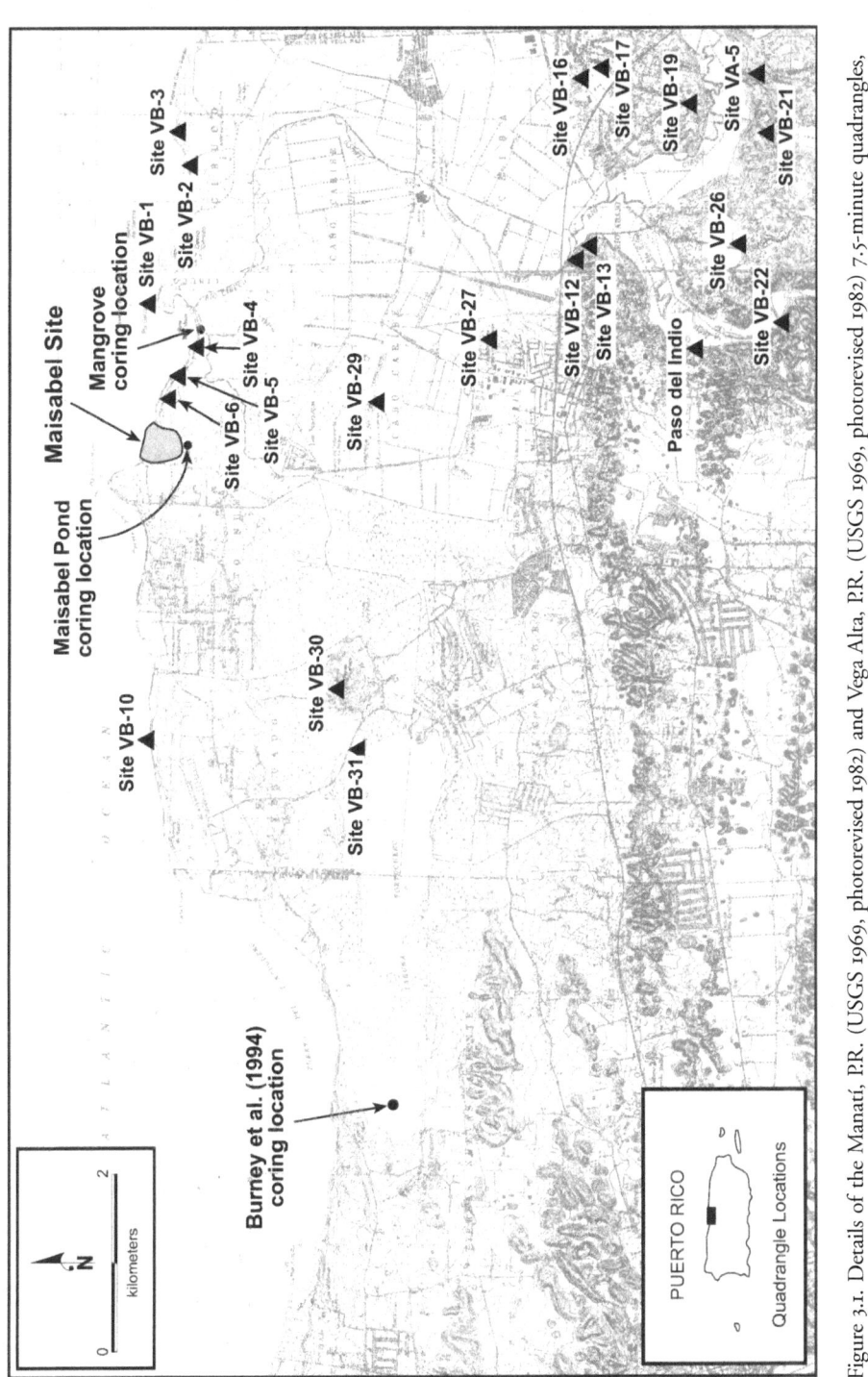

Figure 3.1. Details of the Manatí, P.R. (USGS 1969, photorevised 1982) and Vega Alta, P.R. (USGS 1969, photorevised 1982) 7.5-minute quadrangles, showing the Maisabel site and the coring locations discussed in the text.

Figure 3.2. Photograph of the pond while Core LM-2 is in process. Core LM-1 is in the foreground. John Jones is operating the vibracore motor and Peter Siegel and assistant are holding the core tube. Deborah Pearsall is observing. Photograph by Dan Wagner.

levels are based partially on observed increases in sedimentation rates resulting from elevated amounts of "fluvially derived detrital material from Puerto Rico" (Nyberg et al. 2001a:96). Alternatively, or in addition, increased runoff and erosion from the land into the ocean during the latter 1,000 years of their chronological range may be a product of increasingly intensive forms of horticulture practiced by the residents of the island. In another study, Nyberg et al. (2001b) found that the mean annual sea surface temperatures around Puerto Rico were 2–4°C cooler during the seventh century A.D. than at present. They suggest that these cooler conditions resulted from "regional oceanic and atmospheric circulation differences" (Nyberg et al. 2001b).

Oxygen isotope records of planktonic foraminifera from the Cariaco Basin, Venezuela supplied high-resolution climate data for the Caribbean region from the mid to late Holocene (Tedesco et al. 2001). Tedesco et al. (2001) found that "arid conditions commenced in the region between about 3600–3200 cal. yrs. B.P.," which were most likely related to colder sea surface temperatures. These findings are consistent with the timing of dry conditions documented by Higuera-Gundy et al. (1999), Hodell et al. (1991), and Kjellmark (1996).

On the island of Grenada, a team from the Royal Ontario Museum has cored two lakes and one pond; based on a composite pollen profile dating from 25,000 years ago to recent times, these researchers conclude that "a continuous history of rain forest" is represented (McAndrews 1996:247).

Studies by researchers in the Amazon suggest humid conditions well into the Pleistocene and throughout the Holocene, with natural perturbations or disturbances, such as forest fires, occurring randomly (Colinvaux 1987, 1993), although recent evidence suggests a period of significant drying in much of eastern Amazonia (Behling 1995; Piperno and Pearsall 1998). The latter studies are in agreement with most of the Caribbean sequences (Higuera-Gundy 1999; Hodell et al. 1991; Kjellmark 1996; Nyberg et al. 2001a; Tedesco et al. 2001).

Within the framework of the Caribbean Basin, paleoclimatic studies, in toto, reveal broad patterns of environmental and climatic changes. The late Holocene portions of the climatic sequences are relevant for the ceramic-age occupations of Maisabel. Specifically, a dry episode corresponds to a period shortly before occupation of the site and throughout the Hacienda Grande period. This is followed by a 600-year interval of wetter conditions, spanning the Cuevas and Monserrate occupations. Finally, by the Santa Elena period through to the present, the broad Caribbean-wide pattern reveals a shift to dry and warmer conditions. Within the large region of the Caribbean Basin, however, local variations in edaphic conditions, precipitation patterns, and topographic settings produced unique sets of circumstances that were of particular importance for the human groups that occupied these places. It is at this local level, we argue, that archaeologists, and indeed anthropologists in general, initially will be most successful when attempting to unravel and understand human adaptations and sequences of cultural change. Further, an in-depth understanding of the local environmental setting through time provides an important context and perhaps insight into the nature of interactions between groups. Let there be no confusion, we are not advocating an extreme or myopic form of environmental determinism. Relations between culture and environment clearly are of the two-way variety. Individuals, families, and larger social formations respond to, adapt to, and alter their physical settings.

In the remainder of this chapter we present a reconstruction of the environs of the Maisabel locale, examining in particular microbotanical and pedological data. These data are then viewed against the known prehistoric occupations in the area. In doing so, we envision culture and environment as an integrated context. Environmental data reflect the physical settings available to human groups as well as the changes that human groups made to these settings.

Geological and Pedological Context of the Maisabel Site

The Maisabel site is located on the shoreline of the Atlantic Ocean in the lowlands of Puerto Rico's north-central coastal plain (Figure 3.1). Distributed across a sprawling area that ranges as much as 700 meters south of the ocean, the site landscape encompasses both beachfront and inland positions, each with attendant geology, soil types, and formation processes. The beach strand and associated belt of eolian sand extend about 200 meters south of the ocean, beyond which limit the sand begins to taper sharply, and interior upland positions become the majority of the site terrain. Upland landscapes are tied to the valley of a small intermittent drainage way that roughly bisects the southern quarter of the site area. An approximately 2.5 ha (6.2 ac.) pond that was the central focus of this investigation is contained within this drainage way and occupies a position near its western headwater end. From the pond, the drainage way then courses to its eventual outlet about a half kilometer southeast of the site, where it joins with an expansive mangrove swamp at the mouth of the Río Cibuco. A prominent east-west ridge forms the northern flank of the drainage way, and as a topographic divide across the site intervenes between the ocean and the pond. The southern flank of the drainage way is sharply defined by a steeply rising upland that extends well past the site area (Figure 3.3).

An assortment of calcareous sediments and rocks occur in the northern coastal region. These range from Tertiary limestone in the higher uplands well south of the coast to various Pleistocene and Holocene terrace and beach deposits along the coast itself (Beinroth 1969; Guillou and Glass 1957). In the immediate vicinity of the site the main geologic materials other than the

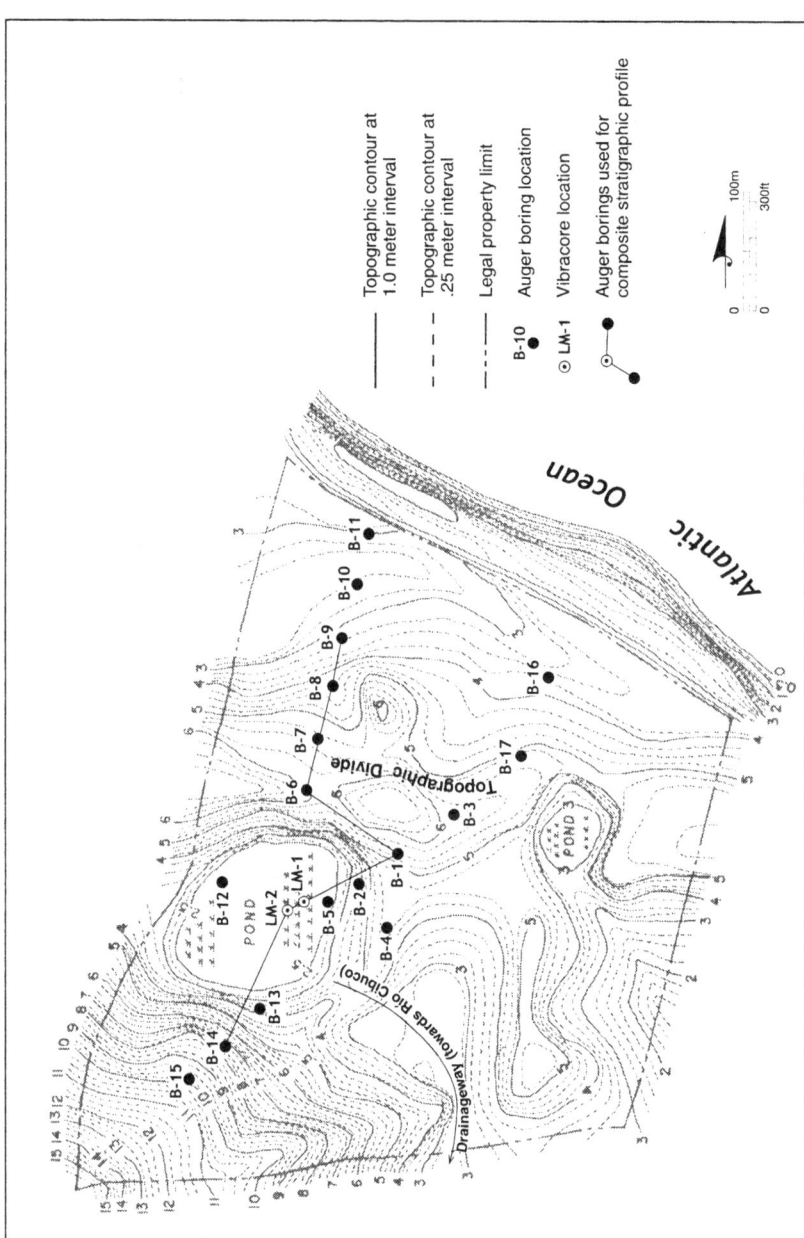

Figure 3.3. Topographic map of the Maisabel setting showing the locations of auger borings and the two pond cores.

eolian sand that would be typical for nearly any low-lying (< 6 m elevation) coastline location are recognized simply as marine terrace deposits. These lithified deposits were originally amassed as beach sand and gravel during the Pleistocene and now occur mainly in the forms of arenaceous limestone or calcium carbonate–cemented sandstone. In recognition of their origin and close proximity to the modern shoreline, early geologic reports referred to these cemented deposits as beachrock (Kaye 1959). Currently, the sandy limestone is almost continuously exposed at the beachfront along the northern edge of the site, and also shows as a surface outcrop on the slope just beyond the northern rim of the pond. A number of auger borings also encountered the rock at subsurface levels, sometimes at depths of less than a meter. The relatively soft rock is susceptible to the same dissolution and disintegration processes typical for other limestone types in moist tropical settings, and karst topographic features, although not as abundant as in the older limestone formations of the interior, are occasionally present in the calcareous rocks of the coast.

The pond, around which much of this investigation was centered, is very likely one such karst feature, specifically a sinkhole (Figure 3.3). Surficial landscape indicators together with the stratigraphic composition of the pond deposits are consistent with a sinkhole form. As collapse features exhibiting roughly circular shapes, sinkholes (dolines) are commonly found in low-lying drainage-way positions, where concentrated water flows contribute to increased dissolution of the underlying limestone (Monroe 1980:22). Indeed, even entire drainage ways themselves can develop along lines of weakened rock that are more vulnerable to carbonate loss. Thus, both the low landscape position and the pond's circular to oval shape are suggestive of a sinkhole. Additionally, occurrences of other nearby features demonstrate probable karst activity in the vicinity. Several similarly circular depressions occur within a few kilometers of the site, and even within the site itself there appear to be two others. One much smaller than the pond but of even more sharply outlined form occurs along a midslope position on the steep slope about 60 meters south of the pond. Another is a somewhat more ephemeral pond occupying a smaller depression about 250 meters northeast of the main pond (Figure 3.3).

Other evidence of karst activity and sinkhole formation is given in the sequence of deposits within the pond. As intercepted by a core near the center of the pond, the general pond stratigraphy consists of an upper 2-meter section of alluvial wash and peat above clayey strata that extend below the 3-meter depth of sampling. The clayey strata are of nearly identical composition to the subsoil horizons developed in the upland limestone soils surrounding the pond. In fact, similarities for particle size distribution as well as major chemical traits are so strong as to suggest a prolonged period of surface-related pedogenic weathering prior to the sinkhole collapse and subsequent accumulation of the overlying peat and wash sediments.

Soil and geomorphological studies of the Maisabel site, pond sediments, and associated upland soils were undertaken in an effort to understand ceramic-age land-use and subsistence practices. Considerations addressed the extent to which natural site conditions may have regulated or directed prehistoric land-use strategies as well as the apparent environmental consequences attributable to the cultural practices themselves.

Soil borings were made across the Maisabel site to identify soil and deposit types and to determine soil and landscape relationships. In total, 32 soil profiles distributed principally along three transects leading from the pond toward the ocean were examined by hand auger borings (Figure 3.3). Standard techniques and nomenclature for the field description of soils were employed (Soil Survey Staff 1993). Samples for laboratory analyses were collected from seven of the profiles. In addition, soils collected from the pond core were sampled and described in detail.

Measurements of soil particle size distribution and a suite of chemical properties were made on selected soil and sediment samples. Soil particle size distributions were determined for 45 samples derived from seven soil profiles and the pond core. Particle sizes measured included total clay and total silt as well as sand fractions of very coarse, coarse, medium, fine, and very fine. Chemical analyses performed on 30 samples collected from four soil profiles and the pond core included pH, percent organic matter (Walkley-Black and loss on ignition), extractable amounts of P, K, Ca, Mg, Zn, Cu, and Fe, and total concentrations of P, Ba, and Sr.

Pedology

Types and distribution of soil parent material

Soil variability across the site is related to soil parent material type and landscape position. Three main parent material or deposit types occur within the site. These consist of the eolian sand concentrated mainly between the Atlantic Ocean and the crest of the interfluve ridge, the sandy residual limestone comprising nearly all of upland landscapes south of the ridge, and alluvial and peat deposits contained within the studied pond (Figure 3.4). In positions near the ridge crest and for distances up to 100 meters north of the crest, soil horizons are formed in both eolian sand and underlying limestone residuum. Subsoil formed from the residual limestone may actually carry northward the entire distance to the ocean, but this could not be ascertained due to a sea-

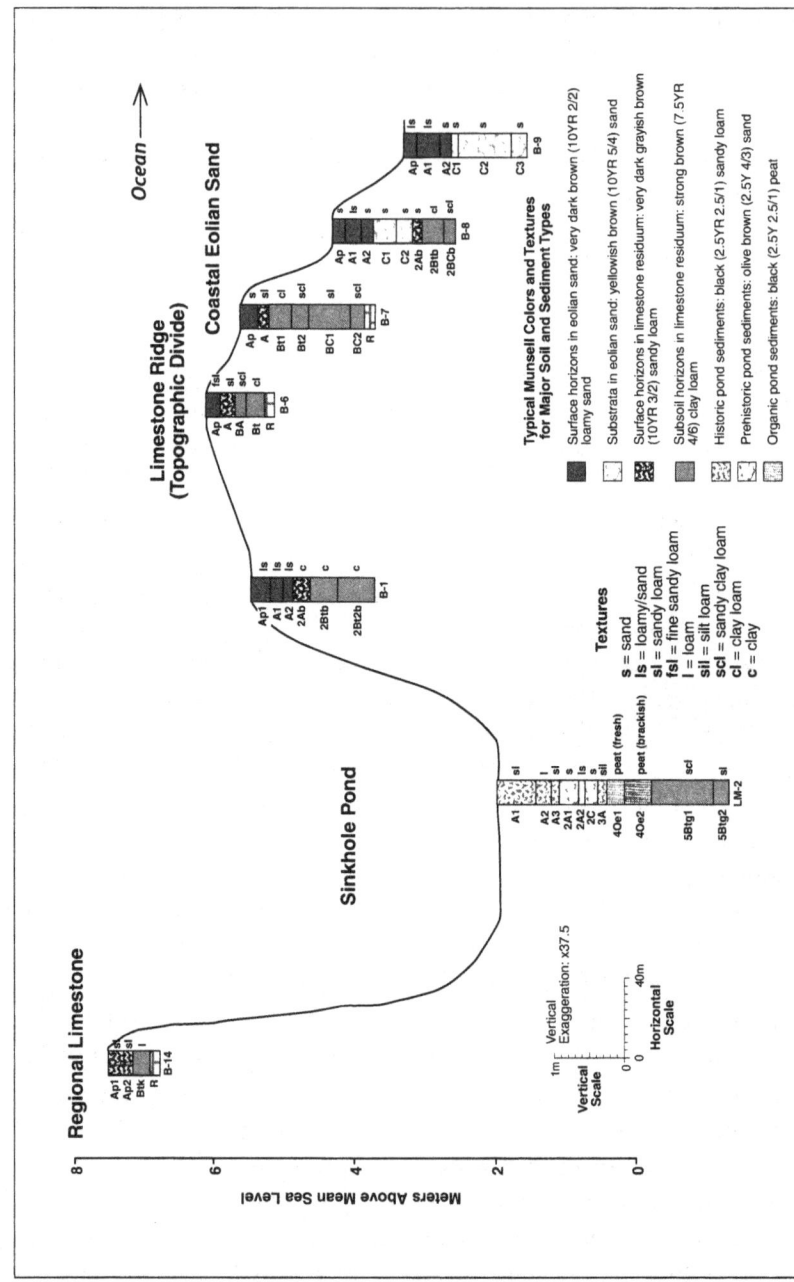

Figure 3.4. Representative soil profiles across the landforms of the Maisabel site and its surroundings.

ward thickening of the eolian cap that eventually exceeded the 1.5-m capability of the auger employed.

Eolian soils

Roughly half of the site area is occupied by soils in which eolian sand is a significant component of the soil parent material. This area is located largely on the north side of the site's topographic divide, where deposits of eolian sand are nearly everywhere in excess of a meter in thickness. As the beach source area is approached, the eolian mantle progressively thickens to over 2 meters. Eolian sand also carries across the ridge to the southern half of the site, but on this leeward side of the ridge it thins to a veneer of 3 to 40 cm, and is often partially mixed with underlying limestone-derived material (Figure 3.4).

Where eolian sand is the dominant parent, soil profiles typically consist of a stacked sequence of three to four surface (A) horizons atop underlying eolian substrata (C) horizons and/or strongly developed subsoil (B) horizons of the residual limestone soil. The modern surface horizon has clearly been plowed, and it is very likely that in most instances the next surface horizon down was formerly plowed as well. The lower two to three of the surface horizons usually contain heavy concentrations of ceramics, but as observed in the relatively small volumes of material retrieved in augering, artifacts either do not occur or have a very low presence in underlying eolian substrata or residual limestone subsoil layers. Low concentrations of artifacts characterize most modern surface horizons, and this is interpreted to represent mixing by tillage with the artifact-rich layer beneath.

The stacking of multiple A horizons is evidence of an active eolian regime during and after the intervals of prehistoric occupation. This would not be unexpected given the oceanfront location of the site, and indeed the amount of activity can actually be considered relatively modest. The sand is distributed as sheet deposits rather than in the undulating dunal forms indicative of highly unstable landscapes continuously undergoing reworking. Also, the sequence of surface horizons demonstrates that major periods of sand mobilization occurred episodically and were interspersed with intervals of essential surface stability of sufficient duration to allow for significant organic matter accumulation and surface horizon differentiation. The episodes may be related to environmental controls such as shifts in wind or precipitation patterns, or they could also have been culturally influenced. Human regulation of the type and density of vegetative cover could readily have affected the trapping and retention of windblown sand as well as the susceptibility of sand to remobilization in response to varying conditions of surface stability or disturbance.

Residual soils

Soils that developed predominantly in limestone residuum occupy the southern half of the site area, exclusive of the pond and drainage-way bottom. As previously stated, surfaces along the descending leeward slope of the topographic divide are thinly mantled by eolian sand, but the major subsoil horizons in all of the upland soils south of the ridge crest are formed entirely in materials derived from weathered limestone. Limestone soils are characterized by fine-textured subsoil horizons of heavy sandy clay loam to sandy clay and clay textures. The textures of overlying surface horizons vary with respect to the degree of eolian influence. Surfaces not strongly influenced by additions of eolian sand have textures of sandy loam. Where the sands are present, textures are either loamy sand or sand.

The fine-textured and dense subsoil horizons are mainly yellowish brown (10YR 4/6, 5/6) to strong brown (7.5YR 4/6) in color, but unless they are shallow and underlain by limestone bedrock they are typically mottled by grayish (2.5Y 6/2, 5Y 7/2) colors indicative of drainage restrictions. In the immediate vicinity of the pond and drainage-way bottom, a high water table could account for the drainage mottling, but even soils occupying much higher landscape positions exhibit mottling indicative of restricted drainage. Due to the impedance of internal water flow through slowly permeable, clayey subsoils, these soils are only moderately well drained.

The distribution of texturally contrasting soil types (sandy vs. clayey) across the site area could well have influenced prehistoric land-use choices. With respect to either horticulture or inhabitability the two principal soil types are distinctly different; sandy soils would have been preferable. In terms of workability for planting, or any type of subsurface excavation, the sandy soils north of the ridge would have been far more desirable. Additionally, the considerably better drainage properties of the eolian soils represented more favorable living surfaces and subsurface storage conditions. These soils are excessively droughty during dry periods, although this is often a limitation in clayey soils as well. If considered solely on the basis of soil conditions, spaces selected for both living and horticulture are likely to have been concentrated to the north of the ridge. The persistence of the sandy mantle atop some of the limestone soils south of the ridge would have given these soils added utility as well, but where the mantle was less than perhaps 40 centimeters in thickness intensive activity is considered to be less likely. The predominantly residual soils of the limestone uplands may well have been utilized only after an increasing population caused depletion of the readily available areas of eolian soils.

Pond Stratigraphy

Sediment composition and chronology

Pond sediments were examined in a single deep core at a point near the pond center and in several less deep hand augers close to the pond edges (Figures 3.2 and 3.3). Based on these observations sediment and soil types occupying the investigated pond basin can be grouped into four main categories. In order of increasing depth these are variably organic peat deposits, very sandy deposits with low organic contents, highly organic peat deposits, and a basal substratum of clayey soil material weathered from the residual site limestone (Figure 3.4). Dates obtained at several levels in the deep core have enabled a detailed chronological reconstruction of the sedimentation record (Table 3.1).

The upper portion of the sediment column is composed of loamy wash deposits accumulated in historic times. This historic sediment is mainly sandy loam to sandy clay loam in texture, contains high to moderately high amounts of organic matter, and thickens from about 30 cm near the pond edge to 84 cm in the center. Although excessively fluid conditions prevented the sampling and thus dating of about the upper 50 cm of this sediment in the pond center, texturally similar but more coherent sediment extending to a depth of 84 cm was collected. Based on a calibrated intercept date of A.D. 1285 (cal A.D. 1255–1380, 2 sigmas) from closely underlying sandy strata (90–95 cm) together with a morphological likeness and similar chemical properties between this material and that near the pond edge, a historic age for the upper 84 cm of the central core may be inferred (Table 3.1).

Beneath the 84-cm historic mantle are very sandy and much less organic deposits that extend to 142 cm. Except for its uppermost layer, nearly this entire sand section was amassed during major prehistoric occupations of the site. That the uppermost layer was possibly accumulated subsequent to the principal occupation period but before the arrival of Europeans is suggested by the age of the 90–95 cm depth increment. With the calibrated intercept date of A.D. 1285 for this increment and assuming a date of A.D. 1500 at the top of the sand section, it appears likely that about 8.5 cm of sand were laid down during the roughly 215 to 300 years between the late Ostionoid abandonment of the site (ca. A.D. 1200) and the onset of the historic period (Table 3.2). All underlying sand deposits extending to a depth of 142 cm accumulated during major prehistoric occupations of the site.

Underlying the sands are peat deposits that extend to a depth of 205 cm. These deposits are almost entirely of biological origin, with loss on ignition

Table 3.1. Maisabel Coring Project Radiocarbon Dates.

Laboratory Sample Number	Provenience	Material Dated	Conventional Radiocarbon Age (B.P.)	Calibrated Date Range (1 sigma)	Calibrated Date Range (2 sigma)	Intercept of Radiocarbon Age with Calibration Curve
Beta-127522	LM-2, 90–95 cm (AMS date)	organic sediment	710 ± 40	A.D. 1275–1295	A.D. 1255–1380	A.D. 1285
Beta-127523	LM-2, 107–109 cm (AMS date)	charred material	1240 ± 40	A.D. 705–855	A.D. 680–885	A.D. 775
Beta-116369	LM-2, 141–146 cm	peat	1660 ± 50	A.D. 370–435	A.D. 260–535	A.D. 410
Beta-127525	LM-2, 151 cm (AMS date)	wood	1450 ± 40	A.D. 585–645	A.D. 545–660	A.D. 625
Beta-127524	LM-2, 160–165 cm	peat	2270 ± 60	390–210 B.C.	405–180 B.C.	375 B.C.
Beta-116370	LM-2, 200–205 cm	peat	2560 ± 50	800–600 B.C.	815–525 B.C.	785 B.C.
Beta-130450	MAN-1, 203–205 cm	wood	2730 ± 70	930–815 B.C.	1020–795 B.C.	845 B.C.
Beta-130451	MAN-1, 274–281 cm	wood	3640 ± 70	2125–1910 B.C.	2200–1780 B.C.	2010 B.C.
Beta-116372	MAN-1, 385–394 cm	wood	3820 ± 70	2350–2140 B.C.	2465–2030 B.C.	2270 B.C.

Table 3.2. Sedimentation Rates and Inferred Landscape and Pond Conditions during Major Cultural Periods.

Depth (cm)	Intercept of Radiocarbon Age with Calibration Curve[a]	Sedimentation Rate (cm/yr)	Landscape/ Pond Conditions	Cultural Affiliation
0	A.D. 2000[b]			
84	A.D. 1500[b]	.168	Major soil erosion	European
92.5	A.D. 1285	.037	Minor soil erosion	Abandonment
108	A.D. 775	.030	Minor soil erosion	Santa Elena
143.5	A.D. 410	.097	Moderate soil erosion	Cuevas/Monserrate
162.5	375 B.C.	.024	Minor soil erosion	Hacienda Grande
202.5	785 B.C.	.098	In situ peat accumulation, tidal influence, minimal erosion	Archaic

[a] See Table 3.1 for the calibrated age ranges.
[b] This age is based on stratigraphic positioning/depositional conditions and not on a radiocarbon date.

measurements of organic matter in the 60 to 70 percent range. The remaining mineral fraction is probably comprised mainly of biogenic silica, with alluvial silt or clay representing only a small portion of the sediment mass. Thus, during the period of peat formation, contributions of eroded sediments due to natural or human agency should be considered minimal.

Age determinations for several levels of the 63-cm peat section indicate that peat production spanned a period of 1,200 years. Based on calibrated dates from the base and top of the peat, this period began in Archaic times (ca. 785 cal B.C. [815–525 cal B.C., 2 sigmas]) and ended well after the establishment of the early ceramic-age occupations (ca. A.D. 340). A sample of organic sediment located about 20 cm below the top of the peat was dated to approximately 375 cal B.C. (405–180 cal B.C., 2 sigmas), indicating that peat accumulation/formation was most rapid earlier in the period (.098 cm/yr) and had slowed greatly (.023 cm/yr) before its final cessation (Tables 3.1 and 3.2). This also corresponds to the shift from large to small sedges as documented in the pollen record. Clark et al. (2003:638, Table I) documented a sedimentation rate of .05 cm/yr from approximately 2580 B.C. to A.D. 1030 in the Paso del Indio site a few kilometers inland from Maisabel.

Beneath the peat are mineral layers derived largely from weathering of the native site limestone. Fine-textured material closely resembling the soils of adjacent uplands extends to the 295-cm base of the deep core. Interestingly, the intervention of a thin layer (205–210 cm) of sandy alluvium between the peat and limestone residuum is suggestive of a catastrophic event associated with a brief higher energy system. Possibilities include an unusually large storm or hurricane or, perhaps, rapid sinkhole formation due to an abrupt collapse of the underlying limestone. The close resemblance of the clayey soil material to surrounding upland soils strongly suggests that this material originally developed via pedogenesis in a near-surface terrestrial environment. That it is now 2 to 3 meters lower than adjacent land surfaces is clear evidence of land subsidence, and the thin sand layer sharply overlain by peat appears to signal a sudden shift from a terrestrial to an aquatic state.

A number of implications for prehistoric site occupation arise from the compositions and ages of the pond sediments. Dates from various sections of the core enable ages to be interpolated for every horizon of the column, thus allowing the column to be partitioned into segments that correspond to major prehistoric periods (Table 3.1). For each major cultural occupation the prevailing environmental conditions can be addressed, as can the specific impacts of each occupational period on the physical and chemical properties of the pond sediments.

The nature of the pond has not remained static throughout its approximately 3,000 years of existence. Peat production during the first 1,200 years evinces heavy vegetative cover, apparently dominated by such emergent aquatic plants as sedges, suggesting that for the first third of its existence the pond was a shallow water system similar to that of today. Water depths of over a half-meter or so would have inhibited the growth of the herbaceous plants that probably produced the peat. Chemical data indicate that the pond was exposed to brackish influences during the first 500 years of its existence. An extremely acid pH of 1.9 for the lower half of the peat section can only be explained by post-sampling oxidation of finely disseminated sulfides that could originally have formed only in a system open to tidal conditions. The elevation of the lower half of the peat is about 50 centimeters above present-day mean sea level, but even 3,000 years ago when sea level would have been slightly lower, this first increment was apparently within the reach of high tide via the drainage-way connection to the Río Cibuco (Figure 3.3).

It may or may not be significant that site occupation began at just about the time the pond was shifting from a brackish to fresh water system. With thickening peat buildup and perhaps some form of plugging sedimentation in the drainage way, the pond eventually became isolated from brackish input. Hodell et al. (1991:792) observed a "sharp increase" in "higher evaporation rates and lower lake level" by approximately 450 cal B.C. Under these conditions, we would expect the saline wedge that defines the extent of estuarine brackish water in the Río Cibuco to be smaller. This trend is evidenced by a higher pH (3.5) in the upper half of the peat, which, as noted previously, was also being produced at a much slower rate. Water in the pond not only became more potable, but may also have been deeper, a product of wetter conditions from approximately cal A.D. 400–1000 (Hodell et al. 1991:Figure 2). As a nearby source of drinking water the pond may have been a major consideration in the selection of this location by the inhabitants of Maisabel.

Upon initiation of site occupation and with the progression of cultural changes, the types and amounts of deposits accumulating in the pond changed. Table 3.2 summarizes the rates of sediment accumulation/formation during the major stages of the pond history. Several important points stand out. The first settlers, the Hacienda Grande people, appear to have had little impact on pond sedimentation. These inhabitants occupied the site during the final stages of peat formation, and since there is only a scant soil presence in the peat they do not appear to have caused much erosion of the land surfaces within the pond watershed. Their areas of horticulture and other land modification activities must therefore have been substantially removed from the pond, and were probably confined to the eolian sand soils to the north of the ridge divide. Landscape and soil disturbances along the approaches to the pond may have been no more severe than those attributable to footpaths. The sediment volume offers no evidence of intensive horticulture within the pond catchment by the Hacienda Grande inhabitants. Indeed, it tends to refute the possibility.

With the emergence of the Cuevas and continuing into the Monserrate occupations, however, the pond sediments registered an impact. A sedimentation rate of .097 cm/yr is the highest for the prehistoric period (Table 3.2). Peat production ceased, possibly due to increasing water depth, and very sandy deposits began washing or blowing into the pond, burying the peat. Texturally, the sandy sediments are similar to the eolian sand that variably caps the upland soils occupying the northern slopes around the pond. However, a distinct tendency toward coarser sand fractions in the pond sediment can probably be credited to minor sorting by water; most of the sand therefore is likely to have been introduced to the pond as slope wash rather than by wind transport. Nevertheless, increased mobilization of sand by wind would be expected with clearing activities, and some of the sand was no doubt carried directly to the pond by wind.

Given that all of the eolian sand located to the south of the ridge is contained within one or more artifact-bearing surface horizons that were apparently formed during the site occupation, it could well be that eolian sand never carried beyond the ridge crest until the landscape was mostly cleared. Under this scenario, the cultural impact is two-staged. Eolian sand was initially able to spread over the ridge due to the removal of blocking vegetation that normally would have contained the windblown sand to the windward side of the ridge (closer to the ocean). Further movement of the sand resulting in its eventual introduction to the pond was then facilitated by slope wash eroding the disturbed land surfaces around the pond.

In response to shifting cultural impacts on the land, and very likely with some climatic influence as well, the influx of sediments into the pond proceeded at varying rates. By the Santa Elena period, sedimentation in the pond dropped so drastically (.030 cm/yr) that considerably decreased human activity within the pond catchment is indicated. Sedimentation continued to be minor (.037 cm/yr) after apparent abandonment of the site, but with the arrival of Europeans increased massively to a rate of .168 cm/yr (Table 3.2). Additionally, the historic sediments are not as sandy and contain higher percentages of clay, presumably reflecting more extensive utilization of the finer textured limestone soils. Clark et al. (2003:638, Figure 6) reported a remarkably high sedimentation rate of .84 cm/yr in Paso del Indio at approximately A.D. 1000. This age corresponds to the Maisabel pond sedimentation rate of about .03 cm/yr (Table 3.2). Clark et al. (2003:640–641) suggest that increasing precipitation at the tail end of a dry period "coupled with a xeric forest composition would likely result not only in enhanced runoff, but also in large contributions of sediment to the streams." At this point, we cannot reconcile the dramatically different sedimentation rates between Maisabel and Paso del Indio for the period around A.D. 1000, especially given the close proximity of the two sites.

Sediment chemistry

A number of the stratigraphic changes are also echoed by the chemical properties of the pond sediments. Given the great differences in composition and chemical retention capacity between sand, peat, and residual limestone soil, much of the variation in soil chemistry can be explained as simply a function of sediment type. However, even considering the significance of natural origin and compositional variation, overprints of human influence are still discernible. For instance, even though increased sedimentation rates are not associated with the Hacienda Grande people, chemical characteristics of the upper peat section appear to be signaling their presence. In comparison with underlying peat, the layer chronologically corresponding to the Hacienda Grande occupation is substantially higher in total-P, total-Sr, and total-Ba, as well as in extractable concentrations of Ca, K, and Mg. Purely on the basis of natural influences, these trends are counter to what would be expected in a transition from a tidal to fresh water system. Concentrations of all of these elements drop appreciably in the sandy portion of the column, although this is largely a function of the low chemical retention capacity of sand relative to organic matter. Within the sand section, higher elemental concentrations are clearly associated with the Monserrate and Cuevas occupations and then undergo declines within the Santa Elena and postoccupational periods. Historic sediments show huge increases in nearly every elemental concentration measured.

Microbotanical Analysis and the Archaic/Ceramic-Age Transition

Of direct relevance to the present study is a coring project conducted by David Burney and his colleagues (1994) in the western end of Laguna Tortuguero, approximately 6 kilometers west of Maisabel. In tracking the concentration of charcoal particulates stratigraphically, combined with radiocarbon dates, these researchers offer inferences into the initial peopling of Puerto Rico. The premise of this research is that "an increase in charcoal values... co-occurs with human arrival" (Burney et al. 1994:279). They found a significant increase in charcoal concentrations around 5300 cal B.P. (3350 cal B.C.). This corresponds to Archaic age occupations on the island, a good 3,000 years prior to the arrival of the ceramic-using colonists. By approximately 3200 cal B.P. the Tortuguero charcoal concentration declined markedly, and by 1504–1307 cal B.P. (cal A.D. 643–446) the presence of charcoal was exceedingly low. Burney et al. (1994:279–280) are at a loss to explain the decrease in charcoal concentration following the initial high values. They suggest that perhaps "human population density or resource exploitation changed, affecting the anthropogenic burning regime" (Burney et al. 1994:279). This is unlikely given what we know about settlement patterns, site densities, and economic strategies during the ceramic age and into the early post-Contact period. Ethnohistoric documents in particular reveal considerable slash-and-burn activities by the Taínos (Colón 1947; Martyr D'Anghera 1970 [1912]; Oviedo 1950; Sauer 1966). Perhaps local settlement shifts and interactions between groups resulted in cycles of occupations, abandonment, and reoccupations of places, which were associated with distinct land-use histories.

We cored a mangrove swamp located to the east of Maisabel (Figure 3.1). A large piece of preserved wood collected from 390 cm produced a date of 3820 ± 70 B.P. (2465–2030 cal B.C., 2 sigmas). This context is associated with a large peak in the charcoal concentration. The concentration of charcoal declined significantly at 275 cm, dating to 3640 ± 70 B.P. (2200–1780 cal B.C., 2 sigmas), and by 2730 ± 70 B.P. (1020–795 cal B.C., 2 sigmas) charcoal values were very low (Table 3.1, Figure 3.5).

Viewing the charcoal distributions documented in the Maisabel, Tortuguero, and mangrove cores together is potentially revealing of shifting areas of landscape modification in the local area. Chronologically, the Maisabel core overlaps the upper portion of the Tortuguero core. A radiocarbon date of 1490 ± 80 B.P. (cal A.D. 446–643, 1 sigma) from 120–139 cm of the Tortuguero core is slightly more recent than the Maisabel date of 1660 ± 50 B.P. (cal A.D. 370–435, 1 sigma) from 141–146 cm, providing a link between the two cores (Table 3.1).

The frequency of charcoal decreased to negligible quantities in Tortuguero when there was a significant spike in the Maisabel charcoal concentration (Figure 3.6). The large increase in the Maisabel charcoal concentration is related to the currently accepted transition between the Hacienda Grande and Cuevas periods, the two earliest ceramic-age occupations on the island. The peak of the Maisabel core charcoal concentration is located approximately 10 cm below the peat sample that was dated to cal A.D. 410 (intercept date).[1] By interpolation, this charcoal peak dated to approximately 65 cal B.C., assuming a constant sedimentation rate (.024 cm/yr) between 143.5 cm and 162.5 cm in

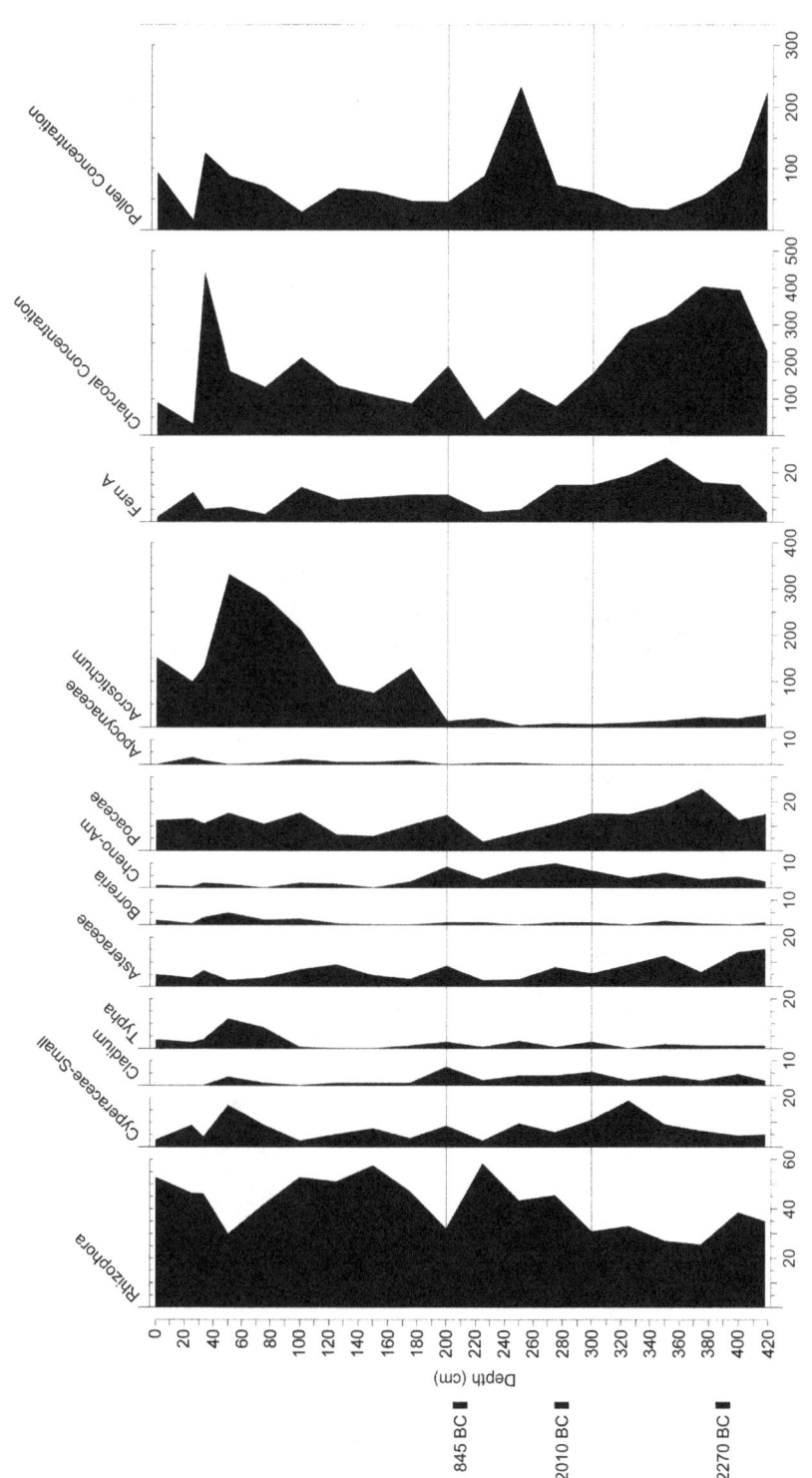

Figure 3.5. Pollen diagram of the Río Cibuco mangrove core.

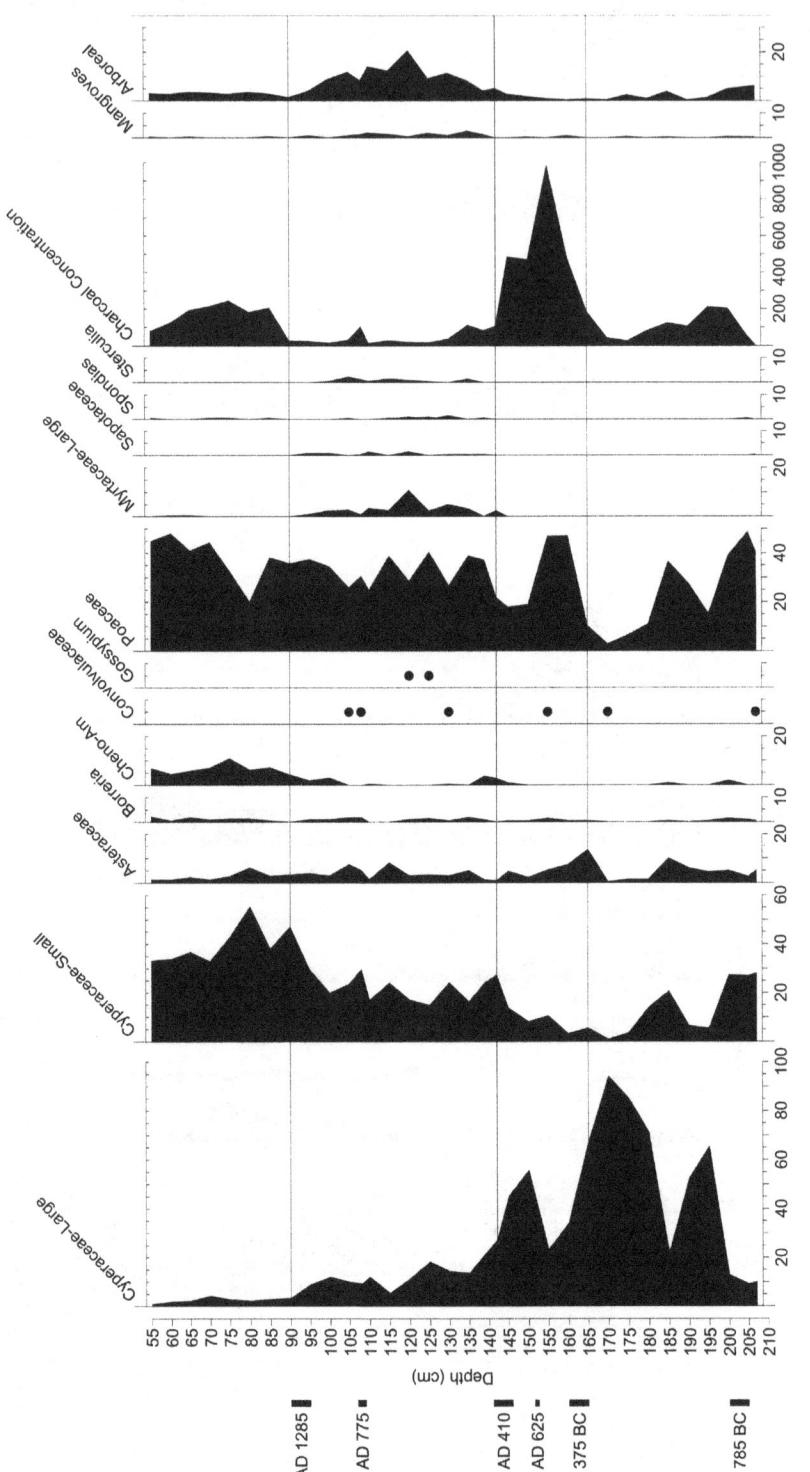

Figure 3.6. Pollen diagram of the LM-2 pond core.

the column. If this is accurate, then the peak in the charcoal concentration is associated with the earliest ceramic-age occupation (Hacienda Grande). Maisabel has a large Hacienda Grande occupation. Typical components of Hacienda Grande assemblages include great amounts of ceramic griddle fragments and small chipped-stone flakes. These are considered to be the durable elements of the aboriginal pancake- or bread-making industry in the West Indies. Lacking any additional data, it is commonly believed that bitter manioc (*Manihot esculenta*) was the crop of choice, which was processed into flour in the industry.

Given that the peak in the charcoal signal from the Maisabel core dates to the early portion of the Hacienda Grande period it is incongruous that the pond sedimentation rate for this period is low (Table 3.2). With the great amount of clearing and burning indicated by the high charcoal concentration we would expect, too, an elevated sedimentation rate resulting from more runoff and erosion. As discussed earlier, it may be that the earliest occupants of Maisabel concentrated their land-clearing activities to the north of the ridge divide in the site, selecting for the easily worked sandy soils. Topographically, terrain located north of the ridge divide is situated outside of the pond catchment (Figure 3.3). However, airborne particulates, like charcoal, still would have settled into the pond, especially with the nearly constant northeasterly winds. The scenario accounting for the high charcoal concentrations and low sedimentation rate in the pond dating to the Hacienda Grande period is that extensive clearing and burning took place in the northern part of the Maisabel site, outside of the pond catchment area. Erosion was minimal within the pond catchment (low sedimentation rate), while at the same time the prevailing northeasterly winds carried charcoal to the pond (high charcoal particulate concentration).

At 164 cm, a depth approximately associated with the earliest ceramic-age occupation in Maisabel, there is a sudden occurrence of Marantaceae (arrowroot) phytoliths, signaling its probable use as a food source. Maize (*Zea mays*) phytoliths were identified in the pond core at 207 cm, predating the earliest ceramic-age occupation of the site (Figure 3.7).

We suggest that charcoal concentrations depicted in the Tortuguero, Maisabel, and mangrove cores reflect local slash-and-burn activities. The dates associated with the Tortuguero and mangrove cores indicate that burning took place during the Archaic period, spanning a calibrated date range from approximately 5300–3500 B.P. (Burney et al. 1994:Figure 3). It would be useful to examine further the Tortuguero coring data for microfossils (pollen, phytoliths). This would provide us with a more complete view of land-use prac-

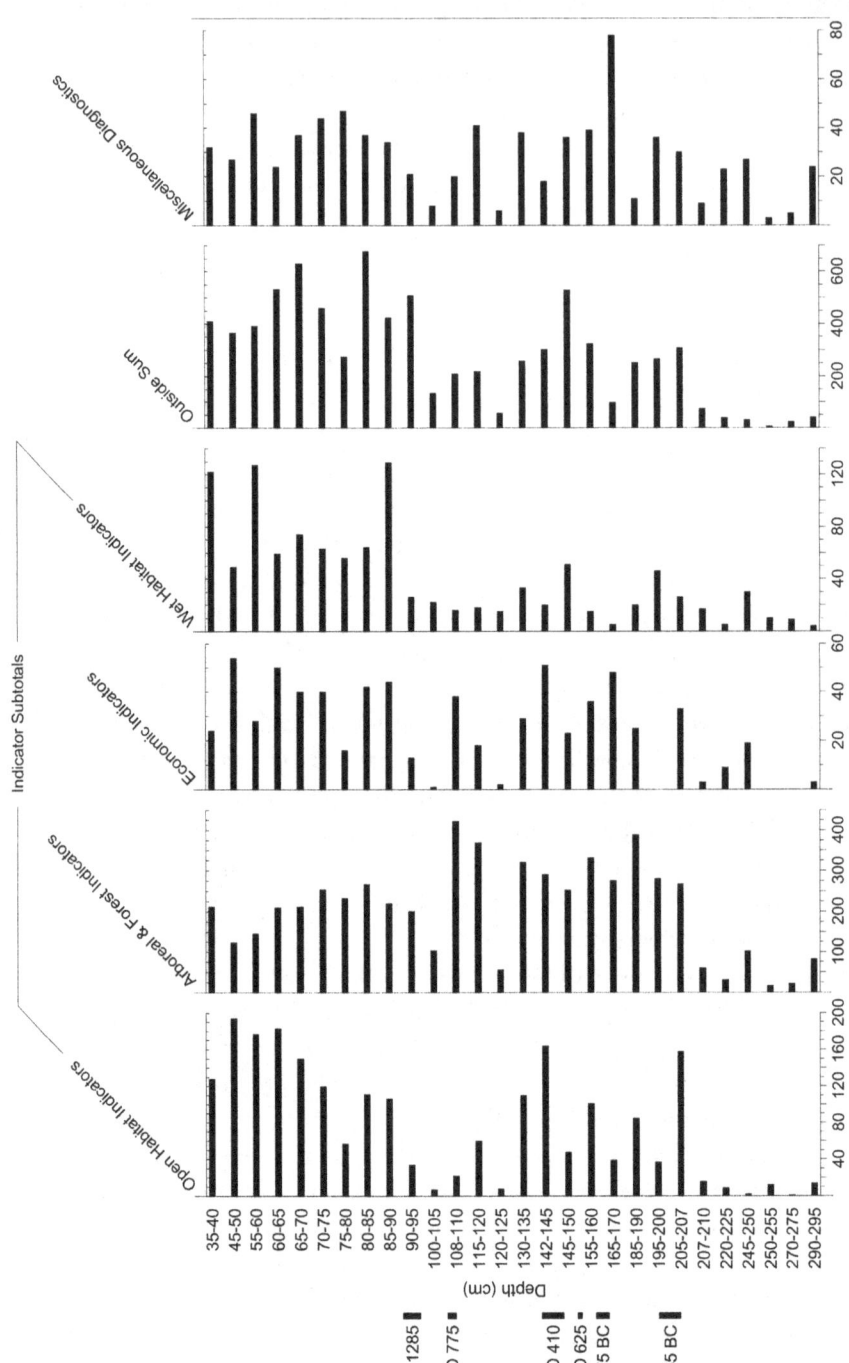

Figure 3.7. Phytolith diagram of the LM-2 pond core.

tices, environmental and climatic changes, and the introduction of cultigens at various times in prehistory along the north-central coast of Puerto Rico.

Until recently, very little has been known about the Archaic period in Puerto Rico. In the last several years a small explosion of research has centered on Archaic sites, including Angostura (north coast, 5960 ± 250 B.P. [5470–4333 cal B.C., 2 sigmas], Ayes Suárez 1988, 1995), Maruca (south coast, 8 dates ranging from 4840–2445 B.P., uncalibrated, Rodríguez López 1997, 1999), and Puerto Ferro (Vieques, 10 dates ranging from 4095 ± 80 B.P. to 2650 ± 90 B.P., [2877–415 cal B.C., 2 sigmas], Luis Chanlatte Baik, personal communication 1999). The Maruca site has yielded post molds, groundstone tools, shell tools, a large assemblage of chipped-stone implements, and 10 burials (Rodríguez López 1999). Other Archaic sites known for Puerto Rico and Vieques include María de la Cruz, Cayo Cofresí, and Caño Hondo (Rouse and Alegría 1990).

In the vicinity of Laguna Tortuguero, at least two Archaic sites have been reported. Angostura is located approximately 8 kilometers to the west-southwest of the lagoon and El Pulguero is situated adjacent to a wetland along the southwest edge of the lagoon. In his excavations at Angostura, Carlos Ayes Suárez recovered implements that indicate intensive processing of plants. These include manos, metates/mortars, and flat grinding tools. In addition, a large igneous stone, approximately 25 cm long by 10 cm wide, pointed at one end and wide at the other, with wide shallow notches along the lateral margins was interpreted by Ayes Suárez to be a hoe (Moscoso et al. 1999:Figure VII). An extended burial was recovered from one of two mounds excavated in the site (Ayes Suárez 1988:25–26). A small fragment of charcoal (.15 g of carbon), collected from the same mound as the burial, produced a ^{14}C date of 5960 ± 250 B.P., with extended counting time (Beta-29778, 5470–4333 cal B.C., 2 sigmas). If this is a reliable date and associated with the cultural occupation then Angostura contains one of the oldest known occupations for the West Indies. We would recommend that additional radiocarbon dates be obtained from other materials in the site. A prime candidate for dating would be a fragment of bone from the extended burial.

Near the base of their sediment core (757–781 cm), Burney et al. (1994) obtained a radiocarbon date of 5960 ± 90 B.P. (Beta-22350, 5057–4617 cal B.C., 2 sigmas), which is included within the range of Ayes's date. The Tortuguero date is associated with negligible quantities of charcoal (Burney et al. 1994:Figure 3), suggesting that if the Angostura occupants were burning, clearing, and cultivating 8 kilometers to the east of Tortuguero no effects of these activities entered the lagoon at this time.

The Archaic period is represented by groups who occupied small settlements that are not easily found and thus may be underrepresented in the literature, especially compared to the large ceramic-age sites documented for the island. The scenario that we are proposing in connection with Tortuguero and Maisabel is that Archaic-period folks occupying the Tortuguero area were responsible for the fires that resulted in large amounts of charcoal in the lagoon. As Saladoid people occupied the Maisabel location during the Hacienda Grande period, Archaic groups were alternatively displaced, exterminated, or absorbed into the ceramic-age groups, resulting in a dramatic decline in the charcoal influx to Laguna Tortuguero.

Microbotanical Analysis and the Saladoid/Ostionoid Transition

By approximately cal A.D. 410 a dramatic shift in the microbotanical record is observed in the Maisabel locale (Figure 3.6). Overall pollen and charcoal concentrations decline, and for charcoal specifically, to the lowest levels observed in the profile. This correlates to the Hacienda Grande–Cuevas transition in the late Saladoid period. Well-documented changes in the material culture record associated with this transition include simplification in the decoration of ceramic vessels (Roe 1989) and an increase in the diversity of site types (Rodríguez López 1990; Rouse 1992). The decline in charcoal production at this time may reflect the large amount of clearing conducted in the earlier Hacienda Grande period, with attendant depletion of soil fertility and increase in erosion in the nearby area. Beginning with Cuevas, and continuing into the Monserrate, Santa Elena, and Esperanza periods numerous small- to moderate-sized sites are documented for the Cibuco watershed (Siegel and Joseph 1993:47–49, Figures 2 and 3); Paso del Indio, a large late Saladoid/Ostionoid-period site is located about 8 kilometers south of Maisabel (Walker, this volume). The Hispaniolan coring data indicate a climatic reversal to moist conditions by approximately cal A.D. 400 (Hodell et al. 1991:Figure 2), which is reflected too in the Maisabel pollen data.

The significant decline in charcoal and pollen concentrations in the Maisabel microbotanical record, combined with the continued occupation of the site and the establishment of additional small camps or settlements in the area suggest that the occupants of Maisabel were traveling farther afield by the late Saladoid and into the Ostionoid periods for their agricultural plots. Many of the sites documented in the Cibuco watershed are located within 6 kilometers of Maisabel (Figure 3.1, Table 3.3). Siegel (Siegel and Joseph 1993) excavated one of these sites (VB-27), which is located on a ridge toe overlooking the Cibuco floodplain. Site VB-27 is a small camp that was intermittently occupied during the Monserrate (A.D. 600–900) and Santa Elena

(A.D. 900–1200) periods and somewhat more intensively during the Esperanza period (A.D. 1200–1500). This site may have been a small farm field camp associated with the occupants of Maisabel, Paso del Indio, or both. La Trocha, located approximately 150 meters from Paso del Indio, was interpreted to be a small camp briefly occupied during the Ostionoid and Chicoid periods (Solís Magaña 1997:91–92). Carlos Solís Magaña (1997:92) suggests that La Trocha was related, economically and socially, to the occupants of Paso del Indio. Sites located near the Río Cibuco in particular are likely candidates for outlying field camps. It is common practice among Amazonian swidden horticulturalists to maintain farm plots within a 6-kilometer radius of their main village. Small houses and cooksheds frequently are present at these plots, especially for some of the more distant locations (e.g., Kuikuru [Carneiro 1961, 1983]; Yaruro [Leeds 1961]; Waiwai [Mentore 1984]; Siona and Secoya [Vickers 1983]).

Although major burning and clearing activities decreased considerably after approximately cal A.D. 410, cultivation continued within the Maisabel settlement. Pollen or phytoliths of maize (*Zea mays*), cotton (*Gossypium*), and sweet potato (Convolvulaceae) were recovered from all of the post-Saladoid occupations of the site (Figures 3.5 and 3.7).

Summary

The relations between culture and environment documented for the north-central coast of Puerto Rico are likely to be a microcosm for the larger island context. Our findings include tantalizing new information concerning interactions and jostling for space between the resident Archaic groups and the early ceramic-age horticultural migrants to the West Indies. Further, the Archaic groups appear to have had a significant impact on the landscape, contrary to previous thoughts about these people in the Caribbean. Lee Newsom and Deborah Pearsall (2003) also discussed the potential for Archaic cultivation practices in the West Indies. This may be consistent with recent findings regarding the Archaic period in Central America. It is worth noting that Belize is one of the likely candidates for the origin of Archaic groups in the northern Caribbean (Rouse 1992; Wilson et al. 1999). By around 3000–2500 B.C., Archaic groups were farming throughout the lowlands of northern Belize (Jones 1994), thus representing another potential avenue of agricultural influence in the West Indies. Whether Archaic-period people were burning for hunting, horticulture, creating open spaces, or some combination of these activities, is unknown and represents an important aspect of continued research.

Table 3.3. Documented Prehistoric Sites in the Vicinity of Maisabel.

Site Number or Name	Context	Description	Reference
VB-1	Rocky headland, near mouth of Río Cibuco.	Prehistoric pottery (late?). About 400 × 200 m.	Walker 1984
VB-4	Lunate embayment, near mouth of Río Cibuco.	Prehistoric and historic pottery. Shell bead. Probably multicomponent, including Saladoid.	Walker 1984
VB-5	Lunate embayment, near mouth of Río Cibuco.	Prehistoric pottery, net sinkers, chert flake, shell. Possibly Ostiones style. Definite Santa Elena style. About 100 × 100 m.	Walker 1984
VB-6	Lunate embayment, near mouth of Río Cibuco.	Prehistoric pottery. Various components. Ostionoid?, Elenoid, possibly Saladoid.	Walker 1984
VB-10	North coast.	Prehistoric pottery. Zoned-incised crosshatching (Hacienda Grande style).	Walker 1984
VB-22	Cave overlooking Río Indio.	Lithics: cores (igneous material, flakes). Petroglyphs. No reported ceramics.	Walker 1984

VB-27	North-south trending ridge on the alluvial fan of the Río Cibuco.	Monserrate, Santa Elena, and Esperanza–style pottery.	Siegel and Joseph 1993; Walker 1984; Weaver and Rodríguez Morales 1991
VB-29	Very low hill on floodplain.	Capá-style pottery. Petaloid celts.	Walker 1984
VB-30	Cave in hill.	Petroglyphs.	Walker 1984
VB-31	Very low hill near Laguna Tortuguero.	Capá-style pottery.	Walker 1984
Paso del Indio	Floodplain of Río Indio.	See Walker, this volume	Walker, this volume
VB-2	North coast.	Late (?) prehistoric pottery eroding into beach. About 20 × 50 m.	Walker 1984
VB-3	North coast.	Mid to late prehistoric pottery. Severe erosion. About 100 × 50 m.	Walker 1984
VB-12	Cave in limestone hills.	Pottery, petroglyphs. Taíno.	Walker 1984
VB-13	Cave in limestone hills.	Pottery, petroglyphs. Taíno.	Walker 1984
VB-16	Cave in limestone hills.	Pottery, petroglyphs. Taíno.	Walker 1984
VB-17	Cave in limestone hills.	Pottery, petroglyphs. Taíno.	Walker 1984
VB-19	Cave in limestone hills.	Pottery, petroglyphs. Taíno.	Walker 1984
VB-21	Cave in limestone hills.	Pottery, petroglyphs. Taíno.	Walker 1984

The Saladoid colonists brought a developed horticultural economy to Puerto Rico, which may have been modified as interactions with the local Archaic groups ensued. Indeed, our data combined with other studies suggest that these Archaic groups may have had their own horticultural economy in place. The transition from the early to late Saladoid period is associated with a dramatic shift in land-use practices and a geographic expansion in local group territory. This trend culminated in the late prehistoric/Contact-period polities that are well documented for Puerto Rico. One of the goals of the present project was to obtain direct evidence of the subsistence economy associated with the transition from egalitarian to ranked society. Cultivated plants documented in the microbotanical record are more prevalent in the portions of the Maisabel pond core that date to the post-Saladoid occupations of the site. These plants include probable sweet potato, maize, and cotton. More sites spanning the Saladoid/Ostionoid transition need to be excavated with an explicit emphasis on fine-grained recovery techniques for micro- and macrobotanical remains in well-dated contexts. As these studies are completed we will obtain increasingly refined views of horticultural production. As such, we will generate ever-more accurate models of the intra- and interpolity linkages that were formalized during the late prehistoric occupations of Puerto Rico.

The present study is part of a larger research program based on multiple lines of evidence, including the micro- and macrobotanical records, zooarchaeology, human osteology and skeletal chemistry, site distributions and stratigraphies, local and regional environmental histories, and ethnographic/ethnohistoric documents (Budinoff 1991; deFrance 1990; deFrance et al. 1996; deFrance and Newsom, this volume; Jones and Pearsall 1999; Newsom 1993; Siegel 1992, 1993, 2004; Siegel et al. 1999; Stokes 1998, this volume). Unraveling the unique circumstances surrounding the prehistoric occupations of north-central Puerto Rico is allowing us to discuss in some detail adaptations by groups to the local landscape, interactions between groups, and environmental changes effected by the groups.

Conclusions

Prior to the present study we knew that ceramic-age inhabitants intensively occupied the Maisabel locale from approximately 200 B.C. to A.D. 1200. We also knew about the existence of a couple of Archaic sites that had been reported to the east of Maisabel. Results of the current investigation provide new insights into shifting patterns of land-use by Archaic and ceramic-age groups, potential interactions between the groups, and environmental changes that occurred naturally as well as those wrought by human activities at various times in prehistory.

The earliest known human occupations of north-central Puerto Rico are characterized by relatively small groups of foragers, collectors, and gatherers. Based on findings from Angostura, Archaic groups may have been cultivating and processing plants as long as 6,000 years ago, although this observation can only be considered suggestive until botanical remains have been collected and additional reporting of artifact contexts and dating of that site have been completed. The environment at this time was characterized by increasingly moist and warm conditions. By approximately 5,200 years ago, Archaic peoples were significantly modifying their landscapes through large-scale burning. Terrain in the vicinity of Laguna Tortuguero was burned, perhaps for horticultural plots or hunting activities, or both, until about 3,500 years ago. Likewise, Archaic people were burning in or near the mangrove swamp located at the mouth of the Río Cibuco about 4,200 years ago. The environment consisted of the wettest conditions documented during the Holocene for this section of the West Indies.

By roughly 200 B.C., or perhaps somewhat earlier, the world, as the Archaic people on Puerto Rico knew it, came to a rather sudden end. The earliest Saladoid colonists to the West Indies arrived on the island, with their technology, lifeways, foodways, and worldview. A group of these colonists, referred to as the Hacienda Grande people, established a village at the Maisabel locale. The environment had shifted to dry conditions compared to earlier periods. At the same time, the local setting included a small pond that had changed from a shallow brackish waterhole to a deeper freshwater pond. The nature of interactions between the colonists and the resident Archaic people in the area is unknown. We do know, however, that burning activities by Archaic people in the vicinity of Laguna Tortuguero and the Cibuco mangrove abruptly ended.

The large assemblage of Hacienda Grande artifacts in the Maisabel site reveals a subsistence economy based on the production and consumption of plants and intensive use of the mangrove and marine resources. In particular, great quantities of land crabs, shellfish, and bony fish were collected and consumed by the Hacienda Grande residents. These people cut and burned much of the forest to establish a clearing for a village and garden plots. The earliest ceramic-age occupants of Maisabel adapted quickly to their setting. Major modifications to the landscape were limited to the immediate area of the village.

The transition from the Hacienda Grande to Cuevas occupations in Maisabel, dated to approximately A.D. 400, is associated with a different impact to the landscape. Large quantities of sand were deposited in the pond and the intensity of burning within and around the village decreased. Human burials and artifacts reveal a continued intensive occupation during the Cuevas period. The scenario accounting for this seemingly paradoxical relation is that clearing and burning within the Maisabel village had removed the majority of vegetation during the Hacienda Grande period. By the Cuevas period, vegetation that previously had been a physical barrier to windblown sand was removed from the topographic ridge divide within the village, thus allowing sand to be deposited into the pond. At this time, too, Cuevas occupants began establishing farm plots and ancillary camps farther afield from Maisabel. By the middle of the Monserrate to the end of the Santa Elena periods, from approximately A.D. 775 to 1285, gradually lower rates of sand deposition were present in the pond, compared to the Cuevas period. Also, at about A.D. 775 a burst of burning and clearing activities occurred within the main portion of the Maisabel village. This period is associated with a brief episode of increased humid conditions before the environment became drier prior to the arrival of the Spaniards.

The Maisabel village was virtually abandoned by around A.D. 1200, or the end of the Santa Elena period. A small assemblage of Esperanza-style pottery in the site indicates that a small group of late prehistoric Indians reoccupied the place, sometime during the period from A.D. 1200 to 1500. The major abandonment of Maisabel was most likely related to larger social and political maneuverings that were occurring across Puerto Rico and, indeed, much of the West Indies at this time.

Acknowledgments

The research reported in this chapter was supported by grants from the Wenner-Gren Foundation for Anthropological Research (Grant No. 6167 to PES) and the H. John Heinz III Fund Grant Program for Latin American Archaeology (to DMP and PES). The site distribution data were compiled for research conducted by PES for New South Associates on behalf of the U.S. Army Corps of Engineers, Jacksonville District (Contract No. DACW17-93-C-0063). Sarah Jane Ruch, Scott Parker, Rob Schultz, and Bill Grimm prepared the graphics. We thank Dan Roberts, Irving Rouse, and two anonymous reviewers for their comments on earlier versions of the paper and Rubén Jiménez for allowing us access to the Maisabel site and the pond.

Note

1. A small fragment of wood collected at 151 cm was dated by accelerator mass spectrometry (AMS) to 1450 ± 40 B.P. (cal A.D. 545–660, 2 sigma). This is out of sequence compared to the dated contexts located immediately above and below this sample. The wood sample that produced this problematic date was most likely translocated from its original context, especially given its small size.

4

The Status of Paleoethnobiological Research on Puerto Rico and Adjacent Islands

Susan D. deFrance and Lee A. Newsom

Recent and ongoing paleoethnobiological research concerning archaeological settlements and biotic resources on Puerto Rico and adjacent islands has begun to illuminate distinctive patterns of resource use by the various prehistoric human groups occupying the area beginning approximately 2,200 years ago. This particular subregion of the Caribbean includes Puerto Rico and the geologically related smaller islands of Culebra and Vieques, immediately to the east of Puerto Rico (Figure 4.1). Archaeobotanical and zooarchaeological studies of several well-preserved assemblages of macrophytic and faunal materials from the island group are providing essential new data on subsistence practices and economic systems associated with the different prehistoric occupations or cultures of the islands. We present an overview of these data and current research, with an emphasis on the distinctive features of the botanical and faunal assemblages, including discernable economic trends in plant and animal use.

The assemblages of plant and animal remains that form the basis of this chapter were recovered from a series of sites in the island group and were independently excavated by archaeologists working on two of the islands: Puerto Rico and Vieques (Figure 4.1 and Table 4.1). In recent years a number of researchers have participated in paleoethnobotanical and zooarchaeological research on these islands, including 10 specialists who were involved in analyses of the biological remains discussed in this chapter (Table 4.1). Overall, these investigations have focused on two basic objectives: (1) identification and interpretation of subsistence remains and patterns of resource use at

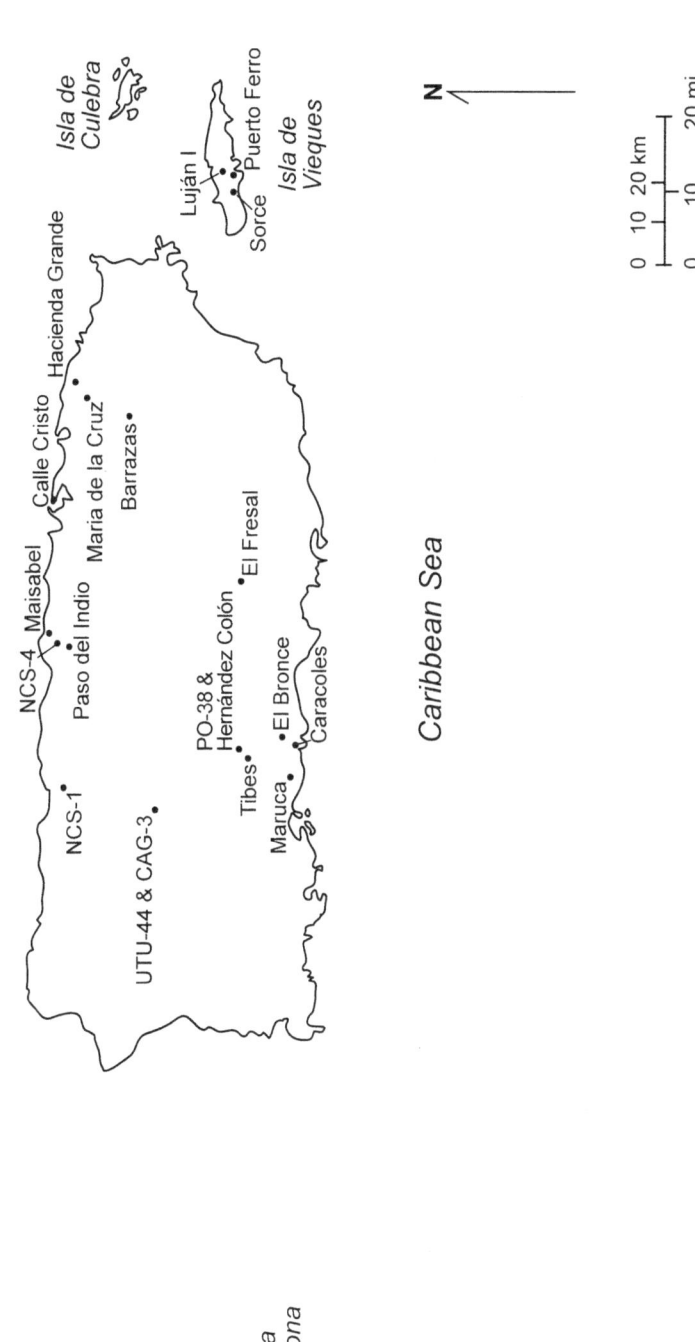

Figure 4.1. Map of Puerto Rico showing the locations of sites discussed in the text.

Table 4.1. Sources of Prehistoric Archaeobotanical and Zooarchaeological Assemblages from Puerto Rico and Vieques.

Site	Municipality	Archaeologist	Analyst/Source
Northern region:			
NCS-1 Finca Valencia	Barceloneta	Solís Magaña et al.	Newsom 1997b; Quitmyer and Kozuch 1996
NCS-4 La Trocha	Barceloneta	Solís Magaña et al.	Newsom 2001; Quitmyer and Brown 2001
Barrazas	Loiza	Rivera Calderón	Newsom 1995b
Hacienda Grande	Loiza	Alegría and Rouse	Wing 1990
María de la Cruz	Loiza	Alegría and Rouse	Newsom 1993 and laboratory data
Maisabel	Manatí	Siegel	deFrance 1990; Newsom 1993
Paso del Indio	Manatí	Solís Magaña et al.	Newsom (laboratory data)
Calle Cristo	San Juan	Solís Magaña et al.	Kozuch n.d.
Central Mountains:			
El Fresal	Aibonito	Meléndez	Newsom 1993
Cueva las Caritas (CAG-3)	Utuado	Oliver, Rivera Fontán, Newsom	Newsom (laboratory data)
UTU-44	Utuado	Oliver, Rivera Fontán, Newsom	Newsom (laboratory data)
Southern region:			
Caracoles	Ponce	López et al.	Colón Parrilla 1997; Narganes Storde 1988
El Bronce	Ponce	Walker et al.	Pearsall 1985; Reitz 1985; Robinson 1985

Hernández Colón	Ponce	Maíz	Maíz López 1996
Maruca	Ponce	Rodríguez	Narganes Storde 1997a, b; Newsom 1999a
PO-38	Ponce	Weaver	Newsom 1992, 1995a, 1999a
Tibes	Ponce	Curet and Newsom	deFrance 1997; Curet et al. 1998; Newsom and Curet 2000, 2003
Vieques:			
Luján I	Vieques	Rivera Calderón	Newsom 1999b; Quitmyer & Wing 2001
Puerto Ferro	Vieques	Chanlatte Baik	Narganes Storde 1994
Sorcé	Vieques	Chanlatte Baik	Narganes Storde 1982

the particular sites, including any detectable changes that might illuminate broader trends, and (2) gather information that contributes to an informed understanding of the environmental context of specific sites, especially during particular periods of occupation. Related questions sometimes addressed in the individual reports (Table 4.1) include human-landscape dynamics, aspects of inherent sustainability of resource-exploitation patterns, plant and animal introductions, and the potential role of biological resources in view of increasing social complexity (e.g., the emergence of chiefdoms) in the region.

Diverse biotic resources were essential to the survival of prehistoric human groups in this centrally located, subtropical region of the Caribbean archipelago (Nieuwolt 1977). In addition to various foods and medicines, plant and animal resources provided numerous products including bone, tooth, sinew, hides, and shell; wooden implements and ornaments; plant extractives such as tannins, resins, gums, and fish stupifiers; fuelwood; fibers for rope and cordage; and various construction materials. Now that a number of archaeological sites on Puerto Rico and nearby Vieques have undergone systematic sampling, collection, and analysis of both plant and animal remains, it is possible to begin to provide a comprehensive picture of the significance of these resources to human settlement in the area. This synthesis indicates that some practices in both plant and animal use, particularly home gardening and aspects of fishing and shellfishing, were initiated during Archaic times and that they were sustained throughout the prehistory of Puerto Rico and neighboring islands. With the migration of ceramic-age horticulturalists various innovations in plant and animal use occurred, including the introduction of new taxa and, eventually, the intensification of production. In contrast to previous models that argued for an initial terrestrial adaptation (i.e., the crab-shell dichotomy [see deFrance 1988, 1989, 1990 for review; Rainey 1940]), marine foods were an important part of the diet at all times. Greater animal protein was acquired through the apparent intensification of existing coastal practices and by the maintenance of some small-sized tended animals. Plant intensification involved greater production of home-garden taxa until very late in island prehistory when more intensive agriculture may have been practiced. There is no indication that maize was a significant component of the diet. Although people engaged in practices unique to local habitats, tropical root-crop horticulture in combination with diverse marine foodstuffs provided a subsistence foundation that required little alteration for several centuries.

The emerging evidence contributes much to clarify prehistoric subsistence and land use. Moreover, now that these data are being systematically collected, we can demonstrate that previous deficiencies in the database are less a problem of preservation than a product of research designs unevenly integrating paleoethnobiological studies.

Paleoethnobiological Background

The sites and assemblages discussed in this chapter are attributed primarily to the Caribbean ceramic age, dating from approximately 300–200 B.C. to around A.D. 1400, uncalibrated (Rouse 1992) (Figure 4.1 and Table 4.1). However, three sites, including Maruca in southern Puerto Rico, María de la Cruz in the northeastern part of the island, and Puerto Ferro on Vieques, are associated with the earlier Archaic (Ortoiroid) occupations of the region; they date between about 3000 and 200 B.C. (Rodríguez López 1997; Rouse 1992; Rouse and Alegría 1990). Seven sites include early ceramic-age Saladoid (Hacienda Grande, Maisabel, Paso del Indio, Hernández Colón, PO-38, and Tibes) and/or Huecoid (Sorcé) components dating from ca. 300 B.C. to A.D. 700 (Table 4.2). Five of these (Maisabel, Paso del Indio, Hernández Colón, PO-38, and Tibes) also contain later Ostionoid components. The remaining sites date predominantly to the Ostionoid series (post ca. A.D. 600).

The Archaic inhabitants of the region are traditionally considered to have been logistically based mobile fisher-foragers, though some may have been relatively or completely sedentary, and certain groups were perhaps low-level cultivators (Newsom 1993; Newsom and Wing 2004; Smith 2001). In contrast, the ceramic-age people were fully sedentary food-producing groups organized as segmentary or chiefdom (later occupations) societies. Among the plants recorded as having been grown by the Taíno Indians of the Greater Antilles at the time of Contact are several root crops: manioc or yuca (*Manihot esculenta*), sweet potato or batatas (*Ipomoea batata*), and yautía (*Xanthosoma* sp.). In addition, gourd/squashes (*Cucurbita* spp.), maize (*Zea mays*), and assorted home-garden taxa, for example, chili peppers or ají (*Capsicum* spp.) and tobacco (*Nicotiana* sp.) were cultivated (Newsom 1993). The early ceramic-age Saladoid and/or Huecoid groups (Oliver 1999) who migrated to the region either directly from northern lowland South America or by way of the Lesser Antilles, seem to have been horticulturists, and they are believed to have emphasized root-crop production, especially manioc, based primarily on the presence of food-processing equipment (Newsom 1993; Petersen 1997). Their cultivation systems are likely also to have included other taxa, especially other root crops and various fruit trees (Newsom 1993; Newsom and Pearsall 2003; Rouse 1992), including some of those mentioned above. Dur-

Table 4.2. Archaeobotanical and Zooarchaeological Assemblages from Commonwealth of Puerto Rico.

Subregion	Site	Material	Archaeobotany	Zooarchaeology
Northern Puerto Rico:	NCS-1 Finca Valencia	Late Ceramic	X	X
	NCS-4 La Trocha	Late Ceramic	X	X
	Barrazas	Late Ceramic	X	
	Hacienda Grande	Early Ceramic	X	
	María de la Cruz	Archaic	X	
	Maisabel	Early-Late Ceramic	X	X
	Paso del Indio	Early-Late Ceramic	X*	
	Calle Cristo (Ballajá)	Late Ceramic	X	X
Central Mountains:	El Fresal	Late Ceramic	X	
	Cueva las Caritas (CAG-3)	Late Ceramic	X*	
	UTU-44	Late Ceramic	X*	
Southern Puerto Rico:	Caracoles	Late Ceramic	X	
	El Bronce	Late Ceramic	X	X
	Hernández Colón	Early-Late Ceramic	X	
	Maruca	Archaic	X	X
	PO-38	Early-Late Ceramic	X	
	Tibes	Early-Late Ceramic	X	X
Vieques:	Luján I	Late Ceramic	X	X
	Puerto Ferro	Archaic	X	
	Sorcé	Early Ceramic	X	

*Sites indicated are currently under analysis, therefore only certain preliminary data are mentioned in this summary.

ing the late ceramic-age Ostionoid series, it appears that additional crops were added to the horticultural base, including maize (see below).

In terms of settlement patterns and site types, two sites were found in rockshelters (María de la Cruz and Cueva las Caritas), while the rest were located in open terrain (Table 4.1). Six of the sites were originally situated in or near coastal environments: Maisabel in northern Puerto Rico, Caracoles and Maruca in the southern part of the island, and Luján I, Puerto Ferro, and Sorcé on the small low island of Vieques. The rest of the sites were located one or more kilometers inland, often within or near river floodplains. Three of these sites (El Fresal, Cueva las Caritas, and UTU-44) occur high in the central mountain region (Table 4.1). Concerning the two rockshelters, María de la Cruz appears to have been used for habitable space, as it includes primarily domestic deposits (Rouse and Alegría 1990), whereas Cueva las Caritas includes both domestic deposits and hearthlike features, as well as a human burial (Oliver et al. 1999). Cueva las Caritas was used primarily for domestic activities; however, it may also have been a venue for ceremonial/ritual purposes. The other sites represent short- to relatively long-term settlements and at least three—Caracoles, NCS-1, and Tibes—may have been the centers of chiefdom activities as they appear to have functioned as civic-ceremonial centers.

In the sections that follow we present an overview of the research that has taken place involving macrophytic assemblages from the various sites, followed by a synopsis of the zooarchaeological research. Some of this research is still in progress and therefore only receives brief consideration here; this concerns specifically Paso del Indio, Cueva las Caritas, and UTU-44 (Table 4.2). Moreover, while we indicate some key aspects of the methods and procedures relevant to both subdisciplines (archaeobotany and zooarchaeology), we refer the reader to individual site reports for details of the sampling strategies, recovery and sample preparations, and laboratory procedures in conjunction with each of the projects (Table 4.1). In general, whole volumetric soil samples of varying sizes (so the samples are not strictly comparable) were collected from the sites, either as columns (zooarchaeology) or as point samples (archaeobotany), focusing in particular on midden deposits and features, especially hearths or fire pits (Table 4.2). Domestic contexts tend to have the greatest probability and potential for preservation of biotic remains from food-related and other subsistence activities. Most samples subsequently underwent fine-sieving procedures (mesh openings of .42 mm for botanical remains and 3.2 mm, or, in some cases, 1.6 mm screen for fauna) or flotation with fine-gauge recovery (ca. .5 mm) to isolate and extract plant and animal remains. The laboratory procedures utilized in the individual analyses were conducted according to established protocols and standards for archaeobotanical and zooarchaeological research, respectively. Most of the sites have undergone sampling and analysis for both plant and animal remains; therefore, these provide complementary aspects of paleoethnobiological research and more complete evidence of prehistoric subsistence practices. Other sites have been studied only in terms of one or the other bodies of data (Table 4.2).

Paleoethnobotany

The plant assemblages discussed in this chapter consist exclusively of macrophytic remains, that is, wood, charcoal, seeds, nut hulls, rind fragments, palm petioles (leaf bases), and other miscellaneous plant remains generally visible without the aid of magnification. With the exception of some of the desiccated wood from the Cueva las Caritas and a few mineralized seeds from El Fresal and Tibes, all archaeobotanical specimens were preserved by carbonization (Table 4.1). All samples were recovered from dry terrestrial (vs. waterlogged or underwater) archaeological deposits.

Seed and rind identifications were made by comparison with modern reference specimens and with the aid of published morphological and/or anatomical data (Delorit 1970; Martin and Barkley 1978). Wood identifications by Newsom were made on the basis of three-dimensional anatomy using a dissecting microscope with enhanced magnification (40x to 125x) to classify individual specimens by anatomical type, in combination with a compound microscope and modern reference slides for direct comparison with representative comparative specimens. All wood identifications were pursued and verified using dichotomous and multivariate computerized keys for wood anatomical structure (Record and Hess 1943–1948; Wheeler et al. 1986).

Each plant identification is specified to the lowest possible taxon. The designation "cf." ("confer," contrast and compare) preceding a given scientific name in the text and tables that follow indicates a very close but not necessarily definitive match with a particular taxon. Identifications may remain provisional due to an insufficient number of specimens with which to verify important morphological and/or anatomical details and/or problems with preservation (excessive fragmentation, incomplete specimens, burn distortion). Typically, archaeological plant taxa were identified to the level of family or genus since problems with preservation, unknown genetic factors, and ecological and/or functional anatomical variation generally preclude definitive species identification. In a few cases, a particular species was indicated as a very strong match based on direct comparison with a modern reference specimen. For example, the wood identification of *Eugenia* sp. from Luján I was based on archaeological specimens that demonstrated a very close structural correspondence with the genus *Eugenia* and specifically with a reference specimen of the modern species *E. confusa* (caracoliollo or red-berry eugenia). Nevertheless, the identification is reported as "*Eugenia (E. confusa)*" to indicate the close affinity evident from the anatomical structure with species *confusa*, while at the same time emphasizing that this does not preclude other, possibly even extinct, species in the genus, given that this finer level of taxonomic resolution is only rarely attainable with archaeological material (Hather 1994:2–4; Newsom 2002).

Macrophytic Data

The complete list of identified plant specimens currently documented from Puerto Rican archaeological sites appears in Table 4.3, with the plant families in the left-hand column, followed by the Latin and vernacular names, and finally specimen type, that is, seed/fruit, rind, petiole (leaf base), or wood. This tally includes 44 plant families and some 69 genera or wood anatomical groups. The majority of the identifications derive from wood charcoal. In general, the assemblage is diverse, including both herbaceous and woody plants, representative of various herbs, vines, shrubs, and trees. This is among the most species rich of archaeobotanical assemblages thus far documented for the Caribbean region as a whole (Newsom and Pearsall 2003).

A number of particularly noteworthy economic taxa are among the plants identified, notwithstanding some provisional identifications. These include edible and other home-garden types, and several exceptional woods for fuel and woodworking operations, for example, guayacán (*Guaiacum* sp.). Among the well-known home-garden trees with edible fruit are guanábana or soursop (*Annona* sp.), lechosa or papaya (*Carica papaya*), guaba (*Inga* sp.), aguacate or avocado (*Persea americana*), guayaba or guava (*Psidium guajava*), tabloncillo or mastic-bully (*Sideroxylon* sp.), yellow sapote and almendrón (*Pouteria* spp.), and possibly caimito or star apple (*Chrysophyllum* sp.), among others. Additional tree taxa that were very likely maintained in garden or other anthropogenic settings are higüera (*Cresentia cujete*), for its gourdlike container fruits and medicinal uses; achiote (*Bixa orellana*), as a source of red dye or condiment; and *cohoba* (cf. *Anadenanthera* sp.), the ground seeds from at least one species of which were the primary source of a narcotic inhalant used in Taíno ritualism (Alegría 1997a). The vine parcha or passionflower (*Passiflora* sp.) is among the identified remains; the citruslike fruits are edible and the pulp can be processed into a beverage, as well as other uses. At least one type of herbaceous plant may have been maintained in prehistoric gardens:

Table 4.3. Macrophytic Identifications from Archaeological Sites on Puerto Rico and Vieques.

Family	Genus/Species	Vernacular	Form*
Aizoaceae	*Trianthema portulacastrum*	verdolaga de hoja ancha	S
Anacardiaceae	cf. *Comocladia* sp.	carrasco, próspera	W
Annonaceae	*Annona* sp.	guanábana, soursop	S, W
Annonaceae	cf. *Oxandra* sp.	haya, lancewood	W
Apocynaceae	—	dogbane family	W
Aracaceae	cf. *Acrocomia media*	corozo, spiny palm	S
Aracaceae	—	palm family	P, W
Bignoniaceae	cf. *Crescentia cujete*	higüera, calabash	R
Bignoniaceae	*Tabebuia* sp.	roble	W
Bignoniaceae	*Tecoma* (*T. stans*)	saúco amarillo	W
Bignoniaceae	*Crescentia* sp. or *Tabebuia* sp.	higüera or roble	W
Bignoniaceae	—	bignonia family	W
Bixaceae	*Bixa orellana*	achiote, anatto	S
Bixaceae/Ebenaceae	cf. *Bixa* sp. or *Diospyros* sp.	achiote or guayabota	W
Boraginaceae	*Bourreria* sp.	palo de vaca, strong bark	W
Boraginaceae	*Cordia* sp., *C. albaldentata*	capá blanco	W
Boraginaceae	*Cordia* sp., *C. laevigata*	capá colorado	W
Boraginaceae	—	borage family	W
Burseraceae	*Bursera simaruba*	almácigo, gumbo-limbo	W

Capparaceae	*Capparis* sp.	burro, sapo	W
Capparaceae	cf. *Cleome* sp.	flor de perro	S
Caricaceae	*Carica papaya*	lechosa, papaya	S
Celastraceae	*Elaeodendron xylocarpum*	guayarote, spoon tree	W
Celastraceae	*Gyminda* or *Crossopetalum* sp.	mala mujer, maravedí	W
Celastraceae	*Maytenus* sp.	cuero de sapo	W
Celastraceae	*Maytenus* or *Torralbasia* sp.	cuero de sapo, boje	W
Chenopodiaceae	—	goosefoot family	S
Combretaceae	*Bucida (B. buceras)*	ucar, black olive	W
Combretaceae	*Conocarpus erectus*	botoncillo, buttonwood	S, W
Convolvulaceae	—	morning glories	S
Erythroxylaceae	*Erythroxylum* sp.	cocaína falsa, false cocaine	W
Euphorbiaceae	*Croton* sp.	lechecillo, pepper bush	W
Euphorbiaceae	*Gymnanthes (G. lucida)*	yaití, tabaco, crabwood	W
Euphorbiaceae	*Jatrophia* sp.	piñón, tártago emético	W
Euphorbiaceae or Rubiaceae	cf. *Hyeronima* sp. or *Genipa americana*	cedro macho or jagua/genip	W
Euphorbiaceae	—	spurge family	S
Fabaceae	cf. *Desmodium/Vigna* sp.	wild herbaceous legumes	S
Fabaceae-Mimosoid	cf. *Anadenanthera (A. peregrina)*	cohoba, cohobilla	W
Fabaceae-Mimosoid	cf. *Inga* or *Pithecellobium* sp.	guaba, cat's claw	W
Fabaceae-Papilio.	*Andira (A. inermis)*	moca	W
Fabaceae-Papilio.	cf. *Andira* or *Lonchocarpus* sp.	moca or palo hediondo	W

Continued on the next page

Table 4.3 *Continued*

Family	Genus/Species	Vernacular	Form*
Fabaceae-Papilio.	cf. *Lonchocarpus* sp.	palo hediondo	W
Fabaceae-Papilio.	*Piscida* (*P. carthagenesis*)	ventura, fish poison	W
cf. Fabaceae	—	tree legumes	S, W
Hypoxidaceae	*Hypoxis* sp.	coquí, stargrass	S
cf. Labiatae	cf. *Ocimum* sp.	albahaca, wild basil	S
Lauraceae	cf. *Aniba, Licaria, Ocotea* spp.	laurel family genera	W
Lauraceae	cf. *Nectandra* (*N. coriácea*)	laurel cigua	W
Lauraceae	*Persea americana*	aguacate, avocado	S
Malpighiaceae	cf. *Byrsonima* sp.	aceituna, candle berry	S, [W]
Malvaceae	cf. *Abutilon* or *Hibiscus* sp.	mallow family genera	W
Malvaceae	*Sida* sp., *Malvastrum* sp.	escoba blanca	S
Malvaceae	*Thespesia* (*Montezuma*) *grandiflora*	maga	W
Malvaceae	—	mallow family	S
cf. Melastomataceae	cf. *Mouriri* sp.	guasávara, mameyuelo	W
cf. Meliaceae	cf. *Trichilia* sp.	cabo de hacha, caracolillo	W
Moraceae	*Ficus* sp.	jagüey, wild fig	W
Myrsinaceae	*Ardisia* sp.	bádula, ausubón	W
Myrtaceae	*Eugenia* (*E. confusa*)	caracolillo, stopper	W
Myrtaceae	cf. *Eugenia* sp.	stoppers	W
Myrtaceae	*Psidium* (*P. guajava*)	guayaba, guava	S, W
Myrtaceae	*Psidium* sp. or *Eugenia* sp.	guava or stopper	W

Onagraceae	*Oenothera* sp.	evening primrose	S
Passifloraceae	*Passiflora* sp.	parcha, passionflower	S
Poaceae	Paniceae, panicoid group	panicoid grasses	S
Poaceae	—	NCS-1 grass morph 2	S
Poaceae	—	NCS-1 grass morph 3	S
Poaceae	—	grass family	S
Polygonaceae	*Coccoloba uvifera*	uva de playa; sea grape	W
Portulacaceae	*Portulaca* sp.	verdolaga, purslane	S
Rhamnaceae	*Krugiodendron* (*K. ferreum*)	bariaco	W
Rosaceae	*Rubus* sp.	fresa de montaña	S
Rubiaceae	*Exostema* (*E. caribaeum*)	alvarillo, quinine bark	W
Rubiaceae	cf. *Randia* (*R. aculeata*)	palo de Navidad, tintillo	W
cf. Rubiaceae		madder family	W
Rutaceae	*Amyris* (*A. elemifera*)	teílla, cuabilla, torchwood	W
Rutaceae	*Zanthoxylum* sp.	espinosa, wild lime type	W
Rutaceae	—	citrus family	W
Sapotaceae	cf. *Sideroxylon* sp.	tabloncillo, mastic-bully	S
Sapotaceae	*Pouteria campechiana*	canistel, yellow sapote	S
Sapotaceae	*Chrysophyllum*/*Sideroxylon*, wood anatomical group I	caimito, tabloncillo, etc.	W
Sapotaceae	*Pouteria* spp., wood anatomical group II	almendrón	W
Sapotaceae	*Manilkara* spp., wood anatomical group III	ausubo, níspero	W

Continued on the next page

Table 4.3 *Continued*

Family	Genus/Species	Vernacular	Form*
Sapotaceae	—	sapodilla family	S, W
Simaroubiaceae	*Picramnia* (*P. pentandra*)	guarema, bitter bush	W
Simaroubiaceae	cf. *Suriana maritima*	guitarán, bay cedar	W
Solanaceae	*Solanum* sp.	yerba mora, nightshade	S
Sterculiaceae	*Guazuma ulmifolia*	guácima	W
Sterculiaceae	cf. *Sterculia* (*S. apetala*)	anacagüita	W
Ulmaceae	cf. *Trema* sp.	guacimilla	W
cf. Vitaceae	cf. *Cissus* sp.	bejuco de gongolí, b. de caro	W
Zygophyllaceae	*Guaiacum* sp.	lignum-vitae, guayacán	W

*P = petiole (leaf base); R = rind; S = seed/fruit; W = wood.

evening primrose (*Oenothera* sp.), which today no longer occurs on the island (though small populations exist on Cuba and in the Dominican Republic). This plant has potential medicinal and/or ritual value as a mild narcotic and sedative (Newsom 1993).

Many of the plant types identified from the Puerto Rican sites have considerable economic and utilitarian potential, not only as food items and medicines but also as dyes, fuelwood, fish poison, and more. Moreover, many have a long history of association with neotropical home gardens throughout the region. In recognition of this potential, Table 4.4 indicates various recorded nonwood, wood, or multipurpose uses of the different taxa from the archaeological sites, according to major use category. Actual archaeological evidence documenting such uses among the sites is difficult to demonstrate conclusively, although the strong associations of some taxa with house posts and others with domestic deposits (hearths, floors, etc.) provide some indications of the importance of individual plant resources to the prehistoric human occupants of Puerto Rico and Vieques.

To consider intrasite variability, we now examine individual plant taxa in terms of their proveniences and distributions among the sites for which analyses are complete. The identifications of various seed taxa and other nonwood plant remains from the sites are indicated in Table 4.5; the data are presented either as presence/absence for sites with few samples or as ubiquity values (percent presence) for sites with sufficient numbers of samples and proveniences analyzed. The taxa are grouped according to whether they are woody or herbaceous, the former including several types of trees with useful fruits, some of which have potential utilitarian or nonfood functions. Among the tree taxa are eight with edible fruit: *Annona*, cf. *Acrocomia*, *Carica*, *Persea*, cf. *Byrsonima*, cf. *Psidium*, cf. *Sideroxylon*, and *Pouteria campechiana* (guanábana, corozo, lechosa or papaya, aguacate or avocado, aceituna, guayaba, tabloncillo, and canistel, respectively). Other noteworthy woody taxa include higüera, with its gourdlike fruits; achiote; and cf. *Zanthoxylum* sp. (espinosa), the fruits of which have the potential to have been used for medicinal purposes (Table 4.4). Most of these identifications come from the ceramic-age site NCS-1, where the seed coats of two edible fruit types closely matched to tabloncillo and corozo (*Sideroxylon* and *Acrocomia* [Table 4.5]) comprised 20 percent and 12 percent ubiquity, respectively (that is, they were found present among 20 percent and 12 percent of the proveniences analyzed). The identifications are provisional (cf.) because the individual seed remains are highly fragmented and very small, generally lacking distinctive diagnostic elements like seed scars. These two taxa are the most frequently represented among the

Table 4.4. Ethnobotany of Plant Taxa from Puerto Rican Sites.

Taxon	Common Name	Recorded Uses*
Edible & Medicinal:		
Acrocomia media	corozo palm	fresh fruit
Amyris sp.	torchwood	fresh fruit
Anadenanthera peregrina	cohoba	narcotic snuff, medicinal
Andira inermis	moca	medicinal
Annona sp.	guanábana	fresh fruit
Bixa orellana	achiote	condiment, dye, medicinal
Bourreria sp.	strongbark, spoon tree	fresh fruit, tea (bark), fermented beverage (flowers), medicinal
Bursera simaruba	almácigo	medicinal
Byrsonima sp.	aceiuna	fresh fruit
Carica papaya	lechosa	fresh fruit, medicinal
Cissus sp.	bejuco de gongolí	fresh fruit
Coccoloba uvifera	uva de playa	fresh fruit, medicinal (bark)
Cordia spp.	capá blanco, c. colorado	some with edible fruit
Cresentia sp.	higüera	medicinal
Croton sp.	lechecillo	medicinal tea (leaves)
Erythroxylum sp.	cocaína falsa	alkaloids and salts beverages
Eugenia spp.	caracolillo, stoppers	fresh fruit, medicinal (leaves)
Exostema sp.	alvarillo	medicinal (bark as febrifuge)
Ficus sp.	jagüey	fresh fruit, medicinal
Guaiacum sp.	guayacán, lignum vitae	various medicinal, guaiac resin
Guazuma ulmifolia	guácima	medicinal
Hypoxis sp.	coquí	entire plant edible
Inga sp.	guaba	edible fruit
Jatrophia sp.	tártago emético	medicinal
Oenothera sp.	evening primrose	whole plant edible, seed oil, medic.
Passiflora sp.	parcha	fresh fruit, beverage, medicinal
Persea americana	aguacate, avocado	edible fruit, medicinal
Picramnia sp.	guarema	medicinal bark
Piscida sp.	ventura, fish poison	various medicinal, sedative (bark)
Psidium guajava	guayaba, guava	fresh fruit, medicinal
Rubus sp.	fresa de montaña	edible fruit

Continued on the next page

Table 4.4. *Continued*

Taxon	Common Name	Recorded Uses*
Sapotaceae, *Sideroxylon Pouteria* etc.	sapote family, mastic-bully, caimito, almendrón	fresh fruit, medicinal
Setaria/Panicum spp.	(Panicoid grasses)	starchy grains (flour, popped grain)
Solanum sp.	yerba mora	medicinal
Trianthema portulacastrum	verdolaga	edible seeds and greens
Zanthoxylum spp.	espinosa	medicinal (bark, roots)
Wood & Multipurpose:		
Acrocomia media	corozo palm	thatching, cordage, needles, posts
Amyris sp.	teílla, torchwood	fuel, torches, resins, ethereal oil
Andira inermis	moca	durable construction, implements
Ardisia sp.	bádula	furniture, general construction
Bourreria sp.	palo de vaca, strongbark	fuelwood, charcoal production
Bucida buceras	ucar	fuelwood, poles, posts, carpentry
Bursera simaruba	almácigo	fragrant oil and resin (incense, copal), glue, fence posts, wood products
Capparis sp.	burro	fuelwood
Coccoloba uvifera	uva de playa, sea grape	fuelwood, implements, furniture
Conocarpus erectus	botoncillo	fuelwood, wood implements
Cordia spp.	capá blanco, c. colorado	joinery, furniture, construction
Cresentia sp.	higüera	container fruits, implements, fuel
Croton sp.	lechecillo	fences, dyes, resins, carpentry
Erythroxylum sp.	cocaína falsa	posts, poles, fuel, turnery
Eugenia spp.	caracolillo, stoppers	fuel, wood implements, cabinetry
Exostema sp.	alvarillo, quinine bark	cabinetry, turnery
Guaiacum sp.	guayacán, lignum vitae	fuelwood, wood implements
Guazuma ulmifolia	guácima	fuelwood, implements, rope (bast)
Gymnanthes sp.	yaití	posts, poles, tool handles, turnery
Krugiodendron ferreum	bariaco	fuelwood
Maytenus sp.	mayten	wood implements, carpentry
Piscida sp.	ventura, fish poison	fish stupifier (bark, leaves, roots), implements, fence posts, fuelwood

Continued on the next page

Table 4.4. *Continued*

Taxon	Common Name	Recorded Uses*
Sapotaceae, *Mastichodendron, Pouteria* etc.	sapote family, mastic-fuel, bully, caimito, almendrón	wood implements, fence posts, construction, latex (some species)
Tabebuia sp.	roble	construction, carpentry
Thespesia grandiflora	maga	furniture, musical instruments, posts
Trema sp.	guacimilla	basketry, bark cordage, fuelwood
Zanthoxylum spp.	espinosa	furniture, carpentry, wood items, dye

*Acevedo-Rodríguez 1996; Ayensu 1981; Brussell 1997; DeBoer 1996; Duke 1992; Honeychurch 1986; Longuefosse 1995; Moerman 2003; Morton 1990; Nuñez Melendez 1992; Scurlock 1987; Record and Hess 1943.

sites as a whole, including Maruca and María de la Cruz, two of the Archaic occupations.

Seeds of the tree taxa listed above, including both avocado (aguacate) and lechosa (papaya), do not differ morphologically from wild forms (Newsom 1993). Thus, all may represent wild species or undomesticated landraces, or at least forms for which evidence of domestication is not apparent from seed morphology alone. Nevertheless, it is worth reiterating that some of these trees are not considered by botanists to be native to Puerto Rico and the Caribbean (Newsom 1993). Therefore, their presence among the plant remains may signify the introduction of important tree taxa, perhaps as components of home gardens, and strengthens the inference of low-level cultivation as a regular component of economic systems. These exotics include achiote, avocado, papaya, yellow sapote, and possibly anacagüita or Panama tree, each of which derive from the Latin American mainland (Liogier and Martorell 2000), and may have been introduced into the Caribbean by prehistoric human groups (Newsom 1993; Newsom and Pearsall 2003). Especially intriguing is that two of these taxa—avocado and yellow sapote—are identifications from María de la Cruz, an Archaic site (Rouse and Alegría 1990). Newsom (1993) has suggested previously that Archaic occupants of the region may have been gardeners or casual food producers (Smith 2001).

A number of potentially edible herbaceous taxa were identified in the sites, including a member of the chenopod or goosefoot family (Chenopodiaceae),

Hypoxis sp. (coquí, also known as stargrass), Panicoid grass, *Rubus* sp. (fresa de montaña, wild raspberry), *Solanum* sp. of the nightshade family (Solanaceae), *Trianthema portulacastrum* (verdolaga, also known as trianthema), and *Oenothera* sp. (evening primroses). As a group, these plants represent weedy herbs that variously possess edible fruits, seeds, greens, and/or rootstocks, some with medicinal or even ritual potential as mild narcotics (Table 4.4), likely to have been utilized by inhabitants of the different sites. For example, verdolaga has edible greens and relatively high-protein seeds (Carr et al. 1985). The potential to use *Oenothera* sp. as a sedative or narcotic was discussed earlier (Newsom 1993; Newsom and Pearsall 2003). It has been documented from five of the 11 sites with seed remains, all associated with ceramic-age occupations, including the civic-ceremonial centers of NCS-1 (where the seeds comprise 20 percent ubiquity) and Tibes (Table 4.5). The remaining herbaceous seed taxa are sporadically present and generally few in numbers of individuals at the individual sites. Consequently, it is difficult to discern significant patterns or differences among sites, except to specify that these taxa—particularly Trianthema, Chenopodiaceae, Hypoxis, and Panicoid grass—commonly occur in ceramic-age deposits, including Paso del Indio and UTU-44. The widespread occurrence of these taxa may be an indication that they represented a set of optimal resources (Kelly 1995). At least some of the seeds, however, may be incidentals, for example, Convolvulaceae and Euphorbiaceae (morning glory and spurge families), that is, they are simply intrusive into the archaeological deposits, not the direct result of human activities.

Macrobotanical evidence of staple crops like maize (*Zea mays*) and manioc or yuca (*Manihot esculenta*) is lacking among archaeobotanical assemblages from Puerto Rico and related islands. However, maize kernels have been identified from Tutu, on the nearby island of St. Thomas, and maize kernels and cupules and manioc tubers were recovered at En Bas Saline, Haiti (Newsom and Pearsall 2003). All of these remains derive from later ceramic-age deposits. Tuber remains and fine fragments of parenchymatous tissues from NCS-1, NCS-4, Tibes, and others of the sites on Puerto Rico may be provisional evidence for the presence of edible roots or tubers in prehistoric subsistence systems of the island. Nearly all of these sites produced artifacts traditionally associated with root-crop processing, indirect evidence for reliance on edible rootstocks. Plant microremains for tubers from a sediment core in the Maisabel site (Siegel et al., this volume) provide additional, albeit provisional, evidence for the presence of such potentially significant taxa. These include pollen grains that compare favorably to *Ipomoea*, which may suggest the presence of *I. batatas* (batata or sweet potato), or any one of some 25

Table 4.5. Seed and Other Nonwood Plant Remains from Puerto Rico and Vieques

FAMILY	GENUS/SPECIES	Northern Region:			
		María	Maisabel	NCS-1	NCS-4
I. Trees & Shrubs:					
Annonaceae	*Annona* sp. (guanábana)			4	
Aracaceae	cf. *Acrocomia media* (corozo)		(frond)	12	X
Bignoniaceae	*Cresentia cujete* (higüera)			8	
Bixaceae	*Bixa orellana* (achiote)			4	
Caricaceae	*Carica papaya* (lechosa)				
Lauraceae	*Persea americana* (aguacate)	X			
Malpighiaceae	cf. *Byrsonima* sp. (aceituna)				
Myrtaceae	cf. *Eugenia* sp. (grajo)				
Myrtaceae	*Psidium guajava* (guayaba)				
Rutaceae	cf. *Zanthoxylum* sp. (espinosa)				
Sapotaceae	cf. *Sideroxylon* sp. (tabloncillo)	X		20	X
Sapotaceae	*Pouteria campechiana* (canistel)	X			
II. Herbs & Vines:					
Aizoaceae	*Trianthema* sp. *(verdolaga)*		5	8	X
Capparaceae	cf. *Cleome* sp.				
Chenopodiaceae	—			4	
Convolvulaceae	—				
Euphorbiaceae	—			4	
Fabaceae	cf. *Desmodium* sp., *Vigna* sp.			12	X
Hypoxidaceae	*Hypoxis* sp. (coquí)			4	X
cf. Labiatae	cf. *Ocimum* sp. (albahaca)			4	
Malvaceae	cf. *Sida* sp. (escoba blanca)				
Onagraceae	*Oenothera* sp. (ev. primroses)			20	X
Passifloraceae	*Passiflora* sp. (parcha)			4	
Poaceae	Panicoid grass			8	
Poaceae	—			4	
Portulacaceae	*Portulaca* sp. (verdolaga)				
Rosaceae	*Rubus* sp. (fresa de montaña)				
Solanaceae	*Solanum* sp. (yerba mora)			12	

NOTE: Presence/absence or site ubiquity values; brackets = provisional.

Central Region:		Southern Region:				Vieques
Barraz.	Fresal	Bronce	Maruca	PO-38	Tibes	Luján
12					X	
4		X	X		X	
[4]						
				X		
					X	
						X
						[X]
						[X]
			X			X
				X		
	X	X		X		
		X				
		X				X
54	X			X		
8		X	X			
	X			X	X	
	X					
[4]						
		X				X
		X				
	X					

wild species documented in the flora of Puerto Rico (Liogier and Martorell 2000:163–165) that may or may not be edible. Also identified from the core samples were phytoliths that suggest Marantaceae and the genus *Canna* sp., which could possibly represent introduced arrowroot (*Maranta arundinacea*) or any of several native wild taxa (lerenes, sweet corn-root, maraca, maraca amarillo, gruya, and such [Liogier and Martorell 2000:262]), some of which are potentially edible.

The wood remains from the sites add significantly to the inventory of identified and potential economic taxa (Table 4.6). Prominent among the wood identifications were several tree legumes (family Fabaceae) and others in the sapodilla family (Sapotaceae). Several woods were conspicuously present at some sites, suggestive of preferential selection and use. *Thespesia grandiflora* (syn. *Montezuma grandiflora*) or "maga," an endemic tree in the cotton family (Liogier and Martorell 2000:121) comprised approximately 25 percent of the sample ubiquities for the ceramic-age sites of Maisabel, NCS-1, and Tibes. *Pouteria* sp. (almendrón; Sapotaceae) wood demonstrated a 56 percent occurrence (ubiquity) at Maisabel, particularly from features including one possible hearth (Newsom 1993). Maga and almendrón are examples of medium to tall trees with durable, straight-grained wood widely used for posts, construction, furniture, and more (Record and Hess 1943:351–352, 501–502). *Bourreria* sp. (palo de vaca) was identified in 62 percent of proveniences at Tibes, while *Guaiacum* sp. (guayacán) was strongly associated with domestic deposits at the site (Newsom and Curet 2000, 2001). Both are exceptional fuelwoods, as are guácima (*Guazuma ulmifolia*) and buttonwood (*Conocarpus erectus*) (Little 1983), prominently represented in the El Bronce and Tibes deposits (Table 4.6). In addition, a legume wood very similar to *Anadenanthera* sp. is conspicuously present (62 percent ubiquity) at Tibes, particularly in a northern sector of the site that may represent an elite compound (Newsom and Curet 2001). Finally, as prominent edible fruit-bearing home-garden trees, for example, níspero and almendrón, these identifications may represent deadwood collection or pruning of trees maintained around dwellings, with the wood then used as fuel.

Zooarchaeology

This section presents a synthesis of previously identified zooarchaeological remains from 13 archaeological sites (Figure 4.1, Table 4.1). These data were collected from published articles, contract reports, theses and dissertations, and unpublished manuscripts, and are presented here as reported in the original documents. Taxonomic names have been corrected for spelling errors.

Table 4.6. Wood Remains from Ceramic-Age Sites on Puerto Rico and Vieques.
(By presence/absence (X) or site ubiquity values; data in brackets indicate provisional taxonomic assignment.)

		Northern Region:			Central Region:		Southern Region:			Vieques
FAMILY	GENUS/SPECIES	Maisabel	NCS-1	NCS-4	Barrazas	Fresal	Bronce	PO-38	Tibes	Luján
Anacardiaceae	cf. *Comocladia* sp.			6						
Annonaceae	*Annona* sp.						2			
Annonaceae	cf. *Oxandra* sp.			3						
cf. Apocynaceae	—				14					
Aracaceae	—		4	3			[2]			
Bignoniaceae	*Tecoma stans*						12			
Bignoniaceae	*Tabebuia* sp.		16							
Bignoniaceae	*Crescentia* sp. or *Tabebuia* sp.			30			28			
Bignoniaceae	—	6								
Bixaceae/Ebenaceae	cf. *Bixa orellana, Diospyros* sp.									7
Boraginaceae	*Bourreria* sp.			9					62	6
Boraginaceae	*Cordia* sp., *C. albal dentata*								25	
Boraginaceae	*Cordia* sp., *C. laevigata*									2
Boraginaceae	—						12			
Burseraceae	*Bursera simaruba*				14					
Capparaceae	*Capparis* sp.						32			2
Celastraceae	*Elaeodendron xylocarpum*	6								
Celastraceae	*Gyminda* or *Crossopetalum* sp.								12	

Table 4.6 Continued

FAMILY	GENUS/SPECIES	Northern Region:			Central Region:		Southern Region:			Vieques
		Maisabel	NCS-1	NCS-4	Barrazas	Fresal	Bronce	PO-38	Tibes	Luján
Celastraceae	*Maytenus* or *Torralbasia* sp.								25	
Celastraceae	*Maytenus* sp.			6					[25]	13
Combretaceae	*Bucida* (*B. buceras*)								37	33
Combretaceae	*Conocarpus erectus*						[70]			
Erythroxylaceae	*Erythroxylum* sp.						2			
Euphorbiaceae	*Croton* sp.				[7]		70			[4]
Euphorbiaceae	*Gymnanthes* (*G. lucida*)				[7]				12	
Euphorbiaceae	*Jatrophia* sp.								12	
Euphorbiaceae or Rubiaceae	cf. *Hyeronima* sp. or *Genipa americana*				[7]					
Fabaceae-Mimosoid	cf. *Inga* or *Pithecellobium*	6	4	21	42			16	37	
Fabaceae-Mimosoid	cf. *Anadenanthera* sp.								62	
Fabaceae-Papilion.	*Andira* (*A. inermis*)						[4]		37	4
Fabaceae-Papilion.	cf. *Andiria* or *Lonchocarpus*				21					
Fabaceae-Papilion.	cf. *Lonchocarpus* sp.				7					
Fabaceae-Papilion.	*Piscida* (*P. carthagenesis*)						[9]			8
Fabaceae	—									
Lauraceae	cf. *Aniba, Licaria, Ocotea* spp.								62	
Lauraceae	cf. *Nectandra* (*N. coriacea*)									1

Family	Taxon						
cf. Malpighiaceae	cf. *Byrsonima* sp.					37	
Malvaceae	cf. *Abutilon* or *Hibiscus* sp.			7			
Malvaceae	*Thespesia grandiflora*	25	24			25	
cf. Melastomataceae	cf. *Mouriri* sp.					12	
cf. Meliaceae	cf. *Trichilia*			[7]		25	
Moraceae	*Ficus* sp.	[6]	6	[X]		12	
Myrsinaceae	*Ardisia* sp.					12	
Myrtaceae	*Eugenia* (*E. confusa*)						2
cf. Myrtaceae	cf. *Eugenia* sp.					12	
Myrtaceae	*Psidium* (*P. guajava*)	[6]					13
Polygonaceae	*Coccoloba uvifera*				32	[12]	
Rhamnaceae	*Krugiodendron* (*K. ferreum*)						1
Rubiaceae	*Exostema* (*E. caribaeum*)				30	25	2
cf. Rubiaceae	cf. *Randia* (*R. aculeata*)					12	1
Rutaceae	*Amyris* (*A. elemifera*)					[12]	1
Rutaceae	*Zanthoxylum* sp.					[25]	1
Rutaceae	—		3				
Sapotaceae*	*Chrysophyllum/Sideroxylon* (wood anatomical group I)	56	21			75	17
Sapotaceae*	*Pouteria* sp. (group II)+			[X]			
Sapotaceae*	*Manilkara* sp. (group III)		9	24	[X]		
Sapotaceae	—				25		

Continued on the next page

Table 4.6 Continued

		Northern Region:			Central Region:			Southern Region:			Vieques
FAMILY	GENUS/SPECIES	Maisabel	NCS-1	NCS-4	Barrazas	Fresal	Bronce	PO-38	Tibes		Luján
Simaroubiaceae	*Picramnia* (*P. pentandra*)										7
Simaroubiaceae	cf. *Suriana maritima*								50		
Sterculiaceae	*Guazuma ulmifolia*				[57]				25		
Sterculiaceae	*Sterculia* (*S. apetala*)	[6]									7
Ulmaceae	cf. *Trema* sp.				7						
cf. Vitaceae	cf. *Cissus* sp.								25		
Zygophyllaceae	*Guaiacum* sp.						9		12		

*Sapotaceae wood anatomical groups according to Record and Hess 1942–1948.
†Also identified from Calle Cristo site (Newsom 1993).

Revisions in taxonomy are denoted by presenting previously recorded and corrected names together. Taxonomic revisions were applied to some taxa of mollusks and aquatic turtles. As stated, the abbreviation cf. stands for "confer." In zooarchaeological usage, it indicates that an element could not be identified definitively to, but was a close approximation of, a specific taxon, similar to the discussion concerning plant identifications. In many cases, specimens were too fragmentary or eroded for positive identifications. If categories were defined as cf. but positive identifications were made at the lower taxonomic levels of family or genus for other elements, then the cf. designation was not included in the table for that time period or location. Cf. designations were included for all species-level identifications (e.g., greater flamingo [*Phoenicopterus* cf. *rubber*]). The summary table includes material regardless of recovery method. Clearly, there are significant differences in types and quantities of faunal remains depending on specific recovery methods employed (i.e., screen-mesh size) and the method of processing (wet-screening, dry-screening, flotation). No assessment is provided herein of the relative effects of recovery methods on the faunal record for these sites.

The faunal data are from sites representing different time periods and contexts. The temporal assignments for the contexts of the faunal assemblages are based on the excavators' interpretations (see Table 4.1). The time periods used are Archaic, Saladoid, Saladoid/Ostionoid, and Ostionoid/Chicoid. The Saladoid/Ostionoid category represents a transitional cultural period, notably associated with the crab-shell dichotomy or subsistence transition (Rainey 1940; Rodríguez Ramos, this volume). Although originally postulated as a migration of new peoples (i.e., replacement) with different economic and ceramic traditions, today the transition is viewed as the merger of existing cultural traits established during the Saladoid period with some new practices. The late deposits associated with Ostionoid and Chicoid contexts are combined for this synthesis. For environmental and spatial comparative purposes, the archaeological contexts are divided into three broad geographic realms of Puerto Rico: north, south, and Vieques. There are no faunal remains included in this chapter from central-mountain interior sites.[1]

The presence or absence of taxa was investigated in this broad analysis of resource use through time on Puerto Rico and Vieques. No measures of relative abundance (e.g., number of identified specimens, minimum numbers of individuals, estimates of edible meat weight) were calculated. Although the range of taxa identified for a site are also dependent on recovery methods, taxa representation is somewhat less sensitive than either primary or secondary measures of relative abundance.

Faunal identifications followed standard zooarchaeological procedures. All but four of the assemblages were identified using the zooarchaeology comparative collections of the Environmental Archaeology Program at the Florida Museum of Natural History.[2] The collections from Maruca and Puerto Ferro were identified using comparative material housed at the Centro de Investigaciones Arqueológicas de la Universidad de Puerto Rico (Narganes Storde 1991a, 1997a, 1997b). Ornithological specimens from the Hernández Colón site were identified by Storrs L. Olson based on collections curated at the National Museum of Natural History, Smithsonian Institution (Maíz López 1996). Finally, the invertebrate remains from the El Bronce (Robinson 1985a) and Caracoles (Colón Parilla 1997) sites were identified based on the analysts' comparative specimens and relevant field guides.

Zooarchaeological Data

The zooarchaeological data consist of vertebrate and invertebrate remains. The invertebrates consist of marine mollusks (gastropods, bivalves, and chitons), crustaceans, and sea urchins. The identification of most terrestrial gastropods was dependent on recovery methods. While some land snails may provide environmental information, the bulk of these are very small nonfood commensal taxa; therefore, they are not included in this synthesis. Terrestrial gastropods believed to have been food items are included. Marine mollusks include a number of taxa represented by very small individuals. Many of them may have entered midden deposits attached to other larger specimens as epibonts. We cannot be certain that small marine mollusks represent food refuse. However, since we are uncertain of food-preparation methods, these specimens cannot be dismissed as sources of sustenance. If boiling was used as a method to extract and cook marine shellfish, then presumably many of the smaller specimens too were included in the diet.

Table 4.7 presents a list of previously identified faunal remains from the 13 sites included in the zooarchaeological analysis. The table indicates geographic locations in Puerto Rico (north, south, Vieques) where the specimens were collected and the cultural periods associated with the taxa. Table 4.8 summarizes the number of taxonomic categories by class for the three geographic locations and four time periods. Totals include identifications of higher taxonomic categories, such as family or genus, as well as species identifications, thus providing an indication of the representation and diversity of the different classes.

Significant differences were documented in the variety of fauna used through time. The two Archaic sites (Maruca and Puerto Ferro) exhibited very little use of vertebrates. Only unidentified rodents and intrusive cattle remains were found in these sites. No exotic fauna were introduced at this

Table 4.7. Zooarchaeological Identifications from Archaeological Sites on Puerto Rico and Vieques.

Taxon		North	South	Vieques	Archaic	Saladoid	Saladoid/ Ostionoid	Ostionoid/ Chicoid
Artibeus jamaicensis	Jamaican fruit-eating bat	X						X
Ehtesicus fuscus	big brown bat	X				X		
Molossus molossus	rat bat	X						X
Nesophontes edithae	West Indian shrew			X		X		X
Nesophontes sp.	shrew		X				X	
Heteropsomys insulans	spiny rat			X		X		
Echimyidae	spiny rat	X					X	
Isolobodon portoricensis	hutia	X	X	X		X	X	X
Plagiodontia sp.	hutia	X				X		
Rodentia	rodent	X	X	X	X	X	X	X
Capromyidae	hutia	X				X		
Cavia porcellus	guinea pig	X	X	X			X	X
Canis familiaris	dog	X	X	X				X
Delphinidae	dolphins and porpoises			X		X		
Trichechus manatus	manatee	X		X		X		X
Equus caballus	horse	X		X		X		
Sus scrofa	domestic pig	X						
Tayassuidae	peccaries			X		X		X
Bos taurus	cow			X	X			

Continued on the next page

Table 4-7 Continued

Taxon		North	South	Vieques	Archaic	Saladoid	Saladoid/Ostionoid	Ostionoid/Chicoid
Puffinus sp.	shearwater							X
Sula sp.	booby			X		X		
Sulidae	boobies			X		X		
Pelecanidae	pelicans			X		X		
Fregata cf. *magnificens*	magnificent frigatebird			X		X		
Egretta alba	great egret	X		X		X		X
Casmerodius alba	great egret		X	X	X	X		X
Nycticorax cf. *nycticorax*	black-crowned hight heron		X		X			
Ardeidae	herons, egrets, and bitterns	X	X	X	X	X		X
cf. *Eudocimus albus*	white ibis			X		X		
Threskiornithidae	ibises and spoonbills	X				X		
Phoenicopterus cf. *ruber*	greater flamingo			X		X		
Phoenicopterus ruber	greater flamingo			X		X		
cf. *Phoenicopterus ruber*	greater flamingo			X		X		
Dedrocygna arborea	West-Indian whistling duck	X				X		
Anserinae	geese			X		X		
Anatidae	ducks, geese, swans	X	X	X	X	X		X
Pandion haliaetus	osprey			X				
Falco sp.	falcon		X		X			
Falconidae	falcons		X		X		X	

Taxon	Common name	1	2	3	4	5	6	7
Falconiformes	falcons					X		
Fulica cf. *americana*	coot			X			X	X
Fulica sp.	coot			X				X
Porphyrula martinicus	purple gallinule			X				X
Porphyrula sp.	gallinule			X				
cf. *Fulica* sp.	coot			X		X		
cf. *Gallinule* sp.	gallinule			X		X		
Rallidae	rails, gallinules, coots	X		X		X		
Scolopacidae	snipes, sandpipers	X				X		
Laridae	gulls, terns			X		X		
Columba sp.	dove	X		X		X	X	
cf. *Zenaida* sp.	dove			X		X		
Zenaida sp.	dove	X		X	X	X	X	
Zenaida asiatica	white-winged dove			X		X		
Columbidae	pigeons and doves	X		X		X	X	X
Amazona sp.	parrot	X		X		X		
Crotophaga ani	smooth-billed ani					X		
Corvus sp.	crow	X		X		X		
Corvidae	crows			X		X		
Muscicapidae	thrushes			X		X		
cf. Muscicapidae	thrushes		X					
Emberizidae	finches	X				X	X	X
Fringillidae	grosbeaks, finches, buntings	X				X		
Passeriformes	song birds	X				X	X	X

Continued on the next page

Table 4.7 Continued

Taxon		North	South	Vieques	Archaic	Saladoid	Saladoid/Ostionoid	Ostionoid/Chicoid
Caretta caretta	Atlantic loggerhead	X		X		X		
Chelonia mydas	green sea turtle	X		X		X		
Lepidochelys kempii	Atlantic Ridley			X		X		
cf. *Lepidochelys kempii*	Atlantic Ridley			X		X		
Cheloniidae	sea turtles	X	X	X		X	X	X
Pseudemys/Trachemys decussata	Antillean painted turtle	X	X	X		X		X
Pseudemys decussata stejnegeri	Antillean painted turtle			X		X		
Pseudemys/Trachemys sp.	aquatic turtle	X		X		X		
Trachemys stejnegeri	Antillean painted turtle	X						X
Ameiva exsul	common ground lizard		X					X
Ameiva sp.	teiid lizard	X	X			X		X
Anguidae	lizard	X				X	X	X
Anolis sp.	lizard	X				X		
Diploglossus sp.	lizard		X				X	
cf. *Diploglossus* sp.	lizard	X				X		
Cyclura pinguis	Anegada iguana	X				X		X
Iguana iguana	common iguana	X				X		X
Iguana sp.	iguana			X				
Iguanidae	iguanid lizards	X		X		X		X
Lacertilia	lizards	X	X			X	X	X
Sauria	lizards		X					X
Alsophis portoricensis	Peurto Rican racer		X			X		X

Taxon	Common name							
Alsophis sp.	racer	X						
Epicrates sp.	pygmy boa	X						
Colubridae	non-poisonous snakes	X	X		X		X	X
Serpentes	snakes	X			X			X
Eleutherodactylus sp.	coqui frog	X						X
Rana sp.	frog		X			X		
Bufo sp.	toad	X				X		
Anura	frog/toads	X	X		X	X		X
Carcharhinus leucas	bull shark	X				X		
Carcharhinus sp.	shark	X	X			X	X	
Carcharhinidae	requiem sharks	X		X	X	X		X
cf. Carcharhinidae	requiem sharks			X		X		
Carcharhiniformes	requiem sharks	X						X
Galeocerdo cuvieri	tiger shark	X				X		
Galeocerdo sp.	tiger shark	X						
cf. *Negaprion brevirostris*	lemon shark			X		X		
cf. *Sphyrna* sp.	possible hammerhead shark	X					X	
Lamniformes	sharks	X					X	X
Dasyatus sp.	stingray			X		X		
Rhinoptera sp.	cow-nosed ray		X				X	
Myliobatidae	eagle rays			X		X		X
Rajiformes	rays	X	X		X	X		X

Continued on the next page

Table 4.7 Continued

Taxon		North	South	Vieques	Archaic	Saladoid	Saladoid/Ostionoid	Ostionoid/Chicoid
Elops saurus	ladyfish	X	X	X		X	X	X
Megalops atlanticus	tarpon	X		X		X	X	X
Elopidae	tarpons			X				X
Albula vulpes	bonefish	X		X		X		X
Anguilla rostrata	American eel	X				X		
Anguilliformes	eels and morays	X				X		
Muraenidae	moray eels	X		X			X	X
Harengula sp.	sardine	X				X	X	X
cf. *Opisthonema* sp.	herring	X						X
Clupeidae	shad, herrings, sardines	X				X	X	X
Clupeidae cf. *Harengula*	sardine	X				X		
Clupeidae cf. *Opisthonema*	herring	X				X		
Engraulidae	anchovies	X						X
Gobiesocidae	cling fishes	X						X
Hemiramphus sp.	halfbeak	X				X		
Exocoetidae	flying fish	X				X	X	X
Exocoetidae/Hemiramphidae	flying fish/halfbeaks	X				X	X	
Strongylura sp.	needlefish	X		X		X	X	X
Tylosurus cf. *acus*	agujon			X		X		
Tylosurus sp.	houndfish	X	X	X		X	X	X
Belonidae	needlefishes	X	X	X		X	X	X
Belonidae cf. *Tylosurus*	houndfish	X				X		

Taxon	Common name					
Atherinidae	silversides	X			X	X
Holocentrus sp.	squirrelfish	X				X
Holocentrus ascensionis	longjaw squirrelfish	X	X	X		
Holocentrus cf. *rufus*	longspine squirrelfish	X		X		
Holocentridae	squirrelfishes	X		X		X
Scorpaena sp.	scorpionfish	X	X	X		
Centropomus parallelus	fat snook	X		X		
Centropomus undecimalis	snook	X	X	X		
Centropomus cf. *pectinatus*	tarpon snook	X		X		
Centropomus sp.	snook	X	X	X	X	X
Centropomidae	snooks			X		
Epinephelus adcensionis	rock hind	X		X		
Epinephelus fulvus	coney	X		X	X	X
Epinephelus guttatus	red hind	X	X	X		
Epinephelus morio	red grouper		X	X		
Epinephelus striatus	Nassau grouper		X	X		
Epinephelus cf. *adscensionis*	rock hind		X	X		
Epinephelus cf. *fulvus*	coney	X		X		
Epinephelus cf. *guttatus*	red hind		X	X		
Epiniphelus cf. *itajara*	jewfish		X	X		
Epinephelus cf. *striatus*	Nassau grouper		X	X		
Epinephelus sp.	grouper	X	X	X	X	X
Mycteroperca bonaci	black grouper		X	X	X	
Mycteroperca sp.	grouper	X	X	X		X

Continued on the next page

Table 4-7 Continued

Taxon		North	South	Vieques	Archaic	Saladoid	Saladoid/ Ostionoid	Ostionoid/ Chicoid
Serranidae	groupers	X	X			X	X	X
Malacanthus plumieri	sand tilefish		X					X
Caranx caballus	jack	X				X		
Caranx crysos	blue runner	X				X		
Caranx hippos	crevalle jack			X	X	X		
Caranx latus	horse-eye jack			X		X		
Caranx cf. latus	horse-eye jack	X		X		X		
Caranx sp.	jack	X	X	X	X	X	X	
Carangidae	jacks	X	X	X		X	X	X
Selene vomer	lookdown	X	X				X	X
cf. Selene sp.	moonfish	X				X		
Trachinotus sp.	pompano	X				X		
Trachurus lathami	rough scad	X				X		
Lutjanus analis	mutton snapper			X		X		
Lutjanus apodus	schoolmaster	X		X		X		
Lutjanus cyanopter	cubera snapper	X				X		
Lutjanus griseus	grey snapper	X		X		X		
Lutjanus jocu	dog snapper					X		
Lutjanus mahogoni	Mahogony snapper			X		X		
Lutjanus synagris	lane snapper			X		X		
Lutjanus vivanus	silk snapper	X				X		
Lutjanus cf. analis	mutton snapper			X		X		

Species	Common name	1	2	3	4	5	6	7
Lutjanus cf. *apodus*	schoolmaster			x				
Lutjanus cf. *buccanella*	blackfin snapper	x				x		
Lutjanus cf. *campechanus*	red snapper	x				x		
Lutjanus cf. *mahogoni*	Mahogony snapper			x		x		
Lutjanus cf. *purpureus*	Caribbean red snapper			x		x		
Lutjanus cf. *synagris*	lane snapper			x		x		
Lutjanus sp.	snapper	x	x	x		x	x	x
Ocyurus chrysurus	yellowtail snapper		x		x	x	x	x
Lutjanidae	snapper	x	x	x		x		x
Diapterus cf. *plumieri*	mojarra	x	x			x		x
Diapterus sp.	mojarra	x	x			x		x
Eucinostomus sp.	jenny	x				x		
Gerres cinereus	yellowfin mojarra	x	x			x		
Gerres sp.	mojarra	x				x		
Gerreidae	mojarras	x	x			x		x
Anisotremus surinamensis	black margate	x	x	x		x		
Anisotremus virginicus	porkfish	x		x	x	x		
Anisotremus cf. *surinamensis*	black margate			x		x		
Anisotremus sp.	porkfish	x		x		x		x
Conodon nobilis	barred grunt	x	x	x		x		x
Haemulon plumieri	white grunt	x		x		x		
Haemulon sciurus	blue stripped grunt			x		x		
Haemulon cf. *sciurus*	blue stripped grunt	x				x		
Haemulon sp.	grunt	x	x			x	x	x
Haemulidae	grunts	x	x			x	x	x

Continued on the next page

Table 4-7 Continued

Taxon		North	South	Vieques	Archaic	Saladoid	Saladoid/Ostionoid	Ostionoid/Chicoid
cf. *Orthopristis chrysoptera*	pigfish	X				X		
Archosargus sp.	porgy			X				X
cf. *Archosargus* spp.	porgy			X		X		
Calamus cf. *pennatula*	pluma			X		X		
Calamus sp.	porgy	X		X		X		
Sparidae	porgies	X	X	X		X		X
Bairdiella ronchus	roncho basto	X				X		
Bairdiella cf. *ronchus*	roncho basto	X				X		
Bairdiella sp.	drum	X				X		
Larimus fasciatus	banded drum		X					X
Micropogonias furnieri	croaker		X					X
Micropogonias undulatus	Atlantic croaker	X				X		
Micropogonias sp.	croaker	X				X		
Sciaenidae	drums	X				X		
Kyphosus sp.	chub	X				X		
Chaetodontidae	butterfly fish	X				X		
Holocanthus sp.	angelfish			X				X
Pomacanthus sp.	angelfish			X				X
Pomacanthidae	angelfishes	X				X		
Abudefduf cf. *saxatilis*	sergeant major	X				X		
Mugil sp.	mullet	X		X		X	X	X
Sphyraena barracuda	barracuda		X	X	X	X		X

Taxon	Common name	1	2	3	4	5
Sphyraena sp.	barracuda			X		X
cf. Sphyraenidae	barracuda	X				X
Bodianus rufus	hogfish	X		X	X	
Bodianus cf. *rufus*	hogfish	X		X	X	X
Bodianus sp.	hogfish	X		X	X	
Halichoeres bivittatus	slippery dick	X			X	
Halichoeres radiatus	puddingwife		X		X	
Halichoeres cf. *bivittatus*	slippery dick	X			X	
Halichoeres cf. *radiatus*	puddingwife	X			X	
Halichoeres sp.	wrasses	X		X	X	X
Lachnolaimus maximus	hogfish		X	X	X	X
Labridae	wrasses	X	X	X	X	
Scarus croicensis	striped parrotfish			X	X	X
cf. *Scarus croicensis*	striped parrotfish			X	X	
Scarus sp.	parrotfishes	X	X	X	X	
Sparisoma rubripinne	redfin parrotfish	X			X	
Sparisoma viride	spotlight parrotfish	X		X	X	X
Sparioma cf. *rubripinne*	redfin parrotfish			X	X	
Sparisoma cf. *viride*	spotlight parrotfish			X	X	
Sparisoma sp.	parrotfish	X	X	X	X	X
Scaridae	parrotfishes	X	X		X	X
cf. *Eleotris* sp.	sleeper	X			X	
Gobiomorus dormitor	bigmouth sleeper	X	X	X	X	X
Gobiomorus sp.	sleeper	X			X	
Eleotridae	sleepers	X	X		X	X

Continued on the next page

Table 4.7 Continued

Taxon		North	South	Vieques	Archaic	Saladoid	Saladoid/ Ostionoid	Ostionoid/ Chicoid
Gobionellus sp.	goby	X				X		
Gobiidae	gobies	X				X	X	X
Acanthurus coeruleus	blue tang	X				X		
Acanthurus sp.	surgeonfish	X		X		X	X	X
Euthynnus alletteratus	little tuna	X		X		X		
Euthynnus sp.	tuna	X				X		
Scomberomorus sp.	tuna	X				X	X	
Thunnus sp.	tuna	X				X		
Scombridae	tuna, mackerels	X	X	X		X	X	X
Balistes vetula	queen triggerfish			X		X		
Balistes cf. *vetula*	queen triggerfish	X		X		X		
Balistes sp.	triggerfish	X		X		X		
Balistidae	triggerfishes	X	X	X		X	X	X
Melichthyes niger	black durgon	X	X			X	X	
Lactophrys sp.	trunkfish	X		X		X	X	X
cf. Ostraciidae	trunkfishes	X				X		
Chilomycterus sp.	burrfish	X				X		
Diodon hystrix	porcupinefish			X	X			X
Diodon sp.	porcupinefish	X	X	X		X	X	
Diodontidae	porcupinefishes	X	X	X		X	X	X

Taxon	Common name	1	2	3	4	5	6	7	8
Macrobrachium sp.	shrimp								X
Coenobita clypeatus	hermit crab		X		X				
Callinectes sapidus	blue crab		X				X		
Callinectes sp.	sea crab		X	X					
Portunidae	swimming crab	X		X		X		X	X
Cardisoma guanhumi	blue land crab	X	X	X	X	X		X	X
Cardisoma sp.	land crab	X			X	X			
Gecarcinus ruricola	land crab		X					X	
Gecarcinus sp.	land crab		X					X	
Gecarcinidae	land crabs	X	X			X	X	X	X
Carpilis corallinus	coral crab		X	X			X	X	
cf. *Panopeus* sp.	swimming crab		X		X				
Epilobocera sinuatifrons	freshwater crab		X		X				
Decapoda	crabs			X		X		X	X
Brachyura	common crabs	X				X		X	X
Panulirus sp.	spiny lobster			X				X	X
Acanthopleura granulata	fuzzy chiton	X		X		X		X	X
Acanthopleura sp.	chiton	X							X
Chiton tuberculatus	common West Indian chiton		X				X		
Chitonidae	chitons		X	X				X	X
Chiton sensu lato	chiton	X			X	X	X	X	X
Neoloricata	chitons	X						X	X
Polyplacphora	chitons			X				X	X

Continued on the next page

Table 4-7 Continued

Taxon		North	South	Vieques	Archaic	Saladoid	Saladoid/Ostionoid	Ostionoid/Chicoid
Brachiodontes exustus	scorched mussel			X	X			X
Brachidontes sp.	mussel			X				X
Ischadium recurvum	hooked mussel		X	X				X
Myrtilidae	datemussel			X				X
Anadara brasiliana	incongruous ark		X				X	
Anadara notabilis	eared ark	X	X	X	X	X	X	X
Anadara ovalis	blood ark	X	X			X	X	X
Anadara sp.	ark	X		X		X		X
Arca imbricata	mossy ark		X		X			
Arca zebra	turkey wing	X	X	X	X	X	X	
Arca sp.	ark		X				X	
Arcidae	arks	X	X	X		X	X	
Glycymeris decussata	desussate bittersweet							X
Pinctada imbricata	Atlantic pearl-oyster		X	X				X
Pinctada radiata	pearl-oyster		X		X			
Pteria colymbus	Atlantic wing-oyster		X					X
Isognomon alatus	flat tree-oyster		X	X	X			X
Pinna carnea	amber penshell		X		X			X
Pinnidae	penshell		X				X	
Lima scabra	rough fileclam	X				X		
Lima cf. scabra	rough fileclam	X				X		
Lima sp.	fileclam	X					X	

Species	Common name							
Aequipecten muscosus	rough scallop						X	
Lyropecten nodostus	Lion's paw						X	X
Pecten ziczac	ziczac scallop		X				X	X
Pecten sp.	scallop		X			X		
Pectinidae	scallops		X			X		
Plicatula gibbosa	Atlantic kittenpaw			X			X	
Spondylus americanus	Atlantic thorny oyster			X				X
cf. *Spondylus americanus*	Atlantic thorny oyster			X				
Crassostrea rhizophorae	Caribbean oyster			X	X		X	X
Ostrea frons	raccoon oysters			X	X			
Ostrea cf. *equestris*	crested oyster	X			X	X		
Ostrea sp.	oyster			X			X	
Anodontia alba	buttercup lucine			X	X			X
Codakia costata	costate lucine			X				X
Codakia orbicularis	tiger lucine	X		X	X	X	X	
Lucina pectinatus	thick lucine	X		X	X	X	X	
Lucina sp.	lucine			X			X	
Lucinidae	lucines	X		X		X	X	
Chama congregata	little corrugated jewel box	X		X	X	X	X	
Chama macerophylla	leafy jewelbox			X		X		X
Chama sarda	cherry jewelbox			X			X	
Chama sp.	jewelbox	X		X	X		X	X
Chamidae	jewelboxes	X			X		X	
Laevicardium laevigatum	eggcockle	X			X			
Laevicardium sp.	eggcockle	X			X			

Continued on the next page

Table 4-7 Continued

Taxon		North	South	Vieques	Archaic	Saladoid	Saladoid/Ostionoid	Ostionoid/Chicoid
Trachycardium isocardia	even pricklycockle		X	X	X			X
Trachycardium magnum	magnum cockle	X				X		
Trachycardium muricatum	yellow cockle		X		X		X	X
Trachycardium sp.	cockle			X				X
Cardiidae	cockles	X		X		X		X
Solen obliquus	jackknife clam		X					
Tellina alternata	smooth tellin		X	X			X	
Tellina fausta	Faust tellin	X	X			X	X	X
Tellina listeri	speckled tellin	X				X		X
Tellina sp.	tellin	X	X			X	X	
Mactrellona alata	Caribbean winged mactra	X				X	X	
Mulinia portoricensis	surfclam	X	X		X			
cf. Mactridae	surfclam	X				X		
Donax denticulatus	coquina	X	X	X	X	X		X
Donax sp.	coquina	X	X			X		
Iphigenia brasiliana	giant false donax		X					X
Asaphis deflorata	gaudy sanguin		X	X				X
Tagelus plebius	stout tagelus	X	X			X		X
Tagelus sp.	tagelus	X						X
Mytilopsis dominguensis	falsemussel		X		X			
Mytilopsis sp.	falsemussel	X						X
Anomalocardia brasiliana	West Indian pointed venus	X	X	X	X	X	X	X

Species	Common name							
Anomalocardia sp.	pointed venus						X	X
Antigona rigida	rigid venus						X	X
Chione cancellata	cross-barred venus	X		X		X	X	X
Chione granulata	venus		X				X	X
Chione intapurpuria	lady-in-waiting venus					X		
Dosinia sp.	dosinia		X					
Pitar arestus	pleasing pitar		X		X			
Pitar dione	venus comb	X					X	
Pitar sp.	pitar	X					X	
cf. *Periglypta listeri*	princess venus	X					X	
Tivela abaconis	Abaco tivela		X	X				
Tivela mactroides	trigonal tivela		X	X				
Teredo incressata	shipworm		X					X
Patelloida pustulata	spotted limpet					X		X
Acmaea antillarium	Antillean limpet	X				X	X	
Acmaea cf. *antillarium*	Antillean limpet	X					X	
Acmaea cf. *leucopleura*	black-ribbed limpet	X					X	
Acmaea sp.	limpet	X					X	
Acmaeidae	limpets	X			X		X	
Diodora cayenensis	Cayenne keyhole limpet		X			X		X
Diodora listeri	Lister's keyhole limpet					X		X
Diodora sp.	keyhole limpet	X				X		
Fissurella barbadensis	Barbados keyhole limpet	X			X	X		X
Fissurella fascicularis	wobbly keyhole limpet	X				X		X

Continued on the next page

Table 4.7 Continued

Taxon		North	South	Vieques	Archaic	Saladoid	Saladoid/ Ostionoid	Ostionoid/ Chicoid
Fissurella nodosa	knobby keyhole limpet	X		X		X		X
Fissurella rosea	rosy keyhole limpet	X				X		
Fissurella sp.	keyhole limpet	X		X		X		
Lucapina sp.	fleshy limpet	X				X		
Hemitoma octoradiata	eight-ribbed emarginula			X	X			X
Fissurellidae	keyhole limpets	X		X		X	X	X
Arene sp.	cyclostreme		X				X	
Astraea/Lithopoma caelatum	carved starsnail		X	X	X			X
Astraea/Lithopoma tuber	green starsnail	X				X		X
Astraea/Lithopoma sp.	starsnail	X		X	X	X	X	X
Astrea phoebia	long-spined star-shell			X				
Astrea tecta	American star-shell			X	X			
Astraeninae	star-shell	X				X		
Turbo castanea	chestnut turban	X	X	X	X	X	X	X
Turbo sp.	turban	X				X		
Turbinidae	turbans, starsnails	X				X		
Cittarium pica	West Indian top-shell	X	X	X	X	X	X	
Trochidae	topsnails	X				X		
Gaza superba	superb gaza	X				X		
Gaza sp.	gaza	X				X		
Tegula fasciata	silky tegula			X	X			
Tegula lividomaculata	West Indian tegual			X	X			

Scientific name	Common name							
Tegula sp.	tegula	X						
Calliostoma sp.	top-shell	X						
Nerita fulgurans	Antillean nerite	X		X	X		X	
Nerita peloronta	bleeding tooth nerite	X	X	X	X		X	
Nerita cf. *peloronta*	bleeding tooth nerite	X			X		X	
Nerita tessellata	checkered nerite	X	X	X	X	X	X	
Nerita versicolor	four-tooth nerite	X	X	X	X	X	X	
Nerita sp.	nerite	X		X	X		X	X
Neritina clenchi	Clenche's nerite			X	X		X	
Neritina piritica	netted nerite			X		X	X	
Neritina punctulata	dotted nerite		X	X	X		X	
Neritina virginea	virgin nerite	X	X	X	X	X	X	X
Neritina sp.	nerite	X		X			X	X
Neritidae	nerites	X	X	X	X		X	X
Alcadia sp.	drop	X						
Alcadia striata subfusca	striate drop	X						
Cerithium algicola	cerith	X	X	X	X	X	X	
Cerithium eburneum	ivory cerith	X	X	X	X		X	
Cerithium litteratum	stocky cerith	X	X	X	X		X	
Cerithium lutosum	dwarf cerith			X	X		X	
Cerithium sp.	cerith	X		X	X	X	X	
Cerithidae	ceriths	X		X			X	
Planaxis nucleus	Black Atlantic planaxis	X					X	
Modulus modulus	Atlantic modulus	X	X	X	X	X	X	
Turritella variegata	variegated turret		X	X	X	X	X	X

Continued on the next page

Table 4.7 Continued

Taxon		North	South	Vieques	Archaic	Saladoid	Saladoid/Ostionoid	Ostionoid/Chicoid
Cenchritis muricatus	beaded periwinkle			X				X
Littorina angustior	slender periwinkle	X				X		
		X				X		
Littorina lineolata	periwinkle	X				X		
Littorina meleagris	periwinkle	X				X		
Littorina ziczac	ziczac periwinkle	X				X		
Littorina sp.	periwinkle	X				X		
Littorinidae	periwinkles	X				X	X	X
Nodolittorina tuberculata	common pricklywinkle	X				X		X
Tectarius muricatus	beaded periwinkle	X		X	X	X		X
Echinius nodulosus	false prickly-winkle	X				X		
Diastoma sp.	bittium	X				X		
Zebina browniana	smooth risso	X				X		
Strombus alatus	Florida fighting conch		X				X	
Strombus costatus	milk conch		X	X	X			X
Strombus gigas	queen conch		X	X	X	X		X
Strombus pugilis	West Indian fighting conch	X		X		X	X	
Strombus raninus	hawkwing conch	X				X		
Strombus cf. *costatus*	milk conch			X	X			
Strombus cf. *pugilis*	West Indian fighting conch	X				X		
Strombus sp.	conch	X	X	X	X	X	X	X
Crepidula aculeata	spiny slipper shell		X	X	X	X		X

Species	Common name						
Crepidula plana	eastern white slipper shell	X					
Crepidula sp.	slipper shell	X					
cf. *Petaloconchus* sp.	wormsnail	X					
Serpulorbis decussata	decussate worm shell		X				X
Vermetidae	worm shell	X					X
Cyphoma gibbosum	flamingo tongue		X				X
Crucibulum auricula	West Indian cup-and-saucer	X				X	
Cypraea cinerea	Atlantic gray cowrie		X				X
Cypraea sp.	cowrie	X		X			
Cypraea zebra	zebra cowry	X			X	X	
Cypraeidae	cowries	X		X			
Natica sp.	natica	X		X			
Polinices hepaticus	brown moonsnail		X	X			X
Polinices lacteus	milk moonsnail			X	X		X
Polinices sp.	moonsnail	X			X		
Tectonatica pusilla	miniature moonsnail			X	X		
Cassis flammea	flame helmet		X	X			X
Cassis tuberosa	king helmet		X	X	X		
Cassis sp.	helmet	X		X			
Cypraecassis sp.	cowriehelmet	X		X			
Phalium granulatum	scotch bonnet			X	X		X
Tonna maculosa	tun			X		X	
Tonna pennata	Atlantic partridge tun			X	X		
Charonia variegata	trumpet triton	X		X	X		X
Cymatium femorale	angular triton		X	X	X		X

Continued on the next page

Table 4.7 Continued

Taxon		North	South	Vieques	Archaic	Saladoid	Saladoid/Ostionoid	Ostionoid/Chicoid
Cymatium moritinctum	triton			X	X			
Cymatium nicobaricum	goldmouth triton			X				X
Cymatium parthaenopeum	giant hairy triton			X	X			
Cymatium poulseni	triton			X	X			
Cymatium cf. *parthaenopeum*	giant hairy triton			X	X			
Cymatium cf. *poulseni*	triton			X	X			
Cymatium cf. *vespaceum*	dwarf hairy triton			X	X			
Cymatium sp.	triton	X		X		X	X	X
Cymatiidae	tritons	X				X		
Ranellidae	triton				X			
Chicoreus brevifrons	West Indian murex		X	X	X			X
Murex brevifrons	West Indian murex		X				X	X
Murex cellulosus leviculus	pitted murex			X	X			
Murex sp.	murex		X				X	
Phyllonotus pomum	apple murex		X		X			X
Plicopurpura/Thais rustica	rustic rocksnail	X	X	X	X	X		X
Thais cf. *rustica*	rustic rocksnail	X	X			X		
Plicopurpura/Thais sp.	rocksnail			X	X			X
Plicopurpura deltoidea	deltoid rocksnail			X				X
Plicopurpura/Purpura patula	widemouth rocksnail			X	X	X		X
Muricidae	murex	X	X	X	X	X	X	X
Engoniophos guadelupensis	Guadeloupe phos		X					X

Species	Common name					
Engoniophos unicinctus	no common name	X	X			X
Engoniophos cf. unicinctus	no common name	X	X		X	
Vasum capitellus	spiny vase		X	X		X
Vasum cf. capitellus	spiny vase		X			
Vasum muricatum	Caribbean vase					X
Vasum sp.	vase			X	X	
Cantharus auritulus	drill			X	X	
Cantharus tinctus	cantharus			X	X	
Pisania tincta	tinted cantharus	X			X	
Pollia auritulus	common cantharus			X		X
Pollia sp.	cantharus			X		X
Nassarius albus	variable nassa	X				
Nassarius vibex	common eastern nassa	X			X	X
Fasciolaria tulipa	true tulip	X			X	
cf. *Fasciolaria tulipa*	true tulip			X	X	
Fasciolaridae	tulips			X	X	
Latirus angulatus	short-tailed latirus			X		
Latirus brevicaudatus	latirus			X		
Leucozonia nassa	chestnut latirus			X		
Leucozonia ocellata	white-spotted latirus	X		X		X
Columbella mercatoria	common dove-shell	X		X	X	X
Mitrella ocellata	white-spotted dove-shell	X				X
Nitidella laevigata	smooth dove-shell	X				X
Nitidella sp.	dove-shell	X				
Oliva reticularis	netted olive		X	X		X

Continued on the next page

Table 4.7 Continued

Taxon		North	South	Vieques	Archaic	Saladoid	Saladoid/Ostionoid	Ostionoid/Chicoid
Oliva sayana	lettered olive	X				X		
Oliva cf. *sayana*	lettered olive	X				X		
Oliva sp.	olive	X		X		X		X
Olivella cf. *nivea*	West Indian dwarf olive	X				X		
Olivella sp.	olive	X				X		X
Marginella sp.	marginella	X		X		X		
Marginellidae	marginella	X		X		X		X
Trigonostoma rugosum	rugose nutmeg			X	X			X
Cancellariidae	nutmegs	X						
Cingulina sp.	pyram			X				X
cf. *Crassispira fuscens*	no common name			X	X			
Conus regius	crown cone	X				X		
Conus cf. *granulatus*	glory-of-the-Atlantic cone			X	X			
Conus sp.	cone	X	X			X		X
Conidae	cones		X		X			
Bulla striata	common Atlantic bubble	X			X			
Melampus sp.	melampus	X				X		
Caracolus sp.	terrestrial snail	X				X		
cf. Cyclophoridae	terrestrial snail	X				X		
Drymaeus sp.	terrestrial snail	X				X		
Guppya sp.	terrestrial snail	X				X		

Lamellaxis micra	terrestrial snail	X	X	
Leptineria sp.	terrestrial snail		X	
Megalomastoma croecum	terrestrial snail	X	X	X
Pleurodonte carocolla	terrestrial snail	X		X
Pleurodonte marginella	terrestrial snail	X		X
Pleurodonte sp.	terrestrial snail	X		X
Polydontes cf. *lima*	terrestrial snail	X	X	
Polydontes lima	terrestrial snail	X		X
Polydontes sp.	terrestrial snail	X		X
Zachrysia auricoma havanensis	terrestrial snail	X		X
Lytechinus variegatus	variegated sea urchin	X		X
Cidaridae	sea urchin	X	X	
Echinoidea	sea urchin	X	X	

Table 4.8. Taxa Totals for Zooarchaeological Assemblages from Puerto Rico and Vieques.

Class	North	South	Vieques	Archaic	Saladoid	Saladoid/ Ostionoid	Ostionoid/ Chicoid
Mammals	12	4	10	2	10	4	8
Birds	14	12	33	8	35	5	13
Reptiles	18	9	12	2	20	5	14
Amphibians	3	2	0	0	3	0	1
Cartilaginous Fishes	8	4	7	1	7	4	8
Bony Fishes	116	40	85	10	142	41	63
Crustaceans	5	8	9	8	7	3	8
Chitons	4	1	4	1	2	1	7
Bivalves	37	53	30	23	35	25	47
Gastropods	98	47	92	74	93	21	84
Terrestrial Gastropods							
Sea Urchins	2	1	0	0	2	1	1
	317	181	282	129	356	110	254

time. Minimal use of birds and reptiles is indicated; however, both doves and aquatic turtles, two resources that remain important through time, were first used during the Archaic. Some marine fish were exploited, but shallow-water collection of mollusks was the primary economic activity. Some use of crustaceans is indicated, including the use of land crabs.

The Saladoid sites contain the greatest diversity of fauna, especially of marine vertebrates. Saladoid contexts (Hacienda Grande, Maisabel, Sorcé, and Tibes) include large multicomponent sites on the northern and southern sides of the island as well as on Vieques. Evidence for the initial importation of nonindigenous *hutías* is present during this time period. Marine mammals, manatee and dolphins or porpoises, occur in some contexts. Probable peccary remains (Tayassuidae) were reported from at least one Saladoid site on Vieques (Sorcé), indicating the importation of this larger mammal in addition to smaller *hutías*.

Saladoid populations, especially those living on Vieques, exploited a variety of aquatic and terrestrial birds. Reptiles used during this time were diverse and included several species of sea turtles and other aquatic turtles. Iguanid lizards and snakes were present in some assemblages. Amphibian remains were also present during the Saladoid period, although it is not known if these were food items, commensal remains, or animals that may have been used in ritual contexts.

The diversity of cartilaginous and bony fishes indicates that fishing technology and knowledge of marine habitats were well developed. Offshore habitats requiring watercraft, reef habitats, and near-shore areas were all exploited. The north coast and Vieques were in close proximity to submerged limestone areas that mimic coral reefs in terms of fish diversity and the predators attracted to them. Coastal mangrove forests that fringe portions of Puerto Rico and Vieques served as nursery grounds for a number of juvenile species and as home habitats for others.

Saladoid peoples also exploited an array of marine shellfish. While the ubiquitous top shell is often viewed as the subsistence staple of early ceramic-age populations, a multitude of other marine gastropods and bivalves were used for food. The most common gastropods are those found in the high-energy surf zone such as limpets, turbans, and nerites. Smaller periwinkles are represented by a number of taxa, however, their overall dietary contribution is open to debate. Chitons, another mollusk found in high-energy surf zones, were also used. The north coast, where Saladoid contexts are clustered, has less available marine habitat (e.g., sandy coastal areas) for bivalves, resulting in somewhat fewer of these remains than univalves.

Terrestrial crabs are a common and visible component of early Saladoid deposits. However, the faunal return from fine-screen recovery methods indicates that the dietary contribution from crabs was a component of a diverse subsistence strategy and does not represent an exclusive adaptation to terrestrial habitats. None of the faunal assemblages associated with Saladoid components indicate a predominant reliance on terrestrial fauna. The earliest Saladoid inhabitants of Puerto Rico and Vieques heavily exploited both marine vertebrates and invertebrates.

Contexts dating to the Saladoid/Ostionoid transition are present in selected deposits from Maisabel (north coast) and from Tibes (south coast). The relatively small faunal samples from these contexts contained a less diverse range of animals compared to other ceramic-age sites. To some degree, this may be a product of poor preservation of vertebrate remains in the deposits dating to this time period. Significantly, in addition to the remains of *hutías*, these deposits contained the earliest occurrence of guinea pigs (*guimo*) from secure archaeological contexts on the island, thus documenting the continued introduction of nonindigenous fauna to the island. Neither birds nor reptiles were common in these transitional contexts. The diversity of marine fish, crustaceans, and chitons was also minimal. Marine mollusks were almost evenly divided between bivalves and gastropods. The southern Tibes samples contained a slightly greater range of bivalves, suggesting, perhaps, greater use of bivalves during the Saladoid/Ostionoid transitional period. However, diversity in all classes is a reflection of small sample sizes for this time period. Fewer land crabs are evident in later periods, although the intensification of existing patterns of procurement of marine fish and other resources offset the decline in food contribution from these crustaceans.

The Ostionoid/Chicoid samples (NCS-1 [Finca Valencia], NCS-4 [La Trocha], Calle Cristo/Ballaja, El Bronce, and Luján I) are from the northern and southern parts of Puerto Rico and Vieques. Mammals included *hutías* and guinea pigs and to a lesser extent dogs and manatees. Aquatic and terrestrial birds were exploited, as well as sea turtles, pond turtles, iguanas, and other lizards. Some amphibian remains were present, but it not clear if these represent food refuse. Cartilaginous fishes included several species of sharks. The assemblage of bony fishes is similar to those from Saladoid contexts in that diversity is high and various inshore and offshore habitats are represented. Crustaceans included some nonfood species and small amounts of land crabs. Mollusks and chitons were both important food items. The greatest diversity of bivalves was associated with sites from this time period and included greater use of mussels and Venus clams. Gastropods were similar to those exploited during Saladoid times.

Interesting patterns in the faunal distributions are related to geographic context of the sites. Most significant was the difference in bird diversity between the three areas: north coast, south coast, and Vieques. The Vieques sample was double that of either sector of Puerto Rico. Although some of the avian identifications are tentative identifications, there is greater diversity of marine birds on the island. With the exceptions of crustaceans and bivalves, other classes of vertebrates are more diverse from the northern sites than the southern sites or those from Vieques. Bivalves were more commonly used for food than gastropods in the southern assemblages. This pattern is a reflection of local habitat: the south coast is characterized by lower-energy sandy shorelines, while the north coast has high-energy surf zones with exposed limestone that is suitable habitat for a greater range of gastropods. The southern assemblages are less diverse in mammals, reptiles, and both cartilaginous and bony fish than elsewhere.

Discussion

Puerto Rico is one of the most diverse landmasses of the Greater Antilles. Archaic and ceramic-age settlers found coastal terrain, interior mountains, tropical and subtropical forests, as well as freshwater rivers, ponds, marshes, and brackish swamps in interior and coastal settings. The adjacent maritime habitats were equally complex. Sandy beaches, protected inlets, offshore reefs, and mangrove coastal habitats could all be found. The ability to exploit the biological resources of the island and adjacent waters depended on cultural knowledge and the possession of technology appropriate to the different habitats, plants, and animals. Although the data are somewhat limited, botanical and faunal remains from Puerto Rico and Vieques provide basic information to address subsistence and settlement dynamics in the island group. Plant and animal identifications provide insights into the vegetation and terrestrial and marine habitats present during the early and later human occupations of the two islands.

Altogether, some 85 plant taxa have been identified in the samples analyzed. At the assemblage level, the native plants recovered from the individual sites on Puerto Rico and Vieques are typical of the general vegetation associated with the northern and southern halves of the island, respectively, and of the smaller arid islands (e.g., Vieques) of the region. For example, tree taxa identified among wood remains from sites in arid southern Puerto Rico and Vieques include a number that commonly occur in the dry limestone and coastal forest regions (e.g., *Bucida buceras* [ucar] and *Guaiacum* sp. [guayacán]) (Liogier and Martorell 2000; Little and Wadsworth 1964). Thus, fuelwood collection and extraction of wood for construction and other purposes predictably appears to have been largely opportunistic, drawn extensively from the surrounding vegetation, perhaps emphasizing locally abundant and/or particularly suitable taxa, or even home-garden species as discussed above.

In general, however, considering in particular the seeds and other non-wood plant remains, the combination of species is indicative of anthropogenic settings. The specific taxa identified in the sites almost certainly resulted from prehistoric plant-use practices involving a number of herbs and trees associated with the villages and their diverse multistrata home gardens. Multipurpose taxa like the palm and tree legumes may have provided edible fruit, fiber, and/or medicinal substances. Most others of the taxa identified were likely the residues of food items. The case of evening primrose (*Oenothera* sp.) is interesting. This plant has a variety of potential uses (Duke 1992; Moerman 2003; Newsom 1997a) and, apparently, the genus no longer occurs on Puerto Rico or elsewhere in the Caribbean, except for limited areas in Cuba and the Dominican Republic. Therefore, it is likely that evening primrose was specifically maintained and cultivated by the ceramic-age inhabitants of the Caribbean, including Puerto Rico (and see below). Thus far the plant has been documented only from later, Ostionoid occupations in the Greater Antilles.

The importation of nonindigenous domesticated plant resources is indicated by indirect evidence in the form of root-crop processing equipment at a number of ceramic-age sites. At least by very late in the cultural sequence, maize was being produced in quantities or varieties that allow for its direct detection archaeologically by the presence of plant macroremains, though not from Puerto Rico. Currently, maize cob fragments and kernels have been identified only from the two archaeological sites mentioned earlier, and in both cases from Chican Ostionoid contexts. It bears repeating that a previous report of Saladoid-age maize kernels from St. Kitts (e.g., see Petersen 1997:127) is false; these specimens were examined by Newsom and Elizabeth Wing and found to be crab or lobster gastroliths, not plant remains (Newsom 1993). We are skeptical about other earlier reports of maize based on limited pollen and phytolith data.

Considering faunal resources, the Archaic settlers were rather restricted in their use of island habitats. There was no importation of nonindigenous fauna. Animal protein was obtained through the use of coastal resources. The Archaic-age technology was relatively simple with a concentration on littoral collecting and little use of offshore habitats. This pattern is in agreement with Archaic settlement throughout the archipelago, especially in the Lesser Antilles.

While human modification of landscapes by burning may have occurred as early as the Archaic age on Puerto Rico (Burney et al. 1994; Siegel et al., this volume), the influx of ceramic-age horticulturists from northern South America brought significant changes in how people used the island habitats. These populations modified the landscape for food production through various means and brought with them nonnative fauna, evidenced in zooarchaeological assemblages.

While wild resources, crop cultivation, and home gardens were important sources of carbohydrates and essential nutrients, our paleoethnobiological data indicate a variety of marine fauna were the primary sources of dietary protein. In all areas of the island and ceramic-age occupations, marine fauna or fauna dependent on marine habitats (e.g., shore birds) were diverse. Although the mainland and Vieques are rich habitats, there are few terrestrial resources that occur in such high frequencies to indicate a focus on a few selected resource patches. Terrestrial resources include land crabs, iguanid lizards, and such ground nesting birds as doves. These fauna are present in ceramic-age deposits, however, the marine taxa, as a group, are more diverse and abundant. The exploitation of marine habitats consisted of both logistical collecting with relatively simple prying tools or digging sticks for bivalves and more complex technology for marine vertebrates. Net technology is indicated, especially for the northern sites where small schooling fishes are common in the assemblages. Marine vertebrates reflect the use of boats or canoes to access offshore waters. Although many deep-water marine fauna will enter shallow waters to feed, the capture of marine mammals, sharks, dolphins, or porpoises presumably would have necessitated watercraft. Expertise in the use of watercraft is not surprising, considering the route of migration to the Greater Antilles and the presumed continued interaction with neighboring islands through and, perhaps, the immigration of new groups to the islands.

One line of evidence indicates human control of faunal resources during the ceramic age, while a second line suggests possible management. Some species of mammals were clearly tended by humans. The now-extinct *hutía* (*Isolobodon portoricensis*) is the earliest nonindigenous animal species to be imported to the island group. Although *hutías* may have been introduced to the islands and released to be later hunted, it is more likely that people tended them locally. *Hutías* are present in the earliest Saladoid contexts on the island. Guinea pigs were also introduced to the islands. Remains of these creatures have been found in secure archaeological contexts from Tibes, Finca Valencia (NCS-1), and from the Luján I site on Vieques. The Tibes contexts are transitional Saladoid/Ostionoid, while Finca Valencia and Luján are later Ostionoid/Chicoid. The presence of guinea pigs on Puerto Rico and Vieques provides the best evidence for both human transport of these animals from South America and the rearing of them in the Antilles (Newsom and Wing 2004; Wing 2001). Increased human dependence on tended animals supports a model of resource intensification associated with greater territoriality and population growth. Small mammals such as *hutías* and guinea pigs are ideal for the tropical habitat. They require neither specialized food nor habitat. The later ceramic-age introduction of guinea pigs into the West Indies is also clear evidence of continued interactions with South America.

It is conceivable that sea turtle eggs were collected from beaches and after hatching the animals were raised until they were of sufficient size to be consumed. Females may also have been captured when nesting. Dogs were also transported to Puerto Rico. Dog remains occur on Vieques in undisturbed archaeological contexts and have been identified in the Tibes deposits. A dog burial and a perforated dog-tooth pendant were found, separately, in one of the mounded middens from Maisabel (Siegel 1992:138, Table 4.2, Figure 3.26); other dog remains were not identified in the general site refuse (deFrance 1988, 1989, 1990).

Another characteristic of the paleoethnobiological data relates to patterns of plant and animal use on Vieques. Through time, the faunal record for the island indicates that the small island provided a range of ecotonal settings with access to diverse fauna, especially birds. In contrast, the archaeobotanical data indicate that the botanical resources were varied but somewhat less diverse on the island in comparison to the mainland (Puerto Rico), which is not surprising as this conforms closely to the predictions of the species-area relationship in island biogeographic theory (Whittaker 1998:115–116). Moreover, the smaller landmass, calcareous soils, general aridity, and restricted freshwater resources of the island may not have afforded people the opportunity for land clearing and cultivation that was possible on the mainland.

Our analyses of the paleoethnobiological data indicate areas of further research important to conduct in the future: more systematic excavations of multicomponent sites in different geographical settings of Puerto Rico and Vieques will enhance our understanding of Greater Antillean subsistence and dietary practices. More information is needed about the basal Archaic occupations of the region. More information is needed on village layout and the locations of specific activity areas related to food production and processing. A better understanding is needed of the extraction and processing technology for both plant and animal resources.

Because the ceramic-age populations were cultivators, there is the tendency to argue that land-based territoriality and/or political control was the singular driving force in cultural development. Throughout the prehistory of

Puerto Rico and Vieques, marine habitats and transport on open waters were important for subsistence and cultural interactions. Our analyses of the paleoethnobiological data indicate that complex systems of plant and animal use characterized the mainland of Puerto Rico and neighboring Vieques. Understanding the depth and nature of this complexity is central to interpretations of economic activities and related social and political dynamics in the region.

Conclusions

The plant and animal assemblages from the various Archaic and ceramic-age sites on Puerto Rico and Vieques are sufficiently intact and distinct enough to begin to suggest subregional patterns of resource extraction and food-production activities. This involved herbaceous and arboreal taxa maintained in garden plots and home gardens; other plants collected from surrounding forests and grasslands; and a variety of faunal resources, including some that were reared and maintained in villages and others obtained from nearby habitats. The general pattern—at least in terms of fishing practices and the presence of home gardens—may have been established very early, perhaps with the Archaic groups. With the influx of ceramic-age populations in the region came a more concerted, though for the most part still low-level, horticultural emphasis revolving around root-crop production. This seems to have been the pattern, at least until the latest of the occupational sequences, when intensification of plant production may have occurred; late prehistoric agricultural terraces located in the mountainous interior of Puerto Rico attest to agricultural intensification (Oliver et al. 1999).

In regard to animal use, early studies emphasized the crab-shell dichotomy and the decline through time in the exploitation of terrestrial crustaceans and other land fauna. Our synthesis indicates that faunal use was never focused exclusively on terrestrial resources. Change in resource procurement was not a simple island-wide phenomenon, but rather, dietary and economic change in animal use was most likely the consequence of a complex set of behaviors involving both technological capabilities and human preference combined with local habitat variability. The maintenance of captive animals and intensive fishing practices were additional developments associated with increasingly complex cultural practices. To what degree is uncertain, but these data demonstrate some level of conservatism or conservation, in part, of subsistence practices developed in the continental mainland source areas (root crops, animals). Fishing techniques and garden practices were modified, as appropriate, to the island habitats. Some degree of food intensification appears to have occurred during the ceramic age, although this is currently poorly understood.

Acknowledgments

We would like to express our gratitude to Peter Siegel for bringing this volume to reality and to the many archaeologists whose superb excavations and careful recovery of samples from the individual sites made this research possible. The Environmental Archaeology Lab of the Florida Museum of Natural History; the Center for Archaeological Investigations, Southern Illinois University, Carbondale; and the Department of Anthropology, The Pennsylvania State University, provided laboratory space, equipment, and other necessary support for this research.

Notes

1. The results of a faunal analysis by Narganes Storde (2001) of material from four cave sites in the Central Mountains of Puerto Rico near Caguana, Utuado, were unavailable to us until this chapter was in revision. These data are not included in the summary presented here. However, the fauna are consistent with the trends in animal use from other areas of the island. The most distinctive aspects of the faunal assemblages are the presence of a large number of snakes, which may not represent food remains, and the consumption of large numbers of the terrestrial crab (*Epilobocera sinuatifrons*). Despite their inland location, some marine foodstuffs, including several species of mollusks, were transported to the cave sites.

2. Identifications completed at the Florida Museum of Natural History also made use of the comparative collections housed in both the Divisions of Mammalogy and Ornithology.

5

Ceramic-Age Dietary Patterns in Puerto Rico
Stable Isotopes and Island Biogeography

Anne V. Stokes

Diet and foodways are among the most fascinating and important aspects of culture. A defining attribute distinguishing cultural groups is based in large part on food habits. Archaeologists seek multiple lines of evidence to identify foods consumed by ancient peoples. These include animal and plant remains, artifacts, settlement patterns, and such distinctive features of the landscape as the remains of ditches, dikes, raised beds, and enriched soils. Each of these topics can provide substantial information on foods, although none by itself can tell the entire dietary story.

Over the past two decades or so, stable isotope analysis has emerged as an important line of evidence in reconstructing past diets. Like other fields of inquiry, stable isotope analysis does not have all the answers. What it uniquely offers, however, is an estimate of the isotopic composition of carbon and nitrogen in the overall diet. This estimate can then be evaluated independently by identifying bones, plant remains, artifacts, and such.

Here I will evaluate the stable isotopes of carbon and nitrogen in human bones recovered from Maisabel and Paso del Indio, two large ceramic-age sites in Puerto Rico (Siegel 1989a, 1992; Siegel et al., this volume; Walker, this volume). I will interpret the results in terms of the isotopic compositions of potential plant and animal foods. Further, the results will be interpreted in the cultural contexts of the sites, locally within Puerto Rico and regionally across the West Indies. The interisland perspective will benefit from principles derived from island biogeography, a fitting way to look at peoples whose cultural ties spanned numerous islands in the Caribbean.

The Process

Stable isotope analysis allows us to measure the relative contribution of food groups to diet. This is possible because animals incorporate the stable isotopes of carbon (C) and nitrogen (N) into their bodies in different relative amounts that reflect the isotopic compositions of their foods. By analyzing the bone collagen and apatite carbonate, a picture of prehistoric diet emerges.

Isotopic ratios are expressed in the delta (δ) notation in parts per thousand (per mil or ‰) relative to a standard using the following equations:

$$\delta^{13}C = \left[\frac{(^{13}C/^{12}C)_{sample} - (^{13}C/^{12}C)_{PDB}}{(^{13}C/^{12}C)_{PDB}} \times \right] 1000‰$$

$$\delta^{15}N = \left[\frac{(^{15}N/^{14}N)_{sample} - (^{15}N/^{14}N)_{AIR}}{(^{15}N/^{14}N)_{AIR}} \times \right] 1000‰$$

The standard used for carbon is *Belemnitella americana,* a marine fossil from the Peedee Formation in South Carolina (Craig 1957). The standard contains more ^{13}C than all dietary items and most human tissues, and therefore the $\delta^{13}C$ values will almost always be expressed as a negative number (Ambrose 1993; DeNiro and Epstein 1978). The standard measure for nitrogen isotope values is atmospheric nitrogen (AIR) (Mariotti 1983). Since most food resources and human tissues have more ^{15}N than the standard, the values normally are reported as positive numbers (Ambrose 1993; DeNiro and Epstein 1981).

Certain food groups differ predictably in their carbon and nitrogen stable isotope values depending on their sources of carbon and nitrogen and their position in the food web (Figure 5.1). Most plants use a Calvin photosynthetic pathway, which produces a 3-carbon molecule, and are thus referred to as C_3 plants. C_3 plants include tubers (such as manioc), fruits, and temperate grasses. A second pathway, more common in hot or arid environments, results in a 4-carbon molecule (Hatch and Slack 1966; Hatch et al. 1967). C_4 plants include tropical grasses such as *Zea mays* (corn), *Seteria* sp. (foxtail grass, rabo de zorra), and some amaranths and chenopods. Some xerophytic succulents and epiphytic plants, such as species of Agavaceae and Bromeliadaceae, use a third photosynthetic pathway, Crassulacean Acid Metabolism (CAM) (Bender 1968; O'Leary 1981; Smith et al. 1979; Troughton et al. 1974). The three pathways vary in how much ^{13}C they fix from atmospheric CO_2, resulting in a separation between the $\delta^{13}C$ values of C_3 and C_4 plants with some overlap in

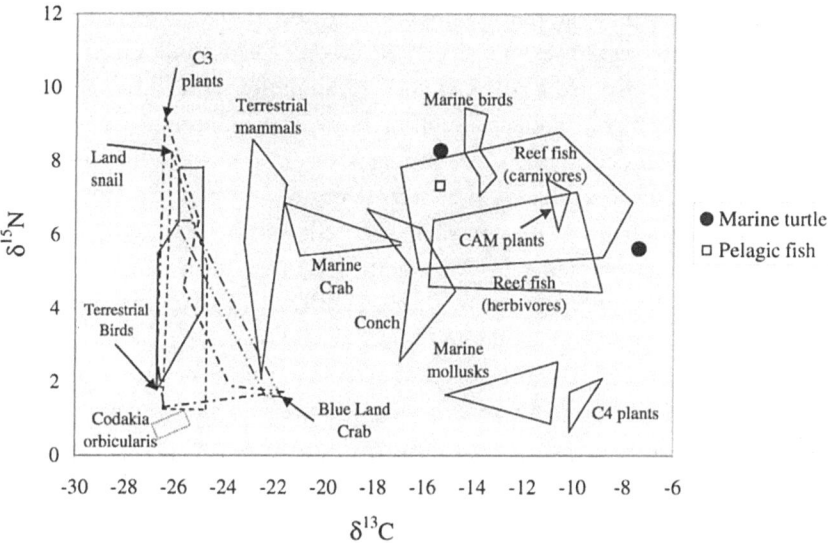

Figure 5.1. General range of isotope values of potential prehistoric food items.

CAM values. In general, C_3 plants range from −23 to −30‰ and C_4 plants range from −8 to −<14‰ (Bender 1968; Bender et al. 1981; Smith and Epstein 1971). CAM plant values depend upon their environment and can overlap either with C_3 or C_4 plants, although in my West Indian studies, CAM plants are more similar to C_4 plants. Thus animals consuming C_3 plants, or that feed on animals that consumed C_3 plants, will have a more negative signature than animals feeding on C_4 or CAM plants or consumers of those animals.

Nitrogen is the more difficult isotope to use in studies that involve terrestrial ecosystems as well as marine ecosystems where coral reefs are present. In terrestrial ecosystems, nitrogen is incorporated into plants either from ^{15}N-enriched soil or by symbiosis with N_2-fixing bacteria. Most plants consumed by humans do not fix nitrogen and have a δ^{15}N value of between 0 to +6‰ (Delwiche et al. 1979; DeNiro and Hastorf 1985). The primary N_2-fixing plants in human diets are legumes, which average from −2 to +2‰. In a marine ecosystem, nitrogen is present as N_2 fixed by bacteria and blue-green algae and as atmospheric nitrogen dissolved in seawater. Typically, these values would be more positive than the δ^{15}N values in terrestrial ecosystems, but because nitrogen fixation occurs in sea grasses and shallow water corals (where reef fish feed; Capone et al. 1977) and in some invertebrates, the δ^{15}N values overlap with those of terrestrial environments. Nitrogen exhibits a trophic level effect with a stepwise increase in δ^{15}N values as one moves up the food chain (Minagawa and Wada 1984; Schoeninger 1985; Schoeninger and DeNiro 1984).

In order to interpret the diets of prehistoric West Indian people, I determined the isotopic signatures in a variety of modern plants and animals that they would have consumed (Stokes 1998). The animals included fishes (estuarine, pelagic, and reef), mollusks, reptiles, birds, and mammals. The plants included corn, manioc, prickly pear, and fig. Corn (C_4) and manioc (C_3) are potential staples, whereas prickly pear represents a CAM plant and fig represents a tropical C_3 fruit. When possible, the flesh and bone of animals and the edible portions of plants from modern specimens were analyzed. For some extinct or threatened animals, such as sea turtle, agouti, rice rat, and some birds, this was not possible and bones from zooarchaeological collections were used instead. For many species, several specimens were analyzed. These data provide a basis for interpreting the isotopic analyses of human bone from the two sites on Puerto Rico.

In complex environments such as the West Indies, diet reconstruction using stable isotope analysis is relatively difficult due to the presence of C_4 grasses, CAM plants, coral reefs, and nitrogen-fixing organisms. Nevertheless, the use of two fractions of bone, collagen and apatite carbonate, leads to interpretive methods that can "tease out" the human diet.

When isotopic reconstruction of human diet was first developed, only the bone collagen portion was analyzed (e.g., Bender et al. 1981). There was disagreement about the utility of apatite because some researchers maintained it was too susceptible to diagenesis to be an accurate indicator of prehistoric diet (Schoeninger and DeNiro 1982), whereas others believed that apatite reflected a true dietary signal (Krueger and Sullivan 1984). In a study of modern rat bone, isotope ratios in the collagen fraction were found to reflect primarily the source of protein in the diet, whereas those in the bone apatite carbonate fraction were seen to reflect more accurately the whole (protein and energy) diet (Ambrose and Norr 1993), with energy (carbohydrates) being derived from plants. Therefore, analyzing collagen estimates the relative contribution of terrestrial vs. marine protein in the diet, whereas analyzing apatite carbonate estimates how terrestrial plants contributed to the diet. Comparing the $\delta^{13}C$ value of collagen to that in apatite serves as a verification of the sources of protein and energy. A small apatite to collagen spacing (ca. +1.7‰) results from a diet of C_4 protein and C_3 energy. A monoisotopic diet (either C_3 energy and protein or C_4/C_4-like energy and protein) shows an intermediate spacing, approximately +5.7‰. A diet primarily of C_3 protein and C_4/C_4-like (marine) energy results in a large spacing of over +7.2‰, and assuming a 20 percent protein diet has a mean of +11.3‰. In maritime cultures, the spacing between the $\delta^{13}C$ values of bone collagen and apatite will differentiate between a diet of marine protein and maize vs. marine protein and other (C_3) plants. The $\delta^{15}N$ values contribute to understanding the trophic level at which humans were feeding and are particularly beneficial when C_4 plants are indicated in the apatite analysis.

Previous West Indian Multi-Island Isotope Studies

Two prior isotope studies utilized human bone samples excavated from Hacienda Grande and Maisabel in Puerto Rico. These studies (Keegan 1985; Keegan and DeNiro 1988; van Klinken 1991) were conducted before apatite was proven to be applicable to interpret diet, and therefore only bone collagen was analyzed. William Keegan (1985) and Keegan and Michael DeNiro (1988) analyzed one individual from the unprovenienced Castillo collection of the Hacienda Grande site along with 17 individuals from sites on various Bahamian islands. This was the first study of nitrogen isotopes in marine environments. Although they lacked radiocarbon dates, Keegan and DeNiro hypothesized that the bones of the earlier (Saladoid) individual from Hacienda Grande should reflect a more terrestrial diet than those from Lucayan sites in the Bahamas that were later in time. This is based on the "optimal path of diet breadth expansion" which is from abundant, easily exploited terrestrial animals to marine animals that take more effort to capture (Keegan and DeNiro 1988:330). Keegan and DeNiro worked from the premise that a similar set of food items was available in the Bahamas and Puerto Rico.

The results of their study showed that the $\delta^{13}C$ value of the collagen from the Hacienda Grande sample was much more negative than those of the Bahamian samples, supporting the hypothesis that diet earlier in prehistory was more terrestrial. For the Bahamas, Keegan distinguished three different diets over time based on the relative locations of the islands, from which skeletal remains were derived. Keegan used a weighted distribution demonstrating that the southern islands were settled first with populations expanding northward through time. The isotope data supported this theory showing that the initial diet was terrestrially based, followed by increased reliance on marine foods, and finally the introduction of maize in the diet (Keegan 1985:185; Keegan and DeNiro 1988).

The high $\delta^{15}N$ values in the Hacienda Grande and some of the Bahamian samples were interpreted by Keegan as evidence of seasonal maize consumption. Keegan based this interpretation on a $\delta^{15}N$ value for maize of 10‰, which was generated from Belize maize (DeNiro and Hastorf 1985). Maize samples that I analyzed from the Turks and Caicos were much lower in $\delta^{15}N$, ranging from .91 to 2.18‰ (Stokes 1998). Also, without the apatite $\delta^{13}C$ values and apatite to collagen spacing values, the potential contribution of C_4

plants cannot be interpreted. Therefore, Keegan's interpretation is questionable on two grounds: first, the $\delta^{15}N$ value he used for the maize may not be accurate for the West Indies, and second, collagen cannot be used to interpret whole diet.

Another study covering six sites in the West Indies and Suriname was performed by G. van Klinken (1991). When conducting isotope studies, it is important to ensure, to the extent possible, the geochemical and taphonomic integrity of each sample. The sample should not have been subject to diagenesis, and it must be prepared in the lab to remove any potential contaminates. Substandard samples do not adequately reflect prehistoric diet and should be eliminated from data sets. Van Klinken's C:N values, the gauge of whether samples have undergone diagenesis or not, are either outside of the acceptable range of 2.9 to 3.6 (see Ambrose 1993; Ambrose and Norr 1992) or are not reported. Some of his $\delta^{15}N$ values are so high (> 50‰) as to be out of the realm of possibility for human samples. Van Klinken blames some of the $\delta^{15}N$ values on contamination from soil humates (van Klinken 1991:96). Through proper extraction of the collagen with NaOH to remove humic contaminates, the results should be consistent and reproducible. For some samples, van Klinken did more than one run and reported different values for each run. This also may be due to improper preparation of the sample collagen. Lastly, van Klinken did not report a "diet $\delta^{15}N$" value and therefore, presumably did not take into account fractionation between collagen and diet (see Stokes 1998:151–152 for further explanation).

In interpreting prehistoric diet, van Klinken was concerned with determining the sources of food eaten by prehistoric populations based on percentages of terrestrial C_3 collagen, C_4 collagen, and reef-food collagen. He ascribed each population to a diet and percentage, for example, Maisabel, which he considered to be 100 percent C_3 consumer diet. In my opinion, such precise interpretations about the contribution of certain food groups to prehistoric diets are unsupportable. Also, as with Keegan and DeNiro, van Klinken's study only involved collagen and therefore should only have been used to interpret the protein portion of the diet.

Results

The isotope analyses of human skeletal materials collected from the Paso del Indio and Maisabel sites indicate very different diets for the settlement occupants. Paso del Indio is located approximately 5 kilometers inland on the north coast and was settled during the late Saladoid and Ostionoid periods, although a precise chronology is not available for the human bones (Walker, this volume). Maisabel is located along the north coast, almost due north of Paso del Indio. The individuals analyzed for stable isotopes lived at the site from the late Saladoid (ca. A.D. 450) to the mid-Ostionoid periods (ca. A.D. 1100) (Siegel 1992:131).

Paso del Indio

Eleven individuals were analyzed from Paso del Indio (Table 5.1). The bone collagen data for $\delta^{13}C$ cluster around −19.5‰, suggesting that most protein in the diet came from either terrestrial sources or marine crab (Figure 5.2). The $\delta^{15}N$ values are intermediate indicating that there may be some contribution from C_4 plants.

The whole diet of the individuals, as reconstructed from apatite values (Figure 5.3), ranges from more marine/C_4 (≈ −18) to more terrestrial protein/C_3 (≈ −22) than the collagen values. This indicates that some individuals obtained substantial amounts of carbohydrates from C_4 plants, whereas other people consumed fewer C_4 plants and depended more on C_3 plants.

The mean values for collagen and apatite reveal considerable overlap in the sources of protein and whole diet (Figure 5.4), suggesting that variability in diet was based on plant foods. Apatite to collagen spacing supports this interpretation. Seven of the 11 individuals tested from Paso del Indio had a large apatite to collagen spacing, resulting from a diet of terrestrial protein and C_4 or CAM energy (Figure 5.5). Because CAM plants probably were not used as staple foods, we can assume that most of the energy was derived from such C_4 plants as corn, *Seteria* sp., or other panacoid grasses. The remaining four individuals do not fit neatly within any category. One falls closest to the monoisotopic range with a diet of either C_3 protein and energy, or marine/C_4 protein and C_4/CAM energy.

Because the whole diet (apatite) data indicate consumption of C_4 or CAM plants, and the apatite to collagen spacing shows seven individuals with C_4 or CAM plants as a large part of their diet, we can assume that the remaining four individuals had some C_4-like energy in their diet. For Paso del Indio, the isotopic data suggest an overall diet of primarily C_3 protein and C_4 energy, with some contribution of either marine/C_4 protein or C_3 plant energy. If this is the case, then three of the four individuals also had a diet of mainly C_3 protein and C_4 energy, with the addition of C_3 energy, marine protein, or both. The final individual closest to the medium spacing had a diet either of C_3 protein and energy, marine/C_4 protein and energy, or some combination of all. That C_4 plants (i.e., corn and perhaps other tropical grasses) were included in the diet at Paso del Indio seems certain from both the $\delta^{13}C$ and $\delta^{15}N$ values.

Table 5.1. Isotope Data for Human Skeletal Samples from Paso del Indio and Maisabel in Puerto Rico.

Site	Provenience	Lab #	Bone	Age	Sex	%N/wt	%C/wt
Paso del Indio	P7W, U5, B2	AS 25	ribs/femur	adult	female	13.77	39.24
Paso del Indio	P7, impact, BD	AS 26	tibia	adult	male	9.03	25.69
Paso del Indio	P8S, U3, B2	AS 27	femur	infant	unk	11.34	32.66
Paso del Indio	P8N, U12, B5	AS 28	femur	infant	unk	10.55	30.42
Paso del Indio	P7W, U5, B1	AS 29	femur	infant	unk	12.35	35.44
Paso del Indio	P7, T1, B4	AS 30	tibia	adult	female	10.46	29.40
Paso del Indio	P6, T1, B1	AS 31	ribs	adult	female	13.39	38.36
Paso del Indio	P8I, U1, B2	AS 32	ribs	adult	male	11.95	33.98
Paso del Indio	P7W, U3, B2	AS 33	humerus	adult	female	9.41	36.61
Paso del Indio	P7W, U5, B5	AS124	tibia	infant	unk	13.40	37.67
Paso del Indio	P7W, U2, B4	AS 55	tibia	infant	unk	12.16	34.04
Maisabel	N44/E3, B7	AS 37	l. humerus	adult	male	11.25	32.48
Maisabel	N84/E72, B17	AS 38	l. tibia	adult	male	10.46	29.93
Maisabel	N40/W10, B18	AS 40	l. femur	adult	female	11.42	32.94
Maisabel	N50/E100, B1	AS 41	metatarsal	adult	female	12.91	37.58
Maisabel	N50/E100, B2	AS 42	rt. fibula	adult	male	13.29	37.52
Maisabel	N82/E72, B4	AS 43	tibia	adult	male	12.98	36.54
Maisabel	N82/E72, B5	AS 44	ulna	adult	female	13.29	38.61
Maisabel	N80/E72, B10	AS 45	rt. femur	adult	female	12.23	35.25
Maisabel	N90/E42, B14	AS 46	l. tibia	adult	female	12.17	34.34
Maisabel	N90/E42/B16	AS 47	l. tibia	child	female	12.15	35.27
Maisabel	N80/E72, B20	AS 48	tibia	adult	male	8.91	24.50
Maisabel	N80/E72, B21	AS 49	ribs	adult	female	8.48	24.59
Maisabel	N84/E72, B22	AS 50	l. radius	adult	female	13.34	38.59
Maisabel	N42/W20, B23	AS 51	fragments	adult	female	13.44	38.29
Maisabel	N42/W21, B25	AS 52	femur	adult	female	14.18	41.21
Maisabel	N44/E3, B26	AS 53	fibula	adult	male	13.84	40.03
Maisabel	N31/W23, B29	AS 54	fragments	adult	female	13.83	38.15
Maisabel	N45/E0, B30	AS126	rt. tibia	adult	male	12.26	35.10

C:N	$\delta^{15}N_{col}$	Diet $\delta^{15}N_{col}$	$\delta^{13}C_{col}$	$\delta^{13}C_{apa}$	$\Delta\delta^{13}C_{apa-col}$	Diet $\delta^{13}C_{apa}$	Yield Col.	Yield Apa.
3.31	9.00	6.50	−19.55	−7.92	11.63	−17.42	9.26	11.76
3.30	9.38	6.88	−19.22	−9.59	9.63	−19.09	3.83	21.70
3.34	9.41	6.91	−19.75	−9.10	10.65	−18.60	4.42	19.64
3.34	9.93	7.43	−19.55	−11.13	8.42	−20.63	5.50	24.46
3.33	9.92	7.42	−19.74	−8.81	10.93	−18.31	6.22	14.70
3.26	8.70	6.20	−18.56	−7.92	10.64	−17.42	3.50	20.09
3.32	8.98	6.48	−19.45	−12.61	6.84	−22.11	8.59	12.54
3.30	8.50	6.00	−19.34	−11.22	8.12	−20.72	6.11	26.06
3.28	8.43	5.93	−19.73	−9.60	10.13	−19.10	3.28	26.44
3.26	9.12	6.62	−19.50	−10.77	8.73	−20.27	7.52	38.05
3.25	10.79	8.29	−19.30	−9.70	9.60	−19.20	3.60	60.88
3.60	9.25	6.75	−18.34	−9.02	9.32	−18.52	4.37	22.48
3.04	8.90	6.40	−18.63	−9.50	9.13	−19.00	3.23	24.79
2.96	9.65	7.15	−18.76	−9.50	9.26	−19.00	12.06	24.42
3.38	11.08	8.58	−15.91	−9.02	6.89	−18.52	10.07	57.60
3.35	9.18	6.68	−15.73	−8.58	7.15	−18.08	4.15	56.39
3.19	9.76	7.26	−19.34	−10.32	9.02	−19.82	7.90	53.58
3.38	10.05	7.55	−18.28	−10.48	7.80	−19.98	8.56	52.76
3.34	9.74	7.24	−18.06	−9.48	8.58	−18.98	6.43	52.57
3.27	9.76	7.26	−18.14	−11.68	6.46	−21.18	6.13	42.65
3.36	11.33	8.83	−17.98	−10.30	7.68	−19.80	5.08	51.40
3.19	9.54	7.04	−18.33	−11.64	6.69	−21.14	17.49	52.54
3.36	9.21	6.71	−18.76	−10.33	8.43	−19.83	6.63	58.11
3.36	9.74	7.24	−17.71	−9.52	8.19	−19.02	4.18	50.80
3.30	8.28	5.78	−19.45	−9.73	9.72	−19.23	6.63	46.44
3.38	9.99	7.49	−17.55	−9.05	8.50	−18.55	6.49	37.74
3.35	9.36	6.86	−18.46	−11.17	7.29	−20.67	6.97	53.44
3.20	9.96	7.46	−18.34	−10.12	8.22	−19.62	3.85	59.38
3.32	7.83	5.33	−17.45	−9.80	7.65	−19.30	3.86	44.45

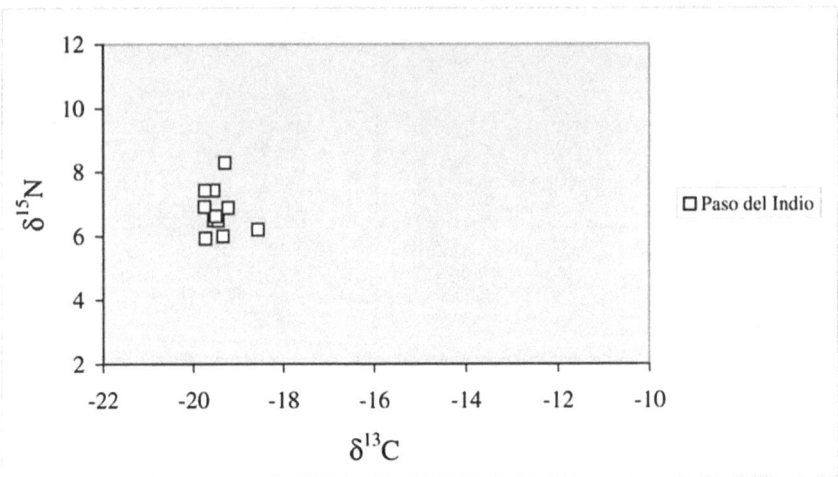

Figure 5.2. Source of protein in the diet of individuals from Paso del Indio.

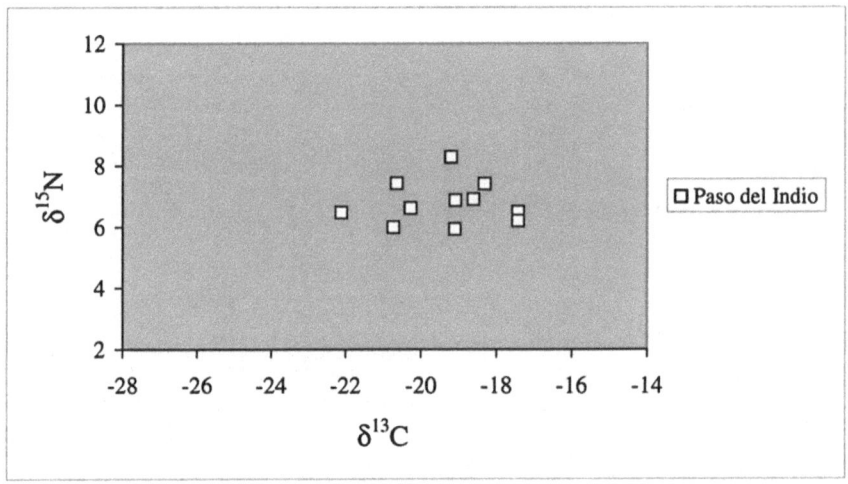

Figure 5.3. Whole diet of individuals from Paso del Indio.

Maisabel

Bone of 18 individuals, spanning the late Saladoid and Ostionoid periods, were analyzed from Maisabel (see Table 5.1). Only those with acceptable glycine depletion ratios (GDR) were used in this isotope study (see Siegel 1999). The GDR is a measure of adequate collagen preservation (Siegel 1999:217). An acceptable GDR is less than 100, with the preferred amount being less than 10. The Maisabel samples I used ranged in GDR from 1.8 to 22.1.

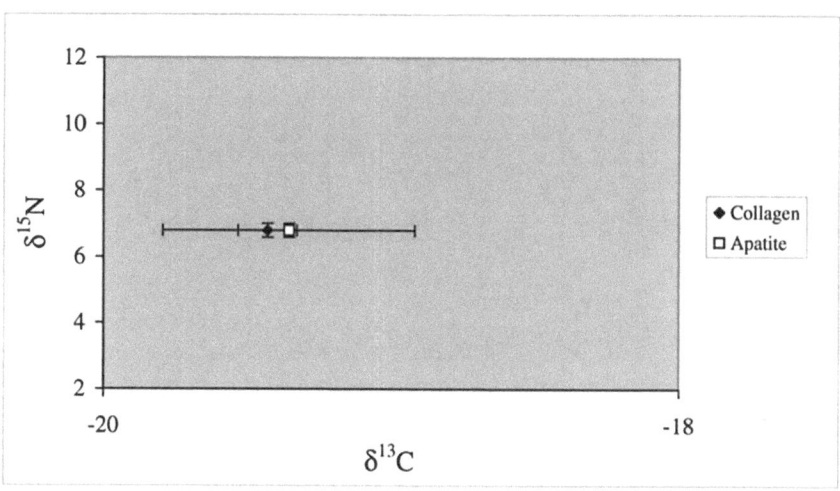

Figure 5.4. Mean $\delta^{13}C$ values (with standard error) for human bone collagen and apatite, Paso del Indio.

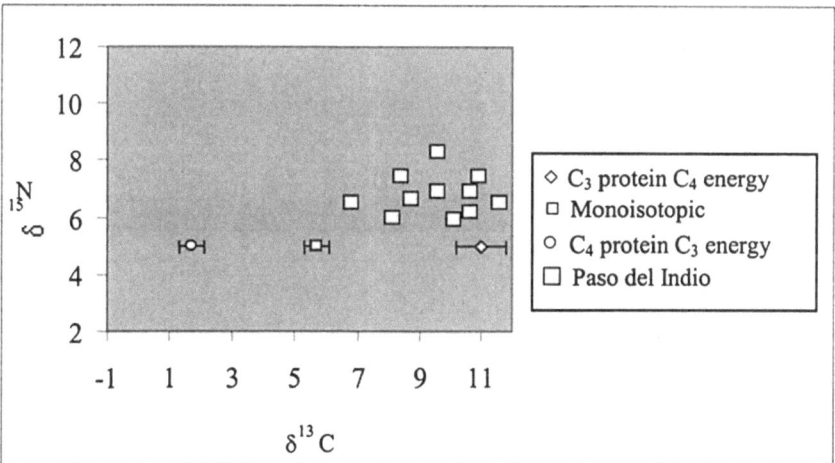

Figure 5.5. Apatite to collagen spacing from Paso del Indio individuals compared to laboratory-derived dietary values.

Two individuals, AS 41 (Burial 1) and AS 42 (Burial 2) have $\delta^{13}C$ collagen values that indicate a diet with substantially more marine/C_4 protein than other Maisabel individuals (Figure 5.6) or any at Paso del Indio. This is reasonable since Maisabel is a coastal site and Paso del Indio is inland. The human $\delta^{15}N$ values are more variable than Paso del Indio but again are rela-

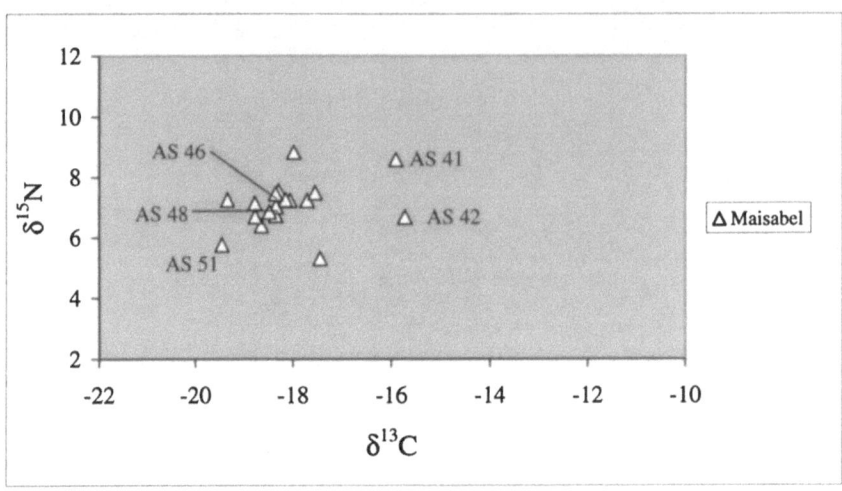

Figure 5.6. Source of protein in the diet of individuals from Maisabel.

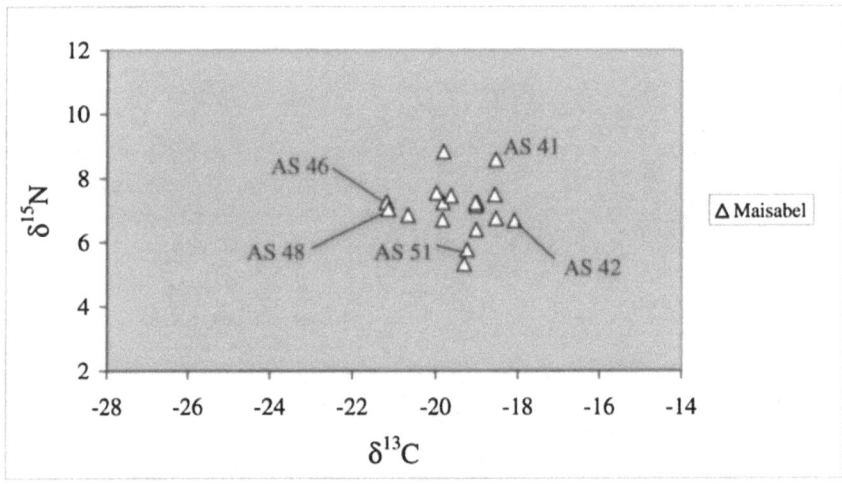

Figure 5.7. Whole diet of individuals from Maisabel.

tively intermediate, falling within the ranges for terrestrial mammals, iguanas, land crabs, reef fishes, and C_4 plants.

The apatite values at Maisabel fall between those for C_3 and C_4 whole diets and are very similar to the Paso del Indio whole diets (Figure 5.7). Considering that plants undoubtedly made up a large part of the prehistoric horticulturalists' diets, the fact that the apatite values are pulled to the left suggests a larger contribution of C_3 plants (such as manioc) than C_4 plants (such as

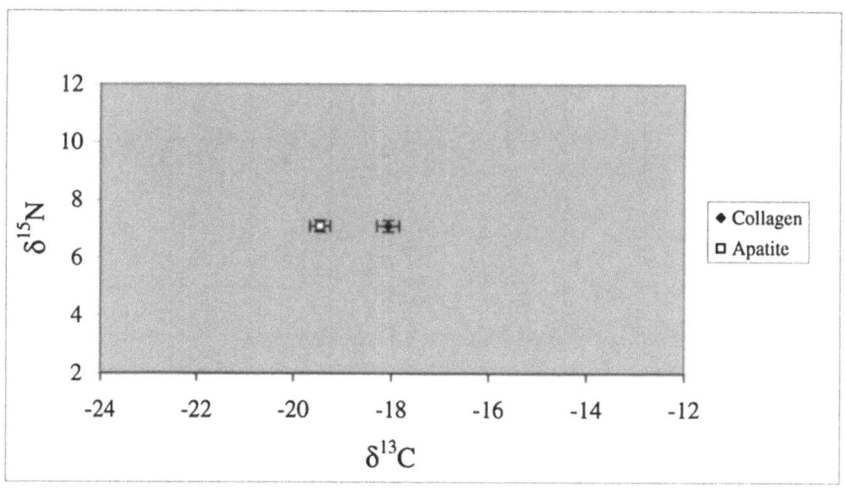

Figure 5.8. Mean $\delta^{13}C$ values (with standard error) for human bone collage and apatite, Maisabel.

corn). However, this pull toward C_3 plants is not as large as that found at certain other West Indian sites, such as those in the Bahamas and Saba (Stokes 1998), suggesting that some C_4 plants may have been consumed.

The mean collagen and apatite values at Maisabel (Figure 5.8) do not overlap like those from Paso del Indio. The protein portion of the diet is less negative than the apatite. Both are in the intermediate range between terrestrial/C_3 diets and marine/C_4 diets, but the less negative mean collagen value may be due to protein in maize rather than solely due to marine protein.

The $\delta^{13}C$ values for apatite to collagen spacing (Figure 5.9) do not fit well into the ranges of experimental diets. One individual, AS 51 (Burial 23), is nearly within the range for a diet based on terrestrial protein and C_4/CAM energy. A second individual, AS 46 (Burial 14), is marginally within the monoisotopic range. The remaining 16 individuals lie somewhere in between. In order to interpret the diets, it is necessary to discuss individuals. The two individuals (AS 41, 42) with the least negative collagen signatures also had the least negative apatite signatures, suggesting a diet based on marine/C_4 protein and at least some C_4 energy. These two samples had apatite to collagen spacings of around 7‰, just to the right of the monoisotopic range. The values have been pulled to the right by incorporation of C_3 protein (terrestrial animals) in the diet.

AS 46 (Burial 14) and AS 48 (Burial 20) are the two individuals closest to the apatite to collagen spacing that would indicate a monoisotopic diet. These

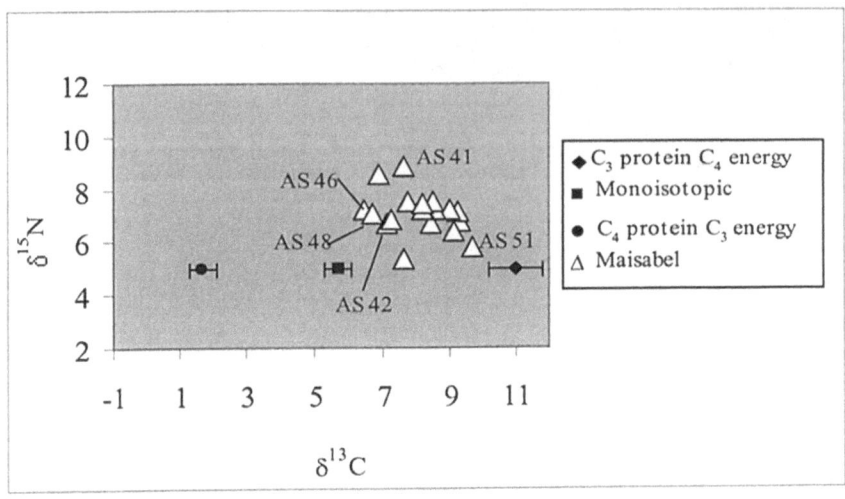

Figure 5.9. Apatite to collagen spacing from Maisabel individuals compared to laboratory-derived dietary values.

two samples also had the most negative apatite signatures, which would suggest a heavily C_3 diet. If AS 46 and AS 48 truly had a C_3-monoisotopic diet, and if samples AS 41 and 42 truly represent a C_4-monoisotopic diet, then it is impossible to determine whether the remaining 14 individuals (which lie between a medium spacing and a large spacing) had a generally C_3-based or C_4-based diet and are being pulled to the right by either terrestrial protein or C_4/CAM plants. Although the individual diets for most samples cannot be well distinguished, the data do suggest that the inhabitants of Maisabel had diverse diets. The different diets do not appear to have temporal trends because AS 41 (marine protein and C_4/CAM plants) and AS 46 (terrestrial protein and C_3 plants) both date to the Saladoid period whereas AS 42 is from the Saladoid/Ostionoid transitional period and AS 48 is Ostionoid.

Discussion

Zooarchaeology and Archaeobotany

Although most protein in both data sets was from marine sources, the isotopic data from bone collagen suggest that the people living at Paso del Indio had more terrestrial protein in their diet than those from Maisabel. This is to be expected since Paso del Indio lies 5 km inland and Maisabel is located on the coast. Unfortunately, the zooarchaeological data from Paso del Indio are unavailable. The faunal evidence from Maisabel suggests a maritime-based economy dominated by fish and mollusks (deFrance 1988) that, in light of the isotopic analysis, may slightly underestimate the contribution of terrestrial animals, especially in the Ostionoid period.

The whole diets, as suggested by bone apatite, were very similar at Maisabel and Paso del Indio. Since the collagen values for Paso del Indio were more negative than those of Maisabel, the similar whole diet values are evidence for a significant contribution of C_4 or CAM plants in the diet at Paso del Indio. In the Maisabel diets, the apatite values are more negative than the collagen values. Therefore, C_3 plants were the major energy source at Maisabel. However, we must keep in mind that the Maisabel individuals had very diverse diets, which are not reflected in mean values. Individual choice or potentially some other factor such as hierarchy or age was responsible for the observed diversity. At Maisabel, Susan deFrance (1988) found that, using edible portions as a measure, 77.2 percent of the recovered specimens were vertebrates (terrestrial and marine) and 22.8 percent were marine invertebrates. Of the vertebrates, approximately 74 percent were bony fishes characteristic of reefs. Therefore, the lower $\delta^{15}N$ value could be due mainly to reef fishes.

That C_4 and/or CAM plants were an important part of the diet of ceramic-age inhabitants of Puerto Rico is almost assured by the isotopic data. The archaeobotanical data support some use of C_4 grasses (Poaceae) by the late ceramic period (deFrance and Newsom, this volume; Newsom 1997b). Maize (*Zea mays*) has been recorded at En Bas Saline in Haiti (Newsom and Deagan 1994) and Tutu in the Virgin Islands (Pearsall 2002) in late ceramic-age deposits.

Although nitrogen values are not always as useful as carbon values in extrapolating diet, in the case of the Puerto Rican samples, the lower $\delta^{15}N$ values indicate that those individuals living at Maisabel had a larger contribution of either C_4/CAM plants or reef fishes than those living at Paso del Indio. Because the apatite values indicate more C_4/CAM plants at Paso del Indio, the lower $\delta^{15}N$ values at Maisabel probably are due to reef fishes.

Temporal Change

Archaeologists have long proposed, based on zooarchaeological samples, a major temporal change in West Indian diet from the Saladoid to the Ostionoid periods (Goodwin 1980; Jones 1985; Roe 1985a). Presumably, during the Saladoid period, land crabs were the primary protein source with a shift through time toward marine resources. At Maisabel, for example, deFrance (1988) found that the density of land crab remains decreased in the Ostionoid levels while the exploitation of marine resources increased. The isotopic data,

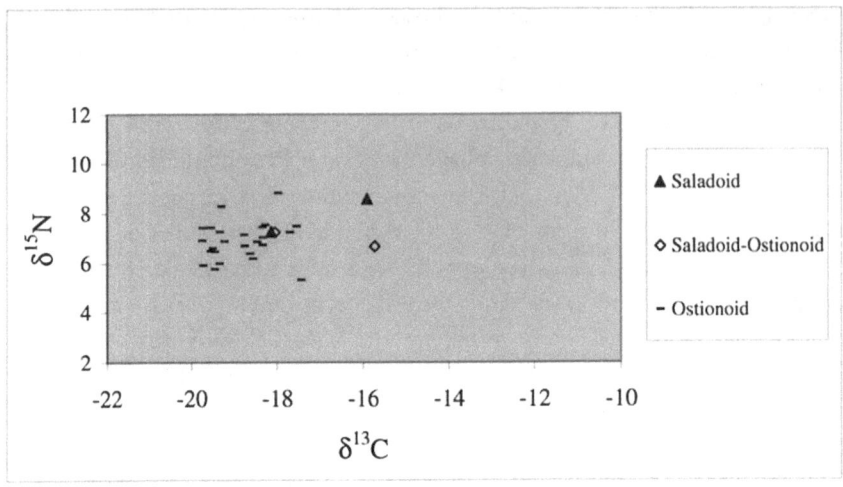

Figure 5.10. Temporal change in diet in Puerto Rico.

albeit limited in number of Saladoid samples, show no evidence of such a shift and even suggest that the protein portion of the Ostionoid diet averaged more terrestrial than during Saladoid times (Figure 5.10).

Biogeography

The Puerto Rican data are part of a larger sample from 13 islands in the West Indies, from the Bahamas to Grenada (Stokes 1998). The Puerto Rican samples cluster with the Hispaniolan sites in having relatively more negative carbon isotopic signatures, indicative of a more terrestrial diet than sites in the Lesser Antilles or the Bahamas. As part of the Greater Antilles, Puerto Rico and Hispaniola are larger, older, and less isolated than islands in the Lesser Antilles or Bahamas. It is logical that the more highly diverse terrestrial flora and fauna in the Greater Antilles would lead to a more terrestrially based human diet.

Acknowledgments

I thank Peter Siegel, Mike Roca, Osvaldo García Goyco, Adalberto Maurás, Edwin Crespo, Jeff Walker, and Bill Keegan for the human bone, and Elizabeth Wing, Betsy Carlson, and David Steadman for the animal bone used in this study. Jason Curtis, Dave Hodell, and Matt Emmons ran the isotope samples. Lynette Norr was instrumental in teaching me the technique and in interpreting the results. Lee Newsom answered numerous questions on plants and her research at various sites. David Steadman provided helpful comments on the manuscript and Bill Keegan and John Krigbaum answered specific, last minute questions. My research was supported by a grant from the Wenner-Gren Foundation for Anthropological Research (Grant number 6001).

6

Deconstructing the Polity
Communities and Social Landscapes of the Ceramic-Age Peoples of South Central Puerto Rico

Joshua M. Torres

The regional organization and development of past societies has been and continues to be a critical component of archaeological research. Investigations at this level contribute to understanding the processes responsible for the growth of complex social systems within the context of the landscapes they occupied. For researchers focusing on the ceramic age of the Greater Antilles (between ca. 300 B.C. and A.D. 1500), regional studies are fueled by an anthropological interest in elucidating the development of formalized social inequality and the dynamics of sociopolitical organization through time and space. Substantiating these avenues of inquiry are ethnohistoric documents that depict territorial paramount chiefdoms existing at the time of European contact, and the rich archaeological record that chronicles their maturation.

Upon arrival to the Greater Antilles, Spanish chroniclers documented the sociopolitical networks of the indigenous Taíno peoples as being composed of a series of *cacicazgos* (or chiefdoms) under the centralized leadership of caciques (chiefs) (Las Casas 1992; Oviedo 1975; Pané 1999). The role of the cacique and the institutionalization of social inequality have been the focal points of contemporary archaeological research of prehistoric Hispaniola and Puerto Rico (Curet 1996; Moscoso 1981; Oliver 1992b; Rouse 1992; Siegel 1999; Wilson 1990). Currently, it is accepted that caciques assumed a multiplicity of political, symbolic, and ceremonial roles serving as intermediaries between the human world and the supernatural realm. Within this context, caciques were instrumental in organizing economic production and the division of labor by controlling religious and political ideology through community-based rituals (Curet 1992a, 1996; Moscoso 1981; Oliver 1992b, 1998; Siegel 1991c, 1996, 1999). The manifestations of caciques' centralized authority and ideological power are evident in the remains of monumental architecture, represented by plazas and ball courts (*bateys*), which began to appear sometime during the first half of the Ostionoid series (ca. A.D. 600–900) on the island of Puerto Rico.

Research regarding the regional sociopolitical organization of Puerto Rico's ceramic-age societies has typically focused on the distribution of monumental architecture to elucidate the temporal and spatial distribution of centers of political power (e.g., Alegría 1983; Siegel 1991c, 1999; Vescelius 1977). Monumental architecture has been a key component in this respect as these features are not only deemed representative of the formalization of centralized authority but also of a certain level of political and decision-making power based on time and labor invested in their construction (Alegría 1983:118; Siegel 1999:221). Spatially, clusters of sites possessing these features are thought to approximate sociopolitical territories (Siegel 1999:221; Vescelius 1977:1). However, even though most researchers would agree that complex, territorial political units characterized Taíno settlement systems of Puerto Rico and Hispaniola (Fewkes 1907:33; Keegan 1997:116–117; Oliver 1998, 1992:11; Siegel 1991c, 1996:236; Wilson 1990), the development, organization, and morphology of ceramic-age social landscapes have not been thoroughly explored.

In this chapter, I present an examination of the ceramic-age social landscapes of south-central Puerto Rico (Figure 6.1). This area is important for consideration as some of the earliest ceremonial architecture in the Caribbean is located here (González Colón 1984; Rouse 1992:112), suggesting the development of a complex regional sociopolitical system prior to the twelfth century A.D. (Oliver 1992b:9) and quite possibly the seat of the first chiefdoms of the Greater Antilles. To facilitate this study, I utilize archival site information from the State Historic Preservation Office in San Juan, Puerto Rico (PRSHPO) and Geographic Information Systems (GIS) technology to explore the spatial distribution of ceramic-age settlements and to model potential spheres of social interaction through time. In doing so, this study addresses conceptual and methodological aspects of communities for examining the development and organization of ceramic-age sociopolitical systems in Puerto Rico and the Greater Antilles in general.

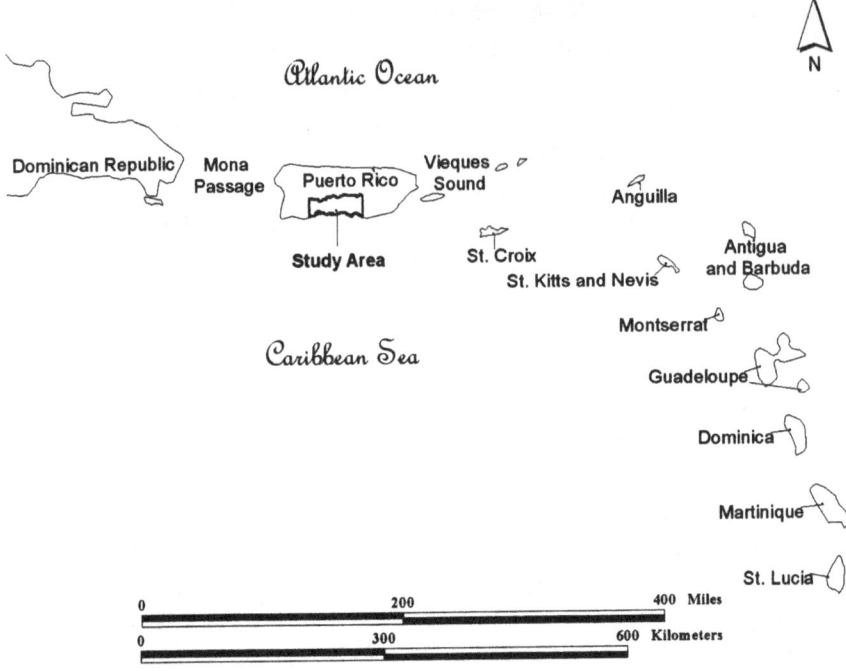

Figure 6.1. Study area.

Exploring Puerto Rico's Social Landscape

Research related to the processes of social change, and the centralization of sociopolitical power on Puerto Rico, has focused on three distinct periods of its prehistory (Periods II, III, and IV). Within the context of Irving Rouse's model (Table 6.1) for the spatial and temporal distribution of cultural traits in the Caribbean, these periods approximate the occupational sequences associated with the ceramic-making peoples of the Saladoid series (ca. 300 B.C.– A.D. 600), the Elenan and Ostionan Ostionoid subseries (A.D. 600–1200) and, the Chican Ostionoid subseries (ca. A.D. 1200–1500) (Rouse 1992:52–53, 107). Broad trends in ceramic styles (Rouse 1992), village morphology (Siegel 1996), households (Curet 1992b), and mortuary (Curet and Oliver 1998; Siegel 1999) and settlement patterns (Lundberg 1985a; Torres 2001) are used to distinguish these periods, which not only denote changes in material culture but also involve fundamental transitions in social organization. Conjunctively, these archaeological data suggest a shift from a communal, relatively egalitarian social system (Saladoid series) to one characterized by social hierarchies (Chican Ostionoid subseries) evident at the time of European contact.

In support of dynamic social changes, regional analyses of ceramic-age sites have shown considerable variation in the temporal distribution, density, and frequency of site types across the island (e.g., Curet et al. 2004; Lundberg 1985a; Oliver 1998, 1999; Maíz López and Questell Rodríguez 1990; Rodríguez 1985, 1990; Torres 2001). Specifically, there is a dramatic increase in the number of sites during the Elenan and Ostionan Ostionoid and subsequent shifts in regional populations during the Chican Ostionoid (Curet et al. 2004; Lundberg 1985a; Torres 2001). Investigations at the regional level have typically been characterized by macrostructural approaches to settlement pattern analysis (see Chang 1968:6–7 for discussion), emphasizing either ecological or sociopolitical perspectives in the interpretation of spatial patterning.[1] Ecological approaches to settlement pattern analyses have been utilized to examine variation in the frequencies of sites and site types relative to ecological settings (Lundberg 1985a; Maíz López and Questell Rodríguez 1990; Rodríguez López 1985; Torres 2001). In contrast, sociopolitical approaches have focused on the distribution of monumental architecture to elucidate the temporal and spatial distribution of sociopolitical units (Lundberg 1985a; Siegel 1991c, 1999; Torres 2001; Vescelius 1977).

Despite conceptual and methodological variability between these types of analyses, both stress the importance of social phenomena at a regional level, and how actors create and negotiate their social realities within the geographic locations they inhabit. In this chapter, I emphasize the social landscape in which the intersections of people and place are seen as "worlds of cultural product... that are not synonymous with natural environments" and as "dynamic constructions that serve as an arena for a community's activities" (Anschuetz et al. 2001:160–161). From this perspective the landscape is considered an anthropogenic entity contextualized by the articulation of social groups within it and through time (Fisher and Thurston 1999).

Yet, in order to discuss the landscape in these terms, it is necessary to thread together observed spatial patterning of the archaeological site data with the organizational dynamics of social groups. In the contexts of this study, I suggest that communities offer an interpretive connection between people, place, and time. Communities are critical to the examination of social landscapes as they represent a central component to sociological and anthropological understandings of social organization above the household (Adler 2002:37; Rouse 1968:23). Further, communities represent the basic elements within a given social landscape for the expressions of group identity and so-

Table 6.1. Chronological Model for Prehistoric Puerto Rico.

Date	Period	Series	Subseries	Complex/Style	
				West	East
ca. 300 B.C.–A.D. 400	IIa	Saladoid	Cedrosan	Hacienda Grande	Hacienda Grande*
ca. 300 B.C.–A.D. 300					La Hueca**
ca. A.D. 400–600	IIb			Cuevas	
ca. A.D. 600–900	IIIa	Ostionoid	Ostionan (West)	Early (Pure)	Monserrate
ca. A.D. 900–1200	IIIb		Elenan (East)	Late (Modified)	Santa Elena
ca. A.D. 1200–1500	IVa		Chican	Capá/Boca Chica	Esperanza

(Table adapted from Curet 1996; Garrow et al. 1995; Rouse 1992).
*In the later portion of Period IIa.
**Huecan Saladoid subseries.

cial organization that are subject to developmental processes at varying scales (Hegmon 2002; Kolb and Snead 1997).

On Puerto Rico, few archaeological studies define or attempt to examine, in very basic terms, the organizational and interpretive implications of communities for examining the formation and interaction of social and political groups through time and space (e.g., Lundberg 1985a; Oliver 1998, 1999). I attribute this in part to shifts in the organization of Puerto Rico's ceramic-age communities through time and the multiplicity of meanings and connotations associated with the term that make them difficult to define both on a conceptual and methodological level (see Hegmon 2002; Kolb and Snead 1997:609–612). In the following discussion, I offer a basic definition of community and a framework for exploring the ceramic-age social and political landscapes of Puerto Rico.

Components of the Sociopolitical Landscape

Within archaeological research contexts, the fundamental concept of "community" is typically conceived of as a self-identifying, residentially based territorial social group that interacts face to face on a consistent basis and is bound together in the shared utilization of local social and natural resources (Adler 2002:29; Chang 1968:2–3; Kolb and Snead 1997:609–612; Murdock 1949:79; Varien 2002:19, 1999:20). Central to this definition, and a critical aspect of the current study, is the notion of community as a socially based organizational unit that possesses decision-making structures directly relevant for the group members.

Communities do not exist in isolation. Regional linkages influence or define roles and behaviors within and across communities. Spatially, the proximity of communities influences the degree to which groups share forms of meaning and behavior relative to their unique contexts (Bourdieu 1977; Varien 1999; Yeager 2000:125). The organization and development of social groups are influenced through these interactions, forming an "arena in which sociopolitical relationships are negotiated or played out" (Kolb and Snead 1997:611; see also Blanton et al. 1996). As a component of the social landscape, communities are culturally constructed organizational units that provide access to resources, social identities, and territorial boundaries (Adler 2002:31). From this perspective, communities, or spatially related groups of them, potentially represent sociopolitical groupings across a given landscape.

Within the context of communities as organizational units, integrative mechanisms in the form of public rituals are utilized to reinforce sociopolitical and religious ideologies, social relationships, and to resolve disputes (Adler and Wilshusen 1990; Curet 1996; Earle 1997:153–154; Hegmon 1989:6–9;

Siegel 1996, 1999). In many cases, this behavior is conducted within areas of spatially segregated public or civic architecture (Adler and Wilshusen 1990; Earle 1997:155–158). The relevance of monumental architecture within a sociopolitical landscape is based on the organizational and behavioral implications of the existence of such features. Monumental architecture often denotes stratified forms of social organization characterized by the formalization of centralized leadership (Earle 1997:157; Kirch 1990; Siegel 1996, 1999). This notion is in part a result of socioeconomic factors related to the construction and maintenance of the structures and the implicit control and use of the spaces associated with them (Earle 1997:155–158).

On Puerto Rico, this space is manifested in the Saladoid period by the clearing of central plazas in villages (Siegel 1991c) and in the Ostionoid periods by the construction of monumental architecture in the form of stonelined plazas/ball courts (Alegría 1983). This shift in how ceremonial space was defined is related to changes in sociopolitical complexity, the centralization of ideological power, and potential territorial competition between sociopolitical groups (Curet 1996; Oliver 1992b, 1998; Siegel 1991c, 1999; Torres 2001). This shift also represents a transition in the organization of local social and community groups.

Functionally, monumental architecture was a forum that allowed individuals to be integrated within the larger social contexts of communities and community groups (Adler and Wilshusen 1990; Alegría 1983:5; Earle 1997:156; Hegmon 1989:5–14; Magness-Gardiner and Falconer 1994:127–128; Varien 1999:22). Regionally, monumental architecture supplies visual reminders of extant ideological systems (Ashmore and Sabloff 2002:203; Earle 1997:156) that denote areas of perceived power and also act as symbols to join people and place. On Puerto Rico, these spaces were utilized to perpetuate elite authority and ideology as group unity and membership were reinforced through the rituals conducted within these spaces (Curet 1996:123; Siegel 1996, 1999).

As a spatial entity, communities are difficult to quantify. Archaeologists have in some cases conceptualized the village and the community synonymously (Chang 1968:2–3; Hegmon 2002:265; Kolb and Snead 1997:612; Lundberg 1985a:L2; Rouse 1968:23). However, there are many factors associated with the appropriateness of this terminological application; namely the scale and complexity of a site within the organizational contexts and the regional settlement system in which it exists (Hegmon 2002:265; Kolb and Snead 1997:612). In many instances, the community consists of multiple domestic groups that do not necessarily reside in the same place. "The community can be nucleated in a single settlement, or it can occur as multiple dispersed settlements that share leadership responsibilities, local resources and a common identity" (Adler 2002:29). Further, communities are dynamic and their compositional structure and spatial morphology may vary through time and space (Hegmon 2002:264).

Typologically, the nomenclatures associated with the ceramic-age sites of Puerto Rico are generic (e.g., Tronolone et al. 1990:459–460). Existing types embody a range of implied functional behaviors based on features, artifacts, and potential occupational duration at a given site. Sites have been classified as ceremonial centers, villages, hamlets, campsites, and rock art. Although these types represent a useful baseline for examining variation of past settlement and behavioral use within the landscape, the utilization of this typological system creates a functional disconnect when examining the organization of communities or community groups based on their constituent components. Specifically, no distinction is made between Ostionoid sites possessing monumental architectural features and evidence of extended domestic occupation and those that do not have these features.[2] This is problematic, since the presence or absence of formalized monumental architecture, with evidence of long-term domestic habitation, is an important aspect for considering the functional and organizational role of a village within the larger behavioral and organizational contexts of its community and sociopolitical unit.

To avoid interpretive problems associated with established settlement typologies and to facilitate examination of the community as a conceptual and spatial entity, I have revised the traditional settlement typology for the region based on evidence of persistent habitation and the presence or absence of ceremonial architecture. My revised nomenclature consists of (1) sites with ceremonial architecture but no evidence of domestic habitation, (2) villages with ceremonial features, and (3) villages without ceremonial features. I use the term "village" in this study to denote the spatial and behavioral location of the constituent components of communities. Villages in this study are defined by sites possessing evidence of multiple, long-term, persistent domestic habitations evinced either by the remains of habitation structures and/or substantial midden deposits. The use of this nomenclature recognizes the potential for independent or concurrent instances of sites with ceremonial features and domestic habitation. This is useful for establishing a baseline for examining the potential interrelationships between contemporaneous social groups and the morphology of the social landscape through time.

Methodology

Geographical Information Systems (GIS) technology is employed as a tool to spatially model related villages and examine the social and political landscape of south-central Puerto Rico. Spatial boundaries were generated for villages for each of the three sociotemporal periods (Periods II–IV) established by Rouse (1992:107). Through an examination of these boundaries and site distributions though time, I model possible spheres of social interaction across the landscape, discuss the potential development and organization of social groups, and offer a discussion of the social and political landscape for the region.

I would be remiss in not pointing out, as others have (Curet et al. 2004; Lundberg 1985a:L9; Siegel 1999:222; Torres 2001), the serious problems associated with the regional study of sites in this area. Affecting the nature of the sample and the data that does exist are the lack of systematic full-coverage surveys, fine-scaled temporal data, and inconsistencies in data collection and recordation of sites in the region through time. Unfortunately, much of the documentation that exists for sites within the study area excludes ceramic data to the level of style for accurate period dating (e.g., Periods IIa, IIb, IIIa, etc.). Hence, there are serious problems associated with ascertaining the contemporaneity of sites. These problems are compounded by the destruction of sites from recent development, resulting in potentially skewed spatial patterns. Yet despite the problems associated with these data, site distributions conform to meaningful relationships between place and behavior, which enable them to be evaluated as a reflection of the social landscape. In this study, I explore observed site patterning to establish a baseline for potential social interaction and for generating hypotheses rather than statistical analysis for testing regional relationships.[3]

The Data

The present study utilizes two geospatial datasets to model potential community groups and regional interaction through time. The first dataset consists of topographic information for the south-central portion of the island derived from a Digital Elevation Model (DEM), which was obtained from the U.S. Geological Survey. The dataset is based on 1:20,000 scale topographic maps for the region and is a raster (grid) based representation of topography. In this format, elevation data are recorded for each 30-x-30-m cell in the model. The DEM for this region represents approximately 1,300 square kilometers (500 square miles) of surface area.

The second GIS dataset was acquired from the State Historic Preservation Office in Puerto Rico (PRSHPO), and represents all documented ceramic-age sites for the region as spatially referenced points. The point data were accompanied by site-specific information from archival field documentation housed at the PRSHPO. Site-specific documentation was examined for temporal affiliation (Periods II, III, or IV), evidence of persistent domestic habitation, presence/absence of ceremonial features, and the number of such features if present (Alegría 1983; Lundberg 1985a; Maíz López and Questell Rodríguez 1990; Rodríguez López 1985; Siegel 1996, 1999). In total, 48 sites could be assigned to periods and possessed evidence of extended domestic habitation and/or monumental architecture (Table 6.2). Sites lacking temporal data and evidence of extended habitation or monumental architecture were omitted from the study. Many of the disqualified sites were classified on the PRSHPO forms as hamlets, campsites, or limited activity areas (n = 50).[4] In a previous study, I used these sites to discuss potential site interrelationships (Torres 2001:112–128).

GIS MODELING OF INTERACTION SPHERES

As previously suggested, the organization and development of communities is in part a result of the ability to access social resources within a given landscape (Adler 2002; Clark and Blake 1994; Varien 1999). Such access depends largely upon topographic characteristics of the region and the spatial positioning of settlements within it (Clark and Blake 1994:19–20; Johnson 1977:492; Varien 1997). Within this context, the intersections of behavior and place determine future growth and social interaction between communities (Flannery 1976:168–169). As communities are inherently connected to others through social contact, the focus of inquiry becomes the delineation of spheres of interaction across the physical landscape (Lundberg 1985a:L2). Identifying spheres of interaction enables us to recognize community aggregates and their organizational contexts within the greater sociopolitical system. Importantly, it is possible to delineate potential focal points of social interaction and places where the processes of social change are potentially intensified (Clark and Blake 1994:20).

Traditionally, the determination of interaction spheres on the physical landscape are generated through the two-dimensional modeling of site boundaries using, for instance, Thiessen polygons or overlapping site catchments based on a fixed radius from the site. Although appropriate for ascertaining general spatial relationships over a uniform surface, this method of determining site territories (or areas of habitual land use) is problematic in that these models do not account for idiosyncrasies in topography and the physical costs for individuals traveling it from one place to another.[5]

As an alternative for modeling social boundaries, cost-based models have been used to establish more realistic territorial units associated with settlements (e.g., Torres 2001; Varien 1999). Cost models measure surface distance based on impedance factors, which take into account characteristics of the

Table 6.2. Site Data.

MAPID	Site Name	PII	PIII	PIV	A	B	C	D	Source
1	Vega del Seboruco	0	1	0	0	1	0	1	Site Form
2	Los Burgos	0	1	1	0	0	1	0	Site Form
3	Las Flores	1	1	0	0	1	0	1	Siegel 1999; Site Form
4	Villon/Cuyon	0	1	1	0	1	0	3	Alegría 1983; Siegel 1999; Site Form
5	Buenos Aires	1	1	0	0	0	0	0	Site Form
6	Tecla	1	1	0	0	0	1	0	Siegel 1999
7	La Vega	1	1	1	0	1	0	0	Siegel 1999; Site Form
8	Santi	0	1	0	0	0	1	0	Site Form
9	Guayabal I	0	0	1	0	0	1	0	Site Form
10	Río Canas	0	1	0	0	1	0	1	Site Form
11	Vengas (Ollas Hondas)	0	0	1	0	1	0	2	Lundberg 1985a; Site Form
12	Collores	1	1	0	0	0	1	0	Lundberg 1985a; Site Form
13	Pe-1	0	1	1	0	1	0	1	Site Form
14	La Jagua	0	1	0	0	0	1	0	Site Form
15	Canas	1	1	0	0	0	1	0	Lundberg 1985a; Rainey 1940; Site Form
16	Duey/Diego Hernández	1	1	1	0	1	0	1	Site Form
17	La Fraternidad	1	0	0	0	0	1	0	Site Form
18	Tibes	1	1	0	0	0	1	9	Siegel 1999; Site Form
19	Hernández Colón	1	1	1	0	1	0	1	Site Form

#	Site						Reference
20	Ana Maria	0	1	0	0	1	1	Rodríguez López 1985; Site Form
21	Caracoles	0	1	1	0	1	1	Rodríguez López 1985; Site Form
22	Camp Santiago P-2 (antes F-4-01)	0	1	0	0	0	1	Rodríguez López 1985; Site Form
23	Camp Santiago P-4 (antes M-14-01)	0	1	0	0	0	1	Rodríguez López 1985; Site Form
24	Camp Santiago P-7	0	1	1	0	1	0	Rodríguez López 1985; Site Form
25	Camp Santiago P-10	0	1	0	0	1	1	Rodríguez López 1985; Site Form
26	Camp Santiago P-12	0	1	0	0	1	0	Rodríguez López 1985; Site Form
27	Camp Santiago P-14 (antes G-15-01)	0	1	0	0	1	1	Rodríguez López 1985; Site Form
28	Camp Santiago P-20	0	1	1	0	1	0	Rodríguez López 1985; Site Form
29	Penuelas	0	1	0	0	1	1	Rodríguez López 1985; Site Form
30	Jauca I	0	0	1	0	1	0	Rodríguez López 1985; Site Form
31	Jauca II	0	0	1	0	1	0	Rodríguez López 1985; Site Form
32	La Jungla	0	0	0	0	1	0	Site Form
33	Las Ollas	0	1	0	0	1	0	Rodríguez López 1985; Site Form
34	El Cayito	0	0	1	0	0	0	Garrow et al. 1995; Lundberg 1985a; Site Form
35	VL-4	0	1	0	0	1	0	Site Form
36	Las Florida/Los Indios	0	1	0	0	1	0	Rodríguez López 1985; Site Form
37	El Bronce	1	1	1	0	0	1	Robinson et al. 1985; Siegel 1999
38	Aguirre	0	1	1	0	1	0	Rodríguez López 1985; Site Form
39	El Coco	0	1	1	0	1	1	Site Form
40	Carmen/Margarita	1	1	0	0	1	0	Rodríguez López 1985
41	El Llano	0	1	0	0	0	1	Rodríguez López 1985; Site Form

MAPID	Site Name	PII	PIII	PIV	A	B	C	D	Source
42	Esperanza	0	1	1	0	1	0	2	Site Form
43	Camp Santiago P-16	0	1	0	1	0	0	1	Rodríguez López 1985; Site Form
44	Maragüez	0	1	0	1	0	0	1	Site Form
45	Camp Santiago P-19	0	1	1	1	0	0	1	Rodríguez López 1985; Site Form
46	La Plena 1	0	1	0	1	0	0	1	Site Form
47	La Iglesia de Maragüez (CT9)	0	1	1	1	0	0	1	Garrow et al. 1995; Site Form
48	Asomante	0	0	1	1	0	0	1	Site Form

Column headings and data values:

(MAPID) Number used to refer to the site on the maps.

(Site Name) Common name given to the site.

(PII) Presence (1) or Absence (0) of Period II temporal components.

(PIII) Presence (1) or Absence (0) of Period III temporal components.

(PIV) Presence (1) or Absence (0) of Period IV temporal components.

(A) Presence (1) or Absence (0) of Monumental Architecture/No Domestic Habitation.

(B) Presence (1) or Absence (0) of Village/Monumental Architecture Present.

(C) Presence (1) or Absence (0) of Village/Monumental Architecture Absent.

(D) Number of Monumental Features.

(Source) Refers to the primary source(s) of the information.

natural topography. Differing from other models of travel based on two dimensional modeling techniques, cost models measure resistance units across a topographically nonuniform plane to calculate a least accumulative surface from a given point location. In the present study, the DEM was used to generate slope for the region, which in turn serves as a resistance surface for measuring cost distances. As the slope increases, cost values increase accordingly (Torres 2001:70–75).

Cost boundaries were generated for 2.5- and 5-km distance intervals for villages by period. The 2.5-km cost interval was used to approximate the extent of lands habitually utilized by a given village for its most basic social and subsistence activities (Chisholm 1970:131; Stone 1991:347, 1992:166; Varien 1999, 2002:174–175). I used the 2.5-km cost distance to delimit areas of potentially consistent face-to-face interaction, and as a baseline for community interrelationships (Varien 1999:153–154). The 5-km interval represented an upper extent of this intensively utilized area (Torres 2001). The resultant boundaries, and areas of overlap at both levels of cost, were used to model possible spheres of interaction, community groups, and potential territorial units.

Results and Discussion

Visual examination of the cost models and site distributions for each period (Figures 6.2–6.4) reveal a series of village clusters varying in density and spatial extent through time. Notably, a persistent trend is apparent in the clustering of villages in the west, central, and eastern portions of the study area. Within these areas, the numbers and locations of villages are variable through time. Changes in spatial patterns of villages through time should reflect shifts in networks of social interaction. Since villages are clustered at a number of inclusive levels (particularly during Period III in the eastern portion of the study area), there arises the question: which level of clustering represents the community (Varien 1997:22)?

At the 2.5-km level, I would suggest that overlapping boundaries represent social spheres characterized by a high potential for interaction among contemporaneous village-based domestic groups. Within this distance, contemporaneous villages would have the most occasions for interaction and sharing of local social and subsistence resources. The overlap of several boundaries at the 2.5-km range may suggest a network of socially related villages and indicate a dispersed community pattern. Conversely, sites with little overlap at this distance interval may reveal more independence between villages and a more nucleated community pattern. The 5-km cost boundaries are used to

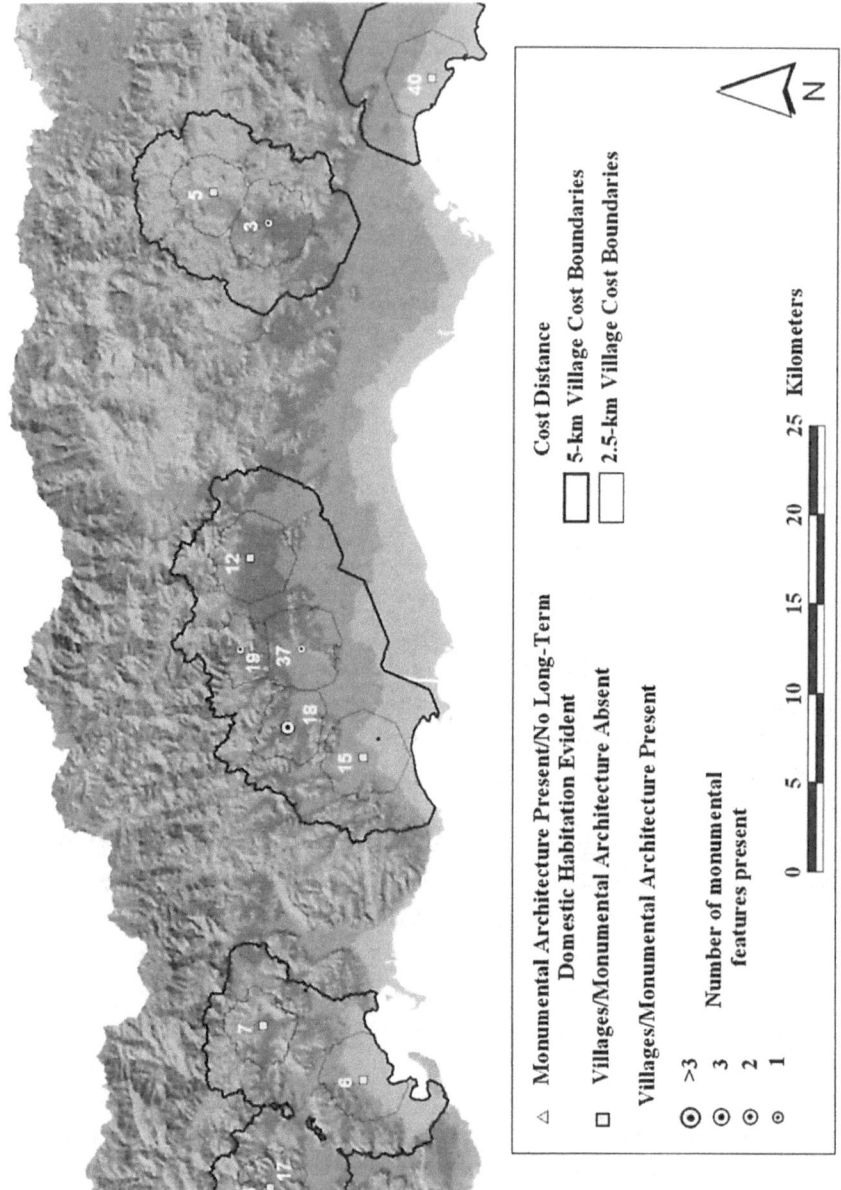

Figure 6.2. Period II site distributions, cost boundaries, and village clusters.

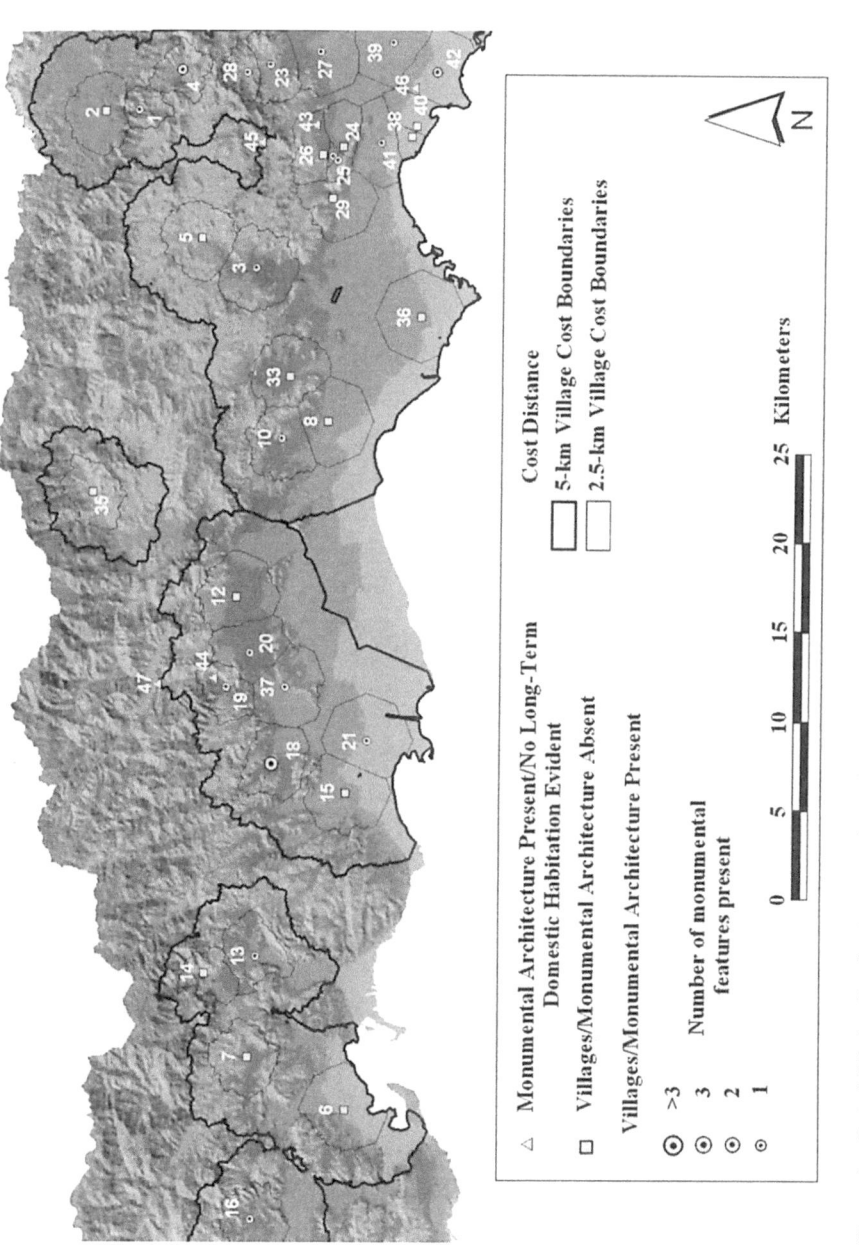

Figure 6.3. Period III site distributions, cost boundaries, and village clusters.

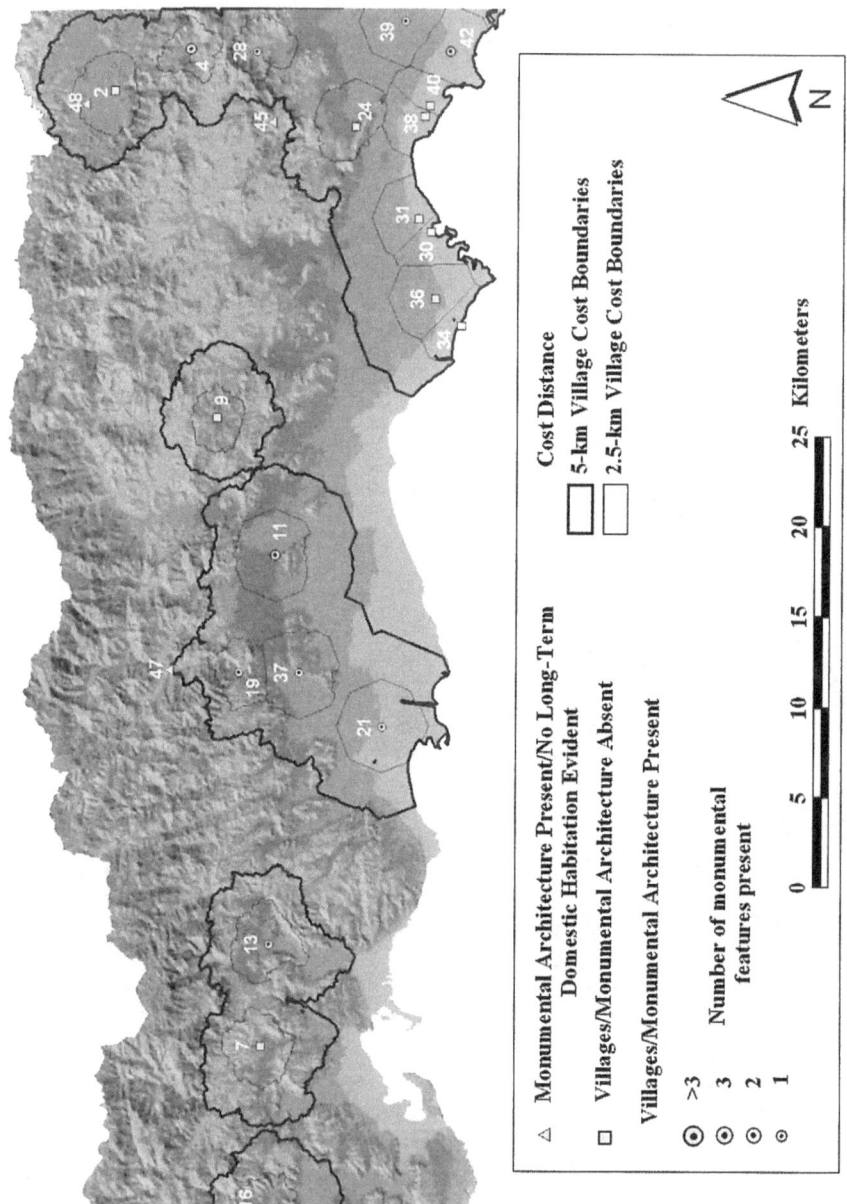

Figure 6.4. Period IV site distributions, cost boundaries, and village clusters.

delimit possible multiple groupings of spatially related village clusters, forming more inclusive spheres of social interaction.

Period II

Examination of the 5-km cost boundaries for the 12 villages during Period II (Saladoid) display three village groupings, located in the west, central, and eastern portions of the study area (Figure 6.2). In general, villages during this time appear to be loosely clustered, and there is no evidence of regional hierarchical organization based on site size. The lack of formalized ceremonial architecture during this period also supports this supposition. Based on the low density of villages across the landscape, the lack of evidence supporting site hierarchies, and the rather even spatial distribution, suggest that villages were relatively autonomous in nature (Siegel 1989a, 1991c, 1996, 1999). These observations, combined with research regarding village organization, suggest that domestic structures consisted of several extended families (Curet 1992b) residing in nucleated communities.

Considering the villages that eventually developed monumental architecture in Period III offers a spatial context for spheres of social interaction, wherein changes in political and ideological structure were forming by the end of the Saladoid period (Period IIb). For example, the 2.5-km boundary in the center of the study area displays a relatively dense clustering of villages and contains some of the earliest occurrences of formalized monumental architecture (Tibes and El Bronce) in the region. Examples at a smaller scale are evident in the eastern (Las Flores) and western (Diego Hernández) portions of the study area. Importantly, these patterns point to the development of multivillage communities.

Period III

Inspection of village clusters during Period III (Figure 6.3) reveals several interesting changes in regional settlement from the preceding period, at both the 2.5- and 5-km levels. In general, this period is characterized by a dramatic increase in the frequency distribution of sites, representing the highest density of habitation loci in the region prior to European contact (Figure 6.5). During this period, the number of villages increased by approximately 200 percent (n = 35) compared to Period II (n = 12), and are concentrated primarily in the eastern portion of the study area. This increase in village frequency was accompanied by the formalization of ceremonial space at most of the sites (n = 20). Finally, several Period III sites possessed monumental architecture but no evidence of domestic occupations (n = 5).

Local interactions during Period III were represented by village clusters identified at the 2.5-km cost boundaries. With very few exceptions, village clusters at this level contained at least one site possessing formalized ceremonial architecture. Sites with little to no monumental architecture appeared to cluster in close proximity to villages possessing more substantial amounts of ceremonial space (e.g., Tibes, Villón, Esperanza, Río Canas, Las Flores). The presence of these architectural features, in conjunction with the localized clustered patterning of habitation sites, implies a degree of interaction and organization encompassing multiple villages. This pattern contrasts to Saladoid social groups that appear to have been concentrated at discrete village locations and relatively autonomous in nature. These contrasts reflect a fundamental shift in the organization of social groups from the Saladoid to the Ostionan and Elenan Ostionoid periods.

Settlement patterns at the 5-km level suggest regional interaction spheres. Within the 5-km cost boundaries, villages were grouped into one, two, and four clusters at the 2.5-km level from west to east. This trend implies an increase in the complexity of local social networks and interactions from west to east through the study area. Variations in the sizes of village clusters and the number of formal ceremonial features among them (particularly in the central and eastern portions of the study area) indicate hierarchical organization of community groups (see also Siegel 1991c, 1999). At this level, proximally related clusters of villages could conceivably indicate the basis of political units whose social centers are designated by substantial amounts of formalized architecture. From this perspective, the 5-km cost boundaries may approximate territorial units associated with these community groups whose local populations shared closer social, political, and ideological ties among themselves than with other less-connected village clusters in the region.

Siegel (1999:227) suggested the existence of territorial social groups based on concurrent and potentially competitive based building episodes of monumental architecture at several site locations across the island. In this context, the growth of monumental architecture within the study area is most noticeable between sites in the eastern (e.g., Villón, Las Flores, G-15-01, and F-3-01) and central (e.g., Tibes, El Bronce, and La Iglesia de Maragüez) portions of the region. This observation, combined with the morphology of spatial clustering, indicates that social and political groups were organized within discrete geographical contexts. The geographical differentiation of social groupings and spheres of interaction is also noted by variation in the stylistic distribution of ceramics that, based on limited data, shift in degrees from Elenan Ostionoid to Ostionan Ostionoid from east to west across the study area (Figure 6.6).[6] Elsewhere, I proposed that this distribution, within the context of regional sociopolitical organization, may indicate the convergence

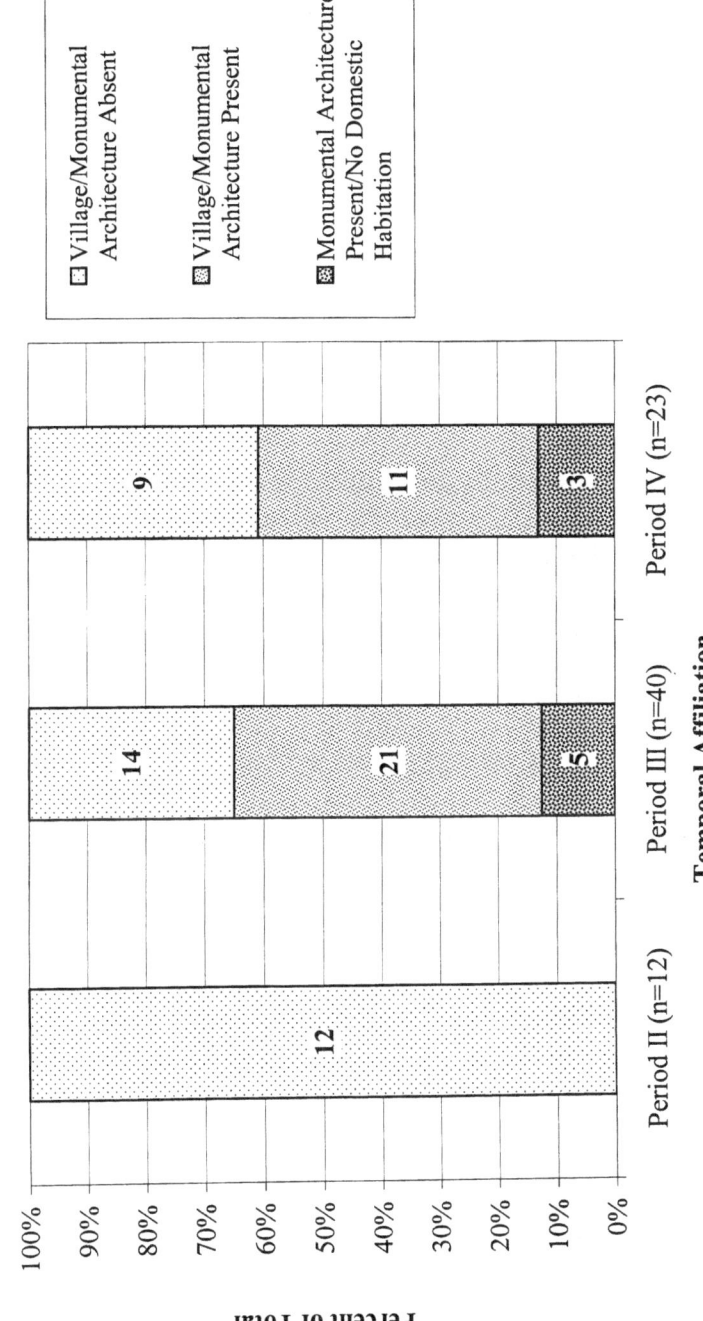

Figure 6.5. Site type frequencies through time. Five of the Period II sites continued to be occupied in Period III and incorporated monumental architecture.

of interaction spheres between social groups, from the Mona Passage to Vieques Sound (Torres 2002).

The increase in social complexity, political competition, and the development of multivillage community groups during the Elenan and Ostionan Ostionoid were not mutually exclusive, and the concurrent developments of these elements were influenced and perpetuated by the spatial dynamics of the social landscape. For instance, increases in site density during Period III would have affected access to and control over locally based natural and social resources.[7] Decreases in the amount of land associated with Period III villages is seen at the 2.5-km level (Figure 6.7). As social relationships between nearby social groups intensified, the development of integrative systems in the form of public ritual would have facilitated local integration and unique conceptualizations of social order that, while potentially being similar in many respects, may not have been completely homogenous to other social groups within the region.[8]

Commonalties between local groups and differences between distant ones would have perpetuated complex social hierarchies, group identities, territoriality, and sociopolitical competition. The organization of groups reveals locally based units, below the level of the traditional conceptualization of the polity (Renfrew 1986). Carole Crumley and William Marquardt observed: "Between human groups contradictions emerge because people occupying particular localities develop models of their landscape based on their specific needs and experiences; these models may be at variance with those of other groups, leading to competition, solidification of group identities, or alternatives in the organizational strategies of related social groups. Importantly, these alternatives and their subsequent effects on neighboring groups constitute the raw material of changes, which occurs in the resolution of conflicts and tensions between and among social networks containing multiple groups" (Crumley and Marquardt 1990:73).

Finally, I would like to discuss the potential implications of sites that possess ceremonial architecture but no evidence of persistent habitation. These sites appear to be located at the boundaries between one or more communities and in some cases at the edges of community clusters. Most notably is a line of these sites running northwest to southeast between sites on the very eastern edge of the study area and the cluster of sites surrounding Camp Santiago P-2. Two more of these sites are arranged in a linear fashion in the Cerrillos River Valley extending from La Iglesia de Maragüez in the north to Maragüez in the south—the latter a short distance north and east of Hernández Colón.

It has previously been suggested that these sites may represent localized

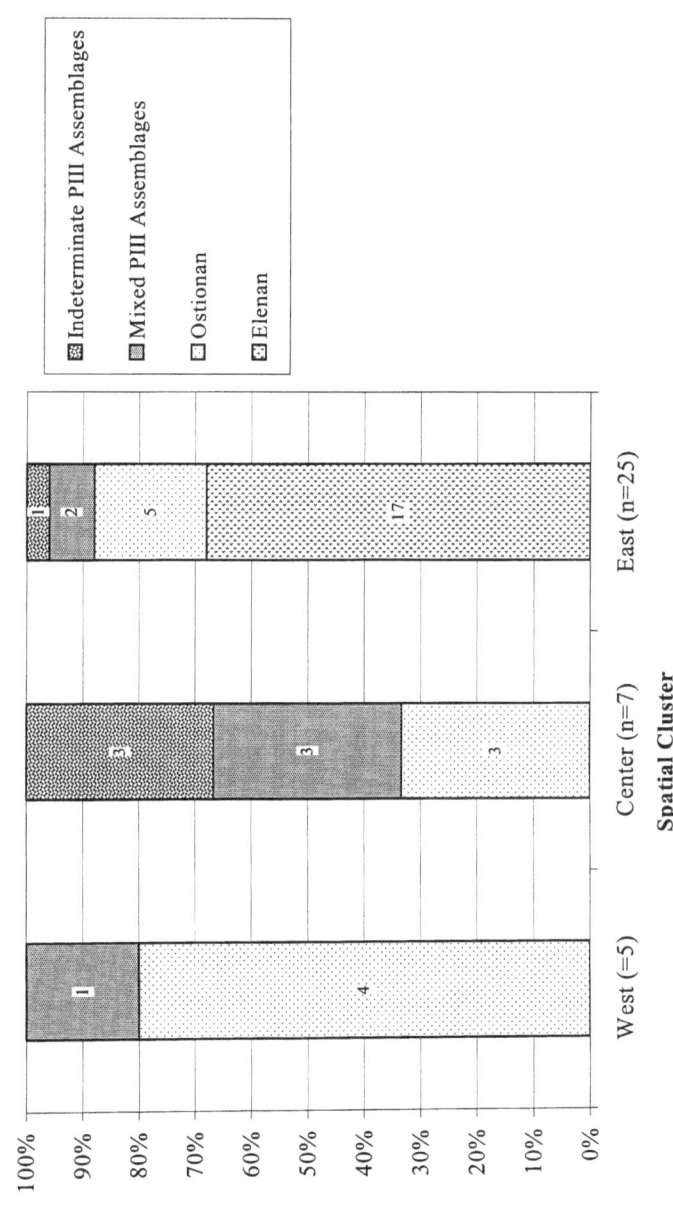

Figure 6.6. General trends in ceramic distributions through the region. (Note: Site VL-4 was not included in this graph as it is located outside of all the main clusters. However, based on the information available, this site purportedly contains both Elenan and Ostionan ceramic styles.)

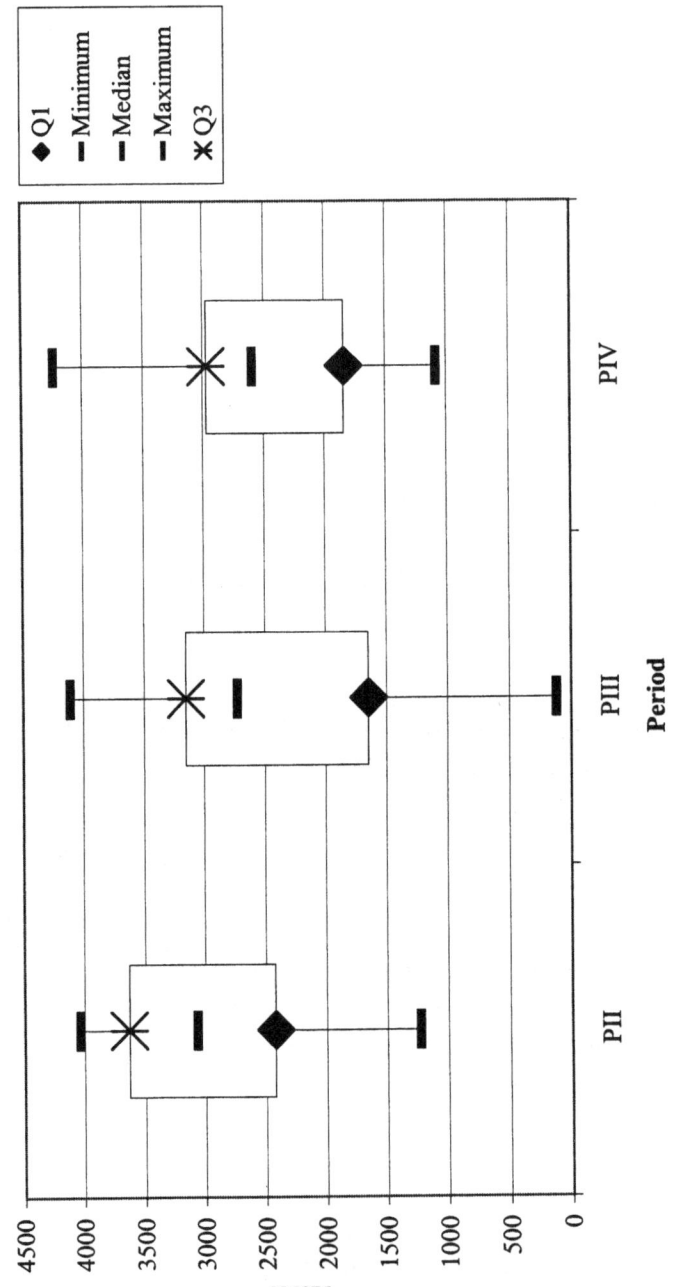

Figure 6.7. Territory associated with villages through time.

ceremonial centers for communities lacking such features (Garrow et al. 1995). However, these sites may also serve to integrate villages at the borders of or outside of primary community groups. And although villages with large amounts of ceremonial space undoubtedly serve the same purpose, the ceremonial sites lacking persistent habitation are an interesting development and provide even greater evidence of social and political activity beyond the level of the single village. This trend was more apparent during Period IV in the mountainous central portions of the island (Oliver 1998, 1999). It is possible, based on observed settlement patterning, that the sociopolitical impetus for this type of organization originated on the south coast during Period III and was the product of increasingly complex social relationships between proximally related villages and community groups.

Period IV

At the 5-km level (Figure 6.4) the morphology of the social landscape during Period IV is in some ways similar to the spatial configuration of village clusters in previous periods. In this respect, habitation sites continued to be concentrated in the west, central, and eastern portions of the study area. However, upon closer examination it is clear that Period IV settlement patterns are quite different from Period III. Specifically, site frequency decreased substantially from the preceding period (n = 23) with habitation sites possessing formalized ceremonial space diminishing by half (n = 10).[9]

In the eastern portion of the study area, changes in settlement were characterized by a shift in the concentration of villages to areas along the coast with less emphasis on foothill and upland locations (Curet et al. 2004; Lundberg 1985a; Rodríguez López 1985; Torres 2001). In this area, there is little evidence of ceremonial architecture at village sites—with few exceptions (e.g., Villón, Esperanza, El Coco, and Camp Santiago P-20). One observation worthy of mention is the presence of Boca Chica style ceramics at a number of sites in the region (specifically at El Cayito, Villón, and Esperanza). This style is typically associated with assemblages from the eastern portion of Hispaniola and western Puerto Rico, suggesting some social interaction with groups from these areas. However, Boca Chica is a minority style in the Villón and Esperanza assemblages.

Within the west and central 5-km boundaries, villages were increasingly segmented with fewer sites clustered at the 2.5-km level. In each area, some sites persisted from Period III—some with formalized ceremonial space (e.g., PE-1, Hernández Colón, El Bronce, and Caracoles). However, both the western (and in particular) the central clusters were characterized by substantially fewer sites with the loss of potentially important villages and community centers (e.g., Tecla and Tibes).

The abandonment of villages throughout the region, particularly those with ceremonial architecture, coupled with shifts in settlements in the east, implies a major realignment of social and political networks by this time. In this context, these changes indicate the depopulation and a potential collapse or "playing out" of the sociopolitical system in this portion of the island (Curet et al. 2004; Lundberg 1985a:L16; Oliver 1992b; Torres 2001). Depopulation of this region is accompanied by the apparent increase in village frequency in the island's mountainous interior, specifically around the ceremonial center of Caguana (Oliver 1998, 1999). However, the pattern of settlement in the south-central portion of Puerto Rico is contrary to what one would expect for this period, which is the presence of very complex regional networks and obvious settlement hierarchies evincing the power of ruling caciques, as discussed in the chronicles (Oviedo 1975).

The reasons for the observed transitions in Period IV community and regional organization are not clear. These changes may have resulted from local or regional processes related to cyclical patterns of change hypothesized to be inherent in chiefdom-based organizational systems (Anderson 1996a, 1996b). Previous work by Curet (1992a) has shown that in the Valley of Maunabo, local populations never reached subsistence carrying capacities—indicating socially based catalysts for the development of formally stratified social structures. Applying this model to the study area one could conclude that social factors were responsible for the observed changes in the region. More research is necessary to determine the reasons for social and political developments during this time.

Conclusions

The complex social landscape that developed during the Elenan and Ostionan Ostionoid appears to have been the result of gradual and consistent social contact between local groups within distinctive and persistent spheres of interaction. Through time these groups formed communities whose members shared social realities defined by history, place, and ritual activities. The construction and use of ceremonial space through time, combined with settlement patterning, supports a shifting pattern in the organization of communities from Saladoid to Ostionoid times. Research presented here shows the contrast between spatial patterns of Saladoid and Ostionoid community organization as a shift from centralized, relatively egalitarian, and independent autonomous village units to multiple dispersed village groups within a hierarchical sociopolitical system.

Saladoid groups were able to select optimum locations for their villages based on access to resources and their preconceptions of territory and space inherited from their South American ancestry. During this time, villages were large and relatively autonomous, with no evidence of regional political units or settlement hierarchies. The distribution of sites during this period appears to influence the location of future sites and the formation of social networks across the landscape through time. As more land was settled during the Elenan and Ostionan Ostionoid, the island's social networks increased in complexity in which "Each cluster of residence, ritual, and local identity was the manifestation of a social strategy designed to integrate and differentiate regional populations" (Adler 2002:32).

In the past, methodological conceptualizations of community and sociopolitical units have typically been considered from a single site perspective characterized by spatial, developmental, and organizational homogeneity through time (Curet 2003). To address these issues I have focused on the utilization of the community as a conceptual and analytical unit to acknowledge the complex social networks and heterogeneity inherent in the organization of regional social groups. Communities are important because they force us to consider the processes of social development at varying scales (e.g., local vs. regional), the fluidity of social interrelationships, and the complexity of human societies.

For archaeologists focused on the ceramic-age societies of Puerto Rico, the concept of community has important implications for understanding regional sociopolitical units. From a developmental standpoint, examining the temporal variability in the location and proximity of villages within the landscape promotes the identification of potentially related social groups and the local contexts influencing trajectories of social change (Curet et al. 2004; Siegel 1999:211). Importantly, it allows archaeologists to break away from previous notions of sociopolitical organization, which tend to focus solely on the location of ceremonial architecture or single village sites by shifting our attention to the interrelationships between multiple groups within a dynamic social landscape.

However, in order to explore regional social systems in this fashion we must refine our methodological and conceptual applications of "community" and clarify the units we use to reconstruct potential prehistoric communities. Consideration of the organizational homogeneity implicit in our characterization of the community and further refinement of its application and conceptualization through time and space are most pressing. I have tried to resolve these issues through revision of established settlement typologies in order to visually display the morphology of the social and political landscape through time. Yet the qualification of social relatedness between villages and community groups is a necessary trajectory of future research in order to better understand the dynamics of social interaction and political development within the Greater Antilles.

Critically, the observations and interpretations presented here must be tempered by further work and the testing of hypotheses aimed at understanding the relationships between social groups through time and space. In particular, future work should focus on the interaction between contemporaneous sites both within and between villages and community groups. Examination of variability in stylistic, compositional, and, production method elements among ceramic assemblages may be used to define local social boundaries and interaction. For instance, little variability in these elements between proximal contemporaneous villages may suggest a high level of social relatedness. Conversely, significant variation of one or more of these elements through space may offer insight into social differences within or between contemporaneous groups. Work conducted by Michele Hayward and Michael Cinquino (2002:33–34) has suggested the utilization of rock art as a potential geographic and stylistic marker between social and political groups. These studies in conjunction could greatly facilitate our understanding of community and sociopolitical landscapes.

The present study has sought to show the promise of communities as a means for refining our approach to Puerto Rico's ceramic-age sociopolitical landscape. In particular, I have tried to show that the processes of change and the organization of social groups that constitute sociopolitical units are potentially based within more localized levels of human behavior and interaction. Further, I suggest that the social landscape was a dynamic and complex entity that was both a manifestation and influential element in the arrangement and growth of regional social groups. Archaeologists in Puerto Rico, and the Greater Antilles in general, need to consider the implications of community-based networks and interaction to expand our understanding of, and explain changes in, the social and political organization of the prehistoric indigenous societies of the region.

Acknowledgments

I want to thank Peter Siegel for his gracious invitation to participate in this publication. My sincere gratitude to Miguel Bonini and the State Historic Preservation Office in San Juan, Puerto Rico, for their continual assistance and support of my research. Special thanks to Antonio Curet, Richard Wilshusen, and Todd McMahon for reading and commenting on a previous draft of this paper and for their invaluable insight over the course of its development. Finally, I would like to thank two anonymous reviewers for their thorough and helpful comments. Any errors or shortcomings in this paper are solely my responsibility.

Notes

1. In some studies ecological and sociopolitical approaches have been utilized jointly (e.g., Lundberg 1985a; Torres 2001).

2. Oliver has, in recent studies (1998, 1999), used a tiered or ordered system primarily based on the number of monumental architectural features at a given site.

3. In a previous study I did conduct an analysis of variance study on the distance of sites in the region through time to suggest increasing social and political interrelationships of sites through time (Torres 2001:112–128)

4. Limited activity areas also included rock-art sites.

5. This is also the problem with conducting nearest-neighbor analysis in an area where topographical characteristics are extremely variable.

6. Based on the paucity of data, this observation is very tentative. Hopefully, future research will elaborate on the stylistic distribution and variation in ceramics for a finer scale examination of regional social groupings, interaction, and refinement of the temporal contexts of villages.

7. Research conducted by Valcárcel Rojas (2001) on Cuba has shown site clustering and potential multivillage community development during Period IV, which he attributes to increases in site density, location of cultivatable land, and increases in agriculture practices.

8. Curet (2003) has cogently presented the case that ceramic-age groups may have been regionally variable, in a critique of homogenetic approaches to understanding the trajectories of social development in the Greater Antilles.

9. The decrease of sites in this area during this period is accompanied by increases in sites in the island's mountainous interior, in the contemporary municipality of Utuado (Oliver 1992b, 1998; Oliver et al. 1999) just north of the western portion of the study area.

7

The Proto-Taíno Monumental *Cemís* of Caguana
A Political-Religious "Manifesto"

José R. Oliver

Without a doubt, Caguana is the iconographically most complex site thus far known in the Caribbean, albeit not the largest in terms of total area of public/ceremonial space (Siegel 1992, 1999). However, the rigorous study and analysis of Caguana's rich iconographic corpus has been slow to develop (Oliver 1981), even though 87 years have elapsed since it was first excavated by J. Alden Mason in 1915 (Mason 1917, 1941). But, by the early 1990s several papers and one monograph devoted to iconographic analyses and interpretations had been published (e.g., Oliver 1998; Roe 1993). Yet these studies remain known to a rather limited circle of Caribbean specialists, and mostly Spanish speaking. This chapter furnishes an excellent opportunity to highlight why Caguana should be of interest to archaeologists beyond the Antilles. To achieve this, the foregoing discussions are framed in terms of how elite political-religious power relates to, articulates with, and is manifested in Caguana's iconography, and how the Precolumbian Taíno people interacted with them. I am confident that readers will recognize "patterns of familiarity" pertinent to their own regional specialty. Power is, after all, a fundamental concept in human endeavor, past, present, and future. The iconography of Caguana has a story to tell, and it is largely about power and empowerment.

The Cultural Landscape of Caguana

The scenario for this chapter is the civic-ceremonial center of Caguana (coded Utu-10), located on an old and partly modified terrace above the

Tanamá River in Barrio Caguana, Municipality of Utuado, in northwestern Puerto Rico (Figure 7.1). Caguana is situated precisely at the boundary between the gently rolling igneous hills to the south and the abrupt karst hilly region to the north (Figures 7.2, 7.3) (Ford and Williams 1994:441–447, 507; Lugo et al. 2001; Picó 1975:69). The Tanamá alluvial terraces and colluvial deposits, where Utu-10 is located, were heavily cultivated with sugar cane in the 1930s, with its attendant consequences in the integrity of archaeological sites. Today, the karst region has almost entirely been reclaimed by a dense Humid Northern Karst Forest (Little et al. 1977) that is frequently perceived, incorrectly, as a "pristine" virgin forest.

The karst topography to the north of Caguana is characterized by a spectacular network of underground caves and rivers that occasionally surface at some locations only to disappear again under the landscape. Tall conical hills (*mogotes*) sprinkled throughout the region surround small circular depressions (dolines) formed by the differential erosion and solution of calcium carbonates (Ford and Williams 1994:441–447, 507).

The *mogotes* are home to numerous caves and rockshelters (Picó 1975:69-ss). Some caves were selected by Precolumbian natives as veritable canvases for painting pictographs with red, black, and/or brown pigments (Dávila 1980), for engraving petroglyphs, and/or for burying humans (Aitken 1917; Oliver et al. 1999; Oliver and Narganes Storde 2003). This cave-studded landscape provided the Taíno numerous gateways between the worlds of the ordinary surface and the extraordinary underground. For the Taíno it was from caves that humanity emerged (Pané 1999:5–6) and, judging by the archaeological data, caves were also the places to where some selected few would return upon death (Aitken 1917; Oliver et al. 1999). And it is also from caves that, according to Taíno mythology, bats, the souls of the nonliving beings (*opías*), emerged every night to roam through the forests and feast on the astringent but sweet guava fruits (*Psidium guajava*) (Pané 1999:18–19). This is why, in the darkness of the night, the Taíno "feared" to walk around the forest alone, lest they might chance an encounter with these dead spirit beings (*operitos, opías*) (Pané 1999:18–19).

The *mogotes* often present a profile that is replicated in the ubiquitous three-pointed stone objects (Figure 7.3), a sculptural shape that was probably imbued with supernatural *cemí* power (Figure 7.4). The karst landscape is more than simply a geomorphic province; it is a vibrant, dynamic (animistic) landscape full of meaning and symbolism (Saunders and Gray 1996). The limestone slabs framing the eastern row of the central plaza at Caguana, once containing about half of the iconography of the site, were quarried, cut, and transported from this karst domain. Likewise, the huge slabs framing the

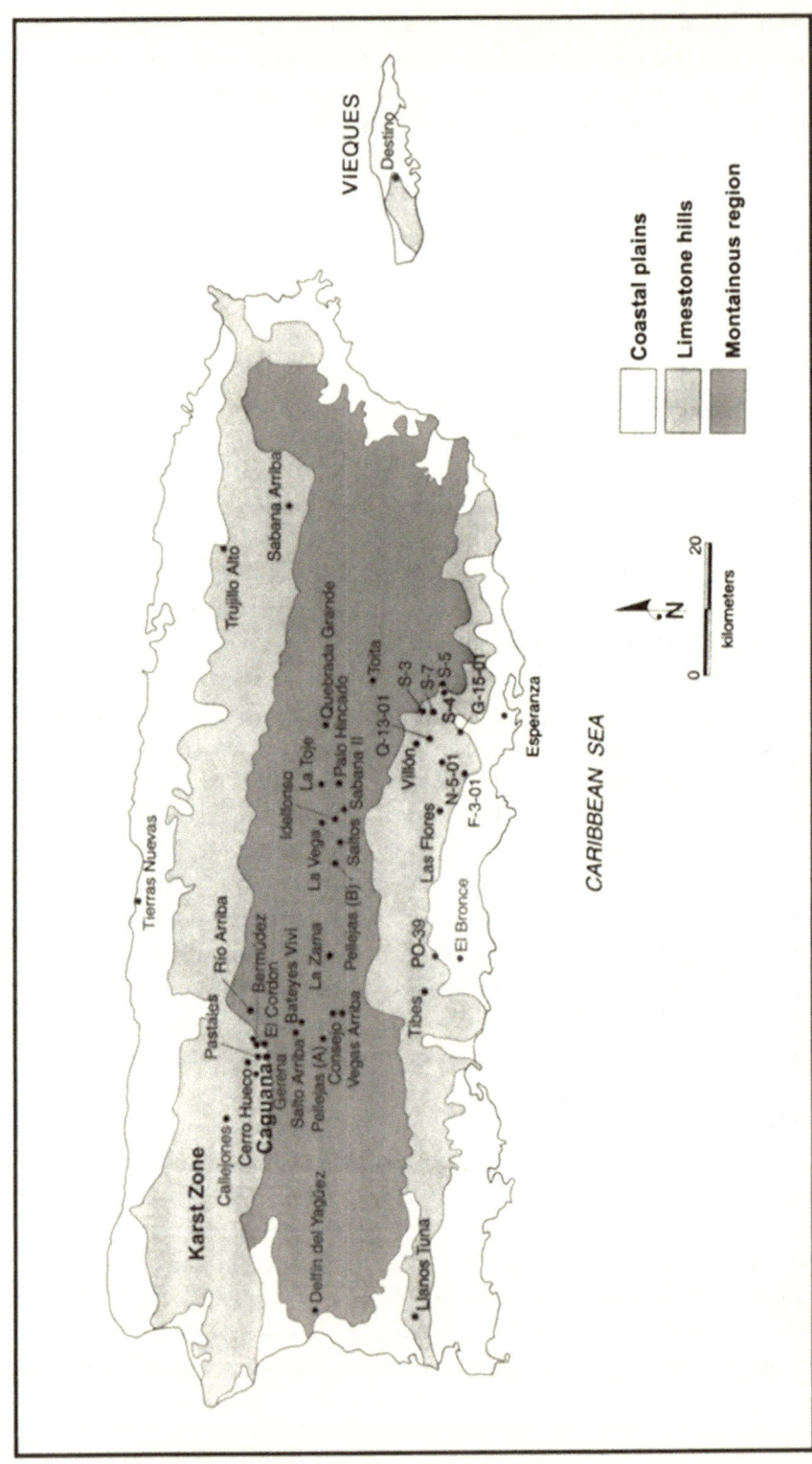

Figure 7.1. Locations of sites with stone-demarcated precincts (plazas and/or ball courts) in Puerto Rico (after Siegel 1999:Figure 4).

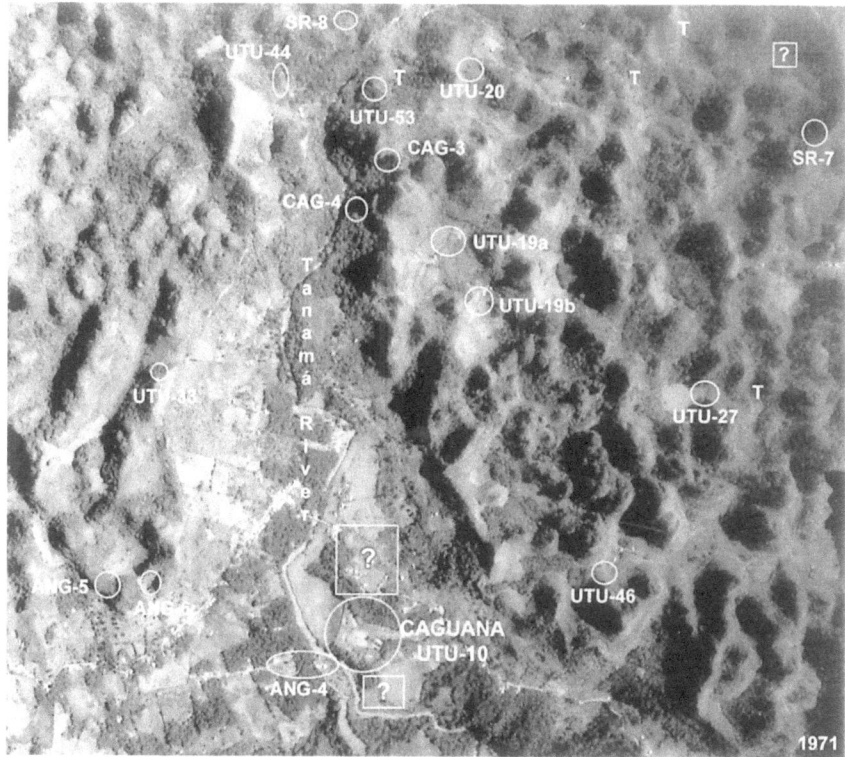

Figure 7.2. Locations of archaeological sites in the vicinity of Caguana (Site Utu-10). Aerial photo 1971. Autoridad de Carreteras de Puerto Rico. Circles and ovals: archaeological site. Squares with "?": confirmed ceremonial precincts, now destroyed. "T": surveyed agricultural terrace complexes. (Courtesy of Agamemnon Gus Pantel Tekakis)

longest of the rectangular precincts in Caguana were also brought down from this limestone domain drilled with caves, portals to the underworld.

By way of contrast, the gentle rolling hills to the south are devoid of any such natural crevices, caves, or passages to the underworld. The river networks meander above ground, its channels littered with metavolcanic rocks and boulders, and always subject to unannounced, dangerous flash floods. The Tanamá and Camuy rivers, originating to the south, flow northward through this landscape of gentle, rolling hills. The Tanamá River flows along the west side of the main plaza of Caguana. The western row of monoliths framing the central plaza of Caguana are all metavolcanic boulders selected and brought from the Tanamá riverbed. The main plaza incorporates stones from both the hilly karst and the riverine igneous landscape domains (Oliver 1998:205). This selective distribution of raw stone materials is not accidental,

Figure 7.3. View to the three-pointed karst hills northwest from the oval Plaza C, Caguana (Site Utu-10). In the background, the three-pointed Cerro El Cemí (compare to Figure 7.4) intimating that the landscape itself displays a sacred topography.

but partakes of the distinct symbolism embedded in these two contrasting landscapes (Oliver 1992a, 1992b, 1992c, 1998).

The river boulders were the main raw resource for the manufacture of many other stone-sculptured objects taken as emblematic of Taíno elite authority, such as the enigmatic spheroliths, elbow stones, stone "collars," elaborate three-pointed stones (Figure 7.4), and stone or *turén* seats (see Figure 7.9)

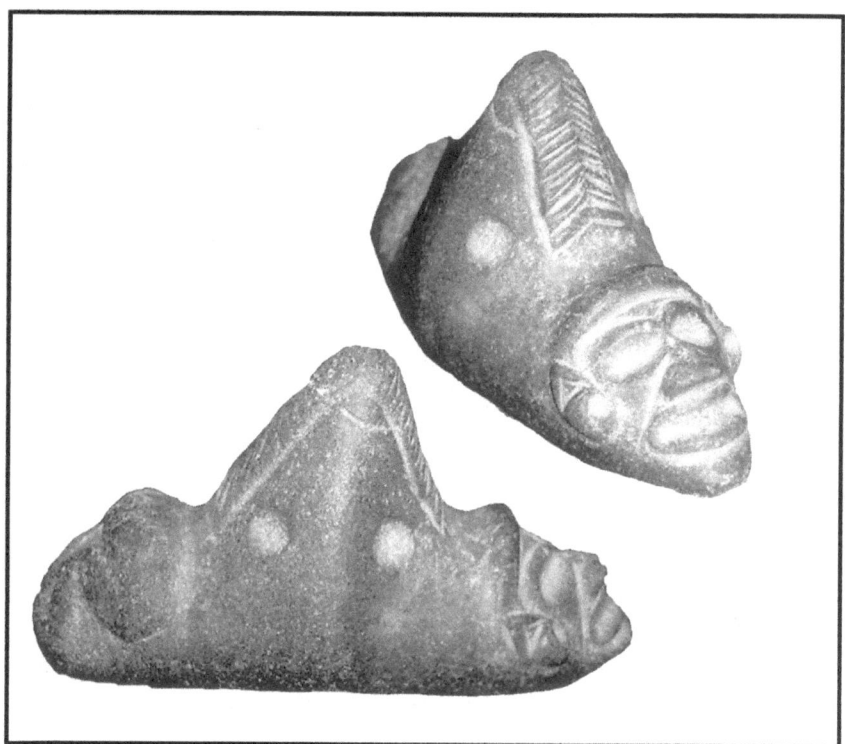

Figure 7.4. Two perspectives of a three-pointed stone carved from metavolcanic rock, from the valley of Caguas, eastern Puerto Rico (W. A. Géigel private collection).

(see Bercht et al. 1997; Walker 1995). Thus, riverbeds were sources of important, powerful objects deployed by the elite.

To date, some 30 archaeological sites of various types have been located in a 15-km² study area within the karst region to the north of Caguana. These range from simple habitation sites to vacant ball courts, and from burial caves and petroglyph stations to possible agricultural terrace complexes (Oliver et al. 1999; Rivera and Oliver 2003). Oddly, no archaeological sites have yet been discovered or reported within the igneous rolling hill landscape, although systematic archaeological surveys have yet to be implemented in this zone. However, it is highly probable that there are neither large nor densely nucleated village sites in the study area, presenting a sharp contrast to the traditional and prevailing semicircular, nucleated ("village") settlement pattern on the coastal plains and broad interior valleys of Puerto Rico (Lundberg 1985a; Oliver 2003; Rodríguez López 1990, 1992a). Habitation in the study region is dispersed and characterized by single household farmsteads. The core of the civic-ceremonial center of Caguana is no exception in regard to habitation: few house structures have been uncovered thus far (Mason 1941; Oliver 1998:15–19; Rivera Fontán 1992:20–28).

Liminality and articulation between different landscape units is an underlying theme in Caguana, one that is reproduced not only in the dichotomous selection of stones for the central plaza but also in the spatial distribution of all of its precincts, and by the thematic ordering and distribution of its iconography. The segregated segments and differentiated social strata that comprise proto-Taíno society, sources of potential tension, were ritually articulated in different ways through the *areíto* (chant/dance) and *batey* (ball game) ceremonies that took place in Caguana. Coherence and articulation to Caguana and its users, not to mention staying power, is to be found in its rich zoo- and anthropomorphic iconography. Of all the petroglyphs depicted in the central plaza, anthropomorphic personages in particular tell us much about Taíno notions of sociopolitical order. The "icons" engraved as petroglyphs are not merely passive, representational rock art, but indeed participating actors in the ceremonial activities taking place in the animated, built landscape of Caguana.

Different perspectives elicit different meanings from the polysemic iconographic ensemble of Caguana (Oliver 1981, 1992a, 1992b, 1992c, 1998; see also Roe 1993). However, one message to emerge is the pivotal role that the cacique (chief) played in the political-religious arena. Both the centrally located plaza and the centrally located icon of a "cemíified" cacique are situated at the axis of cosmos, articulating and mediating what amounts to segregated domains in the cultural and geographical landscape. Moreover, as I shall argue later, the "cemíified cacique" together with four other adjacent anthropomorphic icons (petroglyphs) amount to a proto-Taíno political-religious manifesto, an explicit visual statement of why things have always been and will always be the way they are. Even so, this manifesto is not to be taken merely as political propaganda to maintain or justify the status quo, the rule of caciques, but it also embodies all the elements of instability and change that are inherent to social inequality and chiefdom politics that took place in a frequently unpredictable world.

Cacicazgos and Civic-Ceremonial Centers

The civic-ceremonial center of Caguana must be approached as a site embedded within a framework of complex *cacicazgos* (chiefdoms), and to consider that its participants would have included members of all the social strata within the proto-Taíno and historic Taíno societies of Puerto Rico.[1] Politically, Caguana climaxed between A.D. 1300 and 1450, thus it is appropriate to judiciously use the rich sixteenth-century ethnohistoric documentation written by the Spanish on the Taíno.

With the lone exception of Roberto Cassá (1974, 1995), scholars are in agreement that the historic-period Taíno, and their immediate proto-Taíno ancestors, were organized into several *cacicazgos* of varying degrees of political integration and centralization (Curet 1996, 2002; Moscoso 1986, 1999; Oliver 1998; Redmond and Spencer 1994; Siegel 1999; Sued Badillo 1979b; Wilson 1990). During the initial Contact period (A.D. 1492–1510) there were some very powerful *cacicazgos,* such as Xaraguá in western Hispaniola (Wilson 1990) and Guaynía in southwestern Puerto Rico (Moscoso 1986:397–398; Sued Badillo 1985). At least five major chiefdoms were present in Hispaniola between A.D. 1492 and1503 (Fernández de Oviedo 1944 [1]:132–133; Book III, Chapter 4; Wilson 1990:14–16), although by 1497 at least three of them had collapsed under the weight of Spanish conquest (Wilson 1990). While Royal Chronicler, Fernández de Oviedo y Valdés (hereafter Oviedo), spoke of a single paramount chief for all Puerto Rico, in the *Relación del Memorial del Almirante* (ca. A.D. 1509–1510), Diego Colón insinuated that in Boriquén there were two paramount chiefs (Sued Badillo 2001:57). One was certainly Agüeybaná I (El Viejo), as Oviedo noted, and the other was most probably Guaybanex, ruler of the Caguas-Turabo drainage basins in eastern Puerto Rico.[2]

Research on the political history of Precolumbian Boriquén is still in its infancy to warrant detailed treatment here, although there are several studies that provide insights on the evolution and functioning of Taíno chiefdoms (e.g., Curet 2002; Moscoso 1986, 1999; Oliver 1998:28–49; Siegel 1999; Wilson 1990). Cacique Guarionex, who ruled somewhere in the Otoao (Utuado) region, has been traditionally regarded as the chief who probably ruled Caguana (Fewkes 1907:39; Mason 1941:264; Rouse 1992:113). However, this conclusion is not supported by ethnohistorical documentation. There is simply no information on the location of the seat and extent of Guarionex's chiefdom, and he was not the only cacique mentioned by the Spanish who resided within the province or region of Otoao (Oliver 1998:82–85). All we can document is that "Caguana" existed either as a site or region, as it was appended to the names of several Indian commoners (e.g., Juanillo de Caguana) in the lists of *encomiendas* (assignments) dating to 1515–1519 (Tanodi 1971:125). The Spanish documents never mentioned "Caguana" or a ruling cacique in connection with a major civic-ceremonial center such as Utu-10. In short, no specific cacique can be securely linked to Caguana, nor did the Spanish acknowledge the presence of a major civic-ceremonial center by that or any other name in the region that today we know as Caguana. All evidence suggests that Caguana was abandoned prior to the arrival of the Spanish in 1508.

There is better information about the antecedents of Caguana. To date, there is one site that predates Caguana, and which exhibits the same level and degree of architectural complexity. The civic-ceremonial center of Tibes (Figure 7.5) is situated next to the Portugués River, on the outskirts of Ponce, and at the edge of the semiarid, intermediate limestone hills of southern Puerto Rico (Alvarado Zayas 1981; González Colón 1984). Current evidence, although preliminary, does suggest that Tibes began as a simple early Saladoid village (ca. 200 B.C. to A.D. 600) characterized by a semicircular ring of (domestic) refuse middens and a single, unmarked, multifunctional central plaza (Curet and Rodríguez Gracia 1995; Curet, personal communication 2002; Oliver 1992b, 1998:38–40). This plaza also functioned as a burial ground (González Colón 1984). But by A.D. 900 or perhaps somewhat later, it further developed into the largest civic-ceremonial center known in Puerto Rico at that time (Curet and Rodríguez Gracia 1995; Oliver 1998:38–47).

By this time, pottery style had changed (into early Ostionoid) and Tibes' main plaza ceased to be a locus of human burials. A large quadrangular plaza framed by igneous river boulders was built over and beyond the confines of the ancient, unmarked circular Saladoid plaza. Seven additional rectangular courts were constructed around the periphery of the quadrangular plaza, along with a circular (star-shaped) court, adjacent to the central plaza (Figure 7.5). The central plaza also concentrated the largest number of petroglyphs found in the site. Tibes appears to have declined sometime between A.D. 1200 and 1300, precisely when Caguana (ca. A.D. 1200–1450) was in ascendancy (Oliver 1992c, 1998:37–46). Was Caguana somehow implicated in the decline of Tibes, perhaps as a succeeding seat of chiefly power? Or was it also symptomatic of broader, far-reaching political-religious changes throughout Boriquén, an island-wide realignment of political leadership and of territorial boundaries?

For our purposes, two relevant facts cannot be disputed. First, the spatial arrangement of the precincts in Tibes (Figure 7.5) is nearly a duplicate of Caguana (Figure 7.6); the former may have served as a blueprint for the latter. Second, once the stone-demarcated central plaza was constructed, this space would no longer be used as a burial ground. Instead, petroglyphs framed this central communal space. In Caguana, the central plaza never contained human burials, and like Tibes, it concentrated the iconography in its eastern and western rows of monoliths. These observations will gain significance when the iconography of Caguana is analyzed in detail later on.

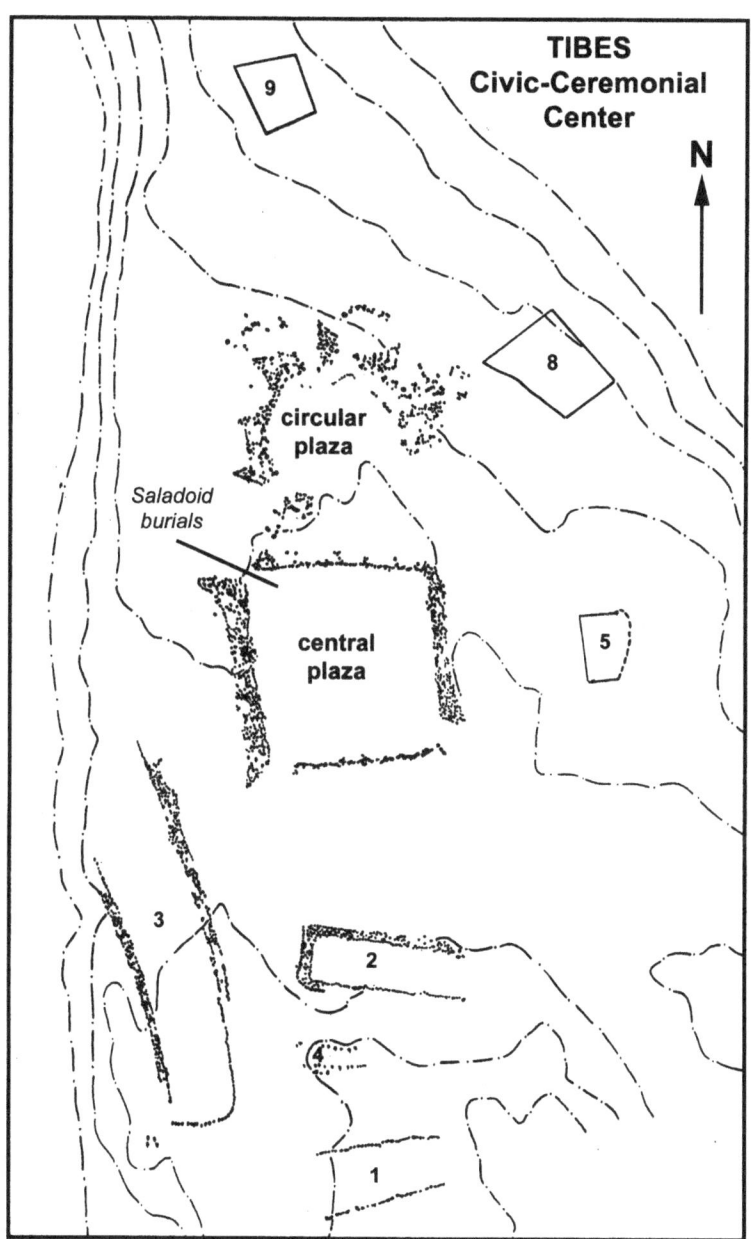

Figure 7.5. Map of the stone-demarcated precincts of Tibes, Ponce (after Oliver 1998:Figura 24).

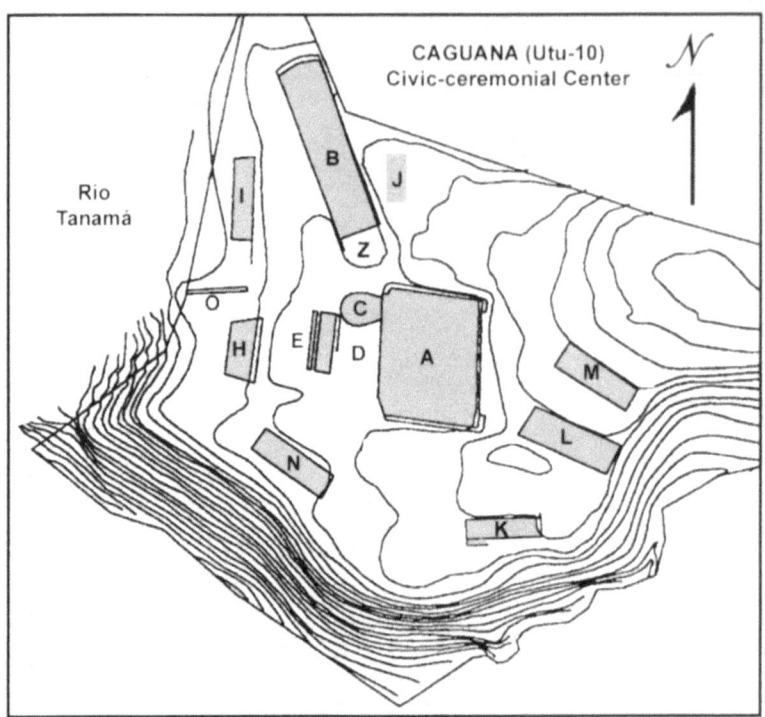

Figure 7.6. Contour map of Caguana (Site Utu-10) locating the various reconstructed precincts, after reconstruction directed by Ricardo E. Alegría in the 1960s.

There are differences in the techniques of selecting, shaping, and setting the slabs and boulders framing the precincts between both sites. The most glaring difference is on the iconographic style and organization (sequencing) of petroglyphs along each row in their respective central plazas. The iconography at Tibes did not develop the artistic Taíno canon so evident at Caguana. Tibes' iconographic ensemble also lacks the order and thematic coherence that characterizes Caguana, suggesting that a succinct, well-structured iconographic political-religious "manifesto" took some time to develop. The crystallization of an official, overt iconographic style lagged behind the actual development of social inequality and centralized chiefdom politics.

Tibes' primacy declined after A.D. 1200 for as yet unknown but apparently nonviolent reasons. The climax period of political-religious power of Caguana is framed between approximately A.D. 1300 and 1450 or 1460. These 150 or so years represent the height of Caguana's maturity, even though there is evidence from pottery style, not iconography or architecture, that the site's origin could be as early as A.D. 1000. Regardless of when the first precincts were constructed, what remains visible today represents Caguana at its peak, just before its abandonment. Caguana's decline seems to have been peaceful: it did not involve the mutilation of petroglyphs or the destruction of precincts. Its decline was probably the result of internal, native politics, rather than as a direct consequence of the initial Spanish conquest of Puerto Rico (in A.D. 1508–1519), although local politics may have been indirectly influenced by the Spanish-Taíno conflicts raging in Hispaniola by A.D. 1494–1497 (Wilson 1990).

What can we learn about the people who ruled over and participated in the ceremonies conducted in Caguana during its climax period, just before its abandonment, ca. A.D. 1450–1460? After all, it was Caguana's proto-Taíno community that ceremonially and ritually interacted with these monumental and numinous icons engraved in stones framing the central plaza. The question of "Who were the social actors in Caguana?" needs to be addressed if we are to elicit the range of meanings from the iconographic ensemble.[3]

The Political Elite: Caciques and Nitaínos

By the time Columbus arrived in San Salvador in A.D. 1492, Taíno societies were already stratified into first/second order *cacicazgos,* with social classes of sorts: cacique (chief), *nitaíno* (elite), *behique, bohíte,* or *buhuittihu* (shaman, medicine-man), and *naboría* (commoner) (Oliver 1998:64–82). Paramount chiefs had subordinated chiefs, sometimes large numbers of them. Bartolomé de Las Casas reported that paramount chieftess Anacaona of Xaraguá (today's Haiti) had some 300 subordinated "caciques" under her command (Sued Badillo 1985:30), 40 to 80 of which were almost certainly second-order chiefs (Las Casas 1929 [1]:164–165, Chapter IX). The duties of a cacique were succinctly spelled out in the Taíno myth pertaining to Guahayona's Journey cycle. It told of how, in primordial times, Mácocael (Without-Eyelids-Son) failed to become a cacique because he neglected his duties of how to "guard, give orders and redistribute" labor and resources (Oliver 2000:215; Pané 1999:6).

Caciques were followed in status by an elite designated as nitaíno. The nitaíno were described by the Spanish as *cosmógrafos,* or surveyors of the *cacicazgo,* charged with gathering data and informing the cacique of the state of affairs of the polity (Curet 1992b:71; Moscoso 1986:325). The nitaíno executed orders and implemented policies emanating directly from the cacique and, when circumstance required, from accords undertaken in council meetings.

Nitaínos organized the commoner labor into work gangs to perform tasks ranging from food production and manufacture to seafaring trade expeditions and warfare. Indeed, the Spanish took advantage of this native system of labor organization, when implementing the short-lived *repartimiento* and *encomienda* systems in the very early conquest years, when placer gold mining was the principal colonial economic activity (Anderson-Córdova, this volume; Moya Pons 1987; Sued Badillo 2001).[4]

Elites were distinguished from commoners in a variety of ways. Caciques were entitled to special foods, such as *xauxau* (or *xabxao*), a fine, pure starch cassava bread, and iguana meat (*Iguana iguana;* perhaps *Cyclura* sp. also?) (Mártir de Anglería 1964 [1516] cited in Oliver 1998:69; Las Casas 1929 [3]:444, Chapter XI). The accouterments of the caciques and nitaíno elites, when in full regalia, also distinguished them from all other social strata (Alegría 1995). One emblem exclusively worn by the cacique was the *guaíza,* meaning "rostrum" or "face," which the Spanish called *caratonas* (large facemasks). The same Taíno term, *guaíza,* also means "soul of the living," in contrast to "soul of the nonliving" (*ma-opíya*). As an artifact, a *guaíza* could be fashioned into a plaque that was either fastened to the forehead or hung from a necklace on the chest (a pectoral) of the cacique. *Guaízas* made of wood, stone, or shell were often covered with hammered *caona* (gold) sheets; in other cases only the eyes-mouths of the icon were inlaid with gold or encrusted with marine shells (Figure 7.7). Still other *guaízas* were made of imported *guanín,* a copper-gold-silver alloy, available only from mainland South America (Bray 1997; Oliver 2000; Siegel and Severin 1993). Large ear spools (*taguagua*), made of *caona* (pure gold) or guanín were also markers of both age and rank.

Another important chiefly emblem was the stone-bead necklace, or cibas (stones), which could also be combined with carved shell beads or plaques (separators; Figure 7.8). Descriptions of chiefly accouterments are invaluable in identifying the rank and status of the zoo- and anthropomorphic petroglyphs of Caguana (Oliver 1998:66–67; 2000). As we shall see, it is in the head and face that the monumental *cemí* icons of Caguana and human beings display their social status.

In life, caciques and elites could also afford (and needed) to be polygamous, thus extending their household's network of political alliances through marriage (Curet 2002; Keegan and MacLachlan 1989; Keegan et al. 1993; Wilson 1990). Upon death, caciques received elaborate burial treatment. They would be interred in an underground roofed burial chamber with some of their most precious "jewels." The body would be wrapped in a cotton bandage (or a hammock) and seated on a *duho,* alongside cassava bread and other offerings (Oviedo 1944 [1]:243–244, Book V, Chapter III; Oviedo in

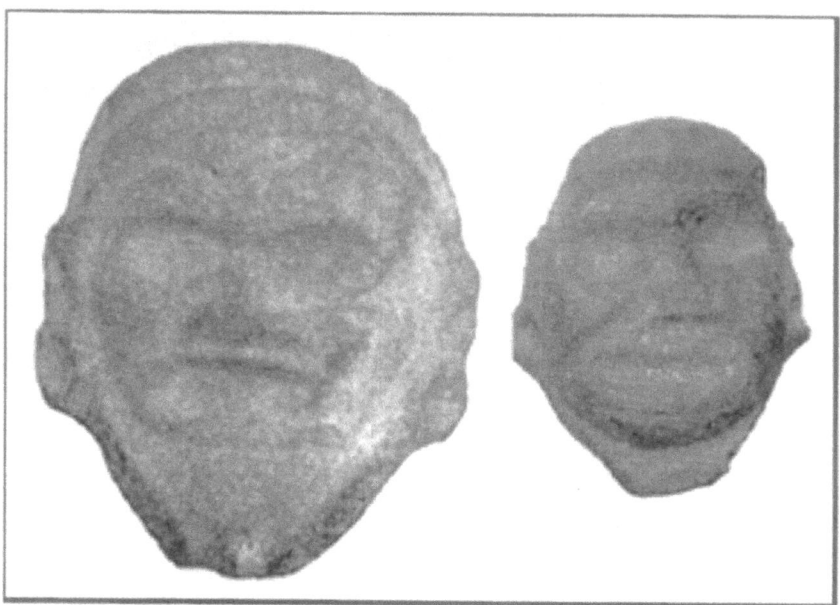

Figure 7.7. A pair of igneous stone *guaízas* (masks) from Puerto Rico (Museum of Art and Anthropology, University of Puerto Rico).

Fernández Méndez 1973:84). Commoners were instead "buried in tombs in the countryside, away from their houses, because of the fear there was of ghosts" (Las Casas 1929 [3]:566–567, Chapter CCIV). In the case of paramount Chief Behechio's death in Xaraguá, his principal wife along with two secondary wives were sacrificed and buried with him, although Oviedo (1944 [1]:244, Book V, Chapter III) clearly noted that this was an atypical funerary practice (see also Veloz Maggiolo 1973:64–72). The funerary *requiem* festivities of an important chief involved the performance of ceremonial chants and dances (*areítos*) by the locals who were joined by: "many others from the region [and] other principal caciques that came to honor him. [It was] among these foreign caciques that the *bienes muebles* [estate] of the deceased cacique were distributed" (Oviedo 1944 [1]:244, Book V, Chapter 3).

That a good portion of the "estate" of the deceased chief would *not* be interred or inherited by the heir to the office, but redistributed among other

Figure 7.8. An incised necklace separator made from *Strombus* spp. shell from Site Utu-27 (dated A.D. 1350–1450).

"foreign" caciques is significant. It is an indication of how important political alliances were for the heir in guaranteeing his/her ascendancy and success as a cacique. It also implies that a portion of the material wealth of the deceased cacique would remain in circulation, among which probably included such portable objects as *cemís*. The latter included *duhos* (seats; e.g., Figure 7.10), wooden *cohoba*-idol-plates, elaborately carved three-pointed objects, stone collars, and elbow stones.

It is the relationship between the elites and the class of numinous and powerful objects commonly known as *cemís* that is central to identifying and decoding the meaning of Caguana's iconography. Taíno concepts of the *cemí* and its relationship to chiefly power are at the core of the meaning of the biomorphic (petroglyph) iconographic ensemble at Caguana, and of the ceremonial activities that took place in the central plaza.[5]

The *Behiques*

Shamans' (*behique, bohíte,* or *buhuittihu*) access to the numinous and their knowledge about nature and the supernatural distinguished them from other members of society (Deive 1978, 1983; Moscoso 1986:329; Pané 1999:19–25).

The term "cemí" literally means sweetness. Elsewhere I have shown that *cemí* is linked not only to sweet things, sweet fragrances, but also to bats and shamans, forming a metaphorical and symbolic chain of references to the "supernatural" forces (Oliver 1998:72–73; on the significance of bats and owls see Arrom 1988; García Arévalo 1988; Morbán Laucer 1988). In sum, notions of shamanism are closely related to the concept of *cemí*.

Behiques were highly respected by the community, perhaps some even feared. Powerful and ambitious *behiques* may have been potential competitors of caciques in the political-religious arena, although the Spanish never recorded an instance where a *behique* had usurped the office of cacique. Since caciques also had to be great shamans, there has been some debate as to the precise roles that each played, and to what extent these overlap (see Deive 1978, 1983; Siegel 1999). The agenda of a cacique in a *cabildo* (council) meeting and *cohoba* (hallucinogen snuffing) ceremony had to do with the politics of governance and the collective well-being of his subjects throughout the *cacicazgo*. To do so, a cacique had to access the supernatural, namely the numinous *cemís*. Ecstasy and shamanistic flight were required by caciques and nitaínos in order to be able to make decisions about, or divine the future of, policies affecting the chiefdom.

By way of contrast, the *behique's* sphere of action revolved around the physical-spiritual health and welfare of individuals (Pané 1974, 1999). Their principal task was to cure by determining what taboos or rules a patient had violated, which supernatural forces were implicated, and how these should be placated. And this the *behiques* also achieved by performing the same ritual activities of the *cohoba* ceremony. While the *cohoba* ceremony led by a *behique* followed a similar, if not identical, ritual formula to that performed by caciques and nitaínos, the purposes for engaging in shamanistic flight were different. In some public ceremonies a *behique* would take an active leading role. Curiously, there is no documentary evidence that explicitly points to *behiques* as leading in two of the most important public Taíno ceremonies: the *areíto* and the *batey* (ball game).

Like the elite, *behiques* also cared for *cemís*. Some of these were minimally modified and used for curing/protecting patients. Others probably were entirely made of unmodified raw materials, such as pebbles or rocks. *Behiques* also handled elaborately sculptured and powerful *cemís*, particularly those associated with the *cohoba* ceremony. It is not clear whether some of the powerful *cemí*-objects were in the exclusive care of the *behique* or were entrusted to him from the arsenal of *cemís* under the control of a cacique and/or nitaíno. There were probably instances of both.

The Rest of Them—*Naborías*

At the bottom of the Taíno society were the commoners, collectively designated as *naboría,* a term literally meaning "the rest of them" (Moscoso 1986:330–355; Oliver 1998:64–82; Redmond and Spencer 1994:Table 1). By early Spanish conquest they were also referred to as house servants (*naborías de casa*) or as "slaves," both terms having led to much discussion among scholars (Oliver 1998:81–82). The *naboría* comprised the majority of the population, perhaps more than nine out of every ten individuals (Moscoso 1986:348).

The Powers of Sweetness—*Cemí*

The exercise of political-religious power by Taíno chiefs and elites is rooted in a reciprocal, yet asymmetrical, relationship with the numinous *cemí*. *Cemí* is primarily a conceptual quality (i.e., sweetens); it does not need to be transformed into an object (artifact). *Cemí* is not equivalent to a morphologically unique class of artifacts. It is better to think of this word as an adjective or adverb than a noun. However, a variety of artifacts could be and were imbued with *cemí*. The monumental iconography (petroglyphs) engraved in Caguana's monoliths, I will argue, are also imbued with *cemí*. This is especially important since many archaeologists think of "cemí" simply as a class of artifacts.

Cemíism entails a corpus of Taíno beliefs about supernatural and multinatural (Viveiros de Castro 2001) forces that had immediate impact upon ordinary people in an ordinary world. *Cemís* are implicated in the affairs of the here and now (Reichel-Dolmatoff 1975:5–6). The overt form (body) of the *cemí* is multiple and diverse. Their immediacy and meddling in the ordinary Taíno world made them agents of causality. All sorts of daily happenstances were attributable, in part, to *cemí* activity. *Cemís* were causal agents, thus they needed to be controlled by humans to obtain desirable outcomes, although without guarantees that the outcomes would be forthcoming. A lot depended on the state of power relations between the *cemís* and their human owners.

The Taíno often portrayed *cemís* as unpredictable and potentially dangerous forces. In nature, their formal "outer skins" concealed their supernatural and spiritual essence (i.e., they were perceived as "beings"). In this sense *cemís* were numinous entities. But, *cemí* was not merely an abstract, generalized concept of everything that was numinous and powerful. Each *cemí* wielded a distinct, highly individualized sphere of power. Their power was often associated with meteorological phenomena: rain, drought, hurricane winds, thunder, clouds, storms, and so on. Some *cemís* also involved ideas of "seminal energy," the ability to reproduce and sustain plants, animals, and humans. Others were manifestations of numinous forces emanating from the domain of the nonliving (dead, ancestors). *Cemís* were also guardians of cosmic order and/or generators of chaos and destruction (see Oliver 1998:110–118).

The Objectification and Materiality of "Cemí"

A *cemí* was frequently manifested in numerous guises in nature (e.g., rock, animal, or tree). Pané observed that,

> they had many cemís of different kinds. Some contained the bones of their father, and of their mother, and of their relatives, and of their ancestors, which are made of stone or wood. There are many of both kinds; there were some that spoke, and others that germinate the things [the Taínos] eat, and others that make rain, and still others that make the winds blow. . . . The stone cemís come in different shapes. There are some that the medicine-men extract from the [patient's] body . . . [which] are said by the patients to be the best for aiding pregnant women in birthing. There are others that speak and have the shape of a thick turnip . . . [and still] others that are three-pointed which they believe make *yuca* [manioc] grow [Pané 1974:34–35, 43; see also Pané 1999:21, 26].

These uncanny manifestations are contextual (place/time) and relational (subject/object). A potential encounter with *cemí* may occur to any ordinary Taíno walking through a forest, who may sense an unusual movement of a branch, an unexpected stench from a rotten fruit, the sudden appearance of a rare bird, the presence of an oddly shaped river boulder that was not there before, or any other sensorial experience that was unusual for that particular environment and that specific time. According to Pané's account, a *behique* was called upon to interpret the significance of uncanny *cemí* manifestations by engaging the *cemí*. Further, *cemís* were transformed into artifacts. As Fray Pané wrote,

> when someone [walking] along a path says that he saw a tree that moved the root, then with great fear he stops and asks it who it is. And it responds, "Call the *behique* for me and he will tell you who I am," And that man, having gone to the said medicine-man, tells him what

he has seen. And then the sorcerer or witch-doctor runs immediately to see the tree that the other man spoke about and performs the *cohoba* [hallucinogenic snuffing ceremony].... The cohoba concluded, he [the shaman] rises to his feet and recites to it all its titles, as if it were a great lord, and he asks: "Tell me who you are, what are you doing here, what do you want from me, and why have you sent for me? Tell me if you want me to cut [fell] you, or if you want to come with me, and how do you want me to carry you [that] I will build a house and a garden for you." Then that tree or cemí, made into an idol or a devil, responds by telling him the form in which it wants to be made. He cuts it [the *cemí*-tree] in the manner he was ordered; he builds it a house and a garden, and many times during the year he performs the cohoba [Pané 1974:43; see also Pané 1999:26].[6]

Any medium in nature would potentially become objectified in this manner and shaped into an icon. The monumental petroglyphs of Caguana were probably the result of similarly context-specific encounters with particular *cemís,* which were then pecked and engraved into iconographic designs. The iconography followed the specific stylistic rules that the shaman discovered through hallucinogenic trance. The iconographic forms were objectified through a culturally defined artistic canon that archaeologists recognize as a "classic" Taíno art style. However, not all the *cemí* manifestations were transformed into artifacts. In some instances the unusual characteristics (e.g., shape, odor, color, resplendence) of the materials imbued with *cemí* would not require any transformation.

Cemís and Altered States of Consciousness (ASC)

Any sensorial experience with the uncanny in nature is insufficient to infer that a *cemí* is manifested. To ascertain its numinous presence, shamanistic knowledge and the *cohoba* ceremony are required. The inhalation of *cohoba* (*Anadenanthera peregrina*) allows shamanistic flight to occur and enables the *behique* to apprehend the numinous *cemí* (Las Casas 1929 [3]:546, Chapter CLXVI; Pané 1999:21; see also Oliver 1998:76). The *behique* establishes a dialogue with "it." In effect, the "it" is not a thing but a personified being. The *behique* speaks to a tree root with more senses engaged than just aural vocalization. Not *any* root, or bird, or rock, in nature would do, rather it has to be one imbued with *cemí*.[7] The "it" (*cemí*) becomes a "he" or "she," an animated being with humanlike properties and personhood. This view is consistent with Alfred Gell's (1998) theories of art and agency regarding "art objects" (he calls indexes) and his concepts of "distributed person" and "extended mind."

Research into Altered States of Consciousness (ASC) indicates that the ecstatic experience may synaptically transform ordinarily inanimate things in nature into sentient beings (Clottes and Lewis-Williams 1998:12–99; Harner 1973; Pearson 2002:29–40; Reichel-Dolmatoff 1978; see also Gregory 1998:194–200). While in an ecstatic trance, associations of particular odors, sights, tastes, sounds, and so on, can trigger memory associations (engrams) of place, events, or situations that may or may not have occurred in the past. Sensorial stimuli can become "enriched" as in the rare case of synaesthesia, where sound is color and vision is taste (Carter 1998:173–180), a phenomenon that can be triggered during hallucinatory trances.[8] Equally common in the early stages of ASC is entopic phenomena, including visualization of luminous shapes (phosphenes), such as light dots, that are universal, although meanings are culturally conditioned (Lewis-Williams 2002:121–130). Although impossible to prove, the dot cluster motif is a common element in rock art in Puerto Rico and is also found in monoliths framing ceremonial plazas (Figure 7.9).

Moreover, to achieve a hallucinatory state it is not necessary to ingest an active psychotropic drug like *cohoba*. Certain repetitive external stimuli, like drumming or the flashing of a strobe of light, may also induce a hallucinatory state. For example, the visionary and dreamy (ASC) states in a patient have been registered in the theta wavelength in an electroencephalogram. This is precisely the same wavelength frequency and amplitude (theta) produced by, for example, the repetitive drumming in Haitian voodoo ceremonies. The theta wavelength stimulus appears to block the sequential processing function of the left lobe of the brain (responsible for logical, rational thought) thus allowing the right lobe (responsible for the holistic, intuitive, and visionary consciousness) to become dominant (Dr. A. L. Oliver, personal communication 2002; see also Carter 1998). The relevance of this information will be appreciated when the Taíno drumming, dancing, and chanting ceremonies known as *areítos* are discussed in relation to the "decoding" of the iconography in Caguana.

The combination of *cohoba* with appropriate external stimuli such as drumming and chanting created the ideal environment in which the rapprochement between *cemís* and humans could be realized. It was in such an ambiance that the iconographic "beings" of Caguana literally became animated and active participants. As such, Caguana's petroglyphs did not just represent a static portrait of a *cemí;* they were *cemí*.

Once objectified, *cemís* would fall into the hands of a human trustee.

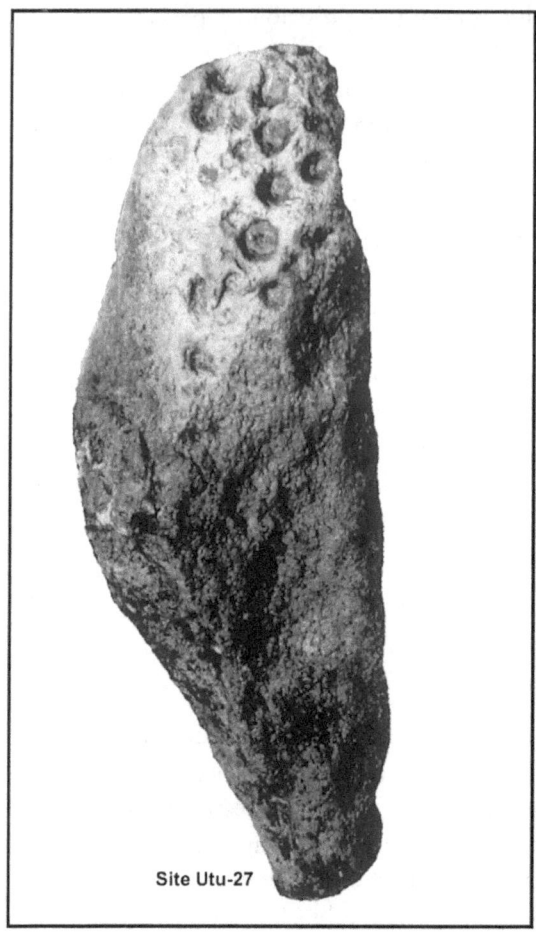

Figure 7.9. A limestone monolith from Site Utu-27. At the top, it displays multiple carved dots, possibly reproducing *cohoba*-induced phosphene patterns.

These *cemís* came in a variety of shapes and materials, and each had different kinds and degrees of powers to wield. Perceived as animated and as organized in society, these beings were ranked according to their power, status, and seniority (ancestry and antiquity), just as in Taíno society. Each *cemí* bore a personal name and title, and indeed had a personal history, just as did every Taíno individual. The Taíno knew the individual history of each objectified *cemí*. The deeds and achievements accrued through a *cemí*'s lifetime (as a materialized object) would thus build its reputation, along with those of its trustees, becoming the stuff of oral legend and lore. Sadly, the vast majority of the *cemís*' personal histories have been lost forever. Fortunately, not all is lost, since the individual histories of one dozen powerful *cemí*-objects from the Taíno chiefdoms Macorix and Maguá in Hispaniola were recorded by Fray Ramón Pané between 1494 and 1497 (see Arrom's forestudy in Pané 1974, 1999; also Arrom 1997).

The Dual Structure of *Cemís* of Maguá-Macorix-Maguá

Fray Ramón Pané (1974, 1999) provides us with an entrée into the organization and legends of a set of *cemís*. In so doing, we are afforded the opportunity to understand the iconographic organization of Caguana's petroglyphs. The structural correspondence between the *cemís* of Hispaniola and Caguana suggests that the same may apply throughout the Greater Antilles.

Stevens-Arroyo (1988) was the first to propose that the 12 *cemís* exhibited a moiety structure or dual order in their organization, through an analysis of their essential characteristics as described by Pané (Table 7.1). Subsequently, I further elaborated upon Stevens-Arroyo's analysis (Oliver 1992b, 1992c, 1998:110–118). One moiety, the "Fruitful Order," included six *cemís* whose principal characteristics were potentially beneficial for ordinary humans. Six other *cemís*, whose qualities were inherently dangerous, belonged to the other moiety, here labeled the "Inverse Order." In addition to a moiety structure, the Hispaniolan *cemís* exhibited a quadripartite, hierarchical structure of high-ranking and low-ranking *cemís*. The hierarchical ranking of *cemís* paralleled Taíno society, reinforcing a concept of socially stratified cultural entities. We shall see that this quadripartite structure underlies, too, the organization of Caguana's iconography.

In sum, the objectified *cemís* of Hispaniola had personal names; were accorded specific statuses and ranks; had genealogical histories, which were linked to their human owners; and accrued prestige. For the Taínos, *cemís* were indeed personified beings. Each one was endowed with a social persona, which was not merely a generalized abstraction, but rather perceived by the Taíno to be an individualized being that lived and acted in society. The relationship between *cemís* and elites (cacique, nitaíno) is of interest, as this has a bearing on the significance of the monumental petroglyph-*cemís* of Caguana.

Caciques and *Cemís:* An Asymmetry of Interlocked Powers

A significant portion of the political economy of a Taíno cacique centered on staple wealth (vast agricultural fields) and prestige items (Moscoso 1986, 1999). This material wealth could only be assured through the cacique's negotiation, manipulation, and interaction with the appropriate contingent of

Table 7.1. The Quadripartite Structure of the *Cemís* of Hispaniola.

Generative Principle	Moiety Order of Fruitfulness	Moiety Order of Inversion
Masculine high-rank *cemís*	**Yokahú Guamá** . . . [etc.] Lord of Fertility & Abundance	**Maquetauire Guayaba** Lord of the Dead
twin auxiliary *cemís*	**Baibrama & Baraguabael** Guardians of *naborías* Replenishers of cultigens, fish, animals and wild plants	**Opiyel-guobirán & Cocorote** Guardians of souls of dead and of the night-forest; libidinous excess, picaresque
Feminine high-rank *cemís*	**Attabey Guácar** . . . [etc.] Lord of Fecundity & Abundance	**Guabancex** Lord of Hurricanes
twin auxiliary *cemís*	**Boinayel & Máhoru** Guardians of beneficial rainfall and calm, sunny, bright weather	**Coatrisquie & Guataúba** Harbingers of Thunder, violent storms, floods and destructive weather

Note. After Oliver (1998:111, Table 5) and Stevens-Arroyo (1988:Table 7).

cemís under that chief's control. For important matters involving decisions of governance, the Taíno elites gathered in council at the chief's *caney* (elite house) to engage with the *cemís*. In the privacy of the caney, the cacique began the *cohoba* ceremony to negotiate with the *cemís* and determine whether his policies would be sanctioned, or to divine what the future held in store, and thus act accordingly. Bishop Las Casas witnessed *cohoba* rituals and also provided samples of the agenda for such council meetings:

> I sometimes saw them celebrate the *cohoba*. . . . The first one to begin was the *Señor,* and while he did it [snuffing] the rest would remain silent. Having inhaled his cohoba [Figure 7.11] . . . while seating in some low and very richly sculptured benches, that they call *duhos* [Figure 7.10], he would remain for a while with his head leaning to one side and his arms resting on his knees. Then he raised his head, with his face looking to the sky, and spoke truthful words, which must have been their prayers to the true God, or the one they had for their god. Then the others responded as when we say "Amen." This they did with notorious voice and sound. Then they thanked him [the *cemí*], and must

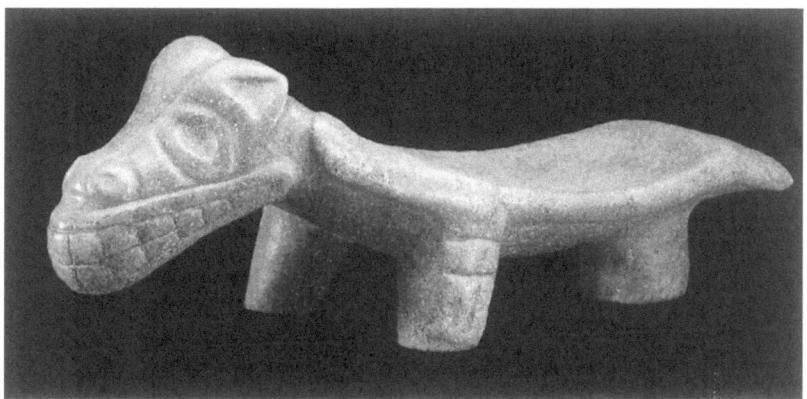

Figure 7.10. The "Duho Oliver," from Dos Bocas Region, Utuado. This stone seat (*turén*) is carved in red marble. The "doglike" creature is very similar to Petroglyph 2 in Figure 7.16 (Instituto de Cultura Puertorriqueña).

have said so in flattering words, thus capturing his [the *cemí*s] benevolence. Then they [the *nitaíno* councilors] begged him [the cacique] to tell them what he had seen. And he would give account of his vision, telling them that the *Cemí* had spoken to him and had confirmed good or adverse times [to come], or that they would have children, or that theirs [the children] would die, or that there would be a conflict or war against their neighbors [Las Casas 1929 [3]:546, Chapter CLXVI].

The political-religious importance of the *cemí*-objects is evident in the way in which caciques bragged about having the best and most powerful ones and how the caciques engaged in stealing the *cemís* from each other. Fernando Colón noted that,

the caciques and their people boasted of having better *cemís* than others [have]. And when they enter into the house where the *cemís* are, they are guarded [hidden] from the Christians and they [Indians] do not let them enter the house. On the contrary, if they suspect of their [Spanish] arrival, they take the *cemís* and hide them in the forests, for fear that they would be taken from them. And what is most hilarious, they have the custom among themselves of stealing the *cemí* from each other [Colón in Pané 1974:89].

Bishop Las Casas echoes Colón:

Figure 7.11. An anthropomorphic *cohoba* inhalator (tubes are lacking), from La Cucama cemetery, Juan Dolio, Santo Domingo (Fundación García Arévalo, Inc.).

they [caciques] bragged about having the most glorious [by] saying that they had the best Cemís, [better] than those from other towns and *Señores,* and they tried to steal them from each other and thus took great care in guarding these statues or idols, or whatever they were, from other Indians from other kingdoms and *señoríos* [Las Casas 1929 [3]:526, Chapter CXX].

The frequency of such acts of "thievery" strongly indicates the level of intensity of factional competition, which I suspect was not just restricted to chiefly lineages from different polities, but was also between chiefs and politically ambitious nitaíno factions within the same *cacicazgo*. To exercise power a cacique had to demonstrate his capability to directly control these powerful *cemís* and also to retain them under his trust. Without the *cemís*, caciques would not be able to make decisions of policy on any matters concerning governance of the *cacicazgo*.

Based on my interpretation of the ethnohistoric texts discussed above, the following argument can be proposed. Since everyone, from *nitaíno* to *naboría*, knew precisely the pedigree, reputation, power, and legends (history) that any given *cemí* had accrued over its lifetime, it makes sense to infer that not even a paramount cacique could order, as needed, the manufacture of a *cemí* to suit his needs (or shortcomings). The most powerful *cemís* were in large measure powerful because of their long histories, including the string of prior human trustees (powerful ancestors). You cannot create on the spot an antique, senior *cemí*. Chiefs bragging about having the most powerful *cemís* can only work up to a point. Ancient (senior) *cemís* with proven reputations and reputable human owners would be coveted by lesser chiefs whose *cemís* were not as powerful. There would have been numerous circumstances and reasons for stealing powerful *cemís* from other chiefs and elites.

Although the "theft" of *cemís* almost certainly intensified in response to the crises of political power vacuums engendered by the Spanish conquest and diseases, it is probable that such crises had occurred too in the Precolumbian past. Policy-making could not function without the appropriate contingent of *cemís* under a chief's control. Caciques and *cemís* were truly interlocked in the exercise of power. To implement policies and divine the future, the cacique had to have powerful *cemís* under his control. The more highly ranked *cemís* would have been more desirable to caciques attempting to solidify their power bases.

While "powerful" *cemís* required "big men" to handle, the reverse would not be true. *Cemís* could and did "abandon" or "run away" from the cacique, become ineffective, or even turn against him, perhaps due to the chief's shortcomings or incompetence (e.g., the cases of *Opiyelguobirán* or Baraguabael [Pané 1999:28–30]). Herein lies the paradox: *cemís* were as much the cause for chiefly power as they were of the cacique's (and/or chiefdom's) failure. *Cemís* were therefore active agents in the changing fortunes of the political landscape of the Taíno.

If a cacique had the misfortune of allowing any or all of his powerful *cemís* to be stolen by competitors, it must have been perceived by the public as a sign of either weakness in his leadership or as a sign of other more powerful *cemís* belonging to competitors who overpowered his own.

While the personal history of the *cemí* and its human trustees were intertwined, each *cemí* accrued power through its lifetime, independently from who owned it at any given time. Since the powers of *cemís* and their human trustees were not static, we may conclude that *cemís* and caciques had asymmetrical yet interlocked power relationships. For example, a neophyte cacique inheriting a *cemí* with a long history of deeds would be more powerful than a new cacique without an experienced *cemí*. However, only with time could the neophyte cacique with neophyte *cemí* provide concrete proof of their political-religious abilities to deliver. Stealing in times of crisis became necessary precisely because no one could instantly invent a credible history of proven powerful deeds for a newly minted *cemí*.

On the one hand, the *cemís* the chroniclers referred to as being stolen had to be portable and of a size that could be stealthily carried away, such as three-pointed stones (see Figure 7.4), *cohoba*-idol-plates, or lithic collars (on collars, see Walker 1995, 1997b). On the other hand, Caguana's petroglyph-*cemís* are monumental, some weighing over a ton, securely fixed on the ground, and practically immovable. None could easily be stolen by foreign caciques or appropriated by competing factions, short of a violent internal revolt or a military takeover of Caguana. Given that they are fixed in space suggests that the central plaza, itself, was a pivot of power. Did the plaza endow the petroglyph-*cemís* with added significance and power? If so, stealing monumental *cemís* alone would deprive them of the appropriate context of empowerment: the sacred plaza.

The central plaza once contained more than 40 monumental petroglyph-*cemís*. No other site within at least 9 km of Caguana has as many. Further, no other site displays a sequence of petroglyphs with an icon of a *cemiified* cacique and ancestors and descendants located at its very center, framed by a contingent of other powerful zoomorphic *cemís*. The petroglyphs of Caguana represent a two-dimensional iconic version of the smaller, three-dimensional, portable *cemís*. This large assemblage of monumental *cemí* icons is direct evidence of a powerful political and religious center.

These observations apply also to other civic-ceremonial centers with monumental petroglyph-*cemís,* such as Tibes, Trujillo Alto, Tierras Nuevas, and Palo Hincado (Dávila 1979; Ortíz Aguilú et al. 2001; Rodríguez López 1995; Figure 7.1). The development of monumental and fixed *cemí* icons would have undoubtedly provided, among other things, an effective way to safeguard powerful *cemí*-objects from theft. I assume that stealing small and portable *cemí*-objects had been a feature of politics since Saladoid times, even if these earlier groups were characterized by an egalitarian ethos (Curet and Oliver 1998; Siegel 1992, 1999).

Cemís and Ancestors

Selected human bones (e.g., skull, long bones) would sometimes be encased in cotton *cemí*-idols or placed inside gourds and baskets (Siegel 1997:107, Plate 82). Primary human burials have been found in caves (in the Caguana area), thus not all of the dead were *cemiified*. *Cemí*-objects were intimately related to a cult of the ancestors (Siegel 1997, 1999). But I would argue not all *cemí*-objects fall into this class of "ancestor-cemís." A statement by Fernando Colón, often used as evidence, does leave the alternative interpretation that the referenced "ancestors" are those of the *cemí*-object in question, and not necessarily those of the human trustee:

> They [Taínos] give a name to this idol; I think it was the name of the father, grandfather or both, because they have more than one [name], some more than ten, in memory as I said, of some of their ancestors [Whose ancestors, Taínos or *cemí*?] [Colón in Siegel 1999:215; my comments in square brackets].

I would restrict the ancestor-*cemís* to the actual bones and their receptacles containing a deceased human who had become *cemiified*. This is different from the notion that all *cemís,* as personified beings with names, ranks, and genealogical histories, did not have a long line of their own ancestors. Some of these may not have been necessarily objects of a cult to the ancestors. To what extent these named ancestor genealogies of a *cemí* also confounded or included that of their human trustees remains open to debate. Two of the set of five anthropomorphic petroglyph-*cemís* located toward the center of the western row of monoliths in Plaza A at Caguana are implicated in this category of ancestor *cemís*. In this case a connection can be made between the living and the dead.

To speak of ancestor-*cemís* (and human bones) is, of course, to speak about death and beliefs about the dead and burial practices. Given the structural order of the *cemís* of Hispaniola (Table 7.1), "ancestor-*cemís*" relate to the Order of Inversion. The treatment of human skeletons is also significant since one of the most notable changes in burial practices between the Saladoid to early Ostionoid periods was that the communal burial grounds would no longer be located under the central plaza (Curet and Oliver 1998; but see Siegel 1992, 1999).

One can reasonably assume that in Saladoid times (pre-ca. A.D. 500) the central unmarked plaza was the arena where actual ancestors (bones below ground) and their living descendants (on the surface) articulated through dance/chant ceremonies, precursors of the later Taíno *areítos*. These buried ancestral skeletons provided the means through which different lineage segments of the village could articulate as an integrated, spatially localized community (Curet and Oliver 1998; Siegel 1997, 1999). In sites with just one communal public space, all activities articulating different segments of society came together as much for mundane (profane) as for solemn (sacred) occasions, but always underlain by the ancestors. I view this as reflecting a kin-based corporate ethos of the Saladoid community, which is defined by their descent ties to specific burials (ancestors) congregated under the central plaza. But as public space became more specialized and sharply distinguished (stone-demarcated) from the peripheral (and private) domestic space, in some but not all the early Ostionoid sites (Oliver 1998:28–49), the direct articulation between the living and the buried skeletons (ancestors) was ruptured. In the region of Caguana, at least some of the dead were buried in caves (e.g., sites SR-1, Cag-3; see Aitken 1917), while others were buried outside the plazas (e.g., site Utu-19a or "Finca Gerena," see Figure 7.2) (see Alegría 1983). This change in burial practices signals a significant change in the spatial locus and conceptual focus of ancestor worship.

In Caguana, there are no burials in the main plaza (Alegría 1983; Mason 1941). The erection of monoliths with petroglyphs suggests that the ceremonial and ritual activities in the main plaza were no longer directly related to human bones but, if anything, were related to the petroglyph-*cemís*. What does the absence of human bones (ancestors) in the plaza imply? Was this a substitution of petroglyph-*cemís* for ancestors (burials), or were these unrelated? The answers to these questions will be suggested later on, but first we must gain an appreciation of what sorts of ceremonial activities were likely to have taken place in the main plaza of Caguana, as it is here where the iconography is assembled.

The Ceremonial *Areíto* Dances and Ritual *Batey* Ball Games

The *areíto* was the principal ceremony enacted in the large central, quadrangular plaza of such civic-ceremonial centers as Tibes and Caguana (Figures 7.5, 7.12, Table 7.2). The complex power relationships between *cemí*-objects and the elites have already been discussed. We now explore the ritual context in which *cemís* and humans interacted and the symbolic themes and functions of the *areítos,* both of which are relevant in decoding the iconography of the petroglyphs. The range of meanings elicited by participants ought to be different in an *areíto* for a wedding than for a funeral.

The ensemble of 40-plus petroglyph icons located in the central plaza of

Figure 7.12. Oblique aerial photograph of Caguana (Site Utu-10). View to the south-southeast. The letters correspond to the map in Figure 7.6 (Photo by A. G. Pantel 1974; after Oliver 1998:Figure 3).

Caguana was articulated in a complex set of ritual interactions with humans (Figures 7.13, 7.15). Rather than the buried community of ancestors of the ancient Saladoids, these protohistoric icons comprised the community of numinous beings. While the message for the Saladoid was to reinforce their kin-based values, in Caguana the message was to reinforce the central institution of cacique as the means to maintain solidarity.

The assembling of a community of petroglyph-*cemís* in Plaza A is striking in contrast to the surrounding precincts, which had either a single petroglyph or none at all (Figure 7.14). Most of the peripheral precincts are small (Table 7.2), suggesting that the associated rituals would most likely have been more exclusive and private than in the central plaza.

The contrast is between the quadrangular central plaza and the various rectangular peripheral precincts. The large central plaza, covering 1,761 m^2 in area, is where the *areíto* activities occurred and articulated the members of the community, including the petroglyph-*cemís*. In executing an *areíto*, cooperation is required of all participants, regardless of the various social segments represented. The peripheral precincts are the arenas for confrontation, competition, and individualism. In these precincts, even the petroglyph commu-

Table 7.2. Precinct Measurements and Number of Associated Petroglyphs.

Precinct	Outline	# Petroglyphs	Dimension (m)	Area (m^2)
A	Quadrangular	22 +	48.7 × 35.5	1,761.0
B	Rectangular	0	61 × 17	1,073.0
C	Ovaloid	1	15 m diam.	17.7
E	Rectangular	1	30 × 7.6	227.0
G**	stepped platform? rectangular	0	15.2 × 28.9	439.0
H	Rectangular	0	40 × 7	280.0
I	Rectangular	0	33.6 × 11.5	386.0
J**	Rectangular	0	24.4 × 7.6	185.0
K	Rectangular	1	26 × 8.4	218.0
L	Rectangular	1	22 × 12	264.0
M	Rectangular	1	26 × 12	312.0
N	Rectangular	0	27 × 9	240.0
O	linear pavement	0	6.7 m length	—
Area Z	Circular	0	18 m diam	28.27
Area D	Rectangular	0		

Note. From Oliver (1998:Table 1).
**These precincts were destroyed before site reconstruction in the 1960s. In Plaza A, only 22 petroglyphs are extant today; in 1915, a similar number of petroglyphs were known for the eastern limestone row of slabs.

nity was segmented and spread over several precincts (see Figure 7.6: K, L, M, N, E, and C). This reflects ideas that originated in the early Saladoid semicircular coastal settlements, where families resided around a communal space in which their buried ancestors came together. Caguana's community was widely dispersed and such semicircular village configuration is neither feasible in the karst topography nor economically effective for an agrarian society. Yet, Caguana, as a civic-ceremonial center did preserve in its elaborate precincts the same spatial concepts and precepts. It also should be noted that in the coastal plains, contemporaneous with Caguana, quite a number of sites originating in Saladoid times continued to be occupied until Capá (Taíno) times, without dramatic changes to the semicircular spatial arrangement. Despite all other changes in society and material culture, the persistence of such spatial configuration is remarkable.

The large rectangular precincts "B," "H," and "I" could hold a large con-

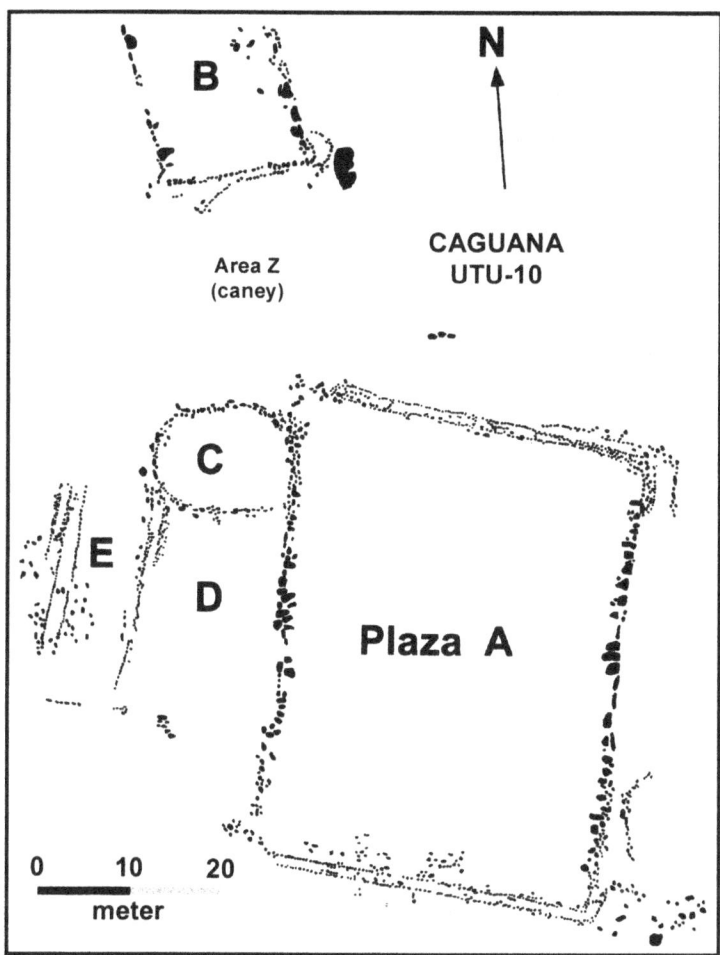

Figure 7.13. Close-up plan view of Plaza A and immediate structural features as mapped by Mason in 1915 (after Mason 1941:Figure 2 and Oliver 1998:Figure 4).

tingent of participants. Their rectangular configurations correlate with the proportional dimensions (3:1) for courts in which the *batey* game was documented ethnohistorically (Las Casas 1929 [3]:570, Chapter CCIV).[9] None of these ball courts have petroglyphs. Their absence is also true for the rectangular (ball) courts identified in Caguana's hinterland, such as at site Utu-54 (Figure 7.2).

Several small precincts in Caguana, however, each contain a single petroglyph-*cemí* located at one of the terminal points in a row of stones (Figure

Figure 7.14. Petroglyph 24. An example of the lonely "terminal icons" located in peripheral, small courts. This specimen comes from Precinct M and depicts a humanlike face surmounted by or covered with a frog head. This motif is identical to the head lugs adorning modified Ostiones and Santa Elena style ceramic vessels.

Figure 7.15. Photo of northern end of Plaza A marking the locations of Petroglyphs 1, 11, and 17–22, and oval Precinct C and its sole petroglyph (23). Area D yielded concentrations of house posts; Area Z yielded an unusually large (18–23 m) round house.

7.14). These include the circular Precinct C, Precinct E, and the three rectangular courts, K, L, and M, to the east of Plaza A (Figures 7.12, 7.13, 7.15). Given the small sizes of these courts (none larger than 300 m² [Table 7.2]), each could only accommodate a small number of people. I believe that these small courts were reserved for intimate ceremonial activities, perhaps for members of particular lineages. The notion of intimate ritual spaces in Courts C, D, K, L, and M correlates with the fact that the petroglyph-*cemís* of these courts are represented as biomorphic heads, lacking full bodies. Social segmentation is reinforced in the iconographic representation.

What did an *areíto* actually entail? The sixteenth-century chroniclers tell us that *areítos* recited histories, which were transmitted through the generations. *Areítos* functioned "like the history books" of Europeans (Oviedo 1944 [1]:232, Part 1, Book 5, Chapter 1).[10] *Areíto* designated a variety of dance-chants that were enacted for diverse purposes, implying that the choreography and lyrical content varied according to the occasion being celebrated (Las Casas 1929 [1]:455–456, Chapter CXIV; Mártir de Anglería in Sued Badillo 1975:12; Pané in Arrom 1974:34; Wilson 1990:120). The thematic content of the chants most likely varied with the function of the *areíto*. Therefore, meanings in the petroglyphs must have been flexible (polysemic), since the monumental icons could not be reordered and shuffled for every occasion.

The success of an *areíto* performance depended on every participant submitting to the lead provided by the "master of ceremony" with precision. The *areíto* can be regarded as a ritualized and choreographed expression of how a society should ideally behave. I do not think this is just about integrating (i.e., homogenizing) all segments of society, but rather of how to effectively articulate that which is normally segregated, divided, or disparate. Articulation respects the identity of each component without implying that they are being integrated into a homogeneous whole.

The *areíto,* in essence, praised the individual achievements of the dead cacique, which were added to those of his/her *cemíified* ancestors. In his or her lifetime the succeeding cacique would add his/her own deeds and achievements to those of the deceased and *cemíified* ancestor-caciques. Every major social, political, and religious event, be it a wedding, a political pact, or an initiation rite, would be marked by an *areíto,* and would both recall prior successes of ancestral chiefs and incorporate into the lyrics the events presided by the living cacique. Thus, *areíto* histories were about aggrandizing/maintaining chiefly power, which could only be achieved if there was cooperation among the different social segments within and perhaps across polities.

Areítos were powerful tools for cementing political alliances. An instance of this was recorded in the famous case of paramount Chief Guarionex, ruler of the Maguana chiefdom in Hispaniola. He cemented an important political-military pact with Cacique Mayobanex of the Macorix chiefdom, in northeastern Hispaniola (Wilson 1990:102–108).

The *areítos* performed in the central plaza of Caguana may have been about histories relating to chiefs and their ancestors, proclaiming their long record of deeds and achievements. They also told and commemorated important events in the life cycle of the society and polity. The nature of *cemí*-objects, their interlocked power relationships with chiefs, and the significance of the *areíto* ceremonial performances provide a context within which to situate Caguana's iconography and, thus, address the question of who are these monumental *cemís*.

The Iconography of Caguana

Eight primary iconographic themes have been identified on the surviving petroglyphs in the western row of Plaza A. These themes correlate well with Taíno mythology and the legends (histories) recorded for particular *cemís* (Oliver 1992b, 1992c, 1998), and comprise the actions and behaviors of personages that occurred in specifiable domains of the cosmos. I will briefly summarize the themes; they have been discussed in detail elsewhere (Oliver 1992b, 1992c, 1998:121–191; see also Roe 1993).

I will arbitrarily begin from the southernmost end of the western row of Plaza A, with Petroglyph 1 and conclude at the north end, with Petroglyph 22. This western (igneous) row is only half of the iconographic ensemble in Plaza A. Mason (1941) published photographs indicating that the eastern (limestone) row also contained a serial or linear arrangement of petroglyphs, with a similar iconographic content as that of the western row (Roe 1993).

The Primordial Domains: Toward a Genesis of Life

Each of the first four domains, starting from the southern end, is dominated by one or more petroglyph-*cemís* whose formal features enable the identification of the scenario. These four discrete spaces, together, referred to a primordial cosmos. I have labeled the primordial domains as: (1) Coaybay, (2) Bagua/Ocean, (3) Guanín Sky, and (4) Ancestors. The number four comprises a whole (two pairs of complementary opposites) for the Taíno, and was a structural principle that underlay the organization of the *cemís* of Hispaniola and the stylistic composition of Taíno artifacts.

The first domain contains two petroglyphs that relate to the domain of

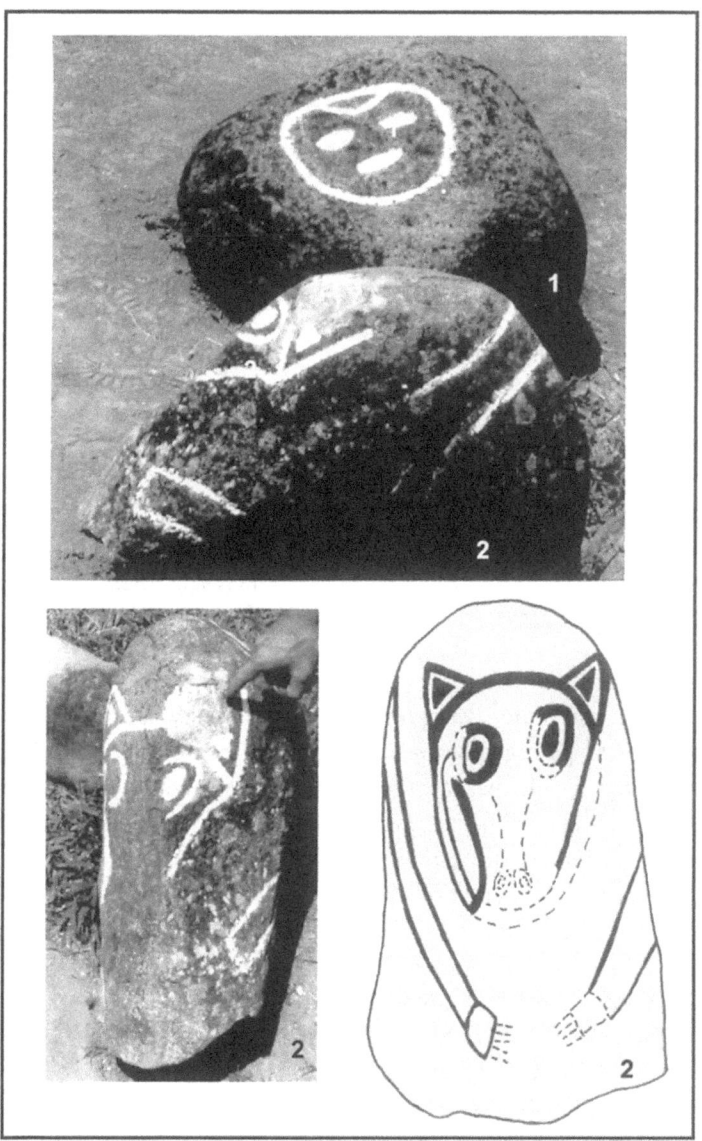

Figure 7.16. A simple face (No. 1 top) and a doglike zoomorphic being (No. 2, top and bottom) related to the Domain of the Nonliving. Compare Petroglyph 2 with the ceremonial *duho* in Figure 7.10.

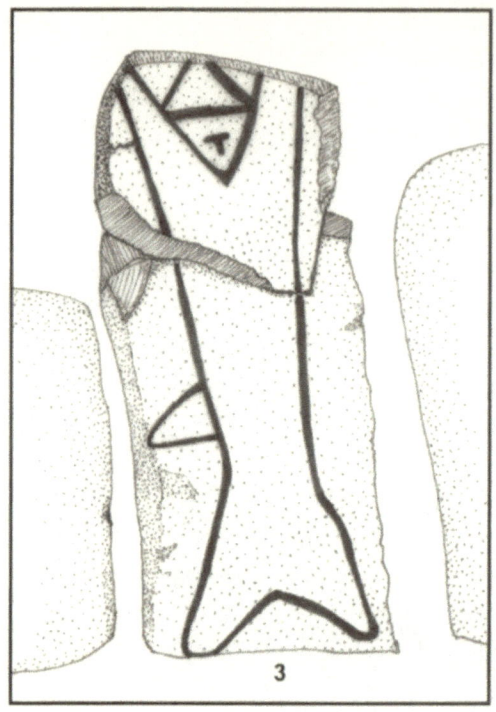

Figure 7.17. Petroglyph 3. An ichthyolmorph petroglyph (head is missing), "Master" of the fish and ocean (*bagua*) resources.

spirits (*opías*) (Figure 7.16: Petroglyph 1) and the nonliving, including a doglike, long-snouted petroglyph-*cemí* (Figure 7.16: Petroglyph 2; compare with Figure 7.10) that recalls the *Opiyelguobirán* of Hispaniolan lore (Roe 1995a). Doglike creatures played the role of guardians of the Nonliving. This doglike petroglyph-*cemí* signals the gateway to the Domain of Coaybay. Coaybay was the island of savannas and full of *jobo* trees (*Spondias* sp.), where the souls of the *opías* lived and were ruled by the Cacique of the Nonliving (the Maquetaurie Guayaba of Hispaniolan lore). The spot where Petroglyph 2 is located in the row marks a boundary between the world of the dead spirits and the primordial forest, where *opías* escaped to at night (Pané 1974:32–33, 45; 1990:39–40, 47; 1999:28–29).

The Domain of Bagua or the primordial ocean is inferred since the next petroglyph displays a fish standing on its tail (Figure 7.17; compare with Oliver 1998:Figure 25). The upper segment (head) was broken long ago. I interpreted the fish-*cemí* to be a guardian or master of the fish and oceans, as a *cemí* involved in replenishing the stock of fish and perhaps other marine resources. Since large terrestrial animals were scarce to nonexistent in the Pre-columbian Caribbean, marine fauna were a vital source of protein. Furthermore, fishing enjoyed a privileged status among the Taíno. I conclude that the powers of the Lord Fish-*Cemí* relate to the economics of fishing and maritime resource exploitation, and things affecting the fish themselves.

Continuing north, we encounter the first set of bird petroglyphs, evoking the domain of the primordial sky, which in Taíno mythology is strongly associated with guanín (*tumbaga* gold), iridescent feathers, astral bodies (Venus, the Sun), and long-beaked birds (Oliver 2000). Birds not only signified the presence of a primordial Guanín Sky domain but also of the ocean, where they feed, and of earth, where they nest and live in colonies. The first two bird *cemís*, Petroglyphs 5 and 6 (Figure 7.17), look like brown pelicans (*Pelecanus occidentalis occidentalis*). These bird-*cemís* may have had powers directly related to fishermen and their skills in harvesting maritime resources, replenished by the preceding Master Fish-*Cemí*.

Also in the Guanín Sky, we find a long-beaked bird-*cemí*, Petroglyph 7 (Figure 7.19) that may represent the rare Antillean great blue heron (*Ardea herodias adoxa*) (Oliver 1992c, 1998; Roe 1993). Herons feed on a range of small terrestrial animals and fish. They are like humans in both fishing in oceans and hunting on land. From south to north there appears to be a process of genesis, as domains and their inhabitants become established. Fish-eating birds must follow the creation of fish and oceans. Indeed the first major act of the Taíno Supreme Being, Yaya, was to create fish and the ocean (*bagua*) (Oliver 1997).

Most long-beaked, head-feathered birds appearing as personages in myths among the Taíno of the Caribbean and Carib-Arawak groups in the Guyanas function as facilitators, as personages that make accessible that which is inaccessible to ordinary humans (Oliver 1998:142–151). In the case of the Taíno of Hispaniola, the long (phallic) beak-bone of the woodpecker (Oliver 1998: Figure 48) was enlisted to carve out a vagina from the treelike, slippery ("like eels") protowomen. In doing so, the category of marriageable women (incest taboo) was established in this primordial domain (Pané 1974:45).

At the northern end of the Guanín Sky domain, the petroglyph-*cemí*—husband-masculine, phallic bird—was related to the making of primordial women accessible for marriage, hence fertile and reproductive, and at the same time carried the eminently masculine symbol of chiefly power, the feathers, which in turn are associated with solar motifs, including guanín gold, Venus, and the Sun.

Finally, this primordial domain dominated by zoomorphic beings and *opías* contains two other petroglyph-*cemís*. One is an exaggerated smiling face—a rendering of emotion that is uncharacteristic of any standard anthropomorphic Taíno rendition, be it petroglyphs or other iconographic media

Figure 7.18. Petroglyph 4. An exaggerated grinning biomorphic face ("jester"), whose unabashed display of emotion and view to the north runs against rigid modes of presentation and behavior among anthropomorphic (and human) beings (Photo by Oliver 1974).

(see Figure 7.18). The unemotional, rigid expression is the expected proper social conduct of a Taíno in a ceremonial context, especially when in the presence of the numinous. An archetypal personage of South American mythology that defies the norms of social conduct is the mischievous, libidinous, and unrestrained jester; the antithesis of cultured behavior. Gerardo Reichel-Dolmatoff (1992; also cited in Oliver 1998:141–142) described this role as a facilitator to provide different means to achieve objectives.

The other petroglyph-*cemí* is located to the north of the Husband-Heron-*Cemí*. It shows an anthropomorphic heart-shaped face, sporting two small

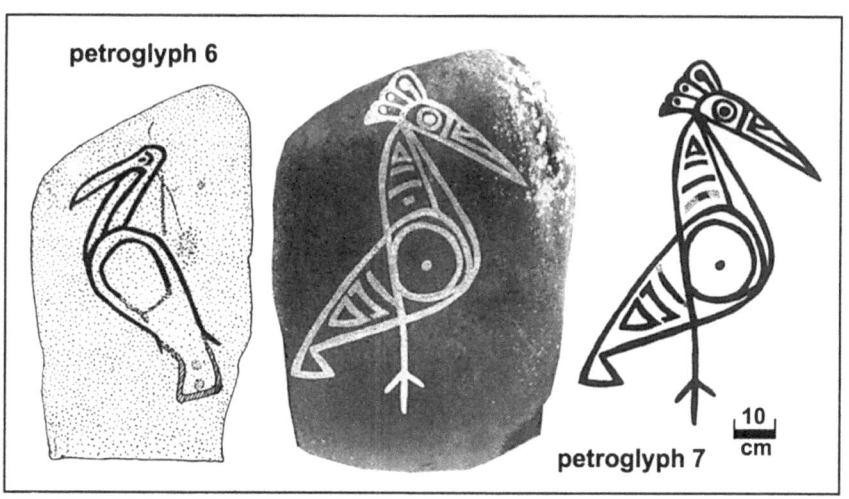

Figure 7.19. Ornithomorphic petroglyphs. Petroglyph 6 (right) is based on the pelican; Petroglyph 7 is based on a heron or egret. Of the two renditions, "B" is the most likely (line and stippled drawing).

ear spools (Oliver 1998:Figure 58[8]). This type of facial contour, which emphasizes the eyebrows while ignoring the hairline, is the same convention used in all Taíno anthropomorphic icons (e.g., Figures 7.4, 7.7, 7.11). It is the first time in the linear sequence where a clearly recognizable human face occurs, although it lacks a full body. These two petroglyphs seem to play auxiliary roles.

The Anthropocentric Primordial Domain: The Ancestor-*Cemís*

Following the Heron-Husband-*Cemí* (Number 7) and the heart-shaped anthropomorphic head (Number 8), for the first time we encounter the full-bodied icon of an anthropomorphic being. Her vulva is clearly marked, leaving no doubt as to her sex (Figure 7.20: Petroglyph 9). This woman-petroglyph is of high status, indicated by her large circular ear spools and the elaborate head dress or cap. On the head dress, there is a semicircular motif that suggests the depiction of a *guaíza,* that emblem worn only by a chief (Alegría 1995). Her coffee-bean-eye and mouth motif suggest closed or slit eyes. On her chest triangular motifs are depicted with line incisions that represent protruding rib bones. If her head displays all the accoutrements and signs of high rank and status, her thorax exhibits all the symbols of age. This is an old, millenarian lady, quite likely a *cemíified cacica* (a chieftess), an ancestor in a

The Proto-Taíno Monumental Cemís *of Caguana* / 269

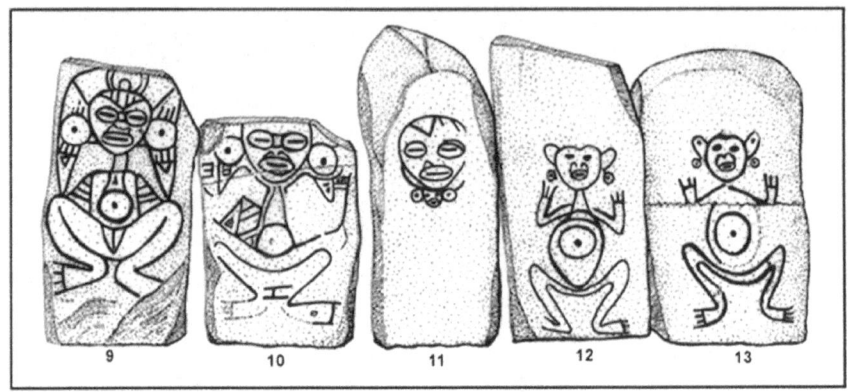

Figure 7.20. Petroglyphs 9, 10, 11, 12, and 13. The facial icon of a cacique sporting the emblematic *guaíza* pectoral (No. 11) is framed to its left by a pair of ancestral and high-ranking personages (Nos. 9–10) and to its right by a pair of lower-ranked descendants (Nos. 12–13).

lineage of chiefs. Yet her lower extremities and abdominal area clearly are not bony, but rather exude an air of fertility. The legs are modeled after batrachians (compare with the leg motifs in Figure 7.4); this is an ancestor-*cemí* of a "Frog Lady," a chieftess, and hence from which a brood of elite descendants were borne. The lower body and abdomen with a navel are fleshy. Having a navel immediately indicates that she is no mere *opía-cemí*, which prompted me to infer her function as a *cemíified* female ancestor. She is the source of human procreation, but as a *cemíified* ancestor (see also Roe 1993).

To her left is the Frog Lady's consort (Figure 7.20: Petroglyph 10). Although his headdress is missing, his large ear spools and nearly identical facial treatment indicate that this is also a high-ranking being. It also has a bony rib-cage motif, signaling old age. The main distinctions are a more elaborate decoration in the chest area and a swiveled H-like motif positioned under the froglike legs. This motif may represent a stylized *duho* (seat). There is no depiction of male organs, although its sexual emphasis is underscored by that most masculine of Taíno objects: the *duho*.

This concludes the segment pertaining to the primordial domains, where the iconography depicts a sequence beginning with creation through the domain of spirits and nonliving to the ocean and sky to a primordial cultural world of *cemíified* (once human) ancestors. Age, rank, and sex are established. Here is where the lyrical-historic and genealogical content of the *areíto* beautifully coordinate with the presence of this pair of *cemí*-petroglyphs. My suspicion that the actual skeletons that were once the focus of ancestor worship were replaced by some of the petroglyphs after about A.D. 900–1000 seems to be supported. My skepticism as to whether all *cemís* are related to the ancestor cult can be partly refuted through logical reasoning, though I remain skeptical. From south to north, the order suggests a food chain sequence starting with a numinous spirit to fish (created by the Supreme Spirit) to fish-eating birds and to women-making birds and human ancestors that create human progeny.

The Anthropocentric in the Ordinary Domain: The Cacique and Descendant-*Cemís*

The next icon (Figure 7.20: Petroglyph 11) is situated at the center of the stone row. All of the petroglyph-*cemís* located to his right refer to beings of the primordial world of spirits (Coaybay) and to *cemís* relating to the process of genesis and creation, including the *cemíified* pair of ancestors. To his right, we find another pair of full-bodied anthropomorphic beings.

These individuals do not have elaborate head dresses. They both sport small ear spools and their eye-motifs are not slits but hollows. Apparently, the pair is asexual. Their bodies show soft fleshy contours, in contrast to the bony features of the ancestor pair. In sum, they are young personages, with flesh, of lower status and rank than the preceding ancestor couplet. They may be regarded as descendants, and perhaps they are objectified-*cemís* associated with the protection of elite children. Or, this pair could represent all living individuals who could trace their ancestry to the couple of ancestors. That they follow the ancestral pair of *cemís* and Petroglyph 11 suggests that there is a genealogical relationship.

The two couples (ancestor *cemís* and descendant *cemís*) potentially represented a single unit. This quadripartite unit may symbolize the constitution of a functioning family, a living pair and their *cemíified* ancestors. Such is the elemental structure underlying a family and lineage group in society. Despite the self-serving elitist overtones of this imagery, the petroglyph couples strike a chord of familiarity and recognition to any *naboría* confronting these petroglyph-*cemís*.

The *areíto* chants praising past (*cemíified*) and present caciques and stressing their genealogical connections articulate nicely with this anthropocentric group of petroglyph-*cemís*. Any rite of initiation may articulate with the two couples. If a deflowering rite or wedding then it is the articulation between the Heron-Husband's seminal power; if a funeral, then the focus is on the icons of Coaybay. If a war victory, then it would likely be the petroglyph-*cemí* of the cacique.

The icon of a cacique is spatially situated between the ancestor and descendant *cemís* (Figure 7.20: Petroglyph 11). Even in the absence of a full body, the depiction of a pectoral *guaíza* (Figure 7.7) hung from a necklace defines him/her as a cacique. Its location at the center of the row of monoliths signals its mediating role. Without the cacique-*cemí* mediating between the primordial/ancestral and the ordinary domains, cosmic, social, political, and religious order would fall apart. In his absence, the two cosmic moieties could not be articulated. This was the idealized role of a cacique in society as well, since it was s/he who mediated between the affairs of this world by negotiating with the *cemís* and supernatural forces of the spirit world.

The *areítos* generally praised the cacique's achievements and that of his ancestors. At a pragmatic level, the entire ensemble (*areíto* dancers and petroglyph-*cemís*) was at once a display of the political religious power of the cacique and a justification of the chiefly institution. The group of petroglyphs is thus a political-religious statement, propaganda if you will, of the flesh-and-bone "cacique of Caguana." While the two pairs of anthropomorphic icons were representative of a constituted society, they were also the *cemified* relatives of the cacique of Caguana.

From the "Ordinary" Back to the "Extraordinary" Domains of Cosmos

The remaining nine petroglyphs, to the left of the cacique (Figure 7.15: Petroglyphs 14–22), repeat the themes and domains encountered in the northern half of the petroglyph row, but with a twist. Rather than stressing the themes of creation, the northern half of the row emphasizes that all life ultimately ends in death and, thus, the domain of Coaybay. I perceive this other half of the cosmos to be an inverse parallel of the primordial domains. The domains are labeled: (1) Descendants, (2) Turey (Bright Sky), and (3) Arcabuco, the forest of the ordinary world. But just because this half of the cosmos is categorized as "ordinary" or "natural," does not mean that the extraordinary, numinous, and supernatural were absent.

The pair of descendants is followed by a bird-*cemí* (Oliver 1998:Figure 61). Farther north we encounter a face with crying eyes (Figure 7.21), a motif that complements the aquatic primordial domain of the fish. Lachrymal waters derived from the eyes of an anthropomorphic being probably related to earthly waters. This is the Domain of Uniabo and contrasts to the primordial Domain of Bagua (Oliver 1992c, 1998:176–178, 192).

The Domain of Uniabo is followed to the north by an anthropomorphic being with an elaborate head dress that signals its high rank (Figure 7.22). Its body lacks arms and legs. The full figure almost certainly is that of the abun-

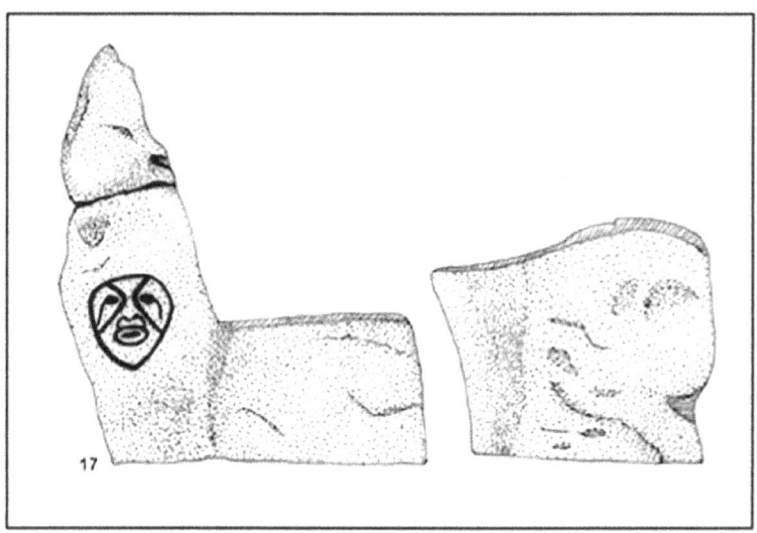

Figure 7.21. Petroglyph 17. A biomorphic face with "crying" motif. The monolith is carved much like a seat.

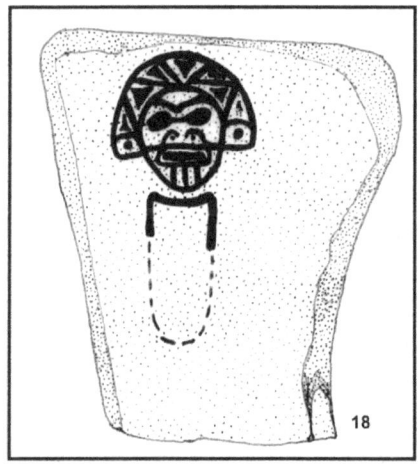

Figure 7.22. Petroglyph 18. An anthropomorphic being with elaborate headdress and its body "wrapped" for burial.

dant "cocooned" petroglyphs of Puerto Rico (Oliver 1998:Figure 26), traditionally labeled as "swaddled infants." These armless/legless petroglyphs refer to deceased individuals that were wrapped in bandages or hammocks for burial (Roe 1993). If so, then we are in a domain that relates to human burial and death.

The next petroglyph may represent the royal owl (*Asio flameus flameus*),

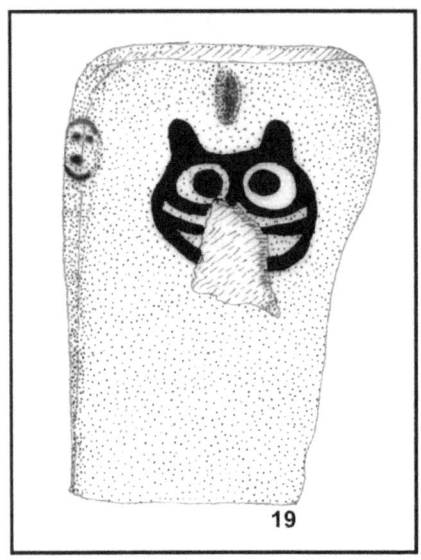

Figure 7.23. Petroglyph 19. A Múcaro Real (royal owl, *Asio flameus portoricensis*), associated with *opías* (souls of the dead).

primarily because of the depiction of ear-tips, which are actually feathers (Figure 7.23). Owls and bats in Taíno mythology are associated with the spirits of the Non-Living, who may leave the land of Coaybay at night to roam in the forests of the Taíno (Arrom 1988; García Arévalo 1988; Morbán Laucer 1988). This location in the plaza incorporates themes related to death and *opías* (souls of the dead): a wrapped dead ancestor and an owl.

Following the royal owl-*cemí* is a possible phosphene image, a spiral engraved in the tallest monolith of the row (Figure 7.24). The spiral is situated between two petroglyph-*cemís* related to the deceased and *opías* (souls of the dead), both of which are in this transitional Domain of Arcabuco (forest). Arcabuco is located in the ordinary cosmos and is, at the same time, an extraordinary domain *at night* (at the time of inversion), when the *opías* emerge from Coaybay to feast on guavas, according to Taíno mythology.

The last petroglyph (Number 22) depicts a high-ranked individual with large ears pools and an elaborate head dress (Figure 7.25). It is the homologue of the ancestral petroglyph-*cemís* (with slit-eyes) and the cacique in Petroglyph 11 (Figure 7.20: Number 11). This petroglyph gives the visual impression that its body is hiding underground, as if the individual is just about to emerge from the underworld, where in ancient times Saladoid peoples used to congregate and bury their deceased relatives. The fact that this last petroglyph is found beyond the Domain of the Arcabuco (forests), with its roaming *opías* (owls), suggests it represents the cacique-*cemí* of the Non-Living, a

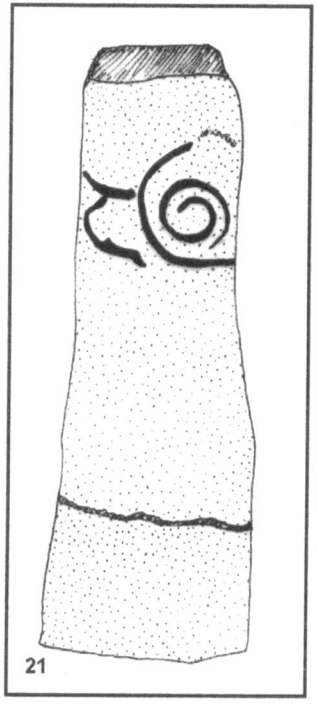

Figure 7.24. Petroglyph 21. A spiral, and the only geometric design in Caguana, perhaps resulting from hallucination-induced phosphenes.

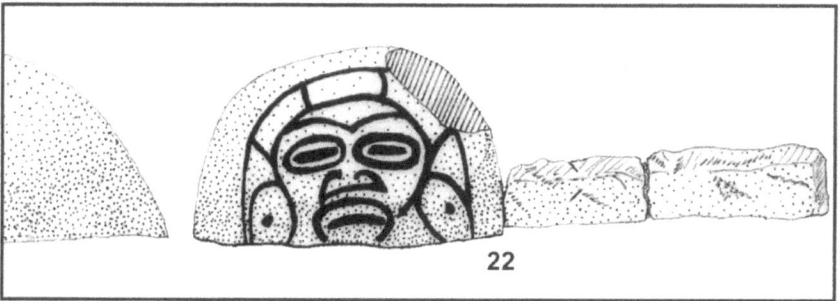

Figure 7.25. Petroglyph 22. An anthropomorphic head of a high-ranking personage, probably analogous to the Cacique of the Non-Living, Maquetaurie Guayaba of Hispaniola. Its ground-level perspective gives the impression that the rest of its body (of a complexity similar to Petroglyphs 9–10) is "hidden" underground. This *cemí*-lord of the dead appears to be emerging from underground.

personage for which the Hispaniolan Maquetaurie Guayaba is a likely archetype (see Table 7.1).

The Political-Religious Manifesto: Powerful Caciques for the Living and the Dead

The linear sequence of petroglyphs could represent the different stages of the life cycle, beginning and ending with the spiritual. But petroglyphs are more than a series of visual mnemonic devices to explain key stages of the cosmic life cycle. It is not just to be "read" or viewed in sequence, as one would a standard story. Rather it is cyclical.

The iconographic sequence suggests an additional underlying structure. By joining the two conceptually adjacent but spatially remote row ends, the structure may become more apparent. The resulting circular model (Figure 7.26) revolves around the central cacique-petroglyph; all of the domains align themselves in a quadripartite set of complementary oppositions. The anthropomorphic, societal domain of ancestors and descendants is in direct opposition to the Coaybay (land of the Non-Living) and Arcabuco (the ambiguous night-forest of *opías*). The sky domains pertaining to a primordial world (Guanín Sky) and the "ordinary" world (Turey Sky), complement each other. Finally, we observe the complementary relationship between the domains of Bagua (ocean-fish) and Uniabo (earthly water, crying petroglyph). At the edges of the circular structure I have placed petroglyphs, which I think function more like auxiliary *cemís* (see Table 7.1) than as fulfilling a preeminent role in the iconographic structure.

The centrally positioned cacique mediates between the two sets (moiety) of quadripartite domains. This model illustrates the same structural principle of complementary opposition that orders the known *cemís* from Hispaniola. The model, locating the cacique-petroglyph (Number 11) at the center (*axis mundi*), has its counterpart in the primordial, extraordinary domain: the homologous Cacique ruling in the Non-Living Domain (Petroglyph 22).

This dual and quadripartite structure was probably repeated in the other, eastern row of limestone slabs. As Peter Roe (1993) noted, the igneous western iconography seems to emphasize feminine motifs, whereas one may speculate that the iconography of the opposite limestone row would have emphasized masculine traits. The stones of the eastern row were quarried from limestone materials coming from the karst hills, a landscape replete with caves and openings to the underworld. In contrast, the igneous rocks originated from the Tanamá riverbed. I am convinced that the contrast between the yellow, soft, limestones and the darker, grayish, hard igneous rocks in-

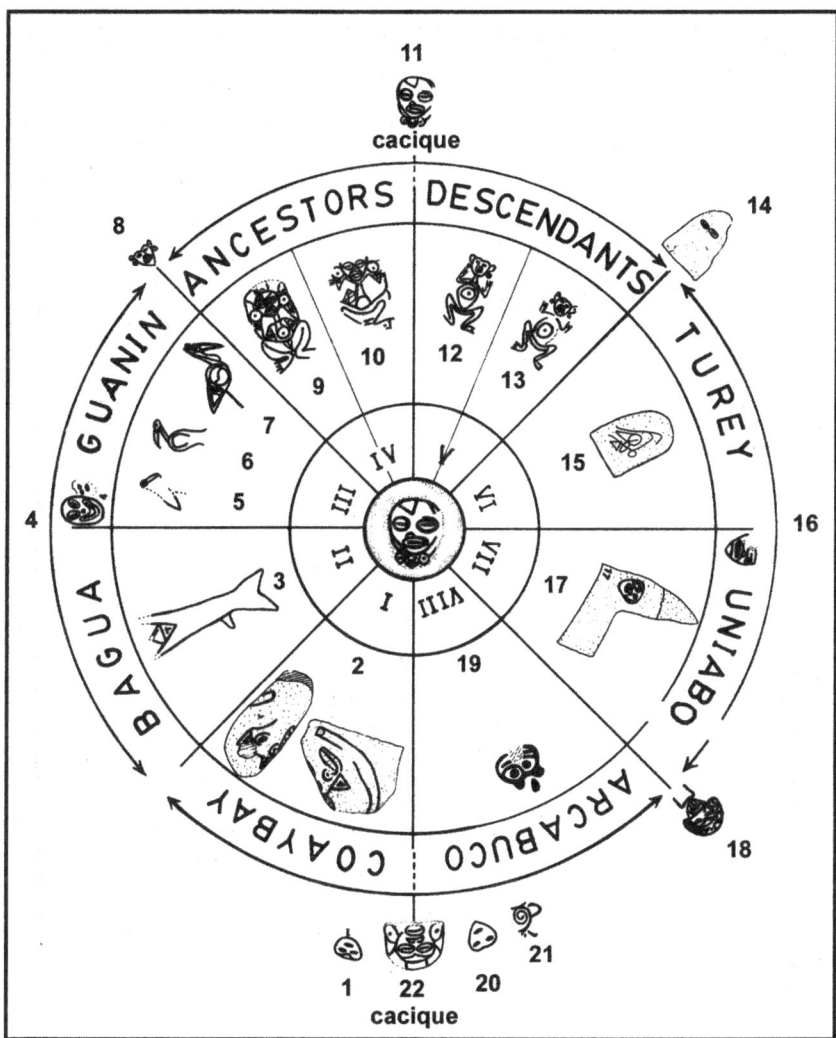

Figure 7.26. A dual and quadripartite structural model of the iconography and their respective domains.

volved Taíno notions of sacred landscapes, which were also structured within a system of duality. It is tempting to suggest that sacred landscapes, society, *cemís,* objects d'art, were all structured by the same principle, reproduced at various spatial scales and ritual activities.

Given the assumption of a sequential, linear order of icons in both rows, combined with the observed western sequence and its underlying dual and quadripartite structure, I decided to transpose the eight domains onto a schematic plan of the plaza (Figure 7.27). Assuming that the west and east rows inverted the sequence of icons and themes (as Taínos would be prone to do), a plaza emerges with a four-part spatial arena. Since the *areíto* moved in a side-step dance (lateral motion and displacement) within the plaza, it is likely that the participants rotated from one domain to the next. Within each spatial domain, the *areíto* dancers were "watched" and perhaps even "joined" (via ASC) by the appropriate contingent of petroglyph-*cemís*. The cacique, symbolically located at the center of the plaza, presided over the *areíto*.

The centrality of the living cacique, located at the axis of sociopolitical and religious life, is reproduced in the linear sequence of the iconography. He mediates between the extraordinary, supernatural, and primordial cosmic domain and the ordinary, yet numinous and natural domain of cosmos. If one removes either the living cacique or the cacique-petroglyph-*cemí*, the structural order collapses, and the mediation of past and present, remote and immediate, natural and supernatural, is no longer attainable. This axiality, as a mediating, coordinating, and articulating pivot is, in essence, a political-religious manifesto. All these petroglyph-*cemís* were entrusted to the living cacique, and only s/he occupies the place and position to access, manipulate, and control the destiny of his/her subjects.

In this circular, structural model, it is only the anthropomorphic domain that was split into a dual and quadripartite structure, composed of ancient, high-ranking ancestors and younger, low-ranking descendants. These ancestors/descendants, positioned in different halves of the world, were articulated by the cacique. Importantly, this vision of the cosmos was defined from the perspective of the cacique, as he holds the key, axial, position at the center of the universe. Thus it is not only a cosmocentric and anthropocentric conceptualization of cosmos, but primarily cacique-centric. At the northernmost terminus of Plaza A, the cacique of the Non-Living (the counterpart of the living chief) emerged from the underground, as if ready to take over its pivotal position at the appropriate, auspicious time of inversion. This petroglyph (Number 22) functioned as an inverse and complementary role to the living chief. Beyond this petroglyph is the space of the large *batey* court, an arena where competition, individualism, and uncertainty of victory/defeat signaled precisely those things that would most worry any political leader: the threat of disorder and his ability to rule. In the *batey*, who would win depended on how the various supernatural powers aligned themselves.

The small exclusive ceremonial peripheral spaces, with their solitary petroglyph-*cemís* were places that1 behaviorally and socially reflected the antithesis of the central plaza and its assemblage of petroglyphs.

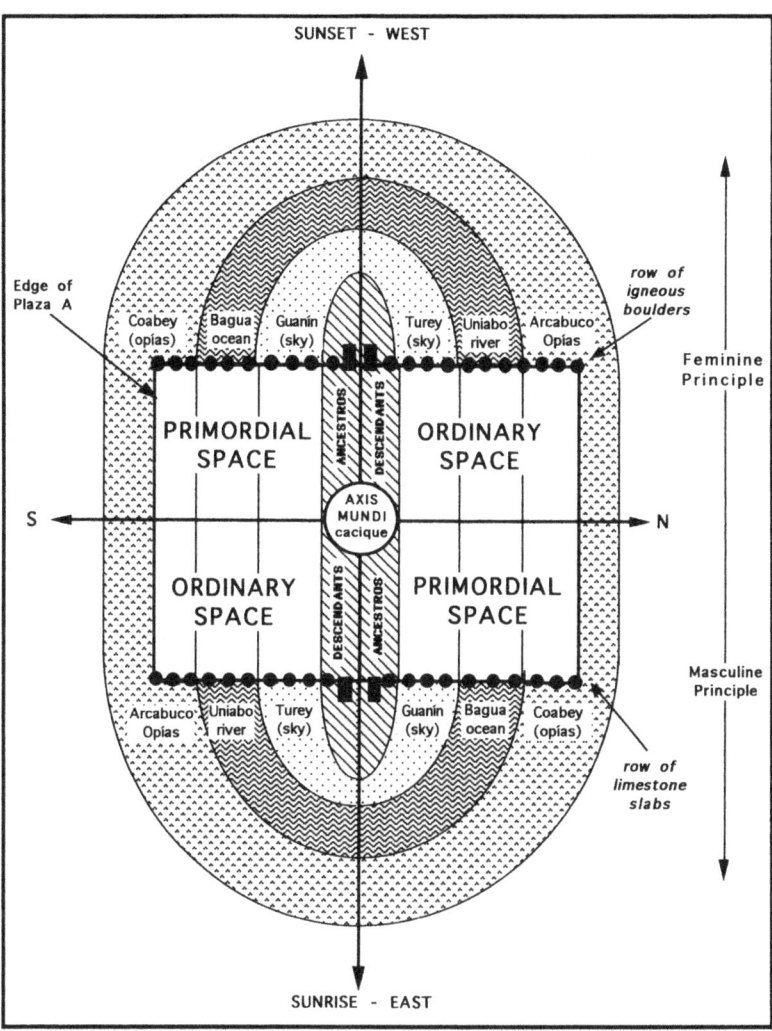

Figure 7.27. A model of the spatial cosmic domains within the central Plaza A, Caguana.

Conclusions

This long "cosmic journey" was necessary to address the three primary questions asked by visitors of all ages and backgrounds in Caguana today: Who are these personages? What do these petroglyphs mean to the Taíno? And, what ceremonies were performed in the precincts of Caguana? However, few people realized the degree to which these seemingly static images were vibrant "beings" (*cemís*), brokers of chiefly power, and, as a group, that they also displayed a manifesto of political propaganda by the elite. Key to any understanding of the iconography is how the Taíno conceived "*cemí*," and the realization that Caguana's monumental art is *cemí*. These petroglyphs were likely to have been the cause for the disgrace and fall of incompetent elites, as were all *cemís* by virtue of their numinous, independently accrued power and prestige. It is interesting to note that the iconography of Caguana has, once more, been endowed with new meanings that speak of empowerment by modern Puerto Ricans in their search for a national root and identity (Figure 7.28). These neotaíno images are used by the populace at large and current politicians in our dialogue to define ourselves (cf. Haslip and Viera 2001).

In the coming years, I hope to keep building on the history of Caguana. This site can only begin to make sense in relation to the pre-Columbian communities widely distributed in Caguana's hinterland. While I think that Caguana articulated a large territorial domain, perhaps a chiefdom, well beyond the hinterland, its immediate neighbors were most likely the ones who formed the core of Caguana. It is their lifestyle, daily activities, subsistence basis, exchange and trade, social status and rank, and their ritual life that our "Utuado-Caguana Archaeological Project" is after. How these communities articulated with each other and to Caguana is the next phase of inquiry. As the archaeological sites are very dispersed and very small (farmsteads), at least by coastal standards, the uncovering of Caguana's role through history will require time, patience, and persistence. That, I have.

Acknowledgments

I wish to dedicate this paper to the memory of my father Dr. Andrés L. Oliver (1928–2003). In the best Caribbean tradition, he was truly an advocate for archaeology; without his guidance I would have not become one. I also thank Peter Siegel for the opportunity he provided me to dwell extensively on the topic of this paper, and in particular for his thoughtful critiques and comments to previous drafts. Combined with the advice of anonymous reviewers, the revisions have notably improved my "Spanglish" syntax; for all of that I am indeed grateful. I wish also to thank Juan Rivera Fontán at the Instituto de Cultura Puertorriqueña for his friendship and participation in the Utuado-Caguana Archaeological Project. For their indefatigable support, I also wish to recognize Lee A. Newsom (Penn State University), Yvonne Narganes Storde (Centro de Investigaciones Arqueológicas-UPR), Diana López Sotomayor and her students from the University of Puerto Rico, Jaime Pagán (UNAM, Mexico City) and Reniel Rodríguez (University of Florida).

Figure 7.28 This iconic image from Caguana has been reinterpreted and integrated into current culture by modern Puerto Ricans in their search for a national root and identity.

I am indebted to the British Academy, the Institute of Archaeology in London, and the Consejo para la Protección del Patrimonio Arqueológico Terrestre de Puerto Rico for their generous financial support toward the investigations in Caguana since 1996. I would be remiss if I did not pay tribute to Professor Emeritus José Juan Arrom (Yale University), a true pioneer in Taíno iconographic research in the Caribbean. As always, I am alone responsible for any and all shortcomings and errors contained herein.

Notes

1. It is worth remembering that the noun "Taíno" (in the past often equated with "Arawak") is essentially a modern anthropological construct that glosses over significant sociocultural, political, economic, ethnic, and linguistic variability in the Greater Antilles. Consistently, the early Spanish documents refer to the native populations as peoples of this Indies, or as Indians of this "island" or that "territory." Taíno

derived from the noun used to designate elite individuals, nitaíno (/ni-taí-no/ or 'us-noble/good-persons), first reported in Columbus's second voyage in 1494 when a native was confronted with the question of "who are you." In San Salvador (Bahamas), the same question resulted in the response, lucayo or "Islander" (a syncope of /luku/ [person] and /kaí-o/ [kay or island]).

2. The relevant quote of Diego Colón's words in reference to Ponce de León's activities in Puerto Rico goes as follows:

> Digo que al Juan Ponce, que vino a la isla con la fuerza de la tormenta que le tomó yendo a Santa Cruz, le dejó el mismo partido que tenía señalándole tantos indios cuanto tenía necesidad para llevar adelante el dicho partido; y esto porque Don Cristóbal [Sotomayor] estaba determinado de le tomar los indios, diciendo que eran mejores y que cabían en su cacique. Esto del cacique de don Cristóbal [who was Agüeybaná II] era mucho más prejucio de Vuestra Alteza y no se poblara la isla porque no hay en ella sino dos [caciques, chiefs], y si el uno él [Agüeybaná II] con los indios a él [Sotomayor] anexos, ningún indio quedará para los pobladores, y por esto se le señaló 300 indios...." [Colón, quoted in Sued Badillo 2001:57–8; clarifications in straight brackets].

> I say that to Juan Ponce, who came to the Island with the force of the storm that overtook him going to Sta. Croix [Virgin Islands], left the same party [of Spaniards], the appointed [group of] Indians, as he had been given and needed to lead the above noted party. And this was so because Don Cristóbal [Sotomayor] was determined to take from these Indians, saying that [it was because] they were better [workers] and because they belonged to his cacique [assigned to Sotomayor]. This [account] about the cacique of Don Cristóbal [who was Agüeybaná II] worked against the interests of Your Royal Highness; [*the Island would not be settled because there but only two [paramount chiefs]*], and if one of them [Agüeybaná II] with the Indians annexed to him [were to be assigned to Sotomayor], then there will remain no more Indians for the [Spanish] settlers [to be given in assignment or *encomienda*]. For this reason he [Sotomayor] was given [only] 300 Indians [Colón, quoted in Sued Badillo 2001:57–8; clarifications in straight brackets; my translation and emphasis].

The context of this quote is Diego's arguments about the effects of the assignment (*encomienda*) of Indian labor, as Sotomayor was his ally, whereas Ponce de León was following the interests of the Spanish Crown. In contrast Oviedo (1944 [3]:192, Book XVI, Chapter 1) unequivocally stated that Boriquén had but one paramount chief, in the person of Agüeybaná I (and later Agüeybaná II).

3. I am aware of the difference between social actor as social types in contrast

to historical individuals and personages. A full discussion of the latter cannot be included due to space, but I have discussed some of this elsewhere (Oliver 1998).

4. The Spanish combined their experience in the Reconquest of Spain (against Moors) and conquest of the Canary Islands with the Taíno *naboría* work-gang system to institute the forced (and the latter is the key distinction) labor systems of *repartimiento* and *encomienda* (distribution and assignment of Indians to specific "conquistadors"). By 1530, during Governor Lando's tenure, the census data clearly indicate that the *naboría encomienda* system was all but extinct. By this time black African slaves and Amerindians from the continental circum-Caribbean and Yucatán had replaced the dwindling Taíno labor force.

5. After finishing this chapter I (finally) came across Alfred Gell's (1998) anthropological theory of art and agency. I was pleased to find that, to a large extent, his approach fits nicely with mine, albeit I rely more on semiotics and linguistics, which Gell explicitly disavowed from his theory. Nevertheless I argue that my analysis of petroglyph and *cemís* is indeed amenable to Gell's "indexes" and their relationships to social actors. Following Gell's argument, art objects (indexes) and human (even animal) actors are both agents enmeshed in mutually binding causal relations. The meanings and roles of the indexes (i.e., petroglyphs-*cemís*) vis-à-vis individuals and society can be understood in terms of Gell's concepts of the "distributed person" and "extended mind," both of which I do tackle here, but without using Gell's terminology.

6. My translation of Pané (based on Pané 1974) has a few differences with Griswold's English version (i.e., Pané 1999), where I have found some errors of subject (pronoun) and case agreements that change the meaning of the original Spanish sentence.

7. A root that can "speak" to humans at once recalls the Taíno characterization of the primordial world in mythological time, when verbal communication (typically an "onomatopoeic" language) and "social" interaction with nonhuman kinds of beings and things were commonplace. It would seem as if, over the eons since creation, Nature had distanced itself from Culture, which reigned in this primordial, animistic, and culturally constructed world (see Viveiros de Castro 2002). Thanks to the Culture Heroes and Guahayona (the primordial cacique), humans in "this" world regained the material means and ritual/ceremonial knowledge to interact with, and gain access to, the numinous and now extra-ordinary forces: the "sweet" *cemís*.

8. Considerable work has been conducted recently on ASC within the theoretical framework of cognitive archaeology (grounded in neuroscience) and most commonly focusing on shaman agency and shamanism, such as the work of James Pearson (2002) and David Lewis-Williams's tightly argued theory accounting for the origin of cave/rock art during the Middle to Upper Paleolithic transition (Aurignacian/Châtelperronian) among *Homo sapiens* (Cro-Magnon) rather than *Homo neanderthalensis*. The discussion by Lewis-Williams (2002:106–135) is particularly relevant to

my discussion of shamanism and hallucinogens in relation to petroglyphs and the numinous objects designated as "*cemí*" by the Taíno.

9. Speaking about Hispaniola, Las Casas noted: "they had a plaza commonly placed before the house of the señor [lord], swept clean, three times longer than wide, framed by *lomillos* of a palm or two in height . . . " (Las Casas 1929 [3]:570, Chapter CCIV).

10. Oviedo's original Spanish text is: "Y en esta isla, a lo que he podido entender, solo sus cantares, que ellos llaman *areytos,* es su libro ó memorial que de gente en gente queda de los padres á los hijos, y de los presentes á los venideros . . . " It translates as follows: "And in this Island, as far as I could understand, only their chants, which they call *areítos,* function as their book or memorial that from people to people remains, from parents to children, and from the present to the future [generations]" (Oviedo 1944 [1]:232, Part 1, Book 5, Chapter 1, emphasis in original).

8

Rivers of Stone, Rivers within Stone
Rock Art in Ancient Puerto Rico

Peter G. Roe

Puerto Rico, the easternmost of the Greater Antilles (Figure 8.1), is a large island characterized by a complex geology, including a spectacular interior karst topography honeycombed with caves and sinkholes, as well as huge boulder-strewn rivers winding from the mountainous center to the coasts. It thus has all the requisite raw materials for rock art, or *arte rupestre* as it is called in Spanish. Indeed, it appears in two media here: pictographs (González Colón 1988), or rock paintings (Figure 8.2), and petroglyphs (Alvarado Zayas 1999), carvings in stone executed by incision and excision, producing shallow relief images (Figure 8.3). The parent raw materials range from hard grano-diorites to limestone and eolinitic sandstone. While the earliest arrivals, "Mesoindian" Archaic Indians circa 4000 B.C., worked in portable stone, there is no evidence they produced rock art. It was the horticultural and ceramic-using Amerindians, ultimately from South America via the stepping stones of the Lesser Antilles, who were the first to capitalize on these abundant lithic resources and produce a voluminous and aesthetically impressive lithographic legacy.

Yet the first of these new arrivals, the Huecan Saladoid populations, followed closely by their "cousins," the more numerous and ultimately more successful Cedrosan Saladoids, appear not to have recognized the rock-art possibilities of their new insular home. From their arrival at roughly 400 or more B.C. and, in the form of the descendants of the Cedrosans, enduring until approximately A.D. 600 (Rouse 1992:Figure 14), theirs was a material culture of "personal presentation" (Roe 1989a). Typical of lowland tribes today, this artifactual assemblage results from an "aesthetic of the pristine."

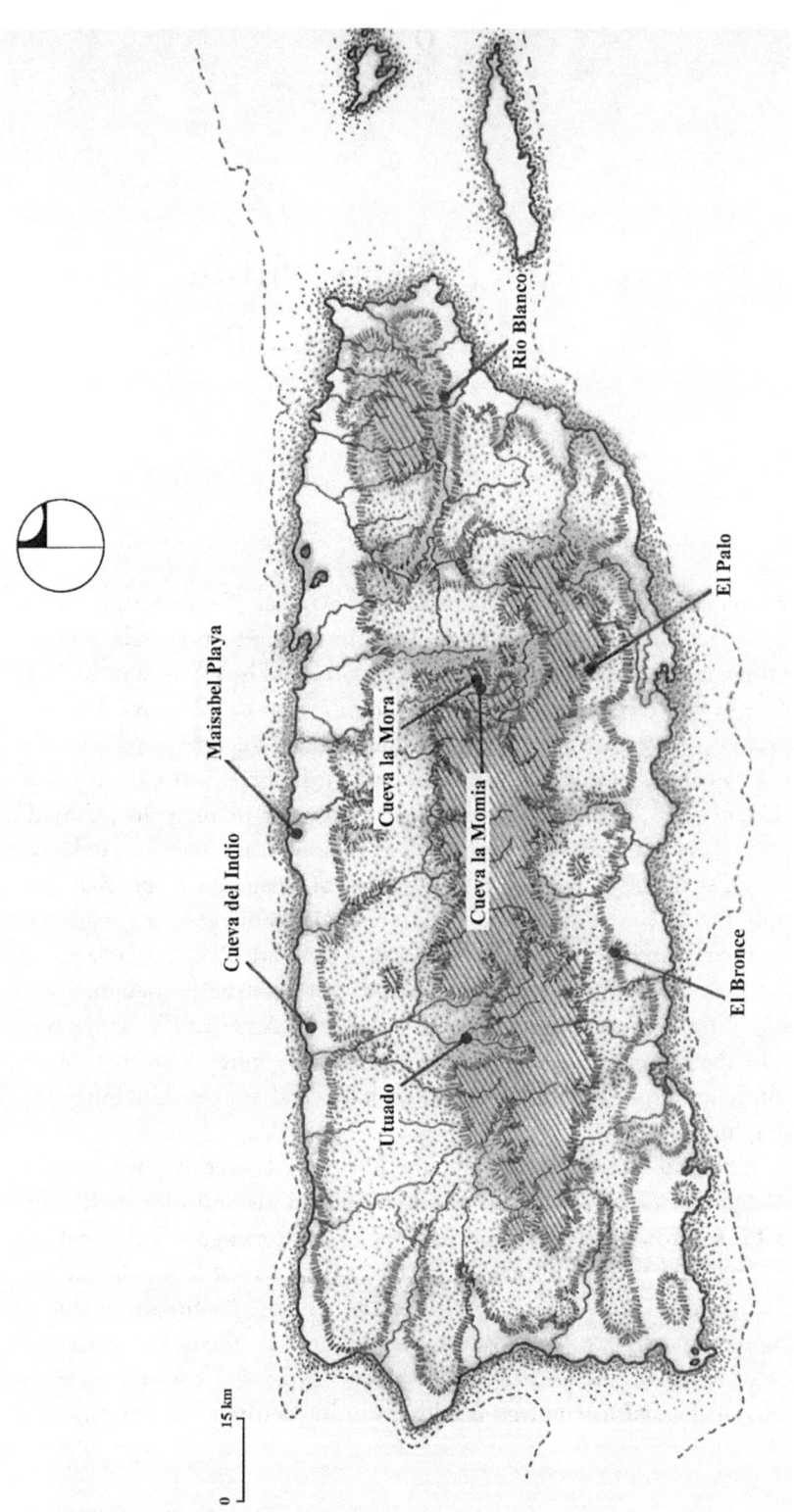

Figure 8.1. A map of Puerto Rico situating the rock art sites discussed in the text (drawn by the author).

Figure 8.2. A close-up of northern ledge pictographs from Chamber 2, Cueva de Mora, Comerío, including the head of a wrapped ancestor and an owl's face (photo from 1998, taken by the author, see Figure 8.19).

Brand new and unique objects are created both for internal consumption and to offer honored guests at feasts. The Saladoids emphasized small, portable, and exquisitely worked objects in multimedia: carving in semiprecious and other decorative stones, work in shell and mother-of-pearl, as well as modeled, incised and, in the Cedrosan phases like Hacienda Grande, white-on-red and true polychrome pottery with effigy and kinetic features (Figure 8.4a). In the latter style these surface decoration modes were combined with vessel shapes characterized by complex silhouettes (pots bristling with labial flanges, *adornos,* or decorative lugs, carinations, and annular bases). All of these jewel-like artifacts were designed to be observed close-up as corporeal art or handled as service ware. Many of these objects, as elements of what Polly Wiessner (1983) has called "assertive style," would have presented an image of the skill and taste of their owners as unique and cultivated persons, and the respect they were required to show their guests.

The "anatropic" (invertible) and rotational imagery (Figure 8.4b) of early Cedrosan Saladoid art conveyed a uniquely South and Antillean Amerindian style of graphic and plastic devices. They indirectly argue for a dualistic animistic worldview based upon the ritual use of hallucinogenic drugs for shamanic curing/bewitching (Roe 2000b, 2000c). That intricate and natu-

Figure 8.3. A ball park petroglyph, the famous "Diosa de Caguana," attributed to the Earth Goddess, Attabeira, a Taíno version of the Frog Lady (photographed in 1978 by the author).

rally modeled cosmology, together with its florid associated mythology, was to endure, albeit with modification, through the middle pre-Taíno pottery styles (Figure 8.4c, e–g), their Taíno descendant's ceramics (Figure 8.4h–i), and its unfortunate encounters with Europeans in 1492 and 1493 (Roe 1997a, 1999). Taíno cosmology continued to survive beyond the initial shock of encounter in certain "hybrid" transculturative artifacts (Roe 1997b) until the cultural extinction of the Taíno by approximately A.D. 1550 (see Anderson-Córdova, this volume).

By the time of the Elenan/Ostionan Ostionoid transformation a gradual (A.D. 600–1200) but dramatic demographic increase took place, resulting in the penetration of the island's interior. This "explosion" of sites derived from a successful adaptation to an insular environment, with a concomitant "complexification" of social structure and organization. To judge from the appearance of the first monumental architectural features like early ball parks such as Tibes (González Colón 1984; Figure 8.5, Phase A: 6), and a size increase for even humble pots, local social evolution was beginning to generate "complex tribes" or "incipient chiefdoms." Ironically, social augmentation was combined with a paradoxical simplification of material culture, in everything from three-pointers to serving bowls (Roe 1995b). Such giant bowls underwent a technical and aesthetic "devolution," losing both skill and surface decoration modes (asymmetry and generally sloppy execution in the former and, in the latter, first the reduction of bi- and polychrome to monochromatic paint and then, ultimately, to ill-prepared plain surfaces). This may have been symptomatic of a changing locus of art (Roe 1995b:Figures 2–6) from small personal items to megalithic expressions of long-distance-visible, and rigidly "frontal" artifacts. I hypothesize that rock art emerged in this more "human-centric" cultural milieu, where artisan's and patron's attention alike shifted from the "lateral view" (shape-shifting were-animal spirits) evocative of the earlier egalitarian society, toward a "vertical view" of more powerful humans above one's station and in control of one's life. Such a change in perspective is a *stigmata* of an emergent rank society (Figure 8.5, Phase B: 12, 13); objects function as so many "billboards" of emergent "public power." Certainly, as Cornelius Dubelaar (1985) pointed out for the Caribbean as a whole, most of the portrayals are anthropomorphic. This is precisely what one would predict for human-centric societies. The scale of public gatherings had apparently increased, as had site density, hierarchy, interdependence (Roe 2000d), and spacing. These factors hint at egalitarian redistribution replacing reciprocity, and the consequent emergence of prominent authority figures using feasting, trade, and marital alliance to build little regional interaction networks. By the time of the demonstrably complex Taíno chiefdom (A.D. 1350–1500), fur-

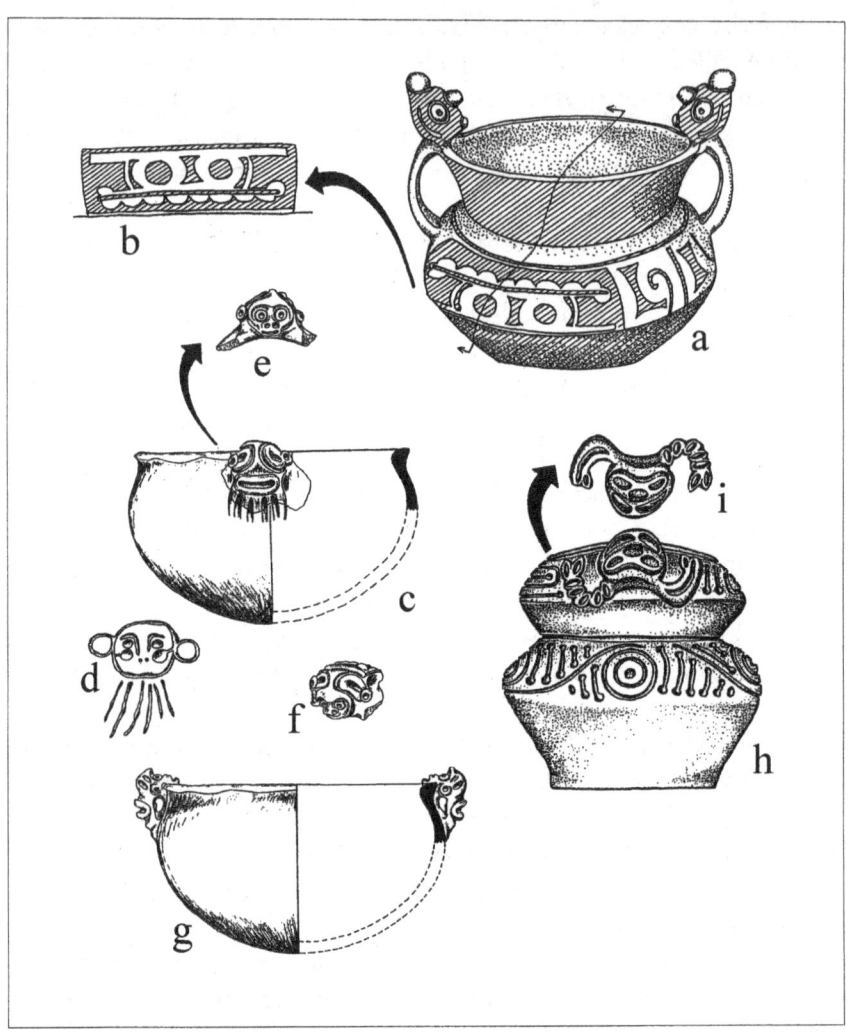

Figure 8.4. Anatropic (reversible) imagery in Puerto Rican prehistoric pottery, together with a "cross-media isomorphism" with petroglyphic art (all reconstructions and drawings by the author). (a.) A Cedrosan Saladoid (Hacienda Grande phase) unrestricted bowl with adorno-topped vertical "D"-shaped strap handles and white-on-red positive-negative painting, from the University of Puerto Rico, Río Piedras, collection, left-side reconstructed (adapted from Roe 1989b). (b.) The anatropic "Saladoid Being" vertically reflected from the shoulder band. (c, e–g.) A restricted Elenan Ostionoid bowl with the modified "D"-shaped adorno handle with a "rayed face," now unpainted, Jardines de Loiza site. The adorno face, when vertically reflected, yields another visage in "double-vision." (d.) An Elenan Ostionoid petroglyph, Barrio Cibuco site (drawn from Rodríguez Miranda 1999), of a similar "rayed face" with circular ear plugs to the ceramic adorno face in "c." (h and i.) A classic Taíno (Chican Ostionoid) biglobular restricted bowl with an anatropic crab appliqué adorno (from the García Arévalo collection, Santo Domingo, adapted from Roe 1999).

ther increases occurred in scale and workmanship throughout all material cultural media. This may have reflected a shift from "village specialist" producers, still partially engaged in the subsistence quest, to full-time, or nearly so, occupational specialists in a two-tier ranked society of nobles and commoners.

One of the mediums reflective of these trends was a now nearly mass-produced, yet also more highly decorated (although exclusively by plastic means such as appliqué and modeling) pottery tradition (Roe 1999). This second "apogee" of ceramics shared surface decoration modes (incision) with specific motifs in similarly incised petroglyphs (compare Figure 8.4c to 8.4d). Such "cross-media isomorphisms" (Roe 1993) highlighted the importance of art in conveying key cultural messages (widespread myths in actual friezes), while at the same time glorifying the "public power" of the *cacical* élite.

We can see this not only in the increased size of the rock art and associated ball parks (huge complexes like Caguana in the western highlands [Oliver 1992b, 1998, this volume]), but also in the complexity of their internal organization and pictorial detail. Specifically, one sees a shift from generic human visages to the accoutrements of dress and corporeal art (Figure 8.5, Phase C: 14–16).[1] The ancillary items of dress (crowns, necklaces, etc.) that assume increasingly complex forms within this seriation appear to be reflective of augmenting social stratification and the imposition of sumptuary codes, with a major shift occurring in late Elenan/Ostionan Ostionoid times (Figure 8.5), and reaching an unmistakable apogee in the plethora of depicted ear spools, crowns, pectorals, belts, and seats of Classic Taíno paraphernalia, as well as added representational corporeal details such as navels, elaborate eye-types, and noses.

In the face of this evident cultural transformation in sociocultural integration (from tribe to chiefdom), I argue for both innovation and conservatism within the belief system (mythology and cosmology). While still reflective to the end of its lowland South American heritage from whence it derived two millennia earlier, one can trace local innovations in animal symbols and, perhaps, ethnoastronomy (Eichholz 2001; Robiou Lamarche 1988). Evidence for this assertion will be found in both the pictographic and petroglyphic assemblages from all over the island that my collaborators and I have recorded and documented in the field and laboratory.

But was this transformation sui generis or the product of outside influences? Diffusionism is still alive and well in the Greater Antilles due to the appearance of both ball parks and yokes in Mesoamerica and on the islands (Alegría 1983). While some contact is probable (Alegría 1986a), the iconography and symbolism of the rock art argue strongly against direct diffusion

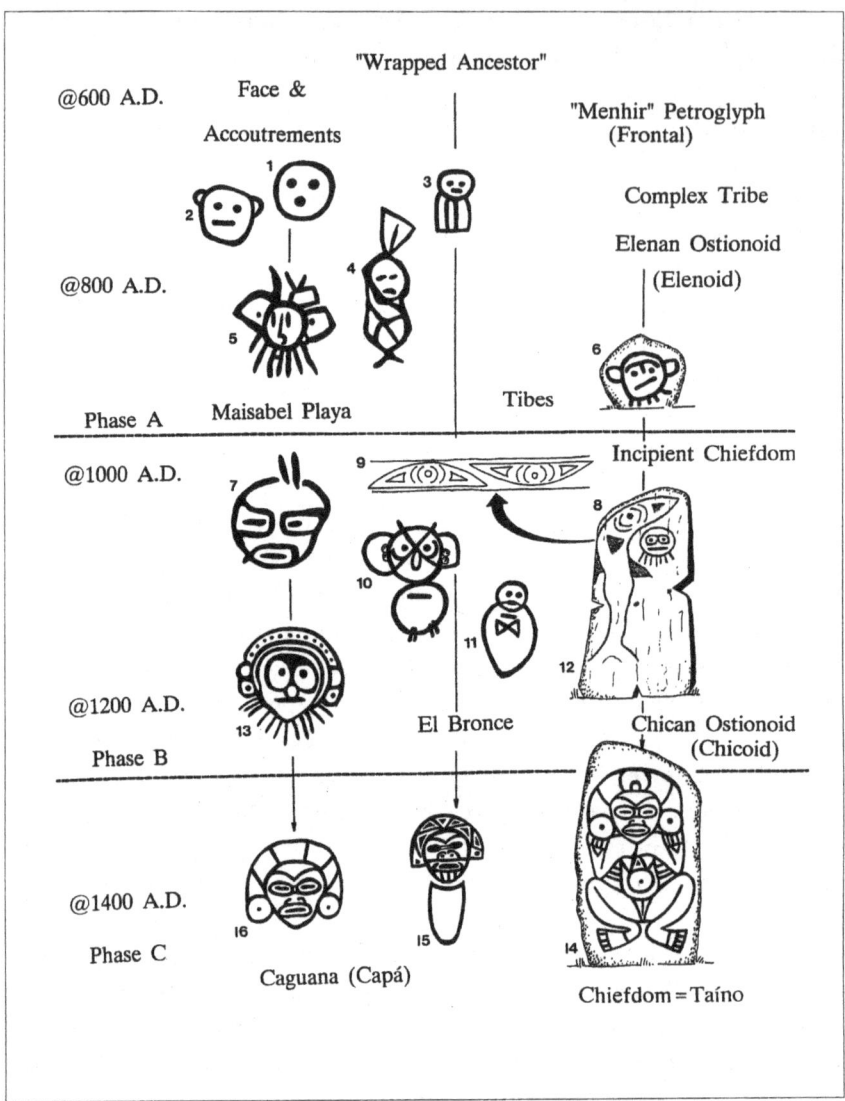

Figure 8.5. A proposed three-phase seriation of Puerto Rican petroglyphs, emphasizing anthropomorphic images (modified from Roe et al. 1999b:Figure 2)

from Mesoamerica (along with the purported borrowing of the ball park and ball game phenomena). It points, instead, to the retention and elaboration of cultural traits and institutions from the ancestral jungles of Guiana-Amazonia. There, detailed similarities in characters, episodes, and mythemes argue for continuity and parallel evolution (see also Alegría 1978; López-Baralt 1977).

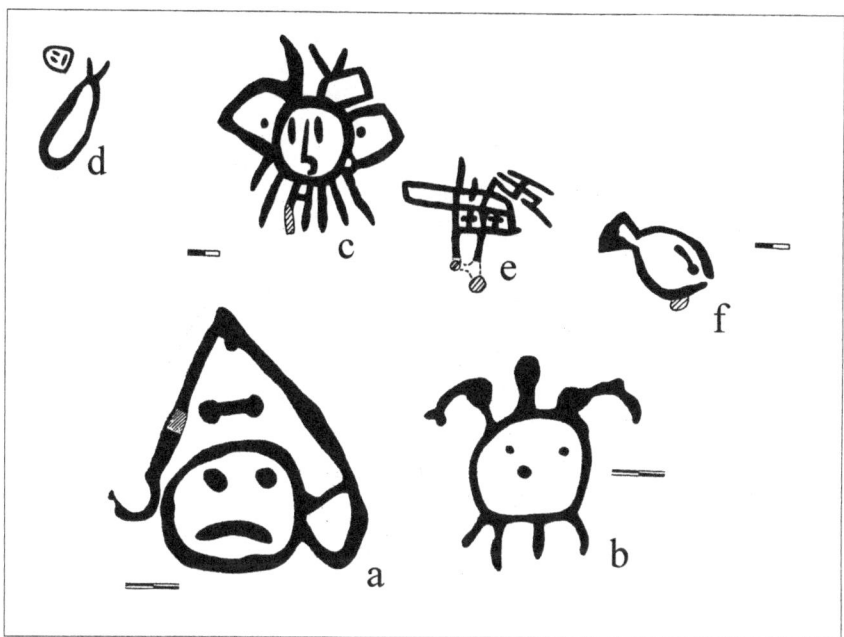

Figure 8.6. A selection of beach rock petroglyphs from the site of Maisabel Playa of possible Elenan Ostionoid cultural affiliation. (a.) A-20, a probable "three-pointer" (adapted from Roe 1991a:Figure 11a), scale = 10 cm. (b.) A-23, a possible hawksbill sea turtle with an internal "simple face" (Roe 1991a:Figure 11d), scale = 10 cm. (c–f.) A-9–13, a petroglyphic "frieze" perhaps illustrating the South Amerindian myth of the "Sun's Fish Trap" (adapted from Roe 1993:Figure 9), scales = 10 cm.

These parallels are evident in many of the texts I have recorded from native informants in their respective languages from both sides of the Amazon Basin, specifically from the Panoan Shipibo of the Peruvian *montaña* to the southeast (Roe 1982), and the Cariban Waiwai of Guyana and Brazil to the northeast (Roe 1985b, 1989b), as well as the entire corpus of comparable recorded modern oral traditions of ethnography in the lowlands (Guss 1989; Kensinger 1995), and the early written ethnohistorical accounts of Fray Ramón Pané (1974, 1992, 1999) and other chroniclers (Griswold 1997a, 1997b, 1997c, 1997d). These same mythemes are present in specific "friezes" of rock art throughout the rock-art sequence, while also revealing the replacement of Amazonian faunal symbols by local insular life forms (mythic substitution), which I have also documented in ethno- and archaeoastronomy (Roe 1983a). Tellingly, most of the insular fauna is aquatic: sea turtles (Figure 8.6b), seals, dolphins, fish (Figure 8.6d, f), and sharks. This is but the natural expression of cultural creativity as people first spread out into, and latter adapted to, a

Figure 8.7. River boulder petroglyphs, Río Caguitas (photo courtesy of Miguel Rodríguez).

distinct and distant environment characterized by an abundance of oceanic protein and a paucity of terrestrial sources (save for inoffensive land crabs and small *anolis* lizards).

I argue too that the two media of this regional rock art, pictographs and petroglyphs, are mutually related, synchronic cultural alternatives rather than diachronic predecessor/descendant forms as was the prior common wisdom. I show how the differentiation and placement of these two media, as well as the iconography and symbolism of the images executed therein, fulfilled a cosmological function, instantiating the structure and connections of a multi-level worldview, cognate with immeasurably more ancient lowland South Amerindian cosmologies (Roe 1982).

Specifically, I document the discovery of a new subtype of petroglyph that completes the hoary triadic classification first recognized by Fewkes (1903) near the turn of the century: Ball Park (Figure 8.3), River (Figure 8.7), and Cave (Figure 8.8) Petroglyphs. The completing venue is "Beach Petroglyph" executed in the lithified sands and dunes of the coast and its semilunar embayments (Figure 8.9). Lastly, and perhaps most challengingly, I take a cue from Oliver's (1998) pioneering study of the symbolic connotations of ball park design at Caguana and unite all four kinds of petroglyphs (and within them the functionally distinct pictographs) as segmental parts of a single

Figure 8.8. A cave petroglyph of a "wrapped ancestor," first chamber, Cueva del Indio, Arecibo (photo taken in 1987 by the author).

Figure 8.9. Group A beach rock petroglyphs from Maisabel Playa of a possible solar image, a fish trap, and a fish. White highlighting done with bread flour to prevent damage to the glyphs (photo taken in 1985 by the author). Scale 15 cm on board, 20 cm on north arrow.

cosmological transformational system. That is, the four subtypes of petroglyphs are merely "way stations" in the journeys of the souls of ancestral figures from their cave portals from/to the dark subaquatic underworld, via the flowing rivers and giant boulders they rest upon in their downward journeys, thence to the broad ball park "sacred lakes" of the highland basins and coastal plain, and ultimately to their "ports" of departure toward the Island of the Dead in the west on the beach rock near where rivers flow into the Caribbean Sea. Along the way they are accompanied by nocturnal/crepuscular birds (owls) and mammals (bats), avatars of the Death Spirits, the dangerous yet seductive *opía* that plagued the night. The *opía* were but malignant "twins" of the beneficent celestially oriented ancestors. The ancestors were also associated with aquatic creatures (fish and turtles) of the "water gyre" they are floating upon. The celestial connection for the chthonic ancestors in their invisible canoes was the same flowing water that courses through the underground caves during the day and the equally cold and dark night sky. As the cosmos turns itself "inside-out" during the diurnal/nocturnal cycle, what was beneath one's feet during the day flows in that foaming river of "fishy" souls, the Milky Way, above one's head at night. The water-gyre flows back upon itself within a triple-tiered universe as these same waters, and the dead carried on its surface, "upwell" from the pools of the caves and *cenotes* in the mountainous interior of the island to start their cycle all over again.

The diurnal/nocturnal, dry/rainy seasons' periodicities thus replay endlessly within this stacked set of platter/domed worlds that others (Siegel 1997:Figure 1; Stevens-Arroyo 1988:Figure 8) and I (Roe 1982:Figure 3) have argued for from evidence as diverse as the ethnohistoric oral tradition and archaeological site structure and process (Siegel 1992). Ideas matter in a systemic view of culture, as do subsistence and the social order. Nowhere do ideas and other dimensions crystallize better than in rock art. As we shall see, it is both curiously "immobile," yet "dynamic," in its structure and function.

Cultural Wholes: Why Study Ancient Puerto Rican Rock Art?

In contrast to the often fragmentary and disturbed nature of archaeological remains, rock art is usually found in situ and intact. Thus it preserves both its original spatial context (Dubelaar 1985) and the cultural "intent," however veiled, of its original makers. Rather than their normal fragmentary fare, rock art thus forces archaeologists to deal with cultural wholes, things that often survive as they were originally executed. Yet that integrity and immobility is sometimes compromised by both the ravages of preservational bias and overt acts of cultural vandalism, especially in the overpopulated insular Caribbean world. The more durable petroglyphs erode, first obscuring and then erasing key identifiable motifs, or whole representations. Sometimes, well-meaning efforts to make them accessible to a visiting public result in their virtual effacement!

Due to this unfortunate combination of factors, rock art has not received the attention it deserves. Matters are made worse by the well-known difficulty of associating it with other classes of artifactual and ecofactual evidence, from which dating and cultural associations are derived. Thus, *arte rupestre* seems to float in time, disconnected from culture, despite its composition of cultural wholes (intended affective statements) rich in stylistic and semantic meaning. I address this issue through a newly proposed seriation, and thus argue for a reintegration of rock-art data into archaeological reconstructions (Figure 8.5). We cannot continue to treat it as a marginal realm of inquiry, sprinkling disconnected images through the literature. Instead, we must attempt to use it as another line of evidence to help understand the past cultures of Puerto Rico. This chapter initiates such an attempt on a series of levels ranging from subsistence to society, art style, and religion.

Not all of the difficulties lie with the medium itself. The materialist orientation of many modern archaeologists has led them to avoid the affective intricacies of art in general (Anderson 1989), and rock art in particular. Since materialism values numerical analysis, and rock art has often eluded quantification (but see Hayward et al. 2001), pictographs and petroglyphs tend not to be regarded as fit subjects for "scientific" study. Because of that abdication, many amateurs have rushed to fill the void, some competent and cautious, others rash and sloppy, reading all sorts of bizarre notions into the "ultimate Rorschach test" that is rock art. Petroglyphs may be regarded as almost a form of pictographic writing, attributing, without much support, precise 1:1 meanings to motifs in petroglyph arrays, and thereby constructing imaginary messages in the process (Blasini 1985). Such views have cast a shadow of inauthenticity over this whole genre, repulsing serious students whose efforts might help to correct the mislabeling and poor documentation (e.g., "swaddled infants," inappropriately taken from North Amerindian ethnography, for wrapped ancestral figures, "bearded faces" for resolutely depilated Amerindian visages adorned with necklaces and breastplates, etc.).

Despite these problems, *arte rupestre* remains an object of great fascination in modern Antillean culture, and a major prop of ethnic identity in Puerto Rico, the Dominican Republic, and Cuba. It is a constant source of inspiration for modern *artesanos* (artisans, folk artists) in every medium from leather belts to jewelry, painting, and sculpture. Naturally, many of the ancient images are modified as artists take liberties with them to create modern designs. Unfortunately, these modified images, a new transculturative art dubbed "neo-taíno" by the prominent Dominican scholar Bernardo Vega (1987), then float in the popular literature as accurate representations of the aboriginal rock art. The process comes full circle when moderns peck new petroglyphs, usually "simple faces," into cave walls where they can be mistaken for ancient images. Part of the imperative for scientific documentation of rock art then becomes a correction of the artistically distorted images by showing accurately their prehistoric models, and distinguishing new from ancient cave carvings.

Carefully recorded, much can be deduced from ancient pictographs and petroglyphs, particularly in the Greater Antilles. We are exceptionally fortunate to be able to utilize direct historical and ethnographic analogy to early ethnohistoric documents such as the small yet precocious volume of Fray Ramón Pané (1974, 1992, 1999), a veritable "Rosetta Stone" of mythic information recorded from Taíno informants before their culture's extinction. In addition, we have abundant comparative mythic data from the better-documented modern lowland ethnography of South Amerindians, from whence the ancestors of the ethnohistoric Taíno came. The combination of both datasets allows the analyst to propose much more detailed iconographic and symbolic decodings of the ancient rock art than would otherwise be possible. Yet, as always, such inferences must be congruent with the data derived from the close visual inspection and analytic "deconstructive" analysis of the actual monuments themselves, as captured with multiple complementary documentary techniques.

Long Known, Little Studied: A Brief History of Puerto Rican Rock-Art Research

The first order of the day is the careful documentation of rock art in its full spatial context, using mutually reinforcing, multimedia techniques. Fortunately, while early studies often were characterized by deplorable freehand versions of Puerto Rican petroglyphs (Bullen 1973; Olsen 1973, 1974; Pinart 1890, 1979), recent advances in the documentation of Greater Antillean rock art have occurred, both in the voluminous "gray literature" of compliance reports (e.g., Ortíz Montañez 1986; Robinson 1985b) and in academic efforts.

The first modern reports on Puerto Rican petroglyphs date to the "father" of the island's prehistory and founder of the Institute of Culture, Ricardo E. Alegría (1941, 1979a), and his protégé, Ovidio Dávila Dávila (1977, 1985a), as well as the pioneering work of Alegría's long-time collaborator, himself the architect of much of Caribbean and northern South Amerindian prehistory's space/time matrix, Irving "Ben" Rouse (1949). A number of Alegría's followers, like Carlos Ayes Suárez (1985a, 1985b, 1986a, 1986b, 1986c, 1986d, 1987; Ayes Suárez and Otero López 1986), Angel Betancourt (1983), and Roberto Martínez Torres (1981, 1988, 1994a, 1994b) began documenting the numerous local assemblages. Unfortunately, their efforts were published in small regional journals of limited circulation (Collazo 1983). Various members of the private La Fundación Arqueológica, Antropológica e Histórica de Puerto Rico have published notes on isolated finds in their newsletter, the *Boletín Informativo,* published during the 1970s (Sued Badillo 1972), but their piecemeal nature has contributed little to a comprehensive study of the island's rock-art riches, and in any case, remains totally inaccessible to researchers outside the island. While valuable, this work was not pursued on a systematic basis, nor were the monuments themselves adequately interpreted.

Therefore, one of my first interests when I began doing archaeology on the island in 1978 was to investigate rock art, a genre unavailable to me in my previous research on lowland South American archaeology. In recent years, my students and others have made the documentation of rock art more careful and systematic (Alvarado Zayas 1999; Delgado Esquilín 1999b; Díaz González 1990; Dubelaar et al. 1999; Hayward et al. 2001; Hayward and Cinquino 2001; Medina Carrillo 1994; Ortíz Montañez 1986; Rivera Meléndez 1996; Rivera Fontán and Silva Pagán 1997; Rivera Meléndez and Ortíz 1995; Rodríguez Alvaréz 1991; Rodríguez Miranda 1999; Walker 1983).

In addition to his work on the menhir petroglyphs and associated ball courts of Caguana, Oliver (1992b, 1998; Oliver et al. 1999) has begun to survey the surrounding area and record additional pieces of rock art that might yield center/periphery stylistic contrasts. Dávila has continued to document the abundant rock art of Mona Island to the west of Puerto Rico (Delgado Esquilín 1999a), but these long-initiated studies have yet to be published.

Drawing It Right: Methodology in Puerto Rican Rock-Art Studies

Most early studies, including the notoriously inept (but thematically precocious) study of the French traveler Alphonse L. Pinart (1890; Alegría 1979a), were based solely on freehand sketches, usually without scale, and were thus prone to misrepresentation (see the highly variable results of my experiment of asking multiple students to draw the same petroglyph, cf. Roe 1993:Figure 2) or outright fantasy. Yet, despite the virtual unintelligibility of Pinart's renderings, Rivera Meléndez (1995) has been able to locate them and provide modern drawings. Indeed, there is still a place for well-made scale drawings made directly from the specimens, particularly to show the relationships between distinct assemblages of petroglyphs within the same site.

The advent of photography has, of course, made documentation easier. I have found that taking photos at night with floods (actually, a detached videocam light), casting illumination at an angle, helps to provide more informative images of even open-air petroglyphs than can be obtained during the day with its diffused or direct light.

Some investigators have also used infrared photography on pictographs, at times to good effect, but none of these images have, so far, been published. Fortunately, recent advances in software for image manipulation and enhancement, such as Adobe Photoshop, Corel Photo House, among others, can dramatically improve photos taken in low-light cave conditions. By changing contrast and producing negative, enhanced images, the computer yields details and isolates features missed by the naked eye. Of course, any photos that have been enhanced should be labeled as such in their presentation. Videotaping with a digital camcorder not only provides a continuous visualization of the spatial context, but the tapes can later be viewed in conjunction with still 35-mm photos (both prints and slides) and rubbings/tracings, to produce final renderings.

A significant advance in graphic documentation was Monica Frassetto's (1960) study of the Cueva del Indio site, located along the north-central coast of Puerto Rico. This spectacular cavern, formed in ancient eolinitic dunes by wave solution, has a great profusion of wrapped figures (Figure 8.8) and more abstract motifs, many connected together in densely packed meandering patterns. She applied the effective (when the parent rock is fairly smooth) technique of roller printing. Large sheets of paper were appended to the walls and then a block-printing roller with ink was rolled over the images, turning the negative cavities and incisions into white and the raised areas into black depictions. This provided accurate 1:1 positive/negative images that are easily transferred into pen-and-ink renderings. Her technique represented a real advance in field methods and interpretation. She argued that periodic retouching of the incised figures was conducted, perhaps as part of cultic practices, evidenced by the extreme depth and width of their component incisions.

By the time I began work in Puerto Rico in 1978, field investigators had added rubbings, either with charcoal on stretched paper or cotton, or the simple, but effective technique of rubbing carbon paper over sheets pegged on top of the incisions. This produced the same sort of 1:1 negative image of the original petroglyph as roller printing, and, again, was most effective on smooth rock surfaces. Yet every crack and irregularity was frequently introduced into the image using this technique, generating considerable noise in the final product. Moreover, if the rock surfaces are irregular, rubbings are virtually unworkable. Even with all but the best surfaces, rubbings are often undecipherable when viewed alone.

In 1986, I pioneered a new technique on the island while at work on the beach rock petroglyphs at Maisabel Playa. To supplement previously mentioned methods, I used heavy-gauge clear plastic. I laid it over both petroglyphs and pictographs, affixing the plastic to the rock, cutting darts where needed to compensate for surface irregularities. The rock art was traced using permanent markers. Clear lines were contrast-coded in black, fugitive sections in hatchures, with depressions and other features coded. Field observations were recorded directly on the plastic. These 1:1 drawings, often connected by clear sheets if spaces existed between images, were simply rolled up and taken back to the lab to be copied on tracing velum with rapidograph. In doing so, the clear plastic drawings could be laid over rubbings to compare methods and add, or correct, details. The images were photographically reduced and the resultant figures redrawn with rapidograph and published. This technique, now common on the island, even compensates for extreme surface irregularities and the high relief that defeat rubbings, provided that the artist keeps his/her eye and hand at 90 degrees over the incised or painted line of the ancient artwork, to prevent parallax errors.

The next technique José Rivera Meléndez and I tried in 1993, sought to combine the surface detail in rubbings with the capture of line in clear plastic tracings. We documented a petroglyphic assemblage incised on a huge river boulder at the El Palo site (Figure 8.12), located in the southeastern highlands near Pueblito Carmen, Guayama. We painted the entire face of the rock with multiple coats of liquid latex modeling compound, allowing appropriate drying time in between. The resulting rubbery sheet is easily transported with no danger of damage. Such latex peels capture every detail of the surface, including the faintest of incised lines, and are invaluable in reconstructing petroglyphs. Later, the peel can serve as a negative master to pour positive plaster casts, thus recreating the entire rock face.

This battery of recording techniques can wrest from the weathered stone the maximum cultural information and aid in the production of accurate drawings. While interpretations may be disputed, the analyst should leave behind a corpus of detailed and accurate field documentation, which is not open to question. That documentation should also include accurate planimetric and topographic maps of the environs of the rock art to provide a spatial context.

Taking the Images Apart: Componential and Statistical Analysis of Rock Art

Using the documentary methods mentioned above, one then produces an inventory of rock-art sites. The Puerto Rico State Historic Preservation Office and the Instituto de Cultura Puertorriqueña are attempting to generate just such an island-wide inventory. After recording this contextual and dimensional data one may try to decipher the formal code of the rock art, itself no easy task. I have found it useful to decompose the images into recurrent, hence arguably meaningful, design elements and the design motifs they form (Figure 8.12), as well as to postulate a number of design rules (Figure 8.13, Roe 1991a:34) that generate meaningful statements (appropriate design layouts), such as a frieze or an association of glyphs.

This analysis first involves culturally problematic etic categories such as geometric vs. representational motifs. Oliver (1998, this volume) has shown that some geometric motifs, such as the "I" under the male menhir petroglyph at Caguana (Roe 1993:Figure 4), actually denotes an artifact, the male's stool or *duho*. The challenge is to decode representational meaning from such geometric designs (Roe 2000c). To initiate study, I compiled a catalog of human body components (wrapped and unwrapped). The images were reduced to their componential subcategories (Figure 8.12a), including diadems, head shape, eyes, ear and ear plugs, noses, mouths, torsos and torso finials,

Figure 8.10. Stalagmite petroglyphs from Cueva de la Momia, Comerío. (a.) A drawing by the author of the stalactite and stalagmite, the latter with petroglyphs (all from 1:1 clear plastic tracings), height of block 1.45 m, width 49 cm at top, 1.17 m at bottom. (b.) The main early Taíno (ca. A.D. 1300) crowned visage of a "wrapped ancestral" figure, utilizing "naturefact transformation" from the stalagmite projection to give a three-dimensional effect. (c.) The "bat" below this figure, both distorted in 2-D as the tracings are laid out flat. (d.) The undistorted appearance of the original 3-D images, scale 5 cm (all from Roe et al. 1999b:Figure 14). (e.) A probable "neotaíno" modern simple face. (f.) Three probable later Elenan Ostionoid (ca. A.D. 800–1100) petroglyphs, the bracket indicating a 37 cm gap, scale 5 cm (Roe et al. 1999b:Figure 12).

Figure 8.11. The petroglyphic assemblage from the Pueblito Carmen river boulder (from a clear plastic 1:1 tracing). (a.) The assortment of 21 spiral motifs, simple faces, and "wrapped ancestral" figures, scale 20 cm (adapted from Roe and Rivera Meléndez 1999:Figure 4). (b.) An enlargement of 21, the "inverted" wrapped figure, apparently drawn by leaning over the top of the huge boulder. (c.) An enlargement of 20, a "right-side-up" wrapped figure, together with 19, an "alter ego" simple face.

arms, legs, and such. Each subcategory was further divided into appropriate elements, such as crowned, scalloped, and plumed. Categories, subcategories, and elements were based on a literature review and the results of my field studies (Roe 1991a:Figures 17–31). This catalog serves as a device to identify consistent patterns (e.g., kind of crown associated with kind of head shape), and to help in delineating stylistic provinces and/or temporal periods. Further, the analysis can assist in distinguishing modern "neotaíno" recreations

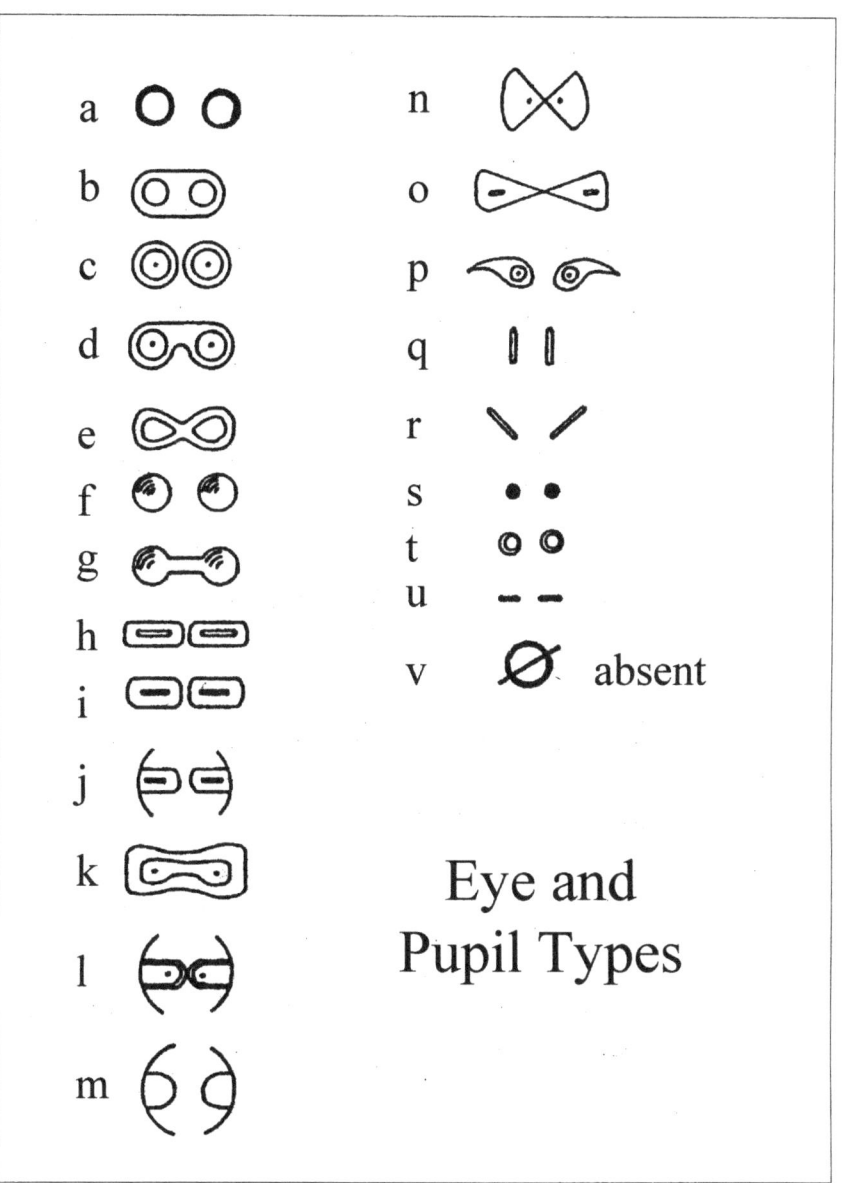

Figure 8.12. A componential approach to the somatic components of anthropomorphic petroglyphs in Puerto Rico.

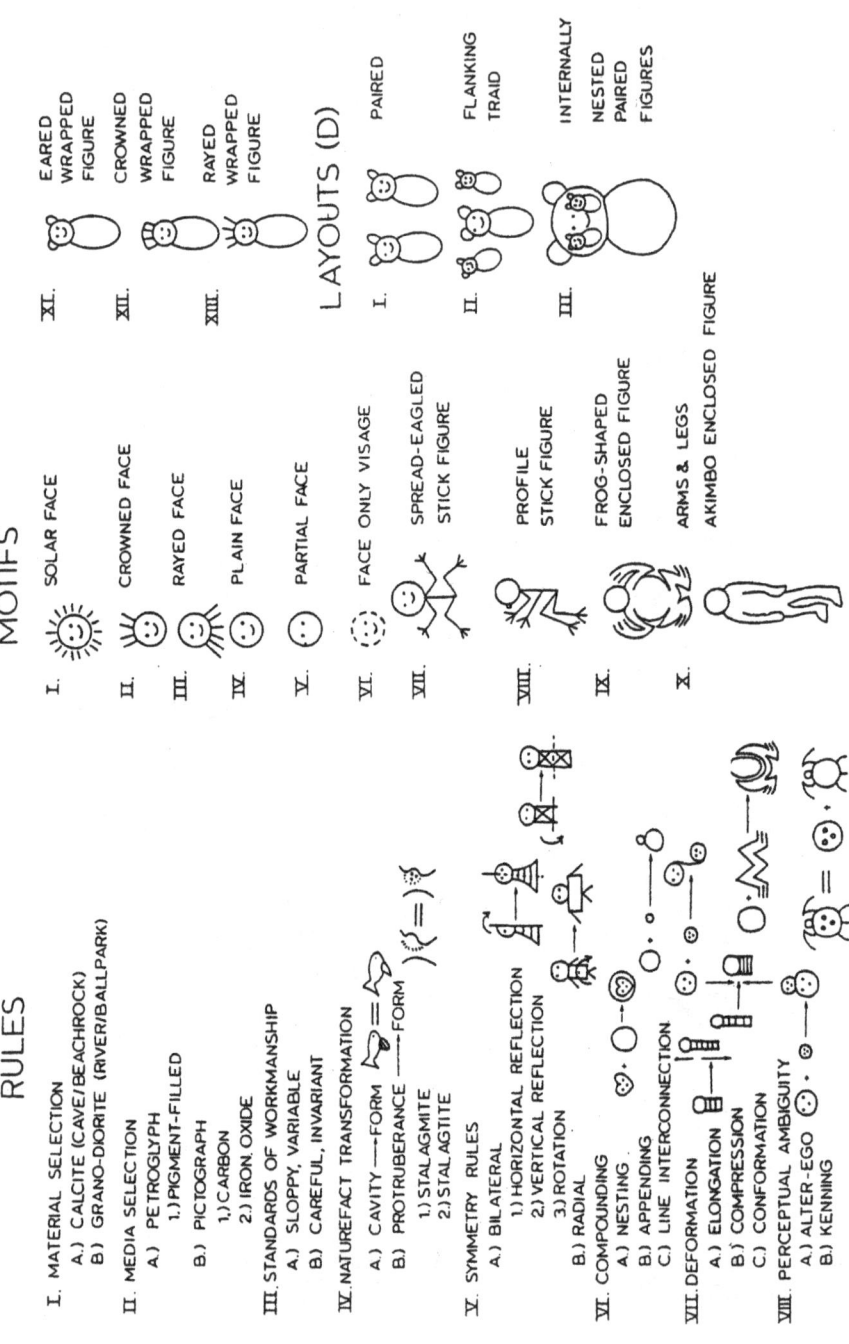

Figure 8.13. The beginnings of a generative grammar for Puerto Rican anthropomorphic petroglyph design (Roe 1991a:Figures 34–35).

from ancient designs by noting the inappropriate combination of motifs. With new finds, or the better documentation of already-known finds, the catalog is revised and updated.

Using cluster analysis, Hayward et al. (2001) grouped categories of designs by site in an effort to identify associations between kinds of petroglyphs and kinds of sites. Tentative associations, like spirals with river boulder petroglyphs (Hayward et al. 2001:Figures 7, 16) as potential representations of eddies or whirlpools, have been suggested for the numerous glyphs at El Palo (Roe and Rivera Meléndez 1995).

Floating in Time: The Problematic Temporal Context of Rock Art

One of the limitations of New World rock-art research has been in dating the images (Veloz Maggiolo et al. 1973). Stylistic cross-ties between datable ceramics and petroglyphs and even ethnographic body paint (Pereira 2001:227), and accidental paint spall spillage from pictographs on datable living floors have been employed to suggest temporal placement for rock art in the lower Amazon (Roosevelt et al. 1996). However, secure time placement for Antillean rock art was lacking until recently (Pagán Perdomo 1988). Some have suggested pictographs to be as early as the Saladoid arrivals (Morbán Laucer 1972:15), while most petroglyphs were assumed to date to the late prehistoric/protohistoric period. Research at the Caguana site in Utuado has provided plausible dating for the elaborate Classic Taíno menhir petroglyphs (Alegría 1983). Juan González Colón's (1984) uncovering of the earlier ball parks at Tibes on the south coast near Ponce, and their associated simpler head-only petroglyphs, began to suggest a seriation, but problems of field recovery and restoration at that site raised serious questions.

A breakthrough in discovering the diachronic dimension of *arte rupestre* in Puerto Rico came from the world of cultural/heritage resource management. The El Bronce excavations, directed by Linda Sickler Robinson, yielded a stone row of menhir petroglyphs in association with a small datable ball park (*batey*) (Robinson 1985b). Among the petroglyphs were two slabs: one depicts an elaborate human head with a complex crown (Figure 8.14a) and the other shows the profile of an entire shark associated with a simple frontal human face (Figure 8.5B8). While cruder and less detailed than the Caguana specimens, they were nonetheless much more elaborate than the Tibes specimens. Culturally, this was significant since their workmanship and imagery not only hinted at increasing hierarchy and stratification but also suggested the greater importance that local fauna represented in pre-Taíno culture, in contrast to the imported symbols from the Amazon-Guianas characteristic of the earlier Cedrosan Saladoid phases. Perhaps this was a form of mythic substitution, where local fauna began to stand for *tierra firme* symbols of their migrant Cedrosan and Huecan Saladoid ancestors (Roe 1989a, 2000a). By associating the formidable shark, pictured accurately down to its parallel gill slits, and which was a sea predator not characteristic of lowland South Amerindian art, with high-status humans, the lithic art of El Bronce mirrored the local ecological success of the pre-Taíno period in terms of both site density and inferable demographic expansion, for which it was a primary symbolic expression. In its development and associated artifacts, El Bronce predated Caguana and postdated Tibes. It also presaged the recent demonstration by Rivera Fontán and Silva Pagán (1997) of the saltwater dolphin, another important local natural symbol of oceanic predation, as part of the iconography of later Taíno provincial ball parks. The El Bronce petroglyphs were incised on the fronts of large boulders, separated spatially from chronologically distinctive artifacts and datable carbon; linkages remain likely but not absolute.

It was against this backdrop of previous work that I embarked on a qualitative seriation of petroglyphic art. I instituted documentary work on all of the recognized types of rock art on the island, as well as serendipitously adding a new subtype to the inventory. The latter emerged at the Maisabel Playa site in conjunction with Peter E. Siegel's Centro de Investigaciones Indígenas de Puerto Rico (CIIPR)–sponsored project at the Maisabel site proper in Vega Baja (Siegel 1992). There, guided by Carlos Ayes, we uncovered a complex of unique petroglyphs incised into the horizontal bedding plane of the soft eolinitic strands. These formations of lithified sands occur within the semilunar embayment fronting the Maisabel site (Figures 8.6, 8.9) (Roe 1991a). This research added the new subtype (Beach Petroglyphs) to the three previously recognized varieties of petroglyphs known for the island: Ball Park, River Boulder, and Cave petroglyphs (Fewkes 1903). Due to the finding of Elenan Ostionoid sherds sedimented *within* the same lithified dunes that the petroglyphs were carved into, combined with local geomorphology and specific componential/stylistic details of the rock art itself, we were afforded a *terminus ante quem*, a chronological point before which the rock art could have not been executed.[2] A tentative three-phase qualitative seriation of Puerto Rican rock art can now be suggested (Figure 8.5). This scheme shows the genre appearing (Figure 8.5, Phase A) in pre-Taíno times (at Tibes and Maisabel), early Elenan Ostionoid (Monserratean times), not during the Saladoid era as had been suggested before (Morbán Laucer 1972), becoming complex in later Elenan times (Santa Elena) (Figure 8.5, Phase B) (e.g., El Bronce [Robinson 1985b]), and then shifting to even greater elaboration, with

Figure 8.14. Two versions of an El Bronce crowned anthropomorphic head, from a clear plastic tracing by the author, scale 5 cm (from Roe 1991a:Figure 14). (a.) The head as traced from the "menhir," incorporating obvious "mistakes" and postexecution damage. (b.) The head as reconstructed by the author according to probable intent.

clear indications of hierarchy, in the Classic Taíno petroglyphs of Caguana, Utuado (Capá) (Figure 8.5, Phase C). The latter site was the seat of one of the most powerful Contact-period *cacicazgos* (chiefdoms) on the island (Rouse 1992:113). For the first time, and rarely for rock-art research generally, we can now suggest dates for many petroglyphs by style and relate them to other media, such as ceramics, in order to discern social and ideological trends over time.

To this end, I produced clear plastic tracings of the menhir-style ball park petroglyphs of Caguana (Roe 1993). Cross-media isomorphisms or stylistic similarities between motifs and design layouts on Chican Ostionoid (Classic Taíno) pottery (Figure 8.15a, g) and those on the menhirs (Figure 8.15e, f) were established. I demonstrated both the importance of these motifs in Taíno cosmovision and the icons underlying the symbols (in the Peircian [1991] sense) of their art, and addressed culture historical reconstructions concerning the possible diffusion of mythological concepts from Central America vs. independent invention derived from lowland South America.

At first glance, geometric layouts composed of roundels and flanking triangular motifs (Figure 8.15b) look purely decorative. However, in many lowland styles (Roe 1990, 1995c) supposedly "geometric" or "nonrepresentational" motifs are not mere decoration, but encode actual "representational" meaning (Roe 1989b). I proposed a similar process for these ubiquitous Antillean incised motifs, such as the roundels; they may be "kennings," or frozen metaphors, for "joints" (Figure 8.15d), among other "bodily portal" referents mentioned by the chroniclers, such as the umbilicus (Figure 8.15f) (Roe 2000c).

In collaboration with José Rivera Meléndez, I followed these coastal and north highland themes farther into the interior by focusing on the southern highlands and the next type of island petroglyphs, those on river boulders. We documented a huge boulder with a series of incised designs (Figure 8.11) at El Palo (Roe and Rivera Meléndez 1995). That study revealed how reversible imagery (Figure 8.11b, c) was as central to rock art as it was to other forms of aesthetic artifacts such as woodcarvings and modeled and incised ceramic depictions (Figure 8.4h, i; Roe 1999). Pictorial dualism was a standard Antillean graphic device dating to Cedrosan Saladoid times (Figure 8.4a, b) (Roe 2000c). It appears to have been derived (literally) from the curiously inverted *cohoba* (*Anadenanthera peregrina*) visions of Taíno (and undoubtedly pre-Taíno) shamans and artists as documented by the chroniclers.

José Rivera, Peter DeScioli, and I (Roe et al. 1999a) then shifted our attention to documenting and interpreting some of the most spectacular petroglyphs and pictographs found in Puerto Rico. These occurred in the last subtype on our agenda: caves. Our lithic "text" was located in the central

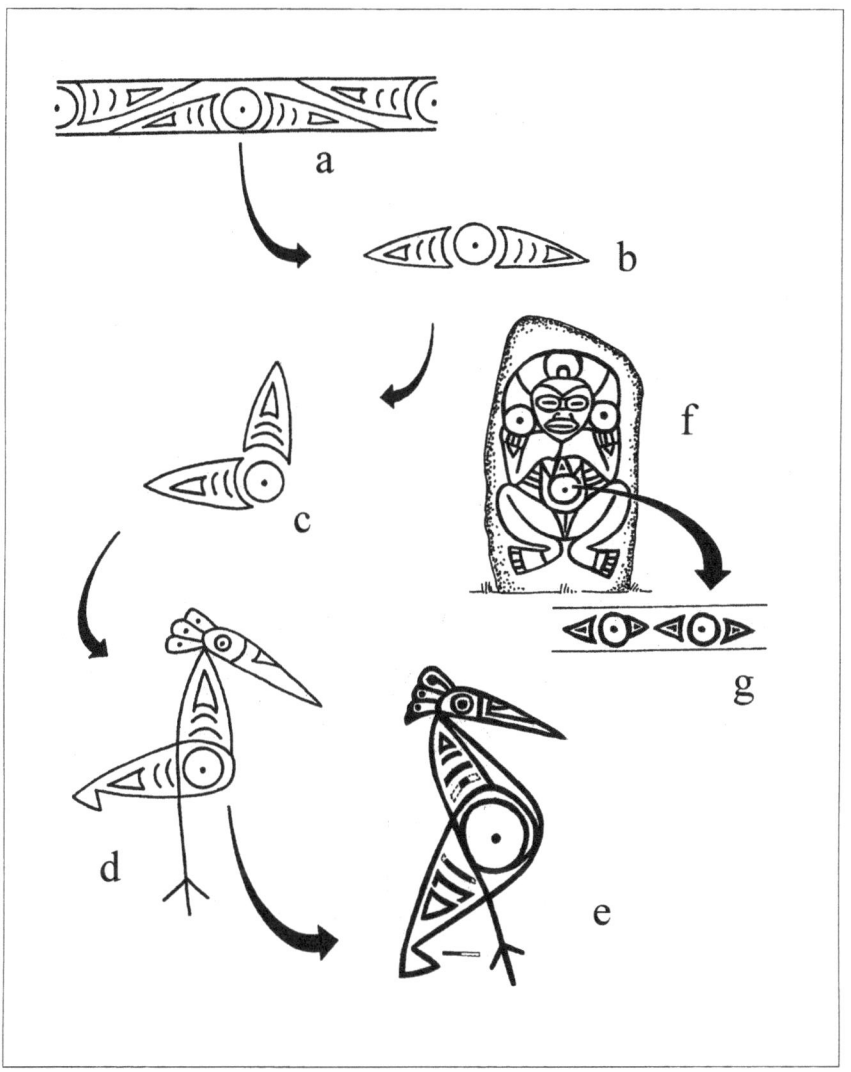

Figure 8.15. Cross-media isomorphisms in Chican Ostionoid (Taíno) incised ceramics and petroglyphs. (a.) A common ceramic design layout of roundels and transverse-reflected triangles. (b.) The isolated repeat module. (c.) One wing of the module rotated 90 degrees vertical. (d.) This "geometric" motif is the core of a "representational" heron (Roe 1993:Figure 8a–d). (e.) The actual great blue heron from the menhir petroglyph row at Caguana, based on a clear plastic tracing by the author (Roe 1993:Figure 7a). (f.) The "Diosa de Caguana," the Frog Lady *Attabeira* Earth Goddess, from a clear plastic tracing by the author. (g.) The "geometric" layout nested within this "representational" image, composed of a belly roundel, inter-breasts triangle and pubic triangle, rotated 90 degrees horizontal, also a common ceramic design layout.

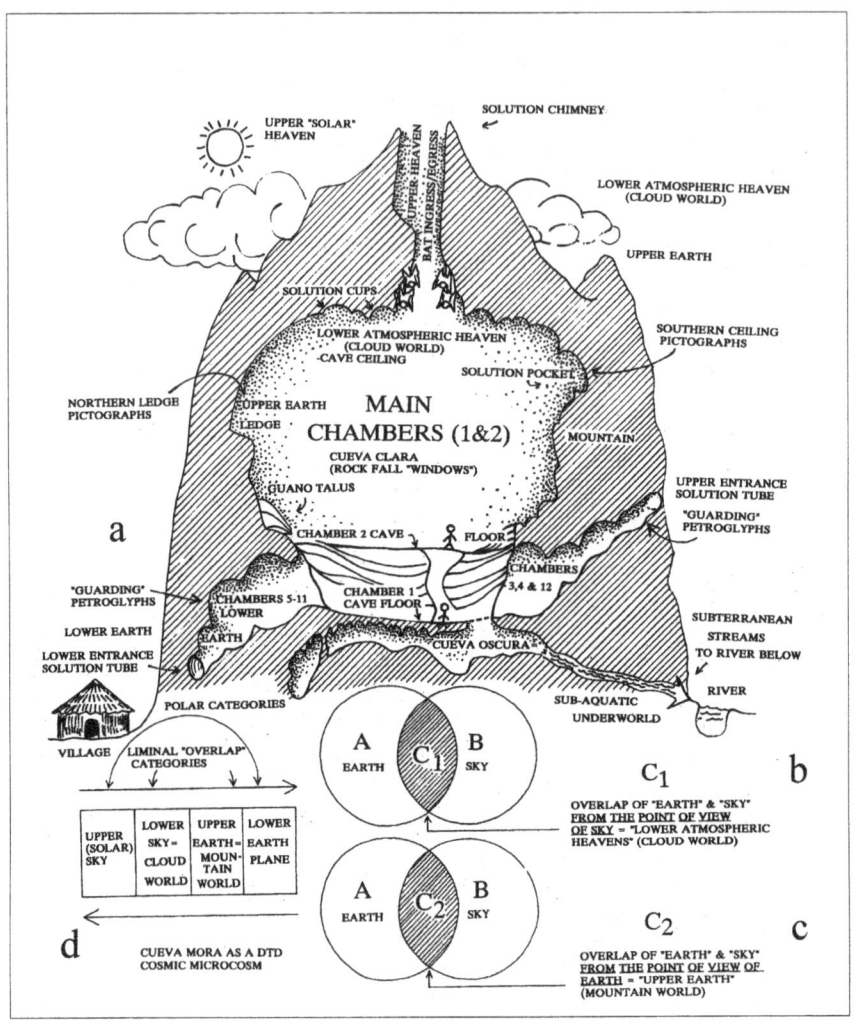

Figure 8.16. The Cueva la Mora, Comerío, as cosmogram. (a.) A cross section of the cave with the main chamber and solution tube entrances, rock art locations plotted. (b.) The DTD (Dual Triadic Dualism) model generating the Cloud World of the southern ceiling pictographs. (c.) The DTD model generating the Mountain World of the lower northern ledge pictographs. (d.) The "chromatic" model of all four realms, including Lower Earth of the "guardian" petroglyphs (Roe et al. 1999a:Figure 38).

highlands cavern of Cueva la Mora in Comerío (Figure 8.16). With the aid of my wife, Amy W. Roe, we initiated the first accurate planimetric map of an entire cave and its rock art in the Greater Antilles (Figure 8.17).[3] This map revealed a functional and spatial division between two rock-art genres: sim-

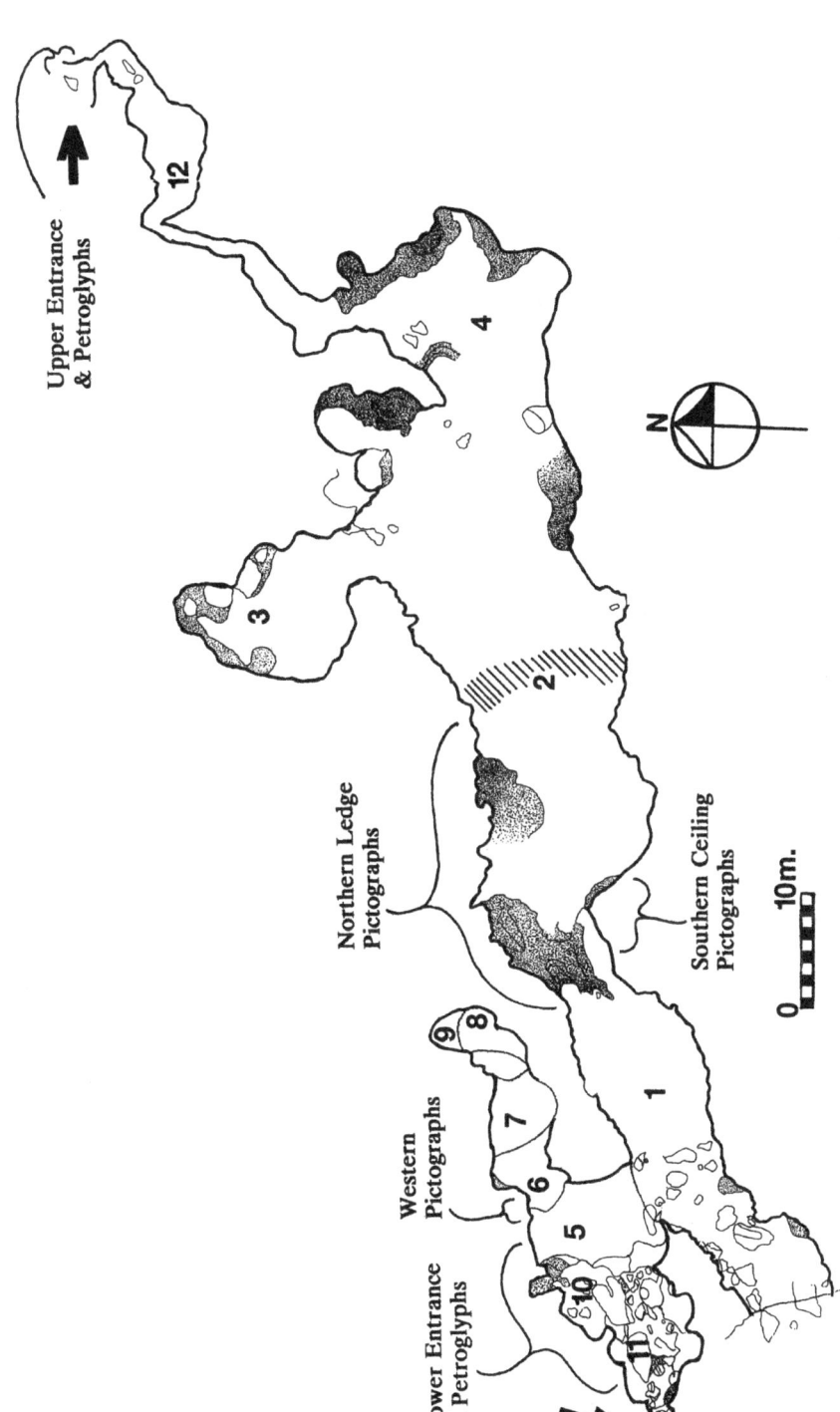

Figure 8.17. A planimetric map of all 12 chambers of la Mora cavern, locating the peripheral and lower "guardian" petroglyphs and the central "cult image," higher, and more elaborate coeval pictographs (adapted from Roe et al. 1999a:Figure 2).

Figure 8.18a. The peripheral "portal guardian" petroglyphs from Cueva la Mora. The upper solution tube entrance petroglyphs, scale 10 cm (Roe et al. 1999a:Figure 12).

pler petroglyphs serving as "portal guardians" on the upper (Figure 8.18a) and lower solution tube entrances (Figure 8.18b, c) to the central chamber and the larger, more elaborate pictographs. These imposing paintings took central stage as the major cult images (Figures 8.19–8.23) in the cavern's main chamber, situated between and above the flanking petroglyphs. Previous dogma, long enshrined in oral tradition, had placed these two media of rock art in a diachronic relationship: earlier (Saladoid) pictographs vs. later (Taíno) petro-

Figure 8.18b. The north wall petroglyphs of Chamber 5, scale 10 cm (adapted from Roe et al. 1999a:Figure 10).

glyphs. It is more likely that the two media functioned as related parts of a whole story rather than as temporally successive expressions.

The iconography, symbolism, and spatial relationships of these portrayals allowed for a detailed demonstration of how rock art may physically instantiate a cosmology. These are some of the most impressive images in the Caribbean, giant life-size pictographs of "wrapped ancestors" (Figure 8.19), executed in a kind of positive-negative painting (Figures 8.19d and 8.20f) in true polychrome that provides stylistic continuity in design rules to Saladoid ceramic decoration, yet without any specific motifs that would date them to that period. They encompass the usual suspects associated with the dead (García Arévalo 1997): bats and owls (Figures 8.19b and 8.20i). They also include the first portrayal of the demonic giant cave spiders, or *guabá* (Figure 8.20b), as well as fish (Figure 8.20d), turtles (Figure 8.20j), and birds (Figure 8.20k). But, by far, the most numerous, penetrating into the light boundary itself, were the multiple, large, wrapped ancestral figures (Figures 8.19a, c, d; 8.20e; 8.21a–d), all painted high up on a natural ledge and out onto the actual curved ceiling (Figure 8.21d). They are located so far above the present floor (and even above the estimated original floor before guano extraction in the last century), that lashed sapling scaffolding would have been necessary to draw them. Indeed, the ceiling glyph could only have been executed by artisans lying on their backs. On the other side of the vast central cavern, whose interior is home to millions of brown bats, is a much higher series of solution concavities, which would have required true rappelling with jungle vine and cave aerial-root ropes to reach. There, a number of humanoid (Figures 8.22 and 8.23d) and turtle effigies (Figures 8.23a, b, f, g) were drawn that evoke

Figure 8.18c. The lower solution tube exit petroglyphs from Chamber 10 pillar, scale 10 cm, all from clear plastic tracings by the author (adapted from Roe et al. 1999a:Figure 7).

Taíno myths of turtle progenitrixes (Pané 1974, 1992, 1999) and even a frontal view of a sacred three-pointer (Figure 8.23c).

The placement of these images vis-à-vis the lower petroglyphs and the presence of an underground wet cave below the dry one (the latter connected in local legend and hydrology to the river far below) hint at a microcosmic recapitulation of the macrocosmos in Taíno art and cosmology (Figure 8.16). Using the same kind of dynamic dualistic thought that is found in the low-

Figure 8.19. The "wrapped ancestor" group from the northern ledge of Chamber 2, Cueva la Mora, from clear plastic tracings by the author, scale 10 cm. (a.) An "eared" ancestor with diamond body wrappings. (b.) An owl face, the Múcaro, herald of the dead. (c.) A fragmentary plumed wrapped ancestor. (d.) Another "eared" ancestor with positive-applied, negative-perception wrapping. (e.) A heart-shaped human face, possibly of a descendant (adapted from Roe et al. 1999a:Figure 26).

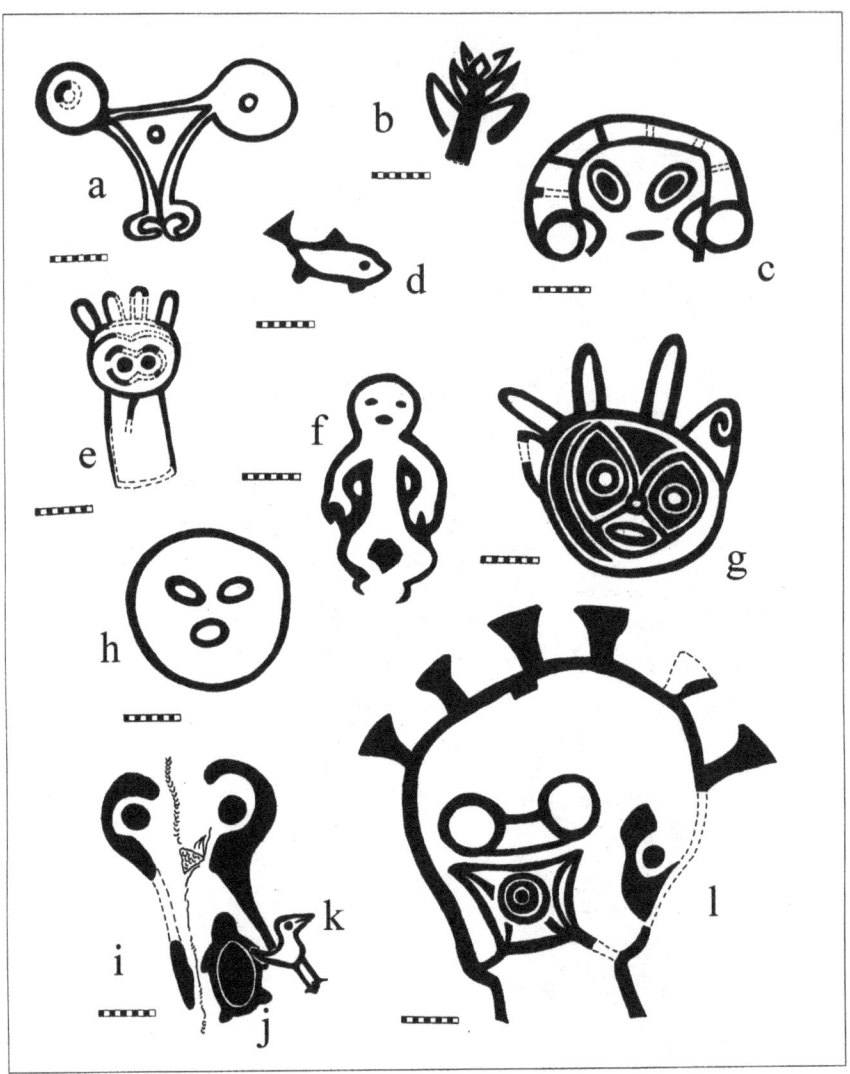

Figure 8.20. A selection of the northern ledge pictographs from Chamber 2, Cueva la Mora, all from clear plastic tracings by the author, scales = 10 cm. (a.) A probable "vaginal-with ovaries" motif (Roe et al. 1999a:Figure 28a). (b.) A possible *guabá* large cave spider, demonic in folk classifications even today (Roe et al. 1999a:Figure 29a). (c.) The crowned head of a "wrapped figure" (Roe et al. 1999a:Figure 29b). (d.) A profile fish associated with the vaginal motif (Roe et al. 1999a:Figure 28b). (e.) A fragmentary plumed, wrapped ancestor (Roe et al. 1999a:Figure 28c). (f.) A naturalistic infant depiction executed in positive-negative paint (Roe et al. 1999a:Figure 29c). (g.) The elaborate plumed face, the internal designs perhaps representing face-paint (Roe et al. 1999a:Figure 31b). (h.) A "simple face" (Roe et al. 1999a:Figure 28d). (i.) The "owl" group, with the "naturefact transformational" use of a seepage line to represent the beak (Roe et al. 1999a:Figure 27a). (j.) An incised turtle (Roe et al. 1999a:Figure 27c). (k.) An associated profile bird (Roe et al. 1999a:Figure 27b). (l.) The huge plumed skull (Roe et al. 1999a:Figure 33).

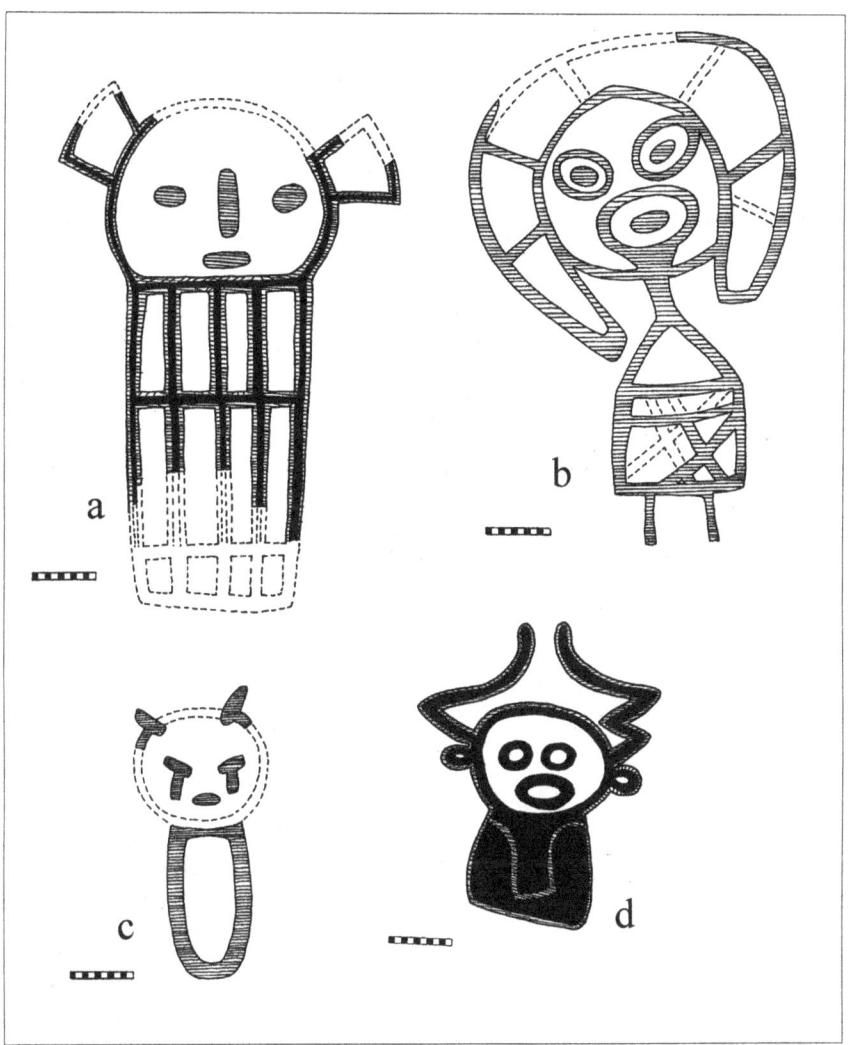

Figure 8.21. A group of "wrapped ancestors" from Chamber 2, Cueva la Mora, all derived from 1:1 clear plastic tracings by the author, scales 10 cm. (a.) A large "eared" wrapped figure with vertically elongated grid body bundle markings in black under-painting and white and red over-painting (Roe et al. 1999a:Figure 35). (b.) The last "wrapped ancestor," a crowned form, almost outside the light boundary in the deep interior, weathered to red monochrome (Roe et al. 1999a:Figure 37). (c.) A small wrapped figure with the remains of a plume headdress, again weathered to monochromatic red. The "tears" may represent *Boinyael*, the Taíno deity of auspicious rains (Roe et al. 1999a:Figure 34b). (d.) The little crowned wrapped figure actually painted on the inclined ceiling above the northern ledge (Roe et al. 1999a:Figure 34a).

Figure 8.22. The central "shamanic" male figure pictograph from the southern ceiling, Cueva la Mora, from a clear plastic tracing by DeScioli, scale 10 cm. Note the erection (Roe et al. 1999a:Figure 18).

lands today, with its emphasis on the liminal overlap categories as conceptual "bridges" to otherwise opposed polar categories (Crocker 1983), the high ceiling of the cave, with its sink-hole apertures for the nightly escape of the immense flights of the resident bats (nocturnal fruit-eating and seductive souls in Taíno belief) may represent the Upper Heavens of the Sky World.

Figure 8.23. A selection of the southern ceiling pictographs, Cueva la Mora, from clear plastic tracings by DeScioli, scales = 10 cm. (a.) A probable "Turtle Woman" effigy with flippers, a stylized head and a carapace face (Roe et al. 1999a:Figure 21). (b.) Another turtle effigy with eroded front flippers (Roe et al. 1999a:Figure 25). (c.) The large three-pointer effigy with a skull face painted on a triangular eminence, the highest depiction in the cave (Roe et al. 1999a:Figure 23). (d.) A small plumed humanoid with a raised hand and a stick body (Roe et al. 1999a:Figure 21a). (e.) The "testicular" face (Roe et al. 1999a:Figure 19a) between the legs of the male shaman (Figure 8.21). (f.) The humanoid were-turtle that flanks the left of the large shaman (Roe et al. 1999a:Figure 19b). (g.) The carapace-face turtle effigy that flanks the right of the shaman, both of these flanking turtles are probable females (Roe et al. 1999a:Figure 17).

Figure 8.24. The "living dead" and their ancestors. (a.) A skeletalized "shaman," with erection, pictograph from a cave on Mona Island, between Puerto Rico and Hispaniola, (photo by the author). The image was *inverted* in the cave (drawn from Roe 1997:Figure 3). (b.) A typical "wrapped ancestor" from Cueva del Indio, Arecibo, drawn from a clear plastic tracing by the author—see Figure 8.8. (c.) The body lozenge of that wrapped figure, minus the head and rotated 90 degrees. (d.) His right-hand lozenge, a transform of "c." (e.) His left-hand lozenge, another analog of wrapped "c," also representing a probable ancestor.

The southern pictographs on the curved sides just below the ceiling might occupy the Lower Atmospheric Heavens of the Cloud World. Their position may have answered a shaman's query, whereby his point of view alternated in a dyadic fashion. This is a cognitive style analogous to the Antillean artist's visual shifting between figure-and-ground in his graphic and plastic art.

For example, the *behique* might have said, in instructing a particularly obtuse neophyte, "what is the overlap between 'Sky' and 'Earth' *from the point of view of Sky*" (Figure 8.16b)? That would be, of course, the Lower Heavens, the atmospheric Cloud World that hangs so low upon the mountains in this part of the Puerto Rican cordillera every morning that it is truly palpable. The even more elaborate lower pictographs on the northern ledge, on the opposite side of the main chamber, may have inhabited the adjacent lower plane, Upper Earth, the Mountain World level (e.g., "what is the overlap between 'Sky' and 'Earth' *from the point of view of Earth*?" [Figure 8.16c]). Those mountain peaks, literally Upper Earth, are frequently wreathed in clouds at these elevations (and Cueva de Mora is formed right in the side of one such peak), an arduous nearly vertical climb from the valley below (so steep that we only ascended in the rainy season on our knees, desperately grabbing roots or even tufts of grass to keep from plummeting back down).

These paired liminal categories: Upper Earth and Lower Sky, are both dynamic dualistic overlaps between Sky World and Earth World in cognate lowland cosmology. Four linked categories (two polar and two liminal) are created from the dual terms (Figure 8.16d), thus providing what Claude Lévi-Strauss (1981) has called "chromatism," the South Amerindian tendency to take small conceptual steps between something and its opposite. The rungs of these steps are generated by overlapping, or bridging, the polar categories. The thinker now progresses in either direction, both to and from either pole (absolutely contrastive), thus turning apparently static dyadic contrast sets into an intercommunicating series. Note that this mental progression recapitulates the journey of the shaman as he flies or climbs through the levels of the universe to cure/bewitch. Thus, like a Taíno shaman, a *behique,* one can get from Earth World to Sky World by first traversing, as in a Sky Ladder or Rope (mythemes abundantly demonstrated in cognate lowland mythology [Roe 1991c]), the intermediary overlap worlds of Upper Earth (the mountain tops), and from thence, via an easy transition, to the Cloud World literally enshrouding such peaks. These crags form the Lower Atmospheric Heavens, the bottom rung of a further ascent to the Upper Sky of the remote Sun and Moon. These may sound like complex doings to a Westerner, burdened as we are by the hoary, and unbridgeable static "Desert Religion" dichotomies of Man/God, Heaven/Earth, Good/Evil, God/Devil, Culture/Nature, and such, but they are old hat for South (and presumably Greater Antillean) Amerindians reared in an ancient "Jungle Religion" based on movement and transformation, not just dyadic opposition.

The guardian petroglyphs extend this chromatism in the opposite direction; the dual liminal overlaps between the Earth World of humans and the subaquatic Underworld of ancestral spirits. Instantiating this descent at Cueva de Mora, the ancient cultists climbed the mountain past the dark and wet unvisited cave below (the Subaquatic Underworld proper), and entered the dry chambers of the upper cave through the narrow lower solution tube entrance (Chamber 11), Inner Earth. A liminal layer, this passage answered the rhetorical question, "what is the overlap between 'Earth World' and 'Subaquatic Underworld' *from the point of view of Earth World?*" The next rung of their ascent/descent, overseen by the small "guardian" petroglyphs of the wrapped dead and their heralds (Chambers 10 and 5), would have represented the Upper Underworld, the soil horizon, (responding to the query "what is the overlap between 'Earth World' and 'Subaquatic Underworld' *from the perspective of Subaquatic Underworld?*"). The same identification marked the upper entrance (Chambers 3, 4, and 12) with its analogous "guardian" petroglyphs.

Scrambling up to the cave floor of Chambers 1 and 2, the humans viewing and paying cult to the large pictographs of the main chamber (2), far above their heads, occupied the surface of the Earth World proper. Thus a trinary system of Sky, Earth, and Underworld would have yielded a complex Lévi-Straussian chromatic continuum of the ascent/descent to and from the cave. (Although, as a Cartesian himself, the master was often blind to such subtleties, save for his discussion of "binary operators" [Roe 1983b], preferring instead typically Western Culture/Nature dyads.) Like a cosmic ladder, these levels could be traveled in either direction, up or down, by shamans and others in their visits to the ancestral animal/avian/fish-turtle spirits. The mountain in Comerío becomes the World Mountain, the shamanic tower-ladder armature anchoring all the levels of the universe and uniting the domains of life and death via the "living dead" *behique.*

To continue the ascent, the eyes of the propitiating human spectators would have taken in the upper rungs of these chromatic worlds, carved by carbolic acid in limestone over eons and by stone axes wielded by artists (and applied in paint by others). The large and imposing lower northern ledge pictographs rising above them to the left represented Upper Earth (chiefly Wrapped Ancestors and their bat-owl avatars). Farther distant and above them to the right loomed the Lower Atmospheric Heavens (occupied by the towering southern ledge, largely showing paired "shamanic progenitor" and "turtle progenitrix" pictographs). Lastly, nearly vertically above and hidden in the gloom of the solution concavity-pocked ceiling, was the chirping Upper Heavens (cave roof apex–nocturnal solution tube exit of bat Death Spirits–*opía*) as they would have poured forth at night into the Middle Earth of the human villages in the valleys below.

It is remarkable that this DTD (Dual Triadic Dualism, cf. Roe 1995b) vision coheres point-by-point with the rock-art images carved and painted within the vertically stratified levels (geomorphological "design fields") of the gigantic Cueva de Mora, Comerío, central highlands, Puerto Rico. Perhaps mute rock art can speak after all?

This work also showed images of other sacred artifacts associated with *cemíism* in the Greater Antilles, such as three-pointers (Figure 8.23c). I obtained an early Elenan Ostionoid image (Figure 8.6a) from Maisabel Playa of this same enigmatic artifact, hitherto only known sculpturally, and now, tucked near the ceiling at more than 30 meters above the cave floor, and accessible to us and the aboriginal artists only via rappelling; we had a late Elenan–early Taíno three-pointer on a much grander scale.[4] The painter who executed this *trigonolito* took advantage of the triangular space in the ceiling to show yet another anthropomorphic image, significantly, the highest of all the images painted in the cave, and one of the largest.

Further work in the vicinity by Rivera Meléndez, James Byerly, Nicole Cornell, and myself (Roe et al. 1999b) documented an additional type of cave formation context (Cueva de la Momia), petroglyphs carved into stalagmites and stalactites (Figure 8.10). We used the same instrumentation to produce the first topographic map of a cave site in Puerto Rico and tested the qualitative seriation by isolating pre-Taíno (Figure 8.10f) and provincial Classic Taíno motifs (Figure 8.10b, c) and matched them with the feature lists already mentioned. This cave illustrates another aspect of Puerto Rican rock-art style, the Boasian (Boas 1955 [1927]) "reading-in" of human visages upon three-dimensional natural cave relief. Here, the natural convexity of a stalagmite was emphasized to give relief and roundness to a carved human visage (Figure 8.10d).

Beyond Documentation: The Hermeneutics of Petroglyphs and Pictographs

Once all of the rock art on the island has been documented and sorted into either stylistic provinces or temporal phases correlated with changing ideological and social phenomena, then the really challenging task begins: that is cultural interpretation (Geertz 1976), and specifically, inferences into the iconic and symbolic significance of the images (Llamazares 1988; Pagán Perdomo 1982). This level of analysis is of fundamental importance, especially since numerous ethnographies are available of living lowland South Amerindians, the survivors of cognate ancient populations that migrated to the Caribbean. These ethnographic descendants demonstrate the centrality of art in their very definitions of human culture (Guss 1989; Roe 1985b, 1989a, 1989b, 1990, 1995b, 1995c, 1997c).

Further, we have available the work of Ramón Pané, which was commissioned by Columbus on his second voyage, and carried out in the field from 1494 to 1496, with the goal of making the Spanish missionization of the Taíno easier by learning about their religion (Bourne 1906). Oliver (1992b, 1998, this volume) and others have used Pané to identify key mythic characters (Gods, Spirits) and episodes (mythemes), with great success (Alegría 1978; Arrom 1986; Deive 1976; Jiménez Lambertus 1983; López-Baralt 1977; Stevens-Arroyo 1988, etc.).

Yet Pané's work is not without problems. The most obvious is a simple artifact of his times, an era long before trained and dispassionate observers. Pané tended to garble what, thanks to contemporary lowland ethnography, we now know to be complete myths. Further, he collapsed several myths into one, such as the tale of *Deminán Caracaracol*. His tale of "sexless beings," for example, conflates elements of both the Wooden Bride and the Mermaid mythic cycles for the origin of women found from the Guianas to the Upper Amazon in South America (Roe 1982). Like authors up to the middle decades of the twentieth century, he is also guilty of the literary conflation of the whole corpus into linear narrative (the tendency of literate Westerners to combine distinct oral myths into an integrated and developmental storyline). To partially compensate for these difficulties, one can best approach his fifteenth-century fragments via the lens of complete mythic cycles derived from modern lowland ethnography (Roe 1992). In this case, the present can illuminate the past. The direct-historical approach, utilizing ethnohistorical and ethnographic analogy, is appropriate for Puerto Rican rock art. Aided by Pané and modern lowland ethnographies, as well as close visual, componential, and syntactical analysis of the artifacts themselves, an attentive student can propose a number of testable iconographic rock-art patterns.

On the level of subsistence, it is clear from the iconography of the images engraved at the Maisabel Playa site, as well as its location near where a freshwater river flows into the ocean, that these petroglyphs marked the zone as the joint property of specific social groups (perhaps lineages and clans) as suggested by "wrapped ancestral" figures (Figure 8.5, Phase A: 4) associated with "solar" images, fish, fish traps, and sea turtles (Figure 8.6b–f). Long called "swaddled infants," based on the false analog of North Amerindian practice. Vega (1976) was the first to recognize, using analogous Dominican Taíno depictions, that these frontal figures with bodies covered in "X"-shaped motifs really indicated the dead wrapped in the strands of their hammocks (Griswold 1997b) prior to carrying them on a burden pole to prepared graves or to caves. But no ordinary dead merited such iconographic depiction; repeated images on rocks from the sea to the interior indicate that these were the "ancestral dead," still absorbed with the fate of their descendants and worshipped by the latter for favors and intercession.

To what resources would such potent ancestors have vouchsafed access for their earthly descendants? The protected semilunar embayments, of which Maisabel Playa is an excellent example, are one of the few places along the storm-lashed northern coast where calm anchorages are offered to dugout canoes, the transport of fishermen in aboriginal times. The submerged eolinitic formations, like coral reefs, also provide haven for innumerable small fish and mollusks, myriad life upon which larger fish depend. Their emergent headlands provide excellent foot access to the deep waters beyond. Indeed, all forms of fish, large and small, are portrayed in the Maisabel petroglyphs, from jacks to snapper and grouper (Figure 8.6f). Moreover, while the fish point to the bay, their habitat, a turtle effigy, whose shell does "double duty" as a frontal human face, points to the shore (Figure 8.6b) where it would have crawled to lay its eggs. These huge marine reptiles are an excellent source of fat and animal protein for insular populations. As well as the turtle unwittingly delivering its own flesh, either to be slaughtered while helpless on land after egg-laying, or captured and kept alive in special ethnohistorically documented flooded shore storage pens for later consumption, it also provides large quantities of soft fat-rich eggs. A geometric basketlike image, which could only be a stylized trap, appears next to the fish (Figure 8.6e), showing the graphic form of their entrapment. Freshwater fish could also have been snared at the mouth of the nearby river. Thanks to ethnohistoric data, we know that such locations were prime fish-netting territories for Contact-period groups, locations requiring protection, both symbolically and socially. Groups were ranked by their access to, and control of, such territories and the resources associated with them. Analogous lowland river petroglyphs have also documented similar associations, linking petroglyphs with prime fishing spots (Lippi 2001), including in the Guianas groups cognate with the ancestors of the Antillean populations (Williams 1978, 1979).

Relevant to the mythic validation of kinship and subsistence-based claims, the spatial positioning of these figural elements within the complete petroglyphic assemblage argues for a recapitulation of mythic syntagmatics. That is, the arrangements of characters into episodes from the oral tradition ("The Sun's Fish Trap") are pictured, similarly arrayed, in a true petroglyphic frieze (Figure 8.6c–f). Perhaps we should not look at rock art as a mélange of isolated images. Instead, they should sometimes be considered as lithographic "friezes" that depict specific episodes from the oral tradition. Thus, it may not be sufficient to accurately depict the single figure. Rather, one should show how that figure is related, spatially and thematically, to surrounding figures, and to the background of decorated space: the beach, the ball park, the river, the cave.

The ideational control of subsistence also implies social competition and hierarchy, the exercise of both power and authority vis-à-vis other populations. Thus, on the level of political evolution, a study of the now-seriated petroglyphs shows a clear shift from the "personal presentation" material culture of the egalitarian early Saladoid arrivals to a material culture of "public power" as complex tribes or incipient chiefdoms initiated two forms of monumental art in tandem: petroglyphs and ball parks (Figure 8.5A6). As the scale of the parks and petroglyphs increased so too did the visual complexity of the rock art, with the emergence of rank society: Classic Taíno paramount caciques, *nitaíno* nobility, and *naboría* commoners. A visual shift occurred away from the physiognomy of the human visage, something all humans possess in common, from the humblest to the most powerful, the "simple face," to status-implying accoutrements such as headdress types, ear plugs, breastplates, and stools (Roe and Rivera Meléndez 1995). Rock art was a clear contributor to social evolution, as visual idioms of hierarchy became fused to ancient shamanistic egalitarian metaphors in a manner parallel to what was happening in cult practices. Thus, the "priest-temple-idol" Intermediate Area–Greater Antilles complex emerged from the formative pattern of egalitarian tribal shamanism (Roe 1997a:157).

That this shamanism was clearly derivative from South America also begins to address a long-festering question of a possible Mesoamerican origin of the Taíno pantheon (Fernández Méndez 1979; García Goyco 1984), and the ball park complex itself (Alegría 1983, 1986a; Roe 1984). While contact clearly occurred, my syntagmatic analysis of the "lithic frieze" formed by the main Caguana alignment of menhir petroglyphs (Roe 1993) shows South American iconography illustrating South American (*not* Mesoamerican) myths. They are of the sort that I have recorded in my ethnographic work on either side of the Amazon, both in the Peruvian jungle and in the Guianas. Thus the visual art conforms to the same lowland South Amerindian pattern as the verbal art of the mythology recorded by Pané (Roe 1982:191). If the ball park was a Mesoamerican innovation why do the images that adorn it speak of lowland South Amerindian sacred tales, specifically the "breaking of the teeth" of the *vagina dentata* of the Frog Woman–*Attabeira* Earth Goddess by the long-beaked phallic aquatic bird, the great blue heron (Roe 1992)? Once again, although now in the fully developed form of élite-commissioned Classic Taíno menhir ball park petroglyphic art at the end of the rock-art sequence, we see the episodic significance of petroglyphic friezes we first encountered at Maisabel Playa at the beginning.

Recently, José Oliver (1992b, 1998, this volume) has shown the cosmological function of the entire ball court of which this alignment is but a component part. His reconstruction allows us to explore in considerable detail the functioning of the entire Taíno religious system. Crucial to the iconography of the *batey* was its association with still and flowing water bounded by the artificial rocky "shores" of its dual stone alignments, and the "play" of forces, telluric and astronomical, that took place therein. Since it clearly played a central role for the people who painted and carved these images adorning the bordering stone, what can rock art tell us about the hallucinogenic "cultural epistemology" of the insular Arawak?

Rock Art as a Conduit to the "Cultural Epistemology" of Extinct Societies

The use of inversion and multiple-view dualism in ancient Puerto Rican rock art (Roe 1997a, 1997b, 1999, 2000c, see Figure 8.4 here) coheres with similar graphic devices in Saladoid (Figure 8.4a, b) to Elenan Ostionoid (Figure 8.4c, e–f) and Taíno (Figure 8.4h, i) pottery, stone, bone, and shell carving, and in wood sculpture. Together, they argue for a worldview characterized by the radical dualism of a waking reality and a realer-than-real (privileged) hallucinogenic reality of Supernatural and proto-Cultural domains. What humans experience in normal rational waking states of consciousness was therefore not really "real." Instead, they were lies invented by malignant spirits to fool and mislead humans (Guss 1989). Real reality is hidden, it lies beyond the Sun, in infinite regress from the terrestrial world humans dwell upon. It hides within the perfect Celestial or Underworld unity of Supernatural/proto-Cultural Species Masters/Mistresses, a sacred world inaccessible to the waking senses. Access to these dual domains is attained via the ritual ingestion of psychotropic drugs like *cohoba* (Schultes and Hofmann 1992). In that spiritual world, shamans became the intermediaries between the dead (the ancestors) and the living (their descendants) via the principle of "genealogical circularity." This is the tendency within unilineal descent systems for the dead to be "recycled" as the newly born replace the recently dead in an infinite circuit of social reproduction that insures the continuity of the lineage or clan. That continuity derives from the fertility of the ancestors and the shamans who communicate with them (note the prominent erections on the two shamanic portrayals pictured here, Figures 8.22 and 8.24a). They are the skeletal/seminal causes of such generational replacement. In Greater Antillean rock art, the ghostly images of the "living dead" shaman yielded fecundity, not mortality, and transferred it to the kin group's women; hence, a skeletal, fasting, and *inverted* (chroniclers describe how initiates under the influence of *cohoba* saw people as walking upside-down) shaman from a Mona Island Taíno period pictograph (Figure 8.24a). Located in a cave on the island, halfway between Puerto Rico and Hispaniola, and within the culturally interacting Mona Passage (Rouse 1992:Figure 8), he holds in his upraised arms the wrapped "eggs" of his lineage's ancestors.

But how do we know he is a shaman, and how do we know he holds his lineage's progeny in his arms? It all sounds like more rock art "reading-in" fantasy. And it would be were it not for congruent imagery derived from cognate living oral continental tradition and recorded ethnohistoric Antillean traditions, as well as close iconographic observation of related archaeological artifacts. We have countless depictions of skeletalized shamanic figures, emaciated from fasting up to four months with only enough nutrition to keep life together (Griswold 1997c), seated on their *duhos* (benches) of power in ceramics (Roe 1997a:Figures 104–105), wood, and stone from the Greater Antilles. Everywhere, skeletalized visages and bodies, sometimes paired in life/death Janus depictions (Roe 1997b:Figures 127–128), signify the fasting shaman, the "living dead" in direct contact, via visions, with the ancestral dead. He visits them as an intermediary, on behalf of the living. In this "jungle religion," attuned as it is to the recycling of the rain forest itself, skeletonized anthropomorphic imagery signifies life (more specifically, the life emergent out of death and decay, gestation springing from rot like the plants and fungi from the leaf litter of the forest floor). These skeletal beings are not symbols of death, as the linear-logic "desert religions" of the West would view them. This Taíno shaman actually stands on his head in the cave wall, as the inverted image of the sacred mirror world of the hereafter, rather than vertically as I have portrayed him here.

But what does he carry in his upward/downward-raised/lowered arms? They are geometric motifs, paired lozenges with internally crossed and curved lines (Figure 8.24d, e). Since such geometric, "nonrepresentational" motifs are frequently, in fact, "representational" in cognate lowland South Amerindian belief (Roe 1995c), what might they stand for? I have decoded the enigmatic lozenges as "eggs," shorthand for "offspring," based on close comparative grounds, this time from Antillean prehistory and ethnohistory, as well as lowland ethnography. My equation derives from the study of cave pictographs and petroglyphs in nearby Puerto Rico, and from the mythic imagery in Pané (El Caribe 1979, referencing Rivera Meléndez's discoveries in Cayey). Marlén Díaz González (1990), in her study of the pictographs of la Cueva de la Catedral, barrio Bayaney, Hatillo, recorded a profusion of drawn lozenges with the same kind of "X" and "+" motifs as are found on the similarly lozengelike (legless) bodies of the classic "wrapped ancestor" figures of pre-Taíno and Taíno rock art (Figure 8.8, redrawn as Figure 8.24b). All one has to do is remove the frontal "head" of the ancestor from his ovoid wrapped body, and rotate the body lozenge horizontally (Figure 8.24c) to generate the encapsulated dead-soon-to-be-reborn (recycled) offspring of this Mona Island pictograph (Figure 8.24d, e). The "living dead" shaman carries his descent group's offspring in his arms as a necessary intermediary to the fecundity of the dead ancestors, defunct but potent with the inseminating power of life, owing, paradoxically, to their affinity with death.

Such graphic conventions derive from "ethnophysiology," a thoroughly "phallocentric" theory of conception common to both the current lowlands and the prehistoric Antilles (Roe 1982, 1991b). In the profound sexual division of labor that characterized South American and Antillean subsistence strategies alike, men : hunters/artisans in solid materials worked subtractively (stone)/warriors/religious specialists :: women : mothers/horticulturalists/artisans in yielding, additively ["gestationally"] produced hollow media (pottery). This Sexual Antagonism Complex was reinforced on symbolic and social levels (men : culture :: women : nature). Men appropriate female fecundity by relegating the female's role to that of passive ambulatory wombs, mere "containers." Indeed, First Women need not even be "women" at all. They appear as artifactual Gourd Women (Roe 1982:63), or Turtle Women (Stevens-Arroyo 1988:95). Even men can give birth via similar hollow, magically induced round bodily protuberances. For example, a hardened hunchback in a male progenitor (*Deminán Caracaracol*) is induced via "spiritual impregnation" from the flung strings of *cohoba-tobacco* induced snot (mislabeled "spittle") of a senior irascible (withholding) male (*Bayamanaco*), seminal in function via the hoary Freudian-Amerindian equation of the nose with the phallus and nasal discharge with semen, to serve as a "dorsal womb." *Deminán's* disfigurement is split by stone axes, and "he" gives birth to the First Woman, the ancestral progenitrix, which happens to be another "round and hollow" ambulatory womb, a female turtle–First Turtle Woman who becomes the mother of all Taíno (Griswold 1997d). This Antillean picture derived from ethnohistory can only be understood in terms of both an act of analogy linking the white viscous fluid emitted from the protuberance above (mucus from the nose) with similar fluids emitted from the projection below (semen from the phallus), and the lowland South Amerindian theory that semen from repeated male ejaculations accumulates within the passive womb of the female to form the "congealed mass" of the fetus. Such a phallocentric theory conveniently robs women of any active role in gestation and assigns it to men; she is just the gourd-pot within which men build babies.

From the point of view of an Antillean archaeologist, this also explains the frontal bone pectorals, represented on the petroglyphs (Roe 1993:Figure 5a), and carved as a species of the "trophy head" curation of portable human bone artifacts associated with Saladoid and pre-Taíno culture. What is a man's skull but a portable bony womb wherein the killer can engender animal fertility and magically give birth to that prey via the "birth canal" of his trophy's *foramen magnum*? Thus the successful homicide not only appropriates his victim's vital life force but his fecundity as well (Roe 1991b)! Pané (1974, 1992, 1999) turns this ethno-logic full circle when he recalls how sequestered bones in suspended gourds break and "give birth" to fish fecundity, how a Turtle Woman, when copulated with by human males, gives birth to human descendants, and how even a hunchbacked man can produce offspring dorsally. All these symbolic vectors intersect to produce life from round and hollow lozenges in the care of a sacred masculine figure, the shaman, who abstains from sexual contact with women when dieting, yet is always depicted, perhaps for that very reason, with a prominent erection (Figures 8.22, 8.24a).

Many Levels, Many Worlds: Rock Art and Antillean Amerindian Cosmology

This sacred Greater Antillean ethnophysiology of conception is situated, as it is in the lowlands of South America (Roe 1982:Figure 3), within a multi-level universe (Siegel 1997:Figure 1) connected by a continuously recycling "water gyre" where life becomes death and death engenders life in a constant cycle that mimics the ecology of the tropical rain forest itself, the same humid biome within which this entire symbol system emerged. In such a dynamic cosmology, a Sky World linked to men and birds hovers over an Earth World associated with society, which, in turn, rests upon, and is surrounded by, a dark Subaquatic Underworld of swimming reptiles and fish linked with women and their theriomorphic seducers (Roe 1982). Studies of both lowland (Roe 1983a) and Antillean (Robiou Lamarche 1988) ethnoastronomy show how this diurnal system is inverted when night falls, the cold and watery Underworld now stretching above one's head as the foaming river of the

Milky Way, the nocturnal domain of beneficent ancestors and maleficent ghosts (*opía* among the Taíno). The watery origin of the night sky explains why the constellations that pass through it are invariably fish-souls, aquatic reptiles, or water-associated artifacts (canoes).

The spatial and thematic analysis of the huge Cueva de Mora petroglyph/pictograph assemblage in the highlands of Puerto Rico (Figure 8.16) directly instantiates this worldview in low-lying simple petroglyphs and intricate, larger-than-life pictographs painted high above them (Figure 8.17), some ten meters beyond the cave floor. The vertical and horizontal layering of these images couple shamanic themes of death-birth and avimorphic transformation with a type of dynamic dualism heretofore only documented from the jungles of South America (Roe et al. 1999a).

Lowland ethnography and Pané's (1974, 1992, 1999) paleoethnology suggest that caves are portals into the dark Underworld from which ancestral figures emerge. The limestone solution caverns of the karst topography of the mountainous interior of Puerto Rico and Hispaniola were formed by running and dripping water. Like Cueva de Mora, they frequently have "wet" lower chambers uninhabited by the living. These lie underneath the "dry" upper chambers visited by Amerindians for ritual purposes, such as to propitiate the ancestors that emerged from these watery and dark depths in mythic space-time (Stevens Arroyo 1988:137–138). These caves are, indeed, filled with representations of the dead wrapped in their hammocks, and the shamans that continue to contact them, together with their frequently avian power animals and, not incongruously, fish. The West, the Land of the Dead in Taíno cosmology, a floating island, is also the site of the mortal (setting) sun, whose body disarticulates to bones and is carried from west to east under the earth in the flowing rivers of the dead. These rivers continue into the Milky Way of the similarly cold and dark night sky. The next day the sun, newly invigorated, ascends as a neonate in the east to mature and climb to the zenith before beginning his aged descent toward the west once again. Thus the sun establishes daily periodicity just as his pale, and mutable, younger brother, the moon, does in the nocturnal river–Milky Way. Together, they form the primordial Magical Twins of Amazonian-Antillean mythology.

Water Falling from Above, Water Upwelling from Below: Rock Art and the Water Gyre

Perhaps all four classes of rock art—cave, river boulder, ball park, and beach—are but connected way-stations on the same watery journey of the souls of the dead ancestors as they too participate in this endless water gyre of birth-death-rebirth? The dead, wrapped in their cotton "canoes," float on their riparian journey, accompanied by fish, aquatic turtles, and water birds, from the mountaintop caves, rivers within stone, to the rivers flowing from their flanks toward the distant low-lying coastal plain and the sea beyond. Those rivers, dry for half the year, are littered with a jumble of cyclopean boulders from the cordillera, stone-within-rivers. Such huge rocks are covered with petroglyphs of the same wrapped ancestors and the spirals that mimic the swirling eddies of the turbulent flowing water. In turn, the rivers lead to the lower mountain plateaus with their *bateys* and from thence to the flat coastal plain where the bulk of the ball parks were located (before their erasure by nineteenth-century sugar cane plowing). There, they flow into the sea next to eolinitic wave-cut caves and lithified strands pocked with the same ancestral petroglyphs.

Oliver (1992b, 1998) is probably correct in reading the parallel lines of boulders and menhir petroglyphs marking the margins of the open rectangular courts, sunken and often filled with standing water during the rainy season, as the same "rivers" that continue to course toward the sea. They are bordered by banks of hand-laid stone filled, again, with "wet" ancestral images: frogs, fish, aquatic mammals (Rivera Fontán and Silva Pagán 1997), and water birds. The ebb and flow of the game itself, Indian soccer, may have been cosmic in its portent, the play canalized within these twin banks, rivers of stone, hurrying on its way to the sea. Further on, the same aquatic and ancestral images greet the river mouths in the form of beach petroglyphs. This mutable rock art goes under water with the tide, and emerges dry, once again, as the tide ebbs, as the dead will submerge, only to upwell once again in the clear pools and lakes within the island's interior. Lowlanders, and perhaps ancient Antilleans too, make a distinction between the dynamic and demonic aspects of flowing water, turbid with sediment, whirlpools and bubbles, vs. the enigmatic and sacred still waters (pools, lakes, ponds), mirrors-doors of standing water. Such lakes and *cenotes* nestle within the karst topography of Puerto Rico's mountainous interior, and flow into caves, only to begin their sacred journey all over again.

Conclusions

As this excursion into the Möbius-strip cosmic linkages of Puerto Rican rock art indicates, *arte rupestre* is not some marginal bailiwick of avocational archaeologists and overly enthusiastic amateurs but a central medium of affective expression among Greater Antillean Amerindians. It must be recorded accurately, and in multimedia, together with its entire spatial and cultural context, to yield unparalleled insights into the subsistence, social, and ideological realms of insular Arawak culture. It can also shed light on culture contact and cultural evolution, addressing questions such as diffusion vs. parallel development, as well as unique cultural epistemologies and the icons and symbols that derive from them. Caribbean insular rock art thus joins the rock art of the Guianas, and other regions of lowland South America, as a major exposition of the animistic "jungle religions" derivable from the ancient Amazonian Formative synthesis. These images, so static and immobile, are really "kinetic art" of a vast circuit of egalitarian shamanic transformation into both eternal life, social continuity, and, ultimately, priestly and chiefly privilege masquerading as a spiritual conduit to "real" (otherworldly) reality for the common weal.

Acknowledgments

I gratefully acknowledge the financial and institutional support of the Centro de Investigaciones Indígenas de Puerto Rico, Inc., and its director, Sr. Gaspar Roca, for making the fieldwork, on which this study is based, possible. I also thank the Centro de Estudios Avanzados de Puerto Rico y El Caribe, and its director, Dr. Ricardo E. Alegría, for providing a venue for working with graduate students on the island in the furtherance of rock-art research. Among my students there, I am most grateful for the continuing help and friendship of Sr. José (Cheo) Rivera Meléndez, M.A., who has proved a tireless collaborator in all my work in *arte rupestre*. I also thank the family of Sr. Juan and Sra. Modesta Torres of Comerío for their friendship and support in the work at Cueva de Mora and Cueva de la Momia. Gratitude must also be expressed toward the University of Delaware (Department of Anthropology and the Undergraduate Research Program), and the CIIPR, for Grants-in-Aid that made possible the participation of a whole set of students in my program of Puerto Rican rock-art research. I conclude by thanking my wife, Mrs. Amy W. Roe, M.A., for her help in mapping caves amidst a shower of bat excrement, and for her aid in computer image processing. She has done more than I can express in this and my other projects.

Notes

1. The preliminary qualitative seriation of the rock art (Roe and Rivera Meléndez 1999) from which this shift becomes perceptible is not based on conjecture, a presumed chronological sequence of designs from simple-old to complex-recent, although such a progression is, in fact, produced by the analysis. Rather, it is anchored

in rare in situ geological associations and the ^{14}C dating of related archaeological sites within which these images are found (i.e., we know that Caguana postdates El Bronce, which, in turn, postdates Tibes and that the Tibes simple faces are closest stylistically to the Maisabel Playa effigies).

2. While it is true that objects are continually being incorporated into the beach rock, and therefore that people may have carved images into the rock prior to the oldest artifact that we saw in the eolinitic formation, except in the precise location of said artifact, there are several factors that lead me to regard the glyphs as being carved shortly after the dune lithified with early Elenan Ostionoid pottery and associated Monserratean artifacts already encrusted within it. First, given the active geomorphic regime on the wind-lashed north coast (at sites like Hacienda Grande and Maisabel) that combines both beach strand progression due to river sedimentation (and there is just such a river feeding into the ocean immediately to the east of the embayment) with equally massive wave erosion of such sediments, it is highly unlikely that the embayment had anything like its present form in Saladoid times (geologist Eduardo Questell, personal communication, 1985). There are no Saladoid sites found along the present coastline of northern Puerto Rico for precisely that reason. They are all located on high ground some distance inland. Moreover, we conducted an exhaustive surface survey of the beach and dunes coupled with only the second underwater archaeological survey along the north coast of Puerto Rico (two scuba divers in a controlled sweep), in front of the beach. While we recorded one incised edge grinder of the sort that persisted into Monserratean times and numerous Elenan Ostionoid sherds, both in situ above and redeposited below water, we found no Saladoid material despite the proximity of a Saladoid component in the Maisabel site proper, just a short distance inland on high ground. Nor did we find any later European material.

3. This survey was accomplished using an altimeter and electronic compass-equipped watches, hand-held electronic compasses, laser levels, and GPS units, all mounted on custom-fabricated, camera tripod-adapted, nonmagnetic aluminum billet stands.

4. These pictographs are cross-dated to Classic Taíno conventions, but are not as hypertrophied, and therefore are arguably somewhat earlier.

9

The Aftermath of Conquest
The Indians of Puerto Rico during the Early Sixteenth Century

Karen F. Anderson-Córdova

In this chapter I will discuss what is known about the first decades of the sixteenth century at the onset of contact between Europeans and the Taínos of Puerto Rico. I will attempt to answer three basic questions:

1. Once the European conquest and colonization of Puerto Rico began, what happened to the Taínos?
2. How did contact between the Spanish and Taínos develop and what were the consequences?
3. Is there anything new and relevant to be gained by the study of this devastating period of New and Old World history?

The short answers to these questions are simple enough: first, the Taínos quickly succumbed to European-introduced diseases and forced labor; second, the historical record provides only limited and European-biased information about the Taínos and their culture, largely extinct by the first half of the sixteenth century; and, third, their demise was so swift that the Contact-period archaeological record is practically nonexistent.

Although it is true that the Taínos have been extinct for at least five centuries, their society, culture, and response to the Spanish conquest and colonization continue to intrigue scholars of history, ethnohistory, anthropology, linguistics, religion, and archaeology. This interest goes hand in hand with the concomitant study of Spanish adaptation to the New World and the genesis of new cultures and societies that sprung from the amalgam of peoples in the Caribbean. Those tumultuous years of the early sixteenth century were the starting point of modern Caribbean society. They witnessed the encounter of peoples whose societies and cultures had developed independently of one another for hundreds of generations and whose mutual "discovery" forever altered the history of humankind. Seen within this broader context, a more complicated story emerges.

Approaches to the Study of Spanish-Indian Contact in the Sixteenth-Century Caribbean

The term Caribbean in this context refers to the Antillean islands explored or settled by the Spanish, and the mainland areas forming an arc along the Caribbean Sea and the Gulf of Mexico, from Florida to Venezuela, also known as the circum-Caribbean. Spanish exploration, conquest, trade, and colonization took place throughout this entire area, and the events in Puerto Rico should not be studied in a geographical vacuum. The literature on Spanish-Indian interactions during the early sixteenth century within the larger circum-Caribbean area is more considerable than that available for Puerto Rico, and is too voluminous to discuss here in detail. However, there are approaches and themes evident in the literature, which are important to discuss with respect to Contact-period Puerto Rico.

Among these are studies that view ethnohistories as narratives, which can inform on the nature of Taíno culture and society during the late prehistoric period. The primary ethnohistoric sources have been used to support alternative conclusions about the level of sociopolitical organization displayed by the Taínos at the time of contact. Following a cultural-evolutionary perspective, José Alcina (1983) argued that the Taínos exhibited a tribal level of organization, in transition to chiefdoms. In contrast, Roberto Cassá (1979) and Samuel Wilson (1990) contend that the Taínos were organized into fully developed chiefdoms, and Francisco Moscoso (1983, 1986) purported that they were well on their way toward social stratification. The primary sources have also been used to reconstruct many aspects of Taíno culture, from religious beliefs, rituals, political organization, agricultural and other subsistence practices, language, mythology, settlements, and so forth (e.g., Alegría 1978, 1979b, 1981, 1997b; Arrom 1975; Cassá 1979; Sued Badillo 1978; Veloz Maggiolo 1983).

Ethnohistoric documents have also been analyzed by historians interested in studying how the Spanish-Taíno encounter was perceived and interpreted by Europeans and what new ways of looking at "the other" developed as a result of this encounter (Jara and Spadaccini 1992; Pastor 1983; Todorov 1984; Varela 1982; Varela and Gil 1984). Scholars have addressed the inherent biases and limitations of the European narratives and descriptions of the Caribbean Indians, both for the reconstruction of late prehistoric Taíno culture and society and for the study of Indian acculturation during the early colonization period (Bucher 1981). However, any discussion of the Contact period in the Caribbean generally and for the Taínos specifically must begin with a consideration of these limited narratives.

The Spanish produced volumes of official documents relating to the conquest, colonization, and governing of their overseas possessions, thus providing a wealth of information that may be used to help understand the context of the period and events. Their penchant for writing things down is a bonus for modern scholars. Many official documents have been published; even more information is available in manuscript form in various archives in Spain, as well as in local archives in countries throughout the Caribbean. Critical analysis of the published and unpublished documents offers an indispensable body of data to assist in the reconstruction of the early history of Spanish colonization, and can provide insights into the responses by the Indians. I have found the sources to be particularly revealing for Indian acculturation in Hispaniola and Puerto Rico (Anderson-Córdova 1990).

An excellent example of the detailed analysis of Spanish documentary sources is Jalil Sued Badillo's (2001) recent volume on the history and economy of Spanish gold mining in Puerto Rico during the first half of the sixteenth century. The primary sources demonstrate the importance and profitability of the gold-mining economy of Puerto Rico for the Spanish. They also show how this extraction economy was largely dependent on forced Taíno labor, which was exhausted before the ore-bearing deposits were. Such new insights on conquest economics and its linkage to Indian labor indicate the wealth of information that can be extracted from a careful and systematic use of manuscript sources.

The careful analysis of Spanish documentary sources can provide a general context and enable more detailed interpretations of the Spanish-Indian interactions (e.g., Sued Badillo 2001:310–338). In addition to supplying information on the use and abuse of Indian labor, the primary documents provide insights into the responses of Indians to contact with the Spanish. In particular, I have found the 1514 Indian *Repartimiento* and the Hieronymite Interrogatory of 1517 to be of great importance (Anderson-Córdova 1990:122–126, 156–177).

The third main body of research available for the study of the early Spanish colonial period is archaeology. Archaeological investigations of the Contact period in the Caribbean have proliferated over the past 10 to 20 years. Studies have emphasized Spanish adaptations in the New World, Indian acculturation and change, Spanish-Indian contact, and multiethnic identities and interactions (Deagan 1985, 1987, 1988, 1995; Ewen 1987; Smith 1986; Willis 1984). Archaeology provides a unique perspective on the material correlates of the Contact period, without the inherent biases of the primary written records. Indian responses to the Spanish potentially are best studied archaeologically, provided that appropriate sites are identified and excavated. Early Spanish settlements may hold evidence of Indian presence or occupation; late prehistoric or protohistoric Indian settlements may have been occupied into the historic period and/or Indians may have occupied some sites in post-Contact times. A reconstruction of what happened in the Caribbean during the early sixteenth century must rely on three major bodies of data: ethnohistoric, documentary, and archaeological. Ethnohistoric sources are the first-hand European accounts of the conquest and colonization of the Caribbean and of Indian cultures and lifeways. Documentary sources are official written records produced by the Spanish bureaucracy, such as royal decrees, census records, and other official correspondence between Spain and its colonies.

Demography is an important aspect of the Contact period, especially in regard to such issues as sources of labor for the Spanish and the general resilience of the Indian population. Reconstructing population figures at the time of contact has been a major area of research (Anderson-Córdova 1990:138–218; Borah 1976; Brau 1966; Cassá 1979; Cook and Borah 1971–1974; Crosby 1972; Denevan 1976; Dobyns 1966, 1983; Fernández Méndez 1984; Henige 1978; Jacobs 1974; Lipschutz 1966; Moya Pons 1978; Ramenofsky 1987; Rosenblat 1954, 1967; Sánchez-Albornoz 1974; Sauer 1966; Smith 1984). This is an important line of inquiry that is most productively evaluated using ethnohistoric, documentary, and archaeological data.

To date, archaeological research has not addressed demography of late Taíno societies in the Caribbean.[1] A major contribution that archaeology can make for Contact-period studies is to provide a baseline body of population estimates. This would not only be significant for the study of demography in Caribbean chiefdoms but would also provide a realistic framework for studying the decline of historic Indian populations.

The Spanish-Indian Contact Period in Puerto Rico

Ethnohistoric Narratives

The islands of Hispaniola (now the Dominican Republic and Haiti), Puerto Rico, and Cuba were the first inhabited areas of the New World colonized by the Spanish and bore the brunt of Spanish conquest and domination. The chronicles of this early period refer generically to the Taínos as the aboriginal groups who inhabited these islands at the time of the Europeans' arrival. Most of the historical descriptions refer to experiences in Hispaniola, the first of the Greater Antilles to be settled by the Spanish. The chroniclers Fray Bartolomé de Las Casas, Gonzalo Fernández de Oviedo y Valdés, and Pedro Mártir de Anglería are the principal sources of information about the events of the conquest and about the Taínos. Fray Bartolomé de Las Casas arrived in the New World in 1502 and had first-hand information about the Taínos of Hispaniola and Cuba. He observed the effects of the Spanish *encomienda* system of forced labor and became a defender of the Indians. Las Casas's detailed narrative, *Historia de las Indias* (1985), benefits from his experiences in the Caribbean during the early historic period, as well as incorporates information from descriptions by Christopher Columbus and his contemporaries.

Gonzalo Fernández de Oviedo y Valdés did not arrive in Hispaniola until 1514, by which time the aboriginal population was already in steep decline (Alegría 1997b:17). Unlike Las Casas, he was not sympathetic toward the Indians, but his multivolume historical work is nevertheless full of very detailed descriptions of the Taínos that are critical for a study of this period. In addition, as pointed out by Alegría (1997b:17), he dedicates an entire chapter of his *Historia* to the island of Puerto Rico, its natural history, conquest, and colonization.

Pedro Mártir de Anglería (1944) (also known by his anglicized name of Peter Martyr) is another important early source. Although he never set foot in the New World, he had personal access to many of the individuals who participated in the events in the Caribbean, and to the accounts of Christopher Columbus, Fray Ramón Pané,[2] Bartolomé Colón, and others. The wealth of information available to Mártir de Anglería and his ability to synthesize and place it into a larger perspective confirms his importance as an early chronicler of late-fifteenth- and early-sixteenth-century Spanish exploration and colonization in the New World.

The Conquest and Colonization of Puerto Rico

These early narrative sources describe the aboriginal inhabitants of the Caribbean and the events of Spanish conquest and colonization in considerable detail, although from a distinctly European viewpoint. Most early narrators relied on what were, for them, primary sources: the diaries of Christopher Columbus's first two voyages (Dunn and Kelley 1989), Fernando Colón's manuscript *Historia del Almirante* (1984), Dr. Diego Alvarez Chanca's letter

(1949) describing Columbus's second voyage, and the *Probanza de Juan González* (Tió 1961:30–109), among others (see Alegría 1997b:15). Primary sources documenting the early conquest and colonization of Puerto Rico are considerably more limited than for Hispaniola.

The events described below have been summarized previously (Anderson-Córdova 1990:88–103) and are based on the Spanish chronicles, official Spanish documents of this period, secondary sources (Brau 1966; Fernández Méndez 1981, 1984; Sauer 1966; Tió 1961), and research of such historians as Murga Sanz (1971) and Otte (1975). The recently published work of Puerto Rican historian Jalil Sued Badillo (2001) was another important source of information.

The purpose here is to summarize what we know about events in Puerto Rico and draw comparisons with what occurred in Hispaniola. Further, this will provide the framework for a discussion of the Indian response to conquest and colonization and the consequences of contact to the ensuing Indian culture, society, and demography. Finally, future avenues of research for Contact studies in Puerto Rico are suggested.

Puerto Rico (or San Juan Bautista de Puerto Rico, as it was christened by Columbus) was discovered by Columbus on his second voyage, on November 19, 1493. Columbus's expedition made a brief stop somewhere along the west coast of the island (the exact location has been both a source of pride and dispute for years among the municipalities of Aguada, Aguadilla, Añasco, and Rincón) but did not encounter any Indians, who ran away from Columbus's landing party. The Spanish fleet of 19 vessels continued on to Hispaniola.

There is some discrepancy as to when the first exploration of Puerto Rico occurred. According to the *Probanza de Juan González* (Tió 1961:30–109), the initial exploration occurred in 1506 when a temporary base was supposedly established near the Bay of Añasco, on the west coast of Puerto Rico (Solís 1988:8). However, most sources indicate that it was not until 1508 that Juan Ponce de León, under the authorization of the Governor of Hispaniola, Don Nicolás de Ovando, began the exploration of Puerto Rico.

The *Probanza* also describes events that were to have occurred in 1508, and it may be just confusion in dates. Nevertheless, the first sustained encounter between the Spanish and Indians was peaceful, and an exchange of gifts occurred. Juan González, a member of Ponce de León's expedition, served as interpreter. The Indians indicated that there was a good bay on the north coast of the island (San Juan harbor). While Juan Ponce de León stayed on the south coast at the village of Cacique Mabo el Grande, Juan González and other Spanish crossed the Cordillera Central and arrived to the Bay of San

Juan, passing numerous Indian villages and continuing the pattern of exchanging gifts (Tió 1961:49, 70).

According to Ponce de León's own testimony of 1509 (*Historia Documental de Puerto Rico [HDPR]* 1973:II:519–522), he left the province of Higüey (his land grant since 1504 on the southeast coast of Hispaniola) on July 12, 1508, with 50 men. He stopped at Mona Island (a small island located half way between Hispaniola and Puerto Rico), which he found was occupied by one or more Taíno polities. He landed on the south coast of Puerto Rico, in the territory of Cacique Agüeybaná I, on August 12, 1508. The expedition encountered at least two storms (most probably tropical storms or hurricanes) on the way to Puerto Rico, and it was running low on food.

The Spanish requested Agüeybaná to plant a *conuco* (the Taíno term for the raised mounds of earth in which they planted cassava) for them, which he apparently agreed to do. Sources indicate that Agüeybaná's mother advised him to be friendly toward the Spanish, in order to avoid the fate of the Indians of Hispaniola (Anderson-Córdova 1990:91; Oviedo y Valdés 1959a:II:90; Fernández Méndez 1981:40; Sued Badillo 2001:61). Most sources agree that of the various chiefdoms that existed on the island of Boriquén (as Puerto Rico was known by the Taíno) at Contact, the principal one, located in the south-central part of the island, was Cacique Agüeybaná's (Sued Badillo 2001:61).

Ponce de León left Agüeybaná's territory and sailed west and north bordering the coast until he arrived at the Bay of San Juan. Here he encountered Indians, including some he identified as Caribs, explored some of the rivers along the north coast, sent some men to prospect for gold, and others back to Mona Island to acquire food (Anderson-Córdova 1990:91; *HDPR* 1973:II:520). Ponce de León also established the settlement of Caparra, which he located a few miles inland from the Bay of San Juan, close to the areas where gold was found.

As had been the case during the conquest and colonization of Hispaniola, the Spanish immediately proceeded to prospect for gold. Their actions in this respect, however, were limited by the lack of food, and Ponce de León again indicates asking five caciques to plant crops to feed the Spanish (Anderson-Córdova 1990:93; *HDPR* 1973:II:521; Murga Sanz 1971:37). The shortage of food may have been a consequence of the two storms that hit the Spanish ships on their way to Puerto Rico. These same storms may have affected the Indians' crops, and the Spanish may have been unable to acquire much food from them. Whatever the reasons, the alleged lack of food inhibited the Spaniards ability to prospect for gold in this early stage of exploration of the island.

Spanish exploration and settlement of the island continued, and Ponce de

León began distributing Indians (*repartimientos*) among Spanish from the mainland and Hispaniola who wished to settle on the island (Anderson-Córdova 1990:94; Murga Sanz 1971:46). In the meantime, Nicolás de Ovando was replaced by Diego Colón (Christopher Columbus's son) as governor of Hispaniola, who proceeded to name Juan Cerón as *alcalde mayor* of the island of San Juan (i.e., Puerto Rico). The Indians who had been distributed by Ponce de León were thereby taken away from their Spanish "owners" (*encomenderos*) and reallocated by Cerón to other settlers late in 1509 (Anderson-Córdova 1990:95; Murga Sanz 1971:47). Diego Columbus instigated this redistribution of Indians because he considered Ponce de León's allocation of Taínos to the settlers as a contradiction to his family's rights to Puerto Rico, based on Christopher Columbus's original discovery of the island.

However, former Governor Ovando, who had returned to Spain, convinced the king to reappoint Ponce de León as Captain Governor of Puerto Rico. Ponce de León proceeded to send both Juan Cerón and Miguel Díaz (who had been named *alguacil mayor* of Puerto Rico by Diego Colón) back to Spain as prisoners on July 10, 1510 (Anderson-Córdova 1990:95; Murga Sanz, 1971:51).

The Indian Rebellion of 1511

As a result of the power struggles between the interests of the Columbus family and the Spanish Crown, the Indians of Puerto Rico were subjected to two *repartimientos* within the span of less than one year. They were moved arbitrarily from one Spanish *encomendero* to another, required to plant crops for the Spanish (Anderson-Córdova 1990:118; *Relación de Ponce de León 1509* in *HDPR* 1973:II:520–521; Fernández Méndez 1984:16–19) and forced to mine for gold. According to Las Casas (1985:II:376; see Anderson-Córdova 1990:95–96), these were the seeds that ignited the Indian rebellion of 1511.

The rebellion started in the territory of Cacique Agüeybaná II, brother and successor of Agüeybaná I, the cacique whom Ponce de León met in 1508 (Anderson-Córdova 1990:194), in whose lands the Villa de Sotomayor settlement had been established. According to the accounts of Las Casas and Fernández de Oviedo, the caciques formed a confederacy to attack the Spanish; Agüeybaná, leader of the rebellion, attacked the town of Sotomayor, killing Cristóbal de Sotomayor and burning the settlement (Anderson-Córdova 1990:96; Fernández Méndez 1981:45; Las Casas 1985:II:388; Tió 1961:52–53).[3] At least 30 caciques participated in the rebellion (Sued Badillo 2001:62). This was the beginning of a general uprising on the island, which probably also involved Indians from neighboring islands (Anderson-Córdova 1990:97; Tió

1961:57–58, 75, 92–93; Sued Badillo 1978:144–145). Sued Badillo (2001:62) indicates that as early as 1510, the Spanish, including Cristóbal de Sotomayor, were bringing Indian slaves from neighboring islands into Puerto Rico.

Spanish retaliation was swift. Ponce de León in Caparra marched against the Indians, attacking them at night (Anderson-Córdova 1990:96; Fernández Méndez 1981:57). He gave an ultimatum to the Indians to surrender, but only two caciques did so (Cacique Caguas of Turabo and Cacique don Alonso of Utuado) (Anderson-Córdova 1990:98; Fernández Méndez 1984:26). The Spanish responded by intensifying their raids of neighboring islands and bringing other Indians to Puerto Rico as slaves (Anderson-Córdova 1990:97; Tió 1961:58, 75–76). In addition, some Spanish captains raided Indian settlements in Puerto Rico, took Indian prisoners, and enslaved them (Anderson-Córdova 1990:98; Murga Sanz 1971:280–288; *Documentos de la Real Hacienda de Puerto Rico* 1971:I:II).

Indians killed at least 100 Spaniards during the uprising (Sued Badillo 2001:63). Spanish retaliatory raids and the ensuing enslavement of Indians amounted to a true military conquest. Sued Badillo (2001:63) cites historian Carlos Pereira: "Puerto Rico was the only one of the Greater Antilles in which there were episodes of true military conquest" (Pereira 1924:V:58, my translation).

As if this were not enough, Miguel Díaz and Juan Cerón were reappointed by Diego Colón to their positions in Puerto Rico and ordered to carry out yet another *repartimiento,* putting the Indians to work in the gold mines (Royal instructions of July 25, 1511, in Murga Sanz 1971:75; Anderson-Córdova 1990:99). The general uprising of the Indians continued, and King Ferdinand authorized all-out war against them. This served as a perfect excuse to acquire Indian slaves, especially among the Spanish settlers loyal to Ponce de León who felt short-changed by the Cerón-Díaz *repartimiento* (Sued Badillo 2001:64).

Spanish expeditions to neighboring islands for the purpose of enslaving Indians and bringing them to Puerto Rico continued. At this time (late 1511), numerous incidents appear in the historical record of so-called Carib Indians raiding settlements in Puerto Rico. The Spaniards tended to use the term "Carib" in very broad terms, referring to any Indians who rebelled against them. Once captured, these "Caribs" could legally be enslaved and forced to work as laborers in the gold-mining operations. The situation on the island continued to be very unstable between the years 1511 and 1515. Cycles of Indian raids followed by Spanish retaliatory raids persisted.

In 1513, an alliance of Indians from Puerto Rico and the Leeward Islands, the latter of whom the Spanish called Caribs, burned the settlement of Caparra, killing 18 (Sued Badillo 2001:64). The Spanish retaliated by attacking caciques under *encomienda,* especially along the eastern and central mountainous areas of the island, specifically against caciques Orocoviz, Don Alonso (Utuado), and Jayuya (Sued Badillo 2001:65).

Amidst all this, under the orders of prosecutor Sancho Velázquez (a Spanish official from Hispaniola), another *repartimiento* was carried out in 1514. Occurring during a time of considerable Indian resistance, and benefiting the established royal authorities rather than the majority of the Spanish settlers on the island, this *repartimiento* caused more resentment and confusion (Anderson-Córdova 1990:100–101; *Memoria de Melgarejo* 1582 in Fernández Méndez 1981:112–113; Murga Sanz 1971:169–170). Only 4,000 Indians were distributed, since pockets of resistance continued (*Boletín Histórico de Puerto Rico [BHPR]* III:67 *Relación de carta a su alteza 8 agosto de 1515;* cited in Sued Badillo 2001:65, 99, footnote 136).

The 1513 Laws for the Protection of the Indians were ignored on the island (Anderson-Córdova 1990:101; Murga Sanz 1971:186). These laws included provisions for adequate food, clothing, and better treatment of the Indians than previously. However, they applied only to *encomienda* Indians, not to Indian slaves. The latter had no legal protection under Spanish laws. The situation in Puerto Rico at this time suggests that numerous Indians were being enslaved, since any Indian pacified on the island or captured as a result of Spanish raiding expeditions immediately lost his/her freedom.

To summarize, in Puerto Rico, as was previously the case in Hispaniola, the seemingly initial peaceful contact between Indians and Spaniards rapidly deteriorated into violence. In Puerto Rico, the period of Indian rebellion was much longer than in Hispaniola. Despite the fact that there are relatively few first-hand accounts of the conquest and colonization of Puerto Rico, compared to Hispaniola and Cuba, the available sources suggest that the Indian rebellion was widespread across the island (Anderson-Córdova 1990:119). Various Spanish sources indicate that Indians on the island were still not subdued as late as 1517 (Sued Badillo 2001:65–66). Carib raids on the island continue to be mentioned through the sixteenth century (Anderson-Córdova 1990:101; Sued Badillo 2001:66). A regional and protracted Indian rebellion was not reported for Hispaniola.

Several factors may have contributed to this situation in Puerto Rico. The smaller geographical area of Puerto Rico, compared to Hispaniola, may have made for easier alliance building against the Spanish (Anderson-Córdova 1990:119). One form of resistance employed by the Indians may have been to take refuge in the neighboring Leeward Islands and then return to raid the Spanish (Anderson-Córdova 1990:101; Brau 1966:258; Sued Badillo 1978:152,

157). Sued Badillo (1978) has discussed the close kinship, trade, and ritual ties that existed among the Taínos of Puerto Rico and the neighboring islands. These connections may have facilitated the flight and fight strategy of Taíno resistance (Anderson-Córdova 1990:120).

Spanish population on the island was relatively sparse during the sixteenth century, and there were only two main settlements: Caparra on the north coast and San Germán on the west coast. A number of Spaniards lived outside of these settlements or were with their Indians mining for gold. In addition, Puerto Rico's mountainous terrain and lack of large interior valleys may have made it easier for the Indians, who knew the territory well, to maintain pockets of resistance for a longer period of time (Anderson-Córdova 1990:102; Sued Badillo 2001:67). The late prehispanic chiefdoms of Puerto Rico may have also situated their civic/ceremonial centers in the extremely dissected mountainous interior as a defensive strategy in response to interpolity feuding (Siegel 2004).

The principal causes of the persistent Indian rebellions on Puerto Rico were probably the manner in which the Spanish authorities established the *encomienda* system (three *repartimientos:* first by Ponce de León, followed by Cerón and Díaz and then Sancho Velázquez) and the enslavement of Indians as mine workers.

The 1530 Census

In 1530, Indian slavery was officially banned. However, this ban excluded the Caribs, which meant that Puerto Rico could legally continue to import Indian slaves, if they were officially designated as Caribs. This same year, Governor Francisco Manuel de Lando carried out the first population census of Puerto Rico. The census documents the small Spanish population of the island, and the fact that of the small number of surviving Indians, the majority were slaves (Anderson-Córdova 1990:102–103; Lluch Mora 1986; Ramírez de Arellano 1934:20–46).

A previous analysis carried out by the author of the de Lando census indicates a total Indian population of 1,543 (Anderson-Córdova 1990:181–187, 208). These were divided between 1,039 slaves and 504 free Indians, a proportion of 2 to 1. Although we do not know the Indian population of Puerto Rico at the time of contact, a conservative estimate ranges between 30,000 and 60,000. (See Anderson-Córdova [1990:180, 1995] for a review of Contact-period Taíno population estimates.) If the Contact-period estimates and the de Lando census are accurate then a precipitous decline in population occurred in 22 years. In addition to documenting this decline, the 1530 census suggests that most of the remaining Indians were captured elsewhere and brought to the island as slaves. In other words, the number of Taíno survivors 22 years after Spanish colonization was considerably less than the total number of Indians documented in the census. The historic Indian population in Puerto Rico was not only very small but also included many non-Taínos.

The Conditions of Spanish-Indian Interaction

The Spanish-Indian Contact period in Puerto Rico effectively spanned a period of 20 to 30 years. Historic documentation about the conditions of contact in Puerto Rico is very sparse. Hostilities developed quickly, and the Indians began a pattern of attacking Spanish settlements and then fleeing into the interior of the island or to neighboring islands. There is no documentation comparable to the 1514 *Repartimiento* or 1517 Hieronymite Interrogatory documents of Hispaniola, so Indian cultural responses cannot be gauged using Spanish sources.

In the past, I have described the cultural processes of Spanish-Indian interaction in the Caribbean as an example of acculturation (Anderson-Córdova 1990). However, the conditions of contact were so destructive to the Taínos and their culture that I now hesitate to use that term. The rapid introduction of the *encomienda* system and the fact that the Indians organized into open rebellion early during the Contact period, which persisted in pockets of sporadic resistance until they had practically disappeared, combined with the use of slave labor to work the agricultural fields and mines created a climate of exploitation and coercion where acculturation may not have been possible.

The use of forced Indian mine labor is one aspect of the Contact-period conditions that was not specifically addressed by scholars in the early history of the Caribbean. Sued Badillo's (2001) recent analysis of the gold economy in Puerto Rico, based on the detailed study of primary archival sources, demonstrated the importance of the gold-mining industry for the economy of the island, as well as of the Spanish mainland. He described the various gold-extraction methods used on the island and indicated that it was based on a rudimentary technology with great reliance on intensive manual labor. Further, Sued Badillo documented that, contrary to conventional wisdom, it was the depletion of labor, not gold, that spelled the end of the gold economy on Puerto Rico. The Spaniards, who immediately exploited Indian labor for its extraction, recognized the plentitude of gold.

The local Taíno population quickly became insufficient to fill this need, so the Spanish resorted initially to raiding neighboring islands and later the wider circum-Caribbean area to import laborers to Puerto Rico. As the pool of Indian slaves became increasingly small, the Spanish resorted to African slaves, a much more expensive form of labor that limited buying power and ultimately their ability to exploit the mineral wealth of the island. Thus the gold-mining industry in Puerto Rico was doomed, owing to the shortage of labor, not to the lack of gold.

Sued Badillo's (2001) analysis includes a description of how the mining operations and labor were organized. Mining was the most important economic activity undertaken by the Spanish during the early sixteenth century. *Encomienda* and enslaved Indians were used intensively in the mines, for periods (called *demoras*) of up to nine months. The basic unit of labor was the *cuadrilla*, which consisted of 10 to 50 Indians (the optimum number was between 12 and 15) under the direction of a Spaniard. These groups would establish mining camps, stake out territories, and prospect for gold (Sued Badillo 2001:310). The mining areas were carefully measured and claimed by individual miners or groups of miners, and prospecting occurred intensively for many months at a time (Sued Badillo 2001:313, citing Oviedo y Valdés 1959a).

Sued Badillo, based on Oviedo y Valdés and other primary sources, describes the following activities that were carried out in the mining camps: "prospecting, weeding, felling of trees, removal of rocks and boulders, excavation, carrying of soil, washing of soil, construction of dikes or canals, tunneling, wells, construction of tents for protection from the elements, construction of corrals for the cattle and pigs, collection of wood, cooking of food, slaughter of animals and food conservation, preparation and conservation of tools, taking care of cattle, breaking and crushing of stones, transportation of equipment" (Sued Badillo 2001:313–314, my translation).

Native patterns of food production were seriously disrupted. The food necessary to feed Spanish and native laborers alike was obtained from the royal *encomiendas* that the Crown established on Mona Island, Toa (northeastern Puerto Rico), and Otoao (central mountains of Puerto Rico); the latter two coincided with areas rich in gold (Sued Badillo 2001:176–177). Many other farms in which cassava was produced were located throughout the island, but local production was insufficient to meet the demands of Spanish and Indian groups, whose labor pools were dedicated mainly to mining. Cassava, among other foodstuffs, was imported into the island (Sued Badillo 2001:149, 286–299). The diet in the mining camps consisted of cassava bread, fish (mainly salted and imported), and pork. Although *encomienda* Indians were supposed to receive adequate food, the physical rigors of work and the high costs to the miners of importing food and equipment into the mountainous regions, where the mines were located, undoubtedly resulted in a less-than-satisfactory diet for the Indians (Sued Badillo 2001:327).

The poor diet combined with hard physical work depleted the number of local Taíno laborers, and the Spanish overseers increasingly depended on imported Indian slaves. Hundreds of "foreign" Indians were brought to the island annually; the preponderance of Indian slaves continued well into the 1530s. They were brought in to replace the dwindling population of local Indians. In addition, the foreigners were preferred by the Spanish, since the Indian-protection laws did not apply to them (Sued Badillo 2001:307–309). As gold production increased in Puerto Rico, beginning in 1519, more Indians were imported; commerce in Indian slaves was conducted throughout the Caribbean by the 1530s (Sued Badillo 2001:358).

Under conditions of intensive forced labor, Indian acculturation was highly unlikely. The disintegration of indigenous social and political organization and of traditional patterns of food production were not conducive for acculturation. Grouping together *encomienda* and slave Indians under extreme working conditions further undermined the survival of traditional cultural patterns. Indians from disparate sections of the circum-Caribbean region were brought to Puerto Rico and communication amongst them would have been difficult. Sources document Indians from the Bahamas, Aruba, Bonaire, Curaçao, the Lesser Antilles, Trinidad, the Gulf and Peninsula of Paria, Cumana, Margarita, and Cubagua, as well as the entire coast of what was known in the sixteenth century as Tierra Firme (from Venezuela to Yucatán, up the coast of New Spain into Florida) were brought to the Spanish Caribbean, including Puerto Rico (Anderson-Córdova 1990:247–258).

Questions persist. Archaeological research in Puerto Rico during the last 20 or 30 years has been considerable. Because of the application of U.S. federal cultural resources protection laws on the island, numerous sites have been surveyed, tested, and excavated. Some of these have been discussed in previous chapters. But, given this amount of archaeological research, why, with the exception of de Hostos's (1938) excavations at Caparra, Mason's (1941) work at Caguana, and Rouse's (1952a) work at the Sardinero site (Mona Island), have no historic-period contact sites been discovered in Puerto Rico?

We know of many more such sites in Hispaniola (e.g., Deagan 1987, 1988, 1995; Ortega and Fondeur 1978) and Cuba (Domínguez 1978, 1980, 1983, 1987; Pichardo Moya 1945; Rivero de la Calle 1978). Puerto Rico is much smaller than these islands, but Taínos, very similar to those who lived in Hispaniola and Cuba, also densely populated it. The Spanish conquest and colonization of these islands was similar as well.

Contact-period sites may still be present on Puerto Rico, and it is only through archaeology that these can be identified. Unfortunately, the areas surrounding Caparra, the first Spanish settlement in Puerto Rico, where ethnohistoric sources indicate that many Indian villages were located, has been highly urbanized. The same may be said, albeit to a lesser degree, for San Germán (the second Spanish settlement, located in western Puerto Rico). If any Contact-period sites remain to be found, these will most likely be found in the mountainous interior. Sued Badillo (2001) indicates that the gold-mining operations were extensive and that camps were occupied nearly year round. Gold prospecting occurred throughout the first three decades of the sixteenth century, and archaeological evidence of these activities may still exist. As development continues to encroach on the mountains of Puerto Rico, many of these sites, if they exist, will be obliterated. According to Sued Badillo, sources mention at least 20 sites where gold was extracted during the first half of the sixteenth century. The principal areas where gold was found include Corozal, Luquillo, Utuado, and San Germán–Lajas (Sued Badillo 2001:333). Localities within these areas that correlate with regions of Utuado, such as Caguana and Don Alonso, among others, are mentioned (Sued Badillo 2001:333–334). A systematic survey of selected areas to locate the early gold-mining sites may be able to provide archaeological evidence of Spanish-Indian interaction. It would be interesting to determine whether Indian ceramic traditions persisted during the early historic period, whether there is material evidence for the influx of foreign Indians into the labor force, and whether there is any indication of Indian modification of Spanish material culture. A study of this type would compare with work done in the Spanish town site of Puerto Real, located in Haiti (Deagan 1995). In Puerto Real, Taíno ceramic traditions were quickly substituted by unidentified plain pottery that appears in the early contexts of the site (pre-1550) and declines through time, and by an undecorated Colono ware called Christophe Plain, interpreted by Smith (1995:373, 374) as being made by Africans.

A complete explanation of what the aftermath of conquest meant to the Indians of Puerto Rico, both native and foreign, may never be possible. Historical research has been conducted, but the necessary archaeological fieldwork that focuses on locating, testing, and excavating Contact-period sites has not occurred. It is sorely needed in order to add pieces to solve the puzzle of Spanish-Indian interaction on Puerto Rico and to compare with the archaeological investigations of this period that have been conducted elsewhere in the Caribbean. The scarcity of Contact-period sites in Puerto Rico remains to be explained.

Notes

1. The exception is Antonio Curet's study of Indian demography in the Maunabo River Valley, which suggests that, at least in this area, the Taíno chiefdoms were below carrying capacity and that demographic pressure could not be considered the cause for their development (Curet 1992a).

2. Fray Ramón Pané was sent by Columbus to live among the Indians of Hispaniola and learn as much as he could about their customs. He is known as the first Caribbean ethnographer for his treatise *Relación acerca de las antigüedades de los indios,* the first and only primary source available about Taíno mythology (Pané 1974).

3. Cacique Agüeybaná had been given in *encomienda* to Don Cristóbal Sotomayor.

10

Multiple Visions of an Island's Past and Some Thoughts for Future Directions in Puerto Rican Prehistory

Peter E. Siegel

My goals in this chapter are twofold: (1) review the salient themes addressed in the previous chapters, and (2) offer some insights into what I think connect the disparate bodies of evidence relating to environment, subsistence, settlements and polities, and religion and cosmology. In the preface, I observed that a book on the prehistory of Puerto Rico is contrived because things that were happening on this island were undoubtedly linked to affairs on neighboring islands and Central and South America. This truism notwithstanding, the chapter authors have demonstrated that from various perspectives there is plenty to say about what happened on Puerto Rico specifically. Some of the authors have explicitly tied the happenings on Puerto Rico to larger Caribbean-wide social, political, and environmental currents. As such, these studies both reflect and illuminate issues of fundamental importance to the Caribbean, lowland South America, and Central America. This overextended justification for a book on the prehistory of Puerto Rico may be summarized by saying "we and the Native Americans who occupied the island were and are not alone."

Themes of the Book

Numerous themes may be identified in the previous chapters. I've chosen three to address: interaction and social change; subsistence, environment, and social change; and cosmology and social change. Social change is the common theme.

INTERACTION AND SOCIAL CHANGE

Historically, the Caribbean has been thought of as a place intersected by peoples of numerous nationalities, ethnic backgrounds, religious and political views, and agendas of various sorts. Sam Wilson discussed the post-Contact blend of Native American and European cultures, producing a distinctively West Indian social and political context: "the essential part of being a Caribbean person is having a multicultural background" (Wilson 1997:212). This observation is equally valid for the pre-Contact Caribbean as well. Archaeologists working in the Caribbean will probably never agree on rates and routes of migrations. And, we will probably eternally disagree on degrees of autochthonous social development vs. influences from elsewhere or successive waves of migration. At least there is agreement on one rather uninteresting truism: at various times in the past, people came to the islands, interacted with those already there, and the ensuing population was different from any of the groups prior to the interaction. Also, as I argued some years ago, I think it's a mistake to think of large pre-Columbian monolithic cultural migrations into the Caribbean (Siegel 1991a:82–83). A more realistic perspective, perhaps, is to think of families, sets of families, or, at most, the occupants of entire villages moving as groups and establishing residences in new places. For the early Saladoid period (ca. 500 B.C.–A.D. 400), the most easily recognizable material correlate of this process is probably the pottery produced by the artisans of the group. At this level, our mind-numbing debates about names applied to cultural complexes (i.e., Hacienda Grande vs. La Hueca), subseries (Cedrosan Saladoid vs. Huecan Saladoid), and series (Saladoid vs. Huecoid) are meaningless. The hard work of trying to tease out stylistic (or microstylistic?) variation in pottery surface decorations and vessel forms, on a regional level, has not been done. It remains to be seen how Caribbean pottery, and its social milieu, relates to ideas of social interaction and information exchange. Given the complexity in Saladoid ceramic assemblages there is potential to further our understanding of underlying social and practical issues related to the migrations that still preoccupy much of Caribbean archaeology by addressing stylistic variation.

Interaction and social change were of fundamental importance at the beginning, end, and during the ceramic age. At the beginning of the ceramic age, we have the interactions that most certainly occurred between Neolithic colonists to the West Indies and the Archaic residents of the islands. These interactions have often been overlooked, largely because of their less-than-obvious traces in the archaeological record. We have a number of clearly identified Archaic sites in the West Indies, based on radiocarbon dates and assemblage characteristics (e.g., Ayes Suárez 1995; Harris 1973; Lundberg 1989; Moscoso et al. 1999; Narganes Storde 1991a; Rodríguez López 1997, 1999; Rouse 1952a, 1952b; Rouse and Alegría 1990). Other sites, often referred to as "aceramic," are not so clear because pottery is not present; they may or may not be preceramic in age (Lundberg 1985b). There are hints of pre-Saladoid Archaic folks producing pottery on Hispaniola (and elsewhere?), reviewed by Rodríguez Ramos in this volume (see Rouse 1992:90–92; Veloz Maggiolo et al. 1974). Then we have the earliest Saladoid sites, with their distinctive assemblages dating to about 500 B.C. in some places (Haviser 1991; Narganes Storde 1991b; Schvoerer et al. 1985; Siegel 1991b). A great many studies have addressed Archaic adaptations and cultures and early ceramic-age (Saladoid) adaptations and cultures (e.g., Armstrong 1980; Carbone 1980; Goodwin 1978, 1980; Siegel 1989b; Veloz Maggiolo 1976; Veloz Maggiolo and Ortega 1973; Veloz Maggiolo and Vega 1982).

Following the lead of Luis Chanlatte Baik (1995) and an early observation by Froelich Rainey (1940:180), Reniel Rodríguez makes the argument that the Archaic people of Puerto Rico didn't go anywhere or disappear when the Saladoid settlers arrived. Indeed, he sees the continuation of Archaic lifeways in Ostionoid (post-Saladoid) assemblages, simply with the addition of the distinctive Ostionoid pottery. In Rodríguez's view, the Archaic peoples evolved into the post-Saladoid Ostionoids, presumably with all of the attendant social and political paraphernalia, like caciques, *behiques,* and so on. It's an interesting idea and one that can only be substantiated with careful excavations of appropriate sites.

In our coring of the Maisabel pond and associated mangrove swamp, John Jones, Debby Pearsall, Dan Wagner, and I obtained tantalizing evidence for shifting use of the landscape dating to the Archaic and early Saladoid periods. Based on relative concentrations of charcoal particulates documented in our cores and in a core taken by Burney et al. (1994) in a nearby lagoon, we concluded that Archaic people were engaged in land-clearing projects, similar to the Neolithic populations that colonized the West Indies. The evidence suggests, too, that with the earliest occupation of the large ceramic-age village (Maisabel), Archaic land-clearing in the vicinity of the village ceased. This may be indirect evidence of Archaic-Saladoid interactions, resulting in Archaic dislocation from the local area. If Rodríguez is correct, then perhaps these Archaic groups became sleeper cells in the interior mountains for the next 600 or so years until developing Ostionoid pottery and ball courts.

Following the earliest ceramic-age Hacienda Grande occupations of Puerto Rico (ca. 200 B.C.–A.D. 400), settlement patterns and, undoubtedly, interaction networks changed. With the late Saladoid Cuevas period (ca. A.D. 400–

600/700), we find middle and upper valley areas being settled (Rodríguez López 1990, 1992b). In the Cibuco valley at this time, Maisabel and Paso del Indio were substantial villages, with formal cemeteries, plazas, and habitation areas. It's hard to imagine that the occupants of these two sizable villages were not intimately involved with each other socially and economically, and matters of political import were probably addressed together by representatives of the villages. The short one- to two-hour canoe paddle down and up the Río Cibuco would have facilitated easy visits between the villages. We see in this scenario the germination of the multivillage polities that became prominent in the ensuing centuries.

At the other end of the chronological spectrum, in the fifteenth and sixteenth centuries A.D., interactions and social change came in the form of the Spanish colonization of the Caribbean islands. Karen Anderson referred to "the conditions of Spanish-Indian interaction" and, in contrast to her earlier thinking (Anderson-Córdova 1990), now believes that the concept of acculturation is not of primary relevance. Clearly, exploitation for labor, resources, and land was the operative process in the sixteenth-century era of the Spanish Inquisition. In that context, interaction, acculturation, and social change might be genteel ways of referring to the depressingly familiar concept of "ethnic cleansing." One reviewer suggested that Anderson should address the archaeology of acculturation in her paper. My dictionary defines acculturation as "cultural modification of an individual, group, or people by adapting to or borrowing traits from another culture; *also:* a merging of cultures as a result of prolonged contact" (Webster's 1991:50). Like any person or group stuck between a rock and a hard place, the Taínos attempted to survive and in some cases resist. Of course, acculturation to some extent happened. Look at the modern Caribbean, with its unique blends of African, European, Native American, and East Asian cultures. However, these outcomes do not provide much insight into the tumultuous times of the sixteenth-century Spanish-occupied islands. For that, we need to sift through the writings of Las Casas, Oviedo, Mártir de Anglería, Columbus, and others.

Between the initial Saladoid and the later Spanish colonization to the West Indies, we have approximately 16 centuries of occupation and social developments. Interaction is relevant for this era as well. Torres discussed "the complex social landscape that developed during the Elenan and Ostionan Ostionoid" as a product of "distinctive and persistent spheres of interaction." His discussion of "the arrangement and growth of regional social groups" is of fundamental importance in understanding the competitive tensions and interactions that fueled the development of the Taíno *cacicazgos*. As I have argued elsewhere, Taíno polities were fluid social formations related to competitive interactions and spatially expansive imperatives (Siegel 2004). Alliances were forged and dissolved, as convenient, with aspiring leaders seeking to accumulate wealth and followers.

Interaction and resulting social change are perhaps magnified in archipelago settings. The availability of land and options are limited by the nearest beach or rocky cliff. From the earliest human occupations to the present, the nature and outcome of interactions within and across groups on Puerto Rico undoubtedly shaped ensuing social formations.

SUBSISTENCE, ENVIRONMENT, AND SOCIAL CHANGE

Inspiration for much of the research into subsistence economics in the pre-Columbian West Indies stems from Rainey's (1940) precocious study of the Crab and Shell cultures. Rainey was interested specifically in cultural systematics and migrations, rather than subsistence patterns per se: "the abrupt change in the type of food refuse substantiates the inference that some time elapsed before the arrival of the immigrating group, since direct contact would undoubtedly result in a carry-over of the food complex, at least for a certain time, before giving way to a gradual change" (Rainey 1940:61). Based on evidence available at the time, Rainey correctly concluded that the Crab culture (now called Saladoid series) originated in lowland South America. Marked distinctions in the assemblages of the Crab and the following Shell cultures (Ostionoid series) indicated to Rainey population replacement, rather than in-place development. Similarities in key aspects of the two assemblages suggested to Rainey that the Shell culture also derived from the same South American heartland: "clay griddles, modeled head lugs on the rims of vessels; rectangular and semi-lunar lugs; the relation between boat-shaped and oval bowls; the relation between loop and D-shaped handles; polished stone implements; and the absence of flint tools.... The similarities can best be explained by a common source of diffusion rather than by direct contact" (Rainey 1940:182). It was for later generations of archaeologists to investigate the implications of the crab and shell remains from the explicit perspective of subsistence adaptations (e.g., Carbone 1980; Goodwin 1980; Jones 1985, 1989; Wing 1989; Keegan 1989; deFrance 1989). In doing so, researchers quickly realized that it was critical "to look in more detail at other quantifiable features of the midden and their faunal material" (Jones 1989:47). Largely following the lead of Elizabeth Wing at the University of Florida, an explosion of detailed ethnobiological studies beginning in the 1960s did just that. In addition to faunal investigations, other lines of inquiry were followed to fill in the picture of subsistence trends, including archaeobotany, human skeletal isotope analysis, human osteology, and paleoecology (e.g., Berman and Pearsall 2000; Budinoff 1991; Carbone 1980; deFrance 1989, 1990; deFrance et al. 1996; Higuera-Gundy 1989, 1991; Keegan and DeNiro 1988; Newsom 1993; Newsom and Pearsall 2003; Stokes 1998; van Klinken 1991; Wing 1989; Wing and Reitz 1982; Wing et al. 1968).

Susan deFrance, Lee Newsom, and Anne Stokes, all University of Florida Ph.D.s, addressed shifting patterns of subsistence, from the domains of animals, plants, and human skeletal isotopes, respectively. John Jones, Debby Pearsall, Dan Wagner, and I looked at pollen, phytoliths, charcoal microparticulates, and sediments to assess land-use patterns and cultivation practices. As might be expected, detailed studies of ethnobiological assemblages, skeletal chemistry, and paleoecological records resulted in patterns less clear than we hoped for, especially compared to the intuitively appealing phrase "crab-shell dichotomy." The theoretical expectations and conventional wisdom linked to the phrase may be simplified to a structural equation: crabs : terrestrial adaptations :: shells : maritime adaptations. The data weren't so accommodating.

One of the common-sense conclusions of deFrance, Newsom, and Stokes is that the organisms collected, some of which were eaten, were largely determined by where people lived. DeFrance and Newsom indicate that there were "subregional patterns of resource extraction and food production," and Stokes found "that the people living at Paso del Indio had more terrestrial protein in their diet than those from Maisabel. This is to be expected since Paso del Indio lies 5 km inland and Maisabel is located on the coast."

Of considerable interest are hints of land, plant, and animal management even during the Archaic period. Discussed earlier in connection with interactions between Archaic and Saladoid groups, there is growing evidence that Archaic peoples were purposely clearing tracts of land, probably for some degree of plant cultivation. This would support Newsom's observation "that Archaic occupants of the region may have been gardeners or casual food producers." There is evidence for human introductions of various animals during the ceramic age: *hutías* in several early Saladoid contexts, guinea pigs in later Saladoid and Ostionoid contexts, and probable peccary in the early Saladoid Sorcé site on Vieques. Dogs have been found in numerous early and late ceramic-age deposits.

People who colonized the Caribbean, dating to the Archaic and ceramic ages, brought their knowledge of previous places, habitats, and lifeways with them. As new places were occupied, colonists undoubtedly reflected on their surroundings vis-à-vis how they did things before. It is plausible that when establishing new places of residence, Archaic and ceramic-age colonists still maintained links with their respective cultural homelands. Vivid expressions of a South American homeland are central in much of the ceramic iconography in Saladoid and Ostionoid assemblages (de Hostos 1919; Roe 1989a). Rather than attempting to reproduce their ancestral homeland in a new place, it could be that colonists selectively introduced plant or animal species, as appropriate. As such, the new colonists, like agricultural extension agents, would evaluate characteristics of the soils, precipitation levels, and topography, as well as their needs, when deciding on the appropriateness of various plants. We may be able to address origins of plant and animal domesticates, directly, by extracting and comparing DNA from botanical and faunal remains excavated in sites from the Caribbean, South America, and Central America.

One of the images, albeit blurry at this point, emerging from studies of ethnobiology and land-use histories is that Archaic foragers, collectors, and cultivators may not have been all that dissimilar to the early Saladoid cultivators, collectors, and foragers. We certainly know more about settlement structure, burial patterns, and associated social organization of the Saladoid than we do for the Archaic, and this lopsided knowledge base may color our interpretations of relative social "complexity." This view may lend credence to Reniel Rodríguez's argument that the Archaic residents of Puerto Rico may have blended into the Saladoid landscape, to emerge some centuries later as the Ostionoid.

We can now safely say, nearly 70 years later, that Rainey got at least one thing wrong. There was no "abrupt change in the type of food" consumed between the Crab and Shell cultures. Nearly 40 years of ethnobiological studies and perhaps 20 years of isotope and paleoecological studies indicate many continuities as well as local variations in diet, between at least the Crab and Shell cultures and perhaps the previous Archaic cultures.

Cosmology, Religion, Ideology, and Social Change

The studies by José Oliver and Peter Roe are monumental in more ways than one. They are long and dense, and they address monumental art and architecture. I will not attempt to summarize these two studies. Suffice it to say, Oliver and Roe, in their unique ways, provide believable and closely argued links between rock art, iconography, ball courts, shamanism, power, social and political organization, cosmology, and myths and ethnohistoric data.

Cosmology, religion, and ideology have been systematically addressed as legitimate and significant components of Greater Antillean archaeology for about the past 25 years (Alegría 1986b; Lopéz-Baralt 1977, 1985; Oliver 1997, 1998; Robiou Lamarche 2002; Roe 1982, 1997a; Siegel 1997; Stevens-Arroyo 1988). These components are sometimes lumped with a larger domain of research called cognitive archaeology, or the "archaeology of mind" (Flannery and Marcus 1993; Pearson 2002; Renfrew and Zubrow 1994). "Cognitive archaeology is the study of all those aspects of ancient culture that are the product of the human mind: the perception, description, and classification of the universe (cosmology); the nature of the supernatural (religion); the principles, philosophies, ethics, and values by which human societies are governed (ideology); the ways in which aspects of the world, the supernatural, or human values are conveyed in art (iconography)" (Flannery and Marcus 1993:261). Flannery and Marcus (1993:266–267) make the important point that cognitive archaeology can only be done under "appropriate conditions," namely with "a great deal of background information." Common sources of background information include ethnohistoric documents or relevant ethnographic observations. Lacking appropriate conditions, forays into cognitive archaeology "border on science fiction" (Flannery and Marcus 1993:267; see also Renfrew 1994).

Others and I have variously addressed cosmology, ideology, religion, and iconography in the development of Taíno chiefdoms or *cacicazgos* (Curet 1996; Curet and Oliver 1998; Oliver 1998; Roe 1989a, 1997a; Siegel 1991c, 1996, 1997, 1999). We seem to agree that leaders, or aspiring leaders, tapped into shared conceptions of the cosmos as a basis for their power. Reading the Taíno myths, we are confronted with a wonderfully tight complex structural system that facilitated order and continuity in the universe. José Oliver (this volume) convincingly argues that the person of the chief or cacique was central to Taíno cosmological structure: "The centrality of the living cacique, located at the axis of sociopolitical and religious life, is reproduced in the linear sequence of the iconography. He mediates between the extraordinary . . . and the ordinary. . . . If one removes either the living cacique or the cacique-petroglyph-*cemí,* the structural order collapses, and the mediation of past and present . . . natural and supernatural is no longer attainable." The materializations of Taíno myths, expressed on the landscape as ball courts, petroglyphs, and cave paintings, are snapshots of cosmic structural organization. However, this cosmic organization has deep roots, extending back 16 or 17 centuries to the earliest Saladoid settlers (Oliver 1998, this volume; Roe 1997a, this volume; Siegel 1996, 1999). In terms of currently accepted definitions of *cacicazgos* and caciques, there is general agreement that during the Saladoid, multivillage polities and chiefs did not exist. So, if Taíno cosmic structure was rooted in the Saladoid past and the person of cacique was central to the cosmic structure, how do we account for the absence of caciques and their associated polities in the Saladoid? I think the answer lies in a process that may be referred to as "mythic recontextualization."[1] If we had a collection of Las Casas/Colón/Pané-like documents written say every 100 years, from about 200 B.C. to A.D. 1400, we might see some continuities in certain themes about gourds, fish, frogs, woodpeckers, spirits, and such. However, there would undoubtedly be some critical differences in how key social institutions, like leaders, were presented and the nature of intergroup relations. At any given time in the trajectory from 200 B.C. to A.D. 1400, the cosmic order of the moment would be maintained by people observing the proper set of structural relations defining the sacred and secular realms. However, as the historical context of their world changed, the nature and scale of many of the structural relations would need to change accordingly. Thus, the archaeologically documented shift from the Saladoid village-bound entity to the post-Saladoid multivillage polity was undoubtedly associated with a number of conceptual shifts in how the universe was structured. Over long trajectories of time, where the very nature of social and political institutions have changed, reconceptualizing myths to accommodate or reflect history may have been necessary.

How Can We Link Subsistence, Settlement and Social Organization, and Cosmology in a Single Believable Story about the Past?

The chapters in this book present detailed studies of various aspects of Puerto Rico's past. All of the studies are empirically based, and some bodies of evidence overlap to some degree from chapter to chapter. By concentrating on the points of overlap, we may construct an empirically based narrative about the past that links seemingly disparate lines of evidence.

The earliest documented settlers of Puerto Rico date to about 6,000 years ago. These Archaic groups appear to have followed a subsistence economy based on hunting, foraging, collecting, and perhaps cultivation. Archaic groups left their mark on the landscape, most noticeably by systematic burning and clearing of surface vegetation. When the earliest Saladoid colonists arrived to the island, around 300 to 200 B.C., it is inconceivable that the groups graciously ignored one another or that the Archaic people conveniently and simply disappeared. Considerably more field research directed to the Late Archaic period is needed before we can offer any more definitive statements about the nature of interactions between the Archaic and Saladoid groups.

For the next six to seven centuries (ca. 300/200 B.C.–A.D. 400), early Saladoid (Hacienda Grande complex) groups occupied sizable villages located in coastal to near-coastal settings. Subsistence was based on slash-and-burn swidden horticulture, combined with collecting, fishing, foraging, and hunting of locally available resources. It is likely that the Saladoid newcomers came to a landscape already modified by the previous Archaic residents. In addition, the new colonists brought with them established ideas for how to make a living, how to organize their villages, and how the universe was structured. Ceramic iconography and village organization are vivid expressions of the Saladoid connection to the South American tropical rainforest.

Settlement patterns and burials indicate that early Saladoid social structure was based on an egalitarian ethic. Institutional social inequality was not a feature of early Saladoid society. By about A.D. 400, we see an increase in the number of sites and habitats occupied compared to previous occupations. The late Saladoid period (A.D. 400–600/700) was associated with continued habitation of coastal areas, in addition to substantial occupations in interior valley settings (Rodríguez López 1990; Siegel 2004). The earliest large deposits in the Paso del Indio site date to this period.

The post-Saladoid occupations of the island are associated with an explosion in the frequency of sites and site types. At this time, formal ball courts and ceremonial plazas were constructed in a number of settlements. Combining lines of evidence from site locations, relative site sizes, architectural and structural organization, and mortuary patterns, there appears to have been a fundamental transformation in social relations beginning around A.D. 700 (Curet and Oliver 1998; Oliver 1998; Siegel 1996, 1999, 2004). Given the rather coarse chronology that we currently work with, where our finest degree of control is no better than two to three hundred years, the underlying shift in social organization was probably more gradual than it appears to us archaeologically. Over the span of about seven centuries, from ca. A.D. 700 to A.D. 1400, the cultural landscape of Puerto Rico progressed through a series of gradual but dramatic shifts. Tracking the locations of ceremonial centers, as a proxy for mapping the political geography of the island, we see power initially broadly dispersed in the south and, through time, increasingly concentrated in the high interior mountains (Siegel 1999; Torres, this volume). This trend was "associated with [the establishment] of well-defined group territories, increased solidarity among group members, and notions of exclusive rights over territories, land, and people" (Siegel 2004:93). Ethnohistoric documents reveal tensions between groups, ranging from low-level rivalries to casual feuding to out-and-out warfare and military campaigns of conquest (Siegel 2004:89–90). The number of sites in general, and ball courts/ceremonial plazas in particular, increased to their greatest levels by the Esperanza (protohistoric) period. From the demographic trends apparent in the regional archaeological database, we might infer that population pressure was responsible for changes in sociopolitical organization. However, when viewing maps of site distributions over time, large portions of the island appear to have been uninhabited. In large part, this is a product of uneven sampling. Yet when we examine individual watersheds for the frequency of sites by time period there are some telling differences. For example, the Loiza and Maunabo valleys experienced population *decreases* during the final prehispanic period, in contrast to the Manatí Valley, whose population increased exponentially during the same period (compare Curet [1992a], Rodríguez López [1990, 1992b], and Siegel [2004]). In the context of interpolity competition, feuding, and campaigns of conquest there may have been subregional patterns of population restructuring. Rather than demography driving other aspects of culture, political maneuverings of leaders and aspiring leaders may have been largely responsible for changes in population across Puerto Rico. Financing for the increasingly competitive polities was undoubtedly a major challenge for aggressive leaders. The ethnohistories describe great caches of sumptuous items. For instance, "Había grandísima abundancia de algodón bien hilado en ovillos, tanto que en una sola casa vieron más de 12,500 libras de algodón hilado" (Colón 1947:101). It's hard to imagine more than six tons of woven cotton kept in a single structure as anything but stored wealth. Understanding the formation, maintenance, and dissolution of individual polities is a critically important line of research for the future.

Closing Note

Over the 6,000 years of human occupations on Puerto Rico, we've documented an increasingly complex mosaic of cultures. Like an impressionist painting, the view of the cultural scene becomes clearer as we step back for the long view. However, we must not forget that the success of the picture hinges on the painstaking work of putting just the right dabs of paint in just the right places; so it is too for good research and data collection. The turgid details of the analysis in this book allow us to variously build on and revise previous conceptions of Puerto Rico's past. As such, the distinct bodies of data and perspectives enable us to view the past from the various vantages of subsistence, environment, settlements, religion, politics, and art.

Note

1. My inspiration for this idea comes from Guss's (1989:14) discussion of "historical incorporation [whereby] verifiable events are recontextualized within an already established mythic universe."

REFERENCES CITED

Acevedo-Rodríguez, P.
   1996   *Flora of St. John: U.S. Virgin Islands.* New York Botanical Garden, Bronx.

Adler, M. A.
   2002   The Ancestral Pueblo Community as Structure and Strategy. In *Seeking the Center Place,* edited by Mark D. Varien and Richard H. Wilshusen, pp. 25–36. University of Utah Press, Salt Lake City.

Adler, M. A., and R. Wilshusen
   1990   Large-Scale Integrative Facilities in Tribal Societies: Cross-Cultural and Southwestern U.S. Examples. *World Archaeology* 22:133–147.

Aitken, Robert T.
   1917   Puerto Rican Burial Caves. *Proceedings of the International Congress of Americanists* 19:224–228. Washington, D.C.

Alcina Franch, José
   1983   La cultura taína como sociedad en transición entre los niveles tribal y de jefaturas. *La cultura taína: Seminario sobre la investigación de la cultura taína,* pp. 69–80. Comisión Nacional para la Celebración del V Centenario del Descubrimiento de América, Madrid.

Alegría, Ricardo E.
   1941   Petroglifos indígenas. *La Torre* 2(55):6.
   1978   *Apuntes en torno a la mitología de los indios Taínos de las antillas mayores y sus orígenes suramericanos.* Centro de Estudios Avanzados de Puerto Rico y el Caribe, San Juan.
   1979a   "Introducción y notas de" Notas sobre los petroglifos y antigüedades de las Antillas Mayores y Menores, by Alphonso L. Pinart. *Revista del Museo de la Universidad de Puerto Rico* 1(1):71–88.

1979b   Apuntes para el estudio de los caciques de Puerto Rico. *Revista del Instituto de Cultura Puertorriqueña* 85:25–41.

1981   *El uso de la terminología etnohistórica para designar las culturas aborígenes de las Antillas.* Cuadernos Prehispánicos. Seminario de Historia de América, Universidad de Valladolid, Valladolid.

1983   *Ball Courts and Ceremonial Plazas in the West Indies.* Yale University Publications in Anthropology No. 79. Department of Anthropology, Yale University, New Haven.

1986a   Nuevas interpretaciones en torno a la parafernalia de los jugadores de pelota en las antillas mayores. *La Revista del Centro de Estudios Avanzados de Puerto Rico y el Caribe* 3:31–42.

1986b   *Apuntes en torno a la mitología de los indios Taínos de las antillas mayores y sus orígenes suramericanos.* 2nd ed. Centro de Estudios Avanzados de Puerto Rico y el Caribe, San Juan.

1988   Apuntes en torno a las culturas aborígenes de Puerto Rico. In *Temas de la historia de Puerto Rico,* edited by Ricardo E. Alegría, pp. 18–53. Centro de Estudios Avanzados de Puerto Rico y el Caribe, San Juan.

1995   La vestimenta y adornos de los caciques taínos y la parafernalia asociada a sus funciones mágico-religiosas. *Proceedings of the Congress of the International Association for Caribbean Archaeology* 15:295–309. San Juan.

1997a   An Introduction to Taíno Culture and History. In *Taíno: Pre-Columbian Art and Culture from the Caribbean,* edited by Fatima Bercht, Estrellita Brodsky, John Alan Farmer, and Dicey Taylor, pp. 18–33. Monacelli Press and El Museo del Barrio, New York.

1997b   The Study of Aboriginal Peoples: Multiple Ways of Knowing. In *The Indigenous People of the Caribbean,* edited by Samuel M. Wilson, pp. 11–19. University Press of Florida, Gainesville.

Alegría, Ricardo E., Henry B. Nicholson, and Gordon R. Willey

1955   The Archaic Tradition of Puerto Rico. *American Antiquity* 21:113–121.

Alvarado Zayas, Pedro

1981   La cerámica del centro ceremonial de Tibes: Estudio descriptivo. Unpublished Master's thesis, Centro de Estudios Avanzados de Puerto Rico y el Caribe, San Juan.

1999   Estudio y documentación del arte rupestre en Puerto Rico. In *Trabajos de investigación arqueológica en Puerto Rico: Tercer encuentro de investigadores,* edited by Juan Rivera Fontán, pp. 97–102. Publicación Ocasional de la División de Arqueología, Instituto de Cultura Puertorriqueña, San Juan.

Alvarez Chanca, Diego

1949   *Navegaciones Colombinas,* edited by Edmundo O'Gorman. Secretaría de Educación Pública, Mexico City.

Ambrose, Stanley H.

1993   Isotopic Analysis of Paleodiets: Methodological and Interpretive Considerations. In *Investigations of Ancient Human Tissue Chemical Analyses in*

Anthropology, edited by Mary K. Sanford, pp. 59–130. Gordon and Breach, Langhorne, Pennsylvania.

Ambrose, Stanley H., and Lynette Norr
- 1992 On Stable Isotope Data and Prehistoric Subsistence in the Soconusco Region. *Current Anthropology* 33:401–404.
- 1993 Experimental Evidence for the Relationship of the Carbon Isotope Ratios of Whole Diet and Dietary Protein to Those of Bone Collagen and Carbonate. In *Prehistoric Human Bone: Archaeology at the Molecular Level,* edited by J. B. Lambert and G. Grupe, pp. 1–37. Springer-Verlag, New York.

Anderson, David G.
- 1996a Fluctuations between Simple and Complex Chiefdoms: Cycling in the Late Prehistoric Southeast. In *Political Structure and Change in the Prehistoric Southeastern United States,* edited by John F. Scarry, pp. 231–252. University Press of Florida, Gainesville.
- 1996b Chiefly Cycling and Large-Scale Abandonments as Viewed from the Savannah River Basin. In *Political Structure and Change in the Prehistoric Southeastern United States,* edited by John F. Scarry, pp. 150–191. University Press of Florida, Gainesville.

Anderson, Richard L.
- 1989 *Art in Small-Scale Societies.* 2nd ed. Prentice Hall, Englewood Cliffs, New Jersey.

Anderson-Córdova, Karen
- 1990 *Hispaniola and Puerto Rico: Indian Acculturation and Heterogeneity, 1492–1550.* Ph.D. dissertation, Yale University. University Microfilms, Ann Arbor.
- 1995 Aspectos demográficos de los cacicazgos Taínos. *Proceedings of the Congress of the International Association for Caribbean Archaeology* 15:351–365. San Juan.

Anschuetz, K. F., R. Wilshusen, and C. Scheik
- 2001 An Archaeology of Landscapes: Perspectives and Directions. *Journal of Archaeological Research* 9:157–211.

Armstrong, Douglas V.
- 1980 Shellfish Gatherers of St. Kitts: A Study of Archaic Subsistence and Settlement Patterns. *Proceedings of the International Congress for the Study of the Pre-Columbian Cultures of the Lesser Antilles* 8:152–167. Arizona State University, Tempe.

Arrom, José Juan
- 1975 *Mitología y artes prehispánicas de las Antillas.* Editorial Siglo xxi, Mexico City.
- 1986 Fray Ramón Pané o el rescate de un mundo mítico. *La Revista del Centro de Estudios Avanzados de Puerto Rico y el Caribe* 3:2–8.
- 1988 La lechuza: Motivo recurrente en las artes taínas y el folclor hispanoameri-

cano. In *El murciélago y la lechuza en la cultura taína.* Fundación García Arévalo, Santo Domingo, Dominican Republic.

1997 The Creation Myths of the Taíno. In *Taíno: Pre-Columbian Art and Culture from the Caribbean,* edited by Fatima Bercht, Estrellita Brodsky, John Alan Farmer, and Dicey Taylor, pp. 68–79. Monacelli Press and El Museo del Barrio, New York.

2000 *Estudios de lexicología antillana.* 2nd ed., revised and enlarged. Editorial de la Universidad de Puerto Rico, San Juan.

Ashmore, Wendy, and Jeremy A. Sabloff
2002 Spatial Order in Maya Civic Plans. *Latin American Antiquity* 13:202–217.

Ayensu, E. S.
1981 *Medicinal Plants of the West Indies.* Reference Publications, Algonac, Michigan.

Ayes Suárez, Carlos M.
1985a Para graduarse de cialeño, hay que subir a las Archillas. *Arqueología* 1(1):2–9, 18.
1985b La cueva de las Ortigas. *Avanzada* 1(1):13–14.
1986a Investigaciones arqueológicas en la cueva de las Guindas. *Horizontes* January-February:12–13.
1986b La Cueva de las Ortigas. *Horizontes* August-September:12–13.
1986c Los petroglifos ostiones de las cuevas. *Horizontes* November-December: 16–17.
1986d Petroglifo, Cueva de las Golondrinas, Barrio Cordillera, Ciales, P.R. *Arqueología* 2(1):Endpiece.
1987 La Cueva de los Burros. *Horizontes* January-February:8–9.
1988 *Evaluación arqueológica tipo fase 2 Angostura, Florida Afuera, Barceloneta, Puerto Rico.* AYES: Investigaciones Arqueológicas e Historicas, Manatí, Puerto Rico. Submitted to Custodio, Roe & Asociados, Hato Rey, Puerto Rico. Copies available from the Instituto de Cultura Puertorriqueña, San Juan.
1989 Excavaciones arqueológicas en Angostura, Barrio Florida Afuera, Barceloneta, Puerto Rico. *Ecos de la Plazuela* 1(3):9–11.
1995 *Mitigacion parcial del monticulo a del yacimiento de Angostura, Barrio Florida Afuera, Barceloneta, Puerto Rico.* AYES: Investigaciones Arqueológicas e Historicas, Manatí, Puerto Rico. Submitted to Autoridad de Carreteras y Transportación, San Juan, Puerto Rico. Copies available from the Instituto de Cultura Puertorriqueña, San Juan.

Ayes Suárez, Carlos M., and Edgar Otero López
1986 La cueva del negro. *Arqueología* 2(1):2–7.

Baena, Javier
1998 *Tecnología lítica experimental.* BAR International Series No. 271. British Archaeological Reports, Oxford.

Bartone, Robert. N., and John. G. Crock
- 1993 Flaked Stone Industries at the Early Saladoid Trants Site, Montserrat, West Indies. *Proceedings of the International Congress for Caribbean Archaeology* 14:124–146. Barbados.

Behling, Hermann
- 1995 A High Resolution Holocene Pollen Record from Lago do Pires, S.E. Brazil: Vegetation, Climate and Fire History. *Journal of Paleolimnology* 14:253–268.

Beinroth, Friedrich H.
- 1969 *An Outline of the Geology of Puerto Rico.* Bulletin 213. Agricultural Experiment Station, University of Puerto Rico, Mayagüez.

Bender, Margaret M.
- 1968 Mass Spectrometric Studies of Carbon 13 Variations in Corn and Other Grasses. *Radiocarbon* 10:468–472.

Bender, Margaret M., David A. Baerreis, and Raymond L. Steventon
- 1981 Further Light on Carbon Isotopes and Hopewell Agriculture. *American Antiquity* 46:346–353.

Bercht, Fatima, Estrellita Brodsky, John Alan Farmer, and Dicey Taylor (editors)
- 1997 *Taíno: Pre-Columbian Art and Culture from the Caribbean.* Monacelli Press and El Museo del Barrio, New York.

Berman, Mary Jane, and Deborah M. Pearsall
- 2000 Plants, People, and Culture in the Prehistoric Central Bahamas: A View from the Three Dog Site, An Early Lucayan Settlement on San Salvador Island, Bahamas. *Latin American Antiquity* 11:219–239.

Betancourt, Angel
- 1983 Investigación arqueológica en la Cueva del Caballo (Parte I). *Revista de la Sociedad para el Estudio de la Arqueología* 1(1):4–5.

Blasini, Antonio
- 1985 *El aguila y el jaguar: Autoradiografía de una civilización.* Publigraph, Hato Rey, Puerto Rico.

Boas, Franz
- 1955 *Primitive Art.* Dover, New York.
- [1927]

Boëda, E.
- 1993 Le débitage discoide et le débitage Levallois recurrent centripéte. *Bulletin de la Societé Préhistorique Française* 90:392–404.

Boletín Histórico de Puerto Rico (BHPR)
- 1914–1927 14 Vols. Edited by Cayetano Coll y Toste. San Juan.

Borah, Woodrow
- 1976 The Historical Demography of Aboriginal and Colonial America: An At-

tempt at Perspective. In *The Native Population of the Americas in 1492*, edited by William M. Denevan, pp. 13–34. University of Wisconsin Press, Madison.

Bourdieu, Pierre
1977 *Outline of a Theory of Practice.* Cambridge University Press, Cambridge.

Bourne, Edward Gaylord
1906 Columbus, Ramón Pané, and the Beginnings of American Anthropology. *Proceedings of the American Antiquarian Society* (n.s.) 17:310–348.

Brau, Salvador
1966 *La colonización de Puerto Rico.* Instituto de Cultura Puertorriqueña, San Juan.

Bray, Warwick
1997 Metallurgy and Anthropology: Two Studies from Prehispanic America. *Boletín. Museo del Oro* 42:3–55. Banco de la República, Bogotá, Colombia.

Brenner, Mark, and Michael W. Binford
1988 A Sedimentary Record of Human Disturbance from Lake Miragoane, Haiti. *Journal of Paleolimnology* 1:85–97.

Brito, Jorge, and Oscar Pereira
2001 Guía bibliográfica del protoagrícola. *El Caribe arqueológico* 5:124–128.

Brussell, David E.
1997 *Potions, Poisons, and Panaceas: An Ethnobotanical Study of Montserrat.* Southern Illinois University Press, Carbondale.

Bucher, Bernadette
1981 *Icon and Conquest: A Structural Analysis of the Illustrations of De Bry's Great Voyages.* University of Chicago Press, Chicago.

Budinoff, Linda C.
1991 An Osteological Analysis of the Human Burials Recovered from Maisabel: An Early Ceramic Site on the North Coast of Puerto Rico. *Proceedings of the Congress of the International Association for Caribbean Archaeology* 12:117–133. Martinique.

Bullen, Ripley P.
1973 Petroglyphs of the Virgin Islands and Puerto Rico. *Proceedings of the International Congress for the Study of the Pre-Columbian Cultures of the Lesser Antilles* 4:13–16. Reduit Plage, St. Lucia.

Burney, David A., Lida Pigott Burney, and R. D. E. MacPhee
1994 Holocene Charcoal Stratigraphy from Laguna Tortuguero, Puerto Rico, and the Timing of Human Arrival on the Island. *Journal of Archaeological Science* 21:273–281.

Callahan, Richard T.
1995 Antillean Cultural Contacts with Mainland Regions as a Navigation Problem. *Proceedings of the Congress of the International Association for Caribbean Archaeology* 15:181–189. San Juan.

Capone, D. G., D. L. Taylor, and B. F. Taylor
   1977   Nitrogen Fixation (Acetylene Reduction) Associated with Macroalgae in a Coral-Reef Community in the Bahamas. *Marine Biology* 40:29–32.

Carbone, Victor A.
   1980   Some Problems in Cultural Paleoecology in the Caribbean Area. *Proceedings of the International Congress for the Study of the Precolumbian Cultures of the Lesser Antilles* 8:98–126. Arizona State University, Tempe.

El Caribe
   1979   Descubren yacimiento de arte rupestre indígena que podría ser caverna citada por Fray Ramón Pané. *El Caribe* July 28:12.

Carlson, Betsy
   1995   Strings of Command: Manufacture and Utilization of Shell Beads among the Taino. *Proceedings of the Congress of the International Association for Caribbean Archaeology* 15:97–109. San Juan.

Carneiro, Robert L.
   1961   Slash-and-Burn Cultivation among the Kuikuru and Its Implications for Cultural Development in the Amazon Basin. In *The Evolution of Horticultural Systems in Native South America: Causes and Consequences,* edited by Johannes Wilbert, pp. 47–67. *Antropológica* Supplement Publication No. 2. Sociedad de Ciencias Naturales la Salle, Caracas.
   1983   The Cultivation of Manioc among the Kuikuru of the Upper Xingú. In *Adaptive Responses of Native Amazonians,* edited by Raymond B. Hames and William T. Vickers, pp. 65–111. Academic Press, New York.

Carr, M. E., B. S. Phillips, and M. O. Bagby
   1985   Xerophytic Species Evaluated for Renewal Energy Resources. *Economic Botany* 39:505–513.

Carter, Rita
   1998   *Mapping the Mind.* Phoenix, London.

Cassá, Roberto
   1974   *Los taínos de la Española.* Colección Historia y Sociedad No. 11. Publicaciones de la Universidad Autónoma de Santo Domingo, Santo Domingo, Dominican Republic.
   1979   *Los taínos de la Española.* 2nd ed. Editorial Alfa y Omega, Santo Domingo, Dominican Republic.
   1995   *Los indios de las Antillas.* 2nd ed. Ediciones ABYA-AYALA, Quito, Ecuador.

Chang, Kwang-Chih
   1968   Toward a Science of Prehistoric Society. In *Settlement Archaeology,* edited by Kwang-Chih Chang, pp. 1–9. National Press Books, Palo Alto.

Chanlatte Baik, Luis A.
   1995   Los arcaicos y el formative Antillano (6000 A.C.–1492 D.C.). *Proceedings of the Congress of the International Association for Caribbean Archaeology* 16:267–274. Basse Terre, Guadeloupe.

Chanlatte Baik, Luis A., and Yvonne M. Narganes Storde
   1980   La Hueca, Vieques: Nuevo complejo cultural agroalfarero en la arqueología antillana. *Proceedings of the International Congress for the Study of the Precolumbian Cultures of the Lesser Antilles* 8:501–523. Arizona State University, Tempe.
   1983   *Vieques-Puerto Rico: Asiento de una nueva cultura aborigen antillana.* Impresora Corporán, Santo Domingo, Dominican Republic.
   1990   *La nueva arqueología de Puerto Rico (Su proyección en las Antillas).* Taller, Santo Domingo, Dominican Republic.

Chisholm, M.
   1970   *Rural Settlement and Landuse.* Aldine, Chicago.

Clark, Jeffrey J., Jeff Walker, and Reniel Rodríguez Ramos
   2003   Depositional History and Evolution of the Paso del Indio Site, Vega Baja, Puerto Rico. *Geoarchaeology: An International Journal* 18:625–648.

Clark, John E., and Michael Blake
   1994   The Power of Prestige: Competitive Generosity and the Emergence of Rank Societies in Lowland Mesoamerica. In *Factional Competition and Political Development in the New World*, edited by E. M. Brumfiel and J. W. Fox, pp. 17–31. Cambridge University Press, Cambridge.

Clottes, Jean, and David Lewis-Williams
   1998   *The Shamans in Prehistory: Trance and Magic in the Painted Caves.* Harry N. Abrams, New York.

Colinvaux, Paul
   1987   Amazon Diversity in Light of the Paleoecological Record. *Quaternary Science Review* 6:93–114.
   1993   Pleistocene Biogeography and Diversity in Tropical Forests of South America. In *Biological Relationships between Africa and South America*, edited by P. Goldblatt, pp. 473–499. Yale University Press, New Haven.

Coll y Toste, Cayetano
   1897   *Prehistoria de Puerto Rico.* Editorial Vasco Americana, S.A., Bilbao.

Collazo, Nelson Rafael
   1983   Petroglifos indígenas. *Revista Cultural "Hequetí"* 5:2–8.

Collins, Michael B.
   1975   Lithic Technology as a Means of Processual Inference. In *Lithic Technology: Making and Using Stone Tools*, edited by E. Swanson, pp. 14–34. Mouton, Paris.
   1999   *Clovis Blade Technology.* University of Texas Press, Austin.

Colón, Fernando
   1984   *Historia del almirante.* Edited by Luis Schneider and translated by Alfonso Ulloa. Crónicas de América, Madrid.

Colón, Hernando
1947   *Vida del almirante don Cristobal Colón escrita por su hijo don Hernando.* Fondo de Cultura Económica, Mexico City.

Colón Parrilla, L.
1997   Las conchas y los caracoles: Sito arqueológico Caracoles, Ponce, Puerto Rico. In *Clasificacion de materiales arqueologicos sito Caracoles, Ponce: Materiales de la fase III,* by D. Molina Feal and D. López, pp. 1–26. Submitted to the Consejo Arqueologico Terrestre, San Juan, Puerto Rico. Copies available from the Instituto de Cultura Puertorriqueña, San Juan.

Cook, Sherburne F., and Woodrow Borah
1971   *Essays in Population History: Mexico and the Caribbean, Volume 1.* University of California Press, Berkeley.

Craig, Harmon
1957   Isotopic Standards for Carbon and Oxygen and Correction Factors for Mass-Spectrometric Analysis of Carbon Dioxide. *Geochimica et Cosmochimica Acta* 12:133–149.

Crespo Torres, Edwin
2000   *Estudio comparativo biocultural entre dos poblaciones prehistóricas en la isla de Puerto Rico: Punta Candelero y Paso del Indio.* Unpublished Ph.D. dissertation, Facultad de Filosofía, Instituto de Investigaciones Antropológicas, Universidad Autónoma de México.
2001   Proyecto arqueológico Paso del Indio, fase III, estudio osteológico de los restos humanos. Manuscript on file, Paso del Indio Laboratory, Canovanas, Puerto Rico.

Crock, John G.
2000   *Interisland Interaction and the Development of Chiefdoms in the Eastern Caribbean.* Ph.D. dissertation, University of Pittsburgh. University Microfilms, Ann Arbor.

Crock, John G., and Robert N. Bartone
1998   Archaeology of Trants, Montserrat. Part 4: Flaked Stone and Stone Bead Industries. *Annals of the Carnegie Museum* 67(3):97–224.

Crocker, William H.
1983   Ultimate Reality and Meaning for the Ramkómekra-Canela, Eastern Timbira, Brazil: A Triadic Dualistic Cognitive Pattern. *Journal of Ultimate Reality and Meaning* 6(2):84–111.

Crosby, Alfred W., Jr.
1972   *The Columbian Exchange: Biological and Cultural Consequences of 1492.* Greenwood Press, Westport, Connecticut.

Crumley, Carole L., and William H. Marquardt
1990   Landscape: A Unifying Concept in Regional Analysis. In *Interpreting*

Space: GIS and Archaeology, edited by Kathleen M. S. Allen, Stanton W. Green, and Ezra B. W. Zubrow, pp. 73–79. Taylor and Francis, London.

Curet, L. Antonio
- 1992a *The Development of Chiefdoms in the Greater Antilles: A Regional Study of the Valley of Maunabo, Puerto Rico.* Ph.D. dissertation, Arizona State University, Tempe. University Microfilms, Ann Arbor.
- 1992b House Structure and Cultural Change in the Caribbean: Three Case Studies from Puerto Rico. *Latin American Antiquity* 3:160–174.
- 1996 Ideology, Chiefly Power, and Material Culture: An Example from the Greater Antilles. *Latin American Antiquity* 7:114–131.
- 2002 The Chief is Dead, Long Live . . . Who? Descent and Succession in the Protohistoric Chiefdoms of the Caribbean. *Ethnohistory* 49:259–280.
- 2003 Issues on the Diversity and Emergence of Middle-Range Societies of the Ancient Caribbean: A Critique. *Journal of Archaeological Research* 11:1–42.

Curet, L. Antonio, and José R. Oliver
- 1998 Mortuary Practices, Social Development, and Ideology in Precolumbian Puerto Rico. *Latin American Antiquity* 9:217–239.

Curet, L. Antonio, Lee A. Newsom, and Susan D. deFrance
- 1998 Report on the 1996–1997 Research at the Civic-Ceremonial Center of Tibes, Ponce, Puerto Rico. Submitted to Latin American Archaeology Program, Heinz Family Foundation, Pittsburgh, Pennsylvania.

Curet, L. Antonio, and Luis Antonio Rodríguez Gracia
- 1995 Informe preliminar del proyecto arqueológico de Tibes. *Proceedings of the Congress of the International Association for Caribbean Archaeology* 16:113–126. Basse Terre, Guadeloupe.

Curet, L. Antonio, Joshua Torres, and Miguel Rodríguez
- 2004 Political and Social History of Eastern Puerto Rico: The Ceramic Age. In *Late Ceramic Age Societies in the Eastern Caribbean,* edited by André Delpuech and Corinne L. Hofman, pp. 59–85. Paris Monographs in American Archaeology No. 14. BAR International Series No. 1273. Archaeopress, Oxford.

Curtis, Jason H., and David A. Hodell
- 1993 An Isotopic and Trace Element Study of Ostracods from Lake Miragoane, Haiti: A 10.5 kyr Record of Paleosalinity and Paleotemperature Changes in the Caribbean. *American Geophysical Union Monograph* 78:135–152.

Dacal Moure, Ramón
- 1978 *Artefactos de concha en las comunidades aborígenes Cubanas.* Publicaciones No. 5. Museo Antropológico Montane, Universidad de la Habana, Havana, Cuba.
- 2001 La industria de la concha en Aruba. Paper presented at the 14th Congress of the International Association for Caribbean Archaeology, Aruba.

Dávila Dávila, Ovidio
- 1977 *Las pictografías de Cueva Maldita.* Sociedad de Investigaciones Arqueológicas e Historicas Sebuco, Vega Baja, Puerto Rico.
- 1979 Excavaciones arqueológicas en Manatí. *Revista del Instituto de Cultura Puertorriqueña* 85:8–16.
- 1980 *La Cueva de John Alden Mason.* PRABE, San Juan, Puerto Rico.
- 1981 Cueva Gemelos: Un yacimiento Arcaico de Morovis, Puerto Rico. Unpublished Master's thesis, Estudios Puertorriqueños, Centro de Estudios Avanzados de Puerto Rico y el Caribe, San Juan.
- 1985a La arqueología de las cuevas de Puerto Rico. *Revista del Instituto de Cultura Puertorriqueña* 89:24–27.
- 1985b El poblamiento aborigen precerámico en las Antillas. *Cuadernos Prehispánicos* 11:5–49.

Deagan, Kathleen
- 1985 Spanish-Indian Interaction in Sixteenth Century Florida and the Caribbean. In *Cultures in Contact,* edited by W. Fitzhugh, pp. 281–318. Smithsonian Institution Press, Washington, D.C.
- 1987 Initial Encounters: Arawak Responses to European Contact at the En Bas Saline Site. In *Proceedings of the First San Salvador Conference Columbus and his World,* edited by Donald T. Gerace, pp. 341–359. College Center of the Finger Lakes, Bahamian Field Station, Florida.
- 1988 The Archaeology of the Spanish Contact Period in the Caribbean. *Journal of Prehistory* 2:187–225.

Deagan, Kathleen (editor)
- 1995 *Puerto Real: The Archaeology of a Sixteenth-Century Spanish Town in Hispaniola.* University Press of Florida, Gainesville.

DeBoer, Bart A.
- 1996 *Our Plants and Trees (Nos Mata-I Palunan; Onze Planten en Bomen).* Dieren Bescherming, Curaçao, Netherlands Antilles.

deFrance, Susan D.
- 1988 Zooarchaeological Investigations of Subsistence Strategies at the Maisabel Site, Puerto Rico. Unpublished Master's Research Project, Department of Anthropology, University of Florida, Gainesville.
- 1989 Saladoid and Ostionoid Subsistence Adaptations: Zooarchaeological Data from a Coastal Occupation on Puerto Rico. In *Early Ceramic Population Lifeways and Adaptive Strategies in the Caribbean,* edited by Peter E. Siegel, pp. 57–78. BAR International Series No. 506. British Archaeological Reports, Oxford.
- 1990 Zooarchaeological Investigations of an Early Ceramic Age Frontier Community in the Caribbean, The Maisabel Site, Puerto Rico. *Antropológica* 73-74:3–180.
- 1997 Faunal Material Recovered from the 1996 Test Excavations at the Tibes Ceremonial Site, Puerto Rico. Submitted to L. Antonio Curet and Lee

Newsom, Tibes Archaeological Project, University of Colorado and Southern Illinois University, Carbondale.

deFrance, Susan D., William F. Keegan, and Lee A. Newsom
- 1996 The Archaeobotanical, Bone Isotope, and Zooarchaeological Records from Caribbean Sites in Comparative Perspective. In *Case Studies in Environmental Archaeology*, edited by Elizabeth J. Reitz, Lee A. Newsom, and Sylvia J. Scudder, pp. 289–304. Plenum Press, New York.

De Hostos, Adolfo
- 1919 Prehistoric Porto Rican Ceramics. *American Anthropologist* 21:376–399.
- 1938 *Investigaciones históricas.* Oficina del Historiador, San Juan, Puerto Rico.

Deive, Carlos E.
- 1976 Fray Ramón Pané y el nacimiento de la etnografía americana. *Boletín del Museo del Hombre Dominicano* 6:133–156.
- 1978 El chamanismo taíno. *Boletín del Museo del Hombre Dominicano* 9:189–207.
- 1983 El chamanismo taíno. In *La cultura taína: Seminario sobre la investigación de la cultura taína*, pp. 81–88. Comisión Nacional para la Celebración del V Centenario del Descubrimiento de América, Madrid.

Delgado Esquilín, Gloribel
- 1999a Mona: Eslabón del Caribe. *El Mundo.* Escenario. Sunday Supplement, 27 December:E18–19. San Juan, Puerto Rico.
- 1999b Cueva Catedral . . . santuario de culto y aventura. *El Mundo.* Escenario. Sunday Supplement, 17 January:E15–17. San Juan, Puerto Rico.

Delorit, R. J.
- 1970 *Illustrated Taxonomy Manual of Weed Seeds.* Agronomy Publications, River Falls, Wisconsin.

Delwiche, C. C., P. J. Zinke, C. M. Johnson, and R. A. Virginia
- 1979 Nitrogen Isotope Distribution as a Presumptive Indicator of Nitrogen Fixation. *Botanical Gazette* 140:65–69.

Denevan, William M. (editor)
- 1976 *The Native Population of the Americas in 1492.* University of Wisconsin Press, Madison.

DeNiro, Michael J., and Samuel Epstein
- 1978 Influence of Diet on the Distribution of Carbon Isotopes in Animals. *Geochimica et Cosmochimica Acta* 42:495–506.
- 1981 Influence of Diet on the Distribution of Nitrogen Isotopes in Animals. *Geochimica et Cosmochimica Acta* 45:341–351.

DeNiro, Michael J., and Christine A. Hastorf
- 1985 Alterations of $^{15}N/^{14}N$ and $^{13}C/^{12}C$ Ratios of Plant Matter during the Initial Stages of Diagenesis: Studies Utilizing Archaeological Specimens from Peru. *Geochimica et Cosmochimica Acta* 49:97–115.

Díaz González, Marlén
- 1990 *Proyecto recuperación arqueológica arte rupestre de la Cueva de la Catedral*

barrio Bayaney: Hatillo, Puerto Rico. Unpublished Master's thesis, Centro de Estudios Avanzados de Puerto Rico y el Caribe, San Juan.

Dobyns, Henry F.
1966   Estimating Aboriginal American Population: An Appraisal of Techniques with a New Hemispheric Estimate. *Current Anthropology* 7:395–416.
1983   *Their Numbers Became Thinned: Native American Population Dynamics in Eastern North America.* University of Tennessee Press, Knoxville.

Documentos de la Real Hacienda de Puerto Rico
1971   2 Vols. Edited and compiled by Aurelio Tanodi. Centro de Investigaciones Históricas, Universidad de Puerto Rico, Río Piedras.

Domínguez, Lourdes
1978   La transculturación en Cuba (siglos 16–17). *Cuba Arqueológica* 33–50. Editorial Oriente, Santiago.
1980   *Cerámica de transculturación del sitio colonial Casa de la Obrapía. Cuba Arqueológica* II. Editorial Oriente, Santiago.
1983   *El Yayal.* Separata de Cesaraugusta, Institución Fernando el Católico, Zaragoza.
1987   La cerámica del sitio arqueológico El Yayal, Cuba. *La Revista del Centro de Estudios Avanzados de Puerto Rico y el Caribe* 4:140–145.

Dubelaar, Cornelius N.
1985   A Comparison between Petroglyphs of the Antilles and of Northeastern South America. *Proceedings of the International Congress for the Study of the Pre-Columbian Cultures of the Lesser Antilles* 10:421–435. Centre de Recherches Caraïbes, Université de Montréal, Montreal.

Dubelaar, Cornelius N., Michele H. Hayward Merkling, and Michael A. Cinquino Argana
1999   *Puerto Rican Rock Art: A Resource Guide.* Panamerican Consultants, Buffalo, New York. Submitted to the Puerto Rico State Historic Preservation Office, San Juan.

Duke, J. A.
1992   *Handbook of Edible Weeds.* CRC Press, Boca Raton.

Dunn, Oliver, and James E. Kelley Jr.
1989   *The Diario of Columbus's First Voyage to America 1492–1493, Abstracted by Fray Bartolomé de Las Casas.* University of Oklahoma Press, Norman.

Earle, Timothy
1997   *How Chiefs Come to Power: The Political Economy in Prehistory.* Stanford University Press, Stanford.

Eichholz, Duane W.
2001   Rock Art and Astronomy at Las Flores, Puerto Rico. *Proceedings of the Congress of the International Association for Caribbean Archaeology* 17:3–19. Rockville Centre, New York.

Evans, Clifford, and Betty J. Meggers
 1976 Some Potential Contributions of Caribbean Archaeology to the Reconstruction of New World Prehistory. In *Proceedings of the First Puerto Rican Symposium on Archaeology,* edited by Linda Sickler Robinson, pp. 25–32. Fundación Arqueológica, Antropológica e Histórica de Puerto Rico, San Juan.

Ewen, Charles Robin
 1987 *From Spanish to Creole: The Archaeology of Hispanic American Cultural Formation at Puerto Real, Haiti.* Ph.D. dissertation, University of Florida, Gainesville. University Microfilms, Ann Arbor.

Febles, Jorge
 1988 *Manual para el estudio de la piedra tallada de los aborígenes de Cuba.* Editora de la Academia de Ciencias de Cuba, Havana.
 1998 Análisis de la lítica de Maruca, Ponce, Puerto Rico. Manuscript in possession of the author.

Febles, Jorge, and Guillermo Baena
 1995 La industria de piedra tallada del sitio arqueológico Medialuna, El Guaso, Provincia de Guantánamo. In *Contribuciones al conocimiento de las industrias líticas en comunidades aborígenes de Cuba,* edited by J. Febles, pp. 4–6. Editorial Academia, Havana, Cuba.

Fernández Méndez, Eugenio
 1973 *Crónicas de Puerto Rico: Desde la conquista hasta nuestros días (1493–1955).* Editorial de la Universidad de Puerto Rico, Río Piedras.
 1979 *Arte y mitología de los indios taínos de las Antillas Mayores.* El Cemí, San Juan, Puerto Rico.
 1981 *Crónicas de Puerto Rico: Desde la conquista hasta nuestros días (1493–1955).* Editorial de la Universidad de Puerto Rico, Río Piedras.
 1984 *Las encomiendas y la esclavitud de los indios de Puerto Rico, 1508–1550.* Editorial de la Universidad de Puerto Rico, Río Piedras.

Fewkes, Jesse Walter
 1903 Prehistoric Porto Rican Pictographs. *American Anthropologist* 5:441–467.
 1907 *The Aborigines of Porto Rico and Neighboring Islands.* Bulletin No. 25. Bureau of American Ethnology, Smithsonian Institution, Washington, D.C.

Figueroa Lugo, Jesús
 1988 *Evaluación arqueológica fase IA, construcción del autopista de Diego, PR22, Vega Alta, Puerto Rico.* Copies available from the Instituto de Cultura Puertorriqueña, San Juan.
 1991 *La fase arcaica Cayo Cofresí y las culturas recolectoras de las antillas.* Unpublished Master's thesis, Centro de Estudios Avanzados de Puerto Rico y el Caribe, San Juan.

Fisher Christopher T., and Tina L. Thurston
 1999 Introduction. In *Dynamic Landscapes and Socio-Political Process: The To-*

pography of Anthropogenic Environments in Global Perspective, edited by Christopher T. Fisher and Tina L. Thurston. *Antiquity* 73(281):630–649.

Flannery, Kent V. (editor)
    1976   *The Early Mesoamerican Village.* Academic Press, San Diego.

Flannery, Kent V., and Joyce Marcus
    1993   Cognitive Archaeology. *Cambridge Archaeological Journal* 3:260–270.

Ford, Derek, and Paul Williams
    1994   *Karst Geomorphology and Hydrology.* 3rd ed. Chapman and Hall, London.

Frassetto, Monica
    1960   A Preliminary Report on Petroglyphs in Porto Rico. *American Antiquity* 25:381–391.

Futato, Eugene M.
    1995   The Lithic Assemblage from Site PO27, Plan Bonito, Cerrillos River Valley, Ponce, Puerto Rico. Paper presented at the 60th Annual Meeting of the Society for American Archaeology, Minneapolis.

García Arévalo, Manuel A.
    1988   *El murciélago en el arte y mitología taínas.* Fundación García Arévalo, Santo Domingo, Dominican Republic.
    1997   The Bat and the Owl: Nocturnal Images of Death. In *Taíno: Pre-Columbian Art and Culture from the Caribbean,* edited by Fatima Bercht, Estrellita Brodsky, John Alan Farmer, and Dicey Taylor, pp. 112–123. Monacelli Press and El Museo del Barrio, New York.

García Goyco, Osvaldo
    1984   *Influencias Maya y Azteca en las Antillas Mayores.* Ediciones Xibalbay, San Juan, Puerto Rico.

García Goyco, Osvaldo, and Adalberto Maurás Casillas
    1993a   *Informe preliminar de la mitigación arqueológica del Área de Impacto de la Carretera PR 22, sector Paso del Indio, Barrio Río Abajo, Vega Baja, Puerto Rico.* August, 1993. Edwin Crespo Torres, Consultor en Antropología Física. Estudio presentado a Autoridad de Carreteras y Transportación, Estado Libre Asociado, San Juan, Puerto Rico. Copies available from the Instituto de Cultura Puertorriqueña, San Juan.
    1993b   *Proyecto extensión del plan de mitigación, yacimiento Paso del Indio, Carretera Puerto Rico 22, Barrio Río Abajo, Vega Baja, Puerto Rico.* October, 1993. Edwin Crespo Torres, Consultor en Antropología Física. Preparado con la asistencia técnica de Jeff Walker, Servicio Forestal de los Estados Unidos, Bosque Nacional del Caribe. Propuesta presentada a Autoridad de Carreteras y Transportación. Estado Libre Asociado de Puerto Rico, Oficina de Estudios Ambientales, San Juan. Copies available from the Instituto de Cultura Puertorriqueña, San Juan.
    1993c   *Addendum a la propuesta de mitigación del yacimiento Paso del Indio, Carretera Puerto Rico 22, Barrio Río Abajo, Vega Baja, Puerto Rico.* December, 1993. Con la asistencia técnica de Jeff Walker, Caribbean National Forest,

Servicio Forestal de los Estados Unidos. Presentada a Autoridad de Carreteras y Transportación. Estado Libre Asociado de Puerto Rico, Oficina de Estudios Ambientales, San Juan. Copies available from the Instituto de Cultura Puertorriqueña, San Juan.

García Goyco, Osvaldo, and Carlos Solís Magaña
1999   *Informe de fin de obras, proyecto arqueológico Paso del Indio, Vega Baja, Puerto Rico*. Prepared for the Department of Transportation and Public Works, Highway and Transportation Authority, Commonwealth of Puerto Rico, San Juan. Copies available from the Instituto de Cultura Puertorriqueña, San Juan.

García Goyco, Osvaldo, Adalberto Maurás Casillas, Edwin Crespo Torres, and Jeff Walker
1995   And the Earth Spoke. . . . Manuscript on file, State Historic Preservation Office, San Juan, Puerto Rico.

Garrison, Ervan E., and Kent A. Schneider
1994   The Results of Ground Penetrating Radar and Electromagnetic Assessments of the Paso del Indio Site, Vega Baja, Puerto Rico. Manuscript on file, Paso del Indio Laboratory, Canovanas, Puerto Rico.

Garrow, Patrick H., Charles H. McNutt Jr., Guy G. Weaver, and José Oliver
1995   *La Iglesia de Maragüez (PO-39): Investigation of a Local Ceremonial Center in the Cerrillos River Valley, Ponce, Puerto Rico*. Garrow & Associates, Atlanta, Georgia. Submitted to the U.S. Army Corps of Engineers, Jacksonville District. Copies available from the Office of the State Historic Preservation Officer, San Juan, Puerto Rico.

Geertz, Clifford
1976   Art as a Cultural System. *Modern Language Notes* 91:1473–1499.

Gell, Alfred
1998   *Art and Agency: An Anthropological Theory*. Clarendon Press, Oxford.

González Colón, Juan
1984   *Tibes: Un centro ceremonial indígena*. Unpublished Master's thesis, Centro de Estudios Avanzados de Puerto Rico y el Caribe, San Juan.
1988   Pictografías indígenas en Puerto Rico. *Actas del Simposio Internacional de Arte Rupestre Americano* 8:133–144. Museo del Hombre Dominicano, Santo Domingo, Dominican Republic.

Goodwin, R. Christopher
1978   The Lesser Antillean Archaic: New Data from St. Kitts. *Journal of the Virgin Islands Archaeological Society* 5:6–16.
1979   *The Prehistoric Cultural Ecology of St. Kitts, West Indies: A Case Study in Island Archaeology*. Ph.D. dissertation, Arizona State University, Tempe. University Microfilms, Ann Arbor.
1980   Demographic Change and the Crab-Shell Dichotomy. *Proceedings of the International Congress for the Study of the Pre-Columbian Cultures of the Lesser Antilles* 8:45–68. Arizona State University, Tempe.

Goodwin, R. Christopher, and Jeffery B. Walker
    1975   *Villa Taina de Boqueron: The Excavation of an Early Taino Site in Puerto Rico*. Interamerican University Press, San Juan, Puerto Rico.

Gregory, Richard L.
    1998   *Eye and the Brain: The Psychology of Seeing*. 5th ed. Oxford University Press, Oxford.

Griswold, Susan C. (translator)
    1997a   Christopher Columbus, Diary of the First Voyage [on the northwest coast of Hispaniola]. In *Taíno: Precolumbian Art and Culture from the Caribbean*, edited by Fatima Bercht, Estrellita Brodsky, John Alan Farmer, and Dicey Taylor, p. 170. Monacelli Press and El Museo del Barrio, New York.
    1997b   The Admiral's Words. In *Taíno: Precolumbian Art and Culture from the Caribbean*, edited by Fatima Bercht, Estrellita Brodsky, John Alan Farmer, and Dicey Taylor, p. 171. Monacelli Press and El Museo del Barrio, New York.
    1997c   Fray Bartolomé de Las Casas. In *Taíno: Precolumbian Art and Culture from the Caribbean*, edited by Fatima Bercht, Estrellita Brodsky, John Alan Farmer, and Dicey Taylor, pp. 175–180. Monacelli Press and El Museo del Barrio, New York.
    1997d   Pietro Martire d'Anghiera. In *Taíno: Precolumbian Art and Culture from the Caribbean*, edited by Fatima Bercht, Estrellita Brodsky, John Alan Farmer, and Dicey Taylor, pp. 171–175. Monacelli Press and El Museo del Barrio, New York.

Grossman & Associates
    1990   *Excavation and Analysis Results of Archaeological Investigations at Medianía Alta (L-23) and Vieques (L-22), Loíza, Puerto Rico*. Final Report. Grossman & Associates, New York. Submitted to Puerto Rico Aqueduct & Sewer Authority, San Juan. Copies available from the Office of the State Historic Preservation Officer, San Juan, Puerto Rico.

Guillou, Robert B., and Jewell J. Glass
    1957   *A Reconnaissance Study of the Beach Sands of Puerto Rico*. Geological Survey Bulletin 1042-I. U.S. Geological Survey, Washington D.C.

Guss, David M.
    1989   *To Weave and to Sing: Art, Symbol, and Narrative in the South American Rain Forest*. University of California Press, Berkeley.

Harner, Michael J. (editor)
    1973   *Hallucinogens and Shamanism*. Oxford University Press, New York.

Harris, Peter O'B.
    1973   Preliminary Report on Banwari Trace, a Preceramic Site in Trinidad. *Proceedings of the International Congress for the Study of the Pre-Columbian Cultures of the Lesser Antilles* 4:115–125. Reduit Plage, St. Lucia.
    1976   The Preceramic Period in Trinidad. In *Proceedings of the First Puerto Rican Symposium on Archaeology*, edited by Linda Sickler Robinson, pp. 33–64.

Fundación Arqueológica, Antropológica e Histórica de Puerto Rico, San Juan.

Haslip Viera, Gabriel (editor)
2001 *Taino Revival: Critical Perspectives on Puerto Rican Identity and Cultural Politics.* Markus Weiner, Princeton.

Hatch, M. D., and C. R. Slack
1966 Pathway of Sugar Formation. *Biochemical Journal* 101:103–111.

Hatch, M. D., C. R. Slack, and H. S. Johnson
1967 Further Studies on a New Pathway of Photosynthetic Carbon Dioxide Fixation in Sugar-Cane and Its Occurrence in Other Plant Species. *Biochemical Journal* 102:417–422.

Hather, J. G.
1994 *Tropical Archaeobotany: Applications and New Developments.* Routledge, London.

Haviser, Jay B.
1991 Preliminary Results of Test Excavations at the Hope Estate Site (SM-026), St. Martin. *Proceedings of the Congress of the International Association for Caribbean Archaeology* 13:647–666. Curaçao, Netherlands Antilles.

Hayward, Michele H., and Michael A. Cinquino
2001 Three Puerto Rican Rock Art Sites. *Newsletter of the Eastern States Rock Art Research Association* 5(4):1, 3.
2002 *Prehistoric Rock Art of Puerto Rico.* Multiple Property Submission. National Park Service, U.S. Department of Interior, Washington, D.C.

Hayward, Michele H., Frank Schieppati, and Michael A. Cinquino
2001 On the Status of Puerto Rican Rock Art Interpretation. *Proceedings of the Congress of the International Association for Caribbean Archaeology* 19:258–280. Aruba.

Hegmon, Michelle
1989 Social Integration and Architecture. In *The Architecture of Social Integration in Prehistoric Pueblos,* edited by W. D. Lipe and Michelle Hegmon, pp. 5–15. Occasional Paper of the Crow Canyon Archaeological Center. Crow Canyon, Cortez, Colorado.
2002 Concepts of Community in Archaeological Research. In *Seeking the Center Place,* edited by Mark Varien and Richard Wilshusen, pp. 263–279. University of Utah Press, Salt Lake City.

Henige, David
1978 On the Contact Population of Hispaniola: History as Higher Mathematics. *Hispanic American Historical Review* 58:217–237.

Herrera Fritot, René
1964 *Estudio de las hachas antillanas.* Empresa Consolidada de Artes Gráficas, Havana, Cuba.

Higuera-Gundy, Antonia
   1989   Recent Vegetation Changes in Southern Haiti. In *Biogeography of the West Indies: Past, Present, and Future,* edited by Charles A. Woods, pp. 191–200. Sandhill Crane Press, Gainesville, Florida.
   1991   *Antillean Vegetational History and Paleoclimate Reconstructed from the Paleolimnological Record of Lake Miragone, Haiti.* Ph.D. dissertation, University of Florida, Gainesville. University Microfilms, Ann Arbor.

Higuera-Gundy, Antonia, Mark Brenner, David A. Hodell, Jason H. Curtis, Barbara W. Leyden, and Michael W. Binford
   1999   A 10,300 ^{14}C yr Record of Climate and Vegetation Change from Haiti. *Quaternary Research* 52:15–170.

Historia Documental de Puerto Rico (HDPR)
   1973   Vol. II. *El juicio de residencia, moderador democrático. Juicio de residencia del Licenciado Sancho Velázquez, juez de residencia y justicia mayor de la isla de San Juan (Puerto Rico), por el Licenciado Antonio de la Gama (1519–1520),* edited by Vicente Murga. Editorial Plus Ultra, Río Piedras, Puerto Rico.

Hodell, David A., Jason H. Curtis, Glenn A. Jones, Antonia Higuera-Gundy, Mark Brenner, Michael W. Binford, and Kathleen T. Dorsey
   1991   Reconstruction of Caribbean Climate Change over the Past 10,500 Years. *Nature* 352:790–793.

Honeychurch, P. N.
   1986   *Caribbean Wild Plants and Their Uses.* Macmillan, London.

Hoogland, Menno
   1995   Settlement Structure of a Taino Site on Saba, Netherlands Antilles. *Proceedings of the Congress of the International Association for Caribbean Archaeology* 16:146–155. Basse Terre, Guadeloupe.

Jacobs, Wilbur R.
   1974   The Tip of the Iceberg: Pre-Columbian Indian Demography and Some Implications for Revisionism. *William and Mary Quarterly* 31:123–132.

Jara, René, and Nicholas Spadaccini (editors)
   1992   *Amerindian Images and the Legacy of Columbus.* Hispanic Issues Vol. 9. University of Minnesota Press, Minneapolis.

Jiménez Lambertus, Abelardo
   1983   Las dos partes de la relación acerca de las antigüedades de los indios, de Fray Ramón Pané. *Boletín del Museo del Hombre Dominicano* 11(18):141–146.

Johnson, Allen W., and Timothy Earle
   1987   *The Evolution of Human Societies: From Foraging Group to Agrarian State.* Stanford University Press, Stanford.

Johnson, Gregory A.
- 1977 Aspects of Regional Analysis in Archaeology. *Annual Review of Anthropology* 6:479–508.

Jones, Alick R.
- 1985 Dietary Change and Human Population at Indian Creek, Antigua. *American Antiquity* 50:518–536.
- 1989 The Dating of Excavation Levels Using Animal Remains: A Proposed Scheme for Indian Creek, Antigua. In *Early Ceramic Population Lifeways and Adaptive Strategies in the Caribbean*, edited by Peter E. Siegel, pp. 43–56. BAR International Series No. 506. British Archaeological Reports, Oxford.

Jones, John G.
- 1994 Pollen Evidence for Early Settlement and Agriculture in Northern Belize. *Palynology* 18:205–211.

Jones, John G., and Deborah M. Pearsall
- 1999 Pollen and Phytolith Evidence for Settlement, Agriculture and Paleoenvironment at the Maisabel Site, a Multicomponent Site in Puerto Rico. Paper presented at the 64th Annual Meeting of the Society for American Archaeology, Chicago.

Joyce, Thomas A.
- 1916 *Central American and West Indian Archaeology Being an Introduction to the Archaeology of the States of Nicaragua, Costa Rica, Panama and the West Indies.* G. P. Putnam's Sons, New York.

Kaye, Clifford A.
- 1959 *Shoreline Features and Quaternary Shoreline Changes, Puerto Rico.* Geological Survey Professional Paper 317-B. Washington, D.C.

Keegan, William F.
- 1985 *Dynamic Horticulturalists: Population Expansion in the Prehistoric Bahamas.* Ph.D. dissertation, University of California, Los Angeles. University Microfilms, Ann Arbor.
- 1989a Transition from a Terrestrial to a Maritime Economy: A New View of the Crab-Shell Dichotomy. In *Early Ceramic Population Lifeways and Adaptive Strategies in the Caribbean*, edited by Peter E. Siegel, pp. 119–128. BAR International Series No. 506. British Archaeological Reports, Oxford.
- 1989b Creating the Guanahatabey (Ciboney): The Modern Genesis of an Extinct Culture. *Antiquity* 63:373–379.
- 1992 *The People Who Discovered Columbus: The Prehistory of the Bahamas.* University Press of Florida, Gainesville.
- 1997 "No Man [or Woman] Is an Island": Elements of Taíno Social Organization. In *The Indigenous Peoples of the Caribbean*, edited by Samuel M. Wilson, pp. 111–117. University Press of Florida, Gainesville.

Keegan, William F., and Michael J. DeNiro
- 1988 Stable Carbon- and Nitrogen-Isotope Ratios of Bone Collagen Used to

Study Coral-Reef and Terrestrial Components of Prehistoric Bahamian Diet. *American Antiquity* 53:320–336.

Keegan, William F., and Morgan D. MacLachlan
    1989   The Evolution of Avunculocal Chiefdoms: The Reconstruction of Taino Kinship and Politics. *American Anthropologist* 91:613–630.

Keegan, William F., Morgan D. MacLachlan, and Bryan Byrne
    1993   Los cimientos sociales de los caciques taínos. *ERES (Arqueología)* 3(1):7–16. Canary Islands, Spain.

Kelly, Robert L.
    1995   *The Foraging Spectrum: Diversity in Hunter-Gatherer Lifeways.* Smithsonian Institution Press, Washington, D.C.

Kensinger, Kenneth
    1995   *How Real People Ought to Live: The Cashinahua of Eastern Peru.* Waveland Press, Prospect Heights, Illinois.

Kirch, Patrick V.
    1990   Monumental Architecture and Power in Polynesian Chiefdoms: A Comparison of Tonga and Hawaii. *World Archaeology* 22:206–233.

Kjellmark, Eric
    1996   Late Holocene Climate Change and Human Disturbance on Andros Island, Bahamas. *Journal of Paleolimnology* 15:133–145.

Knippenberg, Sebastiaan
    1999   Lithics of Sorcé, Vieques. Manuscript on file, Centro de Investigaciones Arqueológicas, Universidad de Puerto Rico, San Juan.

Kolb, Michael J., and James E. Snead
    1997   It's a Small World after All: Comparative Analyses of Community Organization in Archaeology. *American Antiquity* 62:609–629.

Kooyman, Brian P.
    2000   *Understanding Stone Tools and Archaeological Sites.* University of Calgary Press, Alberta.

Kozlowski, Janusz K.
    1975   *Las industrias de la piedra tallada de Cuba en el contexto del caribe.* Serie Arqueológica No. 5. Academia de las Ciencias de Cuba, Havana.

Kozuch, Laura
    n.d.   Status and Food: Faunal Remains from Historic San Juan, Puerto Rico. Manuscript on file, Department of Natural History, Florida Museum of Natural History, Gainesville.

Krause, Richard A.
    1989   *Coffee, Sugar and Baked Clay: From Prehistory to History in Puerto Rico's Cerrillos River Valley.* Submitted to the U.S. Army Corps of Engineers, Jacksonville District. Copies available from the Office of the State Historic Preservation Officer, San Juan, Puerto Rico.

Krueger, H. W., and C. H. Sullivan
- 1984 Models for Carbon Isotope Fractionation between Diet and Bone. In *Stable Isotopes in Nutrition,* edited by J. E. Turnlund and P. E. Johnson, pp. 205–222. Symposium Series 258. American Chemical Society, Washington, D.C.

Las Casas, Fray Bartolomé de
- 1929 *Historia de las Indias.* 3 Vols. Editorial M. Aguilar, Madrid.
- 1985 *Historia de las Indias.* Edited by Guillermo Piña Contreras. Ediciones del Continente, S.A., Hollywood, Florida.
- 1992 *A Short Account of the Destruction of the West Indies.* Edited and translated by Nigel Griffen with an introduction by Anthony Pagden. Penguin, New York.

Leeds, Anthony
- 1961 Yaruro Incipient Tropical Forest-Horticulture Possibilities and Limits. In *The Evolution of Horticultural Systems in Native South America: Causes and Consequences,* edited by Johannes Wilbert, pp. 13–46. *Antropológica* Supplement Publication No. 2. Sociedad de Ciencias Naturales la Salle, Caracas.

Lévi-Strauss, Claude
- 1981 *The Naked Man.* Introduction to a Science of Mythology series, Vol. 4. Translated by John and Doreen Weightman. Harper and Row, New York.

Lewis-Williams, David
- 2002 *The Mind in the Cave: Consciousness and the Origin of Art.* Thames and Hudson, London.

Liogier, Henri Alain, and Luis Felipe Martorell
- 2000 *Flora of Puerto Rico and Adjacent Islands: A Systematic Synopsis.* 2nd ed., revised. Editorial de la Universidad de Puerto Rico, San Juan.

Lippi, Ronald D.
- 2001 Engraved River Boulders and the Native Peoples of Western Pichincha, Ecuador. Paper presented at the 66th Annual Meeting of the Society for American Archaeology, New Orleans.

Lipschutz, Alejandro
- 1966 La despoblación de las Indias después de la conquista. *América Indígena* 26:3.

Little, Elbert L., Jr.
- 1983 *Common Fuelwood Crops: A Handbook for Their Identification.* Communi-Tech, Morgantown, West Virginia.

Little, Elbert L., Jr., and Frank H. Wadsworth
- 1964 *Common Trees of Puerto Rico and the Virgin Islands.* Agriculture Handbook No. 249. USDA Forest Service. U.S. Government Printing Office, Washington, D.C.

Little, Elbert L., Jr., Frank H. Wadsworth, and José Marrero
   1977   *Arboles comunes de Puerto Rico y las Islas Vírgenes.* Editorial Universitaria, Río Piedras, Puerto Rico.

Llamazares, Ana Maria
   1988   Bosquejo metodológico para un analísis semiótico del arte rupestre. *Actas del Simposio Internacional de Arte Rupestre Americano* 8:217–225. Museo del Hombre Dominicano, Santo Domingo, Dominican Republic.

Lluch Mora, Francisco
   1986   Poblamiento de San Germán (siglos XVI–XVIII). *Revista del Centro de Estudios Avanzados de Puerto Rico y el Caribe* 2:62–68.

Longuefosse, J.-L.
   1995   *100 plantes médicinales de la Caraibe.* Gondwana, Trinité, Martinique.

López, Diana
   1975   *Vieques: Un momento de su historia.* Unpublished Master's thesis, Department of Anthropology, Universidad Nacional Autónoma de México, Mexico City.

López-Baralt, Mercedes
   1977   *El mito taíno: Raíz y proyecciones en la amazonía continental.* Ediciones Huracán, Río Piedras, Puerto Rico.
   1985   *El mito taíno: Lévi-Strauss en las antillas.* 2nd ed. Ediciones Huracán, Río Piedras, Puerto Rico.

Lugo, Areil E., Leopoldo Miranda Castro, Abel Vale, Tania del Mar López, Enrique Hernández Prieto, Andrés García Martinó, Alberto Puente Rolón, Adrianne Tossas, Donald McFarlane, Tom Miller, Armando Rodríguez, Joyce Lundberg, John Thomlinson, José Colón, Johannes Schellekens, Olga Ramos, and Eileen Helmer
   2001   *Puerto Rican Karst—A Vital Resource.* General Technical Report WO-65. USDA Forest Service, Río Piedras, Puerto Rico.

Lundberg, Emily R.
   1980   Old and New Problems in the Study of Antillean Aceramic Traditions. *Proceedings of the International Congress for the Study of the Precolumbian Cultures of the Lesser Antilles* 8:131–138. Arizona State University, Tempe.
   1985a   Settlement Pattern Analysis for South Central Puerto Rico. In *Archaeological Data Recovery at El Bronce, Puerto Rico, Final Report, Phase 2,* by Linda S. Robinson, Emily R. Lundberg, and Jeffery B. Walker, Appendix L. Archaeological Services, Ft. Myers, Florida. Submitted to the U.S. Army Corps of Engineers, Jacksonville District. Copies available from the Office of the State Historic Preservation Officer, San Juan, Puerto Rico.
   1985b   Interpreting the Cultural Associations of Aceramic Deposits in the Virgin Islands. *Journal of Field Archaeology* 12:201–212.
   1989   *Preceramic Procurement Patterns at Krum Bay, Virgin Islands.* Ph.D. dissertation, University of Illinois at Urbana-Champaign. University Microfilms, Ann Arbor.

Magness-Gardiner, Bonnie, and S. E. Falconer
  1994 Community, Polity, and Temple in a Middle Bronze Age Levantine Village. *Journal of Mediterranean Archaeology* 7:127–164.

Maíz López, Edgar
  1996 La fauna ornitológica de la familia Columbidae en el sito arqueológico Hernández Colón de Puerto Rico. In *Ponencias: Primer Seminario de Arqueologia del Caribe*, pp. 90–99, edited by M. Veloz Maggiolo and A. Caba Fuentes. Museo Arqueologico Regional Altos de Chavon, Dominican Republic.

Maíz López, Edgar, and Eduardo Questell Rodríguez
  1990 Reconocimiento arqueológico preliminar de la cuenca hidrográfica del Río Jauco. *Proceedings of the Congress of the International Association for Caribbean Archaeology* 11:311–327. San Juan, Puerto Rico.

Mariotti, Andre
  1983 Atmospheric Nitrogen Is a Reliable Standard for Natural ^{15}N Abundance Measurements. *Nature* 303:685–687.

Martin, A. C., and W. D. Barkley
  1961 *Seed Identification Manual.* University of California Press, Berkeley.

Martínez, Aida G., Alexis Rives, and Guillermo Baena
  1993 *Area arqueológica Canimar-Morato-Yaití, provincia de Matanzas.* Editorial Academia, Havana, Cuba.

Martínez, Roberto
  1994 El yacimiento arcaico La Tembladera en Morovis, Puerto Rico. Unpublished Master's thesis, Centro de Estudios Avanzados de Puerto Rico y el Caribe, San Juan.

Martínez Torres, Roberto
  1981 *Pinturas indígenas de Boriquen.* Ediciones "El Mapa," Morovis, Puerto Rico.
  1988 La pintura rupestre en Puerto Rico. *Actas del Simposio Internacional de Arte Rupestre Americano* 8:117–131. Museo del Hombre Dominicano, Santo Domingo, Dominican Republic.
  1994a Nuestros primeros artistas. *Revista Catey* 1(1):2–21.
  1994b El Parque de las Cavernas de Cabachuelas. *Revista Catey* 1(1):22–23.

Mártir de Anglería, Pedro
  1944 *Décadas del Nuevo Mundo.* Editorial Bajel, Buenos Aires.
  1964 [1516] *Décadas del Nuevo Mundo.* Editorial Porrúa e Hijos, Sucesores, Mexico City.

Martyr D'Anghera, Peter
  1970 [1912] *De Orbe Novo: The Eight Decades of Peter Martyr D'Anghera.* 2 Vols. Translated by Francis Augustus MacNutt. Research and Source Works Series 642. Burt Franklin, New York.

Mason, John Alden
 1917 Excavations of a New Archaeological Site in Porto Rico. *Proceedings of the International Congress of Americanists* 19:220–223. Washington, D.C.
 1941 *A Large Archaeological Site at Capá, Utuado, with Notes on Other Porto Rico Sites Visited in 1914–15.* Scientific Survey of Porto Rico and the Virgin Islands, Vol. XVIII, part 2. New York Academy of Sciences, New York.

McAndrews, John H.
 1996 Pollen Analysis on Grenada, West Indies. *Palynology* 20:247.

Medina Carrillo, Norma
 1994 *Muestra de arte rupestre en Puerto Rico.* Universidad Interamericana, Recinto Metropolitano, San Juan, Puerto Rico.

Mentore, George P.
 1984 *Shepariymo: The Political Economy of a Waiwai Village.* Unpublished Ph.D. dissertation, Graduate School in Arts and Social Studies, University of Sussex, Sussex, England.

Minagawa, M., and E. Wada
 1984 Stepwise Enrichment of ^{15}N along Food Chains: Further Evidence and the Relation between δ^{15}N and Animal Age. *Geochimica et Cosmochimica Acta* 48:1135–1140.

Moerman, Daniel E.
 2003 Native American Indian Ethnobotany Database [online]. URL http://herb.umd.umich.edu/.

Monroe, Watson H.
 1980 *Some Tropical Landforms of Puerto Rico.* Professional Paper 1159. Geological Survey, U.S. Government Printing Office, Washington, D.C.

Morbán Laucer, Fernando
 1972 Afirman cultura Igneri en Santo Domingo. *Listín Diario.* Wednesday, 26 January, p. 15.
 1988 El murciélago: Sus representaciones en el arte rupestre y la mitología precolombina. *Boletín del Museo del Hombre Dominicano* 21:37–57.

Morton, Julia F.
 1990 *Wild Plants for Survival in South Florida.* Fairchild Tropical Garden, Miami, Florida. National Academy of Sciences.

Moscoso, Francisco
 1981 *The Development of Tribal Society in the Caribbean.* Ph.D. dissertation, State University of New York at Binghamton. University Micofilms, Ann Arbor.
 1983 Parentesco y clase en los cacicazgos tainos: El caso de los naborías. *Proceedings of the International Congress for the Study of the Pre-Columbian Cultures of the Lesser Antilles* 9:485–494. Centre de Recherches Caraïbes, Université de Montréal, Montreal.

1986   *Tribu y clases en el Caribe antigüo.* Universidad Central del Este, San Pedro de Macorís, Dominican Republic.

1999   *Sociedad y economía de los taínos.* Editorial Edil, Universidad de Puerto Rico, Río Piedras.

Moscoso, Francisco, Carlos M. Ayes Suárez, and Ovidio Dávila Dávila

1999   *Arcaicos de Angostura: Pasado remoto de Puerto Rico.* Sociedad de Investigaciones Arqueológicas e Históricas Sebuco, Vega Baja, Puerto Rico.

Moya, Juan C.

1989   Análisis preliminar de las fuentes de procedencia de las piezas líticas de Punta Candelero, Humacao: Informe sometido al proyecto arqueológico Punta Candelero. Manuscript on file, Museo de la Universidad del Turabo, Caguas, Puerto Rico.

Moya Pons, Frank

1978   *La Española en el siglo xvi: 1493–1520. Trabajo, sociedad y política en la economía del oro.* Universidad Central Madre y Maestra, Santiago.

1987   *Después de Colón: Trabajo, sociedad y política en la economía del oro.* Alianza Editorial, Madrid.

Murdock, George Peter

1949   *Social Structure.* Macmillan, New York.

Murga Sanz, Vicente

1971   *Juan Ponce de León.* Editorial Universitaria, Universidad de Puerto Rico, Río Piedras.

Narganes Storde, Yvonne M.

1982   *Vertebrate Faunal Remains from Sorcé, Vieques, Puerto Rico.* Unpublished Master's thesis, Department of Anthropology, University of Georgia, Athens.

1985   Restos faunísticos vertebrados de Sorcé, Vieques, Puerto Rico. *Proceedings of the International Congress for the Study of the Pre-Columbian Cultures of the Lesser Antilles* 10:251–264. Centre de Recherches Caraïbes, Université de Montréal, Montreal.

1988   Analysis de los restos faunisticos arqueologicos del sito de Caracoles en Ponce, Puerto Rico. Submitted to Arql. Daniel Molina Feal. Caguas, Puerto Rico.

1991a   Los restos faunisticos del sitio de Puerto Ferro, Vieques, Puerto Rico. *Proceedings of the Congress of the International Association for Caribbean Archaeology* 14:94–114. Barbados.

1991b   Secuencia cronológica de dos sitios arqueológicos de Puerto Rico (Sorcé, Vieques y Tecla, Guayanilla). *Proceedings of the Congress of the International Association for Caribbean Archaeology* 13:628–646. Curaçao, Netherlands Antilles.

1997a   Analysis de los restos faunisticos de Maruca, Ponce: Primero parte, vertebrados y invertebrados. Submitted to Arql. Miguel Rodríguez. Toa Baja, Puerto Rico.

1997b   Analysis de los restos faunisticos de Maruca, Ponce: Segunda parte, moluscos. Submitted to Arql. Miguel Rodríguez. Toa Baja, Puerto Rico.

2001   Informe fáunico de cuatro sitios arqueológicos del municipio de Utuado: La Cueva Juan Miguel, La Finca Doña Rosa, La Vega de Nelo Vargas, La Cueva de los Muertos. Submitted to José Oliver Zamorano. Institute of Archaeology, University College, London.

Navarrete, Ramón

1989   *Arqueologia Caimanes III*. Editorial de Ciencias Sociales de La Habana, Havana, Cuba.

Newsom, Lee A.

1992   Archaeobotanical Analysis of Flotation Samples from Site PO-38, Cerrillos River Valley, Puerto Rico. In *Phase II Archaeological Data Recovery at PO-38, El Parking Site, Barrio Maragüez, Ponce, Puerto Rico*, by Guy G. Weaver, Patrick H. Garrow, and José R. Oliver, pp. 318–330. Garrow & Associates, Atlanta, Georgia. Submitted to the U.S. Army Corps of Engineers, Jacksonville District. Copies available from the Office of the State Historic Preservation Officer, San Juan, Puerto Rico.

1993   *Native West Indian Plant Use*. Ph.D. dissertation, University of Florida, Gainesville. University Microfilms, Ann Arbor.

1995a   Archaeobotany at Site PO-38 and an Emerging Picture of Prehistoric Subsistence on Puerto Rico. Paper presented at the 60th Annual Meeting of the Society for American Archaeology, Minneapolis.

1995b   Archaeobotanical Analysis of Feature Deposits from Barrazas Site, Carolina, Puerto Rico. Submitted to M. Meléndez and the Municipio de Carolina, Puerto Rico.

1997a   Mangroves and Root Crops: The Archaeobotanical Record from En Bas Saline, Haiti. *Proceedings of the Congress of the International Association for Caribbean Archaeology* 16:52–66. Basse Terre, Guadeloupe.

1997b   Archaeobotanical Analysis of Site NCS-1, Finca Valencia, Superaqueduct Project: Preliminary report. Submitted to Law Environmental Caribe, San Juan, Puerto Rico.

1999a   Cambios en la estrategias de subsistencia en el área de Ponce, del Arcaico al Taino. Paper presented in the symposium "Arqueología prehistórica de Ponce y sus hallazgos mas importantes." Ponce, Puerto Rico.

1999b   Archaeobotanical Analysis of Plant Remains Site Luján I, Vieques Island, Commonwealth of Puerto Rico. Submitted to V. Rivera Calderón and the Municipality of Vieques.

2001   Archaeobotanical Analysis of Site NCS-4, La Trocha, Superaqueduct Project: Final report. Submitted to Law Environmental Caribe, San Juan, Puerto Rico.

2002   Concerning North America. *Antiquity* 76:287–310.

Newsom, Lee A., and L. Antonio Curet

2000   Report on the 1998–1999 Field Seasons of the Proyecto Arqueológico del Centro Ceremonial de Tibes (Puerto Rico). Submitted to Committee for Research and Exploration, National Geographic Society, Washington, D.C.

2001 Biodiversity and Natural Capital: Toward Understanding the Ecological Economics of the Tibes Archaeological Site. *Proceedings of the Congress of the International Association for Caribbean Archaeology* 19(1):156–167. Aruba.

Newsom, Lee A., and Kathleen A. Deagan
1994 Zea mays in the West Indies: The Archaeological and Early Historic Record. In *Corn and Culture in the Prehistoric New World,* edited by S. Johannessen and C. A. Hastorf, pp. 203–217. Westview Press, Boulder, Colorado.

Newsom, Lee A., and Deborah M. Pearsall
2003 Trends in Caribbean Island Archaeobotany. In *People and Plants in Ancient Eastern North America,* edited by Paul E. Minnis, pp. 347–412. Smithsonian Institution Press, Washington, D.C.

Newsom, Lee A., and Elizabeth S. Wing
2004 *On Land and Sea: Native American Uses of Biological Resources in the West Indies.* University of Alabama Press, Tuscaloosa.

Nieuwolt, S.
1977 *Tropical Climatology.* John Wiley, London.

Nuñez Melendez, Esteban
1992 *Plantas medicinales de Puerto Rico: Folklore y fundamentos científicos.* Editorial de la Universidad de Puerto Rico, Río Piedras.

Nyberg, Johan, Antoon Kuijpers, Björn A. Malmgren, and Helmar Kunzendorf
2001a Late Holocene Changes in Precipitation and Hydrography Recorded in Marine Sediments from the Northeastern Caribbean Sea. *Quaternary Research* 56:87–102.

Nyberg, J., A. Winter, B. Malmgren, and J. Christy
2001b Surface Temperatures in the Eastern Caribbean during the 7th Century AD Average up to 4 Deg C Cooler Than Present. *Eos Transaction, American Geophysical Union* Abstract Number OS51B-0480.

O'Leary, M. H.
1981 Carbon Isotope Fractionation in Plants. *Phytochemistry* 20:553–567.

Oliver, José R.
1981 *A Cultural Interpretation of the Iconographic Art Style of Caguana's Ceremonial Center, Puerto Rico.* Unpublished Master's thesis, Department of Anthropology, University of Illinois at Urbana-Champaign.

1992a *Results of the Archaeological Testing and Data Recovery Investigations at the Lower Camp Site, Culebra Island National Wildlife Refuge, Puerto Rico.* Garrow & Associates, Atlanta, Georgia. Submitted to Southeast Regional Office, National Park Service, United States Department of the Interior.

        Copies available from the Office of the State Historic Preservation Officer, San Juan, Puerto Rico.
1992b   The Caguana Ceremonial Center: A Cosmic Journey through Taíno Spatial and Iconographic Symbolism. Paper presented at the 10th International Symposium of the Latin American Indian Literatures Association, San Juan, Puerto Rico.
1992c   Taíno Iconographic and Spatial Symbolism at the Caguana Ceremonial Center, Puerto Rico. Paper presented at the 91st Annual Meeting of American Anthropological Association, San Francisco.
1997   The Taino Cosmos. In *The Indigenous People of the Caribbean,* edited by Samuel M. Wilson, pp. 140–153. University Press of Florida, Gainesville.
1998   *El centro ceremonial de Caguana, Puerto Rico: Simbolismo iconográfico, cosmovisión y el poderío caciquil Taíno de Boriquén.* BAR International Series No. 727. British Archaeological Reports, Archaeopress, Oxford.
1999   The "La Hueca Problem" in Puerto Rico and the Caribbean: Old Problems, New Perspectives, Possible Solutions. In *Archaeological Investigations on St. Martin (Lesser Antilles),* edited by Corinne L. Hofman and Menno L. P. Hoogland, pp. 253–297. Archaeological Studies Leiden University. Faculty of Archaeology, Leiden University, The Netherlands.
2000   Gold Symbolism among Caribbean Chiefdoms: Of Feathers, Çibas and Guanín Power among Taíno Elites. In *Pre-Columbian Gold in South America: Technology, Style and Iconography,* edited by Colin McEwan, pp. 196–219. British Museum Press, London.
2001   Análisis de los conjuntos cerámicos del sitio Salto Arriba, Utuado, Puerto Rico. Submitted to CSA Architects and Engineers. Copies available from the Office of the State Historic Preservation Officer, San Juan, Puerto Rico.
2003   An Interpretative Analysis and Discussion of the Río Cocal-1 Community of Sabana Seca, Puerto Rico. In *Final Report of Phase-III Excavations at Cocal-1 Site, Sabana Seca, Puerto Rico,* edited by R. Christopher Goodwin, Chapter 9. R. Christopher Goodwin & Associates, Frederick, Maryland. Submitted to the United States Department of the Navy, Atlantic Division. Copies available from the Office of the State Historic Preservation Officer, San Juan, Puerto Rico.

Oliver, José R., and Yvonne Narganes Storde
2003   The Zooarchaeological Remains from "Juan Miguel Cave" and "Finca de Doña Rosa," Barrio Caguana, Puerto Rico: Ritual Edibles or Quotidian Food? *Proceedings of the Congress of the International Association for Caribbean Archaeology.* Santo Domingo, Dominican Republic, in press.

Oliver, José R., Juan Rivera Fontán, and Lee A. Newsom
1999   Arqueología del Barrio Caguana, Puerto Rico: Resultados preliminares de las temporadas 1996–1997. In *Trabajos de investigación arqueológica en Puerto Rico: Tercer encuentro de investigadores,* pp. 7–26. Publicación Oca-

sional de la División de Arqueología, Instituto de Cultura Puertorriqueña, San Juan.

Olsen, Fred
1973 Petroglyphs of the Caribbean Islands and Arawak Dieties. *Proceedings of the International Congress for the Study of Pre-Columbian Cultures of the Lesser Antilles* 4:35–46. Reduit Plage, St. Lucia.
1974 *On the Trail of the Arawaks.* University of Oklahoma Press, Norman.

Ortega, Elpidio J., and Gabriel Atiles
2003 *Manantial de la Aleta y la arqueología en el Parque Nacional del Este.* Academia de Ciencias de la Republica Dominicana Vol. IX. Fundación Ortega Arévalo, Santo Domingo, Dominican Republic.

Ortega, Elpidio J., and Carmen Fondeur
1978 *Estudio de la cerámica del período indo-hispano de la antigua Concepción de la Vega.* Serie Científica I. Fundación Ortega Alvarez, Santo Domingo, Dominican Republic.

Ortega, Elpidio J., and Jose Guerrero
1981 *Estudio de cuatro nuevos sitios paleoarcaicos en la isla de Santo Domingo.* Editora Taller, Santo Domingo, Dominican Republic.

Ortíz Aguilú, Juan José, Edgar Maíz López, Jalil Sued Badillo, and Timothy R. Sara
2001 Palo Hincado, Puerto Rico: New Insights from Ongoing Investigations. Paper presented at the 19th Congress of the International Association for Caribbean Archaeology, Aruba.

Ortíz Montañez, Hernán
1986 *Estudio investigativo sobre el reconocimiento arqueológico del litoral norte de la costa de Dorado y la documentación de diez localidades arqueológicas adicionales en el municipio de Dorado.* Submitted to the Gobierno Municipal de Dorado, Dorado, Puerto Rico. Copies available from the Office of the State Historic Preservation Officer, San Juan, Puerto Rico.

Osgood, Cornelius
1942 *The Ciboney Culture of Cayo Redondo, Cuba.* Yale University Publications in Anthropology No. 25. Department of Anthropology, Yale University, New Haven.

Otte, Enrique
1975 Los jerónimos y el tráfico humano en el Caribe: Una rectificación. *Anuario de Estudios Americanos* 32:187–204.

Oviedo y Valdés, Gonzalo Fernández de
1944 *Historia general y natural de la yndias, yslas y tierra firme del mar y océano.* Editorial Guaranía, Asunción del Paraguay.
1950 *Sumario de la natural historia de las Indias.* Fondo de Cultura Económica, Mexico City.
1959a *Historia general y natural de las Indias.* 5 Vols. Edited by Juan Pérez de Tudela. Biblioteca de Autores Españoles, CXVII, Madrid.

1959b   *Natural History of the West Indies.* Translated and edited by Sterling A. Stoudemire. University of North Carolina Studies in the Romance Languages and Literature No. 32. University of North Carolina Press, Chapel Hill.

1975   *The Conquest and Settlement of the Island of Boriquen or Puerto Rico.* Translated and edited by Daymond Turner. Limited Editions, Avon.

Pagán Perdomo, Dato
  1982   Aspectos ergológicos e ideología en el arte rupestre de la isla de Santo Domingo. *Boletín del Museo del Hombre Dominicano* 10(17):55–94.
  1988   Notas acerca de los problemas metodológicos de la datación del arte rupestre antillano. *Actas del Simposio Internacional de Arte Rupestre Americano* 8:233–237. Museo del Hombre Dominicano, Santo Domingo, Dominican Republic.

Pané, Fray Ramón
  1974   *Relación acerca de las antigüedades de los indios.* Edited by José Juan Arrom. Siglo Veintiuno Editores, Mexico City.
  1990   *Fra Ramón Pané: Relació sobre les antiquitats dels indis.* Nova versió amb notes, mapa i apèndixs per José Juan Arrom. Traduit al Catalá per Nuria Pi-Sunyer de Carrasco. Generalitat de Catalunya, Comissió Amèrica i Catalunya, Barcelona.
  1992   *Relació sobre les antiquitats dels indis.* Edited by José Juan Arrom. Generalitat de Catalunya, Comissió Amèrica i Catalunya, Barcelona.
  1999   *An Account of the Antiquities of the Indians.* Introductory study, notes, and appendixes by José Juan Arrom. Translated by Susan C. Griswold. Duke University Press, Durham, North Carolina.

Pantel, Agamemnon G.
  1975   Progress Report and Analysis, Barrera Mordan Complex, Azua, Dominican Republic. *Revista Dominicana de Antropologia e Historia* 5:161–187.
  1986   The Lithic Remains. In *Monserrate Restudied: The 1978 C.E.A.P.R.C. Field Season at Luquillo Beach: Excavation Overview, Lithic, Malacological and Physical Anthropological Remains,* edited by Peter G. Roe, pp. 47–53. Centro de Estudios Avanzados de Puerto Rico y el Caribe, San Juan.
  1988   *Precolumbian Flaked Stone Assemblages in the West Indies.* Ph.D. dissertation, University of Tennessee, Knoxville. University Microfilms, Ann Arbor.
  1991   How Sophisticated was the Primitive?: Preceramic Source Materials, Lithic Reduction Processes, Cultural Contexts and Archaeological Inferences. *Proceedings of the Congress of the International Association for Caribbean Archaeology* 14:157–169. Barbados.
  1996   Nuestra percepción de los grupos preagrícolas en el Caribe: Cambios en nuestra percepción sobre el modo de vida de los grupos preagrícolas en el Caribe Antillano. In *Ponencias del Primer Seminario de Arqueología del Caribe,* edited by M. Veloz Maggiolo and A. Caba, pp. 86–89. Dominican Republic.

Parry, William J., and Robert L. Kelly
    1987   Expedient Core Technology and Sedentism. In *The Organization of Core Technology*, edited by Jay K. Johnson and Carol A. Morrow, pp. 285–304. Westview Press, Boulder, Colorado.

Pastor, Beatriz
    1983   *Discurso narrativo de la conquista de América.* Havana, Cuba.

Pearsall, Deborah M.
    1985   Analysis of Soil Phytoliths and Botanical Macroremains from El Bronce Archaeological Site, Ponce, Puerto Rico. In *Archaeological Data Recovery at El Bronce, Puerto Rico, Final Report, Phase 2*, by Linda S. Robinson, Emily R. Lundberg, and Jeffery B. Walker, Appendix B. Archaeological Services, Ft. Myers, Florida. Submitted to the U.S. Army Corps of Engineers, Jacksonville District. Copies available from the Office of the State Historic Preservation Officer, San Juan, Puerto Rico.
    2002   Analysis of Charred Botanical Remains from the Tutu Site. In *The Tutu Archaeological Village Site: A Multidisciplinary Case Study in Human Adaptation*, edited by Elizabeth Righter, pp. 109–134. Routledge, New York.

Pearson, James L.
    2002   *Shamanism and the Ancient Mind: A Cognitive Approach to Archaeology.* Altamira Press, Walnut Creek, California.

Peirce, Charles Sanders
    1991   *Peirce on Signs: Writings on Semiotics.* Edited by James Hoopes. University of North Carolina Press, Chapel Hill.

Pereira, Carlos
    1924   *Historia de la América española.* Vol. 5. Madrid.

Pereira, Edithe
    2001   Testimony in Stone: Rock Art in the Amazon. In *Unknown Amazon: Culture in Nature in Ancient Brazil*, edited by Colin McEwan, pp. 214–229. British Museum Press, London.

Petersen, James B.
    1997   Taino, Island Carib, and Prehistoric Amerindian Economies in the West Indies: Tropical Forest Adaptations to Island Environments. In *The Indigenous People of the Caribbean*, edited by Samuel M. Wilson, pp. 118–130. University Press of Florida, Gainesville.

Pichardo Moya, Felipe
    1945   *Los indios de Cuba en sus tiempos históricos.* Academia de la Historia de Cuba, Havana.

Pinart, Alphonse L.
    1890   *Note sur les pétroglyphes et antiquités, les pétroglyphes.* Folio. A. L. Pinart, Paris.
    1979   Notas sobre los petroglifos y antigüedades de las Antillas Mayores y

Menores. Translated by Manuel Cárdenas. *Revista del Museo de Antropología, Historia y Arte de la Universidad de Puerto Rico* 1(1):71–88.

Piperno, Delores R., and Deborah M. Pearsall
    1998   *The Origins of Agriculture in the Lowland Neotropics.* Academic Press, San Diego.

Quitmyer, Irvy R., and Robin K. Brown
    2001   The Zooarchaeology of Site NCS-4: A Native American Farmstead on the Rio Indio, Northwest, Puerto Rico. Submitted to Law Environmental Caribe, San Juan, Puerto Rico.

Quitmyer, Irvy R., and Laura Kozuch
    1996   Phase II Zooarchaeology at Finca Valencia (NCS-1) and Site NCS-4, Northwest Puerto Rico (with a contribution from Elizabeth S. Wing). Submitted to Law Environmental Caribe, San Juan, Puerto Rico.

Quitmyer, Irvy R., and Elizabeth S. Wing
    2001   The Luján I Site: A Record of Native American Animal Use on Vieques Island, Puerto Rico. Submitted to V. Rivera Calderón and the Municipality of Vieques.

Rainey, Froelich G.
    1940   *Porto Rican Archaeology.* Scientific Survey of Porto Rico and the Virgin Islands, Vol. XVIII, part 1. New York Academy of Sciences, New York.

Ramenofsky, Ann F.
    1987   *Vectors of Death: The Archaeology of European Contact.* University of New Mexico Press, Albuquerque.

Ramírez de Arellano, R. W.
    1934   *Cartas y relaciones históricas y geográficas sobre Puerto Rico, 1493–1598.* San Juan, Puerto Rico.

Ranere, Anthony J.
    1975   Tool Making and Tool Use among the Preceramic Peoples of Panama. In *Lithic Technology: Making and Using Stone Tools,* edited by Earl Swanson, pp. 173–209. Mouton, Paris.
    1976   The Preceramic of Panama: The View from the Interior. In *Proceedings of the First Puerto Rican Symposium on Archaeology,* edited by Linda Sickler Robinson, pp. 103–137. Fundación Arqueológica, Antropológica e Histórica de Puerto Rico, San Juan.

Record, Samuel J., and Robert W. Hess
    1943   *Timbers of the New World.* Yale University Press, New Haven.
    1942–1948   Keys to American Woods. In *Tropical Woods* 72:19–29 (1942), 73:23–42 (1943), 75:8–26 (1943), 76:32–47 (1944), 85:1–19 (1946), 94:29–52 (1948).

Redmond, Elsa M., and Charles S. Spencer
    1994   The Cacicazgo: An Indigenous Design. In *Caciques and Their People: Volume in Honor of Ronald Spores,* edited by Joyce Marcus and Judith F.

Zeitlin, pp. 189–225. Anthropological Papers No. 89. Museum of Anthropology, University of Michigan, Ann Arbor.

Reichel-Dolmatoff, Gerardo
- 1975 *The Shaman and the Jaguar: A Study of Narcotic Drugs among the Indians of Colombia.* Temple University Press, Philadelphia.
- 1978 *Beyond the Milky Way: Hallucinatory Imagery of the Tukano Indians.* Center for Latin American Studies, University of California, Los Angeles.
- 1992 Shortcuts into Tukanoan Tropical Rainforest Symbols. Paper presented at the 10th International Symposium of Latin American Indian Literatures Association, San Juan, Puerto Rico.

Reitz, Elizabeth J.
- 1985 Vertebrate Fauna from El Bronce Archaeological Site, Puerto Rico. In *Archaeological Data Recovery at El Bronce, Puerto Rico, Final Report, Phase 2,* by Linda S. Robinson, Emily R. Lundberg, and Jeffery B. Walker, Appendix C. Archaeological Services, Ft. Myers, Florida. Submitted to the U.S. Army Corps of Engineers, Jacksonville District. Copies available from the Office of the State Historic Preservation Officer, San Juan, Puerto Rico.

Renfrew, Colin
- 1984 *Peer Polity Interaction and Socio-Political Change.* Cambridge University Press, Cambridge.
- 1994 Towards a Cognitive Archaeology. In *The Ancient Mind: Elements of Cognitive Archaeology,* edited by Colin Renfrew and Ezra B. W. Zubrow, pp. 3–12. Cambridge University Press, Cambridge.

Renfrew, Colin, and Ezra B. W. Zubrow (editors)
- 1994 *The Ancient Mind: Elements of Cognitive Archaeology.* Cambridge University Press, Cambridge.

Rímoli, Renato O., and Joaquín E. Nadal
- 1980 Cerámica temprana de Honduras del Oeste. *Boletín del Museo del Hombre Dominicano* 15:17–80.

Rivera Fontán, Juan
- 1992 *Proyecto Arqueológico Caguana 92. Reconocimiento sistematico de los recursos arqueológicos del Parque Ceremonial de Caguana, Utuado, P.R.* Submitted to the División de Arqueología, Instituto de Cultura Puertorriqueña, San Juan.

Rivera Fontán, Juan, and José R. Oliver
- 2003 Impactos y patrones de ocupación histórica jíbara sobre componentes taínos: El sitio "Vega de Nelo vargas" (Utu-27), Barrio Caguana, Municipio de Utuado, Puerto Rico. *Proceedings of the Congress of the International Association for Caribbean Archaeology.* Santo Domingo, Dominican Republic, in press.

Rivera Fontán, Juan A., and Daniel Silva Pagán
- 1997 Proyecto arqueológico Bo. Quemado, Mayagüez (Batey Delfín del Yagüez). *Ocho trabajos de investigación arqueológica en Puerto Rico: Segundo*

encuentro de investigadores, edited by Juan A. Rivera Fontán, pp. 53–64. Publicación Ocasional de la División de Arqueología, Instituto de Cultura Puertorriqueña, San Juan.

Rivera Meléndez, José
1995 Reevaluación del estudio sobre el arte rupestre realizado por Alphonse Pinart en el siglo xix en Cayey, Puerto Rico: Datos en torno al arte rupestre de las Planadas (refugio rocoso la Iglesia). *Proceedings of the Congress of the International Association for Caribbean Archaeology* 15:595–606. San Juan.
1996 *Apuntes para el estudio de la prehistoria de Cayey.* Unpublished Master's thesis, Centro de Estudios Avanzados de Puerto Rico y el Caribe, San Juan.

Rivera Meléndez, José, and Lydia Ortíz
1995 Investigación sobre el arte rupestre en dos cuevas en el interior de la Isla Cayey, Puerto Rico. *Proceedings of the Congress of the International Association for Caribbean Archaeology* 16:462–467. Basse Terre, Guadeloupe.

Rivero de la Calle, Manuel
1978 Supervivencia de descendientes de indoamericanos en la zona de Yateras, Oriente. *Cuba Arqueológica* pp. 149–176. Editorial Oriente, Santiago.

Robinson, Linda Sickler
1985a The Invertebrate Fauna from El Bronce Archaeological Site, Ponce, Puerto Rico. In *Archaeological Data Recovery at El Bronce, Puerto Rico, Final Report, Phase 2,* by Linda S. Robinson, Emily R. Lundberg, and Jeffery B. Walker, Appendix D. Archaeological Services, Ft. Myers, Florida. Submitted to the U.S. Army Corps of Engineers, Jacksonville District. Copies available from the Office of the State Historic Preservation Officer, San Juan, Puerto Rico.
1985b The Stone Row at El Bronce Archaeological Site, Puerto Rico. In *Archaeological Data Recovery at El Bronce, Puerto Rico, Final Report, Phase 2,* by Linda S. Robinson, Emily R. Lundberg, and Jeffery B. Walker, Appendix I. Archaeological Services, Ft. Myers, Florida. Submitted to the U.S. Army Corps of Engineers, Jacksonville District. Copies available from the Office of the State Historic Preservation Officer, San Juan, Puerto Rico.

Robinson, Linda S., Emily R. Lundberg, and Jeffery B. Walker
1985 *Archaeological Data Recovery at El Bronce, Puerto Rico: Final Report, Phase 2.* Archaeological Services, Ft. Myers, Florida. Submitted to the U.S. Army Corps of Engineers, Jacksonville District. Copies available from the Office of the State Historic Preservation Officer, San Juan, Puerto Rico.

Robiou Lamarche, Sebastián
1988 Posibles símbolos astronómicos-meteorológicos en el arte rupestre antillano. *Actas del Simposio Internacional de Arte Rupestre Americano* 8:405–429. Museo del Hombre Dominicano, Santo Domingo, Dominican Republic.

2002   La gran serpiente entre los Taínos y caribes de las Antillas. *Latin American Indian Literatures Journal* 18:21–40.

Rodríguez, Marisol, and Carlos Ayes Suárez
1997   El Pulguero, Puerto Rico. Hallazgo de cerámica en el periodo Arcaico. Paper presented at the 16th Congress of the International Association for Caribbean Archaeology, Bahamas.

Rodríguez Alvaréz, Angel
1991   A Preliminary Petroglyph Survey along the Blanco River: Puerto Rico. *Proceedings of the Congress of the International Association for Caribbean Archaeology* 13:898–926. Curaçao, Netherlands Antilles.

Rodríguez López, Miguel
1985   *Cultural Resources Survey at Camp Santiago Salinas, Puerto Rico.* Museum of Turabo University, Caguas, Puerto Rico. Submitted to the Puerto Rico National Guard. Copies available from the Office of the State Historic Preservation Officer, San Juan, Puerto Rico.
1990   Arqueología del Río Loiza. *Proceedings of the Congress of the International Association for Caribbean Archaeology* 11:287–294. San Juan, Puerto Rico.
1991   Arqueología de Punta Candelero, Puerto Rico. *Proceedings of the Congress of the International Association for Caribbean Archaeology* 13:605–627. Curaçao, Netherlands Antilles.
1992a   El jaguar domesticado: Simbolismo del perro en las culturas precolombinas de Puerto Rico y el Caribe. Paper presented at the 10th International Symposium of the Latin American Indian Literatures Association, San Juan, Puerto Rico.
1992b   Late Ceramic Age Diversity in Eastern Puerto Rico. Paper presented at the 57th Annual Meeting of the Society for American Archaeology, Pittsburgh.
1995   Los bateyes de Trujillo Alto: Un nuevo centro ceremonial indígena en Puerto Rico. *Proceedings of the Congress of the International Association for Caribbean Archaeology* 15:27–42. San Juan, Puerto Rico.
1997   Maruca, Ponce. In *Ocho trabajos de investigación arqueológicas en Puerto Rico: Segundo encuentro de investigadores,* edited by Juan Rivera Fontán, pp. 17–30. Publicación Ocasional de la División de Arqueología. Instituto de Cultura Puertorriqueña, San Juan.
1999   Excavations at Maruca, a Preceramic Site in Southern Puerto Rico. *Proceedings of the Congress of the International Association for Caribbean Archaeology* 17:166–180. Rockville Centre, New York.

Rodríguez Miranda, Marisol
1999   Arte rupestre del Cibuco. In *Trabajos de investigación arqueológica en Puerto Rico, tercer encuentro de investigadores,* edited by Juan Rivera Fontán, pp. 37–46. Publicación Ocasional de la División de Arqueología, Instituto de Cultura Puertorriqueña, San Juan.

Rodríguez Ramos, Reniel
- 1999a Lithic Reduction Trajectories at La Hueca and Punta Candelero Sites, Puerto Rico: A Preliminary Report. *Proceedings of the Congress of the International Association for Caribbean Archeology* 18(1):251–261. Grenada.
- 1999b Estudio de la lítica de Turabo Clusters, Caguas, Puerto Rico. Submitted to Marlene Ramos. Copies available from the Office of the State Historic Preservation Officer, San Juan, Puerto Rico.
- 1999c Análisis de la lítica de Isla de Cabras, Toa Baja, Puerto Rico. Submitted to Marlene Ramos. Copies available from the Office of the State Historic Preservation Officer, San Juan, Puerto Rico.
- 2001a *Lithic Reduction Trajectories at La Hueca and Punta Candelero Sites, Puerto Rico.* Unpublished Master's thesis, Department of Anthropology, Texas A&M University, College Station.
- 2001b Dinámicas de intercambio en el Puerto Rico prehispánico. Paper presented at the Quinto Encuentro de Investigadores del Instituto de Cultura Puertorriqueña, San Juan.
- 2001c Análisis de la lítica de La Mina y Martineau, Vieques, Puerto Rico. Submitted to Marlene Ramos. Copies available from the Office of the State Historic Preservation Officer, San Juan, Puerto Rico.
- 2001d Estudio tecnológico de la lítica de Salto Arriba, Utuado, Puerto Rico. Submitted to CSA Architects and Engineers. Copies available from the Office of the State Historic Preservation Officer, San Juan, Puerto Rico.
- 2002 Una perspectiva diacrónica de la explotación del pedernal en Puerto Rico. *Boletin del Museo del Hombre Dominicano* 32:167–192.

Rodríguez Ramos, Reniel, Jeffery B. Walker, and Eduardo Questell Rodríguez
- 2002 La explotación de pedernal en el noroeste de Puerto Rico: Fuentes, técnicas e implicaciones. Paper presented at the Sexto Encuentro de Investigadores del Instituto de Cultura Puertorriqueña, San Juan.

Roe, Peter G.
- 1982 *The Cosmic Zygote: Cosmology in the Amazon Basin.* Rutgers University Press, New Brunswick, New Jersey.
- 1983a Mythic Substitution and the Stars: Aspects of Shipibo and Quechua Ethnoastronomy Compared. Paper presented at the 1st International Conference on Ethnoastronomy, Washington, D.C.
- 1983b Review of *The Naked Man* by Claude Lévi-Strauss. *American Anthropologist* 85:686–687.
- 1984 Review of *Ball Courts and Ceremonial Plazas in the West Indies* by Ricardo E. Alegría. *American Scientist* 72:65.
- 1985a A Preliminary Report on the 1980 and 1982 Field Seasons at Hacienda Grande (12PSj 7-5): Overview of Site History, Mapping, and Excavations. *Proceedings of the International Congress for the Study of the Pre-Columbian Cultures of the Lesser Antilles* 10:151–180. Centre de Recherches Caraïbes, Université de Montréal, Montreal.

1985b   Fiwa's Tales: Waiwai Mythology in Comparative Perspective. Manuscript on file, Centro de Investigaciones Indígenas de Puerto Rico, San Juan.

1989a   A Grammatical Analysis of Cedrosan Saladoid Vessel Form Categories and Surface Decoration: Aesthetic and Technical Styles in Early Antillean Ceramics. In *Early Ceramic Population Lifeways and Adaptive Strategies in the Caribbean,* edited by Peter E. Siegel, pp. 267–382. BAR International Series No. 506. British Archaeological Reports, Oxford.

1989b   Of Rainbow Dragons and the Origins of Designs: The Waiwai *Urufiri* and the Shipibo *Ronin ëhua. Latin American Indian Literatures Journal* 5(1):1–67.

1990   Review of *From Myth to Creation: Art from Amazonian Ecuador* by Dorothea S. Whitten and Norman E. Whitten Jr. *American Ethnologist* 17:401.

1991a   The Petroglyphs of Maisabel: A Study in Methodology. *Proceedings of the Congress of the International Association for Caribbean Archaeology* 12:317–370. Martinique.

1991b   The Best Enemy Is a Killed, Drilled and Decorative Enemy: Human Corporeal Art (Frontal Bone Pectorals, Belt Ornaments, Carved Humeri and Pierced Teeth) in Precolumbian Puerto Rico. *Proceedings of the Congress of the International Association for Caribbean Archaeology* 13:854–873. Curaçao, Netherlands Antilles.

1991c   *Panó Huëtsa Nëtë:* The Armadillo as Scaly Discoverer of the Lower World in Shipibo and Comparative Lowland South Amerindian Perspective. *Latin American Indian Literatures Journal* 7(1):20–72.

1992   Of Frog Seductresses and the Origin of Phallic Fish: A Shipibo Indian Tale of *Páno Ainbo.* In *MACLAS Latin American Essays V: Selected Papers Presented at the 12th Annual Conference,* edited by Alvin Cohen, Juan Espadas, and Vincent Peloso, pp. 40–66. Middle Atlantic Council of Latin American Studies, Lehigh University, Bethlehem, Pennsylvania.

1993   Cross-Media Isomorphisms in Taíno Ceramics and Petroglyphs from Puerto Rico. *Proceedings of the Congress of the International Association for Caribbean Archaeology* 14:637–671. Barbados.

1995a   Eternal Companions: Amerindian Dogs from Tierra Firme to the Antilles. *Proceedings of the Congress of the International Association for Caribbean Archaeology* 15:155–172. San Juan, Puerto Rico.

1995b   Style, Society, Myth, and Structure. In *Style, Society, and Person,* edited by Christopher Carr and Jill E. Neitzel, pp. 27–76. Plenum Press, New York.

1995c   *Arts of the Amazon.* Edited by Barbara Braun. Thames and Hudson, London and New York.

1995d   Utilitarian Sculpture: Pictorial Kinesics and Dualism in Dominican Republic Chican Ostionoid Pottery. *Proceedings of the Congress of the International Association for Caribbean Archaeology* 16:272–291. Basse Terre, Guadeloupe.

1997a   Just Wasting Away: Taíno Shamanism and Concepts of Fertility. In *Taíno: Pre-Columbian Art and Culture from the Caribbean,* edited by Fatima

        Bercht, Estrellita Brodsky, John Alan Farmer, and Dicey Taylor, pp. 124–157. Monacelli Press and El Museo del Barrio, New York.

1997b   The Museo Pigorini Zemí: The Face of Life/The Face of Death. In *Taíno: Pre-Columbian Art and Culture from the Caribbean,* edited by Fatima Bercht, Estrellita Brodsky, John Alan Farmer, and Dicey Taylor, pp. 164–169. Monacelli Press and El Museo del Barrio, New York.

1997c   An Affecting Culture of Beauty and Ephemerality. In *Fragments of the Sky: The Art of Amazonian Rites of Passage,* edited by Ken Yellis, pp. 1–22. Peabody Museum of Natural History, Yale University, New Haven.

1999   Un centro de joyas precolombinas en Vieques. *El Vocero* 12 December:E26. San Juan, Puerto Rico.

2000a   Cóndores andinos . . . buitres reyes de la selva. *El Mundo.* Escenario, Sunday Supplement, 9 January:E26–27. San Juan, Puerto Rico.

2000b   El otro mundo . . . los alucinógenos de los indios. *El Mundo.* Escenario, Sunday Supplement, 12 March:E20–21. San Juan, Puerto Rico.

2000c   The Ghost in the Machine: Symmetry and Representation in Ancient Antillean Art. Paper presented in the symposium "Embedded Symmetries" organized by Dorothy Washburn. Amerind Foundation, Dragoon, Arizona.

2000d   Jardines de Loiza: Analysis of the Ceramic Component. Submitted to Ing. Juan González Colón, Arqueólogo. Ponce, Puerto Rico.

Roe, Peter G., and José Rivera Meléndez
    1995   Recent Advances in Recording, Dating and Interpreting Puerto Rican Petroglyphs. *Proceedings of the Congress of the International Association for Caribbean Archaeology* 16:444–461. Basse Terre, Guadeloupe.

Roe, Peter G., José Rivera Meléndez, and Peter DeScioli
    1999a   The Cueva de Mora (Comerío, PR) Pictographs and Petroglyphs: A Documentary Project. *Proceedings of the Congress of the International Association for Caribbean Archaeology* 17:20–59. Rockville Centre, New York.

Roe, Peter G., José Rivera Meléndez, James Byerly, and Nicole Cornell
    1999b   The Cueva de La Momia Petroglyphs: A Case Study in Field Technology. *Proceedings of the Congress of the International Association for Caribbean Archaeology* 18(2):311–339. Basse Terre, Guadeloupe.

Roosevelt, Anna C., M. Lima da Costa, C. Lopes Machado, M. Michab, N. Mercier, H. Valladas, J. Feathers, W. Barnett, M. Imazioi da Silveura, A. Henderson, J. Sliva, B. Chernoff, D. S. Reese, J. A. Holman, N. Toth, and K. Schick
    1996   Paleoindian Cave Dwellers in the Amazon: The Peopling of the Americas. *Science* 272:373–384.

Rosenblat, Angel
    1954   *La población indígena y el mestizaje en América 1492–1950.* Editorial Nova, Buenos Aires.
    1967   *La población de América en 1492, viejos y nuevos cálculos.* El Colegio de México, Mexico City.

Rouse, Irving
- 1940 Some Evidence Concerning the Origins of West Indian Pottery Making. *American Anthropologist* 42:49–80.
- 1948 The Arawak. In *The Circum-Caribbean Tribes,* edited by Julian H. Steward, pp. 507–546. Handbook of South American Indians, Vol. 4. Bulletin No. 143. Bureau of American Ethnology, Smithsonian Institution, Washington, D.C.
- 1949 Petroglyphs. In *The Comparative Ethnology of South American Indians,* edited by Julian H. Steward, pp. 493–502. Handbook of South American Indians, Vol. 5. Bulletin No. 143. Bureau of American Ethnology, Smithsonian Institution, Washington, D.C.
- 1951 Areas and Periods of Cultures in the Greater Antilles. *Southwestern Journal of Anthropology* 7:248–265.
- 1952a *Porto Rican Prehistory: Introduction; Excavations in the West and North.* Scientific Survey of Porto Rico and the Virgin Islands, Vol. XVIII, part 3. New York Academy of Sciences, New York.
- 1952b *Porto Rican Prehistory: Excavations in the Interior, South, and East; Chronological Implications.* Scientific Survey of Porto Rico and the Virgin Islands, Vol. XVIII, part 4. New York Academy of Sciences, New York.
- 1968 Prehistory, Typology, and the Study of Society. In *Settlement Archaeology,* edited by Kwang-Chih Chang, pp. 10–30. National Press Books, Palo Alto.
- 1974 The Indian Creek Excavations. *Proceedings of the International Congress for the Study of Pre-Columbian Cultures of the Lesser Antilles* 5:166–176. Antigua.
- 1982 Ceramic and Religious Development in the Greater Antilles. *Journal of New World Archaeology* 5(2):45–55.
- 1986 *Migrations in Prehistory: Inferring Population Movement from Cultural Remains.* Yale University Press, New Haven.
- 1992 *The Tainos: Rise and Decline of the People Who Greeted Columbus.* Yale University Press, New Haven.
- 1999 Foreword. In *Archaeological Investigations on St. Martin (Lesser Antilles),* edited by Corinne L. Hofman and Menno L. P. Hoogland, pp. 13–14. Archaeological Studies Leiden University. Faculty of Archaeology, Leiden University, The Netherlands.

Rouse, Irving, and Ricardo E. Alegría
- 1990 *Excavations at María de la Cruz Cave and Hacienda Grande Village Site, Loiza, Puerto Rico.* Yale University Publications in Anthropology No. 80. Department of Anthropology, Yale University, New Haven.

Rouse, Irving, and Louis Allaire
- 1978 Caribbean. In *Chronologies in New World Archaeology,* edited by R. E. Taylor and C. W. Meighan, pp. 432–481. Academic Press, New York.

Rouse, Irving, and José M. Cruxent
- 1963 *Venezuelan Archaeology.* Yale University Press, New Haven.

Rouse, Irving, and Birgit Faber Morse
   1999   *Excavations at the Indian Creek Site, Antigua, West Indies.* Yale University Publications in Anthropology No. 82. Department of Anthropology, Yale University, New Haven.

Sánchez-Albornoz, Nicolás
   1974   *The Population of Latin America: A History.* University of California Press, Berkeley.

Sanders, Suzanne, Ellen Saint Onge, R. Christopher Goodwin, Dave D. Davis, and Christian Davenport
   2001   *Archeological Survey and Evaluation of Selected Sites at NSGA Sabana Seca, Sabana Seca, Puerto Rico.* Draft Report. R. Christopher Goodwin & Associates, Frederick, Maryland. Submitted to Atlantic Division, Naval Facilities Engineering Command, Norfolk, Virginia. Copies available from the Office of the State Historic Preservation Officer, San Juan, Puerto Rico.

Sauer, Carl Ortwin
   1966   *The Early Spanish Main.* University of California Press, Berkeley.

Saunders, Nicholas J., and Dorrick Gray
   1996   Zemis, Trees, and Symbolic Landscapes: Three Taíno Carvings from Jamaica. *Antiquity* 70:801–812.

Schultes, Richard Evans, and Albert Hofmann
   1992   *Plants of the Gods: Their Sacred, Healing and Hallucinogenic Powers.* Healing Arts Press, Rochester, Vermont.

Schvoerer, M., P. Guibert, F. Bechtel, M. Mattioni, and J. Evin
   1985   Des hommes en Martinique vingt siecles avant Christophe Colomb? *Proceedings of the International Congress for the Study of the Pre-Columbian Cultures of the Lesser Antilles* 10:369–397. Centre de Recherches Caraïbes, Université de Montréal, Montreal.

Scurlock, J. Paul
   1987   *Native Trees and Shrubs of the Florida Keys: A Field Guide.* Laurel Press, Bethel Park, Pennsylvania.

Serrand, Nathalie
   1995   Strombus Gigas: Parts and Their Utilization for Artefacts Manufacture: A Case Study from the Tanki Flip Site, Aruba. *Proceedings of the Congress of the International Association for Caribbean Archaeology* 16:229–240. Basse-Terre, Guadeloupe.

Shafer, Harry J.
   1973   *Lithic Technology at the George C. Davis Site, Cherokee County, Texas.* Unpublished Ph.D. dissertation, Department of Anthropology, University of Texas, Austin.

Siegel, Peter E.
   1989a   Site Structure, Demography, and Social Complexity in the Early Ceramic

Age of the Caribbean. In *Early Ceramic Population Lifeways and Adaptive Strategies in the Caribbean,* edited by Peter E. Siegel, pp. 193–245. BAR International Series No. 506. British Archaeological Reports, Oxford.

1989b *Early Ceramic Population Lifeways and Adaptive Strategies in the Caribbean.* Edited by Peter E. Siegel. BAR International Series No. 506. British Archaeological Reports, Oxford.

1991a Migration Research in Saladoid Archaeology: A Review. *The Florida Anthropologist* 44(1):79–91.

1991b On the Antilles as a Potential Corridor for Cultigens into Eastern North America. *Current Anthropology* 32:332–334.

1991c Political Evolution in the Caribbean. *Proceedings of the Congress of the International Association for Caribbean Archaeology* 13:232–250. Curaçao, Netherlands Antilles.

1992 *Ideology, Power, and Social Complexity in Prehistoric Puerto Rico.* Ph.D. dissertation, State University of New York at Binghamton. University Microfilms, Ann Arbor.

1993 Saladoid Survival Strategies: Evidence from Site Locations. *Proceedings of the Congress of the International Association for Caribbean Archaeology* 14:315–337. Barbados.

1995 The Archaeology of Community Organization in the Tropical Lowlands: A Case Study from Puerto Rico. In *Archaeology in the Lowland American Tropics: Current Analytical Methods and Recent Applications,* edited by Peter W. Stahl, pp. 42–65. Cambridge University Press, Cambridge.

1996 Ideology and Culture Change in Prehistoric Puerto Rico: A View from the Community. *Journal of Field Archaeology* 23:313–333.

1997 Ancestor Worship and Cosmology among the Taíno. In *Taíno: Pre-Columbian Art and Culture from the Caribbean,* edited by Fatima Bercht, Estrellita Brodsky, John Alan Farmer, and Dicey Taylor, pp. 106–111. Monacelli Press and El Museo del Barrio, New York.

1999 Contested Places and Places of Contest: The Evolution of Social Power and Ceremonial Space in Prehistoric Puerto Rico. *Latin American Antiquity* 10:209–238.

2004 What Happened after A.D. 600 on Puerto Rico? Corporate Groups, Population Restructuring, and Post-Saladoid Social Changes. In *Late Ceramic Age Societies in the Eastern Caribbean,* edited by André Delpuech and Corinne Hofman, pp. 87–100. Paris Monographs in American Archaeology No. 14. BAR International Series No. 1273. Archaeopress, Oxford.

Siegel, Peter, E., John G. Jones, Deborah M. Pearsall, and Daniel P. Wagner
1999 Culture and Environment in Prehistoric Puerto Rico. Paper presented at the 64th Annual Meeting of the Society for American Archaeology, Chicago.

Siegel, Peter E., and J. W. Joseph
1993 *Archeological Data Recovery at El Palmar de las Animas (Site VB-27) and the Concrete Well Site (Site VB-32), Río Cibuco Flood Control Project, Mu-*

nicipio de Vega Baja, Puerto Rico. New South Associates Technical Report 206. New South Associates, Stone Mountain, Georgia. Submitted to the U.S. Army Corps of Engineers, Jacksonville District. Copies available from the Office of the State Historic Preservation Officer, San Juan, Puerto Rico.

Siegel, Peter E., and Kenneth P. Severin
   1993   The First Documented Prehistoric Gold-Copper Alloy Artefact from the West Indies. *Journal of Archaeological Science* 20:67–79.

Smith, Bruce D.
   2001   Low-Level Food Production. *Journal of Archaeological Research* 9:1–43.

Smith, Bruce N., and Samuel Epstein
   1971   Two Categories of $^{13}C/^{12}C$ Ratios for Higher Plants. *Plant Physiology* 47:380–384.

Smith, B. N., C. B. Otto, G. E. Martin, and T. W. Boutton
   1979   Photosynthetic Strategies of Plants. In *Arid Land Plant Resources,* edited by J. R. Goodin and D. K. Northington, pp. 474–481. Texas Technical University Press, Lubbock.

Smith, Greg Charles
   1986   *Non-European Pottery at the Sixteenth Century Site of Puerto Real, Haiti.* Unpublished Master's thesis, Department of Anthropology, University of Florida, Gainesville.
   1995   Indians and Africans at Puerto Real: The Ceramic Evidence. In *Puerto Real: The Archaeology of a Sixteenth-Century Spanish Town in Hispaniola,* edited by Kathleen Deagan, pp. 335–374. University Press of Florida, Gainesville.

Smith, Marvin T.
   1984   *Depopulation and Culture Change in the Early Historic Period Interior Southeast.* Ph.D. dissertation, University of Florida, Gainesville. University Microfilms, Ann Arbor.

Soil Survey Staff
   1993   *Soil Survey Manual.* Revised edition. Agricultural Handbook 18. United States Department of Agriculture, U.S. Government Printing Office, Washington, D.C.

Solís Magaña, Carlos
   1988   *Colonial Archaeology of San Juan de Puerto Rico: Excavations at the Casa Rosa Scarp Wall, San Juan National Historic Site, Puerto Rico.* Report of Investigations 52. Office of Archaeological Research, Alabama State Museum of Natural History, University of Alabama, Tuscaloosa.
   1997   Proyecto arqueológico superacueducto de la costa norte de Puerto Rico. In *Ocho trabajos de investigación arqueológicas en Puerto Rico: Segundo encuentro de investigadores,* edtied by Juan Rivera Fontán, pp. 85–93. Publicación Ocasional de la División de Arqueología. Instituto de Cultura Puertorriqueña, San Juan.

Solís Magaña, Carlos, and Osvaldo García Goyco
    1998   *Propuesta de análisis de laboratorio e informe final, proyecto Paso del Indio, Vega Baja, Puerto Rico.* Submitted to the Department of Transportation and Public Works, Highway and Transportation Authority, Commonwealth of Puerto Rico, San Juan. Copies available from the Instituto de Cultura Puertorriqueña, San Juan.

Stevens-Arroyo, Antonio M.
    1988   *Cave of the Jagua: The Mythological World of the Taínos.* University of New Mexico Press, Albuquerque.

Stokes, Anne Vaughn
    1998   *A Biogeographic Survey of Prehistoric Human Diet in the West Indies Using Stable Isotopes.* Ph.D. dissertation, University of Florida, Gainesville. University Microfilms, Ann Arbor.

Stone G. D.
    1991   Agricultural Territories in a Dispersed Settlement System. *Current Anthropology* 32:343–353.
    1992   Social Distance, Spatial Relations, and Agricultural Production among the Kofyar of Namu District, Plateau State, Nigeria. *Journal of Anthropological Archaeology* 11:152–172.

Sued Badillo, Jalil
    1972   Los grabados rupestres en Puerto Rico. *Boletín Informativo de la Fundación Arqueológica, Antropológica e Histórica de Puerto Rico* 1(1):5–7.
    1975   *La mujer indígena y su sociedad.* Editorial el Gazir, Río Piedras, Puerto Rico.
    1978   *Los Caribes: Realidad o fábula: Ensayo de rectificación histórica.* Editorial Antillana, Río Piedras, Puerto Rico.
    1979a   La industria lapidaria pretaína en las Antillas. *Revista Interamericana* 8(3):429–462.
    1979b   *La mujer indígena y su sociedad.* Editorial el Gazir, Río Piedras, Puerto Rico.
    1985   Las cacicas indoantillanas. *Revista del Instituto de Cultura Puertorriqueña* 87:17–26.
    2001   *El Dorado borincano: La economía de la conquista 1510–1550.* Biblioteca del Caribe. Ediciones Puerto, San Juan, Puerto Rico.

Tanodi, Aurelio
    1971   *Documentos de la Real Hacienda de Puerto Rico, Vol. I:1510–1519.* Centro de Investigaciones Históricas. Editorial Universitaria, Río Piedras, Puerto Rico.

Tedesco, K., R. Thunell, and E. Tappa
    2001   A High-Resolution Oxygen Isotope Record for the Cariaco Basin, Venezuela over the Last 6,000 Years. *Eos Transactions, American Geophysical Union* Abstract Number PP12A-0484.

Tió, Aurelio
    1961   *Nuevas fuentes para la historia de Puerto Rico.* Ediciones Universidad Interamericana de Puerto Rico, San Germán.

Todorov, Tzvetan
    1984   *The Conquest of America: The Question of The Other.* Harper and Row, New York.

Torres, Joshua M.
    2001   *Settlement Patterns and Political Geography of the Saladoid and Ostionoid Peoples of South-Central Puerto Rico: An Exploration of Prehistoric Social Complexity on a Regional Level.* Unpublished Master's thesis, Department of Anthropology, University of Colorado, Denver.
    2002   Regional Socio-Political Development and Organization of the Saladoid and Ostionoid Peoples of South Central Puerto Rico. Paper presented at the 67th Annual Meeting of the Society for American Archaeology, Denver.

Tronolone, Carmine A., Michael A. Cinquino, and Charles E. Vandrei
    1990   A Discussion of Prehistoric Resources on the Vieques Naval Reservation in Relation to Prehistorical Settlement Pattern of Vieques Island, Puerto Rico. *Proceedings of the Congress of the International Association for Caribbean Archaeology* 11:459–471. San Juan.

Troughton, J. H., P. V. Wells, and H. A. Mooney
    1974   Photosynthetic Mechanisms and Paleoecology from Carbon Isotope Ratios in Ancient Specimens of C_4 and CAM Plants. *Science* 185:610–612.

Ulloa, Jorge, and Roberto Valcárcel Rojas
    2002   *Cerámica temprana en el centro del oriente de Cuba.* Viewgraph Impresos, Santo Domingo, Dominican Republic.

Valcárcel Rojas, Roberto
    2001   *Banes precolombino: La ocupación agricultora.* Ediciones Holguín, Cuba.

van Klinken, G. J.
    1991   *Dating and Dietary Reconstruction by Isotopic Analysis of Amino Acids in Fossil Bone Collagen—with Special Reference to the Caribbean.* Publication No. 128. Foundation for Scientific Research in the Caribbean Region, Amsterdam.

Varela, Consuelo (editor)
    1982   *Cristóbal Colón. Textos y documentos completos.* Alianza Universidad, Madrid.

Varela Consuelo, and Juan Gil (editors)
    1984   *Cartas de particulares a Colón y relaciones coetáneas.* Alianza Universidad, Madrid.

Varien, Mark
    1997   New Perspectives on Settlement Patterns: Sedentism and Mobility in a

        Social Landscape. Ph.D. dissertation, Arizona State University, Tempe. University Microfilms, Ann Arbor.
- 1999   *Sedentism and Mobility in a Social Landscape.* University of Arizona Press, Tucson.
- 1999   Persistent Communities and Mobile Households. In *Seeking the Center Place,* edited by M. D. Varien and R. H. Wilshusen, pp. 163–185. University of Utah Press, Salt Lake City.

Vega, Bernardo
- 1976   Comparison of Newly Found Cave Drawings in Santo Domingo with Petroglyphs and Pictographs in the Caribbean Region. *Proceedings of the International Congress for the Study of Pre-Columbian Cultures of the Lesser Antilles* 6:200–212. Pointe à Pitre, Guadeloupe.
- 1987   *Arte neotaíno.* Fundación Cultural Dominicana, Santo Domingo, Dominican Republic.

Veloz Maggiolo, Marcio
- 1973   La atheabeanenequen: Evidencia de sacrifico humanos entre los taínos. *Boletín del Museo del Hombre Dominicano* 3:64–69.
- 1976   *Medioambiente y adaptación humana en la prehistoria de Santo Domingo.* Universidad Autónoma de Santo Domingo, Santo Domingo, Dominican Republic.
- 1983   Para una definición de la cultura taina. *La Cultura Taina,* pp. 15–21. Comisión Nacional para la Celebración del V Centenario del Descubrimiento de América, Madrid.
- 1993   *Panorama histórico del caribe precolombino.* Edición del Banco Central de la Republica Dominicana, Santo Domingo, Dominican Republic.

Veloz Maggiolo, Marcio, Juan González, Edgar J. Maiz, and Eduardo Questell Rodríguez
- 1975   *Cayo Cofresí: Un sitio precerámico de Puerto Rico.* Ediciones de Taller, Santo Domingo, Dominican Republic.

Veloz Maggiolo, Marcio, and Elpidio Ortega
- 1973   *El precerámico de Santo Domingo, nuevos lugares y su posible relación con otros puntos del área antillana.* Papeles Ocasionales No. 1. Museo del Hombre Dominicano, Santo Domingo, Dominican Republic.

Veloz Maggiolo, Marcio, Elpidio Ortega, and Plinio Pina Peña.
- 1974   *El Caimito: Un antiguo complejo ceramista de las Antillas Mayores.* Serie Monográfica Num. 30. Museo del Hombre Dominicano, Santo Domingo, Dominican Republic.

Veloz Maggiolo, Marcio, Plinio Pina Peña, Elpidio Ortega, and Bernardo Vega
- 1973   Antillean Pictographs and Petroglyphs: Patterns and Procedures Which Can Be Applied in the Study of Their Location in Time. *Proceedings of the International Congress for the Study of Pre-Columbian Cultures of the Lesser Antilles* 4:1–8. Reduit Plage, St. Lucia.

Veloz Maggiolo, Marcio, and Bernardo Vega
- 1982   The Antillean Preceramic: A New Approximation. *Journal of New World Archaeology* 5(2):33–44.

Versteeg, Aad H.
- 1989   The Internal Organization of a Pioneer Settlement in the Lesser Antilles: The Saladoid Golden Rock Site on St. Eustatius, Netherlands Antilles. In *Early Ceramic Population Lifeways and Adaptive Strategies in the Caribbean*, edited by Peter E. Siegel, pp. 171–192. BAR International Series No. 506. British Archaeological Reports, Oxford.

Vescelius, Gary S.
- 1977   Ballcourts and Boundaries in the Eastern Antilles. Manuscript on file, Department of Anthropology, Peabody Museum, Yale University, New Haven.

Vickers, William T.
- 1983   The Territorial Dimensions of Siona-Secoya and Encabellado Adaptation. In *Adaptive Responses of Native Amazonians*, edited by Raymond B. Hames and William T. Vickers, pp. 451–478. Academic Press, New York.

Viveiros de Castro, Eduardo
- 2001   Cosmological Deixis and Amerindian Perspectivism. In *A Reader in the Anthropology of Religion*, edited by Michael Lambeck, pp. 306–326. Blackwell, Oxford.

Walker, Jeffery B.
- 1980a *Analysis and Replication of the Lithic Artifacts from the Sugar Factory Pier Site, St. Kitts, West Indies.* Unpublished Master's thesis, Department of Anthropology, Washington State University, Pullman.
- 1980b Analysis and Replication of Lithic Artifacts from the Sugar Factory Pier Site, St. Kitts. *Proceedings of the International Congress for the Study of the Pre-Columbian Cultures of the Lesser Antilles* 8:69–79. Arizona State University, Tempe.
- 1983   Stylistic Analysis of the Río Blanco Petroglyph Site. Manuscript on file, Department of Anthropology, University of Delaware, Newark.
- 1984   *Final Report for the Systematic Archaeological Reconnaissance of Ten Selected Coastal River Mouths in Puerto Rico.* Investigaciones Arqueológicas del Caribe, Santurce, Puerto Rico. Submitted to the Puerto Rico State Historic Preservation Office, San Juan. Copies available from the Office of the State Historic Preservation Officer, San Juan, Puerto Rico.
- 1985a A Preliminary Report on the Lithic and Osteological Remains from the 1980, 1981 and 1982 Field Seasons at Hacienda Grande (12 PSj 7-5). *Proceedings of the International Congress for the Study of the Pre-Columbian Cultures of the Lesser Antilles* 10:181–224. Centre de Recherches Caraïbes, Université de Montréal, Montreal.
- 1985b Analysis of the Lithic Artifacts from El Bronce Archaeological Site, Puerto Rico. In *Archaeological Data Recovery at El Bronce, Puerto Rico, Final Re-*

port, Phase 2, by Linda S. Robinson, Emily R. Lundberg, and Jeffery B. Walker, Appendix G. Archaeological Services, Ft. Myers, Florida. Submitted to the U.S. Army Corps of Engineers, Jacksonville District. Copies available from the Office of the State Historic Preservation Officer, San Juan, Puerto Rico.

1993   *Stone Collars, Elbow Stones and Three-Pointers, and the Nature of Taíno Ritual and Myth.* Ph.D. dissertation, Washington State University, Pullman. University Microfilms, Ann Arbor.

1995   On the Nature of Taíno Stone Collars: The Production Technology. *Proceedings of the Congress of the International Association for Caribbean Archaeology.* 15:121–129. San Juan.

1997a   *Analysis of the Lithic Artifacts from the Stage II Testing of the Finca Valencia Site, Arecibo, and the La Trocha Site, Vega Baja, Puerto Rico.* Submitted to the Instituto de Cultura Puertorriqueña, San Juan. Copies available from the Instituto de Cultura Puertorriqueña, San Juan.

1997b   Taíno Stone Collars, Elbow Stones, and Three Pointers. In *Taíno: Pre-Columbian Art and Culture from the Caribbean,* edited by Fatima Bercht, Estrellita Brodsky, John Alan Farmer, and Dicey Taylor, pp. 80–91. Monacelli Press and El Museo del Barrio, New York.

Walker, Jeffery B., Eduardo Questell Rodríguez, and Reniel Rodríguez Ramos
2001   *Fuentes de lítica en el noroeste de Puerto Rico.* Submitted to the Puerto Rico State Historic Preservation Office, San Juan. Copies available from the Office of the State Historic Preservation Officer, San Juan, Puerto Rico.

Watters, David R., and Irving Rouse
1989   Environmental Diversity and Maritime Adaptations in the Caribbean Area. In *Early Ceramic Population Lifeways and Adaptive Strategies in the Caribbean,* edited by Peter E. Siegel, pp. 129–144. BAR International Series No. 506. British Archaeological Reports, Oxford.

Weaver, Guy G., Patrick H. Garrow, Charles H. McNutt Jr., and José R. Oliver
1995   *La Iglesia de Maragüez (PO-39): Investigations of a Local Ceremonial Center in the Cerrillos River Valley, Ponce, Puerto Rico.* Garrow & Associates, Atlanta, Georgia. Submitted to the U.S. Army Corps of Engineers, Jacksonville District. Copies available from the Office of the State Historic Preservation Officer, San Juan, Puerto Rico.

Weaver, Guy G., Patrick H. Garrow, and José R. Oliver
1992   *Phase II Archaeological Data Recovery at PO-38, El Parking Site, Barrio Maragüez, Ponce, Puerto Rico.* Garrow & Associates, Atlanta, Georgia. Submitted to the U.S. Army Corps of Engineers, Jacksonville District. Copies available from the Office of the State Historic Preservation Officer, San Juan, Puerto Rico.

Weaver, Guy G., and Herminio R. Rodríguez Morales
1991   *Final Report: A Cultural Resources Reconnaissance and Survey within the Proposed Río Cibuco Flood Control Project, Vega Baja, Puerto Rico.* Garrow

& Associates, Atlanta, Georgia. Submitted to the U.S. Army Corps of Engineers, Jacksonville District. Copies available from the Office of the State Historic Preservation Officer, San Juan, Puerto Rico.

Webster's
1991   *Webster's Ninth New Collegiate Dictionary.* Merriam-Webster, Springfield, Massachusetts.

Wheeler, E. A., R. G. Pearson, C. A. LaPasha, T. Zack, and W. Hatley
1986   *Computer-Aided Wood Identification.* Bulletin 474. The North Carolina Agricultural Research Service, North Carolina State University, Raleigh.

Whittaker, Robert J.
1998   *Island Biogeography: Ecology, Evolution, and Conservation.* Oxford University Press, Oxford.

Wiessner, Polly
1983   Style and Social Information in Kalahari San Projectile Points. *American Antiquity* 48:253–276.

Wilbert, Johannes
1981   Warao Cosmology and Yekuana Roundhouse Symbolism. *Journal of Latin American Lore* 7(1):37–72.
1987   *Tobacco and Shamanism in South America.* Yale University Press, New Haven.

Williams, Denis
1978   Petroglyphs at Marlissa: Berbice River. *Archaeology and Anthropology* 1:24–31.
1979   Preceramic Fishtraps on the Upper Essequibo: Report on a Survey of Unusual Petroglyphs on the Upper Essequibo and Kassikaityu Rivers, 12–28 March, 1979. *Archaeology and Anthropology* 2(2):125–140.

Willis, Raymond E.
1984   *Empire and Architecture at Sixteenth Century Puerto Real, Hispaniola: An Archaeological Perspective.* Ph.D. dissertation, University of Florida, Gainesville. University Microfilms, Ann Arbor.

Wilson, Samuel M.
1990   *Hispaniola: Caribbean Chiefdoms in the Age of Columbus.* University of Alabama Press, Tuscaloosa.
1997   The Legacy of the Indigenous People of the Caribbean. In *The Indigenous People of the Caribbean,* edited by Samuel M. Wilson, pp. 206–213. University Press of Florida, Gainesville.

Wilson, Samuel M., Harry B. Iceland, and Thomas R. Hester
1999   Preceramic Connections between Yucatán and the Caribbean. *Latin American Antiquity* 9:342–352.

Wing, Elizabeth S.
1989   Human Exploitation of Animal Resources in the Caribbean. In *Biogeogra-*

phy of the West Indies, edited by Charles A. Woods, pp. 137–152. Sandhill Crane Press, Gainesville, Florida.

1990   Animal Remains from the Hacienda Grande Site. In *Excavations at María de la Cruz Cave and Hacienda Grande Village Site, Loiza, Puerto Rico,* by Irving Rouse and Ricardo E. Alegría, pp. 87–101. Yale University Publications in Anthropology Number 80. Department of Anthropology, Yale University, New Haven.

2001   Native American Use of Animals in the Caribbean. In *Biogeography of the West Indies: Patterns and Perspectives, Second Edition,* edited by C. A. Woods and F. Sergile, pp. 481–518. CRC Press, Boca Raton, Florida.

Wing, Elizabeth S., C. E. Ray, and Charles A. Hoffman Jr.
1968   Vertebrate Remains from Indian Sites on Antigua, West Indies. *Caribbean Journal of Science* 8(3–4):123–129.

Wing, Elizabeth S., and Elizabeth J. Reitz
1982   Prehistoric Fishing Communities of the Caribbean. *Journal of New World Archaeology* 5(2):13–32.

Yeager, Jason
2000   The Social Construction of Communities in the Classic Maya Countryside: Strategies of Affiliation in Western Belize. In *The Archaeology of Communities,* edited by M. A. Cantuoand and J. Yeager, pp 123–143. Routledge, New York.

Zucchi, Alberta
1984   Nueva evidencia sobre la penetración de grupos cerámicos en las Antillas Mayores. In *Relaciones Prehispánicas de Venezuela,* edited by E. Wagner, pp. 35–50. Fondo Editorial Acta Científica Venezolana, Caracas.

CONTRIBUTORS

Karen F. Anderson-Córdova obtained her undergraduate degree in anthropology from the University of Puerto Rico and received her Ph.D. in Anthropology from Yale University in New Haven. Her dissertation, *Hispaniola and Puerto Rico: Indian Acculturation and Heterogeneity, 1492–1550,* utilized ethnohistoric and documentary sources to study the Spanish-Indian Contact period in the Spanish Caribbean. Dr. Anderson currently works for the Georgia Department of Natural Resources Historic Preservation Division in Atlanta. Previously, she was Assistant Professor in the Anthropology Department, Social Sciences Faculty and the Social Sciences Department, General Studies Faculty at the University of Puerto Rico in Río Piedras and Deputy State Historic Preservation Officer at the Puerto Rico State Historic Preservation Office, San Juan. Her research interests include Caribbean ethnohistory, culture contact studies, Spanish colonial history, and historical demography. She has worked as a teacher, researcher, and historic preservation/cultural resources consultant for more than 20 years.

Susan D. deFrance is an Assistant Professor in Anthropology at the University of Florida in Gainesville. She has conducted field research in the Caribbean, Peru, Bolivia, and the southeastern United States. Her research interests include zooarchaeology, human adaptations to coastal settings, and the cultural role of diet and foodways in the human past.

John G. Jones is an Assistant Professor of Anthropology at Washington State University in Pullman. He has conducted pollen, phytolith, and archaeobotanical studies for over 20 years throughout Central and South America, the Caribbean, and the southwestern United States. Currently, Dr. Jones is addressing early agriculture in the Neotropics.

Lee A. Newsom is a MacArthur Fellow and an Associate Professor of Anthropology at the Pennsylvania State University, with a joint appointment in the Department of Anthropology and Penn State's Institutes of the Environment. Her research is focused on the Caribbean islands and concerns human use of biological resources, particularly economic plants and forest products, and emphasizes the ecological and cultural dynamics associated with native food production and subsistence systems.

José R. Oliver received his Ph.D. in Anthropology from the University of Illinois at Urbana-Champaign and is currently a lecturer in the Institute of Archaeology at the University of London.

Deborah M. Pearsall is The Frederick A. Middlebush Chair in Social Sciences in the Department of Anthropology at the University of Missouri–Columbia. She is a paleoethnobotanist whose research interests center around using archaeological plant remains, especially charred macroremains, phytoliths (plant silica bodies), and starch grains, to investigate the interrelationships between people and plants in the past in the tropics of the New World.

Reniel Rodríguez Ramos is in the Ph.D. program in Anthropology at the University of Florida, Gainesville. He received his M.A. in Anthropology from Texas A&M University, College Station. His major interest is in lithic analysis.

Peter G. Roe received his Ph.D. in 1973 from the University of Illinois at Urbana-Champaign and is currently Professor of Anthropology at the University of Delaware in Newark. He is trained and has published widely in both lowland and highland South American prehistoric archaeology and South Amerindian ethnography. As a prehistorian, he has specialized in the late prehistoric cultures of the Upper Amazon and the related ceramic-age cultures of the Greater Antilles, as well as the first highland Peruvian civilization, Chavín. As a cultural anthropologist, his research brackets the Amazon Basin with fieldwork among the riverine Panoan "Canoe Indian" Shipibo of the Peruvian montaña in the southwest to the interfluvial Cariban "Foot Indian" Waiwai in the Guianas of the northeast. His theoretical interest lies in the relationship between ideology, social structure, and material culture, specifically the reflections of the mythology, cosmology, and ethnoarchaeoastronomy of South Amerindians, both lowland and highland, past and present, from their ancient iconography down to their current ethnic art.

Peter E. Siegel is a Principal Archeologist/Senior Project Manager in the West Chester, Pennsylvania, office of John Milner Associates, a consulting firm specializing in historic preservation and cultural resource management. Dr. Siegel has conducted archaeological investigations throughout much of eastern North America, Puerto Rico, the U.S. Virgin Islands, Antigua, Guyana, Peru, and Bolivia. His major interests are in complex society, community and spatial organization, lithic use-wear analysis, and heritage management.

Anne V. Stokes received her Ph.D. in Anthropology from the University of Florida in Gainesville. She is currently President of SEARCH, a consulting firm specializing in cultural resource management.

Joshua M. Torres is an archaeologist and Geographic Information Systems specialist who received his B.A. and M.A. degrees in Anthropology from the University of Colorado at Denver. His primary areas of interest are communities, social landscapes, and the sociopolitical development of prehistoric societies of the circum-Caribbean. Josh is currently working on his Ph.D. in anthropology/archaeology at the University of Florida in Gainesville.

Daniel P. Wagner is president of Geo-Sci Consultants, Inc., a firm specializing in pedological and geomorphological studies. Dr. Wagner has worked as a consulting pedologist throughout eastern North America, Central America, and the Caribbean for 29 years. He is also on the part-time faculty of Johns Hopkins University, where he has taught an environmental soils course for 13 years. Dr. Wagner has participated in nearly 370 geoarchaeological studies, focusing mainly on Holocene depositional and weathering sequences. He has authored or co-authored 40 professional publications, the most recent of which addresses soil stratigraphy at the pre-Clovis Cactus Hill site in southeastern Virginia.

Jeff Walker was born in Pullman, Washington, and raised in Puerto Rico. He completed his B.A. at Antioch College, and his M.A. and Ph.D. degrees at Washington State University, Pullman. His expertise is in lithic technology. Walker has worked extensively in contract, government, and academic archaeology in the Caribbean, Central America, and the western and southeastern United States. He is currently the archaeologist for the U.S. Forest Service's Caribbean National Forest in Puerto Rico.

INDEX

Alegría, Ricardo E., 8, 10, 77, 299
Amazonian cosmology: conception of universe, xvii; in relation to Taíno society, 88, 268, 287–289, 291, 294–296, 298, 323
Anacaona: chieftess of Xaraguá, 241
ancestor worship: possible evidence for in Paso del Indio burials, 74; and cemís, 255, 257–258, 263, 269–272; and politics, 276–278; in the Saladoid period, 257–259, 274; and social reproduction, 329–334
Angostura site: open-air habitation, 5, 113, 119; ground stone tools, 6–7; hoe, 6–7, 45, 113; biface, 38; in relation to Paso del Indio, 68; manos, metates/mortars, and flat grinding tools, 113; burial, 113
Archaic: possibility of pottery production, xvi, 8; managing and modifying the landscape, xvi, 5, 51, 111–113, 119, 126, 181, 183; land-use history, xviii, 113–114; persistence in the ceramic age, 4; preceramic society, 4; conventional wisdom of, 5; adaptive strategies, 5; ground stone technology, 6–7; problems in identification of, 6; shell tools, 7; influence on late prehispanic groups of Puerto Rico, 9, 10, 51–53; farming in the lowlands of Belize, 115

areíto (ceremonial chant/dance), 236, 243, 249, 257–264, 278, 284n10

Banway Trace site (Trinidad), 48
batey (ball game), 236, 258–264, 291
bats: as souls of the non-living beings, 231, 315. *See also opias*
bead production, 7, 48
behiques, 244–245, 248, 323. *See* shaman/shamanism
Belize: as likely origin of Archaic groups in northern Caribbean, 115
Borinquen (Boriquén, Boriquen, Buriquén, Borinquén), xviii, 237, 238

Cabo San Antonio (western Cuba): cave dwellers of, 4
cacique (chief): role in political-religious arena, 236, 251–256; and *nitaínos,* 241–244; as shaman, 245; memorialized in *areíto,* 264
Caguana site: as civic-ceremonial center, 226, 236, 258–264, 310; political-religious power in relation to iconography, 230, 236, 256–259, 264, 279–280; and Cacique Guarionex, 237; abandonment of, 238; and *areíto,* 258, 264
Caimitoide, 7
Calle Cristo/Ballaja, 178

Camp Santiago P-2 site, 222
Camp Santiago P-20 site, 225
Caño Hondo site: Archaic, 113
Caracoles site, 129, 225
Carbone, Victor A., 11
Caribbean Archaeology Program: of the Yale Peabody Museum, 1
caves: as portals between the earthly plane and the numinous, 231, 233, 276, 296, 316–325
Cayo Cofresi: Archaic coastal open-air site, 5, 113; ground stone tools, 6
Cedeñoide, 7
Cedrosan Saladoid, 2, 9; as ancestors of the Taínos, 2, 310; flaked-stone technology, 9–10; plano-convex adze, 10, 46, 47, 50, 51; general patterns of stone-tool production, 46–47; linkages between Puerto Rico and Lesser Antilles, 50–51; coexistence of Archaic peoples with, 51
celts, 38–39; distinction between Saladoid and post-Saladoid, 40–41; sumptuary value of, 41
cemís: as three-pointed objects, 49, 243–244, 256; as sources of supernatural power, 231, 246–247; as icons of the cacique, 236, 244, 251–256, 271–272, 274–276; and social status, 242, 249–251, 255; as portable wealth, 243–244; as *duhos* (ceremonial stool), *cohoba* plates, stone collars, and elbow stones, 244, 256; meaning of, 245; and shamanism, 244–245; and Ramón Pané, 247–248; and altered states of consciousness, 248–251, 272–276, 283n8; social organization of, 251; and ancestors, 257–258
cemíism: as Taíno beliefs about supernatural, 246–248
ceramic age: colonization of West Indies, xvi; dating of, xvi; culture change during, xvii; land-use history, xviii
ceremonial plazas: idea of, xvii; as materializations of chiefly power, 203, 208, 256; symbolic aspects of 233–234, 276–278; as burial grounds, 257–258; and *areíto* (ceremonial chants/dance) 258–264; as arenas of competition, 259
Cerrillos: lithic assemblages, 6; dating of, 52–53

channel stones, 41
Chief Behechio, 243
chiefly polities: as competitive and territorial social units, xvii, 207–208, 254–255; in the Santa Elena and Esperanza periods, xvii; centralized leadership of, 203, 237; symbolic aspects of elite authority, 234–235, 291; and civic-ceremonial centers, 236–241; Xaraguá (Hispaniola), 237, 241; Guaynía, 237; Agueybana I, 237; Guaybanex, 237; Macorix (Hispaniola), 250–251, 264; Maguá (Hispaniola), 250–251, 264
Ciboney culture, 1
climatic changes: as explanation of Saladoid to Ostionoid transformations, 11; through the Holocene, 90–94; in relation to human adaptations, culture change, and interactions between groups, 93–94. *See also* Holocene environment; sediment coring
Coll y Toste, Cayetano, 47
Colón, Fernando, 253, 257
Columbus, Christopher, 3
conical manos, 6
Crab culture, 1; ceramics of, 1; persistence of the Archaic in the, 51
crab-shell dichotomy, xviii, 3; as evidence of two migrations, 1, 149; continuum of ceramic modes, 2, 3; shifts in material culture, 2; in the Paso del Indio site, xviii, 3; general discussion of, 4–12; as shift in dietary patterns, 11, 149; as demographic explosion, 11; evidence against, 126, 177–178, 183
Cruxent, José M., xvi
cultural landscape: changes in, 10, 118–120, 181; multi-ethnic nature of, 51; of Caguana, 230–236
Cueva de la Momia site, 325
Cueva la Mora site, 312, 323–325
Cueva las Caritas site: paleoethnobiology of, 129
Cueva Gemelos site: Archaic interior rock shelter, 5
Cuevas: complex, xvii; settlement patterns, xvii; plano-convex adze, 38–40
Cueva Tembladera site: Archaic interior rock shelter, 5

dietary changes: skeletal isotopes, 11, 70, 185, 199–200; faunal remains, 183
Diego Hernandez site, 219
demography: age and sex distributions in Paso del Indio burials, 69

edge-grinders, 7, 8, 43–44, 45, 48, 51
El Bronce: paleoethnobiology of, 144, 178; monumental architecture, 219, 220; petroglyphs of, 307–308
El Caimito site (Dominican Republic), 7
El Cayito site, 225
El Coco site, 225
El Fresal site, 129
El Palo site, 302, 307, 310
El Pulguero site: Archaic, 113
En Bas Saline site (Haiti), 141
Esperanza site, 220, 225
ethnohistoric documents: in regard to Taíno chiefly organization, 88, 202, 226; Taíno cultivation practices, 127; and Caguana, 237; and chiefly duties, 241; and Taíno cosmology, 247–255, [see also Pané]; and ball game, 261–263; and the direct-historic approach applied to rock art, 298, 326
evocative links between current residents of Puerto Rico and the pre-Columbian past, xviii, 61, 280, 298

F-3-01 site, 220
Finca Valencia site (NCS-1), 129, 137, 141, 178, 181
flaked-stone technology: freehand flaking, 6, 10, 24, 46, 51; centripetal flaking, 9–10, 35, 47; bipolar reduction, 10, 24, 46, 50; multidirectional freehand flaking, 10, 34; core-flake reduction, 13, 34; micro-flakes as grater-board teeth, 24, 72; parallel flaking, 30; random flaking, 24; distinctions between Saladoid and Ostionoid series, 46–48, 50–51
Flinty Bay (Antigua), 20
funerary practices: in Paso del Indio burials, 70–75

G-15-01 site, 220
Guacayarima peninsula (Haiti): cave dwellers of, 4

Guarionex: chief of Maguana (Hispaniola), 263–264

Hacienda Grande: complex, xvii; settlement patterns, xvii, ceramic style, 2; site, 8; paleoethnobiology of, 127, 177
Hernández Colón site (early Saladoid): paleoethnobiology of, 127; ceremonial space in, 225
Hispaniola: Archaic groups on, xvi; chiefdoms of, 237
Holocene environment: in the West Indies, 90–94. *See also* climatic changes; sediment coring
home-garden plants: edible fruit, guanabána or soursop, lechosa or papaya, guaba, aguacate or avocado, guayaba or guava, tabloncillo or mastic-bully, yellow sapote and almendrón, caimito or star apple, 131; herbaceous plant, evening primrose, 131–137; tree taxa, higüera, achiote, *cohoba*, 131; general discussion of, 180, 183
Honduras del Oeste (Dominican Republic), 7
Huecan Saladoid, 2
Huecoid series: as distinct from Saladoid series, 9

Institute of Puerto Rican Culture: site files, xv, 302; survey and excavation reports, xv, 299. *See also* Puerto Rico State Historic Preservation Office
interactions between Archaic and Saladoid groups, xvi, 3, 4, 8, 53, 89, 113–114, 115–118

Kelbey's Ridge 2 site (Saba), 74
Kozlowski, Janusz K., 8

La Hueca: complex, 9; lapidary iconography, 9; site, 9; long duration of, 50; coexistence of Archaic peoples with, 51
La Iglesia de Maragüez site, 52, 220
Las Casas, Fray Bartolomé de, 241, 252–254, 261, 284n9
Las Flores site, 219, 220
La Trocha site (NCS-4), 115, 141, 178
Lévi-Strauss, Claude, 323
LO-23 site, 52

lithic analysis: changes in raw material selection and tool production, 3, 46–47
Luján I site (Vieques), 129, 178, 181

macrophytic remains: wood, charcoal, seeds, nut hulls, rind fragments, palm petioles, and miscellaneous plant parts, 130; analysis of, 131–144
Maisabel pond: as a karst sinkhole, 96; stratigraphy of, 96–97, 101–107; sedimentation rates as a measure of human impacts on the landscape, 105–107; sediment chemistry, 107
Maisabel site: Archaic forest clearing in vicinity of, 5; in relation to Paso del Indio, 56; dating of, 89; geological and pedological context, 94–101; environs of as a modified landscape, 105–107; paleoethnobiology of, 127, 141, 144, 177, 178, 182; stable isotope analysis, 185, 194–198; petroglyphs of, 301, 308, 327–328
manos, 6; conical form, 42, 51
María de la Cruz site: Archaic, 8, 46, 113, 127, 140
Maruca site: open-air Archaic habitation, 5, 113, 127; postmolds, groundstone tools, and burials, 113; paleoethnobiology of, 140, 150
Mason, J. Alden, 230, 264
Mayobanex: chief of Macorix (Hispaniola), 264
metates, 44–45
mortars, 6, 44, 48
Musiepedro site (Dominican Republic), 7

naborías (commoners), 246
Native American labor organization: use by Spanish (*repartimiento* and *encomienda* systems), 241–242
netsinkers, 42–43, 48, 51
nutting stones, 7

opias (spirit beings), 231, 264–266, 296, 325
Orinoco Valley: source of ceramic-age migrants, xvi
Osgood, Cornelius, 1
Ostionoid: Chican, 2; Elenan, 2; Ostionan, 2; series, 2; as evolution of Cedrosan Saladoid, 10; stone belt fragments, 49, 75

Palmar de Animas site (VB-27), 52, 114–115
Pané, Fray Ramón, 247–248, 250–251, 293, 298, 326
Paso del Indio site: lithic analysis, 12, 75; problems in excavation methods and recording, 24, 62–64, 86; bipolar flaking activity areas, 38, 68; pecked and ground stone artifacts, 38–43; depth of deposits, 55; geographic setting of, 55–56; archaeological history of, 56–57; in relation to Maisabel, 56, 68, 74, 115; deep testing of, 57–58; remote sensing of, 58; public outreach, 61–62; depositional processes and flood sequences, 64–65; house patterns, 65–67; rock pavements, 67; possible ball court or plaza, 67, 68; ditch feature, 67; burials, 68–75; in relation to Angostura, 68; dating of, 77–78; use of GIS, 84–86; paleoethnobiology of, 127, 141; stable isotope analysis, 185, 191
passage ways between islands: loci of intense cultural activity, xv
PE-1 site, 225
petroglyphs: in caves, 231; as actors in ceremonial activities, 236, 258–259, 282–283n3; in Caguana site, 236, 238, 244, 256, 257, 258–259, 264, 310; of Tibes, 238–240, 256; status ranking of, 242; as cemís, 246–247, 256–259, 266, 280; of Trujillo Alto, Tierras Nuevas, and Palo Hincado, 256; iconographic analysis and cosmological interpretation of, 264–276, 294, 310; seriation of, 308; compared to Taíno pottery, 310; as territorial markers, 327
pictographs: in caves, 231, 314; as cemís, 325
plant intensification: home gardens, 126
PO-23 site, 52
PO-38 site, 52; paleoethnobiology of, 127
PO-39 site, 52
post-Saladoid: settlement patterns, xvii, 114–115, 219–222, 225–226; chipped-stone flaking technology, 34–38. *See also* Ostionoid

pre-Columbian animal introductions to Puerto Rico: evidence for, 177, 178, 181, 182
pre-Columbian plant introductions to Puerto Rico: evidence for, 140, 180
Puerto Ferro site (Vieques, Archaic), 113, 127, 150
Puerto Rico State Historic Preservation Office: site files, xv, 203, 210–211, 302; survey and excavation reports, xv, 299; use of GIS, 84–85, 203, 210. *See also* Institute of Puerto Rican Culture

Rainey, Froelich G., 1, 10, 38, 51
Río Canas site, 220
rock art: problems in interpretation, 297–299; methods of recordation and analysis, 300–307; design elements, motifs, and rules of, 302; dating of, 307–310; cosmology in, 315–325; interpretation of, 325–329
Rouse, Irving, xv, xvi, 2, 7–10, 50–53, 77–78, 204, 299

Sabana Seca: Archaic interior rock shelter, 5
Saladero: type site for Saladoid series, xvi
Saladoid: distinctive material culture, xvi, 287; colonists, xvi, 8; invaders, 7; linkages to the Taínos, 88, 259–260, 287–289; root-crop horticulture, 127; ceremonial plazas, 257–260
Santa Elena: complex, xvii; settlement patterns, xvii
Scientific Survey of Puerto Rico and the Virgin Islands, 2
sediment coring: Paso del Indio site, 57; Lake Miragoane, Haiti, 90, 114; south and west coasts of Puerto Rico, 90–93; Caricao Basin, Venezuela, 93; Grenada, 93; Maisabel site, 96, 108; Laguna Tortuguero, 107–108; Río Cibuco mangrove, 108. *See also* climatic changes; Holocene environment
shaman/shamanism: and access to the numinous, 244, 323; and cemí, 245; and altered states of consciousness, 248
Shell culture, 1, 10
Sorcé site (Vieques), 129, 177
stable isotope analysis: explained, 185–189; history of in the West Indies, 189–190; limitations of, 190; Paso del Indio burials, 191; Maisabel burials, 194–198
St. Kitts, 10, 46, 180
stone bowl, 42, 48, 51
syphilis: evidence in Paso del Indio late Ostiones burial, 70

Tecla site, 226
Tibes site: paleoethnobiology of, 127, 141, 144, 177, 178, 181, 182; monumental architecture, 219, 220, 226, 289; civic-ceremonial center, 238; Saladoid component, 238; in relation to Caguana, 238; and *areíto*, 258
tuber processing, 7, 180; pitted stones used in, 44, 51
Tutu site (St. Thomas), 141

UTU-44 site, 129, 141

Veloz Maggiolo, Marcio, 4, 7
Villón site, 220, 225

zone-incised crosshatching (ZIC): as a design element in Huecoid pottery, 9
Zucchi, Alberta, 8

Index / 423